# SCIENCE STORIES YOU CAN COUNT ON

# 51 CASE STUDIES WITH QUANTITATIVE REASONING IN BIOLOGY

# SCIENCE STORIES YOU CAN COUNT ON

# 51 CASE STUDIES WITH QUANTITATIVE REASONING IN BIOLOGY

**CLYDE FREEMAN HERREID**
**NANCY A. SCHILLER**
**KY F. HERREID**

NSTApress
National Science Teachers Association
Arlington, Virginia

NSTA press®
National Science Teachers Association

Claire Reinburg, Director
Wendy Rubin, Managing Editor
Andrew Cooke, Senior Editor
Amanda O'Brien, Associate Editor
Amy America, Book Acquisitions Coordinator

**Art and Design**
Will Thomas Jr., Director
Rashad Muhammad, Graphic Designer

**Printing and Production**
Catherine Lorrain, Director

**National Science Teachers Association**
David L. Evans, Executive Director
David Beacom, Publisher

1840 Wilson Blvd., Arlington, VA 22201
*www.nsta.org/store*
For customer service inquiries, please call 800-277-5300.




17 16 15 14 4 3 2 1



**Library of Congress Cataloging-in-Publication Data**
Herreid, Clyde Freeman, author.
Science stories you can count on : 51 case studies with quantitative reasoning in biology / Clyde Freeman Herreid, Nancy A. Schiller, Ky F. Herreid.
pages cm
ISBN 978-1-938946-05-9 — ISBN 978-1-938946-59-2 (electronic)
1. Biology--Study and teaching—United States--Case studies. 2. Qualitative reasoning. I. Schiller, Nancy A., 1957- author. II. Herreid, Ky F., 1965- author. III. Title.
QH319.A1H47 2014
570.71—dc23
2014009833

# CONTENTS

# CONTENTS

# CONTENTS

# CONTENTS

# CONTENTS

CHAPTER 1

# INTRODUCTION
## The Numbers Game

*Clyde Freeman Herreid*

*There was a young man from Trinity,*
*Who solved the square root of infinity.*
*While counting the digits,*
*He was seized by the fidgets,*
*Dropped science, and took up divinity.*

— *Author Unknown*

There was no need to do that. Drop science, that is. The young man from Trinity could have buckled down and learned the necessary mathematics to have a happy and fruitful career in science. He might even have discovered the physicists' version of the Holy Grail, the "Theory of Everything," or the answer to the biologist's head-scratching question of how consciousness arose. Then again, not everyone needs to be a scientist. In fact, C. P. Snow, British cultural raconteur and author of *The Two Cultures*, argued it would be downright dangerous. We need folks in the arts and humanities, and perhaps a philosopher or two is desirable. But even these individuals should be able to handle a bit of rudimentary mathematics, according to Snow, even the second law of thermodynamics! And if we believe the most recent behavioral studies, crows can count and so can pigeons, and mathematical calculations appear to be within the purview of even the lowly squid. Surely, we can expect as much from our undergraduates.

Our students should be able to at least reason quantitatively: to read and interpret data, graphs, and statistics. They should be astute enough to demand to see the evidence when some politician claims that a new drug cures cancer, job numbers are up, our carbon footprint is too big, the president's budget is the highest ever, and the world is coming to an end on December 21. And once having been shown the data, our intelligent citizen should not cringe if graphs stare him in the face, but fearlessly look at the data, and challenge the purveyor of false doctrines and celebrate the "truth-sayer" when found. But if this is a worthy ideal, how do we achieve numerical nirvana?

Traditional courses do not appear to achieve this ideal goal, for various reasons we will discuss in this chapter. We need to revise our approach to the required courses. In addition, we need to introduce quantitative skills throughout the curriculum as an integral part of courses, especially those that purport to teach STEM students.

Introductory biology seems an ideal place to start. Most students enroll in this course to fulfill their general elective credits required for graduation. They see it as a user-friendly science, integrating information from the physical sciences and the life sciences. Moreover, it is a gateway course for students on the way to health science careers. Teaching biology using real stories with quantitative reasoning skills enmeshed in the story line is a powerful and logical way to teach the subject and to show its relevance to the lives of future citizens, regardless of whether they are science specialists or laypeople. Yet the fundamental questions remain: What kind of education should a student have to deal with today's world? How much of it should focus on quantitative skills, and what kind of quantitative skills should we be teaching? And how should we do it?

## Why Numeracy Matters

*Numeracy* means the ability to reason and to use numbers, and at its simplest level we are talking about arithmetic, adding, subtracting, multiplying, and dividing. This topic, why numeracy matters, was raised at the National Forum on Quantitative Literacy hosted by the National Academy of Sciences in Washington, D.C., on December 1–2, 2001. In the published proceedings (Madison and Steen 2003), Patricia Cohen gives us an historical perspective, reminding us that an informed and quantitatively literate society is essential for democracy. She notes that Massachusetts statesman Josiah Quincy wrote in 1816 about the "growing" importance of what he called the "art" of "Political Arithmetick." He "expounded on the connections … between statistical knowledge and 'the duties of citizens and lawmakers in the fledgling American republic'" (Cohen 2003, p. 7). Cohen notes in her essay that "Arithmetick" connects to democratic government in three distinct ways:

> First, the very political legitimacy of a representative democracy rests on repeated acts of counting: tallying people in periodic census enumerations to apportion the size and balance of legislative bodies, and tallying votes in varieties of elections to determine office-holding and public policies. Second, as Quincy suggested, a government whose goal is the general welfare of its citizens needs good aggregate information about those citizens on which to erect and assess public policy. It is no coincidence, then, that the word "statisticks" was coined in English in the 1790s…. And third, the citizens of democratic governments also need good information, to assess their leaders' political decisions and judge them on election day. (2003, p. 7)

The educational demands for a U.S. citizen have grown enormously since 1816, and the issue of how mathematics impacts our democracy is even more important today.

In their essay "The Democratization of Mathematics," Carnevale and Desrcochers (2003) write that our current system of teaching mathematics across the curriculum is flawed and threatens to undermine our democracy (p. 21). Mathematics acts as a filtering device, playing a significant role in who gets into the best colleges and the best professions even if higher level mathematics is not required for the day-to-day work in those fields:

> The sequence of abstract high school mathematics courses that prepares students for advanced degrees in mathematics and science is still crucial to our advanced economy, but moving the entire school-age population through the academic hierarchy from arithmetic to calculus as a sorting strategy for producing elite mathematical talent required of a small share of college majors and fewer than 5 percent of the workforce does not match well with our more general needs for applied reasoning abilities and practical numeracy .... It means making mathematics more accessible and responsive to the needs of all students, citizens, and workers. The essential challenge in democratizing mathematics applies to the sciences and humanities as well. The challenge is to match curricula to cultural, political, and economic goals rather than continuing the dominance of discrete disciplinary silos. (pp. 28–29)

The obvious follow-up question is tackled by Arnold Packer (2003) in his essay "What Mathematics Should 'Everyone' Know and Be Able to Do?" Packer asks rhetorically, what is wrong with the present system and then answers: "The way middle school teachers teach fractions provides a clue. They teach their students to add fractions by: First finding the lowest common denominator. Then converting all fractions to that denominator. Then adding the numerators. Finally, reducing the answer, if possible" (p. 34). As Packer goes on to point out, "Nobody does that outside the schoolroom. Imagine a school cafeteria in which the selected items totaled three quarters and three dollars and four dimes. The schoolroom method would be to change all these in for nickels."

## What Kinds of Quantitative Skills?

Quantitative literacy and the need for a general education that includes some quantitative reasoning are important. It seems clear that we need to revise the way we teach these skills, placing greater emphasis on practical applications rather than abstract principles. This is the position of the National Council of Teachers of Mathematics (NCTM), which urges teachers to include real-world problem solving into their lesson plans and the need for students to be able to communicate in the language of mathematics (NCTM 2012). But if some quantitative skills are needed for the general public, they are even more important for students entering the fields of science and engineering.

In this section, we take a look at how the K–12 and college communities are grappling with these issues. A number of organizations and committees whose business it is to set standards have been active in this area. In reviewing the educational standards and goals for K–12 and college science education, we find many similarities. Our focus in this book is on the quantitative skills that people training to be biologists need to master. However, we cannot neglect secondary and postsecondary students, for they are all likely to stream through the general biology course, either because it is required for their major or because they have chosen the course as a general education requirement.

After we summarize the requirements, we turn to the question: What can we do in these introductory biology courses to enhance the quantitative skills of the students? We advocate the use of real-world problems, or cases, that teach quantitative skills to students in introductory biology courses via active learning strategies. We have been pioneers in the use of case study teaching for 20 years. In that time, many studies have supported our contention that teaching in context improves learning. Consistent with this view, this book offers many different examples of cases that have been tested in the classroom by both high school and college instructors. Before turning to those examples, let us see what various communities of scholars say about the foundational knowledge and skills students should acquire at different levels of their education. But it will be evident that the definition of numeracy depends upon the educational level considered and the career aspirations of the individual.

## K–12 Students

The Committee on Conceptual Framework for the New K–12 Science Education Standards under the direction of the National Academies has recently published *A Framework for K–12 Science Education: Practices, Crosscutting Concepts, and Core Ideas* (NRC 2012). They state: "We consider eight practices to be essential elements of the K–12 science and engineering curriculum:

1. Asking questions (for science) and defining problems (for engineering).
2. Developing and using models.
3. Planning and carrying out investigations.
4. Analyzing and interpreting data.
5. Using mathematics, information and computer technology, and computational thinking.
6. Constructing explanations (for science) and designing solutions (for engineering).
7. Engaging in argument from evidence.
8. Obtaining, evaluating, and communicating information." (p. 49).

But, of course, the real issue is: How will the school systems implement these elements? For an answer, let's refer to the details of the framework. Here is the overarching vision:

> By the end of the 12th grade, students should have gained sufficient knowledge of the practices, crosscutting concepts, and core ideas of science and engineering to engage in public discussions on science-related issues, to be critical consumers of scientific information related to their everyday lives, and to continue to learn about

science throughout their lives. They should come to appreciate that science and the current scientific understanding of the world are the result of many hundreds of years of creative human endeavor. It is especially important to note that the above goals are for all students, not just those who pursue careers in science, engineering, or technology or those who continue on to higher education. (p. 9)

For our purposes, let's look closer at what they have to say about practices 4 and 5:

### Practice 4: Analyzing and Interpreting Data (pp. 61–63)

Once collected, data must be presented in a form that can reveal any patterns and relationships and that allows results to be communicated to others. Because raw data as such have little meaning, a major practice of scientists is to organize and interpret the data through tabulating, graphing, or statistical analysis. Such analysis can bring out the meaning of the data—and their relevance—so that they may be used as evidence…

#### Goals

By grade 12, students should be able to:

- Analyze data systematically, either to look for salient patterns or to test whether the data are consistent with an initial hypothesis.
- Recognize when data are in conflict with expectations and consider what revisions in the initial model are needed.
- Use spreadsheets, databases, tables, charts, graphs, statistics, mathematics, and information technology to collate, summarize, and display data and to explore relationships between variables, especially those representing input and output.
- Evaluate the strength of a conclusion that can be inferred from any data set, using appropriate grade-level mathematical and statistical techniques.
- Recognize patterns in data that suggest relationships worth investigating further. Distinguish between causal and correlational relationships.
- Collect data from physical models and analyze the performance of a design under a range of conditions.

### Practice 5: Using Mathematics and Computational Thinking (pp. 65–66)

Mathematics (including statistics) and computational tools are essential for data analysis, especially for large data sets. The abilities to view data from different perspectives and with different graphical representations, to test relationships between variables, and to explore the interplay of diverse external conditions all require mathematical skills that are enhanced and extended with computational skills.

## Goals

By grade 12, students should be able to:

- Recognize dimensional quantities and use appropriate units in scientific applications of mathematical formulas and graphs.
- Express relationships and quantities in appropriate mathematical or algorithmic forms for scientific modeling and investigations.
- Recognize that computer simulations are built on mathematical models that incorporate underlying assumptions about the phenomena or systems being studied.
- Use simple test cases of mathematical expressions, computer programs, or simulations—that is, compare their outcomes with what is known about the real world—to see if they "make sense."
- Use grade-level-appropriate understanding of mathematics and statistics in analyzing data.

The material above has been extracted from a large document and the original version should be consulted in order to get the full flavor of the discussion. Further, the *Framework* does not specify a list of standards; rather, it sets forth an overarching vision for achieving quantitative literacy that makes sense at this time in history. Nor does the document give suggestions about how we can reach the stated goals; no specific courses are prescribed. Individual school systems and statewide recommendations are left to their own devices.

Keeping that in mind, let us turn to the standards initiative adopted by 45 states (*www.corestandards.org*). The *Common Core State Standards for Mathematics* (National Governors Association Center for Best Practices 2010) describes the concepts that students should know in mathematics at each grade level. Although they do not specify how these objectives should be reached, they do provide four model pathways that are used by various school systems. State school districts are now grappling with how they wish to implement the standards. New York and other states have adopted the traditional approach, which consists of two algebra courses and a geometry course, with some data, probability, and statistics included in each course (see *www.p12.nysed.gov/ciai/common_core_standards/pdfdocs/ccssi_mathematics_appendix_a.pdf*). Nonetheless, these courses with their familiar titles do not have to be traditional at all, as we will soon discover.

## College Non-Science Majors

Many individuals and organizations have grappled with the question of what quantitative skills college students will need to achieve quantitative literacy (NRC 2003; AAAS 2009). An outstanding collection of papers have documented how various schools have attempted to overcome our mathematical illiteracy (*CBE – Life Sciences Education* 2010). In these 17 articles, 7 essays, and 7 features, we find multiple ways to infuse undergraduate biology with math and computational science. The Association of American Colleges and Universities (AACU) has even developed a rubric for quantitative literacy (*www.aacu.org/value/rubrics/pdf/QuantitativeLiteracy.pdf*). One cannot help but be impressed by the innovative solutions that faculty have come up with, but these are the exceptions.

Too commonly we find that when a school decides that they must overhaul their math requirements, they turn the problem over to their academic departments to mandate which courses they will accept for graduation. Not surprisingly, they often choose a selection of traditional math courses already in existence. The General Education Committees follow suit: They select pre-existing courses from the institution catalogue. Seldom do you find a faculty or an administration willing to start from scratch and work out which quantitative skills they think students need and then refurbish the curriculum.

Carleton College is an interesting exception. They have institutionalized a different approach to quantitative reasoning (QR), which they define as "the habit of mind to consider the power and limitations of quantitative evidence in the evaluation, construction, and communication of arguments in public, professional, and personal life" (Carleton College 2011a). They have attacked the problem head-on with their Quantitative Inquiry, Reasoning, and Knowledge (QuIRK) Initiative. Basically, the program has encouraged a wholesale, schoolwide overhaul of many courses to include quantitative skills in the course work. The school has a website that lists "Ten Foundational Quantitative Reasoning Questions," written by psychology professor Neil Lutsky, which Carleton College wants their students to be able to ask when confronted with data (Carleton College 2011b):

### *I. What do the numbers show?*

- What do the numbers mean?
- Where are the numbers?
  - › Is there numerical evidence to support a claim?
  - › What were the exact figures?
  - › How can seeking and analyzing numbers illuminate important phenomena?
- How plausible is a possibility in light of back-of-the-envelope calculations?

## II. How representative is that?

- What's the central tendency?
    - "For instance" is not proof; it is an example.
    - Mean, Mode, and Median.
- Interrogating averages:
    - Are there extreme scores?
    - Are there meaningful subgroups?
    - What's the variability (standard deviation)?
- What are the odds of that? What's the base rate?

## III. Compared to what?

- What's the implicit or explicit frame of reference?
- What's the unit of measurement?
- Per what?
- What's the order of magnitude?
- Interrogating a graph:
    - What's the Y-axis? Is it zero-based?
    - Does it K.I.S.S., or is it filled with ChartJunk?

## IV. Is the outcome statistically significant?

- Is the outcome unlikely to have come about by chance?
    - "Chance is lumpy."
    - Criterion of sufficient rarity due to chance: $p < .05$
- What does statistical significance mean, and what doesn't it mean?

## V. What's the effect size?

- How can we take the measure of how substantial an outcome is?
- How large is the mean difference? How large is the association?
- Standardized mean difference (d): $d = (\mu 1 - \mu 2)/\sigma$

## VI. Are the results those of a single study or from literature?

- What's the source of the numbers: PFA, peer-reviewed, or what?
- Who is sponsoring the research?

- How can we take the measure of what the literature shows?
- The importance of meta-analysis in the contemporary world of QR.

## *VII. What is the research design (correlational or experimental)?*

- Design matters: Experimental vs. correlational design.
- How well does the design support a causal claim?
- Experimental Design:
  - Randomized Controlled Trials (RCT): Research trials in which participants are randomly assigned to the conditions of the study.
  - Double blind trials: RCTs in which neither the researcher nor the patient know the treatment condition.
- Correlational Design: Measuring existing variation and evaluating co-occurrences, possibly controlling for other variables.
  - Interrogating associations (correlations):
    - Are there extreme pairs of scores (outliers)?
    - Are there meaningful subgroups?
    - Is the range of scores in a variable restricted?
    - Is the relationship non-linear?

## *VIII. How was the variable operationalized?*

- What meaning and degree of precision does the measurement procedure justify?
- What elements and procedures result in the assignment of a score to a variable?
- What exactly was asked?
- What's the scale of measurement?
- How might we know if the measurement procedure is a good one?
  - Reliability = Repeated applications of the procedure result in consistent scores.
  - Validity = Evidence supports the use to which the measure is being put.
- Is the measure being manipulated or "gamed"? The iatrogenic effects of measurement.

## *IX. Who's in the measurement sample?*

- What domain is being evaluated? Who's in? Who's not?

- Is the sample from that domain representative, meaningful, and/or sufficient?
- Is the sample random?
- Are two or more samples that are being compared equivalent?

### X. Controlling for what?

- What other variables might be influencing the findings?
- Were these assessed or otherwise controlled for in the research design?
- What don't we know, and how can we acknowledge uncertainties?

This seems to me to be an eminently reasonable approach to the question of what we wish every citizen to know. Unfortunately, our typical college courses don't come close to achieving these goals. Interestingly, nearly all of these topics are covered in a typical statistics course, yet most schools do not list statistics as a graduation requirement though many have it as an option. So if we really care about teaching our students to be "quantitative reasoners," how do we accomplish that?

A vote for statistics in the required curriculum comes from Marie Davidian and Thomas Louis in their editorial, "Why Statistics," which appeared in the April 6, 2012, issue of *Science*. They remind us that "Statistics is the science of learning from data, and of measuring, controlling, and communicating uncertainty; and it thereby provides the navigation essential for controlling the course of scientific and societal advances." They point out that statistics informs policy development in governmental budgets as well as medical discoveries and science advancement in general. They applaud the new U.S. Common Core K–12 Mathematics Standards, which introduces statistics as a key part of pre-college education, encompassing skills in describing data, developing statistical models, making inferences, and evaluating the consequences of decisions.

Ecologists Carol Brewer and Louis Gross (2003) foreshadowed these arguments, saying science students and the public should have an education that allows them to deal with uncertainty and variability so that they are better able to grapple with topics such as climate change. Ecologists require a background in probability, including the concepts of random variables, stochastic processes, and Bayesian statistics. But the general public needs an education as well, one that will allow them to appreciate important assumptions and limitations that are part of model building and the reasoning involved in predictive forecasting. Brewer and Gross argue that "regular exposure to probabilistic ideas (e.g., weather forecasts, lotteries) does not provide much of a basis for public appreciation of uncertainty in ecological forecasts …. Beyond formal training in schools and universities, education of the general public can be aided by targeted articles in the press, especially when they can be related to local or regional projects (e.g., restoration projects, land-use reviews) for which ecological projections inform decision-making. This implies that scientists involved in the development of these projections have an obligation to disseminate information at a level that is clear to a general audience" (p. 1413).

But they offer no panacea for how to accomplish this; they simply urge faculty to develop new course materials and attend workshops where the emphasis is on better communication of probabilistic models for future students. One solution to the problem has been touted by a group of instructors who teach mathematics using case studies that they have developed using material from newspapers (Madison et al. 2009).

## Pre-Professional Health Students

An inordinate number of students in most introductory biology classes start college dreaming of a career in the medical, dental, pharmacy, nursing, physical therapy, or related health professions. In my general biology course, they make up about 80% of the population. Less than half of them survive the first two years' requirements.

In the March 30, 2012, issue of *Science*, S. James Gates and Chad Mirkin, members of the President's Council of Advisors on Science and Technology, noted that in the United States over 60% of the students who enter college intending to major in a STEM field fail to graduate with a STEM degree. (Read that again: *Over 60% of the students who enter college intending to major in a STEM field fail to graduate with a STEM degree!*) They report that students leave STEM during the first two years for three major reasons: uninspiring introductory courses, difficulty with the required math, and an academic culture in STEM fields that is unwelcoming. The problem is especially acute for women and minorities. (These comments resonate strongly with Sheila Tobias's 1990 and 1992 books on the topic 20 years ago.) Gates and Mirkin recommend that the "federal government catalyze widespread adoption of active learning approaches using case studies, problem-based learning, peer instruction, and computer simulations." They further emphasize hands-on research and laboratory experiences that begin early in the college career.

How do our current standard curricula stack up to the general criticisms made by the President's Council of Advisors? First, there is the problem that 86% of the natural sciences faculty say that lecturing is their primary method of instruction (National Research Council 2003). Then there are the math requirements. Let's take a look at what they are just for pre-professional health students. The curricula across the United States show little variation among schools and disciplines; they have not seriously changed over the last several decades.

From the American Association of Colleges of Pharmacy course requirements (AACP) for 2012–2013 (AACP 2012) we learn that 94% of the institutions require calculus, 60% require statistics, and 9% require computer science applications. Is this the curriculum that we think is ideal for training today's pharmacists—or, for that matter, for physicians, dentists, or for any health professionals? They have similar requirements for mathematics. Virtually everyone thinks they have to have calculus to get into professional health schools.

Appendix A gives a list of "Expectations for Medical Students" developed by the AAMC-HHMI Scientific Foundations for Future Physicians. But when we look at the desired competencies, there seems to be little need for the standard calculus course. Instead, we see statistics and data interpretation are eminently valued. Yet, courses in these subjects are not apparently on the list of required courses developed by the Association of American Medical Colleges. That seems odd.

What is it about calculus that makes it so desirable, when virtually none of the health practitioners will ever integrate or differentiate anything in their life? As a counterpoint: I have been assured by a dean of pharmacy that students in their PharmD program take pharmacokinetics where the kinetics of drug action does often involve differential equations. There are undoubtedly occasions in medical school where similar examples occur. But do students really need two semesters of calculus while statistics is left to languish?

Still, calculus may have unsuspected potential benefits. Philip Sadler and Robert Tai (2007) wondered if courses in high school affected students' grades in introductory college courses. They studied 8,474 undergraduate students enrolled in one of the three introductory science courses at 63 colleges and universities. Not surprisingly, students who had taken physics, chemistry, or biology in high school performed better in those respective subjects than those that did not. But they did not do better in other science subjects; that is, there was no cross-subject benefit for someone who took chemistry and thus improved their performance in say biology or physics. *But here is the kicker: The students who had taken high school calculus did better in the science subjects than those who did not.* This was true even if calculus was not part of the course curriculum in many of these courses. Was there something about the students who took calculus that brought about higher performance, or was it the course material itself that promoted better performance, or were there other causes at work? Cause/effect questions notwithstanding, the evidence is clear. Whatever brought this effect about, whether it was that taking calculus actually improved science performance or whether the effect was caused by another variable, we should take this result seriously and examine what is driving this correlation.

## Professional Biologists

In a 2004 essay Joel E. Cohen emphasized the importance of mathematics to biology, making the point in his title: "Mathematics is Biology's Next Microscope, Only Better; Biology is Mathematics' Next Physics, Only Better." His points were these: Just as the microscope opened up new vistas for biology, mathematics has the potential to do even more for biology. Cohen reminds us that Mendel's discoveries of the general principles of genetics leaned heavily upon mathematics. William Harvey's calculations of blood flow were crucial to his understanding of human circulation. And dozens of other biological principles are undergirded by quantitative reasoning, including the Hardy-Weinberg Equilibrium of evolution, forensic analysis of DNA and the probability of parentage or criminal activity. Conversely, biology will promote new mathematical discoveries, just as Isaac Newton and Gottfried Leibniz were stimulated by physical problems such as planetary orbits and optical calculations and developed calculus. Hastings et al. (2000) in their NSF report *Quantitative Biology for the 21st Century* develops this thread in more detail, as does the National Academies Press publication, *BIO 2010: Transforming Undergraduate Education for Future Research Biologists* (NRC 2003).

What kind of quantitative skills do we want our biology majors to have if they intend to go to graduate school and become research scientists? The standard requirements at different schools include calculus, with statistics running a poor second. Unless a student has a strong penchant for mathematics or computer competency or is a quantitative masochist, that's it for our requirements. Most students take no more than the minimum.

*BIO 2010* (extracts are reprinted in Appendix B) makes these points: (1) "In contrast to biological research, undergraduate biology education has changed relatively little during the past two decades. The ways in which most future research biologists are educated are geared to the biology of the past, rather than to the biology of the present or future" (p. 1). (2) "Much of today's biomedical research is at the interface between biology and the physical, mathematical, or information sciences. Most colleges and universities already require their biology majors to enroll in courses in mathematics and physical science. However, faculty often do not integrate these subjects into the biology courses they teach." (3) "Most biology majors take no more than one year of calculus, although some also take an additional semester of statistics .... While calculus remains an important topic for future biologists, the committee does not believe biology students should study calculus to the exclusion of other types of mathematics. Newly designed courses in mathematics that cover some calculus as well as the other types of math mentioned above would be suitable for biology majors and would also prove useful to students enrolled in many other undergraduate majors." (4) "One way to start is to add modules into existing biology courses. Throughout this report, modules are mentioned as a way to modify courses without completely revamping the syllabus." As an example of this, see the lab MathBench modules that have been developed by the University of Maryland (Thompson et al. 2010). Also note the BioQUEST site with modules on bioinformatics, quantitative biology, molecular biology, and the math behind biology (*http://bioquest.org*). Changes like these will require a major commitment of faculty and administrators, with faculty development being a central part of such a revolution.

What do I make of this? Most of our students in introductory science courses are not going to be scientists—it is not even a close call. They are just fulfilling a general education requirement, unless it is a course that is catering to biology majors or pre-professional health students. Since the overwhelming number of our students will never take another biology class, our goal in the introductory course should be to show students how science is really practiced and convey to them the excitement of the subject. Quantitative material should be introduced, but only in the context of the subject matter. We should leave the heavy-duty mathematics for the higher-level courses, but even then we should change what we are doing. Taking a page from *BIO 2010*, we should revamp or add modules to our courses by weaving quantitative skills into the material in the context of real-world problems. Moreover, since all schools insist that calculus is the *sine qua non* ingredient for any student who is considering anything remotely scientific, then surely the current course content should be changed. Too many calculus courses seem to emphasize memorizing a set of equations without any apparent connection to the real world; rather, they should be like the integrated two-semester course taught at the University of Tennessee that replaces the traditional calculus course (see Appendix B). This is "A new mathematics sequence that exposes students to statistics, probability, discrete math, linear algebra, calculus, and modeling without requiring that a full semester be spent on each topic." Other examples are presented in the series of articles in the special quantitative issue of the journal *CBE—Life Sciences Education* (2010). Especially note Marsteller et al.'s (2010) list of schools that are using biological examples to teach mathematical concepts and the inventory of colleges and universities with mathematical biology education modules.

## Case Studies and Quantitative Literacy

Now we know several things. Experts believe that mathematics is important, not only for a well-rounded education but because they believe that quantitative literacy skills are essential to making intelligent decisions as citizens. Do students need more than the fundamentals taught in K–12? Some higher education institutions apparently do not think so, for they do not have any math requirements. Other schools, such as my own university, require only a semester of "mathematics" as part of their general education requirements. They include statistics as one of the alternatives, but there are more than 25 other possible options that fulfill the requirement! Obviously, the school does not have a clear vision of what constitutes quantitative literacy and has taken the easy way out of the potential controversy.

Nonetheless, there is a general consensus among the experts: If we are going to go with the standard courses that are on the books, then statistics is the one course that all students should have—scientists and laypersons alike. This point is made indirectly by the AAMC-HHMI report (Appendix A), which lists the course expectations for entering medical students. The same point is made explicitly by the CRAFTY Curriculum Foundations Project (Johnson, Peterson, and Yoshiwara 2002) recommending the courses for students graduating from two-year colleges in technical training. However, if we are going to develop a novel approach, then a practical one-semester course can do the job, such as the one used by the University of Arkansas where quantitative skills are taught via case studies from media sources (Madison et al. 2009; Dingman and Madison 2010; Madison and Dingman 2010).

As for most calculus courses, they are not germane to practically anyone. It is typically a plug and chug experience; i.e., they show you an equation; you memorize it, do a few problems, and then go on to the next equation. There are few opportunities for students to really use the skills on real problems they might encounter in the real world—and of course, few ever will. The course needs a major overhaul, perhaps merging other practical mathematics into a new applied course, such as taught at the University of Tennessee (see Appendix B, p. 513).

So here is the bottom line of this book. All students need some mathematics. They receive the fundamentals in their K–12 education. Once they are in higher education, the kind and extent of their quantitative instruction depends upon their career plans. This training should either be statistics or, even better, a specially designed course that deals with mathematics in an applied manner. This would be the end of most students' math education unless they are headed for specific fields like engineering or advanced fields in biology with a mathematical bent, such as ecology or computational biology. Here is the important point: It is especially important that all students, regardless of their major, leave school knowing what questions to ask when they see data rolled out, like the students graduating from Carleton College.

How can this best be achieved? One way to approach this is to use active learning such as case study teaching. And this can be done in all general science courses, introducing cases whenever possible that have quantitative problems embedded within them. Fortunately, several key resources exist, including websites where case studies can be downloaded along with teaching notes, such as the web-based case collection of the National Center for Case Study Teaching in Science (NCCSTS) at the University at Buffalo (*sciencecases.lib.buffalo.edu*). Currently, the NCCSTS website has about 500 case studies across all science disciplines. Other case collections include the Problem-Based Learning Clearinghouse at the University of Delaware (*https://pblc.nss.udel.edu/Pbl*), Emory University's CASES Online (*www.cse.emory.edu/cases*), and the interactive molecular biology laboratory simulations in the Case It! collection (*www.caseitproject.org*). Many of the cases on these sites have quantitative material, such as tables, graphs, numerical data, and equations that are essential to the case story.

This book includes cases selected from the National Center for Case Study Teaching in Science website (*http://sciencecaase.lib.buffalo.edu*) that develop students' quantitative skills and apply them to solve real-world problems. In this book we present each case along with a list of learning objectives for it. Detailed teaching notes for the cases can be found on our website along with answer keys, which instructors can register to access. The book is designed for college and high school AP biology teachers. We expect that teachers who plan to use the cases will download the case PDF from the website and distribute it to students in class rather than direct students to the website itself where the teaching notes are displayed.

The advantage of these cases is that they teach science in context, not as a set of abstract principles and a jumble of terms without rhyme or reason, but as part of a story so that students can see the relevance of the material. Moreover, in using cases to teach quantitative skills and show their applications to real-world situations, we are inculcating in our students the *practice* of questioning data, not just as a classroom exercise, but as a tool for engaging and understanding the world around them. K–12 teachers will find the cases in-line with the recommendations of the *Next Generation of Science Standards* (*www.nextgenscience.org/next-generation-science-standards*), which lists major biological topics as necessary parts of any curriculum: structure and function, matter and energy in organisms and ecosystems, interdependent relations in ecosystems, inheritance and variation of traits, natural selection and evolution, and understanding the nature of science. The cases included in this book also address the overarching framework presented in *Vision and Change in Undergraduate Biology Education: A Call to Action* (*http://visionandchange.org/files/2011/03/Revised-Vision-and-Change-Final-Report.pdf*), a document prepared by the National Science Foundation and the American Association for the Advancement of Science, which calls for enhanced quantitative and computational expertise in core competencies of biologists, "the ability to use quantitative reasoning" and "the ability to use modeling and simulation," to gain a deeper understanding of the dynamics and complexity of biological systems.

Our book is divided into sections. These mirror the topical sections one finds in many introductory biology textbooks. We have organized cases in the following areas: Scientific Method, Chemistry of Life, the Cell, Microbiology, Genetics, Molecular Biology, Evolution, Plant Form and Function, Animal Form and Function, Health, Ecology and Behavior, and Biosphere and Conservation. High school, community college, and undergraduate college teachers can use these cases to illustrate many of the basic principles of biology, but more importantly, how science is really conducted. The cases—most of which are based on real events and problems—should engage students and put quantitative skills to use, hopefully to illustrate just how necessary these competencies are to understanding our world, which is awash with numbers and people who are willing to exploit them for their own particular agendas.

## References

American Association for the Advancement of Science (AAAS). 2009. *Vision and change in undergraduate biology education: A call to action.* Washington, DC: AAAS.

American Association of Colleges of Pharmacy (AACP). 2012. *Summary of pre-professional course requirements by pharmacy degree institution. www.aacp.org/career/grants/Documents/2012-13_PharmacyPre-RequisiteInformation.pdf*

Brewer, C. A., and L. J. Gross. 2003. Training ecologists to think with uncertainty in mind. *Ecology* 84: 1412–1414.

Carleton College. 2011a. What is quantitative reasoning? *serc.carleton.edu/quirk/forstudents/index.html*

Carelton College. 2011b. 10 foundational quantitative reasoning questions. *wiki.carleton.edu/display/itskb/Things+to+Think+About+When+Writing+About+Data*

Carnevale, A. P., and D. M. Desrochers. 2003. The democratization of mathematics. In *Quantitative literacy: Why numeracy matters for schools and colleges*, ed. B. L. Madison and L. Arthur Steen, pp. 21–31. Princeton, NJ: National Council on Education and the Disciplines.

CBE—Life Sciences Education. 2010. *Special issue in quantitative biology*. 9 (3).

Cohen, J. E. 2004. Mathematics is biology's next microscope, only better; Biology is mathematics' next physics, only better. *PLoS Biology* 2 (12): e439. doi:10.1371/journal.pbio.0020439

Cohen, P. C. 2003. Democracy and the numerate citizen: quantitative literacy in historical perspective." In *Quantitative literacy: Why numeracy matters for schools and colleges*, ed. B. L. Madison and L. Arthur Steen, pp. 7–20. Princeton, NJ: National Council on Education and the Disciplines.

Davidian, M., and T. A. Louis. 2012. Why statistics. *Science* 336 (6077): 12.

Dingman, S., and B. Madison, 2010. Quantitative reasoning in the contemporary world, 1: The course and its challenges. *Numeracy* 3 (2): 1–16.

Gates, S. J., Jr., and C. Mirkin. 2012. Engage to excel. *Science* 335 (6076): 1545.

Hastings, A., et al. 2000. *Quantitative biology for the 21st century. www.maa.org/mtc/quant-bio-report.pdf*

Johnson, E., J. C. Peterson, and K. Yoshiwara. 2002. Technical mathematics: Biotechnology and environmental technology. Mathematical Association of America: CRAFTY curriculum foundations project. *Focus* 22 (8): 157–180.

Madison, B. L., and L. A. Steen, eds. 2003. *Quantitative literacy: Why numeracy matters for schools and colleges*. Princeton, NJ: National Council on Education and the Disciplines.

Madison, B. L., S. Boersma, C. L. Diefenderfer, and S. W. Dingman. 2009. *Case studies for quantitative reasoning: A casebook of media articles*, 2nd ed. New York: Pearson.

Madison, B. L., and S. W. Dingman. 2010. Quantitative reasoning in the contemporary world, 2: Focus questions for the numeracy community. *Numeracy* 3 (2): 1–16.

Marsteller, P., L. de Pillis, A. Findley, K. Joplin, J. Pelesko, K. Nelson, K. Thompson, D. Usher, and J. Watkins. 2010. Toward integration: From quantitative biology to mathbio-biomath? *CBE—Life Sciences Education* 9: 165–171.

National Governors Association Center for Best Practices, Council of Chief State School Officers, 2010. *Common core state standards for mathematics*. Washington, DC: National Governors Association Center for Best Practices, Council of Chief State School Officers.

National Research Council. 2012. *A framework for K–12 science education: Practices, crosscutting concepts, and core ideas*. Washington, DC: National Academies Press.

National Research Council, Committee on Undergraduate Biology Education to Prepare Research Scientists for the 21st Century. 2003. *BIO2010, transforming undergraduate education for future research biologists*. Washington, DC: National Academies Press.

Packer, A. 2003. What mathematics should "everyone" know and be able to do? In *Quantitative literacy: Why numeracy matters for schools and colleges*, ed. B. L. Madison and L. Arthur Steen, pp. 33–42. Princeton, NJ: National Council on Education and the Disciplines.

Sadler, P. M., and R. H. Tai. 2007. The two high-school pillars supporting college science. *Science* 317 (5837): 457–458.

Thompson, K., K. Nelson, G. Marbach-Ad, M. Keller, and W. Fagan. 2010. Online interactive teaching modules enhance quantitative proficiency of introductory biology students. *CBE—Life Sciences Education* 9: 277–283.

Tobias, S. 1990. *They're not dumb, they're different: Stalking the second tier*. Tucson, AZ: Research Corporation.

Tobias, S. 1992. *Revitalizing undergraduate science: Why some things work and most don't*. Tucson, AZ: Research Corporation.

CHAPTER 2

# A CASE FULL OF NUMBERS

## The Why and Wherefore of Teaching With Cases

*Clyde Freeman Herreid*

Numbers mean nothing without context. That context might be minimal; after all, students memorize the multiplication tables with little more than a stern voice to drive them on. And problems at the back of a chapter in an algebra or calculus book only give hints that learning how to manipulate equations might have some conceivable use—someday, somehow, somewhere. Still, a more compelling case can be made for numeracy if numbers and other quantitative skills actually fit into the life experiences of a student. That is where case studies come in.

Cases are stories with an educational message (Herreid 2007). That message can be more persuasive if actual data are used, at least with the cognoscenti; but, the audience had better be prepared to appreciate those data, otherwise we are just whistling in the wind. So, the argument is this: cases and numbers are both enriched if they are used together. This book is testimony to that conviction.

This brings me to the point of this chapter. It will be helpful to summarize what we know about case studies. My plan is to cover the evidence for the effectiveness of case-based teaching. Then, I will outline the different types of case studies and how they are used in the classroom. As we go along, it will hopefully become evident which cases might best be used if the teacher's aim is to enhance the quantitative skills of the students. Scottish mathematician and physicist, William Thompson, aka Lord Kelvin (1889, p. 73), was convinced of their importance when with his usual hubris he pronounced: "When you can measure what you are speaking about, and express it in numbers, you know something about it; but when you cannot measure it, when you cannot express it in numbers, your knowledge is of a meagre and unsatisfactory kind." One should be perhaps more modest. This is the same Lord Kelvin who claimed that Darwin (who seldom used numbers) was wrong because by his calculations, the age of the Earth was far too short for evolution to have occurred. Sociologist Bruce Cameron (1963, p. 13) had a clearer perspective, saying, "Not everything that can be counted counts, and not everything that counts can be counted."

### Effectiveness of Case-Based Teaching

When I was first getting started with case-based teaching, I had the good fortune to meet Bill Welty, a master practitioner of the method, who was teaching business courses at Pace University (Welty 1989). He regaled me with the tale that faculty in the law and business schools at Harvard had pioneered the method at the turn of the 20th century with great success and that this practice had swept the country. Donning my cynic's cap, I asked him the obvious question: "What is the evidence that case-based instruction is better than just plain lecturing?" His response, with a twinkle in his eye, was, "Well, Harvard uses it!" Hmmm.

When pressed further, Welty had to admit that there really wasn't, at least back then, much of a serious effort to study the effectiveness of case-based instruction. The situation has dramatically changed, especially once those of us in STEM education became involved. Before rifling through the literature, however, it is well to emphasize that Welty's answer is not as superficial and flippant as it appears at first glance. Harvard does use it and so do hundreds of other law and business schools across the world. There are case repositories of thousands of cases maintained at places like Harvard and the University of Western Ontario, used by faculty across the globe. So, even if the data are meager, evidently there are hundreds, if not thousands, of teachers that are convinced of the case-method's efficacy. And the fact that Harvard does it and so do countless others, does indeed, mean a great deal.

On a more exact level, what do we know? A significant body of literature has accumulated on the assessment of case teaching and active learning strategies, especially since the case method known as Problem-Based Learning has taken root in medical education. Below is a sample of the relevant research. There are three significant take-home messages:

1. Students learn better, more, and at a deeper level from case study and active learning than from lecturing. Moreover, they enjoy the experience more, have better attitudes toward the subject, develop better social skills, become more articulate, and are more tolerant of differing viewpoints than with the lecture method (Johnson and Johnson 1989, 1993; Hoag et al. 2005; Lundeberg et al. 1999; Bergland et al. 2006; Hake 1998; Udovic et al. 2002; Cliff and Wright 1996; Dinan and Frydrychowski 1995; Walters 1999; Bramble and Workman 2007; Goulet 2008).
2. Students underrepresented in science professions, specifically women and minorities, especially benefit from the case study and active learning approach (Lundeberg and Moch 1995; Lundeberg et al. 1998, 2002; Springer et al. 1999; Pai et al. 2010; Wolter et al. 2010; Kang et al. 2012).
3. Students realize these benefits regardless of their major or career path (Lundeberg et al. 2011; Wolter et al. 2010; Kang et al. 2012, plus the above).

## Types of Case Studies

There are various ways to classify case studies. To get a flavor of the various dimensions by which cases may be judged, we asked the 15,000+ members on the Listserv for the National Center for Case Study Teaching in Science what they looked for in a case (Herreid et al. 2012). More than 1,300 responded, with their answers tending to fall into clusters of categories. Their favorite cases deal with a topic pertinent to the courses they teach, not surprisingly. They also told us that to be successful a case should be realistic, relevant to their students, current, and well written; include data; emphasize critical thinking; and have an appropriate classroom teaching method. This "case wish list" can be used as a list of criteria for categorizing and judging cases.

Several systemic approaches have been made to catalog cases. Here are three:

***Case Difficulty.*** How difficult should a case be and how much information should be included? Some years ago I grappled with this issue (Herreid 2005), and I wasn't the first; case study teachers of law and business have been struggling with it for a hundred years. The answer depends upon a host of factors, including the age and sophistication of the students. I concluded if cases are too complex, there is nothing but frustration for everyone, but if they are too simple, they are downright boring. My advice is to look for the Goldilocks solution: Make the cases just right and match the case level to the situation at hand.

Business professors at the University of Western Ontario created a useful tool for designing case studies that they call the "Case Difficulty Cube" (Erskine et al. 1981). The cube, shown in Figure 2.1, has three dimensions: analytical, conceptual, and presentational. Cases can be simple or complex along each dimension.

**FIGURE 2.1.**

Case Difficulty Cube (showing how cases can be created along three dimensions of increasing difficulty: analytical, conceptual, and presentational; Erskine, Leenders, and Mauffette-Leenders 1981).

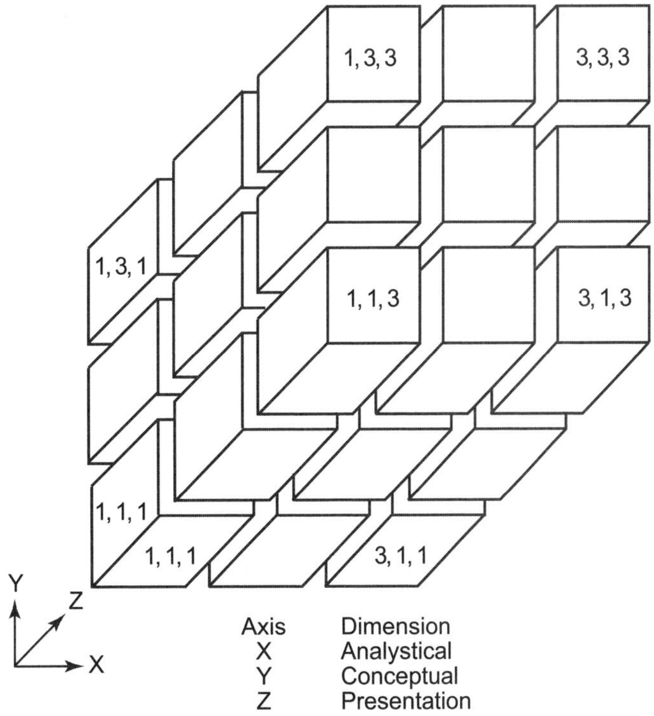

As I summarized in my 2005 article, along the analysis scale, the simplest case would be one where you give the students both a problem and solution and then ask them, does the solution fit the problem or are there alternatives? (Say, a dog is suspected of having rabies and the owner decides to shoot the animal. Is this the appropriate response?) The second degree of difficulty is to give a problem (rabid dog?) and ask the students for a reasonable solution. The third degree of difficulty is to present a situation and ask students to define the problem as well as work out a solution or solutions to it.

The conceptual dimension refers to the level of difficulty of the material presented in the case. The simplest level would be a case that has a single straightforward concept. (Here is a dog that is foaming at the mouth and acting strangely.) The more concepts you introduce, the greater the difficulty. (Maybe the dog has bitten a child, or, at a higher level, the dog has bitten a child and the child loves the animal and the animal is a dog show champion. Still higher: A wolf has bitten your dog and several days later your dog has bitten your child. Neither wolf nor dog is showing symptoms. You are a microbiologist, backpacking out in the wilderness without contact with the outside world and would require several days to get back to civilization. You have waited years to make this trip with your son, who seems okay ….) The third level of difficulty requires significant explanation, clarification, and repetition for most students.

The presentational dimension deals with how much information the case should contain and how clearly it should be presented. The simplest level would be to have only the data that is needed clearly presented in text, table, or graph, and the case would typically be short. For the second level the case is longer and has some irrelevant data in it. For the third level the case would be even longer and may have considerable extraneous information, require significant data sifting, and might have missing pieces of information students would have to research on their own.

So, using the Case Difficulty Cube model, the most difficult case will be at 3,3,3—hard, hard, and hard along all dimensions. Conversely, the simplest would be at the 1,1,1 level. This case you might give to a beginning student who has never seen case studies and is in the early part of an introductory course. As the student matures and the curriculum advances, so would the cases in terms of their complexity.

***Case Purpose.*** Another system is to characterize a case on the basis of its purpose in the classroom (Herreid 2009). Thus, there are cases that can be called "trigger cases" whose primary purpose is to stimulate interest in the subject area of the case. The expectation is that the details of the topic/problem will be developed in later classes and homework. Consequently, when the case is first introduced and discussed, the conversation will be superficial and there will be many matters that need further study. Such cases are typically introduced at the beginning of a class theme or unit to whet the appetite of the students.

At the other end of the spectrum, we find "capstone cases." These are used to summarize, integrate, and review information on a topic, and usually also put this information into a broader context. The case may include a lot of data as well as overarching questions that can be treated with sophistication since at the point they encounter such a case, students should have a wealth of information under their belt.

Although trigger cases and capstone cases may be structured in very different ways, they need not be. In fact, the same case can be used, but very different classroom results should occur, for on the one hand students are naïve about the subject, while on the other hand they are better informed.

***Teaching Method.*** Faculty have strong biases about this. In the survey mentioned above, teachers leaving the lecture method for active learning strategies much prefer that students work in small groups. But there are other ways to tell stories in the classroom (Herreid 1998, 2011).

- ***Lecture method.*** James Conant used this approach to teach historical cases to students at Harvard in the 1940s and 1950s (Conant 1957). He returned from his position as science advisor to President Franklin Roosevelt during World War II, convinced that the average person does not know how science is conducted. Vowing to correct this, he started using the case study approach to teach about the various major breakthroughs in the history of science. Instead of giving a standard lecture about a discovery such as the Second Law of Thermodynamics, he told a story; he put the discovery in the context of the time, detailing the steps and missteps along the way. I do a similar presentation in my general biology class dealing with the theory of evolution where I come to class dressed as Charles Darwin and in an awful English accent relate how I developed the concept of natural selection. It is storytelling, but in the lecture format. Although it may be a compelling narrative, it is still a lecture with all of its advantages and disadvantages, chief among the latter the fact that information flows in one direction: from instructor to student.
- ***Clicker case method.*** Case-based teaching is difficult to use in large classrooms where discussions are important. But with the advent of personal response systems ("clickers"), a new type of case teaching became possible (Herreid 2006). In this approach, the teacher presents a scenario as part of his lecture and then, as the story unfolds, periodically poses multiple-choice questions. The students are then asked to individually choose the correct answer and click it into their handheld, remote-control unit. The data are transmitted via radio frequency to a computer and the results displayed on a PowerPoint slide as a graph. Everyone can see the results and the instructor can then discuss the implications of the answers, calling on students. An example of a clicker case dealing with the Nobel

Prize–winning discovery that most ulcers are caused by bacteria can be seen at *http://sciencecases.lib.buffalo.edu/cs/collection/detail.asp?case_id=483&id=483.* It is loaded with questions that deal with quantitative reasoning. There are another couple of dozen examples of clicker cases also available at *http://sciencecases.lib.buffalo.edu/cs/collection.* Information flow is predominantly from the faculty to the students in the way of a lecture, but because there is feedback from the students as they click in their answers, the professor can clearly modify his or her presentation to match the students' knowledge or lack thereof.

- ***Discussion method.*** This is the classical method of case teaching used in business and law. There are many variants (see Herreid 1998). If we were to drop in on a Harvard law or business class, we would likely see the professor, perhaps wearing a bowtie and blazer with leather patches on his elbows, standing in front of 70 intense students seated in a rows. The professor would have given them a criminal or civil case to analyze and now, as he paced in front of the room, would be asking probing questions of the students as to how they might judge the evidence in the case. He would be relentless as he pressed for their various opinions and justifications. This would last the period, and next time they would move on to another case. Information flow would be a two-way street: back and forth from instructor to students, typically with little interchange between students in the classroom, except in their preparation for class, when they would regularly engage in heated exchanges.
- ***Small-group methods.*** If we were to drop in on a class using this method, it might look chaotic, with students eagerly exclaiming their own viewpoints and challenging everyone else's. The students would be sitting in groups of four or five, perhaps leaping to their feet to write on the board, with their teammates excitedly proclaiming their counter opinions. A faculty or older student facilitator would be in each group to guide the conversation along productive lines. The instructor, in a corner of the room, might be benignly watching the discussions unfold or she might be hailed by a group to adjudicate a dispute. To initiate this discussion, the instructor may have assigned a written case study on global climate change and evidence for and against it. Each of the team members might have been given different perspectives to investigate prior to the lesson, say a paleontologist, a coal mine owner, a meteorologist, a farmer, and an economist. Their job in the small group discussion would be to attempt to come to a consensus about a government policy to establish a carbon tax on companies. Again, the small-group approach has many variations (Herreid 1998), but a favorite is Problem-Based Learning, or PBL, where the problem is presented in stages over several days and students have a chance to make use of various

Good methods, shows how students respond

ues associated with the problem (see Duch et al. 2001).
odel to introduce data into cases. The information
een student members of each group, with a guiding
d a facilitator who might be present.
n flow between methods.

Information Flow in Case Teaching. Student interaction and feedback is least in those methods at the top of the diagram and greatest at the bottom.

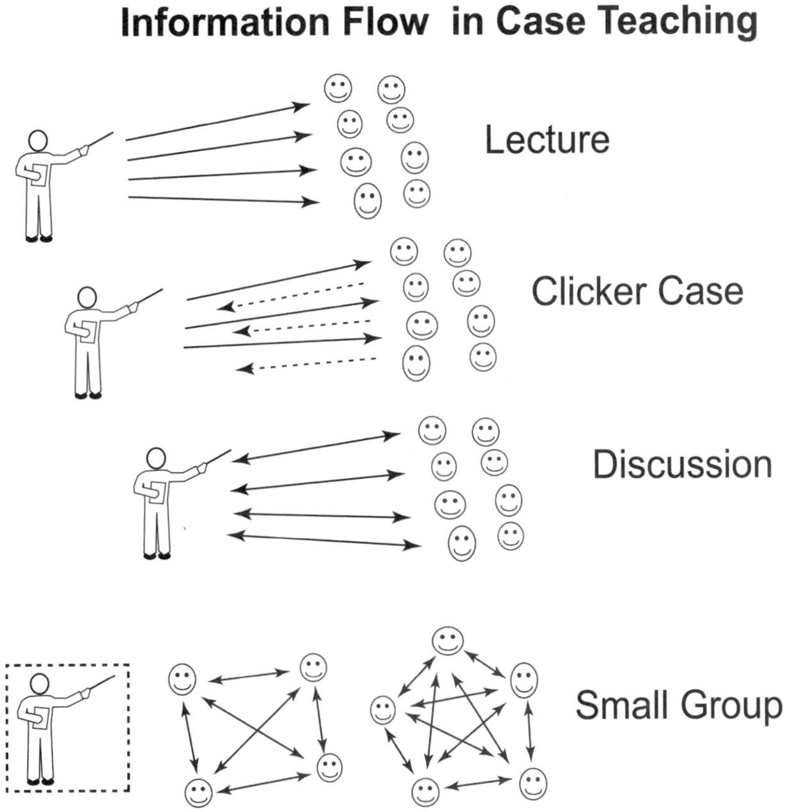


- ***Individual case method.*** Students can work alone on cases. If this is a solitary assignment, students clearly miss out on rich discussions that are present in other classroom formats. Nonetheless, individual cases can be effective. Here is one creative example, called the "dialogue paper." Suppose an instructor wished to consider a controversial topic where there are two reasonable sides to the issue. Of course, there are several formats that might be used to bring the controversy into focus, including public hearing or debate formats, but a dialogue paper functions well. This is how it works: The professor tells the class a little about a controversy, for example, the use of embryonic stem cells. She then assigns everyone the task of writing a dialogue paper that meets these criteria: (1) The paper must be the conversation between two intelligent people on opposite sides of the debate over the use of embryonic stem cells. (2) The first paragraph or two should outline the issue and give the setting for the meeting of two individuals, perhaps in an informal atmosphere. (3) There must be at least 20 substantive exchanges between them; i.e., these should not be comments like, "Sally, you're a jerk." (4) Every time a person makes a claim, there should be an in-text citation to the source and a full citation for it included in the references section of the paper. (5) At the end of the dialogue, there must be a section of the paper that discusses the student's own opinion on the subject with a rationalization spelled out. Examples of dialogue papers can be seen at *http://library.buffalo.edu/libraries/projects/cases/endangered.html* and at *http://library.buffalo.edu/libraries/projects/cases/cloning.html*. This technique is a powerful way to get students to seriously engage with a controversial subject without forcing them into the limelight of a public discourse. But, of course, the professor may have other things in mind; this paper doesn't have to be the end of the story. After the papers have been written, now with the students primed, a vigorous classroom discussion can follow.

## Case Studies and the Cone of Learning

It should be evident that the different case methods can all be used to introduce quantitative skills. But if a teacher wants to know if the skills are really being understood, she must get some feedback. The lecture method is not designed to accomplish that task; the instructor must wait until a homework exercise or an exam to find out the potentially appalling news. Similarly, the individual case method does not inherently have a feedback mechanism built into the process, unless the professor is meeting with the individual student as he or she moves along. All of the other case methods have a feedback mechanism *en suite*. But the degree of interaction among the students and the teacher varies enormously with the different methods. It is no surprise that the small group approach is the one that seems to promise the greatest learning gains and is the one that is favored by most case teachers (Herreid et al. 2011).

One way to visualize the degree of interaction in the class is by superimposing the various case methods alongside the Cone of Learning. The latter has a checkered history that must be mentioned. In 1946, Edgar Dale, a professor in audio-visual learning, proposed what he called the Cone of Experience where he arranged different methods of teaching along a cone-shaped diagram, with the most abstract ways of presenting material at the apex and the most concrete ways at the base (see Figure 2.3). He pointed out that those experiences that were the most concrete were easiest for students to grasp and recall. He presented no evidence to substantiate his claim but appeared not to have stirred any controversy with the model.

**FIGURE 2.3.**

The Cone of Experience as Envisioned by Edgar Dale (1946). Subjects are most easily learned if they are experienced by concrete methods and the most senses are involved.

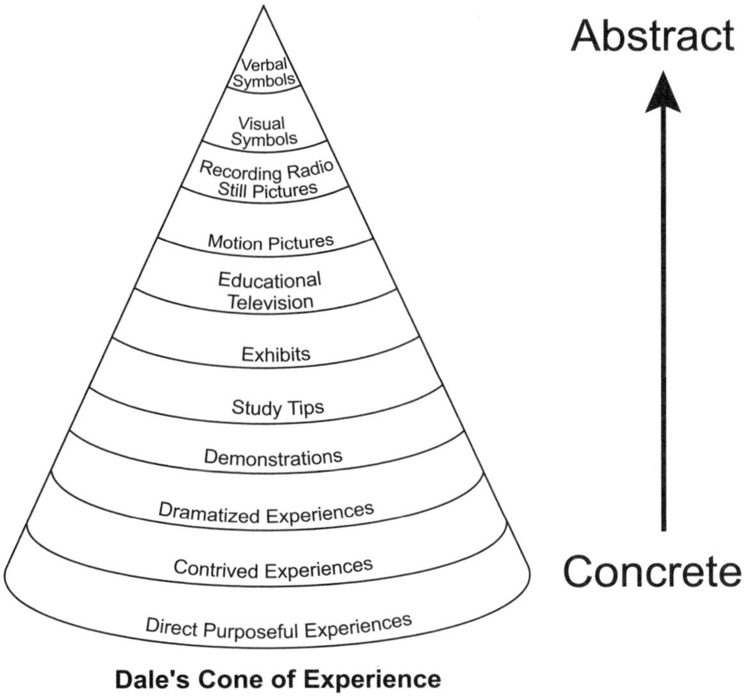


Over the years this cone was modified by a variety of hands, some known and others not, into a very different model, this time with the cone featuring different ways of teaching and often with numerical values attached claiming to express the degree of retention of learning. All of the changes seem to have been made without a lick of evidence. One common version is presented in Figure 2.4 (p. 28) as published by Thomas Lord (2007), but at least in this instance the author had carried out an experiment that gave some sense of validity for the notion that we can quantify the degree of learning. Thus, the lecture method is claimed to yield 4–8% retention of learning after six weeks whereas methods involving cooperative learning interactions can produce up to 98% retention. These values need to be taken with a grain of salt because the experimental data on which the model is based was a simple jigsaw puzzle. But even with the checkered history of the Cone (aka the Pyramid) of Learning, the model makes intuitive sense and seldom has met with serious analysis. Rather, it has uncritically found its way into numerous faculty development workshops. Indeed, the model corresponds to numerous reports that document that the greatest learning occurs in classrooms where active learning is used, a number of which I cited earlier in this chapter. So, in spite of the dubious parentage of the Cone of Learning and the quantitative claims that are made, I have dared to align the various methods of case-based teaching alongside the model in Figure 2.4.

**FIGURE 2.4.**

The Cone of Learning With Data From Lord (2007) and the Major Types of Case Study Teaching Methods Aligned Next to the Cone (after Herreid 2006).

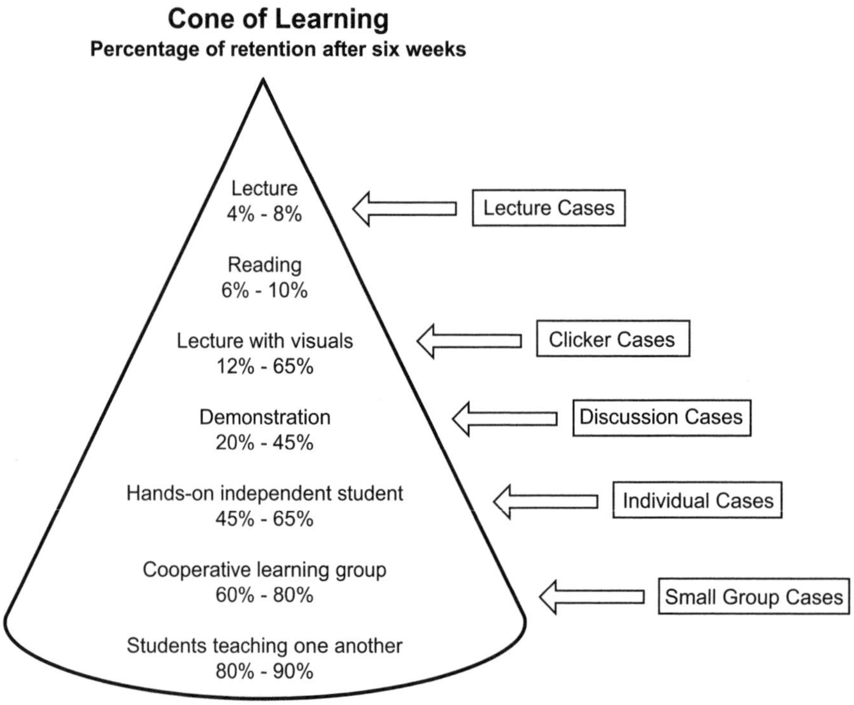


This clearly has implications for those of us who wish to introduce quantitative skills into the classroom. Once again, if you wish to get feedback about how your students are doing, the base of the cone is where your teaching should be. And if you wish to guide the students' quantitative development, the base is where the action is.

## The Flipped Classroom and the Search for the Silver Bullet

Innovations are common in education as we all search for better ways to get our message across. The "flipped classroom" is one of the most recent, but it will sound strikingly familiar. It proposes to get students to prepare ahead of time so that their classroom activities are more meaningful.

The flipped classroom works this way: Students are supposed to read or listen to and watch videos at home on the basic lecture material that they would normally experience in class. Once they are in the class, they encounter exercises and problems they would normally complete outside of class at home and do the work instead under the guidance of their watchful teacher. Thus, the typical classroom activities and home activities are switched or flipped.

There are two problems that must be surmounted. First is the obvious one: you have to get the students to actually prepare at home, which is usually done by watching short videos. This challenge is met by having quizzes or problems that have to be handed in before class starts. The second difficulty is that there must be appropriate material for the students to watch. This challenge is now partially being met with videos that are produced by groups such as the Khan Academy (*www.khanacademy.org*) and BozemanScience (*http://bozemanscience.com/science-videos/*) or by faculty by creating their own using software programs like Camtasia, PaperShow, and ShowMe or apps on the iPad like Educreations and Explain Everything, which they then post to YouTube, iTunes U, and Podcasts (Vodcasting) or on course management systems like Blackboard or Moodle.

What does this have to do with case studies? The answer runs like this: One of the strongest criticisms of the case method is that discussion of cases can take a long time in the classroom. This means that often a teacher may not be able to cover the same amount of subject material as they need to, especially if state or national standards must be met. What to do? Faculty typically forsake the use of case study teaching in order to meet their coverage needs. But with the flipped classroom approach, the difficulty can be surmounted. Students can be assigned the standard lecture material to cover at home by watching videos and then, when they come into the classroom, use their new knowledge by applying it to a real-world case study.

The flipped classroom is not the first innovation that depends upon student outside preparation. In the past couple of decades we have heard of the virtues of "Team Learning," developed by Larry Michaelsen (1992), "Just-in-Time Teaching" (JiTT; Novak et al. 1999), hybrid courses (Buzzetto-More and Sweat-Guy 2006), blended courses (Wu 2010), cooperative learning (Slavin 1990), collaborative learning (Dillenbourg 1999), and process-oriented guided inquiry learning (POGIL; Farrell et al. 1999; Hanson and Wolfskill 2000). These and related methodologies share some of the same advantages as the flipped classroom as well as the two major challenges identified above. Like the flipped classroom, all of these methods allow instructors to cover principles, facts, and terms as part of out-of-class student preparation and to use class time to deliver the application side where students grapple with real-world problems and see the material in context. All of them can be used to introduce students to quantitative reasoning. Regardless of which active learning strategy you might choose, I strongly urge you to take as a serious challenge introducing your students to statistics and numeracy as tools for understanding, analyzing, and solving the many and various problems that beset the planet.

## References


Bergland, M., M. A. Lundeberg, K. Klyczek, D. Hoffman, J. Emmons, C. Martin, K. Marsh, J. Sweet, J. Werner, and M. Jarvis-Uetz. 2006. Exploring biotechnology using case-based multimedia. *American Biology Teacher* 68 (2): 81–86.

Bramble, J., and M. Workman. 2007. Data-rich case studies improve students' abilities to interpret graphs in a large non-majors course. *Teaching Issues and Experiments in Ecology* 5. *http://tiee.esa.org/vol/v5/research/bramble/pdf/Bramble&Workman_2007.pdf*

Buzzetto-More, N. A., and R. Sweat-Guy. 2006. Incorporating the hybrid learning model into minority education at a historically black university. *Journal of Information Technology Education* 5: 153–162.

Cameron, W. B. 1963. *Informal sociology: A casual introduction to sociological thinking.* New York, NY: Random House.

Cliff, W., and A. Wright. 1996. Directed case study method for teaching human anatomy and physiology. *Advances in Physiology Education* 270: 19–28.

Conant, J. B. 1957. *Case histories in experimental science*. Cambridge, MA: Harvard University Press.

Dale, E. 1946. *Audio-visual methods in teaching*. New York: Dryden Press.

Dillenbourg, P. 1999. *Collaborative learning: Cognitive and computational approaches*. New York: Elsevier Science.

Dinan, F., and V. Frydrychowski. 1995. A team learning method for organic chemistry. *Journal Chemical Education* 72 (5): 429–431.

Duch, B., S. Groh, and D. Allen, eds. 2001. *The power of problem-based learning*. Sterling, VA: Stylus.

Erskine, J. A., M. R. Leenders, and L. A. Mauffette-Leenders. 1981. *Teaching with cases*. London, ON, Canada: Research and Publications, Division School of Business Administration, University of Western Ontario.

Farrell, J. J., R. S. Moog, and J. N. Spencer. 1999. A guided inquiry chemistry course. *Journal of Chemical Education* 76 (4): 570–574.

Goulet, T. 2008. The use of case study teaching in a non-majors introductory biology class. Poster abstract at NSF CCLI PI Conference, Washington DC, Aug. 13–15, 2008.

Hake, R. 1998. Interactive engagement versus traditional methods: A six-thousand student survey of mechanics test data for introductory physics courses. *American Journal of Physics* 66 (1): 64–74.

Hanson, D., and T. Wolfskill. 2000. Process workshops: A new model for instruction. *Journal of Chemical Education* 77: 120–129.

Herreid, C. F. 1998. Sorting potatoes for Miss Bonner: Bringing order to case-study methodology through a classification scheme. *Journal of College Science Teaching* 27: 236–239.

Herreid, C. F. 2005. Too much, too little, or just right? *Journal of College Science Teaching* 35 (1): 12–14.

Herreid, C. F. 2006. "Clicker" cases. *Journal of College Science Teaching* 36 (2): 43–47.

Herreid, C. F. 2007. *Start with a story: The case study method of teaching college science*. Arlington, VA: NSTA Press.

Herreid, C. F. 2009. Trigger cases versus capstone cases. *Journal of College Science Teaching* 38 (2): 68–71.

Herreid, C. F., N. A. Schiller, K. F. Herreid, and C. Wright. 2011. In case you are interested: A survey of case study teachers. *Journal of College Science Teaching* 40 (4): 76–80.

Herreid, C. F., N. A. Schiller, K. F. Herreid, and C. Wright. 2012. My favorite case and what makes it so. *Journal of College Science Teaching* 42 (2): 70–75.

Hoag, K., J. Lillie, and R. Hoppe. 2005. Piloting case-based instruction in a didactic clinical immunology course. *Clinical Laboratory Science* 18 (4): 213–220.

Johnson, D. W., and R. T. Johnson. 1989. *Cooperation and competition: Theory and research*. Edina, MN: Interaction Book Co.

Johnson, D. W., and R. T. Johnson. 1993. Cooperative learning: Where we have been, where we are going. *Cooperative Learning and College Teaching* 3 (2): 6–9.

Kang, H., M. A. Lundeberg, B. Wolter, B., R. delMas, and C. F. Herreid. 2012. Gender differences in student performance in large lecture classrooms using personal response systems ("clickers") with narrative case studies. *Learning, Media and Technology* 37 (1): 53–76.

Kelvin, B. W. T. 1889. Lecture on "Electrical units of measurement" (3 May 1883). In *Popular Lectures, vol. I:* 73.

Lord, T. 2007. Revisiting the cone of learning—Is it a reliable way to link instruction method with knowledge recall? *Journal of College Science Teaching* 37 (2): 14–17.

Lundeberg, M. A., and S. Moch. 1995. The influence of social interaction on cognition: Connected learning in science. *Journal of Higher Education* 66 (3): 310–335.

Lundeberg, M. A., B. B. Levin, and H. Harrington, eds. 1999. *Who learns what from cases and how: The research base for teaching and learning with cases*. Mahwah, NJ: Lawrence Erlbaum Associates, Inc.

Lundeberg, M. A., K. Mogen, M. Bergland, K. Klyczek, D. Johnson, and E. MacDonald. 2002. Fostering ethical awareness about human genetics through multimedia-based cases. *Journal of College Science Teaching* 32 (1): 64–69.

Lundeberg, M. A., B. Shearer, M. Bergland, and K. Klyczek. 1998. Fostering scientific inquiry, confidence, and motivation through case-based instructional technology. Paper presented at the Annual Meeting of the American Educational Research Association Conference, San Diego, CA.

Lundeberg, M. A., H. Kang, B. Wolter, R. delMas, N. Armstrong, B. Borsari, N. Boury, P. Brickman, K. Hannam, C. Heinz, T. Horvath, M. Knabb, T. Platt, N. Rice, B. Rogers, J. Sharp, E. Ribbens, K. S. Maier, M. Deschryver, R. Hagley, T. Goulet, and C. F. Herreid. 2011. Context matters: Increasing understanding with interactive clicker case studies. *Educational Technology Research & Development* 59: 645–671.

Michaelsen, L. K. 1992. Team learning: A comprehensive approach for the harnessing of small groups in higher education. *To Improve the Academy* 11: 107–122.

Novak, G. M., E. T. Patterson, A. D. Gavrin, and W. Christian. 1999. *Just-in-time-teaching: Blending active learning with web technology*. New York: Prentice Hall.

Pai, A., T. Benning, N. Woods, G. McGinnis, J. Chu, J. Netherton, and C. Bauerle. 2010. The effectiveness of a case study-based first-year biology class at a black women's college. *Journal of College Science Teaching* 40 (2): 32–39.

Slavin, R. E. 1990. *Cooperative learning*. Englewood Cliffs, NJ: Prentice-Hall.

Springer, L., M. E. Stanne, and S. S. Donovan. 1999. Effects of small-group learning on undergraduates in science, mathematics, engineering, and technology: A meta-analysis. *Review Educational Research* 69 (1): 21–51.

Udovic, D., D. Morris, A. Dickman, J. Postlewait, and P. Wetherwax. 2002. Workshop Biology: Demonstrating the effectiveness of active learning in an introductory biology course. Bioscience 52 (3): 272–281.

Walters, M. R. 1999. Case stimulated learning within endocrine physiology lectures: An approach applicable to other disciplines. *Advances in Physiology Education* 21 (1): S74–S78.

Welty, W. M. 1989. Discussion method teaching. *Change* 26 (4): 41–49.

Wolter, B. J., M. A. Lundeberg, H. Kang, and C. F. Herreid. 2010. Students' perceptions of using personal response systems ("clickers") with cases in science. *Journal of College Science Teaching* 40 (4): 70–75.

Wu, J., R. D. Tennyson, and T. Hsia. 2010. A study of student satisfaction in a blended e-learning system environment. *Computers & Education* 55: 155–164.

CHAPTER 3

# MATH AND DATA EXPLORATION

*Dennis Liu*

Biology is well suited for mathematical description, from the perfect geometry of viruses, to equations that describe the flux of ions across cellular membranes, to computationally intensive models for protein folding. For this short web review, however, I'm going to focus on how mathematics helps us as biologists sort, evaluate, and draw conclusions about our data. Just as computer technology has revolutionized lab work, computers have revolutionized data analysis, in particular with a host of graphically driven methods for sorting, evaluating, and comparing data. The highly technical, often automated, and computationally driven biology of today makes it important to keep students aware of the importance of understanding the underlying mathematics. Computers might seem magical to students, but they only perform the calculations humans tell them to do.

Two independent, ongoing international assessment programs, Trends in International Mathematics and Science Study (TIMSS) and Program for International Student Assessment (PISA), are a perennial source of angst for those who care about education. Students in some wealthy nations, such as the United States, do not perform nearly as well as one might hope on these tests. Those interested in U.S. performance might find it educational to visit the National Center for Educational Statistics (NCES, U.S. Department of Education) website devoted to TIMSS at *http://nces.ed.gov/timss*. TIMSS testing takes place in fourth and eighth grade, so I invite you to "dare to compare" and see whether you are smarter than a fourth or eighth grader. The Dare to Compare section of the NCES website offers tests based on actual assessment items in the TIMSS tests for science and math (*http://nces.ed.gov/nceskids/eyk*; Figure 3.1, p. 34). When you solve a problem incorrectly, you can see the reasoning for the correct answer and even compare your performance to the average performance in various U.S. regions (are you smarter than students in your region?). Dare to Compare is part of the NCES Kids' Zone (Figure 3.2, p. 34) that also has a very nice feature on graphing that includes tutorials and interactive tools for creating graphs.

I took an eighth-grade sample math test, and I missed a question that required me to use a box and whisker plot. The box and whisker plot is in my son's eighth-grade curriculum but was not in mine because it was invented by John Tukey in 1977. My ignorance represents the attitude of many biologists toward math and statistics; if our own research or teaching doesn't require us to be conversant in a particular aspect, we ignore it. Fortunately, several sites offered ways for me to quickly learn this statistical representation. In the K–12 arena, Shodor, a nonprofit organization devoted to improving math and science education

**FIGURE 3.1.**

The U.S. Department of Education Dare to Compare website offers sample tests from the TIMSS math and science test banks for fourth and eighth grades.

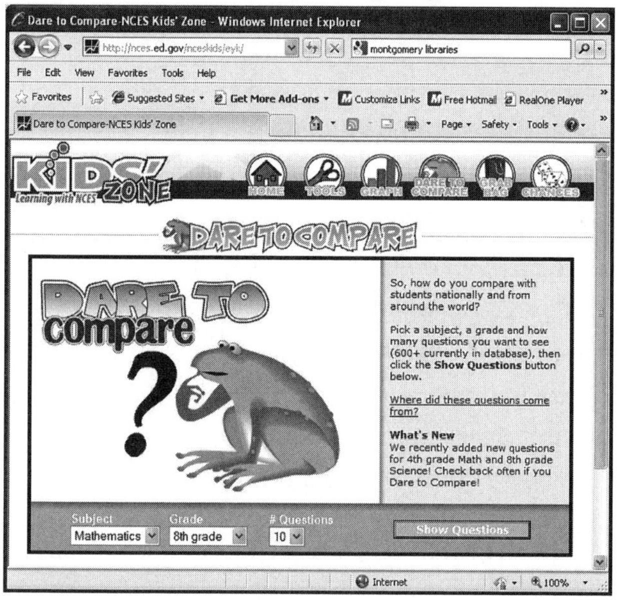


**FIGURE 3.2.**

The U.S. Department of Education Kids' Zone website has an excellent interactive graphing feature.

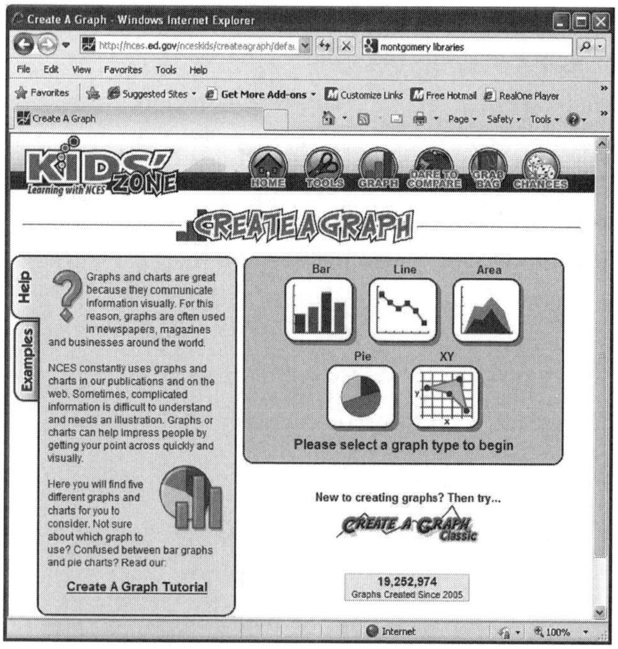


through simulation technology, has a wide variety of excellent math resources. Its "Interactivate" section is a great place to browse for interactive math learning tools (*www.shodor.org/interactivate*; Figure 3.3) and includes a box-plotting tool (*www.shodor.org/interactivate/activities/BoxPlot*) that allows you to enter data and generate box plots with various characteristics. Shodor provides several sample data sets to get you started, such as car mileage and ACT scores. Specific tabs provide support for learners and instructors. I also liked the box plot posting by Fabian Dill on The Information and Visualization blog (*http://informationandvisualization.de/blog/box-plot*). Dill starts out with a good straightforward description of the box plot and then gets into some interesting examples and elaborations. Others might prefer the very clear and concise presentation on the Saint John's University website that also has a place for entering data sets into a box-plotting utility (*www.physics.csbsju.edu/stats/box2.html*). An interesting blog called Junk Chart, by charting maven Kaiser Fung, has a nice treatment of the box plot, including how effective these plots are for looking at the performance of S&P 500 stocks (*http://junkcharts.typepad.com/junk_charts/boxplot*). The box and whisker plot is particularly good at capturing the overall distribution of a data set and clearly showing outlier and potential outlier values.

Have I already spent too much time in a Junior High School mathematical backwater? Tukey did a lot more than just invent the box plot. His text *Exploratory Data Analysis* (EDA; Tukey 1977) is full of ideas and inventions in addition to the box plot. Tukey is credited with revolutionizing statistical approaches to data and their graphical representations. Today, EDA isn't just an abbreviation for Tukey's book but shorthand for an important approach to data analysis. EDA is used extensively in DNA microarray experiments for example. EDA emphasizes generating hypotheses by looking at lots of data in many different ways, as opposed to more "traditional" statistical approaches for testing null hypotheses. The traditional and EDA approaches are complementary and not in opposition. The EDA approach fits particularly well with the massive data sets that are becoming more common with the growing prevalence of various high-throughput methods.

**FIGURE 3.3.**

Shodor has an "interactivate" section on its website devoted to interactive simulations for supporting math learning.

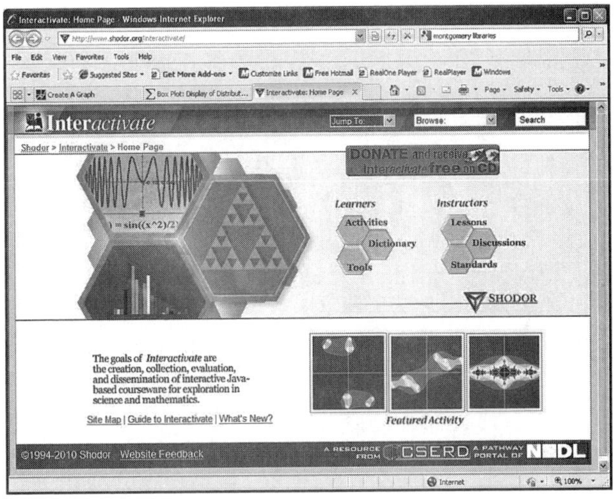


Microarrays have been an exciting research tool for two decades, but what I find so compelling about microarray experiments in the educational context is the broad range of topics and mathematical complexity that microarray experiments generate. The data raise issues such as raw numerical values (signal magnitude), simple ratios for comparing signals, standard data normalization and log transformations, and a large variety of data-sorting methods and algorithms. Malcolm Campbell (coincidentally the editor for this feature) has been a leading proponent of using DNA microarrays for undergraduate education. He cofounded the Genome Consortium for Active Teaching (GCAT; *www.bio.davidson.edu/projects/gcat/gcat.html*). It's hard to do justice to the many accomplishments and activities of GCAT in this short review (see Campbell et al. 2007). You can learn a lot about DNA microarrays by visiting the GCAT website, including a section on Laurie Heyer's MAGIC Tool custom software for data analysis, codeveloped with students (*www.bio.davidson.edu/projects/MAGIC/MAGIC.html*).

The GCAT pages are full of useful information, but they are not what a media critic would call slick. Fortunately, Malcolm teamed up with collaborators at the University of North Carolina several years ago to develop a "MediaBook" on DNA microarrays that is slick enough to have won a Pirelli Prize in 2004 (*http://gcat.davidson.edu/Pirelli/index.htm*; Figure 3.4, p. 36). The section on Data Interpretation covers every major aspect of analyzing array data, from creating heat map images to log transformation and hierarchical clustering of results. The entire MediaBook is beautifully done, with a very attractive design; superior explanatory graphics; and well written, if stiffly read, narration. If you are looking for a single place to start students on an exploration of DNA microarrays, look no further. The MediaBook includes interactive quizzes as well. But, of course, if you want to really engage students in the science of microarrays, you need to join GCAT and have your students do real

**FIGURE 3.4.**

The Microarrays MediaBook is the best place on the web for students to get an introduction to the data analysis methods used to interpret DNA microarray experiments.

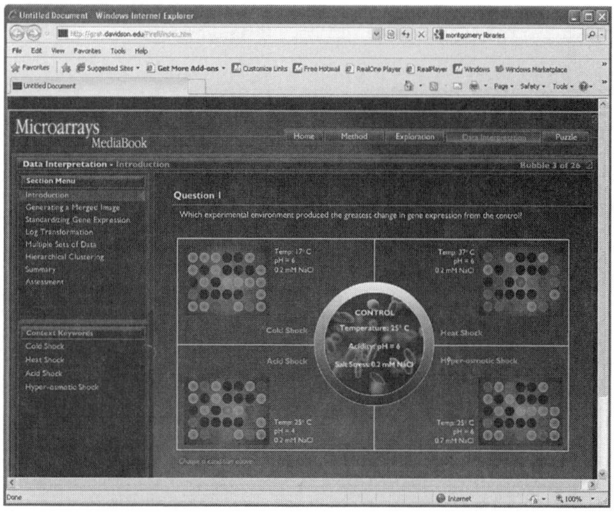


**FIGURE 3.5.**

The R Project for Statistical Computing is an open source package for data analysis and a favorite of EDA aficionados.

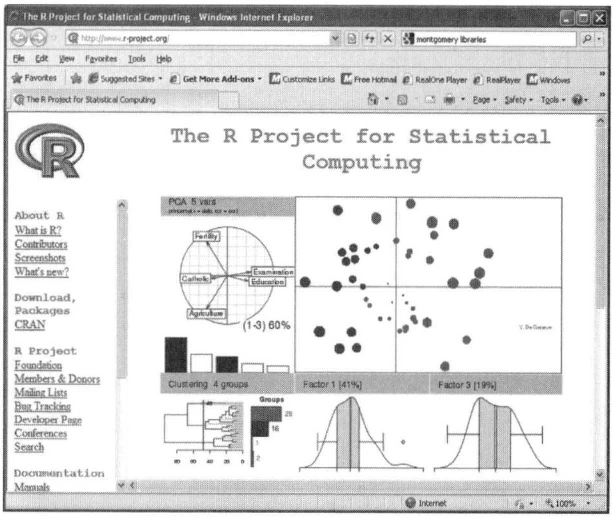


experiments. For a taste of what it's like to work with array data without generating your own, you might visit the University of Barcelona website that presents a lab practical on analyzing microarray data (*www.ub.es/stat/docencia/bioinformatica/microarrays/ADM/practicalMeV.htm*).

It's appropriate that the MediaBook, as an educational tool, very effectively uses graphics to teach about DNA microarrays, because today's state-of-the-art data analysis tools feature powerful graphics capabilities as well. One of the most popular tools for microarray experiments as well as other large data sets is R, an open-access statistical software package (*www.r-project.org*; Figure 3.5). The R project provides users with a complete package of computing environment, language, and graphing tools in a suite that is flexible enough to serve the needs of diverse researchers. R is not as easy to learn as standard desktop software, but a variety of tutorials is available to help (e.g., see *http://mercury.bio.uaf.edu/mercury/R/R.html*). By the way, although the MediaBook does not feature any box plots, the modest graphing method is extensively used in DNA microarray experiments for early quality-control stages of data processing. The box plot is particularly useful for comparing replicate data sets, and for identifying outliers, which can be associated with key findings or the result of experimental errors. Raphael Gottardos's presentations at the 2008 Canadian Bioinformatics Workshops provide a good overview of the EDA approach and the use of R (*www.bioinformatics.ca/workshops/2008/course-content*). Scroll down to Essential Statistics in Biology and look at Module 1 as a PDF or PowerPoint file. Gottardos's lab at The Clinical Research Institute of Montreal and the University of British Columbia focuses on computational biology, especially for high-throughput genomic analysis (*www.rglab.org*).

There are at least two other important software packages that should be mentioned in connection with data analysis, MATLAB, and Mathematica. MATLAB is a product of The MathWorks (Natick, MA) and enjoys wide use in academic and industrial research settings (*www.mathworks.com/products/matlab*). MATLAB began as a numerical computing language but has grown to include symbolic computing capabilities and more sophisticated graphing features. Mathematica is the mainline product of Wolfram Research (Champaign, Illinois), founded by physicist, mathematician, entrepreneur, and computational guru Stephen Wolfram. The best portal into the Wolfram world provides a list and description of his many different websites (*www.wolfram.com/webresources.html*). Wolfram declares that his various insights into computing forced him to invent, not a new science, but "a new kind of science," the title of his book and a website (*www.wolframscience.com*). The central tenant of Wolfram's science is that natural laws are digital, and very simple programming rules are the basis for complex natural systems. He is particularly fond of showing simple "cellular automata" programs that illustrate the complex patterns that can arise from many iterations of a simple set of interactions.

**FIGURE 3.6.**

Gapminder is a website and visualization by Hans Rosling for illustrating aspects of various global health and economics issues.

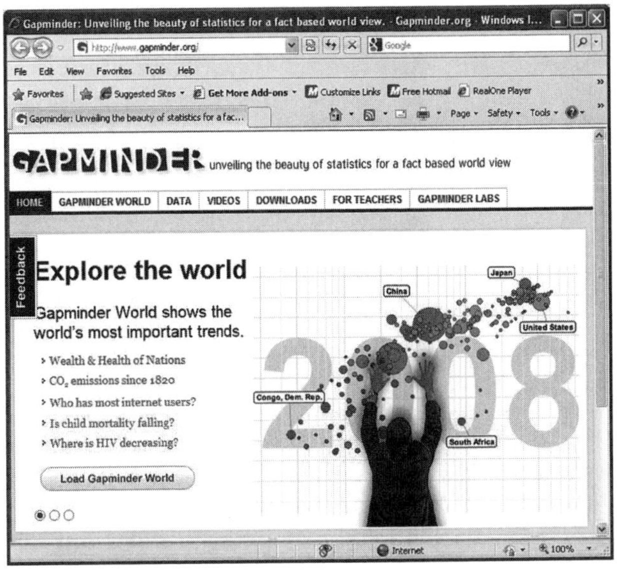


You can get a taste of his style and ideas by viewing his 20-minute talk on the TED website (*www.ted.com/talks/lang/eng/stephen_wolfram_computing_a_theory_of_everything.html*). A hallmark of Wolfram Research products is outstanding graphic capabilities, and the demonstrations website is the best place to get a sample (*http://demonstrations.wolfram.com*). For example, search for "turbulence," an important factor in many real biological systems, and you will find 13 interesting demonstrations. To use the interactive demonstrations, you will have to download the free Mathematica Player. Wolfram calls his latest project WolframAlpha and describes it as an attempt to make all knowledge computable (*www.wolframalpha.com*). I think of WolframAlpha as "Ask Jeeves" (*www.ask.com*), where Jeeves is a robot butler who always answers your questions with data instead of sentences. Interestingly, when I tried to use either Jeeves or WolframAlpha to find out how many offshore oil rigs there are in the world, neither site gave me any useful information, whereas Google gave me some very quick leads. WolframAlpha seems like an interesting idea and produces some thought-provoking results when you try the examples they suggest, such as entering your birthday.

I have been emphasizing graphical representations of data, in particular for exploring the data as opposed to testing hypotheses. Mark Twain warned us about "lies, damn lies, and statistics," and that was before intoxicating computer graphics were added to the mix. Good visuals can be very persuasive, and Hans Rosling has taken his interest in data and statistics in a provocative direction. Wolfram has a TED video, but Rosling has at least five TED videos. His TED talk on human immunodeficiency virus is only 10 minutes and gives you a good idea about how his Gapminder graphing tool works (*www.ted.com/talks/lang/eng/hans_rosling_the_truth_about_hiv.html*; Figure 3.6). To play with Gapminder directly, visit *www.gapminder.org*. Rosling does not ask questions about the data per se but is interested in graphing data sets concerning health, economy, and demographics to look at global issues in ways that provoke critical thinking and challenge conventional wisdom.

In a way, he's taking a looser approach to EDA, where he looks for correlations between health data and economic data. There's no doubt that viewing data this way can make a powerful impression and can provoke critical thinking. The risk, of course, is in confusing correlation and causation.

I think it could be interesting to have students grapple with some of the issues provoked by Rosling's visualizations. You could start by playing with the data and tools called "Gapminder World," but it's probably best to visit one of the "labs" and view some of the animated charts to see how the method works. Gapminder makes the data it uses directly available on the website, and there is also a section devoted to teachers.

I think we can all agree that nothing beats having students grapple with actual data, and struggle to draw meaningful ideas and conclusions from those data. I'd like to close with a short list of some sites that provide access to a variety of data sets worthy of analysis.

- Exploring Data from Education Queensland, Australia (*http://exploringdata.net*) is an excellent website for introductory statistics and includes a large collection of data sets at *http://exploringdata.net/datasets.htm#coedine*.
- Head Start is the once universally hailed early reading program for young children. More recently, enthusiasm for Head Start has been less than unanimous primarily due to controversy over attempts to measure the program's impact. Some of the assessment data are available for you to analyze and draw your own conclusions (*www.acf.hhs.gov/programs/opre/hs/impact_study*).
- Doug Tallamy is an entomologist at the University of Delaware and the best-selling author of *Bringing Nature Home: A Case for Native Gardening* (2007, Timber Press; *http://bringingnaturehome.net*). Part of his argument for restoring landscapes with native plants is that they support more biodiversity. Tallamy has published species lists to support his hypothesis. A "Guide to Lepidoptera on Ornamentals,"

is a downloadable list of plant and insect species (*http://copland.udel.edu/_dtallamy/host/index.html*).

- The Math Forum at Drexel University has a list of websites that have publicly accessible data sets (*http://mathforum.org/library/topics/data_sets*), including websites and data sets aimed more at the K–12 level (*http://mathforum.org/workshops/usi/dataproject/usi.genwebsites.html*).
- The Quantitative Environmental Learning Project from Seattle Central Community College has a wealth of data sets available to support teaching math in the context of environmental science (*www.seattlecentral.edu/qelp*).
- Vanderbilt University Department of Biostatistics makes dozens of mostly medically relevant data sets available in a variety of formats (*http://biostat.mc.vanderbilt.edu/twiki/bin/view/Main/DataSets?CGISESSID_10713f6d891653ddcbb7ddbdd9cffb79*).

## Acknowledgments

I thank Malcolm Campbell for helpful suggestions and edits to this manuscript.

## References

Campbell, A. M., M. S. Ledbetter, L. M. Hoopes, T. T. Eckdahl, L. J. Heyer, A. Rosenwald, E. Fowlks, S. Tonidandel, B. Bucholtz, and G. Gottfried. 2007. Genome consortium for active teaching: Meeting the goals of BIO2010. *CBE Life Sciences Education* 6: 109–118.

Tukey, J. W. 1977. *Exploratory data analysis*. Reading, MA: Addison-Wesley.

Reprinted with permission from *CBE—Life Sciences Education*, Vol. 9, 150–153, Fall 2010.

CHAPTER 4

# REINVENTING THE WHEEL
## Quantifying Cases for Your Classes

*Patricia A. Marsteller and Drew Kohlhorst*

> "I wish it need not have happened in my time," said Frodo."So do I," said Gandalf, "and so do all who live to see such times. But that is not for them to decide. All we have to decide is what to do with the time that is given us."
> —J.R.R. Tolkien, *The Fellowship of the Ring*

Many faculty think that adopting case-based learning strategies is too time consuming and that the time it takes to implement them in class reduces content coverage. At workshops, the first question usually is: "Won't I have to decrease the content coverage if I use cases, especially cases that involve statistics and data sets?" The next questions invariably are: "How do I find the time to write new cases or design new problems that really engage the learners? And how do I find appropriate data sets that address the quantitative skills I want my students to develop?"

Gandalf was right. We have to decide (wisely) how to use the time that is given us. Instead of inventing new lectures, activities, and cases, perhaps we can begin with time-tested case studies and other materials and realign them to suit our students.

Our world is awash in data. College graduates and citizens alike will need to "navigate a sea of numbers on a daily basis" (Grawe 2012). As Clyde Herreid points out in the introduction to this book, all of our students "should be able to at least reason quantitatively, to read and interpret data, graphs, and statistics." Quantitative reasoning competencies include the ability to make sense of graphs, tables, diagrams, and equations and to convert information from one format to another. More importantly perhaps, students need to develop the ability to evaluate evidence and the limits and assumptions that underlie data analysis and models (Dwyer et al. 2003; Hmelo-Sliver 2004). Indeed, data-enhanced learning experiences prepare students for solving complex real-world problems and develop their skills in applying scientific methods. In addition, including critical evaluation of the ways in which data is collected and interpreted develops an appreciation of the ethics of data usage (Manduca and Mogk 2003; Yadav et al. 2007).

Although many cases exist on science topics for undergraduates, there are fewer that incorporate quantitative concepts, data sets, simulations, games, bioinformatics, mathematics, and statistics. When reviewing existing cases to quantify, it helps to have particular concepts, objectives, and course topics in mind. Remember that you can always make a case more or less difficult or complex, so don't hesitate to adapt cases originally developed for another educational level. Sometimes you will find a case or problem that seems to fit your concept, but either is written for a lower level course or for a higher level course, and you'll want to provide more background or structure for students to engage the problem.

*Vision and Change in Undergraduate Biology Education: A Call to Action* (AAAS 2010) can serve as a guide to choosing cases to adapt and make more quantitative. Most faculty agree that to be scientifically literate, students need to understand a few overarching core concepts. These are:

- Evolution
- Pathways and transformations of energy and matter
- Information flow, exchange, and storage
- Structure and function
- Systems

Moreover, as the authors of *Vision and Change* (p. 243) noted,

> As important, undergraduates need to understand the process of science, the interdisciplinary nature of the new biology, and how science is closely integrated within society. Students also should be competent in communication and collaboration, as well as have a certain level of quantitative competency, and a basic ability to understand and interpret data. To be current in biology, students should also have experience with modeling, simulation, and computational and systems-level approaches to biological discovery and analysis, as well as with using large databases.

We have our work cut out for us, as Figure 4.1 shows.

**FIGURE 4.1.**

Quantifying Cases: Easy Steps to Success

1. Identify class characteristics and your own willingness to relinquish control.
2. Identify learner characteristics.
3. Identify learning objectives and curriculum outcomes.
4. Find a case that you want to modify.
5. Find or develop data sets, simulations, websites, scientific papers, or games that provide and scaffold a data-rich learning experience for the case.
6. Develop performance assessments and scoring rubrics.

After providing some detail for the steps outlined in Figure 4.1 in the next section, we will illustrate the process of adapting a case with several cases, some of which are taken from this book. We will also show how existing cases on influenza that have limited quantitative content can be made more quantitative through the addition of data sets, visualization techniques, and simulations to the case.

## Quantifying Cases

### *Step One: Identify Class and Professor Characteristics*

How you begin to adapt a case may depend upon the level and size of the class and upon your own characteristics and comfort with cases and open-ended engagements. An experienced case teacher with the primary goal of engaging students in asking their own questions may choose a very open-ended approach, allowing students to find or create their own data sets and experiments. Most of us, however, have larger classes, with students with a range of backgrounds, information literacy skills, and quantitative experience. In such a case, you may want to approach the task by scaffolding the data-rich experience for your students instead, choosing the dataset or simulation that best fits them and your intended learning outcomes, and developing guided inquiry questions and assignments that direct students to appropriate resources. One way to approach this is to think about how you might modify a case developed for a large class of traditionally aged biology majors for an honors class, for a non-majors class, or for a class that contains large numbers of non-traditional students who may not have had a science class in years or a class whose students have weak quantitative skills. Your approach and level of scaffolding will vary.

Your own characteristics (as indicated in Figure 4.2) are equally important to the path you choose. Are you adventurous and willing to take some risks? Or do you need to have more control of the student experience? Instructors tend to choose differing active learning approaches depending on their training, level of comfort with the topic and overall

**FIGURE 4.2.**

The Active Learning Continuum.

**Where Are You on the Active Learning Continuum?**

**Continuum of course objectives**

Acquisition of knowledge ----------------------------------------Acquisition of skills

**Interaction in your classroom**

Limited interaction ----------------------------------------Extensive interaction

**Levels of control**

Need total control ----------------------------------------Need little control

"Sage on the Stage"----------------------------------------"Guide on the Side"

**Willingness to take a risk**

Cautious----------------------------------------Adventurous

**Level of student experience**

Inexperienced----------------------------------------Experienced

*Note:* Modified from Sutherland and Bonwell 1996.

learning objectives for the course. Often instructors teaching introductory-level courses feel the need to maintain a tighter control over the direction of the course due to the "Continuum of course objectives" and/or "Level of student experience"; however even in introductory-level courses these issues can be balanced by instructor values in "Interaction in your classroom" and/or "Levels of Control." Classroom utilization of quantitative skills and case-based learning can help to elevate any of these active learning continuum issues.

## *Step Two: Identify Learner Characteristics*

To adapt cases to be more engaging for students requires that you have some idea about what they find interesting. Are they primarily interested in one facet of biology or mathematics or computing? What do they like to read, what kinds of movies do they watch, what music do they listen to? What sports do they watch or play? What clubs do they belong to? Who do they admire? Will they be more interested in your case if it is keyed to something recent that happened locally? Are they ready to read primary literature or should your resources focus on general interest publications or news articles? To make cases more quantitative, you need to ask an additional set of questions: What is the students' quantitative background? Have they taken a statistics course? College algebra? Calculus?

How do you find out what students' interests are? There are of course many interest inventories that one can find on the web and many companies that market them. But you can ask your students a short series of questions that will give you ideas about how to engage their interests and connect them to science, mathematics, and computational sciences. Similarly, you can identify the mathematical and computational background of your students through a short assessment of their quantitative skills or by collecting and analyzing information about previous courses they have taken (high school statistics, algebra, calculus, AP courses), their SAT scores, or similar measures.

You might also wish to identify misconceptions that they hold about your course content as well as their understanding of data and evidence. The American Association for the Advancement of Science (AAAS) maintains an assessment site (*http://assessment.aaas.org*) which allows you to create tests and compare your student data to national samples. This can be used to help identify misconceptions that students may hold about the topics in your course. As you consider cases to teach, construct an item bank of the important concepts and list misconceptions you think are relevant to your students here. Additional misconception topics can be found in the "Control of Variables" and "Models" portion of the AAAS Misconception topic list.

Once you have collected all of the information, create a list of the characteristics of your students to guide you—developmental, preferred learning styles, interests, group dynamics, experience with cases, quantitative skills, prior knowledge of concepts, misconceptions, career goals, and so on.

Given that your students have different backgrounds, experiences, and abilities, to meet the learning needs of all of your students, you may need to differentiate instruction, providing entry points for different kinds of learners, accommodating differently abled students, or providing supplemental instruction for those with weaker backgrounds. It also helps to redesign cases to include people from different cultures and perspectives.

***Tip:*** We have found over the years that students, particularly undergraduate and high school students, love stories with continuing characters that talk like they do. They also like embedded information on careers in science, and they love dilemmas and suspense. And, although they can be captured by a more didactic style or a news story, it helps to have local interest.

### *Step Three: Identify Learning Objectives and Curriculum Outcomes*

Student learning is enhanced when courses, assignments, and cases have clear goals and objectives. List specific curriculum outcomes your students will achieve through the redesigned case study. Use different levels of Bloom's taxonomy if you can (*www.odu.edu/educ/roverbau/Bloom/blooms_taxonomy.htm*).

For example, you might choose one or more of these, as shown in Table 4.1 (p. 46).

### *Step Four: What Case Do You Want to Modify?*

Find a case that fits your content objectives. Decide if the level of the case fits your students and your overall goals. Think about how you might modify it for your class. Will you need to add or delete components? Make it more or less open ended? Scaffold the ideas with clicker questions (i.e., using an electronic personalized response system), mini-lectures, or structured assignments?

#### Places to Find Cases

1. **This book.**
2. **The National Center for Case Study Teaching in Science Case Collection** (*sciencecases.lib.buffalo.edu/cs/collection/*)—Searchable collection of over 500 cases in all areas of science with a particular focus on the life sciences. Includes teaching notes and answer keys. Over 50 cases have scientific methods embedded. Seven specifically address statistics. Freely available to the public; teachers must register to access the answer keys.
3. **University of Delaware's Problem-Based Learning (PBL) Clearinghouse** (*https://pblc.nss.udel.edu/Pbl/*)—Collection of problems and articles to assist educators in using problem-based learning. Materials are free but registration is required.

**TABLE 4.1.**

Potential Quantitative Skills-Building Activities Based on Bloom's Taxonomy for Problem-Based Learning.

| Suggested Activity | Bloom's Taxonomy Description | Bloom's Level |
|---|---|---|
| Apply scientific methods. | Apply | Level 3 |
| Apply inquiry and analytical skills. | Apply | Level 3 |
| Calculate Chi square. | Apply | Level 3 |
| Run a correlation analysis and interpret it. | Apply | Level 3 |
| Run an ANOVA and interpret it. | Apply | Level 3 |
| Use graphic analysis tools. | Apply | Level 3 |
| Gather data, either in the lab or in the field. | Analyze | Level 4 |
| Construct and interpret a graph. | Analyze | Level 4 |
| Use DNA sequence data to construct evolutionary relationships. | Synthesis | Level 5 |
| Obtain, critically evaluate, and communicate biological information. | Synthesis | Level 5 |
| Model a complex data set utilizing data visualization software. | Synthesis | Level 5 |
| Evaluate the ethical issues in manipulating photographs or figures or in eliminating data points. | Evaluate | Level 6 |
| Compare/contrast the two differing data visualization means and determine which to use to present complex experimental data. | Evaluate | Level 6 |
| Support your use of evolutionary relationship data in a scientific manuscript. | Evaluate | Level 6 |

4. **Emory University's CASES Online** (*www.cse.emory.edu/cases/*)—More than 400 investigative lessons, or "cases," for K–12, undergraduate, and graduate science. Many incorporate scientific methods, experimental design, and epidemiology. Free registration enables you to download cases and support materials.
5. **Investigative Case-Based Learning from BioQuest** (*bioquest.org/icbl/*)—Case modules developed by faculty participants in BioQuest's Investigative Case-Based Learning workshops.
6. **Case It!** (*www.caseitproject.org*)—Free, open-ended molecular biology simulations and cases based primarily on genetic and infectious disease. The software allows students to virtually conduct experiments using SNP and expression microarrays, restriction enzyme digestion, gel electrophoresis, PCR, ELISA, Southern or Western blot, dot blot, and connection to the NCBI BLAST database.

### Step Five: Find or Develop Data Sets, Simulations, Websites, Scientific Papers, or Games to Provide and Scaffold a Data-Rich Learning Experience for the Case

List the resources you have used in re-designing the case and that you want your students to use in their inquiry. Resources may include simulations, data sources, games, books, articles, websites, videos, people (contact information), agencies, and so on. You will likely add to this list as you develop and implement the case. A Google search for teaching data sets or statistics data sets for your topic may yield fruitful results. See Appendix C for sources for general statistics data sets.

### Step Six: Develop Performance Assessments and Scoring Rubrics

Specify two or three "along-the-way" assessments that you will insert as your students work on the case/problem/concept. This can include clicker questions, Just-in-time quizzes, know/need-to-know charts, and learning issue reports. A Just-in-time quiz is designed to address two/three concept issues that students should have grasped before they begin the case/problem/concept in order to ensure prior learning objectives have been met. Know/need-to-know charts are often helpful in interrupted cases as students are able to determine their current understanding of the case and predict information needed for additional sections of the case/problem/concept (see Appendix C). Learning issue reports ask students to identify important questions that may help them resolve the case and understand background material. These often include primary references that help students identify appropriate source materials and summarize the important points.

Specify the final, authentic performance assessment at the end of your case in which students will demonstrate what they know, can do, and value via presentations of their solution(s) to the problem(s) posed in the case study. Authentic performance assessment is hallmarked by using learning objectives, developed prior to delivering instructional material, and measuring student performance on both lower and higher level Bloom's taxonomy curriculum-driven questions/applications. This often takes the form of short answer, essay or well-developed multiple-choice questions in exams as well as written or oral work.

Sketch out a beginning rubric for assessing students' final performance. What criteria state your expectations for a successful performance? What evidence will demonstrate that students have learned? Be sure that the rubric aligns with your curriculum outcomes and standards.

## Data Sets and Visualization: Applying These Tools to "Inactive Brains"

Incorporating real data to teach analytical skills and data analysis skills is one of the approaches to adapting cases. In this section, we use the case study "Inactive Brains" (Spierer, Williams, and Lyttle 2007) as an example. The case is available online at *http://sciencecases.lib.buffalo.edu/cs/files/inactive_brains.pdf.* "Inactive Brains" was developed for a graduate-level exercise science course or public health course. Let's consider what you might do to use the case for introductory biology, for an upper level data analysis course, or to make it more quantitative in general.

> The case presents a scenario in which two speakers have been invited to a town hall meeting to help decide a hotly contested issue. A grant has been awarded to the school district with the stipulation that the money be dedicated to only one program. School officials want to use the funds to improve the science curriculum, but district parents favor an investment in physical education to improve the health of their children. Since the grant money cannot be divided, students are forced to grapple with the role of science in education, the growing problem of childhood obesity, and related issues of public policy.

The authors' stated learning objectives are to:

- Provide an understanding of how far-reaching childhood obesity is in the United States.
- Encourage discussion on issues of obesity and its physiological consequences.
- Provide a forum in which obesity is seen as a health risk and not just a challenging aesthetic.
- Emphasize the need for critical thinking in deciding how grant money should be spent.

- Provide a forum for a discussion of the challenges we face in reducing obesity in this country and strategies to prevent it.
- Encourage students to look at government as both an enabler and a protector.
- Encourage students to make a choice on a sensitive issue.

Suppose you wanted to familiarize students with data that is available on obesity and you wanted them to analyze data from their own state. You could direct them to explore the Centers for Disease Control and Prevention (CDC) website at *www.cdc.gov/obesity/data/childhood.html,* which contains data and implementation plans for combatting childhood obesity from Minnesota, New Hampshire, New York, Rhode Island, and South Carolina. Or you might insert the map from the site (shown in Figure 4.3) and ask students to consider why the differences in obesity prevalence might occur.

**FIGURE 4.3.**

Sample Map: 2009–2011 County Obesity Prevalence Among Low-Income Children Ages 2 to 4 Years (Centers for Disease Control and Prevention, 2012).

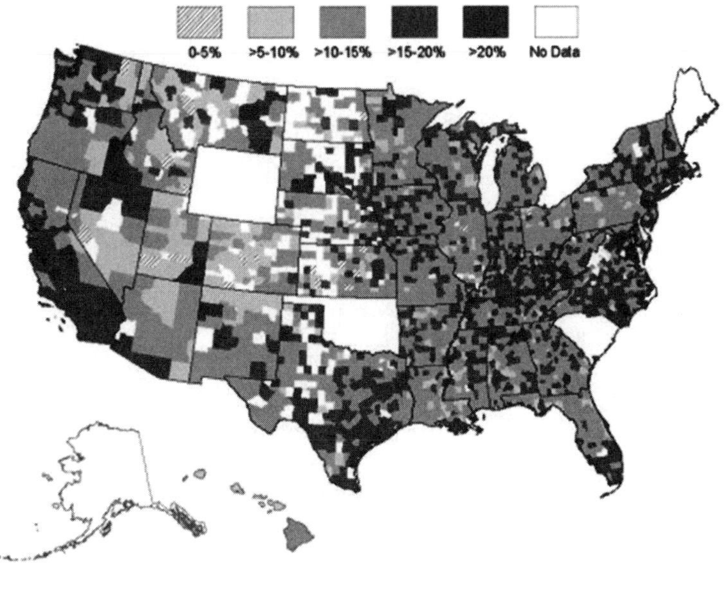


The CDC site contains a number of studies and data that could be incorporated into the case to allow students to see trends in obesity and extreme obesity rates. For example, one study using the Pediatric Nutrition Surveillance System (PedNSS) (CDC *www.cdc.gov/obesity/data/childhood.html)* shows that:

- Obesity and extreme obesity decreased among U.S. low-income, preschool-age children.

- From 2003 through 2010, the prevalence of obesity decreased slightly from 15.21% to 14.94%. Extreme obesity decreased from 2.22% to 2.07%.
- Extreme obesity significantly decreased among all racial groups except American Indians/Alaska Natives.

Examples of questions/assignments generated from the case noted above including Bloom's categorization are listed in Table 4.2.

**TABLE 4.2.**

Potential Quantitative Skills-Rich Activities Using CDC 2009–2011 Obesity Prevalence Data Among Low-Income Children.

| Example Question/Assignment | Bloom's Taxonomy Description | Bloom's Taxonomy Level |
|---|---|---|
| Using proper software, demonstrate the changing trends in child-age obesity from 2003 to 2010. | Application | Level 3 |
| Given the current data, predict child-age obesity trends for the next five years. | Application | Level 3 |
| Compare the child-age obesity rates in the United States with three other economically comparable countries for the same time period (2003–2010). | Analysis | Level 4 |
| Design an experiment to determine the factors involved in the large decrease of extreme obesity in Asian/Pacific Islander children. | Synthesis | Level 5 |
| Based on the data presented, develop an argument for a change in federal, state, or local policies to decrease child-age obesity. | Evaluation | Level 6 |
| Using three other countries as comparators, develop a rating system for the potential effectiveness of means to decrease child-age obesity. | Evaluation | Level 6 |

Other data-rich articles on the CDC site include: "Obesity rates among all children in the United States" (with data from the National Health and Nutrition Examination Survey) and "Obesity rates among low-income preschool children" (with data from the Pediatric Nutrition Surveillance System).

Another potential dataset that could enhance the quantitative nature of this case is from the 2007 National Survey of Children's Health (*www.childhealthdata.org/browse/topic/obesity*).

This data set contains body-mass index (BMI) data, physical activity data, and maps, as well as articles and reports.

For a more advanced class, you might direct students to the Gene Expression Omnibus. Here they can compare two sets of samples, analyze gene expression in obese children, see what genes are involved in obesity, and look at experimental design and cluster maps. The full data set can be downloaded for further exploration at *www.ncbi.nlm.nih.gov/sites/GDSbrowser?acc=GDS3688*.

For more advanced students, you could add specific references or have then reanalyze or interpret data from the primary literature, such as the 2012 article titled "A genome-wide association meta-analysis identifies new childhood obesity loci," by Bradfield et al. in *Nature Genetics* (vol. 44, pp. 526–531; *www.nature.com/ng/journal/v44/n5/full/ng.2247.html*). Since obese children display insulin resistance and other metabolic abnormalities at higher rates than do normal weight children, students could consider the molecular mechanisms of childhood obesity.

For a course focusing on the public health aspects of the case, the CDC site contains a state-based searchable database (*http://apps.nccd.cdc.gov/CDPHPPolicySearch/Default.aspx*) that provides legislation information on nutrition, physical activity, and obesity, including bill numbers, year, and congressional sponsor; a short summary of the legislation; and its current status. This could provide an entry point to developing a policy paper for a public health focus or a debate about strategies using the data.

For a course focused more on exercise science or exercise physiology, one could customize the case using the U.S. physical activity database (*www.cdc.gov/nccdphp/dnpa/physical/stats/index.htm*). This interactive database provides data by demographics and physical activity levels for a metropolitan area, state, or national groups.

To add global perspectives to the case, you might use data from Canada, South America, or other parts of the world. The World Health Organization (WHO) provides interactive maps and downloadable data sets related to obesity (*www.who.int/gho/ncd/risk_factors/overweight/en*). You could have students view the interactive maps and choose countries for comparison to the U.S. data.

***Tip:*** A goldmine of data and statistics, the World Health Organization provides access via *www.who.int/research/en* to data sets, analyses, and interactive graphics that could be used in many other cases on topics ranging from HIV, life expectancy, and communicable diseases to infectious diseases, substance abuse, and many more public health indicators.

## Making Non-Quantitative Cases Quantitative: Quantifying the Flu

The flu fascinates everyone, but especially case writers. Maybe because it arrives every year and we are urged to get yet another flu shot. In Figure 4.4, we show some sources for case studies on influenza.

Many of the cases in Figure 4.4 have learning objectives that focus on the causes of the flu and how it can be spread, as well as some of the genetic differences between flu strains. A common list of learning objectives for them might include:

1. Understand the flu (influenza), its causes, why it occurs yearly, and who is most affected.
2. Explain the genetic makeup and transmission of the influenza virus.
3. Describe host specificity.
4. Define the terms *pandemic*, *epidemic*, and *endemic*.
5. Explain the purpose, production/execution, and procedures for administration, and efficacy of vaccines and quarantines.
6. Describe viral strain variation and immunological naiveté.
7. Discuss the history of influenza (specifically outbreaks of 1918, 1957, and 1968).
8. Summarize the epidemiology of pandemic flu strains versus the typical yearly flu.
9. Consider why avian flu is highly publicized.
10. Discuss the virulence of the influenza virus.

**FIGURE 4.4.**

Cases of the Flu

**From: The National Center for Case Study Teaching in Science**

- **A Case Study Involving Influenza and the Influenza Vaccine** by John S. Bennett
  *http://sciencecases.lib.buffalo.edu/cs/collection/detail.asp?case_id=326&id=326*

  Explores the benefits of the influenza vaccine. Students work in small groups to evaluate arguments for and against vaccination and, in answering the case questions, learn about the general biology of viral infections, treatment of infections, and immunity. Designed for an entry-level course in microbiology for nursing students or first-year biology course for majors.
- **Chickens and Humans and Pigs, Oh My!** by Jeffrey J. Byrd and Samantha L. Elliott
  *http://sciencecases.lib.buffalo.edu/cs/collection/detail.asp?case_id=615&id=615*

Figure 4.4 (*continued*)

Explores important concepts in virology and immunology including antigenic shift/drift, re-assortment of viral antigens, viral entry via sialic acid residues, vaccinations, and pandemics. Appropriate for use in an immunology, virology, or microbiology course.

- **Decoding the Flu** by Norris Armstrong
  *http://sciencecases.lib.buffalo.edu/cs/collection/detail.asp?case_id=597&id=597*

  Designed to develop students' ability to read and interpret information stored in DNA, this case follows the story of "Jason," a student intern at the CDC who uses molecular data collected from different local strains of flu to identify which one may be causing the sickness among his co-workers. Designed for an introductory biology course for science or non-science majors; could be adapted for upper-level courses by including more complex problems and aspects of gene expression, such as the excision of introns.
- **Why Was the 1918 Influenza So Deadly?** by Annie Prud'homme Genereux and Carmen A. Petrick
  *http://sciencecases.lib.buffalo.edu/cs/collection/detail.asp?case_id=636&id=636*

  Examines the causes of the devastation wrought by the 1918 so-called "Spanish" influenza pandemic and consider if the 1918 flu was exceptionally deadly because of its biology or because prevalent geopolitical-socioeconomic conditions led to the negative health outcomes. Students assess the contribution of each factor, consider how they might have interacted, and apply their knowledge to evaluate the risks of current flu outbreaks. Developed for a sophomore undergraduate course on infectious disease; could be adapted for a general biology course if students are given a sufficient background in viral biology.

**From: CASES Online**

- **Bird Flu and the 1918 Pandemic** by Elizabeth Lindsey and Gerda Louizi
  *http://cse.emory.edu/cases/casedisplay.cfm?case_id=1183*

  This case, designed from a NYT editorial, looks at the threat of an outbreak of avian flu, which caught the attention of the public, government, and media. How serious is avian flu? Where did it come from? Scientists from around the world focus on the probability of an outbreak. Students are expected to be able to describe the flu, its causes and who is most affected, describe the epidemiological issues associated with this strain of avian flu and discuss virulence of the influence virus upon completing this case.
- **ACHOO!** by Andrea Liatis and Amanda Lockhart
  *http://cse.emory.edu/cases/casedisplay.cfm?case_id=2705*

  "Jordan" is sick and convinced he needs antibiotics. What if he took some of his girlfriend's leftover pills? Or could it be the flu? Didn't he just get vaccinated? This case, developed for upper-level high school students addresses the difference between viral and bacterial infections, and modes of transmission while discussing the usage and over usage of antibiotics in this country.

**From: Case It!**

- There are nine different flu cases on the site; see:
  *http://caseitproject.org/wp-content/uploads/2012/07/RM2012.html#humanflu*

Most of these objectives are at the lower levels of Bloom's Taxonomy. Could we convert objective #8 into a quantitative or synthesis level by saying "Create, use, or construct a model that predicts a pandemic flu?" A number of tools and data sets exist for doing that including those listed in Table 4.3.

**TABLE 4.3.**

Selected Tools and Data Sets for Quantifying the Flu.

**Google Flu Trends**
*www.google.org/flutrends*
Provides near real-time estimates of flu activity for a number of countries and regions around the world based on aggregated search queries.

**Tracking the Progress of H1N1 Swine Flu**
*http://flutracker.rhizalabs.com*
This map was compiled using data from official sources, news reports, and user-contributions, and is updated multiple times per day.

**Real Science, Real Data**
*http://flu.deciphermydata.org.uk*
Can school absence data be used to detect flu peaks early? Get your students to analyze your school's absence data and report on their findings. While this site is no longer accepting data, it provides students with a means to visualize and manipulate mid-sized data sets of real data collected by fellow students. This site also provides an excellent guide to other teachers/instructors who wish to develop a real-world collection method of data from students to encourage student engagement in discussion and analysis.

**Investigative Case 9: Pandemic Flu Open Ended Investigation**
*http://bioquest.org/icbl/casebook/avian*
This site allows you to develop a scenario of your own (e.g., more virulent flu, different mitigation efforts, targeting certain population segments, etc.) and see how the spread of disease is changed.

**Other Examples of Sources of Data Related to the Flu**

- Taubenberger, J. K., and D. M. Morens. 2006. 1918 Influenza: The mother of all pandemics. *Emerging Infectious Diseases* 12 (1): Online at *www.cdc.gov/ncidod/EID/vol12no01/05-0979.htm*
- Weisstein, A. E.2007. SIR modeling. In: *Biological ESTEEM: Excel simulations and tools for exploratory, experiential mathematics. bioquest.org/esteem/esteem_result.php*
- World Health Organization. Antigenic and genetic characteristics of H5N1 viruses and candidate H5N1 vaccine viruses developed for potential use as pre-pandemic vaccines. *www.who.int/csr/disease/avian_influenza/guidelines/h5n1virus/en/index.html*

**Selected H1N1 Map Links**

- *http://gamapserver.who.int/mapLibrary/Files/Maps/Global_SubNat_H5N1inAnimalConfirmedCUMULATIVE_20070329.png*

Table 4.3 (*continued*)

- *http://gamapserver.who.int/mapLibrary/Files/Maps/Global_H5N1inHumanCUMULATIVE_FIMS_20070329.png*
- *http://calag.ucop.edu/0603JAS/images/avianMap.jpg*
- *http://pbs.org/wgbh/nova/evolution/evolving-flu.html*

## Using Gapminder to Quantify Cases: Investigating HIV and AIDS

To demonstrate how Gapminder can be used to visualize and quantify a case, in this section we use a case study from this book, "Resistance Is Futile ... Or Is It? The Immunity System and HIV Infection" by Annie Prud'homme Genereux. While the majority of people are prone to HIV infection, some individuals remain uninfected despite repeated exposure. This case study is based on the landmark paper by Paxton et al. (1996), which uncovered some of the mechanisms of protection against HIV infection. Students are guided to suggest hypotheses, predict the outcomes of experiments, and compare their predictions with the paper's results.

Designed for lower division undergraduates, specifically a non-majors molecular biology course, the learning objectives for the case state that students will be able to:

- Formulate testable hypotheses given preliminary data.
- Suggest tests to evaluate hypotheses.
- Predict results of experiments that would confirm each hypothesis.
- Interpret data and compare to predicted outcomes.
- Describe cellular and humoral immunity.
- Draw the HIV virus structure and describe the function of each component.
- Describe the interaction of the HIV virus with the immune system.
- Differentiate between resistance and immunity as mechanisms of protection against a foreign particle.
- Debate the pros and cons of personal knowledge of HIV resistance and immunity.

Suppose you wanted to extend this case for an upper division course or for a longer unit on HIV? Or perhaps you just wanted to go deeper for a course on AIDS. One way to do that is to use tools such as Gapminder to adapt the case and make it more quantitative.

Gapminder (*www.gapminder.org*) allows you to visualize complex and large data sets in a user-friendly, interactive environment. The tool is organized into Gapminder World and various Gapminder Labs. Gapminder World uses the largest and most diverse data sets to provide a wide range of uses depending on your data visualization needs and learning goals. Gapminder Labs are more specialized as they focus on specific data sets, allowing users to focus on specific places, issues, and learning goals.

For each graphing variable in Gapminder there is a button shaped like a spreadsheet—this will take you to the data table for that variable. Within this data table is all the data needed to complete the graphing of that variable over the time course. Data is presented first along with tabs for data source ("About"), additional information ("Footnotes"), and the settings Gapminder uses to display the data. Lastly, Gapminder allows users to download the data in various formats ("Download"). Please note some of these data tables can be very large.

Figure 4.5 shows a sample chart generated using Gapminder. Table 4.4 provides more detailed information about the features and use of the tool.

**FIGURE 4.5.**

Gapminder USA.

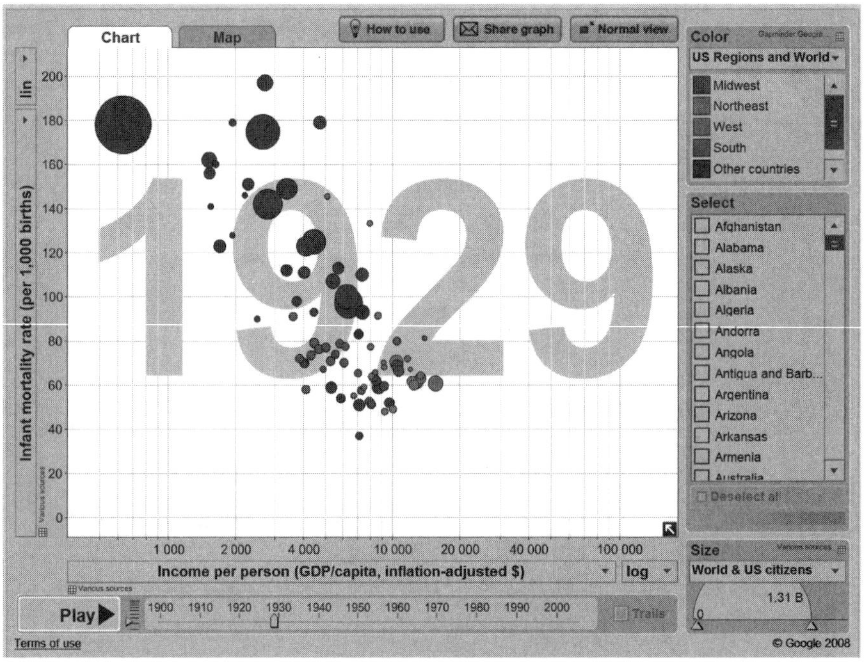


*Source:* Gapminder USA Lab

**TABLE 4.4.**

Gapminder 101.

**Using Gapminder Charts**

Once you have entered Gapminder World or a Gapminder lab you will see the familiar "chart" visualization. This will be the primary tool to use to begin visualizing various data sets. The chart tool is set up as a standard graphing tool with the ability to change both the *X* and *Y* axis depending on the variables of interest. What makes Gapminder unique and powerful is its ability to show data

Table 4.4 (*continued*)

over time; this feature is seen as a timeline at the bottom of the Chart tool. By default, Gapminder World initially displays the "Wealth vs. Health of Nations" graph of Life Expectancy (years) vs. Income per Person (GDP/capita, PPP$ inflation-adjusted) as visualized in 2012; clicking on "Play" will reset the graph and allow users to see the changes to these variables over time.

**Gapminder Selections:** Gapminder allows users to select and change visualizations via the tools presented at the right side of the Chart tool. By selecting any specific region in the world map, users can place emphasis on these regions in the graphing tool. Further, users can select specific countries, regions, or common groupings of countries from the Select box or by using the Geographic Regions drop box. The last box of this panel, labeled "Size," gives users the ability to change the size of all of the visualization "bubbles" based on specific criteria from the Size drop box.

**Additional Chart Features:** Gapminder also allows users to zoom into specific locations of the chart using the Zoom tool located at the bottom right of the Chart tool. This tool can be activated/de-activated using the arrow box at the bottom right of the Chart tool window. Also, Gapminder allows for different means of visualizing data by changing axis displays from linear to log scales, located at the ends of each axis. Lastly, users can visualize data over time for specific countries simply by selecting the country in the Chart tool; this can be further augmented using the "Trails" button, which traces data over time for the selected visualization bubble.

**Exporting Charts:** Gapminder uses a simple URL format in order to allow for embedding or emailing charts created in Gapminder. "Share Graph" allows users to create a unique URL to their current Gapminder chart, including all variables and settings.

**Help:** Gapminder offers a broad-range of help options ranging from "How to Use" on the Chart tool, an FAQ, and even videos on the use of Gapminder to specific information to tips for teachers for incorporating Gapminder into their courses. Help for Gapminder can be found at *www.gapminder.org/faq_frequently_asked_questions*

**Gapminder Map**

In addition to the powerful Gapminder Chart tool, Gapminder provides Gapminder Map in order to visualize data generated using the Gapminder Chart tool on a world map. Using Gapminder Map requires users to add their data to Gapminder Chart tool then use the Gapminder Map tool to see these selections on a time-variable static world map.

**Additional Gapminder Resources**

Gapminder provides a wealth of resources on its website to help integrate Gapminder at all levels. These resources can be found under the "Video" and "For Teachers" tabs on the Gapminder home page. Also see:

- **TED Talk using Gapminder:**
  a. *www.ted.com/talks/hans_rosling_shows_the_best_stats_you_ve_ever_seen.html*
- **Adding Custom Data to Gapminder:**
  b. *http://stackoverflow.com/questions/7179915/adding-custom-data-to-gapminder*
  c. *http://en.wikibooks.org/wiki/Transformative_Applications_in_Education/Gapminder*
  d. *http://singularityhub.com/2010/08/12/gapminder-makes-statistics-awesome-now-on-your-desktop-video*
- **Gapminder Facebook Page:**
  e. *www.facebook.com/gapminder.org*

For our example, on the first page of the Gapminder site, click on "Where is HIV decreasing?" When the map loads, click "Play" to see the changes in numbers of people living with HIV from 1980 to 2011 in different countries. Students can focus in on particular countries or areas of the world in their initial exploration. Then they could pose hypotheses about immunity and access to health care and investigate other questions through the data downloads.

To see other HIV data sets students can explore, click on "Data" or go to *www.gapminder.org/data* and search for HIV. There are 14 separate data sets available for downloading in excel format and for additional visualizations. One could extend the case by looking at when particular treatments were developed and implemented with respect to maternal child transmission. One could speculate about the relationship of HIV and TB using several of the data sets. These kinds of approaches could lead to students reading papers in the primary literature, to presentations or public service messages about HIV, as well as other projects and assignments.

## Another Approach: Using Cases to Navigate Bioinformatics "Problem Spaces"

Problem spaces are rich, open-ended sets of data and analytical tools for exploring biological problems. These problem spaces are developed by professors and science education specialists with the purpose of integrating problems, issues, and concepts with real-world data sets to provide other instructors a framework for implementation into their own courses.

The diagram in Figure 4.6 shows the role of problem spaces in the classroom and development methods of these spaces. As shown, problem spaces rely on the tight integration of principles/concepts with analytical tools and pre-developed data sets in order to further student understanding of the principle while developing analysis/quantitative skill(s).

**FIGURE 4.6.**

Problem Spaces: Integration of Concepts, Tools and Data Sets Improving Student Quantitative Skills.

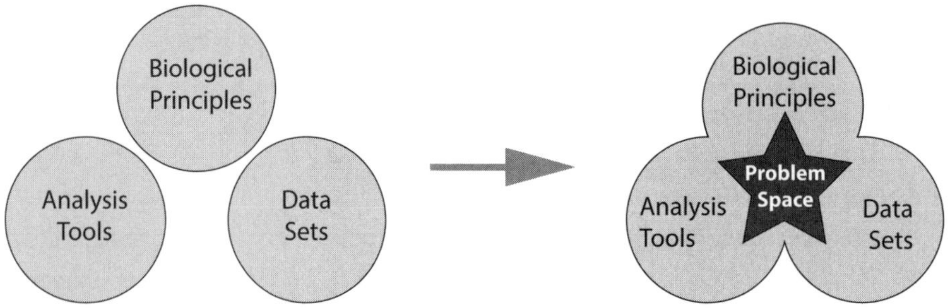


Adapted from *http://bioquest.org/bedrock/problem_spaces*

University of Pittsburgh professor in Biological Sciences and Science Educator Sam Donovan is leading the development of problem spaces as well as the teacher training of this model for quantitative skills integration in the classroom. He states:

> The basis for this vision of how teachers and students might interact with web based curricular resources involves emphasizing the use of molecular data to address biological research questions. In contrast to a more traditional lab approach where the students may be asked to follow a highly structured series of procedures to confirm an experimental result, our view of biology education emphasizes the development and exploration of students' questions as they come to understand biological principles, analytical procedures, and the ways that inferences are made from the collection and analysis of data. This approach does not dismiss the importance of learning foundational biological knowledge and skills. In fact, background knowledge and skills are viewed as essential stepping stones to applying one's knowledge to address new problems. So often, in our experience, it is in the application of factual and procedural knowledge to research questions that we come to understand more deeply both that background knowledge and how scientific claims are developed and justified. (*BEDROCK: Introduction to Problem Spaces, http://bioquest.org/th/bedrock/problem_spaces/index.php*)

Problem spaces provide:

- A brief introduction to an area of research, data set or applied biological problem.
- A collection of "open research questions" that might be addressed.
- Examples of handouts, assignments, and other curricular materials used by other faculty.
- Data and other research resources.
- References and links to background materials.
- Examples of student work and other projects that explore the problem space.

Problem spaces are meant to be flexible tools for teachers. Since they contain background material, tools to explore data as well as examples of how others have applied the materials in classes, teachers can adapt the material in many ways. We have personally used them to allow students to directly explore their own questions. Available problem spaces are listed in Table 4.5 (p. 60).

The case *Blind Spot* by Sam Donovan at the University of Pittsburgh sets the stage for students who will pursue scientific understanding by working collaboratively on answering a question of their own choice using the **Plasmodium Problem Space.** The case can be used to encourage students to share what they know and need to know as well as to develop

**TABLE 4.5.**

Problem Spaces.

- **Chimpanzee Conservation** *(species conservation/biodiversity)*
  *http://bioquest.org/bedrock/problem_spaces/chimp/index.php*
- **Desiccation Tolerance** *(phylogenetic analysis of gene families, biodiversity, species distributions)*
  *http://bioquest.org/bedrock/problem_spaces/desiccation_tolerance/index.php*
- **Enolase** *(phylogenetics protein structure, database exploration)*
  *http://bioquest.org/bedrock/problem_spaces/enolase/index.php*
- **HIV** *(viral evolution, natural selection)*
  *http://bioquest.org/bedrock/problem_spaces/hiv*
- **Prion**
  *http://bioquest.org/bedrock/problem_spaces/prion*
- **Tamarix** *(invasive species, geographical distribution, gene flow)*
  *http://bioquest.org/bedrock/problem_spaces/tamarix/index.php*
- **TRP Cage** *(protein structure/function, pharmacology, protein folding)*
  *http://bioquest.org/bedrock/problem_spaces/trpcage*
- **West Nile Virus** *(infectious disease, bioinformatics, viral structure)*
  *http://bioquest.org/bedrock/problem_spaces/wnv*
- **Whippo** *(evolution, tree reading, whale evolution)*
  *http://bioquest.org/bedrock/problem_spaces/whippo*
- **Identifying Biocontrol Agents** *(invasive species, evolution)*
  *www.nescent.org/courses/2008/workshops/PAEMST.php*
- **Plasmodium**
  *http://sites.google.com/site/plasmodiumproblem*

their own questions about humans, chimpanzees, mosquitoes, and malaria. Students will then gain access to the **Plasmodium Problem Space** that provides resources (such as data sets, tools, and links to diverse materials for studying malaria biology) to explore these questions.

More information on Plasmodium Problem Spaces can be found at: *http://sciencecasenet.org/2012/08/using-investigative-cases-to-explore-the-plasmodium-problem-space*

We suggest that you consider using cases to introduce students to these rich resources for asking questions and exploring biological data. For example, returning to our case study about HIV, we could use the problem space at *http://bioquest.org/bedrock/problem_spaces/hiv.* This problem space contains data from a published study by Markham et al. on HIV evolution within individual patients. The study involved 15 injection drug users in Baltimore, Maryland, who became infected with HIV between 1989 and 1992. Patients came in at approximately six-month intervals ("visits") to have blood samples taken. From these samples, the researchers extracted and sequenced multiple copies of proviral DNA. Patients' CD4 counts were also measured at each visit to assess their level of immune function.

In this problem space, you have access to the following materials:

- Background information on HIV/AIDS.
- The original Markham et al. reference and other primary literature.
- Viral sequences from each visit of each patient.
- Patients' CD4 counts at each visit.
- Phylogenetic trees of the virus sequences from each patient.
- A phylogenetic tree of each patient's starting consensus viral sequence.
- A published activity using this data from the book *Microbes Count!*
- Additional materials prepared by other users of the problem space.

You can use these data to explore a number of different questions. Here are a few general questions to get you started:

- Does the virus evolve the same way in different patients?
- Are there any specific mutations that cause rapid immune decline?
- What types of natural selection might be influencing HIV evolution?
- Is HIV being transmitted between patients after initial infection?

This particular problem space includes five faculty-generated ways of using the problem space in class. For example, go to *bioquest.org/bioinformatics/edgridbeloit/activities.html* to see three of these to use as models:

1. Seven Scenarios: A Context-Setting Activity for Studying Bioinformatics & Biotechnology
2. Is He Guilty? An Introduction to Working With Sequence Data and Analysis
3. Exploring HIV Evolution: An Opportunity to Do Your Own Research

## Molecular Biology Simulations

Another alternative is to use a molecular biology simulation in lab in conjunction with a case study. Case It! is an NSF-supported project for collaborative case-based learning in molecular biology. The Case It software is an open-ended simulation that reads nucleotide or amino acid sequence files, and includes methods for analyzing DNA (restriction digestion and mapping, polymerase chain reaction (PCR), DNA electrophoresis, Southern blotting and dot blotting, microarray analysis) and proteins (protein electrophoresis, Western blotting, ELISA) (Klyczek et al. 2012). Detailed tutorials that describe the various features and the steps for using them can be accessed from Case It! at *www.caseitproject.org*.

Version 6 of the software has several new features, including separate, movable windows and automated loading features for gels, blots, and ELISAs. In addition, bioinformatics capabilities (sequence alignment, tree building) have been added via integration with MEGA software. Several existing cases have bioinformatics extensions that utilize these new features. The site contains many tutorials and explorations beyond HIV. However, visit *www.caseitproject.org/wp-content/uploads/2012/07/RM2012.html#hivmain*. The site contains 13 case scenarios based on real people infected with HIV. Each case includes a video, accessed from the Case It website, showing that person discussing their experience with the disease. It also contains detailed instructions for professors that wish to implement the free software in lecture and lab. As you study the cases, here are some general questions you might consider:

- How did this person become infected with HIV?
- Have others also been infected? Who else should be tested?
- How reliable are the tests?
- How often should someone be tested?
- Why do people engage in risky behaviors?
- What impact is the infection having on this person's life?
- How can this person prevent further transmission of the virus?
- What other ethical decisions does this person face?
- How common is this case?
- Are there cultural differences regarding attitudes about HIV and prevention?

## Conclusion

So many resources, so little time. We hope that this chapter has introduced you to a number of sites that can provide materials for you to begin to use and adapt cases for your classroom. One way to get started is to join the Science Case Network (*sciencecasenet.org*). This is an online network dedicated to building a community of science educators, learners, researchers, developers, and professional organizations interested in furthering the accessibility, development, and use of cases and Problem-Based Learning (PBL). Another way might be to attend one of the national workshops sponsored by any of the case groups. A current calendar is maintained on the Science Case Network site. Of course, you could just dive in and try a case.

Last but not least, when you use a case, please make sure you give credit to the authors. Most sites use creative commons attributions, but be sure you check for copyright and reuse restrictions. When adapting a case, this is even more important. Many sites request that adaptations are resubmitted with credit given to the original authors, adaptations identified, and credited appropriately to the new authors. We are a community that wants to share and learn from each other. Please join us!

## References

American Association for the Advancement of Science (AAAS). 2010. *Vision and change in undergraduate biology education: A call to action*. Washington, DC: AAAS.

Centers for Disease Control and Prevention. 2012. Trends in the prevalence of extreme obesity among US preschool-aged children living in low-income families, 1998–2010. *JAMA* 308 (24): 2563–2565.

Donovan, S. Using problem spaces in the classroom. *http://bioquest.org/bedrock/problem_spaces*

Dori, Y. J., R. T. Tal, and M. Tsausu. 2003. Teaching biotechnology through case studies: Can we improve higher order thinking skills of non-science majors? *Science Education* 87 (6): 767–793.

Dwyer, C. A., A. Gallagher, J. Levin, and M. E. Morley, 2003. *What is quantitative reasoning? Defining the concept for assessment purposes*. Princeton, NJ: Educational Testing Service.

Grawe, N. D. 2012. Achieving a quantitative literate society. Resources and community to support national change. *Liberal Education* 91 (2): 30–35.

Hmelo-Silver, C. E. 2004. Problem-based learning: What and how do students learn? *Educational Psychology Review* 16 (3): 235–266.

Klyczek, K., M. Bergland, and M. Lundeberg. 2012. Computer simulations connecting molecular biology laboratory techniques with bioinformatics analysis and student research. *The International Journal of Learning* 18 (6): 291–330.

Manduca, C. A., and D. W. Mogk. 2003. Using data in undergraduate science classrooms. Final report on an interdisciplinary workshop. *http://serc.carleton.edu/usingdata/index.html*

Spierer, D., S. Williams, and J. Lyttle. 2007. Inactive brains: An interrupted case study. National Center for Case Study Teaching in Science. *http://sciencecases.lib.buffalo.edu/cs*

Sutherland, T., and C. Bonwell, eds. 1996. Using active learning in college classes: A range of options for faculty. *New Directions for Teaching and Learning 67.*

Tolkien, J. R. R. 1954. *The lord of the rings.* Volume I. *The fellowship of the ring.* New York: Ballantine Books.

Yadav, A., M. A. Lundeberg, M. DeSchryver, K. Dirkin, N. A. Schiller, K. Maier, and C. F. Herreid. 2007. Teaching science with case studies: A national survey of faculty perceptions of the benefits and challenges of using cases. *Journal of College Science Teaching* 37 (1): 34–38.

# SECTION I

# THE SCIENTIFIC METHOD

# CELL PHONE USE AND CANCER

*Wilma V. Colón Parrilla*

## Abstract

Based on a scientific article on cell phone use and the risk of acoustic neuroma (Lönn et al. 2004), this case study provides students with an opportunity to review and analyze data about a topic that holds a great deal of interest for them. Students first analyze news articles reporting on the research study and then read the original research article.


## Learning Objectives

- Identify the basic elements of a scientific research study.
- Evaluate a scientific study and offer suggestions for improvement.
- Analyze the appropriateness of the headlines of news articles in relation to their content.
- Compare the accuracy of information offered to the public in a news article with the information presented in a scientific paper.

## Quantitative Reasoning Skills/Concepts

- Use graphs to formulate predictions and explanations.
- Articulate, complete, and correct claims based on data.
- Use appropriate reasoning to support the validity of data-based claims.

## The Case Study

### *Part I: Hang Up!?*

"Alisa, please, get off your cell phone already," said her mother.

"But mom! I want to talk with my friends! Plus all my friends use it!" Alisa whined in response. Annoyed by her mother's impatience, she mumbled: "Anyway, weekends are for free, you know."

"This is not about the money. This is about your health. I've heard that there is a link between cell phones and cancer," Alisa's mother explained.

"You're right!" said Alana, Alisa's sister, cutting in. "In my scientific journalism class we are going to discuss some articles about a study that has been performed on cell phone use and its effect on health. The professor asked us to analyze the titles of those articles," Alana added.

"And what did the study reveal? Has such a link been proved?" asked her mother, interested in hearing more.

"Well, we haven't read the articles yet, but I have their titles here. You can read them," Alana said as she handed a paper to her mother with the following list:

1. Long-Term Cell Phone Use Spurs Tumor Growth
2. Study Indicates Mobile Phones Increase Tumor Risk
3. Mobile Phone Use and Acoustic Neuroma
4. Study Links Mobile Phones, Benign Tumors
5. Cell Phone-Tumor Link Found?

"Now I'm even more confused. Do cell phones cause cancer or not? Can I use mine or not?" asked Alisa impatiently.

"In my next class we're going to read the articles, so I will tell you everything then," concluded her sister.

## Questions

1. What information about the scientific research can be inferred by reading the headlines?
2. Compare headlines 4 and 5. Why is there a difference in the two headlines even when they outline the same scientific research?
3. What questions arise about the methodology and conclusions of the experiment when analyzing the headlines?

## *Part II: Journal Groups*

You will be organized into groups of three or four and given copies of the news articles to read, which your instructor will provide you with. Each member of the group has to read one of the articles. Afterward, you should be able to answer the following questions.

## Questions

1. What is the purpose of the research outlined in the news articles?

2. Who are the researchers involved in the scientific work and in which institution was the research conducted?
3. What methods did the researchers use?
4. Explain the difference between an observational study like this and a controlled experiment.
5. State the results of the study.
6. What conclusions were drawn from the study?
7. Compare the scientific information described in articles 4 and 5: "Study Links Mobile Phones, Benign Tumors," and "Cell Phone-Tumor Link Found?" Which of the two headlines better describes the results of the scientific research? Why?
8. How much credibility do you give to the results of the study? Why?
9. Give suggestions on how to improve the study.
10. How do scientists report the results of their experiments? Why is it important to disseminate this information?

## Part III: A Scientific Article

Your assignment is to read the *Epidemiology* research paper (Lönn et al. 2004) for the next class. The next time class meets, there will be a class discussion led by the instructor. The questions below will help you prepare for this discussion.

### Questions

1. Compare the scientific data given in the press articles with those in the scientific paper.
2. Do you think cell phone use is hazardous to human health?
3. Based on this information, are you going to avoid using cell phones in the future?

## Web Version

Detailed teaching notes, the case PDF, an answer key, and copies of the news articles are available on the NCCSTS website at *sciencecases.lib.buffalo.edu/cs/collection/detail.asp?case_id=210&id=210*.

## References

Lönn, S., A. Ahlbom, P. Hall, and M. Feychting. 2004. Mobile phone use and the risk of acoustic neuroma. *Epidemiology* 15 (6): 653–659.

# IS HIGH-FRUCTOSE CORN SYRUP BAD FOR THE APPLE INDUSTRY?

*Jeffri C. Bohlscheid*

## Abstract

This case is based on a scientific journal article that found that mishandling high fructose corn syrup (HFCS) by allowing it to be exposed to elevated temperatures for excessive periods could lead to the formation of lethal concentrations of toxic sugar by-products such as hydroxymethylfurfural. Students analyze the article and apply the scientific method to solve an agricultural mystery in which a fictional apple farmer and his son are trying to determine if HFCS has led to the loss of beehives necessary for pollinating their apple trees.

## Learning Objectives

- Critically analyze a peer-reviewed scientific article.
- Determine major issues addressed in a scientific article.
- Decipher trends in graphical data presentations.
- Develop recommendations from the conclusions drawn from the research presented.

## Quantitative Reasoning Skills/Concepts

- Represent data in graphs.
- Use graphs to formulate predictions and explanations.
- Articulate complete and correct claims based on data.
- Use appropriate reasoning to support the validity of data-based claims.
- Create experimental designs to test hypotheses.

## The Case Study

### *Part I: Demise of the Hives*

Dad snapped shut his cell phone and his shoulders slumped. "Now we've got a real problem," he sighed.

Life as an apple farmer in Wenatchee, Washington, could be challenging, but Dad was looking particularly depressed.

"What is it now?" Bruce asked.

"Seems that the last beekeeper in the area has lost almost all of his hives," Bruce's dad replied.

After a semester of introductory entomology at Washington State University and a childhood spent in an apple orchard, Bruce knew that this was bad. Bees were necessary to pollinate apple trees to produce the fruit. They pollinated over 130 different food crops, such as berries, beans, nuts, melons, and tree fruit. In fact, bees were responsible for over $15 billion in agricultural products in the United States alone. Without bees, there would be none of these foods. And that included *apples*—which were paying for Bruce's college education!

Bruce thought for a moment. "Can you call anyone from outside the area?" he asked.

"*If* we can find someone—but, even if we could, it might be too late. We only have a window of a week for pollination," Bruce's dad answered. "With the loss of so many hives around here, beekeepers from outside the area might be reluctant to come up here."

Bruce pondered this. Colony Collapse Disorder (CCD), the phrase used to describe the unexplained death or disappearance of a hive, could have over 60 different factors involved. Pesticides and herbicides used in the fields, fungal infections, viruses, and gut-eating mites all had been implicated.

Dad looked perplexed. "The thing is … this just happened over the last three weeks. Our local beekeepers' hives have had a clean bill of health these last few years. I've got money invested with one keeper and there were no signs of infections or chemicals. We've been watching this very closely."

"I'm going to run some errands," said dad. "I think I'll stop by the library and extension office and see if I can find anything out."

Dad came back much later in the day. "Bruce, what do you know about high fructose corn syrup? I found a research article written by scientists at the U.S. Department of Agriculture that seems to say it could be involved with CCD. Can you help me figure this thing out? Recently we have been feeding high fructose corn syrup to our hives."

Bruce had gone over a few scientific articles in school his senior year—hopefully that would help him analyze the data in the article his father handed him. "Well, let's just give this a look," he said. Sitting down, Bruce pulled out a note pad and began to read.

"So … what are your questions?" he asked his father.

Pulling out his own notes, Dad said, "Well, this could be pretty controversial and damaging stuff, so I really want to understand what is going on."

## Your Task

Read the following abstract of the scientific article (LeBlanc et al. 2009) as well as the introduction section of the same article (which your instructor will provide you) and then answer the questions that follow. To help you with your reading, a list of terms and their definitions is included in Table 6.1 (p. 74).

> ***Abstract***
>
> *In the United States, high-fructose corn syrup (HFCS) has become a sucrose replacement for honey bees and has widespread use as a sweetener in many processed foods and beverages for human consumption. It is utilized by commercial beekeepers as a food for honey bees for several reasons: to promote brood production, after bees have been moved for commercial pollination, and when field-gathered nectar sources are scarce. Hydroxymethylfurfural (HMF) is a heat-formed contaminant and is the most noted toxin to honey bees. Currently, there are no rapid field tests that would alert beekeepers of dangerous levels of HMF in HFCS or honey. In this study, the initial levels and the rates of formation of HMF at four temperatures were evaluated in U.S.-available HFCS samples. Different HFCS brands were analyzed and compared for acidity and metal ions by inductively coupled plasma mass spectroscopy. Levels of HMF in eight HFCS products were evaluated over 35 days, and the data were fit to polynomial and exponential equations, with excellent correlations. The data can be used by beekeepers to predict HMF formation on storage. Caged bee studies were conducted to evaluate the HMF dose–response effect on bee mortality. Finally, commercial bases such as lime, potash, and caustic soda were added to neutralize hydronium ion in HMF samples, and the rates of HMF formation were compared at 45°C.*

## Dad's Questions

1. What are the major issues that the authors are addressing in the article?
2. Why is acid added to the syrups? Are there consequences to this?
3. What is the hypothesis and what are the objectives of the authors in this article? Is this relevant to our problem?

Bruce had his own questions after quickly scanning the introduction of the article.

## Bruce's Questions

1. Who would be most interested in the results of this scientific study?

2. With what I know about the scientific method, what should the researchers' next steps be to test their hypothesis and meet their objectives? How would I outline the experiments required to answer the researchers' questions?
3. How long do honeybees live?

"Dad, I think I'll get back to you in the morning."

**TABLE 6.1.**

Definitions of Terms.

| Term | Definition |
|---|---|
| Codex Alimentarius Commission | Organization within the United Nations and Food and Agriculture Organization that develops international food standards to protect health and ensure fair trade. |
| Dissolved solids | Material dissolved in water that can be recovered by drying. In HFCS these would primarily be sugars. % dissolved solids = g dissolved material/100 ml of solution. |
| Dysentery | Inflammation of the intestinal tract that can lead to diarrhea and death. |
| Enzymes | Specialized proteins that speed up chemical reactions (catalysts). |
| Fermentation | Conversion of sugar into alcohol and other substances by microorganisms such as yeast. These compounds can be toxic to bees. |
| Heavy metals | Cadmium, mercury, and lead, for example. |
| Hydrolyze | To break a molecule apart chemically by the addition of water. |
| Invertase | Enzyme that hydrolyzes sucrose into glucose and fructose (the mixture is called invert sugar). |
| Kinetics | Study of the rate of chemical reactions, commonly expressed as unit of product per time. |
| First order kinetics | The rate of a chemical reaction is proportional to the amount of the starting materials, i.e., the sugars. |
| Mineral acids | Acids that do not contain carbon, e.g., HCl (hydrochloric acid) and $H_2SO_4$ (sulfuric acid); generally much stronger acids compared to organic acids. |
| Organic acids | Acids that contain carbon, e.g., citric acid (lemons), tartaric acid (cream of tartar), and lactic acid (yogurt). |

Table 6.1 (*continued*)

| Term | Definition |
|---|---|
| Pasteurization | Heat treatment given to foods to kill off pathogens (disease causing) microorganisms, but not all microorganisms; much more mild than sterilization. |
| ppm | Parts per million, unit of concentration, i.e., microgram/gram or milligram/kilogram. |
| Sucrose | Table sugar, composed of chemically bonded glucose (blood sugar) and fructose (fruit sugar). |
| Thermal effect | The results of heating; increased temperatures generally result in faster chemical reactions. |
| Transition metals | Cobalt, copper, iron, and manganese, for example. |

## *Part II: Analysis of Commercial High-Fructose Corn Syrup Samples*

"OK, Dad, let's go through this paper. What are your questions?"

Dad pulled out his notes again. "So I was looking at this table here and I don't get it."

### Your Task

Examine Table 6.2 (p. 76), taken from the article, and then answer Dad's questions.

**TABLE 6.2.**

Hydronium Ion Concentration, Hydroxymethylfurfural Concentration, and Elemental Analysis of Domestically Produced High-Fructose Corn Syrup.

The D-blend sample was a HFCS-55-sucrose syrup blend that is specifically formulated for beekeepers. The higher pH of this D-blend syrup is due to its high sucrose concentration. Sucrose is less stable at pH values <8.3 and particularly at even lower pH values (18). *Note:* The HFCS samples were gifts from Roquette, Archer Daniels Midland, Mann Lake, Inc. (Cargill HFCS), and Tate & Lyle. All of the HFCS samples were received in quart containers, with the exception of Mann Lake, Inc. (Cargill HFCS), which were provided as 5 gal (18.5 L) samples.

| HFCS | pH | % HCl | $HMF_0$ (µg/g) | % Fructose[a] | % C, H, N, S* |
|---|---|---|---|---|---|
| A-42 | 4.15 ± 0.04 | 0.0104 ± 0.0013 | 20.75 ± 0.004 | 42 | 29.30 ± 0.09, 5.55 ± 0.08, 0.0, 0.0 |
| B-42 | 3.86 ± 0.02 | 0.0108 ± 0.0007 | 3.07 ± 0.002 | 42 | 29.50 ± 0.06, 7.65 ± 0.04, 0.0, 0.0 |
| C-42 | 4.18 ± 0.04 | 0.0092 ± 0.0005 | 8.13 ± 0.000 | 42 | 29.53 ± 0.11, 7.55 ± 0.04, 0.0, 0.0 |
| A-55 | 4.86 ± 0.17 | 0.0776 ± 0.0004 | 28.65 ± 0.005 | 55 | 31.72 ± 0.14, 7.39 ± 0.04, 0.0, 0.0 |
| B-55 | 4.16 ± 0.04 | 0.0092 ± 0.0030 | 20.77 ± 0.006 | 56 | 31.56 ± 0.08, 7.42 ± 0.0, 0.0, 0.0 |
| C-55 | 5.02 ± 0.02 | 0.0074 ± 0.0004 | 7.89 ± 0.004 | 56 | 31.69 ± 0.13, 7.43 ± 0.07, 0.0, 0.0 |
| D-55 | 4.34 ± 0.06 | 0.0085 ± 0.0005 | 27.47 ± 0.003 | 55 | 31.70 ± 0.09, 7.41 ± 0.01, 0.0, 0.0 |
| D-blend | 6.09 ± 0.06 | 0.0062 ± 0.0008 | 4.05 ± 0.001 | 50 | 32.79 ± 0.05, 7.19 ± 0.03, 0.0, 0.0 |

* C = Carbon, H = Hydrogen, N = Nitrogen, and S = Sulfur

## Dad's Questions

1. What do 42, 50, and 55 stand for?
2. What do A, B, C, and D indicate?
3. What does Table 6.2 tell us about the relationships between HFCS samples, HFCS composition, acidity, and HMF content?

"The table doesn't make much sense to me," Dad continued. "Is there another way to present the data that is more meaningful?"

"Let's get some graph paper and see if there is a pattern," suggested Bruce.

### Your Task

Graph the data in Table 6.2 using the graph paper that your instructor will give you. Each student should graph the data individually; then compare your results with your group, after which we will discuss the data as a class.

Bruce constructed a graph of the data in Table 6.2 and handed it to his father. Not surprisingly, Dad had some questions for Bruce about it.

### Dad's Questions

1. Explain why you chose the particular axes on the graph.
2. What are the dependent and independent variables?
3. What conclusions can you draw from the resulting graph?

After answering Dad's questions, Bruce moved on to the figures in the article. "Well, it seems that the scientists looked at how heat affected HMF production in the syrups," he noted.

## *Part III: Formation of Hydroxymethylfurfural in High-Fructose Corn Syrup*

Looking at the figure from the article, Bruce began to consider the ways in which the specific graphs were similar and different.

### Your Task

Examine the graphs in Figure 6.1 (p. 78) and then answer Bruce's and Dad's questions.

**FIGURE 6.1.**

Rates of increase of HMF (ppm) with respect to time over 35 days at 31.5, 40.0, 49.0, and 68.8 °C.

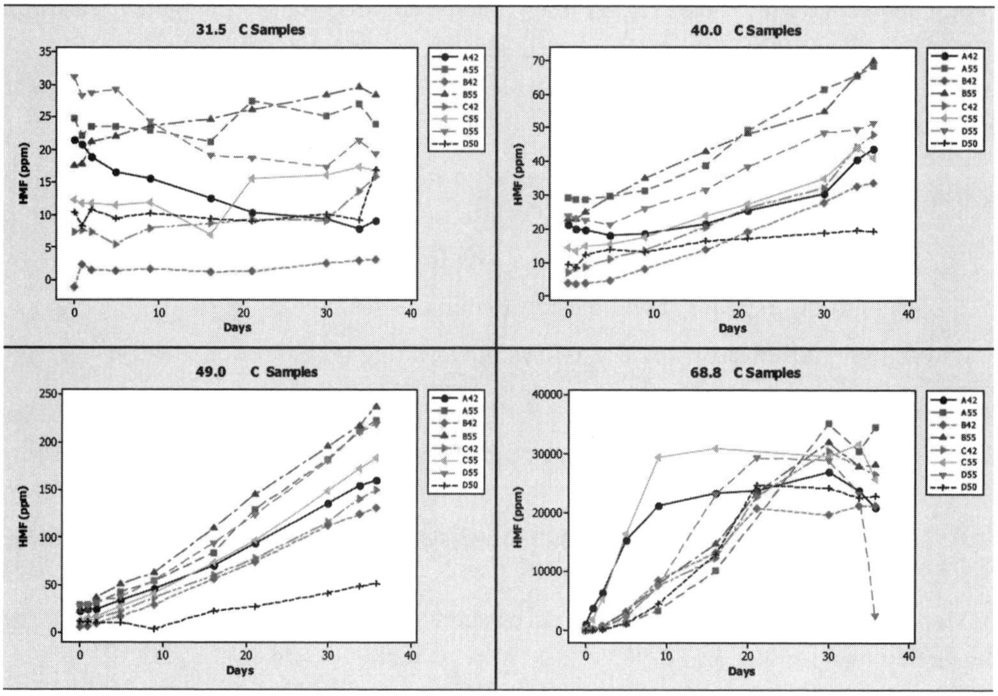


## Bruce's Questions

1. What are the overall trends?
2. How are the graphs similar?
3. How are the graphs different?
4. How are the axes different and what are the implications?

"OK, Bruce, my turn to ask some questions."

## Dad's Questions

1. Why did the researchers select these times and temperatures?
2. What do the temperatures 40°C and 49°C equal in °F?
3. What can we conclude from these graphs?"

Bruce was really getting intrigued by the study.

## Bruce's Question

1. Given the hypothesis I developed earlier, what as a researcher would I want to test next to determine if HMF is an issue in HFCS?

## *Part IV: Caged Bee Studies*

"Well, it seems that heat can really influence the rate of HMF formation," Dad concluded. He started reading the next section of the article, titled "Materials and Methods," which was associated with two figures in the article (Figures 6.2 and 6.3).

> ***Caged Honey Bee Experiments***
>
> *As previously reported, a caged bee method was used (17). Approximately 100 freshly emerged Italian honey bees were placed into the cage for each caged bee trial (conducted in triplicate). Current research laws use committee approval for honey bee research. The caged trials were recorded in multiples of four, so that average and standard deviation counts can be reported. For all trials, the bees were fed water, ad libitum, and a plug of pollen–sugar. For the HFCS syrup formulation, we used A-55, which was determined to have 57 ppm HMF. For the higher HMF concentration solutions (100, 150, 200, and 250 ppm), pure HMF was added to the 57 ppm HFCS to obtain the desired concentrations.*

"What does *ad libitum* mean?" asked Dad.

"I think it means that they could eat as much as they like," Bruce suggested.

"Okay, but I have some other questions about these figures," Dad continued.

## Your Task

Examine Figures 6.2 and 6.3 (pp. 80–81) and then answer Dad's questions.

**FIGURE 6.2.**

Consumption of HMFS in Milligrams of HFCS per Bee at 3 Days (A) and Over 27 Days (B). Different letters in the bar graph indicate significant differences in mortality between different HMF dosages, ANOVA, Dunnet two-sided ($P < 0.005$).

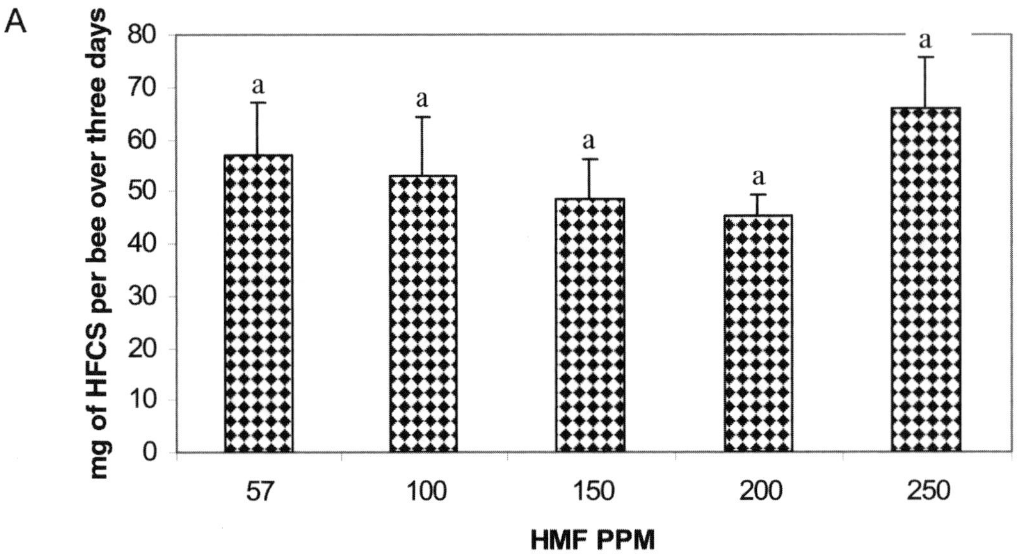


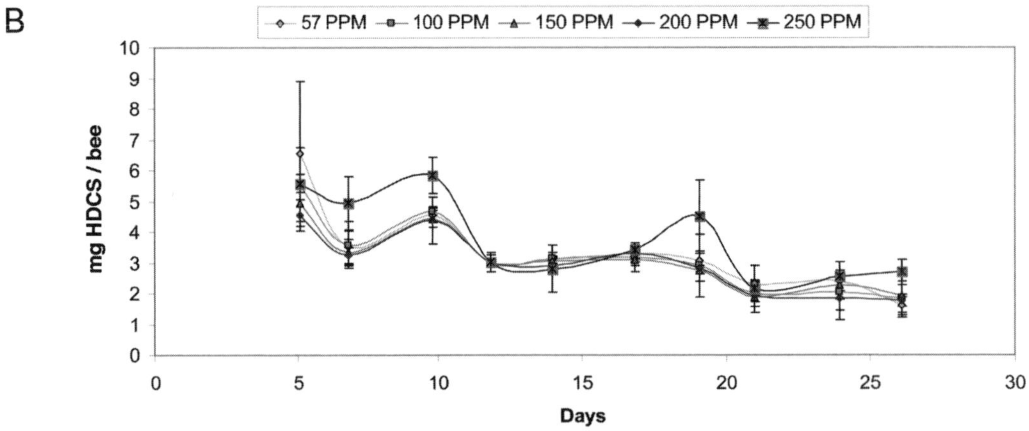

**FIGURE 6.3.**

Mortality Data From Caged Bee Studies for Bees Dosed With 57, 100, 150, 200, and 250 ppm HMF. Different letters indicate significant differences in mortality between different HMF dosages, ANOVA, Dunnet two-sided ($P < 0.005$).

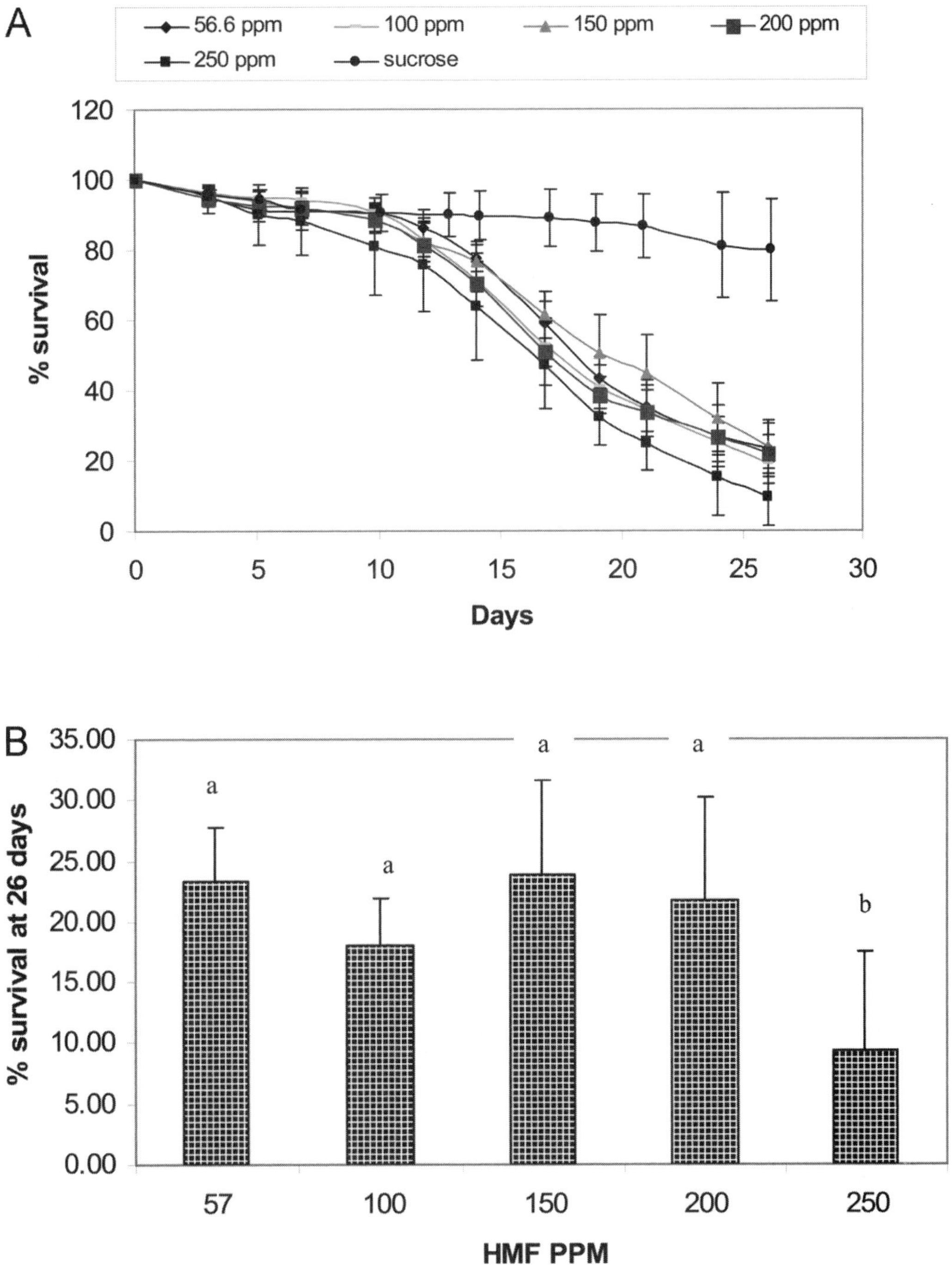

## Dad's Questions

1. What is the purpose of the sucrose (table sugar) in Figure 6.2A?
2. Why did the researchers choose % survival at 26 days?
3. Why were these levels of HMF selected?
4. What do these graphs tell us?

"Whoa, slow down," said Bruce.

## *Part V: Industry Response*

"So Bruce, do we have a problem here?" asked Dad.

Bruce thought to himself.

## Questions

1. Given all of the results presented, what overall conclusions can I draw from this study?
2. Did the researchers meet their objectives and demonstrate enough evidence to support their hypothesis?
   a. If not, what other studies may need to be done?
   b. Would these assist in answering the most important questions facing Dad, or just be of interest?

Dad came back into the room after being on the internet. "Seems the high fructose corn syrup producers were not that happy with this article. I found a response by the HFCS manufacturers."

> ***Humans, bees not at risk from heated HFCS, says CRA*** *by Jess Halliday, 01-Sep-2009*
>
> *Storage standards and temperature control for HFCS mean human health is not at risk from the formation of hydroxymethylfurfural (HMF), the Corn Refiners Association asserts, which also refutes suggestions that the toxin could be a factor in honeybee colony collapse disorder.*
>
> *In a new study published in the Journal of Agriculture and Food Chemistry, USDA researchers measured HMF levels in samples of HFCS over a 35 day time frame, at temperatures of 31.5, 40.0, 49.0 and 68.8°C.*
>
> *Study leader LeBlanc and team saw that HMF levels increased steadily with temperature, and that there was a dramatic jump at 49°C—a finding they said is important for commercial*

*beekeepers, for manufacturers of HFCS, and for purposes of food storage.*

*But the CRA has called the study "flawed," and emphasized that its members have safety measures and best practices in place.*

*Dr John White of White Technical Research, a consultant whose clients include the CRA, told FoodNavigator.com that there are well-established and widely-available industry storage standards for HFCS: for HFCS 55 the temperature standard is between 75°F and 86°F (23.9°C to 30°C), and for HFCS 42 between 95°F and 106°F (35°C to 41.1°C).*

*Moreover, the standards specify use of containers made with stainless steel or mild steel coated with stainless steel material.*

*"Clearly LeBlanc used extreme conditions aimed at maximizing HMF formation which contradicted both temperature and vessel composition specifications. It should be noted that any syrup source subjected to such harsh treatment would produce elevated levels of HMF," White said, on behalf of the Corn Refiners Association.*

***No danger to bees or humans***

*The CRA and White say the risks of HMF to humans presented by the new study are also over-egged. They say that a 2000 study by Janzowski et al. discounts HMF as posing a serious health risk to humans.*

*The new study also suggested that the formation of HMF could be a factor in the decline in honey bee populations, known as colony collapse disorder (CCD). It leant on a study published in 1966 by Bailey to support claims that the toxin that causes gut ulceration and dysentery-like symptoms in bees.*

*HFCS is given to bees to stimulate brood rearing and boost honey production. But according to White, properly stored HFCS would not pose a risk for honeybees.*

*He cites a study by Jachimowicz et al, published in 1975, which saw that concentrations of up to 3mg HMF per 100g of solution was harmless for bees. This would mean that the base HMF level established by LeBlanc, of 30 parts per million (ppm) is also harmless.*

*"Honeybee producers clearly violate published storage recommendations when they expose HFCS to excessive temperatures and store it for prolonged periods in unapproved containers."*

*Nor was HFCS cited as a potential cause of CCD published this year in the Proceedings of the National Academy of Sciences; rather, ribosomal RNA degradation was seen to be the likely cause.*

***References***

*Apidologie 1975; 6:121–143. "Problems of invert sugar as food for honeybees." Authors: Jachimowicz, T.; El Sherbiny, G.*

*Journal of Agriculture and Food Science 2009, 57, 736907376. DOI: 10.1021/jf9014526. "Formation of hydroxymethylfurfural in domestic high fructose corn syrup and its toxicity to the honey bee (Apis mellifera)." Authors: LeBlanc, B.; Eggleston, G.; Sammataro, D.; Cornett, C.; Dufault, R.; Deeby, T.; St Cyr, E.*

*Food Chemical Toxicology 2000; 38:801-809. "5-Hydroxymethylfurfural: assessment of mutagenicity, DNAdamaging potential and reactivity toward cellular glutathione." Janzowski, C.; Glaab, B.; Samimi, E.; Schlatter, J.; Eisenbrand, G.*

Article published at *www.foodnavigator-usa.com/Science/Humans-bees-not-at-risk-from-heated-HFCS-says-CRA*

After reading the article, Bruce asked: "Dad, how long did the beekeepers have the HFCS, and where did they get the HFCS from?"

## Final Questions

1. Given all of the information presented, what overall conclusions can you draw from the study and response by the HFCS manufacturers?
2. What is the probability that the beekeepers may have killed off their own bees?

## *Homework Assignment*

The local Washington State apple growers association has asked Bruce's father to draft a position paper on the potential problems of continued use of HFCS as bee food. Your job is to write the paper for him, summarizing the major issues and findings of the articles in order to provide a fair and balanced assessment of the threat of the use of HFCS to apple growers. You should address the concerns of the various stakeholders in your decision (apple growers, beekeepers, HFCS manufacturers, and the general public). It is important to consider what is known, what is speculation, and what needs to be determined.

## Web Version

Detailed teaching notes, the case PDF, and an answer key are available on the NCCSTS website at *sciencecases.lib.buffalo.edu/cs/collection/detail.asp?case_id=642&id=642*.

## Reference

LeBlanc, B. W., G. Eggelston, D. Sammataro, C. Cornett, R. Dufault, T. Deeby, and E. St Cyr. 2009. Formation of hydroxymethylfurfural in domestic high-fructose corn syrup and its toxicity to the honey bee (*Apis mellifera*). *Journal of Agricultural and Food Chemistry* 57: 7369–7376.

CHAPTER 7

# FEELING DETOXIFIED

## Expectations, Effects, and Explanations

*Giselle A. McCallum* and *Annie Prud'homme-Généreux*

## Abstract

This case uses ionic foot baths to examine how placebo treatments can affect our health and wellness. Inspired by a student's real visit to a spa, the story begins with a description of the experience of an ionic foot bath and then debunks the chemical explanation given by the spa as to how the foot bath works. The case then introduces placebo treatments and the placebo effect, and discusses how placebos can affect our health.


## Learning Objectives

- Describe the causes of the phenomena observed during an ionic foot bath treatment.
- Propose plausible hypotheses to explain the effects of the treatment on the human body.
- Critically review claims about the mechanism of action of ionic foot baths.
- Analyze data presented in tabular form from a research study.
- Describe a placebo and its effects on the outcome of any medical treatment.

## Quantitative Reasoning Skills/Concepts

- Carry out basic mathematical operations.
- Depending on how students choose to analyze the data, represent data in graphs.
- Use numerical data to formulate null and alternative hypotheses.
- Accept or reject null hypotheses based on statistical tests of significance.
- Articulate complete and correct claims based on data.
- Use appropriate reasoning to support the validity of data-based claims.
- Create experimental designs to test hypotheses.
- Identify the best way to interpret data when not presented in a standard way (e.g., presented in a table instead of a graph, presented as more "raw data" rather than summarized statistics, where there are two independent variables rather than only one, and so on).

## The Case Study

### *Part I: The Detoxifying Ionic Foot Bath Experience*

Stressed and tired, you look forward to your monthly visit at the *A New You!* spa. Upon arrival, you are given an information booklet about a new treatment that is being offered. It is an ionic foot bath. You are seduced by the assurances that it will leave you feeling refreshed and opt for this treatment. The spa's technician tends to you, ensures that you are comfortable, and directs you to sit and place your feet in a bath of salt water. She then switches on the electrical box connected to two metal rods that rest in the foot bath.

"This machine's iron electrodes ionize the water in the bath. This creates a negative bio-charge in your body and draws unwanted toxins out of special pores on the soles of your feet. You'll actually see it working," the attendant explains enthusiastically.

"Oh, right," you reply. A few minutes later, reddish-brown streaks appear in the bath water. By the time your half-hour treatment nears its end, the whole bath has a dark brown-reddish tinge, and bubbles cover the surface of the water, which smells faintly of chlorine. You ask the spa's attendant about the smell.

"It's from all the chlorine that we consume in our tap water. It can also be left over in your body from swimming pools. The foot bath pulls it out of your feet. It detoxifies your body."

You leave the spa feeling refreshed. When you return home, you are intrigued. You read with interest the pamphlet that the spa provided you:

> *Electricity is used in this treatment to create positive and negative ions from the water molecules in the foot bath. These ions can penetrate your body. Their positive and negative charge allows them to act as a molecular sponge to soak up and sequester particles of opposite charge. These neutralized toxins then leave the body through the surface of the feet that are in contact with water in the foot bath, leaving you cleansed and refreshed.*

### Questions

1. Why might you be tempted to believe what the pamphlet and spa attendant say? What aspects are convincing?
2. Why might you be skeptical? What are some of the problems with the explanation provided?
3. Design an easy experiment to test whether the explanations provided by the spa are accurate.

## *Part II: A Proposed Chemistry of Foot Baths*

After your spa foot bath, you feel refreshed. You are mentally alert, and that persistent pain in your right knee has faded considerably. Despite your skepticism about the scientific explanation behind it, you feel so fantastic that you sign up for another foot bath the following week.

Over lunch one day, you tell your friends about this experience. Your friends question your foot bath experience.

"But how does it *actually* work? How do you know that it is working? Have you tried taking your feet out and seeing what happens?"

Those questions nag at you when you visit the spa the next time. You resolve to do the experiment that your friends suggest. You are comfortably seated with your feet in the ionic foot bath. The attendant turns the machine on. However, this time, when she leaves the room, you look around cautiously and then slowly slide your feet out.

As time passes, the water slowly turns brown, the faint chlorine smell becomes detectable, and bubbles appear in the water. Your feet are not in the water, so obviously the bath is not drawing unwanted toxins out of your feet. Where do the chlorine smell, the reddish-brown color, and the bubbles come from?

Determined to solve the mystery, you call on your friends for their help. Michael starts things off by drawing on Figure 7.1 as he says: "Let's start with the salty water. The most common salt is table salt, sodium chloride (NaCl), so let's assume that's the salt used in the foot baths. When it is dissolved in water, the two atoms in salt dissociate into their constituent ions: $Na^+$ and $Cl^-$. There always exist a small number of water molecules ($H_2O$) that are

**FIGURE 7.1.**

Proposed Reduction-Oxidation Reactions in the Ionic Footbath.

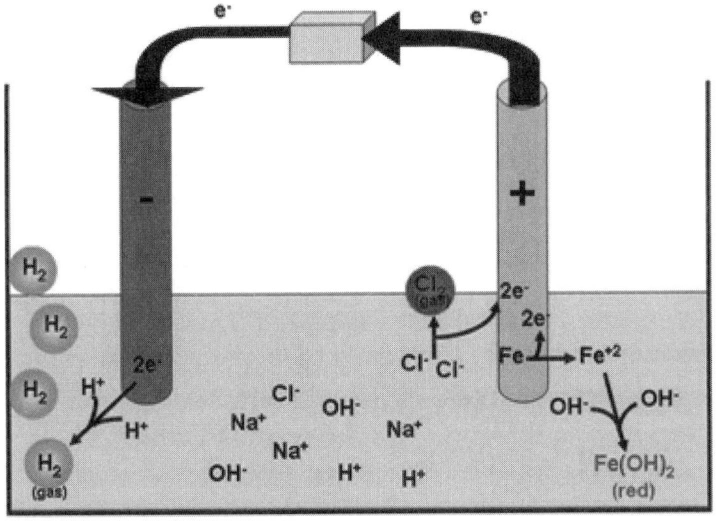


Anode: $Fe_{(s)} \rightarrow Fe^{+2} + 2e^-$

$2Cl^- \rightarrow Cl_{2(g)} + 2e^-$

Cathode: $2H^+ + 2e^- \rightarrow H_{2(g)}$

In the bath: $Fe^{+2} + 2OH^- \rightarrow Fe(OH)_2$

dissociated into $H^+$ and $OH^-$ ions. In other words, you have the following ions in the foot bath: $H^+$, $OH^-$, $Na^+$, and $Cl^-$."

Allison, a chemistry major, thinks she holds another piece of the puzzle.

"What you have here is a simple electrochemical cell where oxidation and reduction reactions take place. Don't panic about the jargon: Let me explain. There were two rods made of metal that were plunged into the water and through which an electrical current was running. An electrical current means that electrons ($e^-$) were flowing in one direction through the wires. In solution, the current is carried by migrating ions. The electrons are induced to move by a force that is provided by the power supply that the foot bath is connected to."

"Metals conduct electricity because they have electrons that can be freed from their atoms to move to other atoms. If we follow the path of an electron through the system, it might look like this: An electron starts in the metal of one of the rods; we'll call this rod the anode. As the anode loses electrons, the metal acquires a positive charge (because it lost some negatively-charged electrons). The electrons flow through the wire and end up in the other metal rod (the cathode), which has a negative charge (because it accepted negatively charged electrons)."

You and Michael nod in agreement. Allison continues as she draws on Figure 7.1.

"The spa attendant told you the metal rods are made of iron. When an electrical charge is run through the cell, the anode loses electrons in the following reaction:

$$Fe_{(s)} \rightarrow Fe^{+2} + 2e^-$$

In other words, the electrode dissolves over time. While the Fe found in the electrodes cannot dissolve in water, the $Fe^{+2}$ ions that are being created by the current are able to interact with other ions in the water."

"In the foot bath, some of the positively charged $Fe^{+2}$ ions react with negatively charged $OH^-$ ions to form $Fe(OH)_{2(s)}$, which is reddish-brown in color (see Figure 7.2). You may also have seen flecks of rusty metal floating in the water."

$$Fe^{+2} + 2OH- \rightarrow Fe(OH)_{2(s)}$$

Allison continues this idea, as she adds to Figure 7.1.

"The negatively charged cathode attracts the positive H+ and Na+ ions in the water. Because H+ accepts electrons more easily than Na+, the Na+ ions do not react at the cathode. They stay in the solution. The H+ ions, however, do react. They gain electrons to become hydrogen gas: $2H^+ + 2e^- \rightarrow H_{2(g)}$

Following the same line of thought, you tentatively propose the following explanation.

"Another reaction occurs at the anode. Its positive charge attracts negatively charged ions. Thus, $Cl^-$ ions are drawn to this electrode. Once they reach the anode, they donate their extra electron, and combine to form chlorine gas:

$$2Cl^- \rightarrow Cl_{2(g)} + 2e^-$$

"Wow!" interjects Allison. "Did you know that chlorine gas is poisonous and was used during World War I as a chemical weapon?"

**FIGURE 7.2.**

$Fe(OH)_2$ is a red-brown substance that forms in the bath.

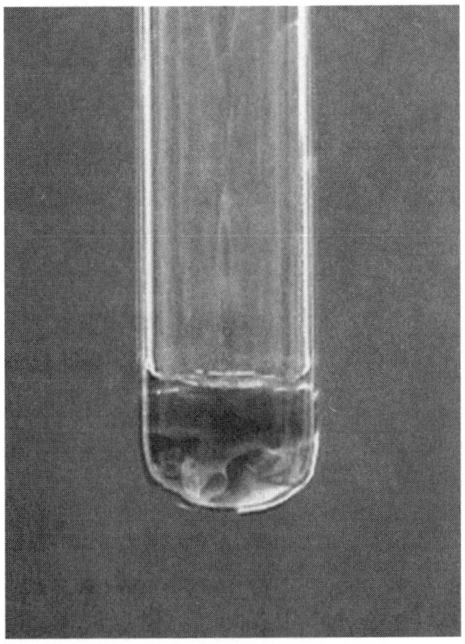

*Credit:* Reprinted with permission of James P. Birk, Arizona State University, *www.public.asu.edu/~jpbirk/qual/qualanal/iron.html*.

## Questions

1. What causes the red-brown color that you saw in the foot bath? The chlorine smell? The bubbles?
2. Should you be concerned about your foot bath's production of a chemical used in warfare?
3. If simple chemistry in the foot bath (that does not involve changes to your body) can explain what you observed, then why do you feel so much better after the treatment? Think of as many possibilities as you can to explain this phenomenon.

## *Part III: Feeling Better After Treatment*

A few weeks go by. Despite being able to explain everything that you observed in the foot bath as a phenomenon that did not involve your body, you definitely felt better after the treatment. You wonder why.

One day over lunch, you share these concerns with Michael. He immediately becomes excited.

"We just read a landmark paper in my psychology class on a phenomenon that may shed some light on your question. In this experiment, two hundred patients with symptoms that could not be diagnosed because they had no obvious physical signs were selected for the study. They were divided into four groups:

- One group received a positive consultation with an empathetic doctor, but received no treatment.
- One group received a positive consultation with an empathetic doctor and received treatment.
- One group received a negative consultation with an unfriendly doctor and received no treatment.

- One group received a negative consultation with an unfriendly doctor and received treatment.

When a treatment was provided, it was in the form of a pill containing no medicinal ingredient (a sugar pill). All patients were surveyed two weeks later to determine the outcome on their symptoms. I happen to have a copy of this article right here. Take a look at the results table" (see Table 7.1).

**TABLE 7.1.**

Effect of Compassion on Treatment. Note that not every patient responded to all sections of the post-doctor-visit survey.

| | Positive consultations | | Negative consultations | |
|---|---|---|---|---|
| | Treated (n=50) | Not treated (n=50) | Treated (n=50) | Not treated (n=50) |
| *How much better do you feel having seen the doctor?* | | | | |
| Completely | 7 (15) | 10 (21) | 2 (5) | 3 (6) |
| Much | 21 (44) | 18 (33) | 12 (30) | 10 (21) |
| A little | 14 (29) | 18 (37) | 15 (38) | 12 (25) |
| No better | 6 (12) | 2 (4) | 11 (27) | 22 (47) |
| *Have you been helped by seeing the doctor?* | | | | |
| A lot | 23 (79) | 35 (73) | 13 (52) | 10 (30) |
| A little | 4 (14) | 10 (21) | 7 (28) | 10 (30) |
| Slightly | 1 (3) | 3 (6) | 2 (8) | 8 (24) |
| Not at all | 1 (5) | | 3 (12) | 5 (15) |

*Source:* Data extracted from rows 3 and 4 of Table 2 from Thomas (1987).

## Questions

1. What do the two columns of numbers for each experimental group represent (the numbers and the numbers in parentheses)?
2. How do you propose to analyze the data (i.e., how will you compare the treatment groups)? Defend why you think your method is the best way of analyzing the data.

3. Based on this table, what do you suspect that the researchers were investigating? What was their hypothesis?
4. Which group(s) is/are the control? Explain your answer.
5. Complete the following form. Repeat as many times as necessary: When I compare Group ___ with Group ___, I learn that ____________.
6. Which of the two variables tested in this study appears to have the largest effect on improved health?
7. What can you conclude from this experiment?
8. Based on these results, propose a mechanism that might explain your improved health upon leaving the spa.

## *Part IV: The Effect of Expectations*

After you have absorbed the data in the table, Michael looks at you expectantly. To recap, he adds: "Empathy is a big part of receiving an effective treatment. Feeling catered to and pampered can go a long way towards making you feel refreshed and de-stressed, independently of any form of treatment."

Pondering these thoughts, you ask: "OK, I buy that, but is there anything else that might be at work here?"

"Well, there is the placebo effect, as it is classically defined."

"I've heard about this. Isn't it when patients are given a sugar pill and it cures them?"

"That's one form of it. Placebos are sham treatments that mirror the experience of undergoing a treatment but do not provide the active ingredient or therapy. In other words, it's the part of the treatment that causes an effect based on human expectations."

"So, if I believe I am receiving a treatment that can make me feel refreshed, that's enough to make me feel refreshed?" you ask, a bit incredulously.

"Yes! The placebo effect does not work for all conditions, but anxiety, depression, pain, swelling, and stomach ulcers all seem to respond to a placebo."

"I guess in my situation I was feeling stressed, which is a form of anxiety, right?"

"Sure. The placebo effect is bizarre. We studied it in class. Did you know that the color of the pill, the presence of a brand name on it, the number of doses to take each day, the route of administration (e.g., orally or intravenously) all affect the size of the placebo effect? Even more striking, the effectiveness of a treatment seems to decrease as new (and, people believe, more effective) treatments become available. There is even evidence that the placebo effect shows differences in strength within different geographical regions, and that in recent years the strength of the placebo effect is increasing."

## Questions

1. Describe a situation where the placebo effect may have played a part in your response to a treatment (other than your experience at the "A New You!" spa).
2. What's the difference between (1) conventional and (2) complementary and alternative medicine? What role does the placebo effect play in each type of therapy?
3. Propose a hypothesis to explain why the strength of the placebo effect might be increasing in recent years.
4. You were inclined to accept the spa attendant's explanations for the foot bath on your first visit, but you felt differently during your second visit. If you had soaked your feet in the bath, should you still expect to feel better after your second treatment? Do you expect the placebo effect to work when you know it's a placebo?
5. If the placebo effect is real, where's the harm in letting people remain uninformed (or falsely informed) about the mechanism of action of ionic foot baths?
6. Why do people sometimes turn away from evidence-based medicine and scientifically trained experts in the treatment of their health?

## Web Version

Detailed teaching notes, the case PDF, and an answer key are available on the NCCSTS website at *sciencecases.lib.buffalo.edu/cs/collection/detail.asp?case_id=626&id=626.*

## References

Thomas, K. B. 1987. Practice research: general practice consultations: Is there any point in being positive? *BMJ* 294 (6581): 1200–1202.

CHAPTER 8

# RABBIT ISLAND AND THE SEARCH FOR TUBERCULOSIS TREATMENT

*Karen M. Aguirre*

## Abstract

This case introduces students to Dr. E. L. Trudeau, who performed a seminal early experiment validating the germ theory of infection. Students learn about tuberculosis and some of the rudiments of experimental design and graphic analysis as well as examine the social context of the disease. Students also learn about the recent resurgence of tuberculosis with the AIDS epidemic, the emergence of drug-resistant strains, and the peculiar contribution of mass incarceration to the global crisis.


## Learning Objectives

- Describe the history of tuberculosis, its social context, and its importance in global health.
- Analyze experimental data presented in a survival graph.
- Identify dependent and independent variables in a simple experiment.
- Select a single independent variable, and design an experiment within a defined experimental system.
- Construct survival curves.
- Critique experimental designs.
- Consider ways in which scientific information can be put to use in formulating public policy.
- Draw parallels between historical experimental data and current real-world data related to incarceration and tuberculosis.

## Quantitative Reasoning Skills/Concepts

- Carry out basic mathematical operations.
- Represent data in graphs.
- Articulate complete and correct claims based on data.
- Use appropriate reasoning to support the validity of data-based claims.
- Create experimental designs to test hypotheses.

## The Case Study

### *Part I: The Rabbit Island Experiment*

Imagine that it is 1874 and you have just been diagnosed with consumption, which we now call tuberculosis. That's what happened to Edward Livingston Trudeau. A few years earlier, he had nursed a brother who ultimately died of the disease. Now, he had a fresh doctor's degree, a young wife, a new baby, and a terrible problem—a diagnosis that, in his time and place, was often a death sentence.

Dr. Trudeau knew all too well that a large number of people diagnosed with consumption ultimately died. Crowded together in cities like New York, where he was living with his young family, were tens of thousands of immigrants who were very glad to have their back-breaking factory jobs, but came home each night to inadequate housing, food, ventilation, sanitation, and little or no leisure or relaxation time. Consumptives labored for as long as they could draw breath as the bacterial infection in their lungs worsened and spread, eroding blood vessels and causing bleeding and poor oxygenation, or causing the lungs to fill with fluid until the sufferer might literally drown. Finally, exhausted consumptives would retire to their dank, crowded apartments to be nursed by their families until they died. Often family members would themselves become infected from their close contact and constant inhalation of organisms expelled by their sneezing, coughing, bleeding loved one.

E. L. Trudeau, however, was not poor, nor was he a member of the factory-worker class. He decided to travel to a place where he had spent a lot of time as a boy and a young man, the Adirondack Mountains of upstate New York. There he could rest a bit, think, take long walks in the open air, and make a plan.

Dr. Trudeau's condition worsened during the arduous trek north by rail and carriage. In fact, the young man was so frail and sick that he had to be carried into the house of an Adirondack outdoorsman and wilderness guide. But a remarkable thing happened. Dr. Trudeau began to feel better. In time, he could hike and hunt and enjoy life with his friends. He resumed his correspondence with doctors and scientists. He sent for his wife and child, and began to build a medical practice in the distant little outpost of Saranac Lake. And he began to think about the cause and cure of what more and more scientists called not consumption, but tuberculosis.

In the 19th century, a portion of the medical community believed that diseases like consumption were caused by an unfortunate combination of bad "family blood" (after all, the poor were certainly not well-bred, and they were more likely to become sick and to die early) and mysterious causative agents as ill-defined as dank conditions, bad "humours," obnoxious smells, and miasmas. But, in 1882, Robert Koch demonstrated to most of the scientific establishment's satisfaction that the tiny bacterium *Mycobacterium tuberculosis* (MTb) caused the disease known as consumption. Moreover, he could grow pure cultures of the finicky MTb and infect cells of experimental animals, and ultimately the animals themselves, causing the disease. Koch said: "If the importance of a disease for mankind is measured by the number of fatalities it causes, then tuberculosis must be considered much more important than those most feared infectious diseases, plague, cholera, and the like. One in seven of all human beings die from tuberculosis. If one only considers the productive middle-age groups, tuberculosis carries away one-third, and often more." Koch's work, along with Louis Pasteur's, led to the more general "germ theory of infection," which stated that infectious diseases were caused by germs, which was the name given to the microscopic organisms (we know them now as viruses, bacteria, fungi, and parasites) that cause disease in people and animals.

Dr. Trudeau had followed Dr. Koch's work with interest. He worked hard to learn how to culture MTb organisms, and was the first to do so in the United States. Intrigued by the correlation between healthy outdoor lifestyle and efficient anti-tubercular defense in his own case, he devised a simple experiment. The experiment spoke to both the MTb "germ" as sole causative agent of tuberculosis and a possible therapy for the disease. The experiment was described in his 1886 paper, "Environment in its Relation to the Progress of Bacterial Invasion in Tuberculosis." The following is an excerpt from that paper.

> *First. What results ensue when both bacillary infection and unhygienic surroundings are made to coexist in tuberculosis?*
>
> *Second. Are unhygienic surroundings when every known precaution has been taken to exclude the bacillus sufficient of themselves to bring about the disease?*
>
> *Third. Is bacillary infection invariably progressive in animals placed under the best conditions of environment attainable?*
>
> *EXPERIMENTS.—Fifteen rabbits were made use of and divided in three lots, each set of animals being placed under conditions best adapted to answer in the results noted [in] the three questions already referred to.*
>
> *Experiment No. 1. Five rabbits were inoculated in the right lung and in the left side of the*

*neck with five minims of sterilized water in which was suspended a sufficient quantity of a pure culture (third generation) of the tubercle bacillus to render the liquid quite perceptibly turbid. The needle of the Koch's inoculating syringe was inserted subcutaneously on the left side of the neck and in the third intercostal space to a depth of thirty millimetres on the right side. These animals were then confined in a small box and put in a dark cellar. They were thus deprived of light, fresh air and exercise and were also stinted in the quantity of food given them while being themselves artificially infected with the tubercle bacillus.*

*Experiment No. 2. Five healthy rabbits were placed under the following conditions: A fresh hole about ten feet deep was dug in the middle of a field, and the animals having been confined in a small box with high sides but no top, were lowered to the bottom of this pit, the mouth of which was then covered with boards and fresh earth. Through this covering a small trap door was cut which was only opened long enough each day to allow of the food, consisting of a small potato to each rabbit, being thrown to the animals. So damp was the ground at the bottom of this pit that the box in which the rabbits were confined was constantly wet. Thus these animals were deprived of light, fresh air, and exercise, furnished with but a scanty supply of food while breathing a chill and damp atmosphere, though free from disease themselves and removed as far as possible from any accidental source of bacterial infection.*

*Experiment No. 3. Five rabbits having been inoculated in precisely the same manner as the animals in the first experiment, were at once turned loose on a small island in June, 1886. It would be difficult to imagine conditions better suited to stimulate the vitality of these animals to the highest point than were here provided. They lived all the time in the sunshine and fresh air, and soon acquired the habit of constant motion so common in wild animals. The grass and green shrubs on the island afforded all the fresh food necessary and in addition they were daily provided with an abundant supply of vegetables. Thus, while artificially infected themselves they were placed in the midst of conditions well adapted to stimulate their vital powers to the highest point attainable.*

## Questions

1. The data from the experiment Dr. Trudeau describes is shown in Figure 8.1. Graphs like Figure 8.1 are called survival curves. Write a narration of the figure describing the results of the experiment. Explain why the rabbits are emaciated in groups 1 and 2. (Please note: What Dr. Trudeau called Experiments 1, 2, and 3 are more like what modern scientists would call treatment groups 1, 2, and 3, and that terminology is used in Figure 8.1.)

**FIGURE 8.1.**

Analyzing the Rabbit Island Experiment.

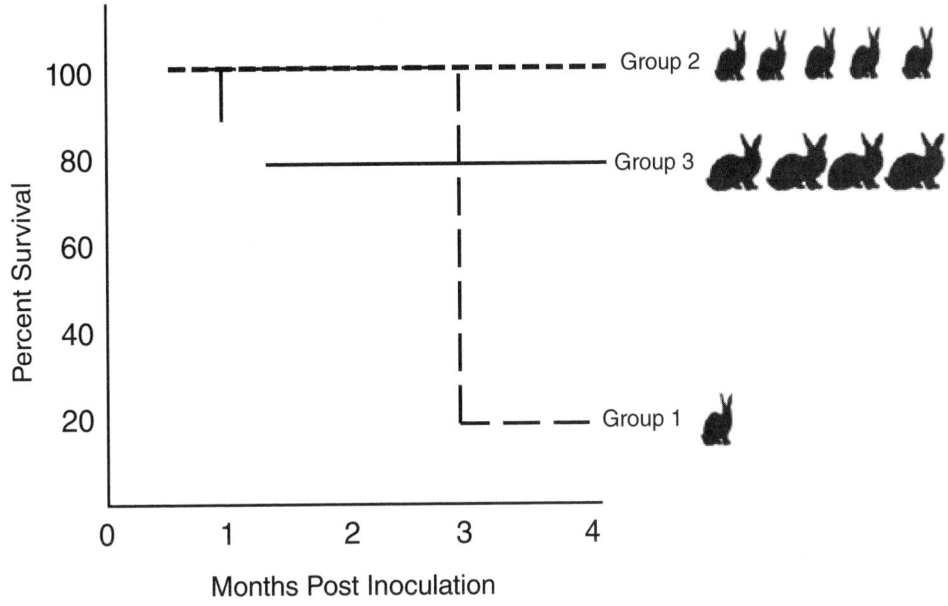


2. Use your results to write an overall conclusion to the Rabbit Island Experiment. Also develop an answer to each of Dr. Trudeau's questions.
3. Do Dr. Trudeau's results support the germ theory of infection? Why or why not?
4. What do the data suggest might be good environmental conditions for tuberculosis patients?
5. What might be the effect of crowding on effective exposure rate of individual animals to MTb? (Hint: Would you rather board an airplane for a three-hour trip where 2 out of 300 passengers had the flu or board an airplane where 200 out of 300 passengers had the flu?)

Dr. Trudeau's little experiment had a big impact on medical thinking at the time. His experiment offered a rationale for opening his Adirondack Cottage Sanitarium, which offered rich and poor alike a regimen of abundant nourishing food, lots of sunlight, plenty of rest, and as much fresh air as a person could tolerate. Hundreds were helped, and many similar establishments were opened.

Perhaps the experiment was so successful because of the care with which Trudeau had designed its components. It is important to identify an interesting and potentially approachable question or set of questions before undertaking an experiment. But it is just as important to devise a clever experimental design.

When we design an experiment, we choose the treatments that will be received and we control or manipulate them in appropriate ways. These treatments or manipulations are the independent variable(s). The observed or measurable differences in outcome for the treatment groups are the dependent variable(s). Suppose I want to know how much sunlight is needed to produce the sweetest oranges? Based on what I know about sunlight and photosynthesis, I hypothesize that the greater amount of sunlight an orange plant gets, the sweeter the juice of the orange. To investigate whether this is true, I might place one group of plants in the sun for two hours per day, another group for 4 hours per day, and another group for eight hours per day. At the end of the experiment, I could test for the amount of sugar in the juice of the oranges. The amount of time in the sun is the independent variable. The sugar in the juice is the dependent variable.

## Questions

1. What is the dependent variable in the Rabbit Island Experiment? Also, list all of the independent variables you can think of in the experiment. (Hmm, maybe Dr. Trudeau's experiment was not so simple after all!)
2. Note: This exercise is to be done at home. Often, scientists like to hold all conditions constant except one. Just varying one thing at a time makes it easier to analyze the results. Select any one of the independent variables you have listed above and design an experiment similar to Dr. Trudeau's. State your experimental question, i.e., what are you trying to find out. Formulate a hypothesis. Then decide upon and write out a description of how you will manipulate your treatment groups (there needn't be three; you could have two, or four—just design a good experiment!), and then imagine the possible outcomes, assuming survival is the dependent variable. Now generate two survival curves based on those imagined outcomes—one that supports your hypothesis and one that does not.
3. We respect Dr. Trudeau and all those earlier scientists who did the best they could within the contemporary understanding of the problem they addressed and utilizing the materials and technology they had at hand. Modern-day biologists like to talk about resistance/susceptibility genes and patterns of inheritance, rather than family blood. They think about infectious disease in terms of microbes and pathogenicity, rather than speaking of bad humors. They have identified vitamins and other nutrients that are abundant in some foodstuffs and lacking in other that are essential for optimal immune function. Without the benefit of such modern formulations, Dr. Trudeau, by a disciplined application of scientific curiosity and careful, clever methodology, shed light on each of these concerns, light that helped to illuminate the minds of scientists who came after. Still, a look at his original paper leaves us wondering, were the rabbits genetically identical? Probably not!

Why? Were they all of the same sex and age? Couldn't he have given the animals kept on short rations just a smaller amount of the same varieties of food available to the animals fed abundantly—after all, there might be some important nutrient missing in potatoes. In light of the title of the paper, why not measure bacterial numbers in the rabbits on post mortem rather than just survival time? (In a subsequent paper, he did exactly that.) Once you start critiquing an experiment from 100 years ago, or 10 years ago, or sometimes even last year, it's hard to stop. Can you think of anything else you would have changed about the Rabbit Island Experiment?

4. Suppose you were the Mayor of New York City in the 1890s/early 1900s and were convinced by Dr. Trudeau's experiments that in your city a transmissible bacterium was causing tuberculosis and that poor living conditions and inadequate diet were adversely affecting the ability of hundreds of people to fight the infection. What sort of public policies might you try to enact in order to combat the public health menace? What obstacles might you encounter?

## *Part II: Tuberculosis in Social Context*

E. L. Trudeau was quick to distinguish between a helpful therapy and a cure. He opened the Adirondack Cottage Sanitarium, where poor and rich alike could come and receive the benefits of fresh air, plenty of sunlight, rest, and abundant but simple nourishing food. Hundreds benefited. Similar institutions opened up in the United States, and the movement was already well underway in Western Europe. But the cure would only come in the 1950s with the discovery of antibiotics that were effective against the mycobacterium.

### Question 1

The curve shown in Figure 8.2 (p. 102) has three parts, from 1700 to 1800, 1800 to approx. 1955, and 1955 to approximately 1985. The data used to produce the curve are from Western Europe, but a similar one could be expected for the United States. From what you know of the history and culture of the United States and Western Europe, write a sentence telling why each part of the curve looks the way it does. In looking just at this graph, what would you predict about the death rate from TB in 2000 and 2005?

**FIGURE 8.2.**

Western European Mortality Statistics: TB Deaths Over Time (based on Murray 2001).

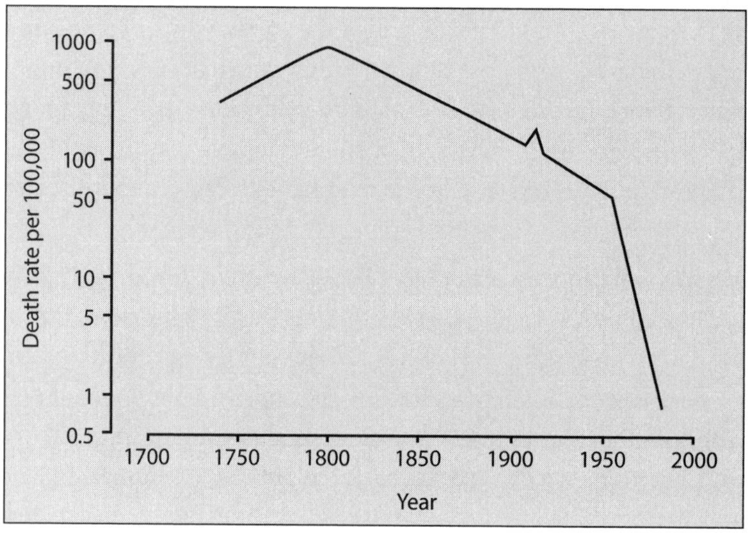


In recent years, a combination of development of antibiotic resistant strains of MTb along with the creation of a reservoir of immunocompromised people by the worldwide AIDS epidemic have contributed to a resurgence of tuberculosis in the United States and a worldwide upswing in TB cases and deaths. This resurgence has been accompanied by a resurgence of interest in the disease by scientists asking new questions about the nature of true host genetic susceptibility/resistance genes for tuberculosis, about virulence genes within the mycobacterium itself, which might offer new drug targets, and about the epigenetic factors that may influence disease predisposition and outcome in people with tuberculosis.

## Question 2

Tuberculosis causes nearly 2 million deaths worldwide each year. Between 1985 and 1992, cases of TB in the United States increased by 20%, as shown in Figure 8.3. Write a paragraph suggesting a few reasons why this resurgence of TB might have occurred in the United States.

**FIGURE 8.3.**

TB Cases in the United States.

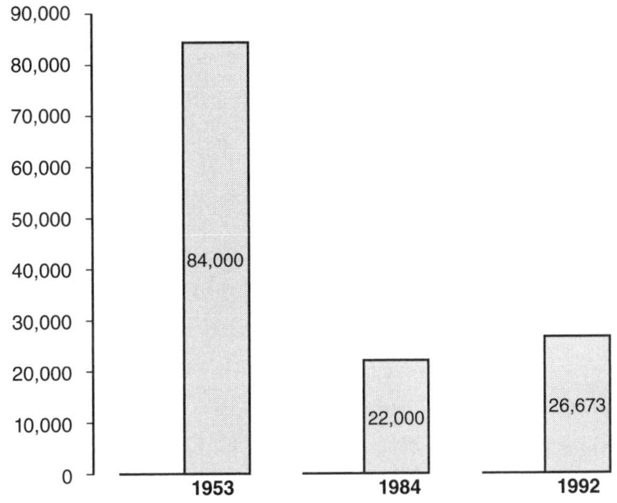


## Question 3

The resurgence lasted until approximately 1992, then, in the United States, it began to abate. In 2005 the TB case rate in the United States was 4.8 per 100,000, as the U.S. medical community brought the epidemic under control (CDC National Prevention Information Network, n.d.). However, in U.S. prisons and all over the world TB remains a serious health problem. In the U.S., zero tolerance drug laws have resulted in a burgeoning incarcerated population, which constitutes a significant reservoir of disease, with a far higher incidence rate than the general population. In New York prisons, the incidence rate of TB is 156.0/100,000 compared to the rate of 10.4/100,000 in the general population (U.S. Agency for International Development, 2009). Considering all you have learned in Parts I and II, discuss why these rates may be so much higher in prison.

In 2006, there were 9 million new cases of tuberculosis worldwide, many of these caused by drug-resistant strains of the mycobacterium. Scientists struggle to find new drugs that will be effective against the resistant strains and to propose better treatment regimens involving more direct observation of treatment (DOT) to ensure patient compliance. Additionally, many have called for public acceptance and physician support for more responsible dispensing of antibiotics. These are difficult and complex problems that require a resolve on the part of many sectors coupled with a willingness to devote adequate resources to a fight a disease that most often strikes people in the poorest of places.

Additionally, it is certainly the case that many modern TB cases occur in a global incarcerated population of approximately 8 million (USAID 2009). Many of those incarcerated were political prisoners taken prisoner in war zones. Conditions in the prisons include inadequate ventilation, poor nutrition, negligent healthcare, HIV co-infection, and rampant despair. How does this resonate with what you've learned of E.L. Trudeau's experience in the late 19th century?

We know a lot about how to prevent and treat tuberculosis. There is much more to be learned. In 2010, 8.8 million people in the world fell ill with TB and 1.4 million died (World Health Organization, 2012).

### Question 4

All of the following factors are important in causing the worldwide resurgence of tuberculosis: (a) emergence of strains that are resistant to one or more of the available antibiotics effective against MTb; (b) incomplete or inadequate understanding by scientists of the details of the host/pathogen interaction in MTb infection; (c) lack of a universally accepted vaccine; (d) lack of financial support for science and for public health initiatives in developing countries; (e) famine; (f) geopolitical instability in the developing world; and (g) inadequate public awareness of public health issues. If you were a billionaire philanthropist like Warren Buffet or Bill Gates, where would you focus your efforts against tuberculosis?

## Web Version

Detailed teaching notes, the case PDF, and an answer key are available on the NCCSTS website at *sciencecases.lib.buffalo.edu/cs/collection/detail.asp?case_id=669&id=669*.

## References

CDC National Prevention Information Network. The Changing Epidemiology of TB. *www.cdcnpin.org/scripts/tb/tb.asp*

Murray, J. F. 2001. A thousand years of pulmonary medicine: Good news and bad. *European Respiratory Journal* 17 (3): 558–565.

Robert Koch and Tuberculosis: Koch's Famous Lecture. *www.nobelprize.org/educational/medicine/tuberculosis/readmore.html?downloadURL=true&loId=BCCBBF73-1B0D-42EA-B590-FF3EA8AA5FDF*

Shampo, M. A., R. A. Kyle, and D. P. Steensman. 2010. Edward L. Trudeau: Founder of a sanatorium for treatment of tuberculosis. *Mayo Clin Proc* 85(7): e48.

Trudeau, E. L. 1887. Environment in its relation to the progress of bacterial invasion in tuberculosis. *American Climatological Society Proceedings* 4: 131–136.

U.S. Agency for International Development (USAID). 2009. Guidelines for Control of Tuberculosis in Prisons. *pdf.usaid.gov/pdf_docs/PNADP462.pdf*.

World Health Organization (WHO). 2012. Tuberculosis Fact Sheet. *www.who.int/mediacentre/factsheets/fs104/en*.

# SECTION II

# CHEMISTRY OF LIFE

# SWEET INDIGESTION
## A Directed Case Study on Carbohydrates

*Peggy Brickman*

### Abstract
This case teaches students how to recognize carbohydrates in the foods they eat and to differentiate between different classes of carbohydrates. In addition, students learn how the body utilizes carbohydrates and consider whether eliminating them from their diet can be healthful.


### Learning Objectives

- Practice recognizing carbohydrates from a list of ingredients to identify their pre-existing knowledge and misconceptions.
- Construct "rules" for determining if foods contain carbohydrates.
- Practice differentiating between the different classes of carbohydrates on a food label.
- Use the fact that undigested carbohydrates cause gas, investigate carbohydrate utilization by the body and tackle the issue of whether or not eliminating carbohydrates can be healthful.

### Quantitative Reasoning Skills/Concepts

- Carry out basic mathematical operations.

### The Case Study

#### *Part I: Of Cows and Carbs*

"What's so funny?" Gwen asked as she slid next to her friends Sara and Emily at the library.

"Read this," Sara said. "I'm thinking about getting my dad vaccinated."

S Y D N E Y, Australia, June 7, 2001
Reuters

Australian farmers are signing up their sheep and cattle in droves to take part in a vaccine program aimed at reducing harmful methane gas emissions from their animals and help take the heat off global warming. Methane is a greenhouse gas more potent than carbon dioxide and farm animals produce a lot of it. Australian scientists said today early results show they may be able to reduce methane emissions per animal by about 20 percent a year, or the equivalent of 300,000 tons of carbon dioxide a year if they can vaccinate three million animals. The methane vaccine discourages Methanogenic archae, organisms which inhabit the animal's digestive system and which produce methane by breaking down feed.

Gwen laughed. "Your dad? What about your dog? He's got the real problem. But seriously, is farting a major cause of global warming?"

"Well, not all of it, but greenhouse gases could be reduced if people stopped eating meat. Cows actually produce the vast majority of methane released in the United States," Emily replied.

"Three-hundred thousand tons of $CO_2$ in Australia alone," Gwen said. "I wonder how much people produce?"

"When I visited Space Camp we learned about how the astronauts deal with noxious fumes," Sara said. "The average astronaut expels about a half liter of gas a day from bacterial breakdown of undigested carbohydrates in the large intestine. Maybe we all should be vaccinated. You both have been dieting. I bet you think you're eating a lot less carbohydrates than before. You could be our first test subjects."

"But what are carbohydrates exactly?" Emily asked, looking at Gwen. "And which are undigested?"

Here is a list of what the girls had eaten so far:

- *For breakfast:* Cheerios with oat bran, a tall Latte with skim milk, and a PowerBar®.
- *For lunch:* Soda and a salad with lettuce, cabbage, tomato, shredded carrot, green peas, kidney beans, and tuna fish.

## Questions

1. Underline all foods containing carbohydrates.
2. Come up with a rule to help you identify foods containing carbohydrates.

3. How are carbohydrates made normally (i.e., what organism makes them)?
4. Which ingredient would cause gas? Why are some foods digestible, and others are not?

## *Part II: Label Analysis*

The girls checked out a textbook on nutrition and learned that almost all of the foods they were eating contained carbohydrates. But how much gas is produced in your intestine depends on the type of bacteria you are harboring and whether or not you eat the following carbohydrates that aren't well digested.

Gwen's list of carbohydrates that are not well digested:

- Simple sugars:
    - Dried beans, peas, and lentils containing the tri- and quatro-saccharides Raffinose and Stachyose
    - Lactose
    - Fructose
    - Sorbitol, found in fruit but also an artificial sweetener
- Starches
- Insoluble fiber

Analyze the PowerBar food label in Figure 9.1 and then answer the questions.

**FIGURE 9.1.**

PowerBar Food Label.

THE ORIGINAL PERFORMANCE ENERGY BAR™

| **Nutrition Facts** | **Amount/Serving** | **% DV** | **Amount/Serving** | **% DV** |
|---|---|---|---|---|
| Serving size 1 bar | **Total Fat 3.5g** | **5%** | **Total Carb 45g** | **15%** |
| | Saturated Fat 0.5g | **3%** | Dietary Fiber 3g | **12%** |
| **Calories** 240 | **Cholesterol** 0mg | **0%** | Sugars 14g | |
| Calories from Fat 30 | **Sodium** 120mg | **5%** | Other Carb 28g | |
| | **Potassium** 130mg | **4%** | **Protein** 10g | **20%** |

*Percent Daily Values (DV) are based on a 2,000 calorie diet

INGREDIENTS: HIGH FRUCTOSE CORN SYRUP WITH GRAPE AND PEAR JUICE CONCENTRATE, OAT BRAN, MALTODEXTRIN,MILK PROTEIN ISOLATE, RICE CRISPS (MILLED RICE, RICE BRAN), PEANUT BUTTER (ROASTED PEANUTS, SALT), BROWN RICE, GLYCERIN

©POWERBAR INC., BERKELEY, CA 94704 MADE IN USA ® REGISTERED TRADEMARK

## Questions

1. What percentage of the carbohydrates in the bar is simple sugar?
2. Can the girls omit all carbohydrates that are not well digested (like those in Gwen's list) from their diet? What are these carbohydrates used for?
3. What are the differences between simple sugars, starches, and fiber?
4. Use this PowerBar label to find all the ingredients that are carbohydrates of the following classes: (a) simple sugars, (b) complex carbohydrates like starches, (c) complex carbohydrates that contain fiber, and (d) carbohydrates that would produce gas according to the list.

## Web Version

Detailed teaching notes, the case PDF, homework questions, a sample exam, and an answer key for the case are available on the NCCSTS website at *sciencecases.lib.buffalo.edu/cs/collection/detail.asp?case_id=375&id=375.*

## References

Partnership for Essential Nutrition. 2004. Opinion survey executive summary: The impact of the low-carb craze on attitudes about eating and weight loss. *web.archive.org/web/20120218101740/http://www.essentialnutrition.org/survey.php*.

CHAPTER 10

# DUST TO DUST

## The Carbon Cycle

*Jennifer Y. Anderson, Diane R. Wang, and Ling Chen*

## Abstract

Students learn how carbon, an essential element of life, is transformed from carbon dioxide to carbohydrate to animals, and then back to carbon dioxide while reinforcing a number of chemistry concepts including atomic structures, carbon isotopes, radiocarbon dating, beta decay, half-life, and photosynthesis.


## Learning Objectives

- Emphasize the importance of photosynthesis to animals on Earth.
- Highlight the concept that carbon is the building block of all living organisms.
- Reinforce atomic structure: subatomic particles (protons, neutrons and electrons).
- Enhance the concepts of radioactive isotope, radiation, and $\beta$ decay.
- Provide practice in balancing nuclear equations.
- Apply the concept of half-life to the carbon dating technique.

## Quantitative Reasoning Skills/Concepts

- Carry out basic mathematical operations.
- Articulate complete and correct claims based on data.

## The Case Study

Tom was visiting his grandfather, a retired high school chemistry teacher, who lived in a nearby adult community apartment. Tom, a freshman in college, wanted to talk to his grandfather about something he had seen on TV.

"Grandpa, have you been watching the National Geographic channel lately? I saw a program on it called *Waking the Baby Mammoth*," Tom said excitedly. "It's a documentary about the discovery of a baby mammoth from 40,000 years ago!"

"Oh, yes," said Tom's grandfather. "I saw that program. The people who found her in Siberia named her Lyuba. She's the oldest and best preserved woolly mammoth discovered so far."

"I wonder how scientists determined Lyuba's age," said Tom.

"Well, they probably used carbon dating."

"What's that?" asked Tom.

"Radiocarbon dating, or carbon dating, is a technique used to determine time passed after a living organism died or the age of a specimen according to the radioactivity of its remaining carbon, found in any organic matter that makes up the specimen—for example, bones, cloth, wood, or plant fibers."

"How does it work?"

"Well, all living things are made up of carbon. Some of the carbon is unstable and breaks down over time after organisms die; you can measure the unstable (radioactive) carbon levels in fossils to determine how long ago the individuals died. Carbon is the basis of life on earth, you know, Tom. Where do you think carbon in our bodies comes from?"

"From food, of course," said Tom.

"You're right on the money. There are two kinds of food sources: plant and animal. A plant combines $CO_2$ (captured from the air), water (from the ground), and solar energy (in the form of light with two wavelengths: 680 nm and 700 nm) to produce carbohydrates and oxygen. This process is called photosynthesis, and it is essential to all life on Earth."

Tom's grandfather continued: "Through photosynthesis, plants produce carbohydrates and oxygen; both are vital to sustain life for all animals, including humans. The carbohydrates provide carbon and energy; oxygen is essential in releasing the energy stored in the carbohydrates in the metabolic process."

Tom's grandfather paused, then asked him a question, like they were in class: "Tom, did you know that a very small amount of $CO_2$ in nature contains the unstable kind of carbon atom and therefore is radioactive?"

"Really?" said Tom. "Does it have something to do with the carbon dating technique?"

"Yes. There are three kinds of carbon atoms: carbon-12, carbon-13, and carbon-14. Although C-12 and C-13 are non-radioactive and stable, C-14 is the opposite; it's radioactive and unstable. In chemistry, we call C-12, C-13, and C-14 isotopes since they are all carbon; they just have different numbers of neutrons in their nuclei. $CO_2$ containing all of these isotopes is obtained by plants during photosynthesis. When animals eat plants, they in turn assimilate C-12, C-13, and C-14, and then that carbon is passed up the chain to any animals that eat these animals, and so on. Radioactive C-14 is found in all living things, including you and me."

"Oh, I get it. According to the amount of remaining carbon, archaeologists can determine the age of a fossil," said Tom.

"C-14 to be exact."

"But I thought C-12, C-13, and C-14 were all carbon." Tom was a little confused.

"It's true that they all have six electrons and the same chemical properties," explained Tom's grandfather. "But they are different at the subatomic level, the nucleus, to be precise. Atoms, the smallest particles of a substance, can be further divided into three subatomic particles: protons, neutrons, and electrons. Protons and neutrons are found inside the nucleus, a very dense region within an atom, while the electrons are outside the nucleus region."

"So, that means six electrons can be found outside the nucleus regions in all three carbon isotopes. But how are C-12, C-13, and C-14 different in the nucleus?" asked Tom.

"They have different numbers of neutrons even though each has six protons in the nucleus. C-14 has eight neutrons, giving it a total of 14 particles (six protons plus eight neutrons) within the nucleus, making C-14 unstable, or radioactive. Over time, the nucleus of C-14 breaks down via spontaneous decay, and releases particles and energy to be in a more stable form. Radiation, the released energy, can be measured during the decay process. On the other hand, C-12 has only six neutrons, a total of 12 particles (six protons plus six neutrons) inside the nucleus, which make C-12 atoms stable, so its nucleus does not break down. As a result, there is no energy released. Same goes for C-13, which contains a total of 13 particles in the nucleus (6 protons plus 7neutrons)."

"I see," said Tom. "So, after the decay, is C-14 still carbon?"

"Nope," said his grandfather. "One of the neutrons in C-14 splits into a proton and electron. The proton remains in the nucleus, but the electron is released from the nucleus with high energy or radiation. The addition of a proton makes the resultant atom a non-radioactive N-14."

"High energy electrons released from the nucleus? That's interesting," said Tom. "Do these high energy electrons have a special name to distinguish them from those found outside the nucleus region?"

"Good question. The high energy electrons emitted from the nucleus are called beta ($\beta$) particles or $\beta$ radiation. Measuring and comparing the intensity of $\beta$-radiation is the basis of the carbon dating technique. The higher the radiation, the more C-14 remains."

"So, can I say that the older an object is, the less C-14 remains; therefore the weaker the radiation it emits?" said Tom.

"Mm-hmm." His grandfather nodded his head. "After an organism dies, it cannot obtain more C-14. Therefore, the level of C-14 in its body begins to decline. By comparing the amount of C-14 left in a fossil with that of a living organism, scientists can figure out how long that fossil has been around. In addition, the half-life concept is needed to pinpoint the age of the fossil. Lyuba is a perfect example to understand the carbon dating half-life, and thus the age of her remains."

"What's *half-life?*" asked Tom.

"The half-life is the time needed for half the total amount of a radioactive element to break down. The half-life of C-14 is known to be approximately 5,730 years. Let's round it up to 6,000 years for simplicity. A fossil of 6,000 years old, which is one half-life, will then have half of its C-14 left as compared to a living organism."

"So if a quarter of the C-14 remains in the fossil, then two half-lives have passed, and the fossil is about 12,000 years old," Tom said.

"Excellent, Tom! Can you tell me how many half-lives of C-14 in Lyuba's remains have gone through?"

"Let me see. Her remains are about 40,000 years old; one half-life of C-14 is approximately 6,000 years. It's almost seven half-lives."

"Well done! Tell me how did you calculate it so quickly?" Tom's grandfather asked.

"I divided 40,000 years (the age of her remains) by 6,000 years (the half-life of C-14); I then rounded the result to 7. Grandpa, I have another question for you: Where does radioactive carbon originally come?"

"It's from the upper atmosphere. Since cosmic rays from outer space bombard the atmosphere constantly, when a neutron attacks nitrogen-14 (with 7 protons and 7 neutrons), one of the protons is knocked out and replaced by the neutron, as a result radioactive C-14 (which has 6 protons and 8 neutrons) is produced."

"Wow. So, in β-decay, C-14 becomes N-14, but in the bombardment, N-14 is transformed back to C-14. Carbon and nitrogen are next-door neighbors in the periodic table with only one proton and one electron difference. Now I see how they're related at the atomic level. Awesome!"

"Yep. This process is called nuclear chemistry in which new elements are produced. Did you know that another source of C-14 in the air is from the burning of fossil fuels?"

"What are fossil fuels?" asked Tom.

"They're fuels when dead plants and animals from millions of years ago decompose. An example of a fossil fuel is crude oil," explained his grandfather.

"Cool! Carbons transformed from ancient life to crude oil, to $CO_2$, and then incorporated into the food chain, back to life again.

"As the old saying goes: from dust to dust. It would be fair to say, Tom, that we are a collection of carbon. Life is a process of recycling chemicals, like carbon, oxygen, hydrogen, and nitrogen. All living organisms are chemically related to one another because we all share the same pool of elements."

"Does it mean that part of me might come from stars or dinosaurs?" asked Tom.

"Sure. We are part of the universe and a part of the universe is in us too. Life is a chemical process and a precious gift, so eat well and live your life to the fullest."

"Will do, Grandpa."

## Questions

1. What is photosynthesis?
2. Is photosynthesis an endothermic or exothermic reaction? Show the chemical equation.
3. Why is photosynthesis essential to the lives of animals on Earth?
4. Compare isotopes of carbon, C-12, C-13, and C-14; what do they have in common and how are they different?
5. In the upper atmosphere, high energetic neutrons in cosmic rays constantly collide with nitrogen-14 to produce carbon-14 (radioactive). Write the nucleus equation for this bombardment process, the origin of C-14.
6. What is *half-life*? (Use carbon as an example.)
7. Write the β decay nuclear equation of C-14. Explain the origin and the nature of the β particle.
8. What is the purpose of radiation in food industry? Is it safe to consume irradiated foods?
9. Why is $CO_2$ called one of the greenhouse gases?
10. Yttrium 90 (Y-90) is a beta emitter and a valuable clinical tool in internal radiation therapy for treating liver tumors. Y-90 has a short half life (less than three days). Implanted in a patient's tissue, it penetrates 2.5 mm, with a maximum range of 11 mm, which minimizes side effects to adjacent tissues. Write the Y-90 β-decay equation in which zirconium-90 is produced.
11. Diamond is also made of carbon. Can the carbon dating technique be used to determine the age of a diamond? Explain why or why not.

## Web Version

Detailed teaching notes, the case PDF, and an answer key are available on the NCCSTS website at *sciencecases.lib.buffalo.edu/cs/collection/detail.asp?case_id=246&id=246*.

# A CAN OF BULL

## Do Energy Drinks Really Provide a Source of Energy?

*Merle Heidemann and Gerald Urqhuart*

## Abstract

This case teaches students about large biomolecules, nutrition, and product analysis. Students conduct a biochemical analysis of several popular energy drinks on the market and determine whether these products nutritionally match their marketing claims.


## Learning Objectives

- Describe and categorize chemically the components of various popular "energy drinks."
- Determine the physiological role of these components in the human body.
- Explain scientifically how the marketing claims for these drinks are supported (or not).
- Determine under what conditions each of the "energy drinks" might be useful to the consumer.
- Write an analysis of energy drinks for a popular magazine.

## Quantitative Reasoning Skills/Concepts

- Articulate complete and correct claims based on data.
- Use appropriate reasoning to support the validity of data-based claims.

## The Case Study

### *Case Scenario*

After spending several years working the Sport's Desk of the *Lansing State Journal*, Rhonda had landed the job of her dreams as a writer for *Runners' World* magazine. The job was fantastic! Since high school, where she had excelled in cross country, Rhonda had been a consistent runner, participating in local races and those assigned to her for her job. For her last assignment, she had run and reported on the Leadwood, South Dakota, marathon—*it was a blast!*

As if reading her mind, her boss Charley walked in just then with a can of XS Citrus Blast® in one hand and a list of several other energy drinks in the other.

"We've been getting a lot of inquiries about the different energy drinks on the market, including XS Citrus Blast. Do you know anything about them?" Charley asked.

"I know that people use them for various reasons," replied Rhonda. "It seems they're primarily used by athletes to provide some 'fuel' as they practice and compete. Other people use them more casually as a way to become 'energized.' That's about all I know."

"That seems to be about all any of us knows," Charley said. "For your next assignment," Charley continued, "I want you to find out what each of the ingredients in these drinks is and what it does for a runner or for a non-athlete. You need to be very accurate in your analysis—determine what each component really does for the body, not what the marketers want you to believe it does. Then look at the marketing claims of some of these drinks and see if the scientific facts match up to them. Many of our readers are using these drinks with some general notion that they're helpful, but they're basing their use of them on no scientific information. I've got the marketing claims, a list of ingredients and nutrition facts provided on the cans for consumers, and a short list of questions that should get you started. When you research these, be sure to document all your sources of information, keeping in mind that all resources are not equal. Here's the information."

With that, Charley left the office. Rhonda looked over the list. "Guess I'll have to brush up on my biochemistry. No problem. I'm interested in knowing if my running would be improved by drinking this stuff." Rhonda recalled that a food's calorie content was the simplest reflection of its energy content. Looking at Charley's list she saw that the different energy drinks contained the *numbers of calories* in Table 11.1.

**TABLE 11.1.**

Calorie Content for a Sample of Energy Drinks.

| Energy Drink | Calories |
|---|---|
| XS Citrus Blast® | 8 |
| Red Bull® | 110 |
| Sobe Adrenaline Rush® | 140 |
| Impulse® | 110 |
| *For comparison:* Coca Cola® (12 oz.) | 140 |

## *Marketing Claims*

Next, Rhonda perused the marketing claims for each drink, shown in Table 11.2.

**TABLE 11.2.**

Marketing Claims for a Sample of Energy Drinks.

| Energy Drink | Marketing Claims |
|---|---|
| Red Bull | • The Red Bull energy drink is a functional product developed especially for periods of increased mental and physical exertion.<br>• It can be drunk in virtually any situation: at sport, work, study, driving and socializing.<br>• Improves performance, especially during times of increased stress or strain.<br>• Improves concentration and reaction speed.<br>• Stimulates the metabolism. |
| XS Citrus Blast | • There is less than 1/2 calorie of sugar in XS Citrus Blast. This qualifies for the government-approved statement "No Sugar." The 8 calories in XS Citrus Blast are from amino acids and are protein calories that aid your body's natural metabolic process.<br>• Most 8-ounce energy drinks in the market today have over 100 calories and from 27 to 30 grams of sugar, which is a simple carbohydrate. Most 12-ounce non-diet soft drinks have 170 calories from 40 grams of sugar. Most 5.5-ounce juice drinks have 80 calories from 20 grams of sugar.<br>• Calories from sugar and carbohydrates may increase fat deposits. Simple carbohydrates are also called high glycemic (high sugar) foods. High glycemic foods cause your body to pump insulin to digest the sugar, which sends a message to your body to store calories as fat. Low glycemic foods do not pump insulin to the same degree and aid in your body's natural metabolism of fat, using your body's fat resources as fuel. Many experts fear that the epidemic incidence of diabetes in North America today may be significantly contributed to by high-glycemic diets. The 8 calories in XS Citrus Blast are from amino acids and are protein calories that aid your body's natural metabolic process.<br>• XS Citrus Blast uses a proprietary blend of Sucralose, Acesulfame Potassium (Ace K), and fruit essences to give the drinks their great flavor without sugar or empty calories. In fact, the 8 calories in the drink come from the 2 grams of amino acids, which are protein calories. |

Table 11.2 (*continued*)

| Energy Drink | Marketing Claims |
|---|---|
| Sobe Adrenaline Rush | • This maximum energy supplement delivers an energy boost with a natural passion fruit flavor. It's lightly carbonated with a clean smooth feel.<br>• This maximum energy supplement is fortified with a unique blend of natural energizing elements, including d-ribose, l-carnitine and taurine. It's pure, concentrated energy in an 8.3-fluid-ounce can. |
| Impulse | • Elevate Your Performance<br>• Impulse Energy Drink contains special supplements to immediately enhance mental and physical efficiency and give you the energy boost you deserve... replenishing your strength.<br>• Impulse gets its energy from a simple source: nutrients, minerals, and vitamins that occur naturally in the body and foods we eat. Enjoy: the wake-up power of caffeine, the alertness-inducing properties of taurine, the lift you get from vitamins B6 and B12. Combined with Impulse's other ingredients, these are known to increase mental focus and physical well-being, enhance performance, and accelerate metabolism. |

## *Charley's List of Questions*

Rhonda realized that before she could start analyzing the energy drinks, she needed to know the answer to the following question: "When we say that something gives us 'energy,' what does that mean? What is a biological definition of energy?"

After satisfying herself that she had a good definition, she turned to the first set of questions on Charley's list:

1. What is the nature (sugar, amino acid, vitamin, etc.) of each ingredient listed on the cans?
2. What is the physiological role of each in the human body?
3. Which ingredients provide energy?
4. Which ingredients contribute to body repair, i.e., which help build or rebuild muscle tissue?

## *Ingredients and Nutrition Facts*

Rhonda was determined to wade through the confusing labeling of the drinks. For example, XS Citrus Blast boasted that it had no calories but still provided "energy." That made absolutely no sense based on what Rhonda knew about biological energy! The first thing she needed to do was sort out the various ingredients on the labels—a task that consumers rarely undertake. Her findings are summarized in Table 11.3. As in most labels, ingredients are listed in order of mass in drinks, from highest to lowest.

**TABLE 11.3.**

Energy Drink Ingredients and Nutrition Facts

| Energy Drink | Ingredients and Nutrition Facts |
|---|---|
| XS Citrus Blast | • *Ingredients:* carbonated water, l-taurine, l-glutamine, citric acid, adaptogen blend (eleutherococcus senticosus, panax ginseng, panax quinquefolium, echinacea purpurea, schisandra, astragalus, and reishi), natural flavors, acesulfame potassium, caffeine, sodium benzoate, potassium sorbate, sucralose, niacin, pantothenic acid, pyridoxine HCL, yellow 5, cyanocobalamin<br>• *Nutrition Facts:* serving size: 8.4 fl oz; servings per container: 1; calories: 8; fat: 0 g; sodium: 24 mg; potassium: 25 mg; total carbs: 0 g; sugars: 0 g; protein: 2 g; vitamin B3: 100%; vitamin B6: 300%; vitamin B5: 100%; vitamin B12: 4900% |
| Red Bull | • *Ingredients:* carbonated water, sucrose, glucose, sodium citrate, taurine, glucuronolactone, caffeine, inositol, niacin, D-pantothenol, pyridoxine HCL, vitamin B12, artificial flavors, colors<br>• *Nutrition Facts:* serving size: 8.3 fl oz; servings per container: 1; amount per serving: calories: 110; total fat: 0 g; sodium: 200 mg; protein: 0 g; total carbohydrates: 28 g; sugars: 27 g |
| Sobe Adrenaline Rush | • *Ingredients:* filtered water, high fructose corn syrup, citric acid, taurine, d-ribose, l-carnitine, natural flavor, inositol, sodium citrate, ascorbic acid, caffeine, monopotassium phosphate, salt, gum arabic, ester gum, siberian ginseng root extract, pyridoxine hydrochloride, guarana seed extract, caramel color, beta-carotene, folic acid, cyanocobalamin<br>• *Nutrition Facts:* serving size: 8.3 fl oz; servings per container: 1; amount per serving: calories: 140; total fat: 0 g; sodium: 60 mg; protein: 1 g; total carbohydrates: 36 g; sugars: 34 g; taurine: 1000 mg; d-ribose: 500 mg; l-carnitine: 250 mg; inositol: 100 mg; siberian ginseng: 50 mg; guarana: 50 mg |
| Impulse | • *Ingredients:* carbonated water, sucrose, taurine, glucuronolactone, caffeine, inositol, niacinimide, pyridoxine HCL, vitamin C (citric acid), vitamin B12, artificial flavors, colors<br>• *Nutrition Facts:* serving size: 8.3 fl oz; servings per container: 1; calories: 110; fat: 0 g; sodium: 200 mg; total carbs: 28 g; sugars: 27 g; protein: 1 g; niacin: 100%; vitamin B6: 250%; vitamin B12: 80%; pantothenic acid: 50%: vitamin C: 100% |
| Coca Cola<br>(for later comparison) | • *Ingredients:* carbonated water, high fructose corn syrup and/or sucrose, phosphoric acid, natural flavors, caffeine<br>• *Nutrition Facts:* serving size: 12 fl oz; servings per container: 1; calories: 140; fat: 0 g; total carbs: 38 g; sugars: 38 g; protein: 0 g |

## *Your Task*

Research each ingredient found in these energy drinks. This information can be found in biochemistry and nutrition textbooks. Web sources may provide valuable information, but be critical in their use. Many will make unsubstantiated claims. One that can get you started for basic information is *www.chemindustry.com.* Basic information can also be garnered from *www.usda.gov/wps/portal/usda/usdahome?navid=FOOD_NUTRITION&navtype=SU.* Determine the chemical structure, the type of chemical each is, and the physiological role played by each compound. You should have sufficient information to answer Charley's list of questions as well as the additional questions listed below.

## *Post-Research Analysis*

Using the information that your group gathered, fill out Table 11.4, placing each of the ingredients for your drink under the proper heading, and answer the questions that follow. Cite any websites that you used in your analysis.

**TABLE 11.4.**

Results of Your Research

| Sources of Energy | Amino Acids | Stimulants and Vitamins | Other (please categorize) |
|---|---|---|---|
| | | | |

## Questions

1. When we say that something gives us "energy," what does that mean? What is a biological definition of energy?
2. What is the physiological role of each of the molecules in your table?
    a. Which ingredients provide energy? How do they do that?
    b. Which ingredients contribute to body repair, i.e., which help build or rebuild muscle tissue?
3. In what ways might the one(s) that does (do) not have a metabolic energy source (caffeine) provide the perception of increased energy after consumption?
4. How are the ingredients in these drinks helpful to someone expending a lot of energy, e.g., a runner?
5. Does your analysis substantiate the claim that this is an "energy drink"? If so, what molecules are the sources of energy?
6. Could your drink serve different purposes for different consumers? Explain.
7. What is the normal physiological response to increased intake of sugars? to increased intake of caffeine?
8. Is there such a thing as a "sugar high"? Explain your answer.
9. Evaluate, in terms of basic physiology and biochemistry, the statement: A lack of sleep causes a lack of energy.
10. Are the product claims legitimate? Why?
11. Should you simply buy a can of Coke rather than one of these energy drinks? Why/why not?

### *Assessment*

Individually, or as a group, write an evaluation of the marketing claims for your drink. You may write the evaluation in the form of an article for readers of *Runner's World*. Be sure to include answers to the questions above.

## Web Version

Detailed teaching notes (including a table with biochemical information for ingredients commonly found in energy drinks), the case PDF, and an answer key are available on the NCCSTS website at *sciencecases.lib.buffalo.edu/cs/collection/detail.asp?case_id=203&id=203.*

# SECTION III

# THE CELL

# THE MYSTERY OF THE SEVEN DEATHS

## A Case Study in Cellular Respiration

*Michaela A. Gazdik*

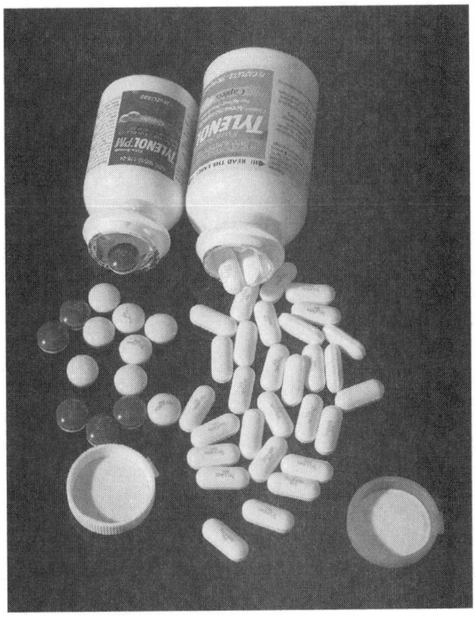



## Abstract

Students learn about the function of cellular respiration and the electron transport chain—and what happens when that function is impaired—in this case study based on the real-life 1982 Chicago Tylenol murders where seven people died when Tylenol capsules were laced with cyanide.


## Learning Objectives

- Explain the overall purpose of cellular respiration.
- Describe the intermediate metabolites of cellular respiration.
- Explain the function and importance of the electron transport chain.
- Describe the role of oxygen in cellular respiration.

## Quantitative Reasoning Skills / Concepts

- Use numerical data to formulate null and alternative hypotheses.
- Articulate complete and correct claims based on data.
- Use appropriate reasoning to support the validity of data-based claims.

## The Case Study

### *Part I: The Symptoms*

Imagine that you work at the medical examiner's office for a major metropolitan city. As Chief Medical Officer, you investigate suspicious deaths and provide toxicology services for the county. Unfortunately, it's been a busy week. In the past five days, seven people have died, all with similar symptoms. It is your job to examine the data and determine the cause of death for these victims.

The first was a 12-year-old girl. Her parents said that she was awake in the middle of the night complaining of a stuffy nose and sore throat. They gave her an extra strength Tylenol and sent her back to bed. At 7 a.m. the next morning, the parents discovered that the girl had collapsed on the bathroom floor. An ambulance rushed the girl to a nearby hospital, where she was pronounced dead.

That same day, paramedics found the second victim unconscious on his kitchen floor after what they thought was an apparent heart attack. Sadly, the victim's brother and fiancée also collapsed later that night while the family gathered to mourn his passing. Both had taken Tylenol to help them cope with their loss shortly before collapsing; neither survived.

In the next four days, four other similar deaths were reported, all in the same neighborhood and all with similar symptoms, including dizziness, confusion, headache, shortness of breath/rapid breathing, and vomiting.

Most deaths were very rapid, occurring within a few hours of symptoms. Are these seven deaths related? What is causing these people to die? It is your job to answer these questions before more deaths are reported.

## Questions

1. Are there any similarities or connections between these seven individuals? What questions would you want to ask the families to answer these questions?
2. In your opinion, are these seven deaths connected? Why or why not?

### *Part II: Autopsy Report*

- Immediate cause of death was hypoxia (suffocation or lack of oxygen).
- Tissue sections from heart, lung, kidney, and liver all show massive cell death.
- Staining with specific dyes showed major mitochondrial damage within the affected tissues.
- Oxygen levels in the patients' blood were approximately 110 mm Hg (normal range is 75–100 mm Hg).

## Questions

1. Recalling your knowledge of the function of organelles, what function of the cells was interrupted in these patients? Could this loss of function lead to the death of these individuals? Why or why not?
2. Given the data in the autopsy, were there any reports that seemed inconsistent with the immediate cause of death?

## Part III: Subcellular Metabolite Analysis

Detailed analysis of the damaged cells showed that ATP levels in the mitochondria were very low. Levels of pyruvate and acetyl coenzyme A (CoA) were normal. You begin to suspect a malfunction of a specific cellular metabolic pathway and so you request a more detailed analysis of the sub-cellular components of the affected cells from the autopsy. The levels of key metabolites are reported in Table 12.1.

**TABLE 12.1.**

Average Metabolite Levels

| Metabolite | Average Patient Levels | Normal Levels |
|---|---|---|
| Glucose | 99 µM | 100 µM |
| Pyruvate | 27 µM | 25 µM |
| NAD+ | 10 µM | 75 µM |
| NADH 400 | 400 µM | 50 µM |

### Questions

1. For each metabolite listed in Table 12.1, describe its role in cellular respiration. Are they substrates or products? What is their main function?
2. Are there any abnormalities in the levels of these metabolites in the victims? Develop a hypothesis about which pathway may be affected based on these abnormalities.
3. Explain your reasoning for your hypothesis.

## Part IV: Role of Cyanide

You are now convinced that you know the cause of death for these victims and quickly report it back to the police as this is a very dangerous situation. After realizing that the electron transport chain was no longer functioning, you started to suspect poisoning and ran a blood test for various poisons that you knew affected the electron transport chain. The test of all seven patients came back positive for cyanide. Cyanide irreversibly binds to cytochrome c oxidase (CcOX) of the electron transport chain and prevents the transfer of electrons to oxygen, the final electron acceptor.

## Questions

1. What effect would cyanide have on the electron transport chain and the production of ATP? Explain your answer.
2. Given what you now know about the action of cyanide on cellular respiration, explain why the patients died of lack of oxygen while their blood oxygen levels were normal.
3. Would artificial respiration or oxygenation have saved these people? Why or why not?
4. Looking back at the information you have about the people before they got sick, can you suggest a possible source of the cyanide poisoning? How should public health officials and police respond to this tragedy?

## Web Version

Detailed teaching notes, the case PDF, and an answer key are available on the NCCSTS website at *sciencecases.lib.buffalo.edu/cs/collection/detail.asp?case_id=431&id=431*.

## References

Beck, M., S. Monroe, and L. Prout. 1982. The Tylenol scare. *Newsweek,* October 11.

Tifft, S. 1982. Poison madness in the Midwest. *Time,* October 11.

CHAPTER 13

# WRESTLING WITH WEIGHT LOSS

## The Dangers of a Weight-Loss Drug

*Susan M. DeSimone and Annie Prud'homme Généreux*

## Abstract

In this case students learn about membrane permeability and the proton motive force in mitochondria in order to understand how DNP acts in mitochondria and how it may lead to various physiological effects.


## Learning Objectives

- Know the order and linkage of the biochemical processes involved in ATP synthesis in mitochondria (glycolysis, TCA cycle, electron transport chain, proton pumping, ATP synthase activity).
- Describe how mitochondria may generate heat to maintain body temperature.
- Apply concepts underlying mitochondrial function to the mechanism of action of a specific diet pill.
- Extract data from a graph, and use that data to make inferences about the action of DNP.
- Relate fundamental principles of mitochondrial function to their own health.
- Extend an understanding of mitochondria function to the mechanism of action of mitochondrial uncoupling protein in thermogenesis in brown fat.
- Explain how altering the function of mitochondria may result in health conditions such as male infertility and degenerative disorders.

## Quantitative Reasoning Skills/Concepts

- Interpret the meaning of simple statistical descriptors.
- Use graphs to formulate predictions and explanations.
- Articulate complete and correct claims based on data.

## The Case Study

### *Part I: Too Weighty One*

"I am tired of not making the wrestling team. I know I'm a good enough wrestler to do it," thought Connor as he walked to the gym one spring afternoon. "If I could just lose a few pounds, I would be able to make a lower weight class, and with my skills I would succeed! "But how?" he wondered. Maybe his friends could help.

Over dinner in the dining hall, Connor asked his friends at the table if they had any suggestions for a quick way to lose weight.

"Well," said Becky, "I read about this stuff called 281 (pronounced "too-weighty-one") that they used to take in the 1930s before there were all these regulations on drugs. People lost weight quickly and easily, and the effects lasted as long as they took it."

"Is it still available?" asked Connor.

"Yeah, I saw an ad for it online. The website said it works great, but you have to be careful with dosage."

That night in his dorm Connor went online and found lots of websites offering to sell this diet pill, now called DNP. According to the information, DNP had helped several people lose weight.

Some of the side effects included a fever, cataracts, and rashes. There were even some reports of deaths. DNP was said to be a "mitochondrial uncoupler."

"What's that?" Connor wondered.

### Question

1. What do you know about mitochondria?

### *Part II: Mitochondrial Function*

Figure 13.1 illustrates mitochondrial function. The image on the left in Figure 13.1 depicts the inside of a mitochondrion. Notice that there are two membranes. This creates two compartments within the mitochondrion. The innermost space, called the matrix, is where ATP (the energy currency in the cell) is generated. The space between the inner and outer membranes is called the intermembrane space.

The image on the right in Figure 13.1 is a magnification of the spaces on either side of the inner membrane. In the right-hand image, the red circles represent hydrogen ions (H+, also called protons), the dark blue box shape represents the four complexes of the electron transport chain, and the green tube shape is ATP synthase.

Through the processes of glycolysis (in the cytosol) and the TCA cycle (in the mitochondrial matrix) energy captured in the breakdown of sugars and fats is used to generate a small amount of ATP. A much larger quantity of ATP can be produced by respiration. In this process, NADH and FADH2 that were generated by glycolysis and the TCA cycle are used by the electron transport chain (ETC) to reduce oxygen to water and to generate a proton gradient across the inner mitochondrial membrane. In other words, sugars and fats provide the energy to pump protons to the intermembrane space. The ETC is the proton pumping mechanism.

**FIGURE 13.1.**

Mitochondrial Structure and Function.

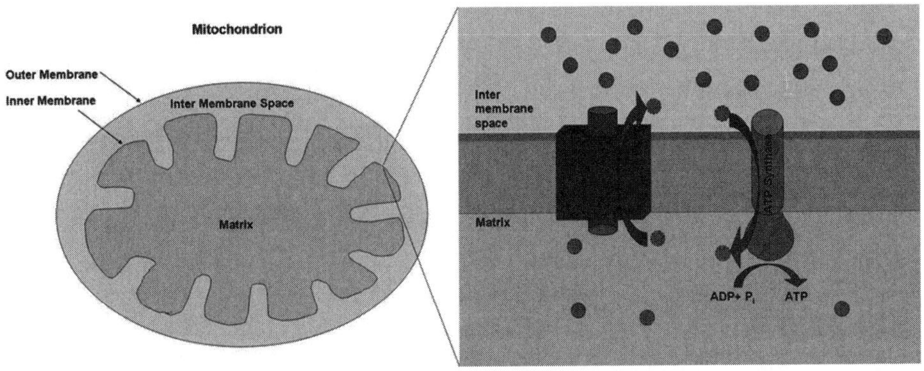


*Note:* The left panel diagrams the double membrane structure and the biochemically distinct spaces that result. The right panel is a magnified diagram of the inner membrane and adjacent spaces; red circles are protons, blue box represents the electron transport chain complex, green tube represents the ATP synthase complex, arrows across the membrane indicate the direction of proton movement through each complex.

A protein within the inner membrane called ATP synthase acts as a turbine through which protons can move down their concentration gradient back to the matrix. The dissipation of the proton gradient (traveling from the intermembrane space to the matrix) releases energy. ATP synthase captures the energy released by the protons and uses it to create ATP. Note that the synthesis of ATP requires energy, which is provided by the movement of protons, so this is an energy transfer reaction. The movement of protons back and forth across the inner membrane is one way that the energy released from the breakdown of fats and sugars is *coupled with* the production of ATP.

## Questions

1. What are the consequences of a proton gradient and how could a gradient be used in the mitochondrion? List all the possibilities that come to mind.
2. What must be an important characteristic of the inner membrane in order for this gradient to be established and maintained?
3. If you "poke a hole" in the inner membrane such that protons can freely move across it, what would happen:

a. To the proton distribution across the inner membrane?

b. To the amount of ATP produced by the mitochondria?

c. To the energy released in the movement of the protons?

4. Most ATP is consumed soon after its production. The cell has ways of detecting how much ATP is produced and needs to keep its supply constant. If you poke a hole through the inner membrane, what might the cell do to try to adapt to the change and reestablish previous levels of ATP? List all the possibilities.

## Part III: What Does This Have to Do With DNP?

**FIGURE 13.2.**

Glycolysis and ATP Synthesis in DNP Treated Myotubules. The data are expressed as a percent of the untreated control; error bars show the standard error ($n$ = 3 for ATP analysis, $n$ = 8 for glucose oxidation). Data are extracted from Figures 1 and 3 of Gaster 2007.

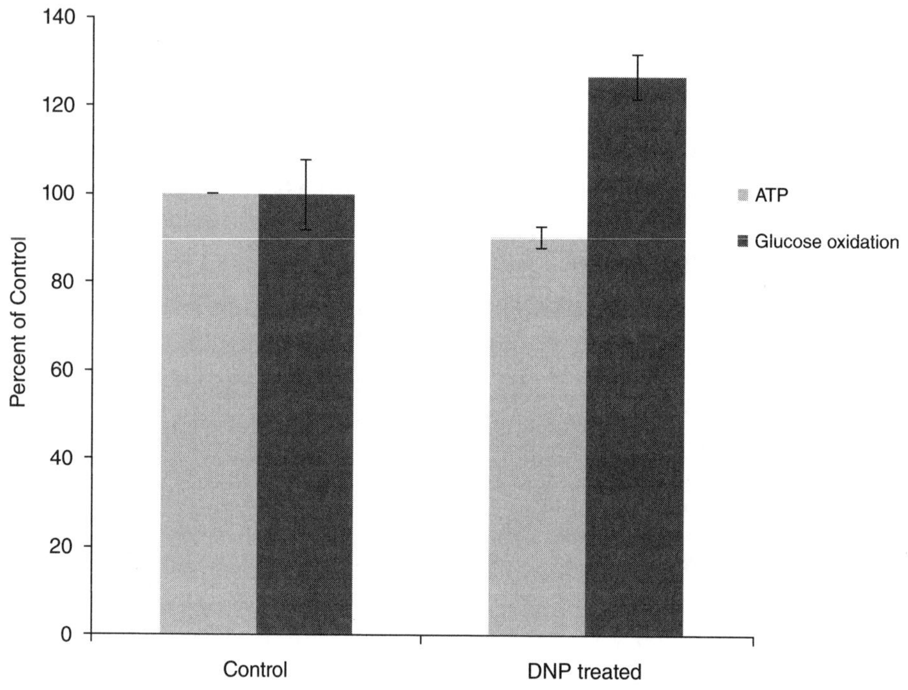

## Questions

1. Summarize what happens to ATP and glucose oxidation levels in response to treatment with DNP.
2. What could cause the effects shown in the graph? Propose as many mechanisms as possible.
3. Remember that DNP is a "mitochondrial uncoupler." An uncoupler is a chemical that disconnects two linked biological processes. Draw a diagram showing the linked processes that lead to mitochondrial ATP synthesis. Mark your diagram to show where DNP could uncouple.
4. Review the list of physiological effects that DNP has on the body (list as many as possible). Which of these effects are energy-related? Using your proposed mechanism of action of DNP, can you explain them?
5. Which linked processes do you think DNP is uncoupling taking into account the physiological effects that you listed in Question 4 above?

## *Part IV: What Should Connor Do?*

DNP (2,4-dinitrophenol) inserts into the inner mitochondrial membrane and shuttles protons between the intermembrane space and the matrix (Figure 13.3). The energy released as the protons move down their concentration gradient is dissipated as heat. This is manifested physiologically by a rise in body temperature (i.e., fever). Without the protein gradient, ATP synthase is not able to maintain ATP production.

The mitochondrion tries to adjust its ATP production by increasing the rate of glycolysis and burning more energy reserves (fats). The energy from the fat burning is used to pump protons to the inter membrane space. However, as long as DNP is in the membrane, this is a futile effort as many of the protons flow back into the matrix. This is how DNP works as a weight-loss drug. It uncouples the energy derived from the breakdown of fats and sugars (which pumps protons to the matrix) from the production of ATP.

**FIGURE 13.3.**

DNP function. Inner membrane and surrounding areas as depicted in Figure 13.1 with the addition of pink tube representing DNP and its effects on proton movement across the inner membrane.

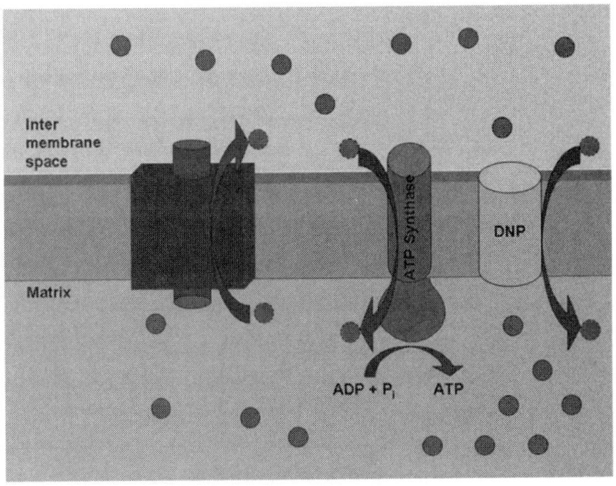


DNP is but one known mitochondrial uncoupler. Acetylsalicylic acid (Aspirin) and the drug 3,4-methylenedioxy-N-methamphetamine (MDMA, or ecstasy) are also mitochondrial uncouplers (Mingatto et al. 1996; Rusyniak et al. 2005). In human cells, there are also proteins (called UCPs—uncoupling proteins) that can uncouple the breakdown of sugars and fats from the synthesis of ATP in order to generate heat. Variant forms of these proteins have been linked with obesity (Crowley and Vidal-Puig 2001). In the course of his web research, Connor encounters a 2006 report of two people dying as a consequence of DNP use.

"Surely, they wouldn't be able to sell DNP online if it were dangerous. I'll bet they had another condition."

But the report in the *Journal of Analytical Toxicology* states that "Death in both cases was attributed to 2,4-DNP toxicity" (Miranda et al. 2006).

## Questions

1. Based on your understanding of the mechanism of action of DNP, how dangerous do you think DNP really is?
2. For an athlete, what are the consequences of ATP depletion?
3. Should Connor take DNP to lose weight?

## Web Version

Detailed teaching notes (including an optional laboratory investigation to accompany the case), the case PDF, and an answer key are available on the NCCSTS website at *sciencecases.lib.buffalo.edu/cs/collection/detail.asp?case_id=563&id=563*.

## References


Crowley, V., and A. J. Vidal-Puig. 2001. Mitochondrial uncoupling proteins (UCPs) and obesity. *Nutrition, Metabolism & Cardiovascular Diseases* 11 (1): 70–75.

Gaster, M. 2007. Insulin resistance and the mitochondrial link. Lesson from cultured human myotubes. *Biochimica et Biophys. Acta.* 1772:755–765.

Mingatto, F. E., A. C. Santos, S. A. Uyemura, M. C. Jordani, and C. Curti. 1996. In vitro interaction of nonsteroidalanti-inflammatory drugs on oxidative phosphorylation of rat kidney mitochondria: Respiration and ATP synthesis. *Archives of Biochemistry and Biophysics* 334 (2): 303–308.

Miranda, E. J., I. M. McIntyre, D. R. Parker, R. D. Gary, and B. K. Logan. 2006. Two deaths attributed to the use of 2,4-dinitrophenol. *Journal of Analytical Toxicology* 30: 219–222.

Rusyniak, D. E., S. L. Tandy, S. K. Hekmatyar, E. Mills, D. J. Smith, N. Bansal, D. MacLellan, M. E. Harper, and J. E. Sprague. 2005. The role of mitochondrial uncoupling in 3,4-methylenedioxymethamphetamine-mediated skeletal muscle hyperthermia and rhabdomyolysis. *Journal of Pharmacology and Experimental Therapeutics* 313 (2): 629–639.

# NANOBACTERIA

## Are They or Aren't They Alive?

*Merri Lynn Casem*

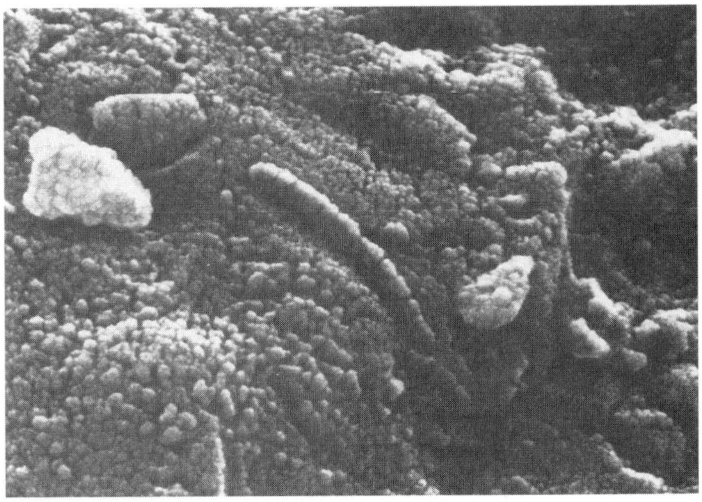


## Abstract

This case is based on two conflicting reports in the scientific literature on the status of nanobacteria as living organisms in order to explore basic concepts related to the biological definition of life and the process of scientific investigation. In addition to engaging students with these topics, the case highlights the ambiguities inherent in science and creates a forum for debate and discussion regarding the ability to arrive at "right answers."


## Learning Objectives

- Develop an accurate biological definition of life.
- Propose an experiment to test one property of life.
- Discuss evidence provided from light and electron microscopic data.
- Formulate associations between specific properties of life and the data that provides evidence for that property.
- Analyze and interpret experimental data.
- Evaluate a hypothesis.
- Recognize the role of replication of results in the scientific process.
- Support conclusions based on evidence.
- Identify the evidence supporting conflicting hypotheses.

## Quantitative Reasoning Skills/Concepts

- Use graphs to formulate predictions and explanations.
- Articulate complete and correct claims based on data.
- Use appropriate reasoning to support the validity of data-based claims.
- Create experimental designs to test hypotheses.

- Electrophoresis analysis.
- Analysis of light, fluorescence, and electron microscopy images of cells.

## The Case Study

### *Part I: What Does It Mean to Be Alive?*

Biology is the study of living things. Whether a single cell or a sequoia tree, a humpback whale or a human being, you have an intuitive sense of what it means to be a biological organism. Sometimes, however, the designation of something as a living thing is not so obvious. A recent example of this is the discovery of *nanobacteria*, which some scientists believe are not bacteria at all.

Bacteria are *prokaryotic* cells. Prokaryotes lack the internal, membrane-bound structures associated with *eukaryotic* cells (your body is made up of eukaryotic cells). Bacteria are extremely abundant and versatile, occurring in every environment on Earth (including inside and outside your body). The name, *nanobacteria*, refers to the very small size of these alleged organisms (on the order of 0.2µm to 0.5µm). They were originally isolated from human and cow blood.

It has been proposed that these bacteria function to stimulate a process called biomineralization.

*Biomineralization* is the formation of inorganic crystalline structures in association with biological macromolecules. This process is responsible for the production of bone and dental enamel. This process is also referred to as *calcification*.

Biomineralization is a good thing when it occurs in the correct location, but often this process occurs in the wrong place at the wrong time. The formation of kidney stones is a good example of this kind of pathological (disease-related) form of biomineralization. Nanobacteria have been isolated from within human kidney stones, leading to the suggestion that these bacteria may be the cause of this disease.

Over the next several class meetings we will be considering the evidence for the existence of nanobacteria and their role in the process of biomineralization.

### Assignment for Part I

The fundamental issue under consideration is whether nanobacteria are alive. How would you decide this question? To answer this you need to think about the properties common to all living things and how you would test whether the nanobacteria possessed these properties.

## Homework

- What are the properties of a biological organism? Think of at least THREE properties of life.
- Fill out the table on the worksheet for Part I (Table 14.1) and bring it with you to the next class period.
- Choose ONE property of life and propose a way you could test for that property.

**TABLE 14.1.**

Worksheet for Part 1: What are the properties of a biological organism?

| Property of life | Is this property common to ALL living things? | How would you test for this property? |
|---|---|---|
| | | |
| | | |
| | | |

## *Part II: What Is the Evidence That Nanobacteria Are Alive?*

Nanobacteria were originally discovered by two researchers from Finland, Drs. E. Olavi Kajander and Neva Ciftcioglu. They isolated very small (0.2 to 0.5µm) coccoid (round) particles from human and cow blood. They found that they were very difficult to work with and did not behave like typical bacteria. They reported: "Nanobacteria are poorly disruptable, stainable, fixable and exceptionally resistant to heat" (i.e., none of these standard techniques worked on the nanobacteria).

The researchers determined that a culture of nanobacteria will double in size in three days and high doses of gamma radiation or antibiotics will prevent this multiplication. They claim to have isolated a "16S rRNA gene sequence that falls within the α-2 subgroup of Proteobacteria," a class of bacteria that includes several human pathogens.

In a research report published in the *Proceedings of the National Academy of Sciences, USA* (*PNAS* 95: 8274-8279, 1998), Kajander and Ciftcioglu present additional information about nanobacteria. The data presented on Data Sheet 1 (Figure 14.1 on p. 140) and Data Sheet 2 (Figure 14.2 on p. 141) are excerpted from this article.

**FIGURE 14.1.**

Data Sheet 1: Light and Electron Microscopic Images of Nanobacteria.

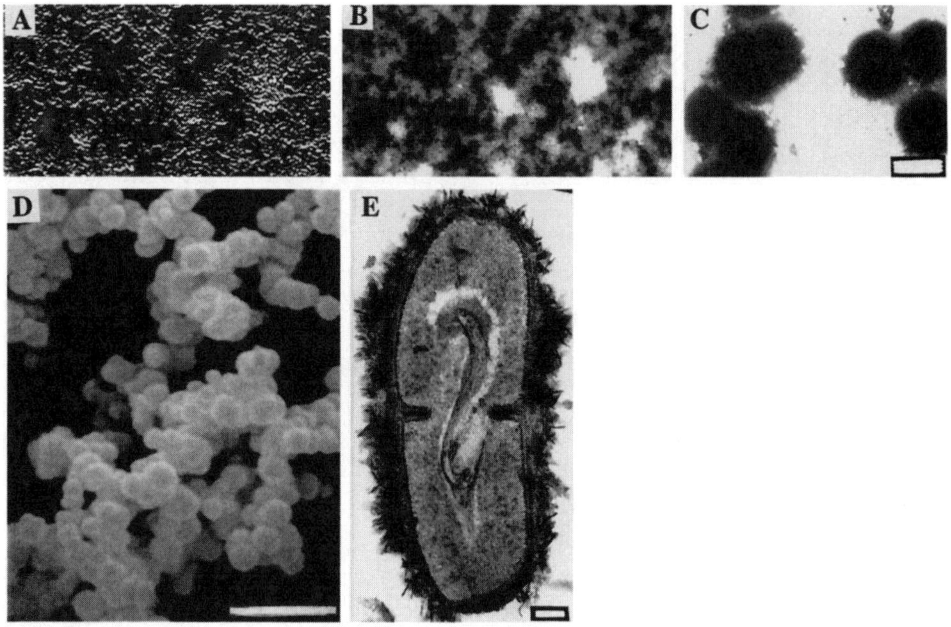


**Key:**
(A) DIC image of bottom-attached nanobacteria after a 2-month culture period.
(B) DNA staining of the same area (X1600) with the modified Hoechst method.
(C) Negative staining of nanobacteria isolated directly from FBS. (Bar = 200 nm.)
(D) SEM micrograph showing their variable size. (Bar = 1 µm.)
(E) A dividing nanobacterium covered with a "hairy" apatite layer. (Bar = 100 nm.)

*Source:* Kajander and Ciftcioglu 1998 (*PNAS* 95: 8274-8279). Copyright 1998 National Academy of Sciences, USA.

**FIGURE 14.2.**

Data Sheet 2: Nanobacteria Cultured Under SF Conditions and Their Interaction With Cells.

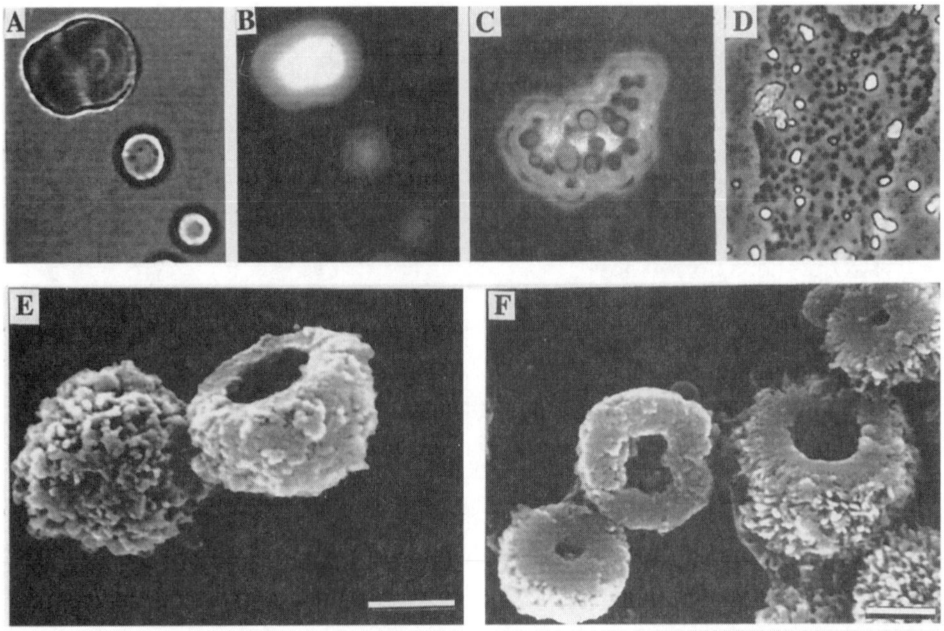


**Key:**
(A) Light microscopic micrograph.
(B) DNA staining of the same area with the modified Hoechst staining method.
(C) DIC images of nanobacteria inside a common apatite shelter.
(D) A partly demineralized nanobacterial group (A-D, X860).
(E and F) SEM micrographs of nanobacterial dwellings detached from the culture vessel.
(Bars = 1 µm.)

*Source:* Kajander and Ciftcioglu 1998 (*PNAS* 95: 8274–8279). Copyright 1998 National Academy of Sciences, USA.

## Assignment for Part II

Scientists conduct experiments in an attempt to answer specific questions. Once they have analyzed their results, they write up their findings for publication. Scientific information is shared through publication in scientific journals. Other scientists can then read and evaluate the research. The scientific process can be complicated by the use of specialized language.

## Homework

- Read over the summary information presented above and examine the data.
- What terms or concepts are new or unclear to you?
- What questions do you have?
- List these on the work sheet for Part II (Table 14.2) and bring them with you to class.

**TABLE 14.2.**

**Worksheet for Part II.**

| |
|---|
| Terms and Concepts I Don't Know: |
| Questions I Have: |

## *Part III: More Evidence of Life*

In their 1998 paper, Kajander and Ciftcioglu describe various experimental results to support their hypothesis that nanobacteria are living organisms. In addition to the evidence you have already considered, these authors describe three key experiments that they feel greatly strengthen their hypothesis.

- *Experiment 1: Transferability*

  When nanobacteria are cultured for a period of time (1 month), the process of biomineralization that they trigger results in the formation of a "biofilm" on the surface of the culture container (much like a hardwater deposit around a faucet). It is possible to scrape up this biofilm, dilute the components (1:10), and transfer the nanobacteria into a new culture container. After another month, the culture container is once again coated with a biofilm. The authors report that they were able to repeat this 1:10 dilution and transfer protocol on a monthly basis for five years. They describe this property as "transferability."

- *Experiment 2: Gamma Radiation*

  Nanobacteria could be isolated from culture as described above. When these isolated cells were exposed to high energy, gamma radiation and then added to a culture container, no growth or formation of a biofilm was observed.

- *Experiment 3: Kidney Stones*

  Kidney stones were examined from 30 different human patients. When these stones were treated to slightly dissolve them, it was possible to isolate nanobacteria-like particles. When placed in culture, these particles behaved exactly like nanobacteria isolated from serum. That is, they formed a biofilm on the surface of the culture container.

### Assignment for Part III

A very important aspect of science is how to interpret the results you get from an experiment. What does the data tell you? How much can you conclude from an experiment?

### Activity

- Consider the results from each of the three experiments previously described.
- What does each experiment tell you?
- How does the experiment support the hypothesis that nanobacteria are living?
- Use the table on the worksheet for Part III (Table 14.3) to record your thoughts.

**TABLE 14.3.**

Worksheet for Part III.

| Experiment | What can you conclude from this experiment? | Does the experiment support the hypothesis? |
|---|---|---|
| **Experiment 1:** Transferability | | |
| **Experiment 2:** Gamma Radiation | | |
| **Experiment 3:** Kidney Stones | | |

## *Part IV: Corroborating Evidence?*

A key requirement in the process of scientific investigation is the repetition of experimental results by other scientists. If others can repeat your work, then it is likely (although not guaranteed) that your conclusions and hypotheses are correct. In October of 2000, Cisar et al. published a paper (*PNAS* 97:11511-11515; 2000) that examined the original work of Kajander and Ciftciolglu.

Cisar's team repeated the experiments described by Kajander. They isolated and cultured the nanobacteria in the same way and observed many of the same behaviors. Despite this, Cisar et al. believe that their evidence does not support the hypothesis that nanobacteria are living and play a role in the development of kidney stones in humans.

One difference between the papers focuses on the evidence for DNA. DNA can be identified by its staining properties (Hoechst or ethidium bromide) or by its ability to absorb light at a wavelength of 260nm (ultraviolet). Another method is to use the technique of Polymerase Chain Reaction (PCR). This technique uses short sequences of DNA called primers to trigger a chemical reaction that results in the amplification or increase in the concentration (number) of pieces of a specific region of DNA from a sample. In this example, the primers were specific for 16S rDNA and the sample was the isolated nanobacteria. Following the PCR reaction the authors could use other techniques to see the PCR product (agarose gels) and they could isolate and sequence the product to determine the exact genetic code or language associated with that PCR product.

The data from these and other experiments are presented in Table 14.4 as well as Data Sheets 3 and 4 (Figures 14.3 and 14.4 on pages 146 and 147).

## Assignment for Part IV

The critical analysis of data becomes even more important when different groups reach conflicting conclusions. Scientific results are meaningless if they cannot be repeated and validated. The inability to repeat results could arise from unknown variables (quality of water, and so on), from minor changes in technique or procedure, from differences in interpretation (researcher bias), or from serious flaws with the original research.

### Homework

Consider the data from the work by Cisar et al. and answer the questions below:

- Which terms or techniques are new or unclear to you?
- How do these data compare to that of Kajander and Ciftcioglu? (To help you answer this question, refer back to Parts II and III of this case study).

### In Class

- Which of the new results are supportive of Kajander and Ciftcioglu?
- Which of the new results contradict Kajander and Ciftcioglu?
- Use the table on the worksheet for Part IV (Table 14.5, p. 148) to critique the work of Cisar et al.
- Circle the result that you believe is most damaging to the hypothesis that nanobacteria are living organisms. Explain why you think this.

**TABLE 14.4.**

Results of Experiments.

| Experiment | Results |
|---|---|
| Culture of Nanobacteria | Nanobacteria maintained in culture generate a biofilm on the surface of the culture container within three weeks. |
| Gamma Radiation | Exposure to gamma radiation prevents the formation of a biofilm. |
| Transferability | When a biofilm (nanobacteria) isolated by scraping the surface of an established culture was diluted 1:10 and transferred into a new culture container, it grew—generating a new biofilm. This could be repeated for several months. |
| Cell-like Appearance | The nanobacteria isolated from the biofilm has a coccoid (round) appearance. See (a) and (c) on Figure 14.3. |
| DNA Staining | Hoechst staining is diffuse (not focused) - does not appear to specifically localize to the cells. See (d) on Figure 14.3.<br>There was no ethidium bromide staining material following standard DNA isolation techniques (not shown). |
| DNA Isolation | There is no evidence of DNA based on absorption at a wavelength of 260nm.<br>See (a) on Figure 14.4. |
| Protein Isolation | Protein gel electrophoresis (a technique that allows you to see all the proteins in a sample) show only a few proteins.<br>See (b) on Figure 14.4. |
| PCR for 16S rDNA | PCR reactions amplified a product of the expected size and with a sequence that was 85% identical to the published nanobacteria sequence.<br>-The same PCR reaction product was found in samples that lacked the nanobacteria.<br>- The sequence of the PCR product was 99% identical to that of *Pseudomonas*, a common bacterial contaminant.<br>- The published sequences of 16S rDNA from nanobacteria are 99% identical to 16S rDNA from *Phyllobacterium*, another common contaminant. |

**FIGURE 14.3.**

Data Sheet 3: Electron and Light Microscopic Images of Nanobacteria-Like Particles Scraped From DMEM-Containing Subcultures Of 0.45-μm Membrane-Filtered Saliva.

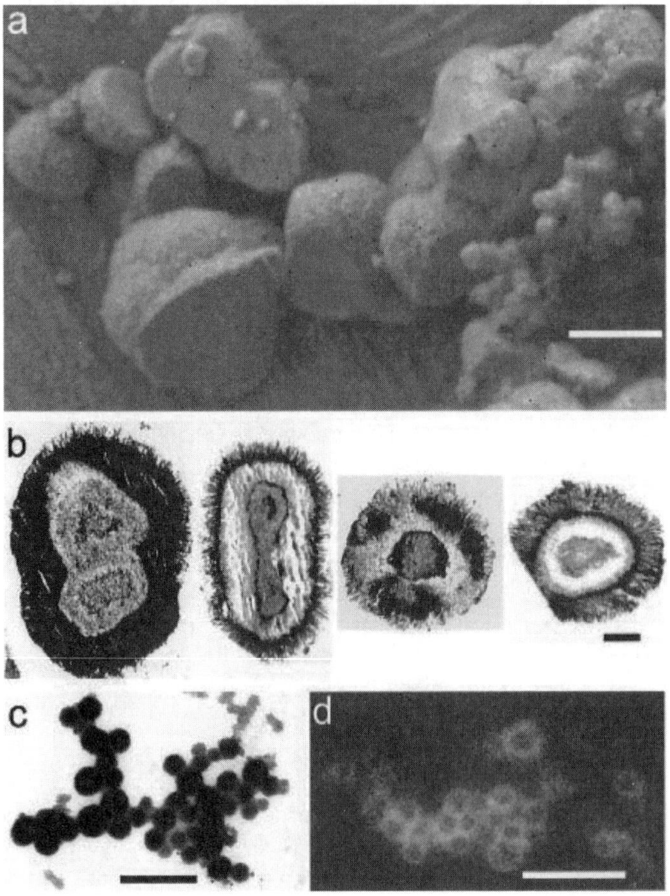


**Key:**
(a) SEM of biofilm material. (Bar = 5 μm.)
(b) TEM of nanobacteria-like particles observed in thin sections of biofilm material. (Bar = 1 μm.)
(c) TEM of negatively stained biofilm material showing small coccoid-shaped particles. (Bar = 0.2 μm.)
(d) Light micrograph of biofilm material stained with Hoechst 33258 showing nonspecific surface fluorescence of coccoid-shaped particles. (Bar = 1 μm.)

*Source:* Kajander and Ciftcioglu 1998 (*PNAS* 95: 8274–8279).

**FIGURE 14.4.**

Data Sheet 4: Biochemical Examination of Biofilm-Associated Macromolecules. Biofilm Material From Subcultures Of 0.45-μm Membrane-Filtered Saliva Was Washed With PBS and Solubilized by Dialysis Against Excess EDTA Followed by PBS.

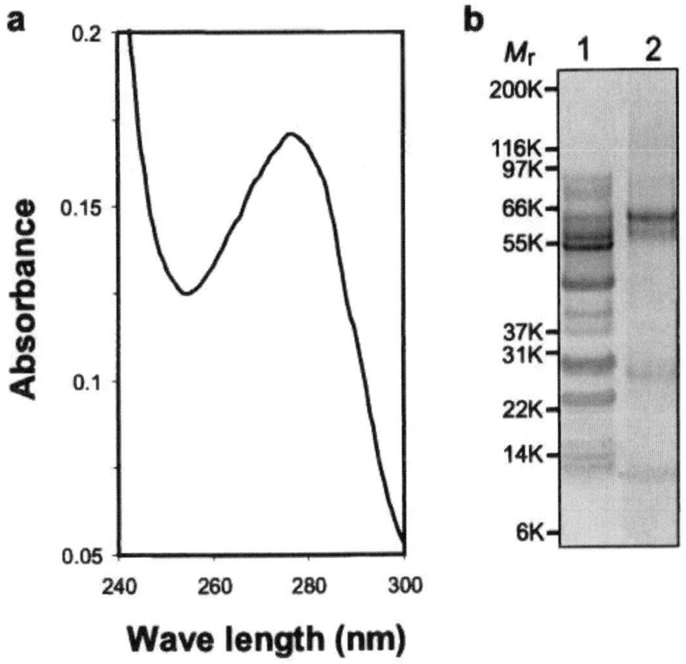


**Key:**

(a) UV absorbance spectrum of the dialyzed preparation.

(b) SDS/PAGE of the dialyzed preparation showing the Coomassie-stained profiles of membrane-filtered, whole human saliva (lane 1) and a comparable amount of biofilm-associated protein (lane 2). $M_r$ of each molecular weight marker is indicated in thousands (K).

*Source:* Kajander and Ciftcioglu 1998 (*PNAS* 95: 8274–8279).

**TABLE 14.5.**

Worksheet for Part IV: Check the correct box to indicate whether you believe that the corresponding experiment by Cisar et al. supports or contradicts the hypothesis that nanobacteria are alive.

| Experiment | Supports | Contradicts |
|---|---|---|
| Culture of nanobacteria | | |
| Gamma radiation | | |
| Transferability | | |
| Cell-like appearance | | |
| DNA staining | | |
| DNA isolation | | |
| Protein isolation | | |
| PCR for 16S rDNA | | |

Then:

- **Circle** the experiment that you think is most damaging to the hypothesis that nanobacteria are living.
- **Explain** your answer here:

## *Part V: Final Chapter (or Is It?)*

When Cisar et al. tried to repeat the experiments described by Kajander and Ciftciolglu, they did not believe that the results they obtained supported the hypothesis that nanobacteria were living. Cisar et al. claim to provide evidence that (1) there is no DNA associated with the nanobacteria based on DNA staining and lack of absorbance at 260nm, (2) that the number and type of proteins isolated from nanobacteria are insufficient for a living cell, and (3) that evidence of nanobacterial 16S rRNA is likely a result of contamination of the PCR results by other common bacteria.

While these results seemed to support the idea that nanobacteria are not biological organisms, there was a problem. Cisar et al. were able to repeat some of Kajander and Ciftciolglu's data. Specifically, Cisar et al. found that:

1. Nanobacteria maintained in culture would generate a biofilm.
2. Exposure to gamma radiation prevented the formation of the biofilm.

3. The ability to form a biofilm could be transferred (transferability).

What could account for these results if nanobacteria were not alive? Cisar et al. needed to explain these results if they wanted their conclusion to be accepted by the scientific community. They attempted to do this by designing an additional set of experiments.

### Assignment for Part V

It is not enough to simply suggest that someone else's research is wrong. The finding of "negative evidence" (not finding something) is usually not sufficient. You must provide compelling, positive evidence that offers an alternative explanation of the published observations.

### Activity

Look over the final set of experimental data provided by Cisar et al. and displayed on the worksheet for Part V (Table 14.6, p. 150).

- What conclusions can you make?
- Decide if these experiments explain the observations of:
    1. the formation of the biofilm,
    2. the ability of gamma radiation to prevent the formation of the biofilm, and
    3. the transferability of biofilm formation.

## *Conclusion: The Debate*

Scientific hypotheses are based on our best understanding of the evidence. These hypotheses must either be modified or abandoned when new evidence is made available that challenges our understanding. In this case study you have been asked to consider experimental results from two competing labs. The contradictory data reported by the two groups resulted in the publication of an independent news item titled "Researchers fail to find signs of life in 'living' particles" by Allison Abbott (*Nature* (408: 394) 2000). In this article, Cisar is quoted as saying, "There is a need for hard molecular evidence" to support a claim of life, while Ciftcioglu is quoted as saying, "We have evidence that the particles are living. We are not fanatics, we are scientists." Who is right?

### Activity

- Discuss which set of evidence (Kajander and Ciftcioglu 1998 or Cisar et al. 2000) you find most convincing.
- Decide whether you believe nanobacteria are alive or not!
- Next class period we will be debating the status of nanobacteria as a living organism.

**TABLE 14.6.**

Worksheet for Part V.

| Experiment | Results | Cisar Lab Conclusion | Alternate Conclusion |
|---|---|---|---|
| Energy use by nanobacteria | Cultures of nanobacteria were exposed to 0.1% *sodium azide*—a powerful inhibitor of cellular respiration. The formation of a biofilm continued even in the presence of this poison. | | |
| "Growth" of dilute cultures | Cultures of nanobacteria were diluted to a higher degree than that used by Kajander. Dilutions of 1:100 or 1:1000 were cultured as before. At these high dilutions there was no evidence of biofilm formation even after eight weeks. | | |
| Biofilm formation in the absence of nanobacteria | Sterile DMEM culture media will not form a biofilm on its own. When purified phosphotidyl inositol (a phospholipid common to biological membranes) was added to the culture, biofilm formation occurred within two weeks. The appearance of the particles was very similar to those found in nanobacterial cultures. This ability for a phospholipid to induce biofilm formation was prevented when the phospholipid was exposed to gamma radiation. | | |

*Source:* Cisar et al. (2000)

## Web Version

Detailed teaching notes, the case PDF, and an answer key are available on the NCCSTS website at *sciencecases.lib.buffalo.edu/cs/collection/detail.asp?case_id=179&id=179*

## References

Campbell, N. A., J. B. Reece, and L. G. Mitchel. 1999. *Biology*. 5th ed. Menlo Park, CA: Benjamin Cummings.

Cisar, J. O., D-Q Xu, J. Thompson, W. Swaim, L. Hu, and D. J. Kopecko. 2000. An alternative interpretation of nanobacterial-induced biomineralization. *Proceedings of the National Academy of Sciences* 97 (21): 11511–11515.

Kajander, E. O., and N. Ciftcioglu. 1998. Nanobacteria: An alternative mechanism for pathogenic intra- and extracellular calcification and stone formation. *Proceedings of the National Academy of Sciences* 95 (14): 8274–8279.

# SECTION IV

# MICROBIOLOGY

# FECAL COLIFORMS IN ANTARCTICA

*Stephen C. Nold*

## Abstract

Students explore the environmental consequences of Antarctic research as they design experiments to assess the impact of disposing untreated sewage from a research station into the ocean. As part of this, they review experimental methods to measure coliform bacteria, examine data, and decide what actions, if any, should be taken.

## Learning Objectives

- Learn how scientists generate and use data to solve everyday problems, including experimental design, appropriate use of controls, data collection, and data interpretation.
- Understand how scientific data informs policy makers.
- Learn about fecal coliform detection methods.

## Quantitative Reasoning Skills/Concepts

- Use graphs to formulate predictions and explanations.
- Articulate complete and correct claims based on data.
- Use appropriate reasoning to support the validity of data-based claims.

## The Case Study

### *Part I: McMurdo Station*

Sally Freeley bounced in her seat as the C-130's powerful turboprops screamed to life, pulling the cargo plane down the runway. After months of planning, she checked her mental lists, knowing it was too late to go back. She took comfort in knowing her scientific equipment was secure in the hold. Sally was heading to Antarctica for the field season. Re-supply was impossible, so she needed everything in perfect order for the next three months of field work.

The brief austral summer is October through January. Only then does the midnight sun warm the coast to -15°C (5°F), balmy enough for a dedicated group of scientists to study the coldest continent on Earth. Scientists like Sally have alerted us to the growing hole in the ozone layer, discovered cold-loving life forms, and demonstrated the importance of polar oceans in global carbon and oxygen cycles.

Sally would spend her next three months at McMurdo Station. This facility offers 1,100 seasonal scientists warm meals, a place to sleep, logistical support such as air and surface transportation, and laboratory space. Funded by the U.S. government, the National Science Foundation (NSF) oversees the management of McMurdo's daily operations.

Several months before, Sally's boss had stopped outside her office. "Sally, I just got a call from NSF. The polar programs office is concerned about how McMurdo Station is managing its waste. It turns out that Greenpeace has been poking around the facility. Those environmentalists raised a big stink over McMurdo's sewage. They collected samples at the sewage outfall and claim that the United States is polluting the international waters of McMurdo Sound!"

Sally knew how to measure fecal coliforms, indicator bacteria that suggest the presence of pathogenic organisms from human waste. After researching the subject, she learned that raw sewage collected from the laboratory and housing facilities is pumped through a masticator (literally, "chewer") that purees the sewage before it is piped into the waters of McMurdo Sound. She also learned that offshore ocean currents that stir McMurdo Sound water rarely mix water with it, limiting the potential for dilution (Figure 15.1). If fecal coliforms survived the ice-cold salt water (-1.8°C), bacterial contaminants could accumulate, posing health risks to Antarctic researchers and polluting pristine waters.

"What can we do to help?" Sally asked.

"We need to get down there pronto. Let's get some background data so we can make some informed decisions," was the reply.

## Questions

1. Why is Greenpeace concerned that McMurdo Station is releasing raw sewage into McMurdo Sound?
2. What type of sampling scheme would you design to see how much of McMurdo Sound is contaminated by fecal bacteria?
3. What are the potential results you might obtain from the sampling scheme you designed? Do they help you answer the research question?
4. What experimental controls did you include? Why?

**FIGURE 15.1.**

Prevailing Ocean Currents in Mcmurdo Sound and the Locations of the Sewage Outfall and Drinking Water Intakes

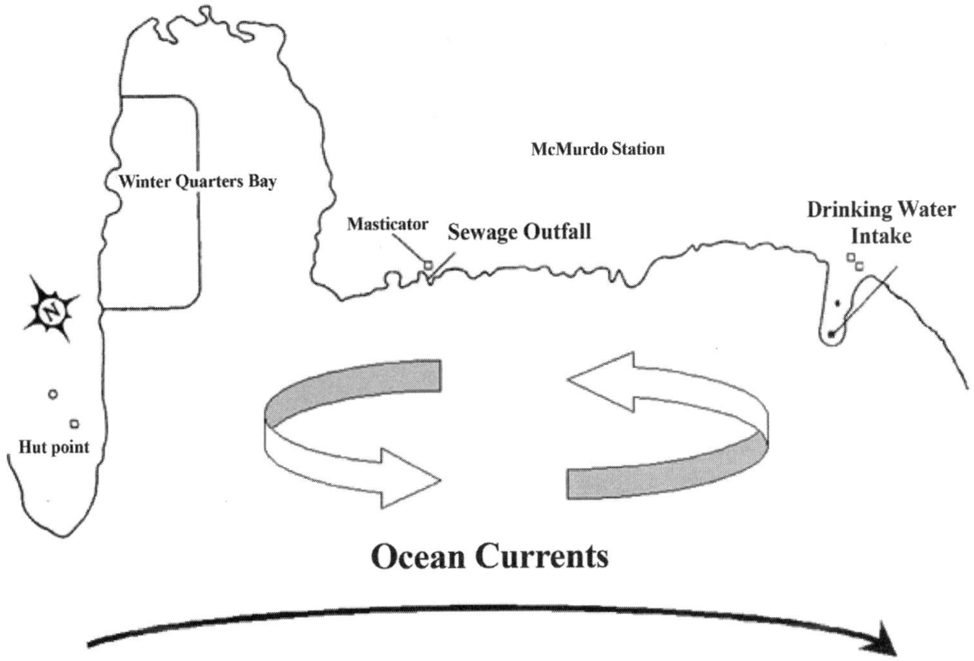


## *Part II: Counting Environmental Bacteria*

Bacteria are everywhere—on our skin, in our food, suspended in our drinking water. Although the microbial majority is benign, a few bacterial species can make us sick. To safeguard against food- and water-borne disease, microbiologists routinely screen our drinking water for bacterial pathogens.

Animal feces contain *coliform bacteria,* microorganisms that inhabit the intestines of warm-blooded animals. Many coliform bacteria are also found on plants and in soil and water. Coliform bacteria are not pathogens themselves, but their presence indicates the possibility of finding pathogens. In contrast, *fecal coliform bacteria* such as *Escherichia coli* are found in feces, and their presence in drinking water indicates fecal contamination. *E. coli* can also be a pathogen itself, so if *E. coli* is found in drinking water, there is a good chance that other pathogens are present too (U.S. Environmental Protection Agency 2012).

To detect *E. coli* and other coliform bacteria, microbiologists filter water samples and place the filter in a petri dish containing growth medium such as Endo agar. Microorganisms from the water grow and form colonies, giving an estimate of the number of bacteria in each milliliter of water. *E. coli* forms colored, shiny colonies on Endo agar while other coliforms grow as white or clear colonies (shown in Figure 15.2).

**FIGURE 15.2.**

Bacterial Colonies Growing on Endo Agar.

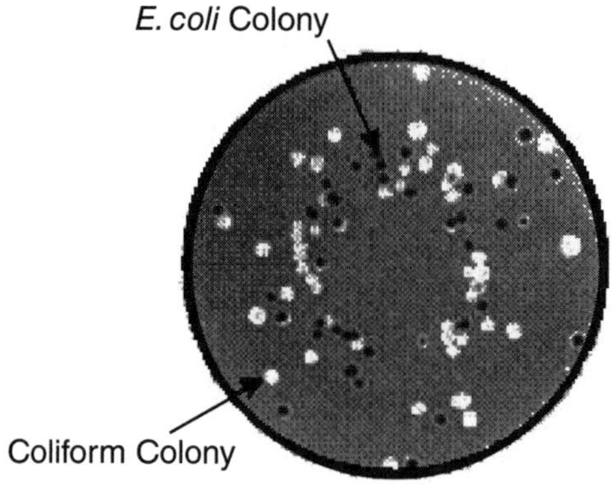


**Key:** Dark colonies = *E. coli*
White/clear colonies = coliform bacteria
White + dark colonies = total coliform bacteria

The guidelines of maximum allowable limits for total coliforms in drinking and recreational waters vary by state. Representative limits appear in Table 15.1.

**TABLE 15.1.**

Maximum Allowable Limits of Fecal Coliform Bacteria (cells/100 ml).

| | Total coliforms | *E. coli* |
|---|---|---|
| Drinking water | 0 | 0 |
| Recreational waters | 400 | 235 |

*Sources:* "Drinking water contaminants," *http://water.epa.gov/drink/contaminants/index.cfm* (USEPA maximum allowable limits for fecal coliforms and other contaminants in drinking water) and Wisconsin Environmental Health Division, *www.slh.wisc.edu/ehd/watermicro* (fecal coliform and *E. coli* acceptable limits for swimming beaches in the State of Wisconsin).

## Questions

1. Why would we want to count the number of fecal coliforms in a water sample?
2. Do 400 coliforms per 100 milliliters strike you as very many?

3. How many other types of bacteria might be present in a normal water sample?
4. What problems might Sally encounter when she uses these techniques in Antarctica?

## Part III: Data Prediction

Sally had spent the day drilling 56 holes through two meters of sea ice to collect her water samples (see sampling scheme in Figure 15.3). Sally needed to quickly return to the station before her samples froze so she could filter the water, place the filters on Petri dishes, and incubate them. Right now, though, she needed help. The snow machine, her only transportation, wouldn't start in the bitter cold. She was three kilometers out and the temperature was quickly dropping. Luckily, the two-way was working when she called for helicopter support to bring her and her valuable samples to the lab. Two days later, Sally counted the colonies growing on her petri dishes.

**FIGURE 15.3.**

Locations of Sally's Sample Collection Sites in McMurdo Sound.

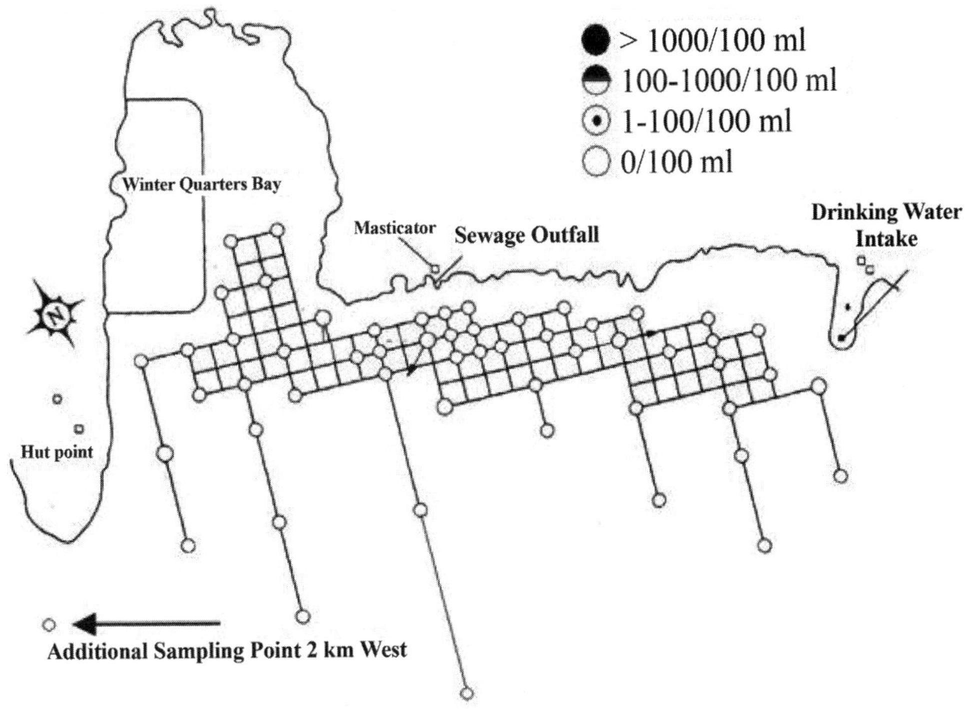


### Questions

1. Why did Sally sample the sites you see on the map in Figure 15.3?

2. Using the scheme, fill in the sampling sites with the number of fecal coliforms you think Sally found.
3. What would you consider to be the "Action Level" of fecal coliform contamination in McMurdo Sound? At what levels would you like to see the National Science Foundation take remedial action?

## *Part IV: Decision Time*

Sally's results appear in Figure 15.4. From these she had to prepare her report in order to make a recommendation to the National Science Foundation. (These are actual results obtained from McMurdo Sound waters; McFeters, Barry, and Howington 1993.)

**FIGURE 15.4.**

Actual Fecal Coliform Data From McMurdo Sound.

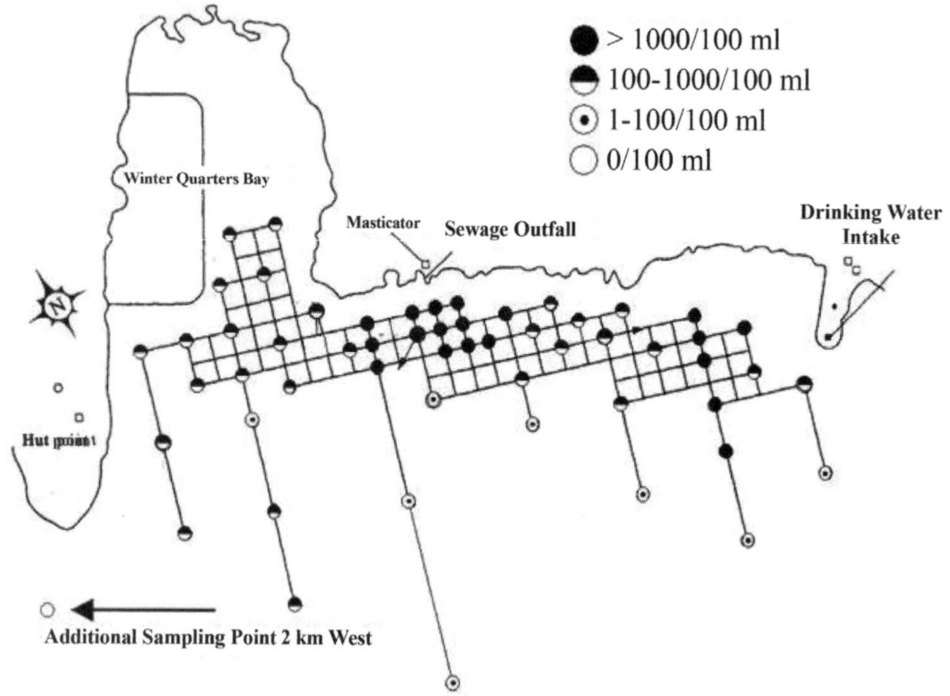

## Questions

1. What do you think Sally should recommend to the National Science Foundation?
2. What roles should scientists play in forming environmental policy?

## Web Version

Detailed teaching notes, the case PDF, and an answer key are available on the NCCSTS website at *sciencecases.lib.buffalo.edu/cs/collection/detail.asp?case_id=330&id=330*.

## References

McFeters, G. A., J. P. Barry, and J.P. Howington. 1993. Distribution of enteric bacteria in Antarctic seawater surrounding a sewage outfall. *Water Research* 27: 645–650.

U.S. Environmental Protection Agency. 2012. Water: Monitoring and assessment. 5.1.1. Fecal bacteria. *http://water.epa.gov/type/rsl/monitoring/vms511.cfm*

# ELVIS MELTDOWN!

## Microbiology Concepts of Culture, Growth, and Metabolism

*Richard C. Stewart, Ann C. Smith, and Patricia A. Shields*

## Abstract

Students assume the role of microbiologists working at a fictional chemical company responsible for providing polyurethane materials for a space mission designed to collect samples from a nearby previously invisible planet. When the collection unit returns to earth, much of the polyurethane material has been degraded. Students must analyze the samples and isolate and characterize the extraterrestrial microbes that may be responsible for the polyurethane degradation.


## Learning Objectives

- Understand and apply knowledge of bacterial structure and function.
- Understand the isolation and growth properties of microorganisms.
- Understand and apply principles of microbial metabolism.
- Understand the mechanisms of microbial growth and how to control growth.

## Quantitative Reasoning Skills/Concepts

- Articulate complete and correct claims based on data.
- Use appropriate reasoning to support the validity of data-based claims.
- Read tabular data, and identify and analyze relevant aspects of those results and make recommendations based upon the evidence.
- Interpret the results of a growth experiment and make recommendations as to the conditions and precautions that the next space mission should make to prevent contamination by earth microorganisms.
- Perform a few simple calculations of ATP yields for microbes growing on different carbon sources under different conditions.

## The Case Study

### *Part I: Return to Sender*

Fresh out of college, with your degree in microbiology, you have landed your "first real job" as a scientist with DuPunt, a company that specializes in development and production of polyurethane derivatives (specialized plastics). You (and your boss) are not quite sure why DuPunt has a microbiologist on staff, but you are both about to find out why the company desperately needs one now. Your boss has called you into his office. "Read this article!" he says, pushing the front page of a major national newspaper across his desk to you.

> **Elvis Naked, Skinless Upon Return from Outerspace!**
>
> The recent return to Earth of the unmanned exploration probe ELV from the Nearby Previously Invisible Planet (NPIP) has provided scientists with important information about conditions on the surface of this recently discovered planet. Although physicists have made great advances in understanding how NPIP recently was "uncloaked," perhaps the most interesting discoveries are yet to come as biological scientists begin to analyze the soil samples collected by the probe's Extraterrestrial Landing Vehicle Integrated Sampler (ELVIS). Designed to gather samples and maintain them in their normal atmospheric and temperature conditions, this collection unit is a sophisticated robot and is the most expensive component of the ELV probe. Inspired by the acronym for the unit (ELVIS), workers constructed this robot to resemble music legend Elvis Presley, and even fashioned a white Spandex jumpsuit to clothe it.
>
> These design features have proven to be a public relations coup, endearing the 2-foot-tall robot to the public and making it the unofficial mascot of the NASA space exploration program. This "human connection" has been instrumental in convincing Congress to provide the necessary funding for the ELV and many related space exploration programs.
>
> However, the successful completion of the ELV mission has generated a mystery, one that has led to accusations of contractors providing substandard materials (in particular

defective plastics) used in the ELV or of someone intentionally sabotaging the plastic components of the ELV in an attempt to embarrass the U.S. space exploration program.

Upon its return to Earth, the ELV capsule was opened to allow scientists to recover the soil samples. This was done as part of a special, televised "welcome home" ceremony, in which ELVIS was supposed to "dance" down the ELV exit ramp and speak his trademark words, "Thank you, thank you very much, for supporting this critical space exploration mission."

NASA scientists and on-lookers at the ceremony were shocked to find that ELVIS's jumpsuit had been reduced to a slimy puddle. Even more distressing was the deterioration of ELVIS's "skin" (a version of Lycra specially developed to resemble human skin). This too was reduced to a slimy residue that dripped from the metal "skeleton" of the ELVIS unit. The deterioration of the plastic components of ELVIS ruined what organizers had planned to be a touching ceremony at the mission's completion. ELVIS's exit from the otherwise intact spacecraft was met by gasps and screams from the gathered audience. "It was a terrible sight!" said one member of the audience. "We expected to see the King, but we saw a horrible mess, a grotesque parody of Elvis. Without his plastic lips, I couldn't understand a word he said, and the smell was horrible!" said one NASA official who wished to remain anonymous.

Television viewers were spared much of the trauma of these sights as networks quickly switched to new episodes of Sponge Bob Squarepants in which a cartoon version of the ELVIS unit was featured. An investigation is underway.

Stifling your initial reaction ("Oh yeah, new Sponge Bob!") you manage to mumble, "What a tragedy!"

"Yes. Yes. And this could take an ugly turn for DuPunt!" your boss says. "I'm not sure what caused this mess, but I do know a couple of things that didn't make it into that news article: (1) the only plastics showing damage in the ELV were polyurethanes; and (2) our company provided those polyurethane products to NASA at a cost of $15,000,000. We're in big trouble if we can't prove that something from that planet is responsible for destroying ELVIS."

He continues, "The polyurethane products we provided were first-rate. We didn't cut any corners with this stuff. Products from the same batches of polyurethane have been into outer space before, and they returned just fine. There must be some explanation other than our incompetence. This is where you come in. I need you to find that explanation!"

"Why me?" you ask.

"Because of the stink!" your boss answers. "Some of the scientists present at the ELVIS disaster said the smell reminded them of an old fermenter or an autoclave. Those are microbiology terms, aren't they?" says your boss. "Those comments tell me that this whole stinking mess might be caused by microorganisms—you know, bacteria, fungi, viruses, germs ... something like that. Get right to work on this! You and I will have to work closely on this, you know. I'll handle all the communications with the press, and you handle the science. Just make sure that you explain everything to me so that I can speak about it to the press without making a fool of myself and DuPunt!"

Okay. You are a trained scientist, you can do this! What do scientists do? They answer questions by testing specific hypotheses. As a microbiologist at DuPunt you must determine what has happened to the polyurethane. Here is your hypothesis: *The degradation of polyurethane products was caused by a microorganism or microorganisms present in the soil samples collected by ELVIS.*

## Questions

1. Using light microscopy, you examine the soil samples and the "goo" from the degraded polyurethane. Will this approach allow you to observe all microorganisms present in the samples? Why or why not? What are the limitations of this approach?
2. You use phase contrast microscopy to observe a wet mount of a soil sample (Figure 16.1) and a "goo" sample (Figure 16.2) from the ELVIS. In what ways are the potential ET microbes similar to microbes previously characterized on Earth? In what ways are they different? How could you determine whether the microbes present in the soil or goo samples are phylogenetically similar or distant from known microorganisms on Earth?
3. Your boss has done a little reading about microorganisms, but he finds it all pretty complicated. "It's like a foreign language!" he complains. "I have to face the press to explain our idea that microbes might be responsible for all the damage to ELVIS. I think that it will help my press conference presentation a lot if I can use some visual aids. What I want to do is explain to my audience what bacteria look like. You know, the functional architecture of bacteria and how they might be able to degrade

**FIGURE 16.1.**

Soil Sample.

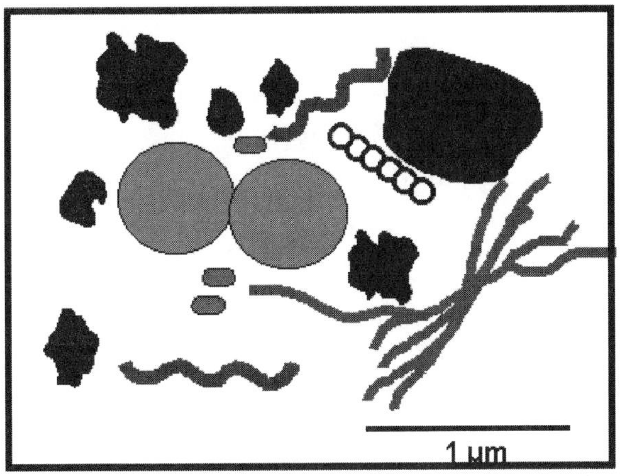


**FIGURE 16.2.**

Goo Sample.

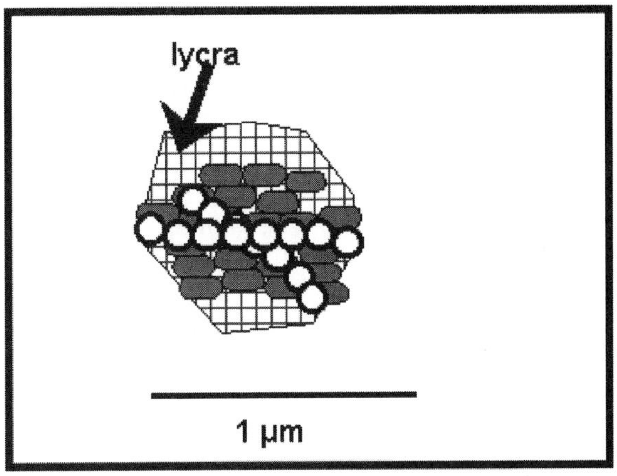


**FIGURE 16.3.**

Uncorrected Sketch of a Typical Gram-Negative Cell.

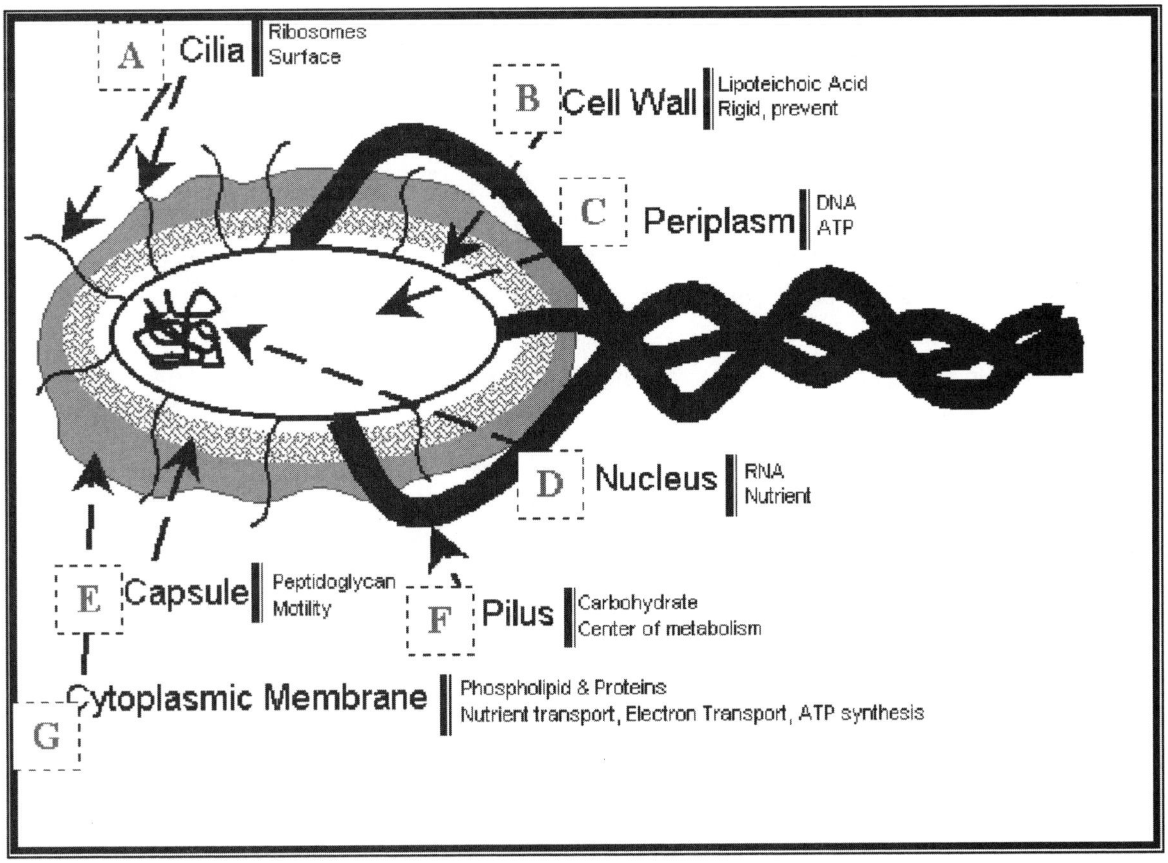

polyurethane. I think that eukaryotes might be too complicated for this audience, so I just want to show them what Gram-negative bacteria look like in a schematic diagram. I've put together this diagram of a typical Gram-negative cell (Figure 16.3). Take a look at it and make any corrections you think are necessary. Notice that I not only labeled the features, I also indicated the major biochemical composition and function(s) of each main feature. Oh yeah, this figure will probably make it into lots of newspapers, magazines, and web sites, so it needs to be scientifically correct. We wouldn't want to make DuPunt look stupid, would we? I've already done most of the work. Just proofread it and make any necessary corrections."

## Part II: Suspicious Minds

Your direct microscopic observation of microorganisms in the soil samples has sparked your boss's interest. He is eager to determine what type of microorganism(s) is present: eukaryotic or prokaryotic, Gram-positive or Gram-negative, or maybe even something new, never before seen on Earth. He sends a sample of the soil off to a biochemistry laboratory for direct analysis.

You are equally interested in the nature of the microbes, but instead of directly analyzing the soil, you first isolate a pure culture of a microorganism that you demonstrate has the ability to degrade polyurethane. You send a sample of this pure culture to the same biochemistry laboratory for analysis.

Later, you receive the results of the analysis (Table 16.1) of your boss's sample and your pure sample.

"I'm not sure what's wrong with your sample, but my results prove that we are dealing with a new kind of life form here. I'm calling it the "proeuk-aryote" because it has components characteristic of both prokaryotes and eukaryotes. It's time for a press conference!" boasts your boss.

Later on, as you are getting ready to head home after a long day in the lab, you hear your boss bellow, "What the H-E-double hockey sticks is going on here!"

You ask him what happened.

"This morning I put a few thousand cells from your pure culture of Extraterrestrial PolyUrethane-Degrading Microbe (ETPUM) onto two slides in some water, but then I had to go to that press conference, and I didn't have enough time to look at the cells carefully except to notice that they were uniformly distributed under the coverslip. I didn't want the slides to dry out so I sealed the edges of the coverslips. On this slide I used a rubber gasket to make the seal, and on this slide I used a Lycra gasket. Now look at the cell distribution! On the rubber-sealed slide, the cells are still uniformly distributed, but on the Lycra-sealed slide all the cells have congregated around the edge of the coverslip. Look. They are all over at the edges; none are left in the middle part of the slide. Could somebody have come in here and moved all those ETPUM cells over to the edges? But who? Maybe someone small with really tiny tweezers. Did you see anyone like that lurking around this scope? Nah, I need to get a grip on reality here. No tweezers could be that small."

**TABLE 16.1.**

Results of Sample Analyses.

| Test | Boss's Sample | Your Sample |
|---|---|---|
| 80 S ribosomes | + | - |
| 70 S ribosomes | + | + |
| Circular DNA | + | + |
| Linear DNA | + | - |
| RNA | + | + |
| Phospholipid membranes containing electron transport membranes | + | + |
| Peptidoglycan | + | + |
| LPS | + | + |
| Lipoteichoic acid | + | - |
| Flagellar basal body proteins | + | + |
| Pilus proteins | + | + |
| Nuclear pore proteins | + | - |
| Histone proteins | + | - |

## Questions

1. How would you go about isolating your pure culture?
2. If your goal is to characterize the ETPUM, whose results are more informative: yours or your boss's? Why? What do your results indicate about the nature of this microbe? Does its biochemical composition most closely resemble that of a prokaryote or a eukaryote? Gram-positive or Gram-negative? Do you agree with your boss's conclusion that the ETPUM is a prokaryotic-eukaryotic hybrid? Why or why not?

3. Come up with at least two possible alternative explanations for the "amazing" redistribution of the ETPUM on the Lycra-sealed slide. Both of your explanations should consider how the microbes "sensed" the presence of polyurethane. One of your answers should not involve flagella.

## *Part III: All Shook Up*

You have found media that support growth of pure cultures of ETPUM in your laboratory. The recipes for these media are shown in Table 16.2.

**TABLE 16.2.**

Media Recipes.

| Medium #1 | Medium #2 |
|---|---|
| 5 g yeast extract | 10.5 g $K_2HPO_4$ |
| 20 g tryptone | 4.5 g $KH_2PO_4$ |
| 0.5 g NaCl | 1 g $MgSO_4$ |
| 3.6 g glucose | 10 g polyurethane |
| 1 l $H_2O$ | 1 l $H_2O$ |

Growth in these media is shown in Table 16.3.

**TABLE 16.3.**

Results of Growth Experiment.

| Growth | Medium #1 | Medium #2 |
|---|---|---|
| ETPUM growth - aerobic | + | + |
| ETPUM growth - anaerobic | + | - |
| *E. coli* growth - aerobic | + | - |
| *E. coli* growth - anaerobic | + | - |

You are excited because, in Medium #2, ETPUM utilizes polyurethane as its energy source and its sole source of carbon and nitrogen, a finding that raises the possibility that ETPUM could be a useful tool for bioremediation of polyurethane-containing wastes (in landfills, for example). You have also made some progress in characterizing the central metabolic pathways and related biochemical activities of ETPUM. In particular, you have discovered that:

- ETPUM secretes an enzyme (polyurethanase) that catalyzes degradation of polyurethane, generating citric acid (citrate) as a product.
- The cytoplasmic membrane of ETPUM contains an ABC transport system capable of transporting citrate across the membrane at the expense of four ATP molecules (hydrolyzed to form ADP and phosphate) per molecule of citrate transported.
- The cytoplasm of this organism contains all of the enzymes required for glycolysis, and for the TCA cycle.
- The cytoplasmic membrane of ETPUM contains proteins that form a functional electron-transport pathway (that uses $O_2$ as the terminal electron acceptor).

## Questions

1. Which medium would you consider to be "complex" and which "defined"? Which is "rich" and which is "minimal"? Explain your answers.
2. Given that polyurethane is a huge polymer (MW >> 100,000 Daltons), why is it important that the polyurethanase is a secreted enzyme? If we assume that the polyurethane is the source of energy for the organism, how can material (carbon atoms) from it find its way into the central metabolic pathways of this microbe? What is the "entry point"? What happens after its entry into the metabolic pathway?
3. Why does growth of ETPUM in Medium #2 require oxygen? Think about this in terms of how ETPUM can generate a net gain in ATP by processing polyurethane. Remember that the degradation of polyurethane by polyurethanase does not expend ATP. In order to answer this question, address each of the following questions in your answer:
    a. Is there a net gain or loss of ATP during the transport of the citrate?
    b. Consider the ATPs that can be generated via substrate-level phosphorylation. Will glycolysis be useful for generating any ATPs during growth on polyurethane? How many ATPs can be generated via TCA? Is this enough to support growth (is there a net positive in the ATP tally)?
    c. Now consider how else ETPUM can generate ATPs (if not by substrate-level phosphorylation). Can this process generate a net positive in the ATP tally?
    d. Now explain the importance of oxygen as relates to the ATP tally.

## *Part IV: A Little Less Conversation*

### Questions

1. At a press conference announcing your company's successful isolation and characterization and cultivation of ETPUM, a reporter raises an important question: "How do you know that this microbe actually came from NPIP (the Nearby Previously Invisible Planet) and not from Earth? Could this microbe really be an Earth microbe that was present in/on ELVIS before it was launched into space?" That's impossible," your boss answers. "Prior to launch, we wiped down the entire ELV and ELVIS with the disinfectants ethanol and triclosan. In addition we used plastics impregnated with disinfectant chlorhexidine. I had our chemists check! These chemicals do all kinds of nasty things to cells: coagulate proteins and destroy membranes. No microbes could have survived that." What do you think? Were these treatments adequate to rule out the possibility raised by the reporter?
2. You are a consultant for a second ELVIS mission to NPIP. Describe what physical and/or chemical treatments you would require prior to liftoff to minimize the opportunity for contamination of the ELV (the landing module of the spacecraft) and ELVIS (a new version of the robot) by Earth microbes. HINT: Keep in mind the following: ELVIS's skin cannot withstand temperatures above 90°C; the ELV itself is approximately the size of a minivan and includes many metal parts. Use scientific terminology as you discuss this answer: e.g., are you trying to achieve disinfection or sterilization? Are you recommending use of antiseptics or disinfectants? Specify how each of your treatments would achieve killing of microbes.
3. In your opinion, is EPTUM an earthly isolate or an extraterrestrial isolate? Some things to think about: Have bacteria been isolated from outer space to date? What is this field of study? What agencies fund this field? What is "Planetary Protection"? Are there earthly microbes that have not yet been isolated and grown in culture? If so, what is the predicted percentage? Are there methods to study microbes that cannot be cultured?

## Web Version

Detailed teaching notes, the case PDF, and an answer key are available on the NCCSTS website at *sciencecases.lib.buffalo.edu/cs/collection/detail.asp?case_id=248&id=248*

# RESISTANCE IS FUTILE ... OR IS IT?

## The Immunity System and HIV Infection

*Annie Prud'homme Généreux*

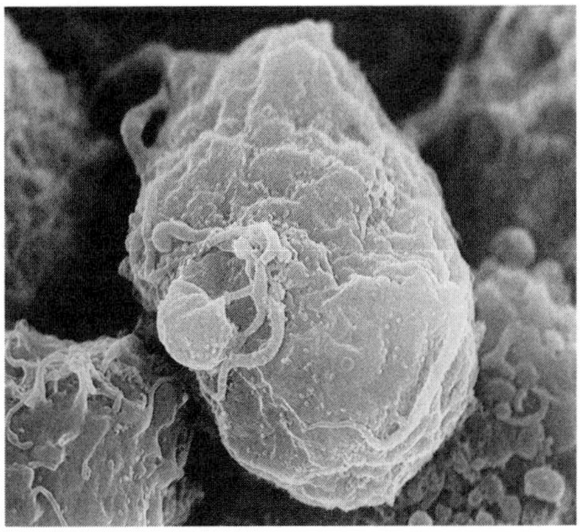


## Abstract

This case uses the results of the landmark paper by Paxton et al. (1996) that offered the first breakthrough in understanding why some people are protected against HIV infection. Students are guided to suggest hypotheses, predict the outcomes of experiments, and compare their predictions with the research paper's results.


## Learning Objectives

- Formulate testable hypotheses given preliminary data.
- Suggest tests to evaluate hypotheses.
- Predict results of experiments that would confirm each hypothesis.
- Interpret data and compare to predicted outcomes.
- Describe cellular and humoral immunity.
- Draw the HIV virus structure and describe the function of each component.
- Describe the interaction of the HIV virus with the immune system.

## Quantitative Reasoning Skills/Concepts

- Represent data in graphs.
- Use graphs to formulate predictions and explanations.
- Use numerical data to formulate null and alternative hypotheses.
- Articulate complete and correct claims based on data.
- Use appropriate reasoning to support the validity of data-based claims.

## The Case Study

### *Part I: HIV and the Immune System*

The vast majority of people are susceptible to HIV infection. However, in the 1990s, several individuals noticed that despite repeated exposure to the HIV virus they remained HIV negative. This could be due to the fact that these individuals were extremely lucky, or perhaps there was something different about them that made HIV infection less likely.

William Paxton and his colleagues at the Aaron Diamond AIDS Research Center in New York became interested in this phenomenon of HIV protection. In this case study, you will retrace the steps and experiments that these researchers performed to understand the mechanism underlying the protection against HIV (Paxton et al. 1996). To this end, you must first review a few facts about HIV, the immune system, and HIV infection.

## HIV

The virus particle is spherical in shape. Its structure consists of multiple enclosed layers, like the skin of an onion (Figure 17.1). It is considerably smaller than human cells. At the center of a virus particle are two copies of its genetic material. HIV encodes its nine genes using the nucleic acid molecule RNA (by comparison, our cells use DNA for this capacity). At the core of the virus particle are also proteins important for the replication of the virus (reverse transcriptase, integrase, protease, ribonuclease). The RNAs and proteins are wrapped in a protein coat (called the capsid) made of the protein p24. The capsid in turn is wrapped in a double layer of phospholipids. Finally, there are proteins that stick out of the lipid layer, such as gp120 (sometimes called Env). This latter protein gives HIV its specificity: gp120 interacts with specific proteins found only on certain human cells (like a lock and key mechanism), allowing HIV to infect specific cell types.

**FIGURE 17.1.**

Structure of HIV.

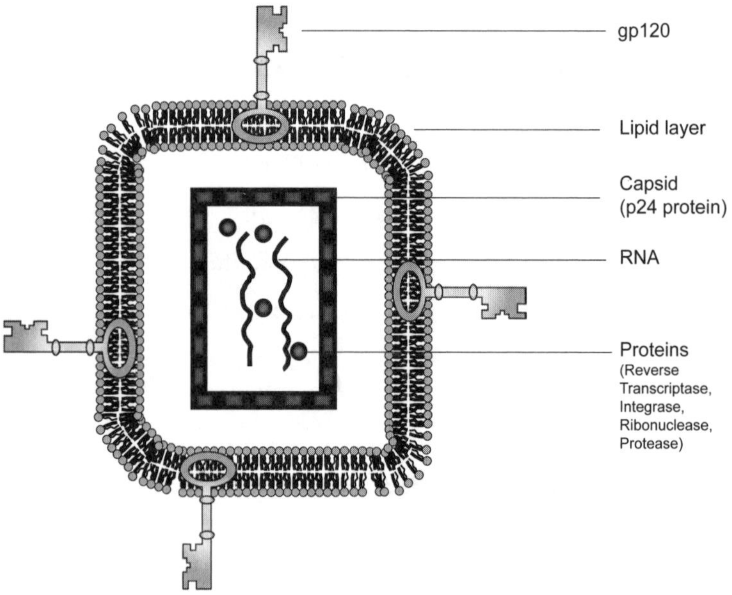

## The Immune System

The adaptive immune system (the part of the immune system that mounts a specific response to each invading pathogen) is a very complex system. Here, we review only those aspects that are relevant to this case (Figure 17.2).

**FIGURE 17.2.**

The Adaptive Immune System: T Cells and B Cells.

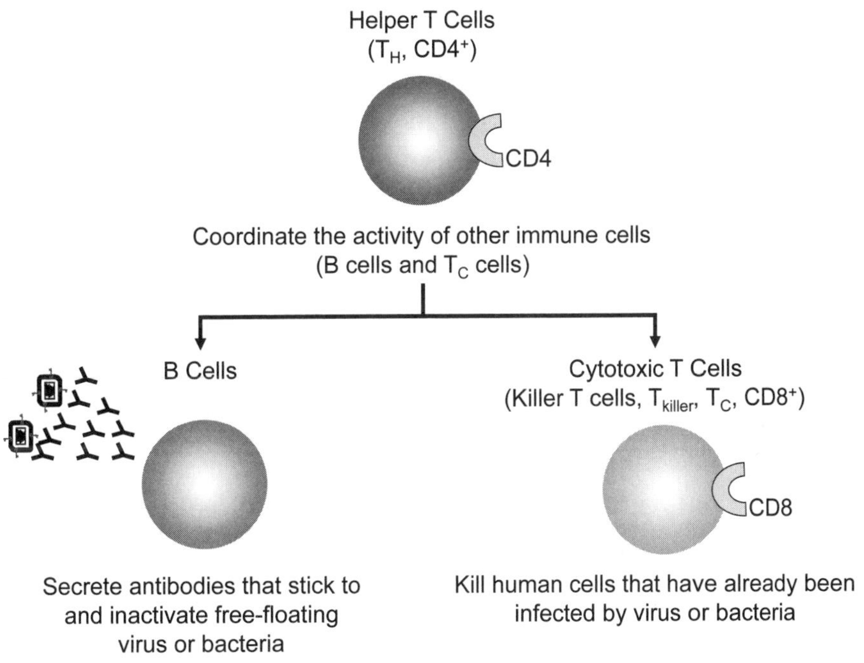


*B cells* (sometimes called B lymphocytes, plasma cells, plasma B cells, plasmocytes, or effector B cells) are white blood cells involved in neutralizing a virus or bacteria that have not yet infected a cell and are "free floating" in the body (this is called the *humoral immune response*). B cells secrete a protein called an antibody into the circulatory system. Each antibody binds to a particular virus or bacteria very specifically and strongly. When antibodies bind to a virus or to bacteria, the foreign object is inactivated. Therefore, when B cells secrete antibodies, they "take out" free-floating foreign invaders.

*Cytotoxic T cells* (sometimes called killer T cells, or TC or T killer or cytotoxic T lymphocytes CTL or CD8+) recognize human cells that have already been infected by a foreign virus or bacteria (this is called the *cellular immune response*). Their job is to kill infected cells. So while B cells remove free-floating virus particles, TC cells remove virus particles that have already made their way inside human cells by killing the infected cells. On their cell surface is a protein called CD8, which is why they are sometimes called CD8+ cells.

*T Helper cells* (sometimes called TH, or CD4+ cells) do not directly interact with foreign bodies. They are the "organizing centers" of the immune system, coordinating the action of cytotoxic T cells and B cells. Without them, TC and B cells do not work effectively. On their cell surface is the protein CD4, which is why these cells are sometimes called CD4+ cells.

## HIV Infection

HIV targets and infects TH cells (Figure 17.3). On the surface of the HIV particle is the protein gp120. This protein recognizes and binds (with a lock and key specificity) the CD4 protein on the surface of T helper cells. Once a virus particle has docked, its lipid membrane either fuses with the human cell's membrane, or the virus is brought in by endocytosis, and the contents of the virus are released inside the cell.

**FIGURE 17.3.**

HIV Replication Cycle Inside Human TH Cells.

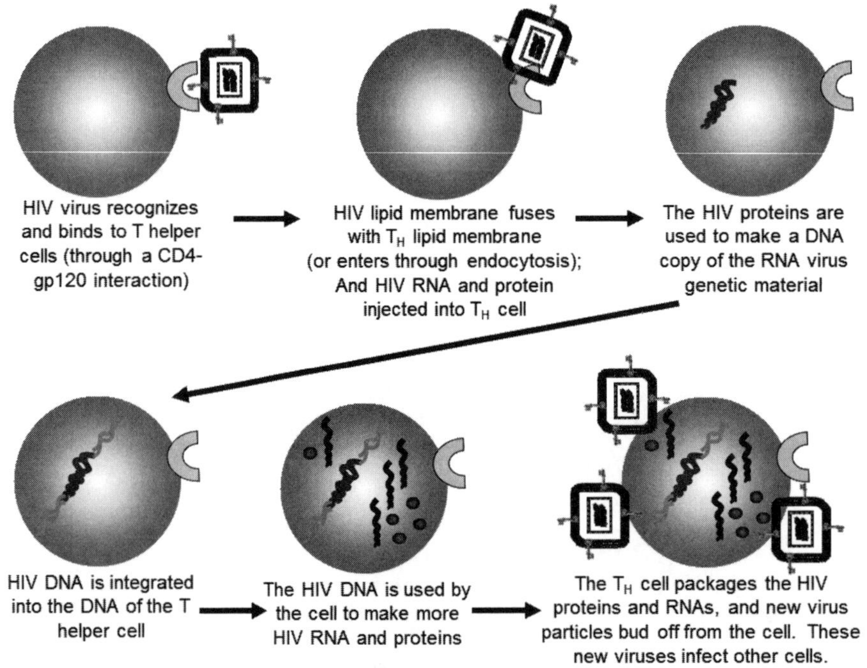

HIV virus recognizes and binds to T helper cells (through a CD4-gp120 interaction)
HIV lipid membrane fuses with $T_H$ lipid membrane (or enters through endocytosis); And HIV RNA and protein injected into $T_H$ cell
The HIV proteins are used to make a DNA copy of the RNA virus genetic material
HIV DNA is integrated into the DNA of the T helper cell
The HIV DNA is used by the cell to make more HIV RNA and proteins
The $T_H$ cell packages the HIV proteins and RNAs, and new virus particles bud off from the cell. These new viruses infect other cells.


Recall that the HIV virus has an RNA genome. If the virus is to highjack the cell machinery, its genetic information must first be converted into the genetic information used by the cell (i.e., DNA). This is the job of the protein reverse transcriptase, which the virus brought into the cell. Reverse transcriptase makes DNA copies of the RNA virus. This newly made

DNA is then integrated into the genome of the human cell. The human cell then uses the nine viral genes as it would its own. It therefore produces all the proteins and RNA needed to make more virus particles. The newly-made virus particles bud off of the T helper cell, which is now a virus-producing factory.

Let's review this information and think of its implication for the study of individuals with an apparent resistance to HIV infection.

## Questions

1. HIV is a retrovirus (a virus that uses reverse transcriptase).
    a What is reverse transcriptase?
    b. How is a retrovirus different from other viruses?
    c. How does a retrovirus infect a cell and reproduce itself?
2. Review of the immune system.
    a. What is a T cell?
    b. What varieties of T cell exist? How are they functionally different?
    c. What are their roles in the human body?
    d. How is each T cell variety differentiated from the others (molecularly)?
3. Immune system and HIV
    a. Which type(s) of immune cells is/are targeted by HIV?
    b. Why are other cells not targeted by the virus?
    c. How should cytotoxic T cells respond to the initial phase of HIV infection (when some T helper cells are still functioning)? Explain your reasoning.
    d. As time progresses, why do the cytotoxic T cells stop responding to the HIV infection?
    e. Propose an explanation.
    f. What happens to the immune system after HIV infection? Why? Can this account for the symptoms of AIDS (i.e., immunodeficiency, or the inability to defend against any foreign invaders like viruses and bacteria)?
    g. Why do you suppose that there is a delay between the time of HIV infection and the appearance of symptoms (and AIDS)?
    h. How does HIV evade the immune system?
4. HIV protection
    a. Consider how HIV infects cells and reproduces. Also consider how the immune system fights off HIV infection. Humans differ by having

mutations that result in slightly different proteins and immune function. Suggest as many hypotheses as possible to explain why some individuals might be protected against HIV infection. In other words, where and how might new viral infections be stopped? What could be different about the people who seem protected against HIV that caused viral replication to stop? Come up with at least three possibilities.

## *Part II: Paxton's Hypotheses About HIV-Protected Individuals*

Paxton and his colleagues had a few hypotheses about why some of the individuals exposed to HIV were protected against this virus.

*CD8+ lymphocyte inhibition of HIV-1 replication ("Super Cytotoxic T Cells" Hypothesis)*

Perhaps the reason that some individuals were protected against HIV is because they had cytotoxic T cells that were better and faster at recognizing infected T helper cells. This ability allowed the immune system to rid the body of any HIV infection before the virus could replicate inside T helper cells and transform these cells into HIV factories.

*CD4+ infectibility and efficiency of viral replication ("Super T Helper Cells" Hypothesis)*

Perhaps the T helper cells of the protected individuals were different, preventing the infection and replication of the virus inside the cell. There are many steps necessary for viral infection and replication inside T helper cells and any of them could be impeded.

### Questions

1. Classify each of *your* proposed hypotheses into the two categories proposed by Paxton and his colleagues (*Note:* some hypotheses may fit into neither category).
2. How might you test each of your hypotheses? Propose an experiment. What are your controls? Experimental conditions?

## *Part III: Predictions From Paxton's Two Hypotheses*

Paxton and his colleagues recruited 25 volunteers who claimed to have had repeated exposure to the HIV virus and yet were not infected with HIV. He also enlisted the help of nine individuals not exposed to the HIV virus (and who tested negative for the virus). This latter group is the control, whose response to HIV should be the same as the response of the majority of people.

Paxton and his colleagues wanted to identify which of their two hypotheses might be correct. The problem with working *in vivo* is that it is unethical to expose individuals to HIV. In addition, the human immune system is complex, with multiple interactions. To isolate the action of T helper cells, cytotoxic T cells, and the HIV virus, Paxton and his colleagues worked in test tubes.

Paxton isolated T helper cells and cytotoxic T cells from individuals in each group. He then performed the following experiments:

- In one tube, he mixed HIV virus and T helper cells.
- In another tube, he mixed HIV virus, T helper cells, and cytotoxic T cells.

He monitored the accumulation of virus in the test tube over time by measuring the amount of p24 proteins produced.

## Questions

1. Design of the experiment:
    a. Why were HIV and T helper cells mixed in the presence and absence of cytotoxic T cells?
2. For control individuals:
    a. If you mix HIV and T helper cells in a test tube, what would you expect to happen? Why?
    b. If you mix HIV, T helper cells, and cytotoxic T cells in a test tube, describe what you would expect to happen and why it occurs that way?
3. For protected individuals:
    a. Assuming that the "Super Cytotoxic T Cells" Hypothesis is correct, then when you perform the experiment using T helper cells and cytotoxic T cells from protected individuals:
        i. If you mix HIV and T helper cells in a test tube, what would you expect would happen? Why?
        ii. If you mix HIV, T helper cells, and cytotoxic T cells in a test tube, describe what you would expect to happen and explain your reasoning.
    b. Assuming that the "Super T Helper Cells" Hypothesis is correct, then when you perform the experiment using T helper cells and cytotoxic T cells from protected individuals:
        i. If you mix HIV and T helper cells in a test tube, what would you expect to happen? Why?
        ii. If you mix HIV, T helper cells, and cytotoxic T cells in a test tube, describe what you would expect to happen and explain your reasoning.
4. How is this experiment able to differentiate whether the mechanism of protection against HIV is through "Super T Helper Cells" or "Super Cytotoxic T Cells"?
5. Use Figure 17.4 to illustrate the results you would expect to obtain for:

a. a normal/control person
b. a protected individual, assuming that the "Super Cytotoxic T Cells" Hypothesis is correct
c. a protected individual, assuming that the "Super T Helper Cells" Hypothesis is correct

Please note that each graph requires two lines (the two test tubes).

**FIGURE 17.4.**

Predictions From Paxton's Experiment to Differentiate Between the *Super Cytotoxic T Cells* Hypothesis and the *Super T Helper Cell* Hypothesis.

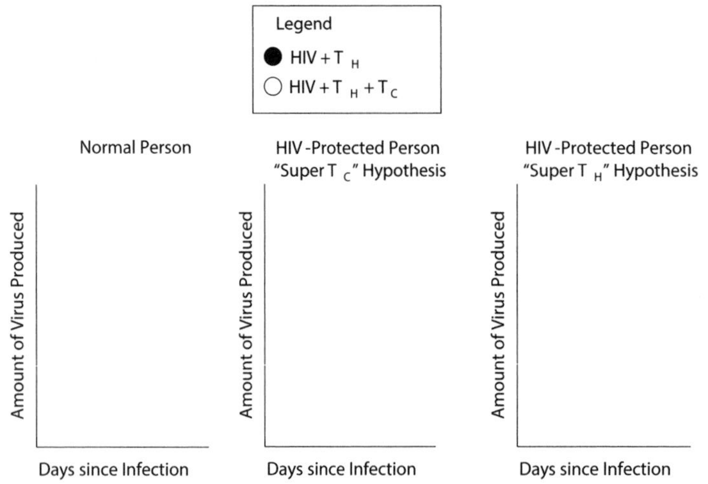


## *Part IV: Paxton's Results*

Figure 17.5 shows Paxton's results (from Figure 1 of his paper). The graphs produced in the top part come from control individuals (each graph represents the results of experiments performed using cells from one person) (Note: LP = Leukopac Preparation, or blood obtained from random blood donors; LW = Laboratory Workers, i.e., people working in the lab). The bottom graphics show 10 selected results from people claiming to be protected against HIV infection (Note: EU = Exposed Uninfected individuals). The filled circles (•) represent the results of experiments in which HIV was incubated with T helper cells, and the empty circles (o) represent experiments where HIV + T helper cells + cytotoxic T cells were mixed in the test tube.

**FIGURE 17.5.**

Results From Paxton's Experiment to Differentiate Between the *Super Cytotoxic T Cells* Hypothesis and the *Super T Helper Cell* Hypothesis.

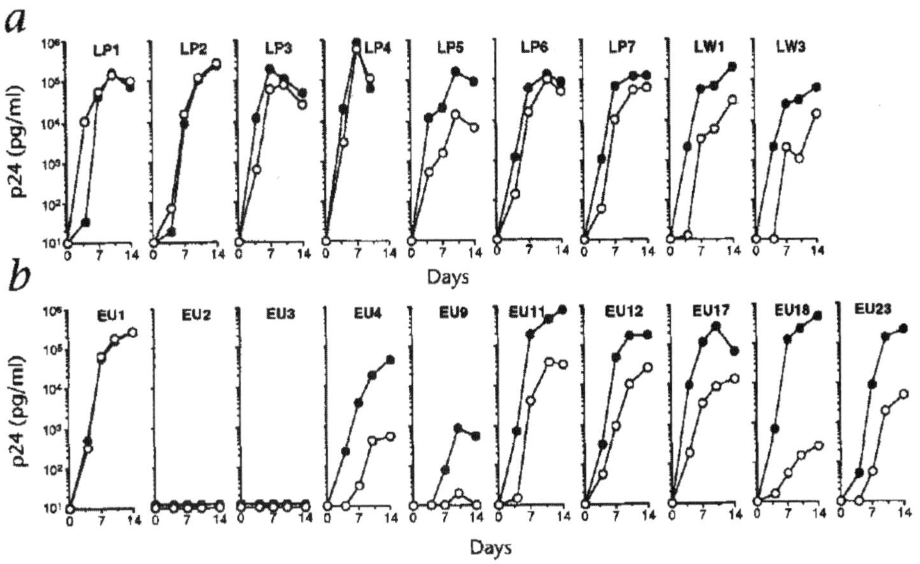


## Questions

1. Do cytotoxic T cells provide protection from HIV in control individuals?
2. Try to identify patterns in the results. Can the individual experiments performed using cells from protected individuals be grouped into categories? If so, how many? Classify each subject into the different categories.
3. Compare these results with what you had predicted in the previous section.
    a. Are the results of the controls as you expected?
    b. Which of Paxton's hypotheses seem to be validated by the results of the protected individuals? Why?
    c. What do you make of EU1? How do you account for his unusual response?

## *Part V: The "Super T Helper Cell" Mechanism*

From the results of this experiment, it is apparent that EU1 has either been lucky so far, or exhibits a mode of protection not anticipated by Paxton's team. EU2 and EU3 do not appear to be infected by the HIV virus at all ("Super T Helper Cells"). The remaining protected individuals exhibit different degrees of infection with very active cytotoxic T cells to slow down the progression of new infections ("Super Cytotoxic T Cells").

Paxton's team was particularly interested in protected subjects EU2 and EU3 and in investigating the mechanism of action of their protection against HIV. To investigate this, they performed an experiment where they mixed purified T helper cells from control or protected individuals with different strains of HIV-1. The goal was to determine whether all HIV-1 strains could infect the T helper cells from protected individuals. HIV-1, the most common form of the virus and the one responsible for the pandemic, can be classified into two different types:

- M-tropic (also called non-syncitia-inducing (NSI) or R5 HIV-1) strains, and
- T-tropic (also called syncitia-inducing (SI) or X4 HIV-1) strains.

This turned out to be a very informative experiment. About the same time, two other papers were published that clarified some of the differences between these two strains of virus.

- M-tropic HIV-1 strains must bind to two cell surface proteins to enter and infect a cell (Dragic et al., 1996):
  - the *CD4 protein* and
  - the beta-chemokine receptor *CCR5*.
- Conversely, T-tropic HIV-1 strains use slightly different proteins to enter and infect a cell (Feng et al., 1996):
  - the *CD4 protein* as well as
  - the alpha-chemokine receptor *CXCR4* (at the time called fusin).

Armed with this information, we can look back at the experiment performed by Paxton's team and investigate whether CD4, CCR5, CXCR4, or another protein is mutated and "different" in individuals that are protected against HIV.

Here is the design of this experiment:

- In one tube: Mix HIV-1 (T-tropic strain) + T helper cells from a control person.
- In another tube: Mix HIV-1 (T-tropic strain) + T helper cells from a protected person.
- Monitor the appearance of p24 in the test tube (i.e., production of new virus) over time.
- In one tube: Mix HIV-1 (M-tropic strain) + T helper cells from a control person.

- In another tube: Mix HIV-1 (M-tropic strain) + T helper cells from a protected person.
- Monitor the appearance of p24 in the test tube (i.e., production of new virus) over time.

## Questions

1. Let's assume that protected individuals have an altered CD4 protein (a mutation in the CD4 gene) compared to controls that renders the protein unrecognizable by gp120. Use Figure 17.6 to draw the results you expect to obtain from the abovementioned experiment. Remember that each graph should have two lines, and review which proteins are required for infection by the two strains.

**FIGURE 17.6.**

Predictions From Paxton's Experiment if HIV-Protected Individuals Have a Mutated CD4 Gene.

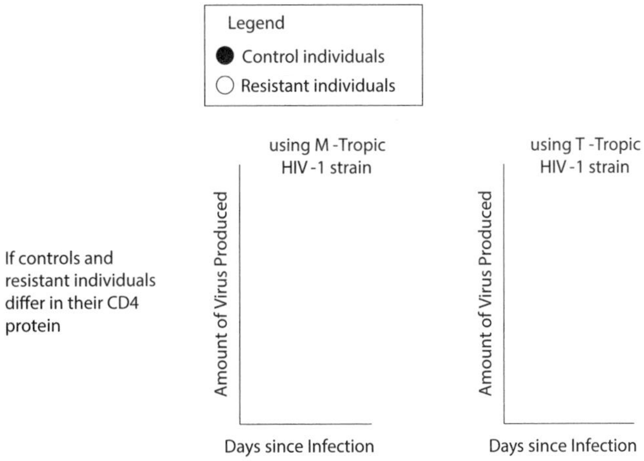


2. Let's assume that protected individuals have an altered CCR5 protein (a mutation in the CCR5 gene) compared to controls. Use Figure 17.7 (p. 184) to draw the results you expect to obtain from the abovementioned experiment. Remember that each graph should have two lines, and review which proteins are required for infection by the two strains.

**FIGURE 17.7.**

Predictions From Paxton's Experiment if HIV-Protected Individuals Have a Mutated CCR5 Gene.

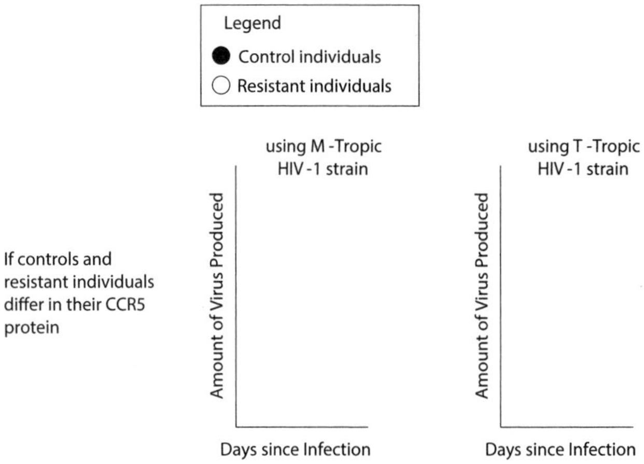


3. Let's assume that protected individuals have an altered CXCR4 protein (a mutation in the CXCR4 gene) compared to controls. Use Figure 17.8 to draw the results you expect to obtain from the above-mentioned experiment. Remember that each graph should have two lines, and review which proteins are required for infection by the two strains.

**FIGURE 17.8.**

Predictions From Paxton's Experiment if HIV-Protected Individuals Have a Mutated CXCR4 Gene.

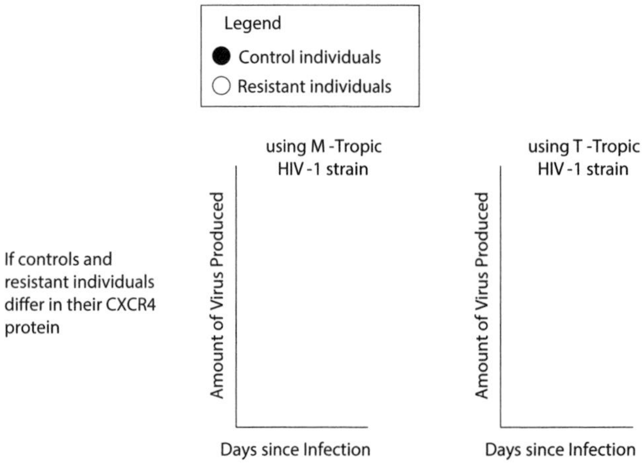

## Part VI: Why Some People Are Protected Against HIV

Figure 17.9 shows Paxton's results from this experiment. The filled circles (•) represent results using T helper cells from controls, and empty circles (o) using T helper cells from protected individuals. The letters and numbers above each graph show the name of the HIV-1 strain used in the experiment.

**FIGURE 17.9.**

Paxton's Results.

M-Tropic strains:

- JR-CSF
- GT
- SF162
- AD-6
- 92US657

T-Tropic strains:

- NL4-3
- SF2
- SF162dbl
- SF162 R3H

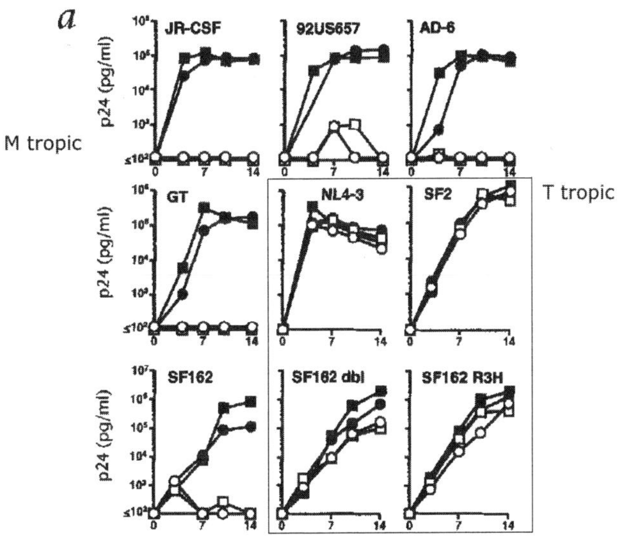


### Questions

1. Infection:
    a. Which strain(s) of HIV-1 can infect and replicate in the TH cells of protected individuals?
    b. Which co-receptor is used by this strain(s) of HIV-1 to infect these cells?
2. No infection:
    a. Which strain(s) of HIV-1 cannot infect and replicate in the TH cells of protected individuals?
    b. Which co-receptor is used by this strain(s) of HIV-1 to infect the cells?
3. Which of your theorized graphics do the results most resemble?

4. Based on this information, what is the mechanism of HIV protection in EU2 and EU3?
5. Are these people protected against all forms of HIV out there? What are the implications?

## Web Version

The case PDF, detailed teaching notes, and an answer key are available on the NCCSTS website at *sciencecases.lib.buffalo.edu/cs/collection/detail.asp?case_id=393&id=393.*

## Reference

Paxton, W. A., S. R. Martin, D. Tse, T. R. O'Brien, J. Skurnick, N. L. VanDevanter, N. Padian, J. F. Braun, D. P. Kotler, S. M. Wolinsky, and R. A. Koup. 1996. Relative resistance to HIV-1 infection of CD4 lymphocytes from persons who remain uninfected despite multiple high-risk sexual exposures. *Nature Medicine* 2 (4): 412–417.

# AN INFECTIOUS CURE

## Phage Therapy

*Dustin J. Eno and Annie Prud'homme Généreux*

## Abstract

Students are introduced to treatments for bacterial infection and discuss the appropriateness of imposing a medical treatment on a group of people. They also learn about the anatomy and life cycle of bacteriophages, evaluate the risks associated with using live agents as treatments, and compare the relative advantages and disadvantages associated with antibiotics and phage therapy.


## Learning Objectives

- Describe the anatomy and life cycle of bacteriophages.
- Deduce the implications of using live agents capable of replication as a form of treatment.
- Assess the health risks of using phage therapy to treat bacterial infections.
- Compare and contrast the use of antibiotics and bacteriophages for the treatment of bacterial infections.
- Weigh the personal and public concerns in selecting treatments that impact the health of a population.

## Quantitative Reasoning Skills/Concepts

- Use graphs to formulate predictions and explanations.
- Articulate complete and correct claims based on data.
- Interpret log scales.

## The Case Study

### *Part I: A Suspicious Treatment for Cholera*

#### India, 1926

It was cholera season again. Cholera struck twice a year; once after the springtime runoff from the high Himalayas, and once after the monsoons. Dinesh was walking home from the fields when his friend, a merchant at the lassi stand, called him over.

"It's started," he said in a mournful tone.

"What?" asked Dinesh.

"Harpriet just died of cholera."

And so this year's outbreak had begun. Cholera was a fact of life in this small village. Several people died of this disease every year. Dinesh would know all of them. Perhaps he would even be one of the victims this year. Cholera was a horrible disease that was dreaded by all. The afflicted endured severe abdominal pain, vomiting, and diarrhea, and some unfortunate people died from dehydration after several days.

A few days later, as Dinesh was walking toward the fields, he noticed a group of European men pouring something into the village well. Coming closer, he overheard one of them explaining to the village elder that this was going to prevent and cure cholera. A similar treatment had apparently helped to treat Europeans. Dinesh had no reason to believe these claims and was suspicious.

The elder was similarly unimpressed by the promises made by the Europeans. Later that day, he called all the able-bodied men in the village to drain the village well. They instructed all the villagers to take water from other wells surrounding the town.

A few days later, the European men returned and asked about the state of the cholera outbreak. Cholera had claimed more lives and new people were getting sick. The foreigners seemed surprised. Their surprise turned to outrage when they discovered that the well in which they poured their treatment had been drained.

In the evening, the European men added a purple dye to all of the town's wells except for one, in which they poured their treatment. The colored water would be avoided by the town's people, forcing them to drink from the "treated" well.

After a couple of days, Dinesh noticed that affected individuals were improving, and there were no new cases reported. Despite his misgivings and anxiety about the contents of the water, the treatment seemed effective.

### Questions

1. Cholera is caused by bacteria that infect the small intestine. These bacteria are typically contracted by drinking contaminated water. The symptoms are brought

about by the secretion of a toxin that disrupts the functioning of the cells of the small intestine. Given this information, what might the European men have poured into the wells? Be as specific as you can in explaining how your proposed treatment cured and prevented cholera. Come up with more than one hypothesis.

2. What ethical issues does imposing a treatment on the villagers without their consent raise? Are there factors that make it more or less acceptable?
3. At the time, the Europeans did not fully understand how their well treatment worked. They only had indications that it worked once in Europe. Were they justified in imposing their treatment? Are there steps they could have taken that would have made the situation more acceptable?
4. Is it ever appropriate to force a "cure" on a population? Remember that in North America many municipalities put fluoride in the water supply to prevent tooth decay.
5. What do you make of the validity of the results from this historical experiment? What conclusions can be drawn? Were the results scientifically reliable or should they be regarded as indicative or anecdotal?

## *Part II: Big Fleas Have Lesser Fleas on Their Backs to Bite Them, and So on Infinitum*

In nature, every organism is part of an ecosystem. It feeds on prey and is preyed upon by its predators. Bacteria (including the cholera-causing bacteria) are no exception. Their enemies are bacteriophages, tiny viruses that use them as virus-making factories, often killing them in the process.

A bacteriophage is composed of genetic information (RNA or DNA) and proteins. It is shaped like a moon lander and has three distinct regions (Figure 18.1). The head contains the genetic material. Proteins form a protective coat around it, giving the head a roundish appearance. The neck and helical

**FIGURE 18.1.**

Bacteriophage Structure.

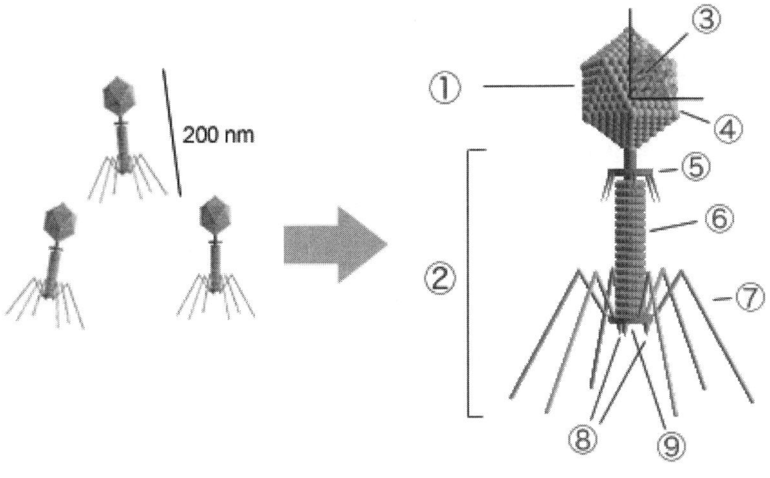


**Key:** (1) Head, (2) Tail, (3) Nucleic acid, (4) Capsid, (5) Collar, (6) Sheath, (7) Tail fiber, (8) Spikes, (9) Baseplate

Credit: *commons.wikimedia.org/wiki/File:Bacteriophage_structure.png* sheath are also composed of proteins and serve as a conduit for injecting the genetic material into a bacterium—like a syringe. Finally, the base plate and the tail fibers are responsible for recognizing and binding to target bacteria. Since they are composed of proteins, they have unique three-dimensional shapes that fit into specific targets on a bacteria's surface, in a lock-and-key fashion.

Like all viruses, bacteriophages are inert and can only replicate inside a cell, using the cell's energy and machinery. Infection begins when the bacteriophage base plate and tail fibers come into contact with its specific bacterial target (Figure 18.2).

**FIGURE 18.2.**

Bacteriophage Life Cycle.

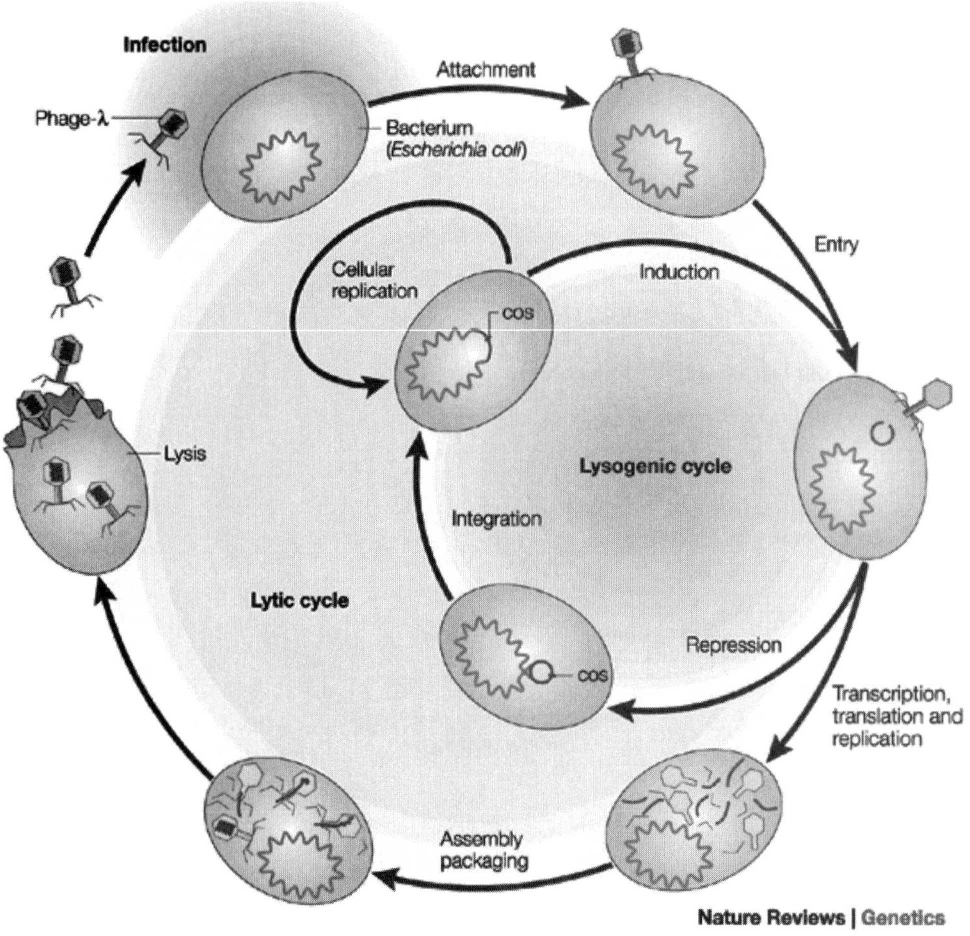


Credit: Campbell, 2003.

The bacteriophage attaches to the bacteria, makes a hole in the bacterial cell wall, and injects its genetic material into the cell. The genetic material can then follow one of two fates. It may use the bacterial machinery to replicate its genome and make more of its proteins. In effect, the bacterium becomes a virus-producing factory. Eventually, the bacteriophage directs the production of two proteins that cause the cell wall of the bacterium to rupture, killing the bacterium and releasing the newly synthesized viral particles into the environment to infect other cells. This process is called the lytic cycle. Other times, once inside the cell the bacteriophage's genetic material pursues another path called the lysogenic cycle. Here, the viral genome integrates into the bacterial genome. Each time the bacterium replicates, its progeny contains a copy of the viral genome. In time, perhaps when the bacteriophage detects that nutrients are depleted, it resumes a lytic life cycle and exits the bacteria.

Each bacteriophage binds to, infects, and kills only specific target bacteria by virtue of the specificity conveyed by its proteins. Bacteria that suffer mutations that change the proteins displayed on their cell surface will escape infection. Through natural selection, these bacteria will thrive and their genome will become the most prevalent one in the bacterial population. However, these bacteria constitute fertile grounds, and natural selection predicts that mutations in the bacteriophage proteins that allow the virus to recognize and infect these bacteria will develop over time. Through this process of co-evolution, bacteriophage can adapt to bacterial defenses.

Although not completely understood by the Europeans at the time, this was the basis of the treatment poured into the wells of Dinesh's village.

## Questions

1. Would the villagers need to drink repeatedly or only once from the treated wells to obtain a sufficient dose to serve as a cure? What is the basis of your answer?
2. Once a person ingests a dose of phages, how long will the treatment remain effective in his or her body? In other words, what is the time course of the treatment? Would you expect the effectiveness of this treatment to increase or decrease over time? Why?
3. Will the process of viral and bacterial co-evolution continue indefinitely?
4. Should the villagers be concerned that this bacterial virus will be harmful to their microbial flora (such as their intestinal bacteria)? Why or why not?
5. What might be a negative health consequence of killing many cholera bacteria with bacteriophage in a short time? Hint: Think about what causes the symptoms of cholera (see Part I, Question 1).
6. The villagers should not be concerned that the bacteriophage will lyse and infect their cells. Bacteriophages are not believed to be able to infect human cells.

Propose why this might be. Hint: Consider the structural differences between human and bacterial cells.

7. What would be the effect on treatment if the bacteriophage that was poured into the wells adopted a lysogenic life cycle?
8. What will happen to the bacteriophages once the supply of cholera bacteria in the intestine of an infected person has run out?
9. What do you think are some of the risks of "phage therapy" (using bacteriophage to treat bacterial infections)?
10. Imagine the following scenario. A bacteriophage taken for the treatment of cholera infects a cholera-causing bacterium and temporarily enters the lysogenic stage. When the virus re-enters the lytic cycle, it includes some pieces of the bacterial DNA in its own genome. Specifically, this DNA encodes information for making the cholera toxin. Imagine some of the possible consequences of this scenario. What will happen to the next bacteria that the virus infects? What will happen to the human in which this bacteriophage exists?
11. From this information, would you subject yourself to bacteriophage therapy for the treatment of cholera? How safe and effective is this form of treatment?

## *Part III: Why Not Use Antibiotics?*

The potentials of phage therapy as a treatment for bacterial diseases were overshadowed by the discovery of antibiotics in the early 20th century. Antibiotics are chemicals that can prevent the growth of bacteria or even kill them. Typically, a range of bacterial species are susceptible to the effects of an antibiotic.

Unfortunately, bacteria are evolving in response to the pressures imposed by antibiotics. When an antibiotic is applied to a population of bacteria, some bacteria have inherent mutations that make them less susceptible to the antibiotic. These bacteria survive, multiply, and eventually make up the majority of bacteria in the population. Thus, we are now facing a situation where bacteria are evolving resistance to our antibiotics faster than we can find new antibiotics to challenge them (Levy and Marshall 2004).

Figure 18.3 shows the result of an experiment where the growth of a bacterial population was monitored over time.

*Staphylococcus aureus* bacteria were grown with all the required nutrients. These common bacteria are the culprit of a range of infections from pimples to pneumonia. Growth was monitored by measuring the turbidity of the culture (the more turbid a culture, the more cells are present). At one hour, the bacteria were divided into seven different flasks. The bacteria in each of these flasks were subjected to different treatment (see Figure 18.3), and the bacteria were incubated and their growth monitored.

- The open circles show the growth of bacteria when nothing was added to the flask.
- The open rhomboids, triangles, and squares show the growth of the culture when rifampicin, vancomycin, and oxacillin, respectively, were added to the culture at time = one hour. All three of these chemicals are antibiotics.
- The closed circle, triangle, and square show the growth of the culture after the addition of bacteriophages that target *Staphylococcus aureus*. Different amounts of phage were added in the three flasks: 0.1, 1, and 10 MOI, respectively. An MOI is a Multiplicity of Infection and corresponds to the ratio of infectious agent to bacteria.

**FIGURE 18.3.**

Comparative effects of bacteriophages and antibiotics on the number of bacterial cells in culture.

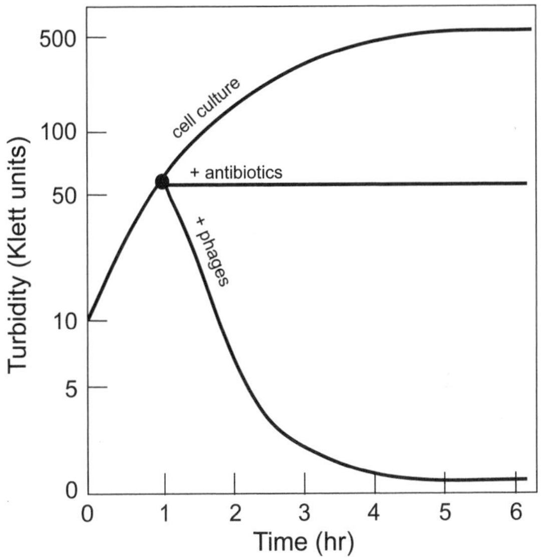


*Source:* Figure 3 from Matsuzaki et al. (2005).

## Questions

1. Based on the results of this figure, comment on the comparative effectiveness of antibiotics and phage on the growth of *Staphylococcus*.
2. This experiment does not capture some of the complexities of administering treatments in a human body. What are some of the factors that would affect the effectiveness of these treatments in a human body that are not measured in these flasks? How might these factors affect treatment?
3. What are some advantages of antibiotics over phages in the treatment of infections in humans?
4. What are some advantages of phages over antibiotics in the treatment of infections in humans?

## *Part IV: Why Not Use Phage Therapy?*

Phage therapy is not an approved treatment for human use in North America. It has yet to pass a rigorous clinical trial to show its effectiveness. Some pharmaceutical companies are showing interest in developing it, but phage therapy offers a few challenges. First, since phages only kill specific bacteria, phage therapy is an extremely individualized treatment. Bacteria must be isolated from the patient and an appropriate virus found. This runs contrary to the current pharmaceutical company model, which is based on the mass production and marketing of products that work for everyone. In addition, given the individualized nature of the cure, it is very difficult to patent each virus used. The patent process ensures that the companies that develop these treatments can recuperate their costs. Finally, such individualized treatment would require a fundamental shift in our medical practices, which is geared toward a one-disease, one-treatment model. Phage therapy requires personalized treatment and customized medicines. It is very laborious, time intensive, and costly. In addition, the time taken to select an appropriate virus may not be possible with certain bacterial diseases that progress rapidly. However, phages are able to access areas of the body that antibiotics cannot, and viruses are produced in those areas where they are most needed (the maximal viral dose is in the area of greatest bacterial infection), ensuring continued interest in this treatment.

Despite the challenges, phage treatment of bacterial infections is routinely used in other applications. Meats are sometimes treated with solutions of phages to kill off potentially harmful bacteria such as *Salmonella* (Hausler 2006). Certain high-value crops, such as tomatoes, are now sprayed with phage solutions. There is a very good chance that you have already eaten phages.

### Questions

1. Given this new information, review the advantages and disadvantages of each form of treatment. Create a table that summarizes your answer.
2. Are there some diseases that lend themselves more to phage therapy than antibiotics? Are there types of infections for which the reverse is true? Explain your reasoning.
3. Do you think restrictions on the use of phage therapy in North America should be loosened? Why or why not?

## Web Version

Detailed teaching notes, the case PDF, and an answer key are available on the NCCSTS website at *sciencecases.lib.buffalo.edu/cs/collection/detail.asp?case_id=608&id=608*.

## References

Brown, K. 2005. *Penicillin man: Alexander Fleming and the antibiotic revolution*. Stroud, Gloucestershire: Sutton Pub.

Campbell, A. 2003. The future of bacteriophage biology. *Nature Reviews Genetics* 4: 471–477.

Hausler, T. 2006. *Viruses vs. superbugs*. New York: Macmillan.

Levy, S. B., and B. Marshall. 2004. Antibacterial resistance worldwide: Causes, challenges and responses. *Nature Medicine Supplement* 10 (12): S122–S129.

Matsuzaki, S., M. Rashel, J. Uchiyama, S. Sakurai, T. Ujihara, M. Kuroda, M. Ikeuchi, T. Tani, M. Fujieda, H. Wakiguchi, and S. Imai. 2005. Bacteriophage therapy: A revitalized therapy against bacterial infectious diseases. *Journal of Infection and Chemotherapy* 11: 211–219.

# SECTION V

# GENETICS

CHAPTER 19

# THE "BLUE PEOPLE" OF KENTUCKY

*Celeste A. Leander and Robert J. Huskey*

## Abstract

Students construct a pedigree based on information they receive about a clan of "blue people" and then are asked to decide whether the condition (methemoglobinemia) is a heritable trait. Students are then exposed to a different perspective of this condition and have to re-evaluate the inheritance pattern.

## Learning Objectives

- Generate a hypothesis.
- Construct and analyze a pedigree.
- Evaluate inheritance patterns.
- Reconcile changing inheritance patterns, depending on perspective.

## Quantitative Reasoning Skills/Concepts

- Use graphs to formulate predictions and explanations.
- Articulate complete and correct claims based on data.
- Create and analyze family pedigrees.
- Create experimental designs to test hypotheses.

## The Case Study

### *Part I: "Blue People"*

Ruth had never been as astonished as she was the day she encountered the first of the "blue people" from Troublesome Creek. The blue woman simply walked into the rural health clinic where Ruth was a nurse. Ruth suspected the woman was having a heart attack, but the woman wasn't concerned at all.

"I'm one of the blue Combses," she explained to Ruth, as if it was all perfectly logical. "And my mother-in-law is a Fugate."

As their conversation continued, Ruth learned from her patient that there were, in fact, many blue people living in the isolated community around Troublesome Creek.

## Questions

1. Why might these people be blue? Generate at least two hypotheses.
2. How might you test your hypotheses?

## *Part II: Pieces of the Family Puzzle*

So began an adventure that lasted nearly a decade. Ruth and a physician, Dr. Cawein, who had heard rumors of blue people in the region, spent the next summer fighting off bugs and dogs as they trudged through the region piecing together a family tree of the reclusive Fugates, a large clan living in the valleys and hollows of the Appalachian Mountains in eastern Kentucky. Several of the relationships that Ruth and Dr. Cawein established have since been challenged by modern-day descendants of Martin Fugate. Nevertheless, the major lineages that they were able to establish helped to answer some of Ruth's questions.

The Fugate clan in the Troublesome Creek region could be traced back to the arrival of Martin Fugate, an orphan from France, in 1820. Legend has it that Martin may have been blue, but reports vary. For this case, we'll assume that Martin was blue. Martin settled in the area and married the pale, red-headed Elizabeth Smith. Over the years, they had at least seven children. Four of them reportedly were blue.

Zachary, one of Martin and Elizabeth's blue sons, married Elizabeth's sister. (Because of the isolation in this region, it was not uncommon to simply marry someone from next door. As the generations passed, this led to sometimes marrying a cousin or other relative as the family continued to grow.)

They had several children. One of their sons was Levy. Levy married a girl from the Ritchie clan, another prominent family in the region. Together, they had eight children, including Luna. Luna is legendary for having had nearly purple skin.

Luna was courted by and married John Stacey. Together they raised 13 children. None of them were blue. One of Luna and John's children had a son, Alva Stacey. Alva and his wife, Hilda, came from separate branches of the extensive clan. Alva remembered his maternal blue grandmother and also tells the story of his infant son, Ben, who had caused quite a stir at the hospital when he was born with a blue tinge. Ben's blue color faded soon after birth, and he now reports only his fingernails and lips turning blue at times. Ben has since gone on to graduate from the Eastern Kentucky University in Richmond, Kentucky. He married soon after graduation and has moved to another state.

## Questions

1. Construct a family tree (pedigree) from the information provided.
2. Evaluate your pedigree. Can you decide if "blueness" is a heritable trait?
3. If so, what pattern of inheritance do you suspect? If not, what other hypotheses might you suspect? Explain your answer.
4. Provide allele designations for each person in the pedigree.

## *Part III: A Different Shade of Blue*

The mutation you have evaluated is located in the gene that codes for the enzyme called NADH diaphorase (or NADH dependent methemoglobin reductase). It is found in large concentration in red blood cells (RBC), where the enzyme functions to return hemoglobin to a normal oxygen binding state after it has been oxidized to methemoglobin (metHb). MetHb cannot bind oxygen or carbon dioxide (because iron, the oxygen binding part of the heme group, is in the ferric state and binds water instead of oxygen), and gives the blood a blue tint. This oxidation process is slow, but requires enzyme mediated reduction to return to hemoglobin as shown below in Figure 19.1.

**FIGURE 19.1.**

Oxidation and Reduction.

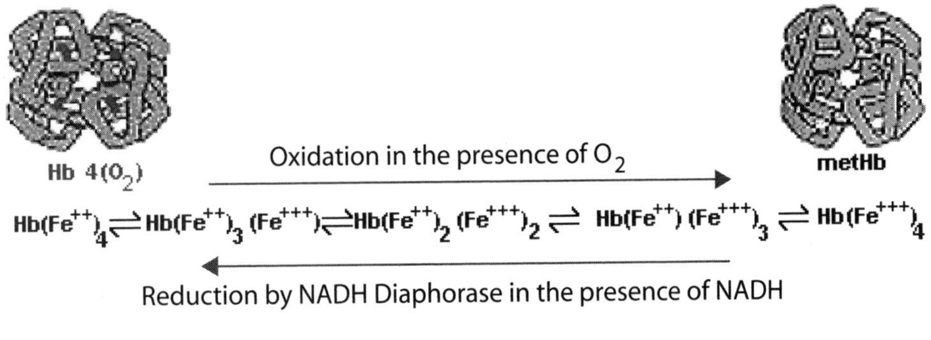


The graph in Figure 19.2 (p. 200) shows enzyme activity over time in people that are blue, people that are not blue but may have blue children, and people that are not blue and never have blue children.

**FIGURE 19.2.**

RBC NADH Diaphorase Activity.

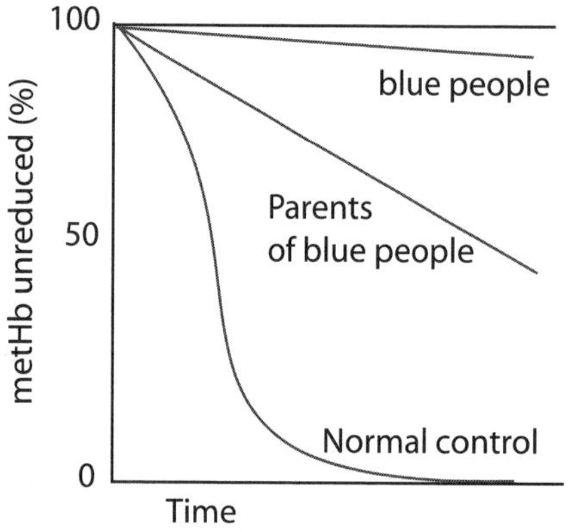


Red blood cell extracts from three different groups assayed for ability to reduce metHb to Hb.

## Questions

1. What are the three lines on the graph in Figure 19.2 telling us?
2. Provide genotype designations for each line on the graph in Figure 19.2.
3. After evaluating the data above, what can you say regarding pattern of inheritance for this scenario?
4. Compare your conclusions on pattern of inheritance with those from Part II. Is one perspective more correct than another? Explain.

## Web Version

Detailed teaching notes, the case PDF, and an answer key are available on the NCCSTS website at *sciencecases.lib.buffalo.edu/cs/collection/detail.asp?case_id=208&id=208*.

# TO THE BITTER END
## The Genetics of PTC Sensitivity

*R. Deborah Overath*

## Abstract
This case dramatizes the discovery of a Mendelian trait in humans, namely the variation in the ability to taste the chemical phenylthiocarbamide (PTC). By examining data and questions related to this trait, students draw connections between Mendel's principles of inheritance and variation at the DNA level by learning about the phenotypic differences due to the single nucleotide polymorphisms in a major gene influencing the ability to taste PTC.


## Learning Objectives
- Understand how Mendelian traits are inherited and studied in humans.
- Explain the role of DNA sequences and mutations in determining protein structure and function.
- Understand how DNA mutations that compromise protein function may be inherited as a recessive allele.
- Understand the connection between Mendelian and molecular genetics by generalizing the specific facts learned in this case to other examples.

## Quantitative Reasoning Skills/Concepts
- Carry out basic mathematical operations.
- Use numerical evidence to formulate null and alternative hypotheses.
- Articulate complete and correct claims based on numerical data.
- Use appropriate reasoning to support the validity of data-based claims.
- Create and interpret Punnett squares (Author's note: Although this is one possible way to obtain answers to some of the questions in this case, I encourage my students to use probability rules instead.)
- Perform DNA analysis.

## The Case Study

### Part I: Discovery

"Arthur," said C. R. Noller in an irritated voice. "What the heck are you doing over there? Why did you let that awful-tasting stuff get into the air? It's so bitter that I want to vomit!"

Drs. Arthur Fox and C.R. Noller were working separately in a lab at the DuPont Chemical Company's facilities in Wilmington, Delaware.

"What do you mean, C.R.?" snapped Arthur. "I don't taste anything, and I'm right on top of this stuff."

"It's got to be that powder you've got there," retorted C.R. "I'm not working with anything bitter, and I'm too far from the door for it to be coming from outside the lab."

Arthur was transferring some phenylthiocarbamide (PTC) into a bottle. During the transfer, some of the white powder had dispersed into the air.

"Look," said Arthur as he licked his finger, picked up a few PTC crystals, and licked his finger again. "I don't taste anything."

"Arthur," said C. R., "give me some of that stuff. I really don't want to taste it, but I'll do it just to prove you're wrong!"

Arthur Fox brought the bottle of PTC over to C. R. Noller, who picked up a few crystals. As soon as the crystals touched his tongue, C. R. exclaimed, "Yuck! Quick—get me something to rinse out my mouth! That stuff is just too bitter!"

After C. R. rinsed out his mouth with some water, Arthur said, "Let's see if we can find some other folks to taste this PTC to see if they taste anything."

For several days Arthur asked all his co-workers, friends, and acquaintances to taste his PTC powder and found that neither he nor C. R. were unique. Regardless of gender, age, or ethnicity, about 60% of people tasted PTC as bitter, like C. R. The other 40% were, like Arthur himself, taste blind: PTC had no taste to them. Arthur also tested closely related chemicals with the same results.

News of Arthur's discovery was published in *Science*, the premier American science journal (Anonymous 1931). Shortly thereafter Arthur received the following letter:

Dear Dr. Fox,

I read the news of your discovery of variation in the ability to taste phenylthiocarbamide (PTC) and related compounds with great excitement. I am studying Mendelian markers in human populations. Unfortunately, we have few examples of such traits in humans, as you can see from my article recently published in the *Eugenical News* (1931b), which I have enclosed. Would you please send me some PTC? I would like to study this variation in tasting ability to see if it is inherited and, therefore, can be used as a Mendelian marker.

Sincerely yours,

L. H. Snyder, PhD

Professor of Genetics

Ohio State University

## Questions

1. What does L. H. Snyder mean by the term "Mendelian marker"?
2. What question(s) will Dr. Snyder address in his study?
3. What is his hypothesis?

## Part II: Mendelian Genetics

After obtaining some PTC from Arthur Fox, L. H. Snyder determined the PTC phenotype (can taste or cannot taste) for the members of 100 nuclear families. He first verified that gender was not a factor by comparing the number of male tasters and non-tasters to the number of female tasters and non-tasters. Because there was essentially no difference between sexes, Snyder grouped families by the phenotypes of the parents, disregarding the gender of each parent, and tabulated his data (see Table 20.1, p. 204; Snyder 1931a):

**TABLE 20.1.**

PTC phenotypes of children from 100 nuclear families grouped by parent phenotype combinations (from Snyder 1931a).

| | | Phenotypes of Children | |
|---|---|---|---|
| **Parent-Phenotype Combinations** | **No. of families** | **Can taste** | **Cannot taste** |
| Both parents can taste | 40 | 90 | 16 |
| One parent can taste, the other cannot | 51 | 80 | 37 |
| Neither parent can taste | 9 | 0 | 17 |

## Questions

1. What kind of evidence would indicate that the ability to taste PTC is inherited?
2. Why was it important for Snyder to verify that males and females had similar proportions of tasters and non-tasters?
3. Why do couples who can taste PTC have children who cannot?
4. What is the significance of the fact that couples who cannot taste PTC never have children who can?
5. Based on these data, what can you conclude about PTC taste blindness? What is your evidence?
6. The second parent-phenotype combination would appear to represent a group of testcrosses. What ratios are expected from testcrosses and what does each ratio represent? These data don't seem to fit either of these expected ratios. How can you explain this?

## *Part III: Molecular Genetics*

More than 70 years after Arthur Fox serendipitously discovered that humans vary in their sensitivity to PTC and related chemicals, researchers from the National Institutes of Health, Stanford University, and the University of Utah together discovered the main gene for PTC sensitivity in humans. This gene is a member of a gene family that encodes bitter taste receptors in the mouth called the *TAS2R* gene family (Kim et al. 2003).

*TAS2R38*, the gene responsible for PTC taste sensitivity, is on chromosome 7 and codes for a receptor protein responsible for bitter taste perception that binds PTC. The two common alleles differ by three SNPs, causing three amino acid changes. One common allele or haplotype has proline (P), alanine (A), and valine (V) for these three amino acids and therefore is called PAV. The other common allele is called AVI because the amino acids are alanine (A), valine (V), and isoleucine (I). The PAV allele codes for a form of the receptor protein that binds PTC, conferring the ability to taste this chemical. The protein product of the AVI allele cannot bind PTC, and thus this allele confers the inability to taste PTC. However, the fact that the AVI and PAV alleles are expressed equally at the RNA level and that the AVI allele contains no frameshifts or other mutations that would result in early termination of the protein suggests that the AVI-coded receptor protein binds another bitter chemical that has not yet been identified (reviewed in Wooding 2006). Other haplotypes, presumably due to recombination between the three SNPs, occur but are rare. These rare haplotypes also showed functional responses in *in vivo* studies and, thus, these alleles appear to code for functional proteins (Bufe et al. 2005).

## Questions

1. What is a gene family? What mechanism generates them?
2. What is a SNP? What is a haplotype? How can SNP haplotypes be determined?
3. Assuming the PAV allele is the original one, what types of mutations (silent, missense, nonsense, and so on) have changed the PAV allele into the AVI allele? Explain. Based on the information given, how do these changes fit with what you have learned about the "functional enzyme hypothesis"?
4. You repeat Snyder's experiment, but instead of determining the ability of each family member to taste PTC, you determine what alleles they carry: 2 PAV (PAV/PAV), 2 AVI (AVI/AVI), or 1 PAV and 1 AVI (PAV/AVI). Using Table 20.2, what are the possible outcomes for offspring if the parents have the genotypes described in the first column? Below the genotype, write the phenotype (taster or non-taster) of each kind of individual.

**TABLE 20.2.**

Possible genotypes and phenotypes of children from parents of different genotype combinations. (to be filled in by students)

| Parent Genotype Combinations | Possible Genotypes / Phenotypes of Children |
|---|---|
| Both parents PAV/PAV | |
| Both parents PAV/AVI | |
| One PAV/PAV, the other PAV/AVI | |
| One PAV/PAV, the other AVI/AVI | |
| One PAV/AVI, the other AVI/AVI | |
| Both parents AVI/AVI | |

1. Go back to Snyder's results in Table 20.1 and give all the possible genotypes for the phenotypes listed in that table.
2. For each step of gene expression, explain how DNA differences lead to phenotypic differences in the ability to taste PTC.
3. Generalizing from this example, what can you say about the connection between Mendelian and molecular genetics? What type of reasoning are you using here?
4. Hypothesize about some consequences of PTC-tasting ability in the daily lives of tasters and non-tasters.

## Web Version

Detailed teaching notes, the case PDF, and an answer key are available on the NCCSTS website at *sciencecases.lib.buffalo.edu/cs/collection/detail.asp?case_id=595&id=595.*

## References

Anonymous. 1931. Science news: tasteblindness. *Science (Suppl.)* 73: 14a.

Bufe, B., P. A. S. Breslin, C. Kuhn, D. R. Reed, C. D. Tharp, J. P. Slack, U.-K. Kim, D. Drayna, and W. Meyerhof. 2005. The molecular basis of individual differences in phenylthiocarbamide and propylthiouracil bitterness perception. *Current Biology* 15: 322–327.

Fox, A. L. 1932. The relationship between chemical constitution and taste. *Proceedings of the National Academy of Sciences USA* 18: 115–120.

Kim, U.-K., E. Jorgenson, H. Coon, M. Leppart, N. Reisch, and D. Drayna. 2003. Positional cloning of the human quantitative trait locus underlying taste sensitivity to phenylthiocarbamide. *Science* 299: 1221–1225.

Snyder, L. H. 1931a. Inherited taste deficiency. *Science* 74: 151–152.

Snyder, L. H. 1931b. Linkage in man. *Eugenical News* 16: 117–119.

Wooding, S. 2006. Phenylthiocarbamide: A 75-year adventure in genetics and natural selection. *Genetics* 172: 2015–2023.

# IN SICKNESS AND IN HEALTH
## A Trip to the Genetic Counselor

*Barry Chess*

## Abstract
Students construct a pedigree from the information presented in the case about a young couple planning a family. Based on the pedigree, students determine if they are carriers for any recessive genetic diseases and the likelihood of their passing those diseases on to their children. Students learn about the inheritance of single gene dominant, recessive, and sex-linked disorders, as well as the significance of carrier frequency.


## Learning Objectives
- Construct a pedigree from a written narrative.
- Determine, from a pedigree, carriers of recessive genetic diseases and the probability that they will pass those diseases on to their offspring.
- Understand the rules governing the inheritance of single gene dominant, recessive, and sex-linked disorders and be able to apply them to analyze simple genetics problems.
- Determine the carrier frequency of a trait given the prevalence of the trait in the population, as well as understand the significance of carrier frequency.

## Quantitative Reasoning Skills/Concepts
- Carry out basic mathematical operations.
- Use numerical evidence to formulate null and alternative hypotheses.
- Articulate complete and correct claims based on data.
- Use appropriate reasoning to support the validity of data-based claims.
- Create and analyze family pedigrees.
- Create and interpret Punnett squares.
- Interpret probabilities in Hardy-Weinberg equation.
- Perform DNA analysis.

## The Case Study

### Part I: Pedigree Construction

Greg and Olga were a little worried. Starting a family presented choices and responsibilities far more long-reaching and complex than anything either of them had encountered before, and sitting here in the reception area of the genetic counselor's office they were beginning to feel the pressure. They had met four years earlier in the hemophilia clinic where Greg was waiting for his brother Jeff to get an injection of factor VIII, a protein that helps the blood to clot. When a person's factor VIII level is very low (less than 1% of normal), even the smallest cuts can be troublesome and uncontrolled internal bleeding is common. Complications include swelling, joint damage, and an increased likelihood of neurological complications due to intracerebral bleeding. Even simple surgical procedures such as tooth extractions become far more risky. Jeff's condition was noted by his pediatrician shortly after birth when his circumcision bled profusely. Since then, Jeff has received monthly injections of factor VIII, either at home or (twice a year) at a clinic where his physical condition is reviewed by a physician's assistant. At first these injections contained clotting factor isolated from the blood of human donors but, for the last 10 years or so, he has received recombinant clotting factor, which is genetically engineered.

It was in that clinic waiting room that Greg struck up a conversation with Olga, who was waiting for her uncle to finish his exam and receive an injection of clotting factor. Like Jeff , Olga's uncle also suffered from hemophilia A due to factor VIII deficiency. Beginning with this common experience, Jeff and Olga quickly fell in love and were married the following year.

They are now thinking about starting a family of their own, but are concerned about the risks of passing on genetic diseases to their children. They know for example that hemophilia A is an inherited disease, and several of Greg's relatives suffer from myotonic dystrophy, a muscle weakening disease that also runs in families.

As a first step, the genetic counselor has asked them to fill out a narrative history listing their relatives, relationships, and if they were affected by any genetic diseases that they know of. The forms are seen below.

> **Name:** *Greg P.*
>
> I have one brother and one sister, neither of whom is married. My brother suffers from factor VIII deficiency, but no one else in my family does. My mother has two brothers and one sister. One of my uncles and one of my aunts are affected by myotonic dystrophy. My affected aunt married an unaffected man and they have a young, seemingly unaffected daughter. My other uncle is unaffected, as is my mother. Our primary care doctor has said that because both my mother and uncle

are over fifty years old and show no symptoms, they do not have the disease. My father is completely normal. He was adopted from an orphanage and nothing is known about his family. My maternal grandmother was an only child who also suffered from myotonic dystrophy. Her husband (my grandfather) was one of seven children (four boys and three girls). No one in the family seems to know much about the health status of my grandfather or his brothers. Both of my parents are alive but all of my grandparents are deceased

**Name:** *Olga P.*

I have two brothers, one of whom has factor VIII deficiency. The brother with the disease is married to a woman who does not have the disease. They have two young boys, both normal. My father is an only child who does not suffer from anything and his parents also are only children who do not suffer from any diseases. They are all still living. My maternal grandmother is healthy and had a sister who died just after birth. She married my grandfather who was one of four children, all boys, none of whom were affected by any disease that anyone is aware of. My grandparents had two children, my mother and my uncle. My uncle has hemophilia but my mom doesn't. My uncle married my aunt (who is unaffected) and they had two children, neither of whom showed any sign of any disease. Their boy is still single but their girl got married, to a normal man, and had a son, who has hemophilia A.

"Good afternoon" said the woman rising to greet them, "I'm Dr. Ciletti. It's good to finally meet you in person."

"Nice to finally put a face to the voice. I'm Greg and this is my wife Olga."

"Nice to meet you," Olga said, taking a seat across the desk from Dr. Ciletti. "This whole having-kids thing is more nerve-wracking when you really start to think about it."

"You're doing exactly the right thing. There is no sense in worrying about things unless you have to. Maybe I can set your mind at ease a little bit. To begin with, I know that you're both concerned about factor VIII deficiency and myotonic dystrophy because of the family history. Is there anything else that you'd like to know?"

"Well," began Olga, "the fact that we both have these diseases in our family and there is a chance that we could pass them on to our children has opened our eyes a little bit, but we'd also like to know if you can predict other diseases that don't run in our family. Like my best friend in high school had cystic fibrosis and she died when she was only twenty four, and was sick almost all the time."

"Okay, well, cystic fibrosis doesn't look like it is in either of your family histories so it's probably not worth worrying about. But, we can spend a little time going over the chance that you both carry a gene that has never before shown its face. The first step is we have to convert the family information you two have provided into a graphical representation called a pedigree. From there we can begin to correlate family relationships with the appearance of specific diseases."

## Question

1. What would a pedigree of Greg and Olga's families look like? Concentrate simply on family relationships and affected persons.

## *Part II: Autosomal Dominant Traits*

"Great, so this looks like an accurate representation of your family, right?" Dr. Ciletti asked.

"Looks good to me," replied Greg.

"My family is so small, there's not much to miss until you get to my grandparents," said Olga.

"Well, factor VIII deficiency and myotonic dystrophy are inherited in completely different ways. Come to think of it, you asked about CF as well and…," said Dr. Ciletti.

"CF?" asked Greg, interrupting the doctor.

"Cystic fibrosis," Dr. Ciletti continued. "I was about to say that cystic fibrosis is inherited in a manner different than both of the other diseases you are concerned about, but let's tackle them one at a time."

"Myotonic dystrophy is an autosomal dominant disease and it is the easiest to pick out of a pedigree. Now, Greg, even though you have an uncle and aunt as well as a grandmother who all have the disease, you don't and there is no way that you will pass this disease on to your children. So that is the first piece of good news."

"But don't a lot of genetic diseases skip a generation?" Greg asked. "And even if it doesn't, my mom has two siblings with the disease. Could she be a carrier and just pass the disease on to me? For that matter, could I be a carrier?"

"Yes, could he be a carrier?" Olga added.

"Absolutely not," Dr. Ciletti said. "Let me show you why."

## Questions

1. Do autosomal dominant disorders skip generations?
2. Could Greg or his mother be carriers of the gene that causes myotonic dystrophy?
3. Is there a possibility that Greg's aunt or uncle is homozygous for the myotonic dystrophy (MD) gene?
4. Symptoms of myotonic dystrophy sometimes don't show up until after age fifty. What is the possibility that Greg's cousin has inherited the MD gene?
5. What is the possibility that Greg and Olga's children could inherit the MD gene?

## *Part III: Autosomal Recessive Traits*

"Well, I certainly feel better about that," said Greg. "I guess there is no reason to worry about passing on MD to our children. They'll just have to worry about inheriting their father's incredible good looks, fabulous sense of humor, creativity…"

"And modesty…. Hold on a second, God's gift to the world," Olga chimed in. "We still haven't talked about factor VIII deficiency, which is why we came here in the first place."

"Well," Dr. Ciletti began, "factor VIII deficiency is what's known as a sex-linked disease. Before we get to that, let's take a look at a disease with a slightly simpler mode of inheritance. Many traits, whether or not they are considered to be diseases, are described as autosomal recessive traits. These are the ones you alluded to earlier when you talked about diseases that skip generations and about people being carriers. Some common recessive traits include albinism, sickle cell disease, and cystic fibrosis, which I promise we will get to, Olga. Now, let's look at some of the rules governing these types of traits."

### Questions

1. What are the hallmarks of an autosomal recessive trait?
2. What does consanguineous mean? Why is this concept especially important when discussing recessive genetic disorders?
3. What is it about the inheritance pattern of factor VIII deficiency seen in Greg and Olga's pedigree that point toward it not being an autosomal recessive trait?

## *Part IV: Sex-Linked Inheritance*

"Alright," Olga began, "so factor VIII deficiency is sex-linked because it only affects men. Does it require the presence of testosterone or something like that?"

"No, but there are many traits that do depend on the presence or absence of sex hormones. We call them sex-influenced traits. Sex-linked traits get their name from the fact that the genes that cause them are carried on the X chromosome, which is one of the chromosomes responsible for determining what sex a person will become. Let's take a look at how factor VIII deficiency runs in both your families."

### Questions

1. What are the characteristics of X-linked recessive inheritance?
2. Why does a son never inherit his father's defective X chromosome?
3. What is required for a woman to display a sex-linked recessive trait?
4. Return to the pedigree drawn earlier for Greg and Olga; mark those persons who are carriers of the factor VIII deficiency gene.

5. What is the chance that Olga carries the gene for factor VIII deficiency? Calculate the probability that she will pass it to her offspring. Will male children be affected in a different way than female children?
6. What is the chance that Greg carries the factor VIII gene? Can he pass the gene on to his sons? His daughters? How will each be affected?

## Part V: Population Genetics

"Finally," Dr. Ciletti began, "let's talk about cystic fibrosis. Now I mentioned that it is probably not something to worry about since neither of you has it in your family history, but there is a way to figure out the odds of being a carrier even without a past family history. Remember that in the case of a recessive autosomal disease like CF, for the disease to show up unexpectedly in your offspring both you and Greg would have to be carriers. We can estimate the probability of each of you being carriers by looking at the population as a whole."

"You mean all the people on Earth?" Olga asked.

"No. For purposes of genetics you each belong to different populations," Dr. Ciletti began. "Now Olga, you're of European descent, correct?"

"Yes, Swedish and German."

"And obviously Caucasian. Now I can look up the carrier frequency, that is, the fraction of people in your population group that carry the most common cystic fibrosis allele. As it happens, one of every twenty-three Caucasians of European descent carries a recessive allele for CF."

"That doesn't sound very encouraging," Olga interjected. "I have a 1 in 23 chance of having a child with cystic fibrosis."

"Not at all. You just have a 1 in 23 chance of carrying the CF gene." Dr. Ciletti replied. "Now Greg is Asian American and within his population group the carrier frequency is 1 out of 180. Making the odds even longer is the fact that if you are a carrier you have only a 50-50 chance of passing on your disease causing allele. So the chance of you two producing a baby with CF is actually $1/23 \times 1/180 \times ½ \times ½$ or 1 out of 16,560. So, just how big a family are you planning to have?"

"But wait," said Greg. "If a carrier is someone who doesn't display any of the features of a disease, how can you know how many carriers are in a population?"

"Good question, Greg. As an old professor of mine once said, 'It all comes down to minding your P's and Q's.' In a large population, the carrier frequency can be estimated by looking at the number of persons with the disease and then doing a little algebra. There are two equations we need to remember. The first describes all the alleles in the population and it just says that $p + q = 1$. In other words, of all the alleles in the population, a percentage of them are the healthy version, which we can call $p$. So if 65% of the alleles in a population are healthy, then $p$ must be 0.65. The rest of the alleles must be the disease causing form, or $q$. If $p$ is 0.65, then $q$ must be 0.35, so that $p + q = 1$.

"But how do you know the percentage of q alleles in a population?" asked Olga. "The only people you can really identify are the people with the disease."

"Exactly, and that brings us to the second equation we need to look at."

## Questions

1. What is the second equation?
2. The incidence of cystic fibrosis in Hispanic Americans is 1/14500 while in African Americans cystic fibrosis is seen in 1 of every 15,000 births. What is the carrier frequency for each of these populations?
3. What is the probability of two Hispanic Americans having a child with cystic fibrosis, given that there is no history of the disease in either's family?
4. Carol is an African American woman who does not suffer from CF. Both of her parents are healthy but her brother has cystic fibrosis. Carol is planning a family with her husband Marcus, who is also African American but who has no history of CF in his family. What is the probability of their having a child with CF?

## *Part VI: Unsettled Issues*

"So, is it possible to test for each of these diseases?" asked Greg.

"Yes, but for the sake of practicality, or expense, as some would say, we only test for those diseases that are reasonably likely based on a patient's history. We wouldn't for example test either of you for the presence of the CF allele."

"Wait a minute," Olga began, "what about a disease that doesn't show up until later in life. Greg's uncle didn't show any symptoms of myotonic dystrophy until he was something like forty…"

"Forty three," Greg corrected.

"Yeah, anyway, if a genetic test shows that you are going to get a genetic disease and it becomes part of your medical history, could an insurance company exclude it as a pre-existing condition, even though you don't have it yet?"

"Well, the law is actually quite unsettled about the issue. Genetic testing has the power to predict the occurrence, or at least the likelihood of occurrence, of many diseases—cancer, Alzheimer's disease, and diabetes just to name a few. Many people are not comfortable with that information being part of their medical records because they are afraid it could lead to a loss of insurance, losing out on a job, or some other form of discrimination. But," Dr. Ciletti said with finality, "that is a subject to take up with lawmakers. It is entirely possible that after the conversation we've just had that you two know far more about the subject of genetic testing than your congressman or senators. If you're concerned about the legal ramifications of genetic testing, you should let them know. It was a pleasure meeting both of you."

"Likewise, Doctor. You really helped to put my mind at ease," Olga said.

"Yeah, I think we both feel a lot better, thanks," said Greg.

## Questions

1. What are some of the risks and benefits of genetic testing as it relates to legal (not medical) issues?
2. Do you think an unintended consequence of genetic testing could be that people would be less liable to seek medical care out of fear that they could later be denied life or health insurance? What laws should be used to govern the use of genetic data of this type?

## Web Version

Detailed teaching notes, the case PDF, and an answer key are available on the NCCSTS website at *sciencecases.lib.buffalo.edu/cs/collection/detail.asp?case_id=291&id=291.*

CHAPTER 22

# THE CASE OF DESIREE'S BABY

## The Genetics and Evolution of Human Skin Color

*Patricia Schneider*

## Abstract

This case is based on Kate Chopin's short story "Desiree's Baby," a tragic tale of race and gender in antebellum Louisiana first published in 1893. Students read the story and then answer a series of questions about the genetics and evolution of skin color.


## Learning Objectives

- Explain polygenetic inheritance.
- Describe the inheritance of skin color.
- Discuss the "sunscreen" and "vitamin" hypotheses of skin color evolution.
- Write a short essay summarizing the key points in a popular science article.

## Quantitative Reasoning Skills/Concepts

- Carry out basic mathematical operations.
- Use numerical evidence to formulate null and alternative hypotheses.
- Create and interpret Punnett squares.
- Create and interpret family pedigrees.

## The Case Study

### *"Desiree's Baby" by Kate Chopin, Vogue Magazine, January 4, 1893*

As the day was pleasant, Madame Valmonde drove over to L'Abri to see Desiree and the baby.

It made her laugh to think of Desiree with a baby. Why, it seemed but yesterday that Desiree was little more than a baby herself; when Monsieur in riding through the gateway of Valmonde had found her lying asleep in the shadow of the big stone pillar.

The little one awoke in his arms and began to cry for "Dada." That was as much as she could do or say. Some people thought she might have strayed there of her own accord, for she was of the toddling age. The prevailing belief was that she had been purposely left by a party of Texans, whose canvas-covered wagon, late in the day, had crossed the ferry that Coton Mais kept, just below the plantation. In time Madame Valmonde abandoned every speculation but the one that Desiree had been sent to her by a beneficent Providence to be the child of her affection, seeing that she was without child of the flesh. For the girl grew to be beautiful and gentle, affectionate and sincere—the idol of Valmonde.

It was no wonder, when she stood one day against the stone pillar in whose shadow she had lain asleep, eighteen years before, that Armand Aubigny riding by and seeing her there, had fallen in love with her. That was the way all the Aubignys fell in love, as if struck by a pistol shot. The wonder was that he had not loved her before; for he had known her since his father brought him home from Paris, a boy of eight, after his mother died there. The passion that awoke in him that day, when he saw her at the gate, swept along like an avalanche, or like a prairie fire, or like anything that drives headlong over all obstacles.

Monsieur Valmonde grew practical and wanted things well considered: that is, the girl's obscure origin. Armand looked into her eyes and did not care. He was reminded that she was nameless. What did it matter about a name when he could give her one of the oldest and proudest in Louisiana? He ordered the corbeille from Paris, and contained himself with what patience he could until it arrived; then they were married.

Madame Valmonde had not seen Desiree and the baby for four weeks. When she reached L'Abri, she shuddered at the first sight of it, as she always did. It was a sad looking place, which for many years had not known the gentle presence of a mistress, old Monsieur Aubigny having married and buried his wife in France, and she having loved her own land too well ever to leave it. The roof came down steep and black like a cowl, reaching out beyond the wide galleries that encircled the yellow stuccoed house. Big, solemn oaks grew close to it, and their thick-leaved, far-reaching branches shadowed it like a pall. Young Aubigny's rule was a strict one, too, and under it his negroes had forgotten how to be gay, as they had been during the old master's easy-going and indulgent lifetime.

The young mother was recovering slowly, and lay full length, in her soft white muslins and laces, upon a couch. The baby was beside her, upon her arm, where he had fallen asleep, at her breast. The yellow nurse woman sat beside a window fanning herself. Madame Valmonde bent her portly figure over Desiree and kissed her, holding her an instant tenderly in her arms. Then she turned to the child.

"This is not the baby!" she exclaimed, in startled tones. French was the language spoken at Valmonde in those days.

"I knew you would be astonished," laughed Desiree, "at the way he has grown. The little cochon de lait! Look at his legs, mamma, and his hands and fingernails—real fingernails. Zandrine had to cut them this morning. Isn't it true, Zandrine?"

The woman bowed her turbaned head majestically, "Mais si, Madame."

"And the way he cries," went on Desiree, "is deafening. Armand heard him the other day as far away as La Blanche's cabin."

Madame Valmonde had never removed her eyes from the child. She lifted it and walked with it over to the window that was lightest. She scanned the baby narrowly, then looked as searchingly at Zandrine, whose face was turned to gaze across the fields.

"Yes, the child has grown, has changed," said Madame Valmonde, slowly, as she replaced it beside its mother. "What does Armand say?"

Desiree's face became suffused with a glow that was happiness itself.

"Oh, Armand is the proudest father in the parish, I believe, chiefly because it is a boy, to bear his name; though he says not,—that he would have loved a girl as well. But I know it isn't true. I know he says that to please me. And mamma," she added, drawing Madame Valmonde's head down to her, and speaking in a whisper, "he hasn't punished one of them—not one of them—since baby is born. Even Negrillon, who pretended to have burnt his leg that he might rest from work—he only laughed, and said Negrillon was a great scamp. Oh, mamma, I'm so happy; it frightens me."

What Desiree said was true. Marriage, and later the birth of his son had softened Armand Aubigny's imperious and exacting nature greatly. This was what made the gentle Desiree so happy, for she loved him desperately. When he frowned she trembled, but loved him. When he smiled, she asked no greater blessing of God. But Armand's dark, handsome face had not often been disfigured by frowns since the day he fell in love with her.

When the baby was about three months old, Desiree awoke one day to the conviction that there was something in the air menacing her peace. It was at first too subtle to grasp. It had only been a disquieting suggestion; an air of mystery among the blacks; unexpected visits from far-off neighbors who could hardly account for their coming. Then a strange, an awful change in her husband's manner, which she dared not ask him to explain. When he spoke to her, it was with averted eyes, from which the old love-light seemed to have gone out. He absented himself from home; and when there, avoided her presence and that of her child, without excuse. And the very spirit of Satan seemed suddenly to take hold of him in his dealings with the slaves. Desiree was miserable enough to die.

She sat in her room, one hot afternoon, in her peignoir, listlessly drawing through her fingers the strands of her long, silky brown hair that hung about her shoulders. The baby, half naked, lay asleep upon her own great mahogany bed, that was like a sumptuous throne, with its satin-lined half-canopy. One of La Blanche's little quadroon boys—half naked too—stood fanning the child slowly with a fan of peacock feathers.

Desiree's eyes had been fixed absently and sadly upon the baby, while she was striving to penetrate the threatening mist that she felt closing about her. She looked from her child to the boy who stood beside him, and back again; over and over. "Ah!" It was a cry that she could not help; which she was not conscious of having uttered. The blood turned like ice in her veins, and a clammy moisture gathered upon her face.

She tried to speak to the little quadroon boy; but no sound would come, at first. When he heard his name uttered, he looked up, and his mistress was pointing to the door. He laid aside the great, soft fan, and obediently stole away, over the polished floor, on his bare tiptoes.

She stayed motionless, with gaze riveted upon her child, and her face the picture of fright.

Presently her husband entered the room, and without noticing her, went to a table and began to search among some papers which covered it.

"Armand," she called to him, in a voice which must have stabbed him, if he was human. But he did not notice. "Armand," she said again. Then she rose and tottered towards him. "Armand," she panted once more, clutching his arm, "look at our child. What does it mean? Tell me."

He coldly but gently loosened her fingers from about his arm and thrust the hand away from him.

"Tell me what it means!" she cried despairingly.

"It means," he answered lightly, "that the child is not white; it means that you are not white."

A quick conception of all that this accusation meant for her nerved her with unwonted courage to deny it. "It is a lie; it is not true, I am white! Look at my hair, it is brown; and my eyes are gray, Armand, you know they are gray. And my skin is fair," seizing his wrist. "Look at my hand; whiter than yours, Armand," she laughed hysterically.

"As white as La Blanche's," he returned cruelly; and went away leaving her alone with their child.

When she could hold a pen in her hand, she sent a despairing letter to Madame Valmonde.

"My mother, they tell me I am not white. Armand has told me I am not white. For God's sake tell them it is not true. You must know it is not true. I shall die. I must die. I cannot be so unhappy, and live."

The answer that came was brief: "My own Desiree: Come home to Valmonde; back to your mother who loves you. Come with your child."

When the letter reached Desiree she went with it to her husband's study, and laid it open upon the desk before which he sat. She was like a stone image: silent, white, motionless after she placed it there.

In silence he ran his cold eyes over the written words.

He said nothing. "Shall I go, Armand?" she asked in tones sharp with agonized suspense.

"Yes, go."

"Do you want me to go?"

"Yes, I want you to go." He thought Almighty God had dealt cruelly and unjustly with him; and felt, somehow, that he was paying Him back in kind when he stabbed thus into his wife's soul. Moreover he no longer loved her, because of the unconscious injury she had brought upon his home and his name.

She turned away like one stunned by a blow, and walked slowly towards the door, hoping he would call her back. "Good-by, Armand," she moaned.

He did not answer her. That was his last blow at fate.

Desiree went in search of her child. Zandrine was pacing the somber gallery with it. She took the little one from the nurse's arms with no word of explanation, and descending the steps, walked away, under the live oak branches. It was an October afternoon; the sun was just sinking. Out in the still fields the negroes were picking cotton.

Desiree had not changed the thin white garment nor the slippers which she wore. Her hair was uncovered and the sun's rays brought a golden gleam from its brown meshes. She did not take the broad, beaten road which led to the far-off plantation of Valmonde. She walked across a deserted field, where the stubble bruised her tender feet, so delicately shod, and tore her thin gown to shreds.

She disappeared among the reeds and willows that grew thick along the banks of the deep, sluggish bayou; and she did not come back again.

Some weeks later there was a curious scene enacted at L'Abri. In the centre of the smoothly swept backyard was a great bonfire. Armand Aubigny sat in the wide hallway that commanded a view of the spectacle; and it was he who dealt out to a half dozen negroes the material which kept this fire ablaze.

A graceful cradle of willow, with all its dainty furbishings, was laid upon the pyre, which had already been fed with the richness of a priceless layette. Then there were silk gowns, and velvet and satin ones added to these; laces, too, and embroideries; bonnets and gloves; for the corbeille had been of rare quality. The last thing to go was a tiny bundle of letters; innocent little scribblings that Desiree had sent to him during the days of their espousal. There was the remnant of one back in the drawer from which he took them. But it was not Desiree's; it was part of an old letter from his mother to his father. He read it. She was thanking God for the blessing of her husband's love:—

"But above all," she wrote, "night and day, I thank the good God for having so arranged our lives that our dear Armand will never know that his mother, who adores him, belongs to the race that is cursed with the brand of slavery."

## Part I: A Mendelian Approach

"Desiree's Baby" is a very moving story that shows us the horror of racism, but is it scientifically accurate?

## Questions

1. According to the story, Madame Valamonde and Armand noticed the baby's dark skin several weeks before Desiree. Can you offer a possible explanation for this gradual increase in pigmentation over the course of three months?
2. Assuming the inheritance of skin color in "Desiree's Baby" follows the simple dominant/recessive pattern described by Mendel, is dark pigmentation best explained as an example of a dominant or recessive allele?
3. Assign suitable symbols for each allele and use the information in the story to develop possible genotypes for Desiree, Armand, and the baby.
4. Consider the skin pigmentation of biracial individuals, such as Halle Berry, Lenny Kravits, Mariah Carey, or "The Rock." Can these phenotypes (skin colors) be explained by the same Mendelian model?

## *Part II: Skin Color Is Polygenetic (Multiple Gene) Trait*

Differences in skin color are largely due to differences in the amount of melanin, a dark pigment produced by skin cells. At least three genes control the synthesis of melanin. Each gene has two forms: an allele for high melanin production, or dark skin (A,B,C), and an allele for low melanin production, or light skin (a,b,c). Each dark skin allele (A,B,C) in the genotype adds a small but equal amount of pigment to the skin. There are seven different shades of skin color ranging from very dark (AABBCC) to very light (aabbcc). Most individuals produce a medium amount of melanin and are of intermediate skin color (AaBbCc).

The Punnett square in Table 22.1 shows the possible offspring from a cross between two individuals of intermediate skin color.

The offspring of this cross exhibit seven shades of skin color based on the number of dark skin alleles in each genotype.

**TABLE 22.1.**

Punnett Square for AaBbCc X AaBbCc
Each square shows the number of dark skin alleles in the genotype.

| Gametes | ABC | ABc | AbC | Abc | aBC | aBc | abC | abc |
|---|---|---|---|---|---|---|---|---|
| ABC | 6 AABBCC | 5 AABBCc | 5 AABbCC | 4 AABbCc | 5 AaBBCC | 4 AaBBCc | 4 AaBbCC | 3 AaBbCc |
| **ABc** | 5 AABBCc | 4 AABBcc | 4 AABbCc | 3 AABbcc | 4 AaBBCc | 3 AaBBcc | 3 AaBbCc | 2 AaBbcc |
| **AbC** | 5 AABbCC | 4 AABbCc | 4 AAbbCC | 3 AAbbCc | 4 AaBbCC | 3 AaBbCc | 3 AabbCC | 2 AabbCc |
| **Abc** | 4 AABbCc | 3 AABbcc | 3 AAbbCc | 2 AAbbcc | 3 AaBbCc | 2 AaBbcc | 2 AabbCc | 1 Aabbcc |
| **aBC** | 5 AaBBCC | 4 AaBBCc | 4 AaBbCC | 3 AaBbCc | 4 aaBBCC | 3 aaBBCc | 3 aaBbCC | 2 aaBbCc |
| **abc** | 4 AaBBCc | 3 AaBBcc | 3 AaBbCc | 2 AaBbcc | 3 aaBBCc | 2 aaBBcc | 2 aaBbCc | 1 aaBbcc |

## Questions

1. Each parent produces eight different types of gametes, which can combine in 64 different ways. Complete Table 22.2:

**TABLE 22.2.**

Phenotypic ratio for AaBbCc X AaBbCc

| # dark skin alleles in genotype | 0 | 1 | 2 | 3 | 4 | 5 | 6 |
|---|---|---|---|---|---|---|---|
| Phenotype: Skin color | | | | | | | |
| Phenotypic ratio: # offspring/64 | | | | | | | |

2. How many of these 64 possible offspring have skin that is darker than their parents?
3. Each of these three genes has two alleles. Are the dark skin alleles dominant to the light skin alleles?
4. There are more than seven shades of skin color. Can you offer an explanation?
5. Use this model of skin color inheritance and the information provided in the short story to develop possible genotypes for each of the following characters: Monsieur and Madame Aubigny, Armand Aubigny, Desiree's mother and father, Desiree, and Desiree's baby.

## *Part III: The Evolution of Skin Color*

DNA analysis indicates that we are all descended from a single ancestral group of Africans If we are all "out of Africa," why are there so many different skin colors?

To complete your group's analysis of the case, read the article "Skin Deep" (Jablonski and Chaplin 2002). Then, using information from the article, write a one-page essay that answers the above question, discussing both the "sunscreen" and "vitamin" hypotheses.

## Web Version

Detailed teaching notes, the case PDF, and an answer key are available on the NCCSTS website at *sciencecases.lib.buffalo.edu/cs/collection/detail.asp?case_id=454&id=454*.

## Reference

Jablonski, N. J., and G. Chaplin. 2002. Skin deep. *Scientific American* 278 (4): 74–81.

# A SICKENINGLY SWEET BABY BOY

## A Case Study on Autosomal Recessive Inheritance

*Jacqueline Washington and Anne Zayaitz*

### Abstract

This case explores the genetics of the disease and the ultimate dilemma of treatment options through the story of a baby boy suffering from a recessively inherited metabolic disorder.


### Learning Objectives

- Explain the relationships between family members and the disease incidence using a pedigree chart.
- Understand the rules governing the inheritance of a single gene recessive disorder.
- Calculate the probabilities of inheriting recessive traits and passing them on to off spring.
- Explain the dietary restrictions associated with Maple Syrup Urine Disease (MSUD).
- Discuss the risks associated with liver transplants.
- Discuss the options of genetic screening and genetic testing in this case.
- Compare the advantages and disadvantages associated with gene therapy and more conventional treatment means, i.e., transplants.
- Explore genetic drift effects on small populations (e.g., the Mennonite community) including other possible conditions resulting from a founder effect in similar communities.

### Quantitative Reasoning Skills/Concepts

- Carry out basic mathematical operations.
- Interpret Punnett squares.
- Interpret family pedigrees.

## The Case Study

### *Part I: Failure to Thrive*

Emma and Jacob Miller were so excited at the birth of their baby Matthew.

"Jacob, he's just so perfect! Just one problem though, it looks like he has your hairline!" Emma teased her husband who, though only 32, was balding.

"Emma, I spent all that time painting the baby's room and I just hope that he's not color blind like your father or he won't be able to see it!" Jacob responded.

Both the pregnancy and delivery had been uneventful. But in the back of their minds, they really were worried because their first child, Samuel, died at the age of nine days.

By the fifth day after birth, Matthew began to have trouble nursing and by the seventh day he had completely stopped feeding. Emma and Jacob were frantic because it seemed to them that Matthew might also die.

"What is going on with our family? Another sick baby?" Jacob thought to himself.

Emma and Jacob rushed him to the emergency room. Although Mathew's limbs were rigid and he had had a seizure, the examination showed no infection and his x-rays were normal. The doctor also did routine lab tests on his blood and urine.

"Doctor, do you think that this funny smell in Matthew's diapers has anything to do with his problem?" Emma asked. "I brought one along so that you could smell it too."

#### Questions

1. What additional information would you want to know to understand Emma and Jacob's panic?
2. What is meant by "failure to thrive"?
3. What are some reasons why newborns fail to thrive?
4. What do you think the smell is?

### *Part II: Pedigree Analysis*

Matthew's urine did have a sweet, maple syrup smell and lab results revealed elevated levels of the branched chain amino acids (BCAA)—valine, isoleucine, and leucine. Skin biopsies from the baby and his parents were taken and cultured. The ability of the cultured skin fibroblasts to metabolize BCAA was determined. While his parents' enzyme activity levels were nearly normal, Matthew's was less than 2% of normal.

"Given the medical information and the smell of the urine, Matthew has Maple Syrup Urine Disease (MSUD)," reported Dr. Morton of the Clinic for Special Children. "He will not be able to breast feed or drink regular formula. What is really important is that Matthew eats a low protein diet. This diet must continue for the rest of his life or else the amino acids will accumulate in the body creating a situation that leads to brain swelling, neurological damage, and death. In spite of dietary intervention, the disease may cause several complications, the most notable being mental retardation. You need to know that dietary intervention does not cure the disease."

Emma and Jacob were Mennonites and their family history revealed that Emma's mother had two sisters who died in their first year of life; no one knew why. Jacob's father had a sister who died at seven months of age from unknown causes. Could the gene for MSUD run in both of their families?

MSUD is due to a recessive gene. For an individual to be affected, he or she would need to inherit a defective nonworking copy from each parent (see Figure 23.1). The individual would then be described as being homozygous recessive.

**FIGURE 23.1.**

Autosomal Recessive Inheritance When Both Parents Are Unaffected Carriers. They have a 25% chance of having a normal child, a 50% chance of having an unaffected child who is a carrier and a 25% chance of having a child with the recessive disorder.

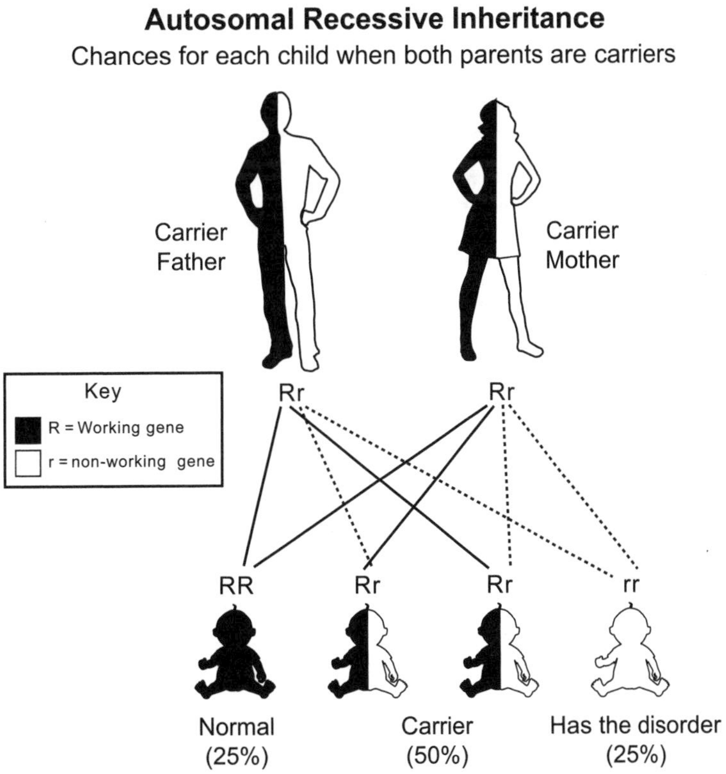

## Questions

Pedigree charts are useful tools used by genetic counselors to look for the incidence of disease within multiple generation families. Each generation is shown on a separate row.

1. Label the pedigree chart in Figure 23.2 to explain the relationships and the disease incidence within this family. Be sure to include Emma, Jacob, Samuel, Matthew, Emma's father, Emma's mother, Emma's aunts, Jacob's mother, Jacob's father, and Jacob's aunt.
2. Indicate on your pedigree chart the individuals who are carriers by shading half of each circle or square.
3. Define the terms *genotype, phenotype, homozygous* and *heterozygous.*
4. How could their son have inherited MSUD even though neither parent suffers from it?
5. What is the probability that they would have another affected child? A carrier?
6. Could Emma and Jacob have children who do not have MSUD (i.e., phenotypically normal)? Explain. What is the probability?
7. If MSUD were a dominant disorder, what would be the probability that Matthew would inherit the disease?
8. *Challenge Question:* Why were Emma's and Jacobs's enzyme levels nearly normal?

**FIGURE 23.2.**

Pedigree Chart for Emma and Jacob's Family.

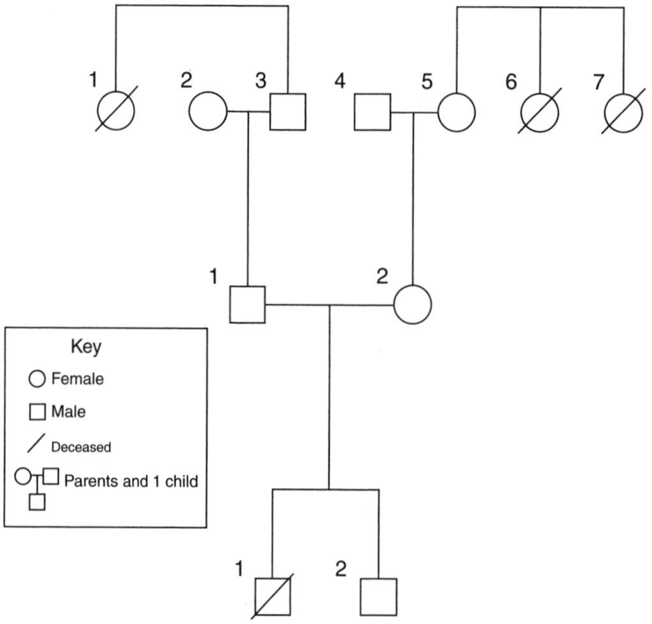

## Part III: Treatment Options

Over the next four years, Matthew's metabolism was controlled by giving him an extremely regimented low protein diet. His staple was potatoes, which he enjoyed with ketchup. He was not able to eat meat, dairy, or poultry products. Unlike most kids, Matthew never ate traditional birthday cake or ice cream. Despite the family's strict adherence to this MSUD diet, Matthew continued to suffer approximately three metabolic crises a year. These crises occurred when amino acids accumulated in his blood leading to the swelling of his brain. Even something as simple as a cold or the flu affected his amino acid levels and sent his metabolism into crisis.

"We cannot continue to live in constant fear that a minor infection or a simple cold or ear infection could kill our son. Even though we are doing everything we are supposed to, he is still getting sick and we are afraid we may lose Matthew," Emma said as she dried her tears. "When I think about how we lost our first child and I see other parents of kids with MSUD grieving over the loss of their child, I'm so afraid of losing Matthew. I do not want to watch him become brain damaged or dead because of a simple sore throat or even having just one too many french fries."

Jacob agreed. "We know that some children with MSUD have had a liver transplant and they are effectively cured. But that is major surgery and he is so small and frail. Would he survive the surgery? On the other hand, the alternative for my son is a life of uncertainty that could end in death at any moment."

The family was directed by Dr. Morton to Children's Hospital of Pittsburgh, where transplant experts agreed to list Matthew for a liver transplant. Jacob and Emma learned that children who received a liver transplant would have to take strong immunosuppressive drugs for the rest of their lives. It was also clear there was a 40% possibility that Matthew could reject the liver and need a second transplant (which also might be rejected) or he could die from surgical complications. Jacob and Emma had to decide what to do.

### Questions

1. What options do these parents have for the care of their son?
2. What are the pros and cons of each choice?
3. Where would a donor liver come from?
4. MSUD is found in one newborn in 200,000 throughout the United States, but one newborn in 200 in the Amish and Mennonites of Lancaster County, Pennsylvania, has the disease. Why is there such a difference in the prevalence of the disease?
5. If Matthew was your son, what would you do?

## Web Version

Detailed teaching notes, the case PDF, and an answer key are available on the NCCSTS website at *sciencecases.lib.buffalo.edu/cs/collection/detail.asp?case_id=241&id=241*.

# SECTION VI

# MOLECULAR BIOLOGY

CHAPTER 24

# "NOT EXACTLY"
## The Complexity of a Human Genetic Disease

*William Morgan and Dean Fraga*

Chromosome 7

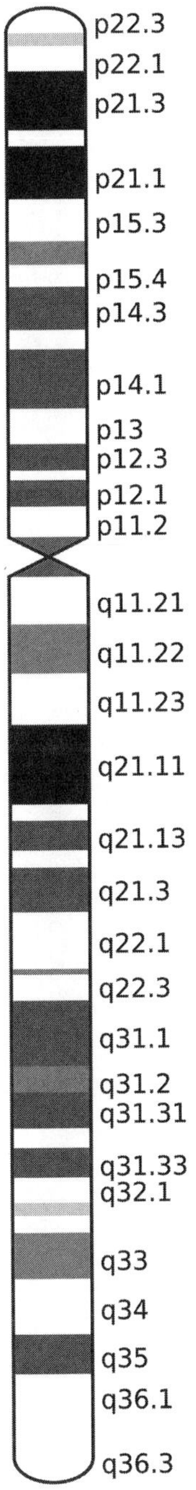


### Abstract
This case follows a young couple with a family history of cystic fibrosis as they consult with a genetic counselor about their plans to have a child. The case reviews the basics of Mendelian and molecular genetics, briefly examines the possibilities and limitations of genetic testing, and introduces students to online bioinformatics databases.

### Learning Objectives

- Construct and analyze a human pedigree and a Punnett square.
- Predict the effect of a mutation on the expression of a gene, specifically whether the mutation will alter the amount of the gene's mRNA, the structure of the gene's mRNA, the amount of the encoded protein, or the structure of the encoded protein.
- Explain why a gene can have many alleles within a population.
- Sketch the typical structure of a eukaryotic gene.
- Explain the trade-offs in developing a genetic test for a complex genetic disease and the consequent limitations of testing for a subset of alleles.
- Explain how a mutation outside of the coding region of a gene can cause a genetic disease.
- Access the OMIM, a commonly used online database of human genetic diseases and other traits.
- Based on a knowledge of genetics, propose a possible explanation (hypothesis generation) and formulate a simple test (experimental design).
- Read a scientific paper to access information relevant to a specific question.

### Quantitative Reasoning Skills/Concepts

- Carry out basic mathematical operations.
- Use graphs to formulate predictions and explanations.
- Use numerical evidence to formulate null and alternative hypotheses.
- Accept or reject null hypotheses based on statistical tests of significance.

- Articulate complete and correct claims based on data.
- Use appropriate reasoning to support the validity of data-based claims.
- Create and interpret Punnett squares.
- Interpret the results of DNA analysis.
- Create and analyze family pedigrees.
- Create experimental designs to test hypotheses.

## The Case Study

### *Part I: The Meeting*

Sarah stared blankly at the blue paisley wallpaper. Her husband Mike sat by her side, bending and unbending a small paper clip.

"Sarah and Michael, it's good to meet you," welcomed the genetic counselor, as she entered the room. "I apologize for being late, but I was just meeting with another couple. Let's see, you'd like to have a child, but you're concerned because of your family history of cystic fibrosis."

"Yes," Sarah replied softly. "Mike and I met at a CF support group meeting a few years ago. He had a younger brother who died of cystic fibrosis, and I had a younger sister. We saw the painful lives they had—difficulty breathing, the constant respiratory infections. Although the treatments for CF are better now, we just don't know if we can...," she trailed off.

"I can certainly understand your concern," the genetic counselor responded sympathetically. "That's where I hope to help, by providing as much information and advice as I can. I'm glad that you came to see me before you became pregnant so I can fully advise you of all options beforehand."

"To start, let's go over what we know about your case so far," continued the genetic counselor. She pulled out a pad of paper, which she placed on the table in front of Sarah and Michael, and began to draw a series of circles and squares connected by lines. "As I recall, both sets of parents did not display any of the symptoms of cystic fibrosis, right?"

"Yes," said Sarah and Michael in unison.

"OK, well that means ...," said the counselor.

### Questions

1. Which organs are affected by cystic fibrosis? What are the disease symptoms?
2. Draw a pedigree showing the family history for CF in Sarah's and Michael's families. Be sure to distinguish between individuals with the disease, those that

are carriers for the disease, and individuals who do not possess a copy of the disease allele.

## *Part II: Punnett Squares*

"So, what's next?" asked Mike.

"First, we'll collect DNA samples from both of you," said the counselor. "We'll then analyze your CF genes for the most common mutations to see if you are carriers for this recessive genetic disease."

A few weeks later, the genetic counselor welcomed back Sarah and Mike. "We've received the results of your genetic tests for common CF mutations. Michael, you're a carrier of the most common disease allele, delta-F508, and Sarah, you tested negative for the most common CF mutations."

"Thank goodness," Sarah replied with relief. "That means it's safe for us to have a child, right?"

"Not exactly," cautioned the genetic counselor.

### Questions

1. Construct a Punnett square to demonstrate why Sarah concluded that she and Michael could not have an affected child (assuming that she does not carry a CF mutation).
2. If Sarah were a carrier, what would be the chance that she and Michael would have an affected child? Show the Punnett square.

## *Part III: CFTR Mutations*

"Since Sarah tested negative for CF, it seems we don't have much to worry about, right?" said Michael, pointing to the pedigree in which Sarah is not a carrier. "So, what did you mean when you said not exactly?"

The genetic counselor grabbed her laptop computer and positioned it in front of the three of them. Her fingers quickly typed out a web address and the words "OMIM—Online Mendelian Inheritance of Man" stretched across the browser window.

"We can learn a lot more about this disease from this site. It will begin to explain why I said not exactly when Sarah asked if it was safe to conceive a child."

### Questions

The Online Mendelian Inheritance of Man (OMIM) is a catalog of known human genetic diseases. Go to OMIM at *www.ncbi.nlm.nih.gov/sites/entrez?db=OMIM* and search with the keyword "cystic fibrosis." Examine the OMIM record entitled "cystic fibrosis transmembrane conductance regulator."

1. Look closely at the section on "Allelic Variants." Is the delta-F508 mutation the only known alteration of the CFTR gene?
2. As you look at the list of Allelic Variants (starting with .001), how does the information in brackets (e.g., [CFTR, PHE508DEL]) describe each mutation?
3. The CFTR gene contains how many exons? How many introns? Sketch a rough diagram of the exon/intron structure of the CFTR gene.
4. For each mutation (allelic variant) listed below, explain how the mutation would affect the production of (1) the mRNA and (2) the protein encoded by the CFTR gene. As an example, the first case is completed for you below.
   - .0001 CYSTIC FIBROSIS [CFTR, PHE508DEL]

   The 508th triplet codon, which normally codes for phenylalanine, is deleted. Consequently, the CFTR mRNA is 3 nucleotides shorter than normal, and the CFTR protein is one amino acid shorter, missing its 508th unit.

   - .0003 CYSTIC FIBROSIS [CFTR, GLN493TER]
   - .0004 CYSTIC FIBROSIS [CFTR, ASP110HIS]
   - .0019 CYSTIC FIBROSIS [CFTR, 2-BP INS, 2566AT]
   - .0008 CYSTIC FIBROSIS [CFTR, IVS10, G-A, -1]
   - .0064 CYSTIC FIBROSIS [CFTR, IVS12, G-A, +1]
   - .0123 CYSTIC FIBROSIS [CFTR, 21-KB DEL]
5. Sarah wondered how all these different mutations can cause the same disease. As the genetic counselor, how would you explain this to Sarah and Michael?

## *Part IV: The Test*

Sarah and Michael looked confused.

"But ..." Michael started to say.

"How can the test say I'm not a carrier, but you say that I could still be a carrier?" Sarah finished.

The counselor pursed her lips and said, "Well, because of cost, no test is as comprehensive as we would like. This research article describes the genetic test used to determine your CF genotypes and explains its limitations," she continued, handing them a printed article.

### Questions

Read the research article by Strom et al. (2006) to learn about the test used for CF genotyping, and then answer the questions.

1. How many different mutations had been found in the CFTR gene when this article was written?
2. How many of these CFTR mutations can be detected by the Tag-It CFTR 40 + 4 Luminex-based reagent system from Tm Biosciences?
3. What criteria did researchers use when determining which mutations to include in the Tag-It test?
4. What is the chance that Sarah is actually a carrier for a CFTR mutation, even though her Tag-It test results came back negative?
5. As the genetic counselor, explain to Sarah and Michael why you said "not exactly" when Sarah asked if it was safe to conceive a child.

## *Part V: Further Analysis*

After hearing the counselor explain the limitations of the test that was used, Sarah and Michael discussed whether to receive further testing. While the cost was significantly more, they felt the added knowledge would help them make an informed decision and so they elected to have Sarah's DNA further analyzed. A week later they met again with the genetic counselor to discuss the test result.

"So do I have a mutation in my CF gene?" asked Sarah

"Not exactly," the genetic counselor replied. "You have a mutation in the region just before the part of the gene that codes for the CF protein. You might want to recall some of your introductory biology lessons, as it will get a little technical here."

### Questions

First let's examine a more comprehensive catalog of known CFTR mutations found at the Cystic Fibrosis Mutation Database at *www.genet.sickkids.on.ca/Home.html* under "Statistics."

1. Are there any mutation types that you haven't seen previously? Which? What are some of the potential effects that they could have on protein expression?
2. Under "CFTR Gene," choose "Genomic DNA Sequence." Compare the image with the sketch of the CFTR gene structure that you prepared for Question 4 in Part III of the case. How are they similar? How do they differ?

The subsequent analysis of Sarah's sample determined the DNA sequence of the CFTR introns and the regions upstream and downstream of the exons. The DNA sequence indicates that Sarah has a single base pair difference about 100 bases before the ATG start codon of the CFTR gene.

1. How might this mutation cause CF?
2. How could you test your hypothesis?

Now let's look at a scientific paper that examines a CFTR promoter variant. Although the paper is more advanced (and contains grammatical errors), we can still distill some useful information relevant to understanding Sarah's CFTR mutation. Examine the following research paper and answer the questions that follow.

> Taulan et al., 2007. First functional polymorphism in CFTR promoter that results in decreased transcriptional activity and Sp1/USF binding. *Biochemical and Biophysical Research Communications* 361: 775–781.

3. Looking at the abstract and introduction, what hypothesis did the authors wish to test?

In their first experiment, the authors joined the wild-type (WT) or -94 mutant (M) CFTR promoter to the luciferase reporter gene. They then tested the transcription levels of each fusion gene in three different cell lines.

4. Examining Figure 1A in the article, does the mutation affect the transcription levels of this gene? Explain.
5. As the genetic counselor, explain fully to Sarah and Michael how this mutation before the protein-coding gene raises the possibility that they could have a child with cystic fibrosis.

## *Part VI: The Final Decision*

While the discussion about the implications of the mutation Sarah harbored was complicated, the young couple was able to grasp the essential elements. The counselor summed up the discussion when she said, "Well, I'm disappointed to inform you that a future child of yours could have cystic fibrosis."

Both Michael and Sarah were visibly upset, but the counselor continued, "But you do still have some options. After natural or in vitro conception, we could test any embryos to determine the genotype, and then you could choose not to proceed with the pregnancy if needed."

"What are we going to do?" asked Sarah and Michael to each other.

### Question

1. If you were Sarah or Michael, what would you choose to do? Why?
   a. Not have children.
   b. Adopt children.
   c. Get pregnant and continue with the pregnancy no matter what.
   d. Get pregnant, test the embryo within 9 weeks via chorionic villus sampling (CVS), and terminate if the embryo has CF.
   e. Undergo in vitro fertilization by harvesting eggs, fertilizing them, and screening the embryos for CF prior to implantation.

## Web Version

Detailed teaching notes, the case PDF, and an answer key are available on the NCCSTS website at *sciencecases.lib.buffalo.edu/cs/collection/detail.asp?case_id=564&id=564.*

## References

Cystic Fibrosis Mutation Database. Cystic Fibrosis Centre, Hospital for Sick Children, Toronto, Canada. *www.genet.sickkids.on.ca/Home.html*

Online Mendelian Inheritance of Man. National Center for Biotechnology Information. *www.ncbi.nlm.nih.gov/sites/entrez?db=OMIM*

Strom, C. M., R. Janeszco, F. Quan, W. Sheng-biao, A. Buller, M. McGinniss, and W. Sun. 2006. Technical validation of a Tm Biosciences luminex-based multiplex assay for detecting the American College of Medical Genetics recommended cystic fibrosis mutation panel. *Journal of Molecular Diagnostics* 8: 371–375.

Taulan, M., E. Lopez, C. Guittard, C. René, D. Baux, J. P. Altieri, M. DesGeorges, M. Claustres, and M. C. Romey. 2007. First functional polymorphism in CFTR promoter that results in decreased transcriptional activity and Sp1/USF binding. *Biochemical and Biophysical Research Communications* 361: 775–781.

CHAPTER 25

# THE CASE OF THE DRUID DRACULA

*Peggy Brickman*

## Abstract

Based on a real crime that was featured on the BBC television program *Crimewatch* in December 2001, this case teaches students about how the structure of DNA and the mechanism used by cells to duplicate is used in forensic analysis. They then determine the statistical validity of the forensic data in the same way a prosecutor would prepare a case for the courtroom.


## Learning Objectives

- Understand the similarities and differences in the DNA of humans and how those differences can be exploited for forensic identification.
- Understand the structure of DNA and how hydrogen bonds between the nucleotide bases dictate the complementary nature of the double helix. Students will be able to predict the nucleotide sequence of one strand of DNA in a double helix if given its complementary strand.
- Describe the technique of polymerase chain reaction (PCR) and relate it to the normal cellular process of DNA replication. Students will be able to predict the sequence of PCR primers that would amplify just one short stretch of DNA out of an entire genome.
- Understand how short tandem repeats (STRs) within human chromosomes can be used to generate fingerprints and how to interpret these fingerprints to match the DNA to a specific person.
- Use statistical prevalence of STRs to determine the probability that someone else at random in the population could have DNA that matched a sample found at a crime scene.

## Quantitative Reasoning Skills/Concepts

- Carry out basic mathematical operations.

- Articulate complete and correct claims based on data.
- Explore DNA analysis.
- Explore electrophoresis analysis.

## The Case Study

### *Part I: DNA Structure and PCR*

In the northernmost corner of the Isle of Anglesey in Wales in a village called Llanfairpwll, the windswept beaches and ancient Druid ruins provided a surreal backdrop for the murder of 90-year-old Mabel Leyshon. Her murder was not only brutal (her heart had been cut out), but also creepy; it appeared as if the killer had collected Mabel's blood in a small kitchen saucepan that had lip marks on the rim, indicating the contents had been tasted. The murder showed other signs of the occult: a candlestick and a pair of crossed pokers had been arranged near the body. Further investigation however indicated that this was no supernatural villain at work. The murderer had worn tennis shoes, which had left distinctive footprints under the glass door that had been shattered with a piece of broken garden slate in order to gain entrance to the victim's home. Inside the house, a windowsill had bloodstains on it. With luck, the evidence recovery unit hoped to use it to find the killer.

### Questions

1. DNA differences can be used to identify people. For example, there is a gene found on both the X and Y chromosomes called amelogenin, but the version of the gene found on the X and Y chromosomes differs in length, so it can be used to tell if a blood stain, such as the one found on the windowsill inside Mable Lyshon's house, was left by a man or woman. This stretch of nucleotides shows one strand of the DNA double helix for the amelogenin gene:

   5'CCCTGGGCTCTGTAAAGAATAGTGTGTTGATTCTTTATCCCAGATGTTTCTAAGTG3'

   What is the sequence of the other complementary strand? Choose the correct answer below.

   a. 3'ACTGTTAGATTTCCCTTTTTAGGTCTAGGTCCGTCGGCCTTATTTCCGAGGAATAA5'
   b. 3'GGGACCCGAGACATTTCTTATCACACAACTAAGAAATAGGGTTTACAAAGATTCAC5'
   c. 5'GGGACCCGAGACATTTCTTATCACACAACTAAGAAATAGGGTTTACAAAGATTCAC3'
   d. 3'CCCTGGGCTCTGTAAAGAATAGTGTGTTGATTCTTTATCCCAGATGTTTCTAAGTG5'
   e. 5'CCCTGGGCTCTGTAAAGAATAGTGTGTTGATTCTTTATCCCAGATGTTTCTAAGTG3'

2. To assist the investigators with the crime, you will need to perform Polymerase Chain Reaction (PCR) to create copies of this gene so the sizes can be compared to determine if the blood was from a man or woman. During PCR it will be necessary to break the hydrogen bonds of the base pairs. Where are those hydrogen bonds normally found?
    a. Between two nitrogen-containing bases in a single strand of DNA.
    b. Between the phosphate and sugar of the same nucleotide.
    c. Between the sugar of one nucleotide and the phosphate of a different nucleotide.
    d. Between one nitrogen-containing base on a single strand of DNA and another nitrogen-containing base on the complementary strand of DNA.
    e. Between one phosphate on a single strand of DNA and a sugar on the complementary strand of DNA.
3. PCR creates copies of DNA using the exact same mechanism used by your cells to copy their own DNA (replication). Place the steps listed below in the order in which they occur during replication:
    a. Two strands, one new and one original template, wind together to form the double helix.
    b. Short stretch of primer (~20 nucleotides exactly complementary to the gene that is going to be copied) is made.
    c. Separation of the double helix from two parental DNA strands.
    d. Use of parental DNA as a template so that nucleotides are covalently bonded together to form a new chain that is complementary to the bases on the original template.

        (i) A, B, C, D

        (ii) B, C, A, D

        (iii) D, B, C, A

        (iv) C, B, D, A
4. PCR can be used to selectively duplicate one single gene out of thousands because the only primers available to start replication are the one unique pair that is complementary to the regions on both sides of the gene. Which of these primers below (one for each strand) could you use to copy just the stretch (in bold type) of the amelogenin gene that differs between the X and Y chromosomes?

3’GGGACCCGAGACATTTCTTATCAC**ACAACTAAGAAATAGGGTCTACAAAGAGTTCACCAGG**
**ACTTTACAGTTCCTACCAC**CAGCTTCCCAGTTTAAGCTCTGAT5’

5′CCCTGGGCTCTGTAAAGAATAGTG**TGTTGATTCTTTATCCCAGATGTTTCTCAAGTGGTCCT GAAATGTCAAGGATGGTG**GTCGAAGGGTCAAATTCGAGACTA3′

a. 3′GGGACCCGAGACATTTCTTATCAC5′ and 5′CCCTGGGCTCTGTAAAGAATAGTG3′

b. 5′CCCTGGGCTCTGTAAAGAATAGTG3′ and 5′GTCGAAGGGTCAAATTCGAGACTA3′

c. 5′CCCTGGGCTCTGTAAAGAATAGTG3′ and 3′CAGCTTCCCAGTTTAAGCTCTGAT5′

## *Part II: The Report*

The results are shown in Figure 25.1.

**FIGURE 25.1.**

Electrophoresis of PCR Products Fom the Amelogenin Gene.

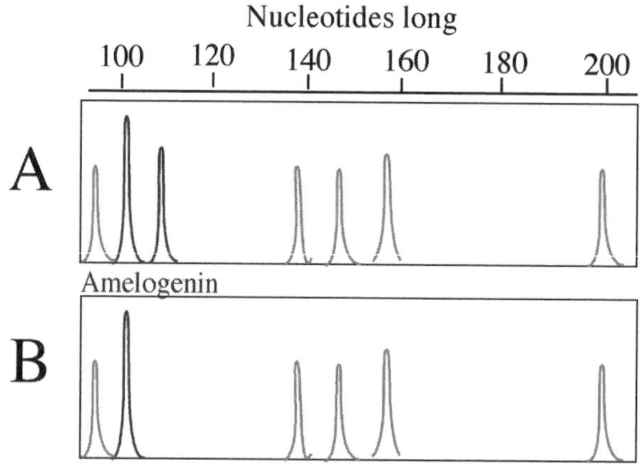


### Question

1. Which of the above (A or B) represents the profile of a man?

## *Part III: More Analysis*

The crime was featured on BBC's *Crimewatch* program in December 2001 and North Wales Police received over 200 calls. Following up on reports of a teenager who had attacked a German student, the police went to the home of Matthew Hardman (suspect 1), who gave police a cheek swab. During this visit, officers found a pair of Levi shoes. Forensic Science Service (FSS) scientists matched Hardman's shoes to the footwear marks found at the murder scene.

Profiling suggested a much older offender, so another suspect was also asked to give a cheek swab (suspect 2). Since both suspects were men, the officers needed to test for other genetic differences. They focused on STRs (short tandem repeats), stretches of DNA that exist in all people, but in different numbers of repeats. The allele ladder in Figure 25.2 shows all varieties in a population.

**FIGURE 25.2.**

DNA Footprinting Analysis of Evidence From the Crime Scene.

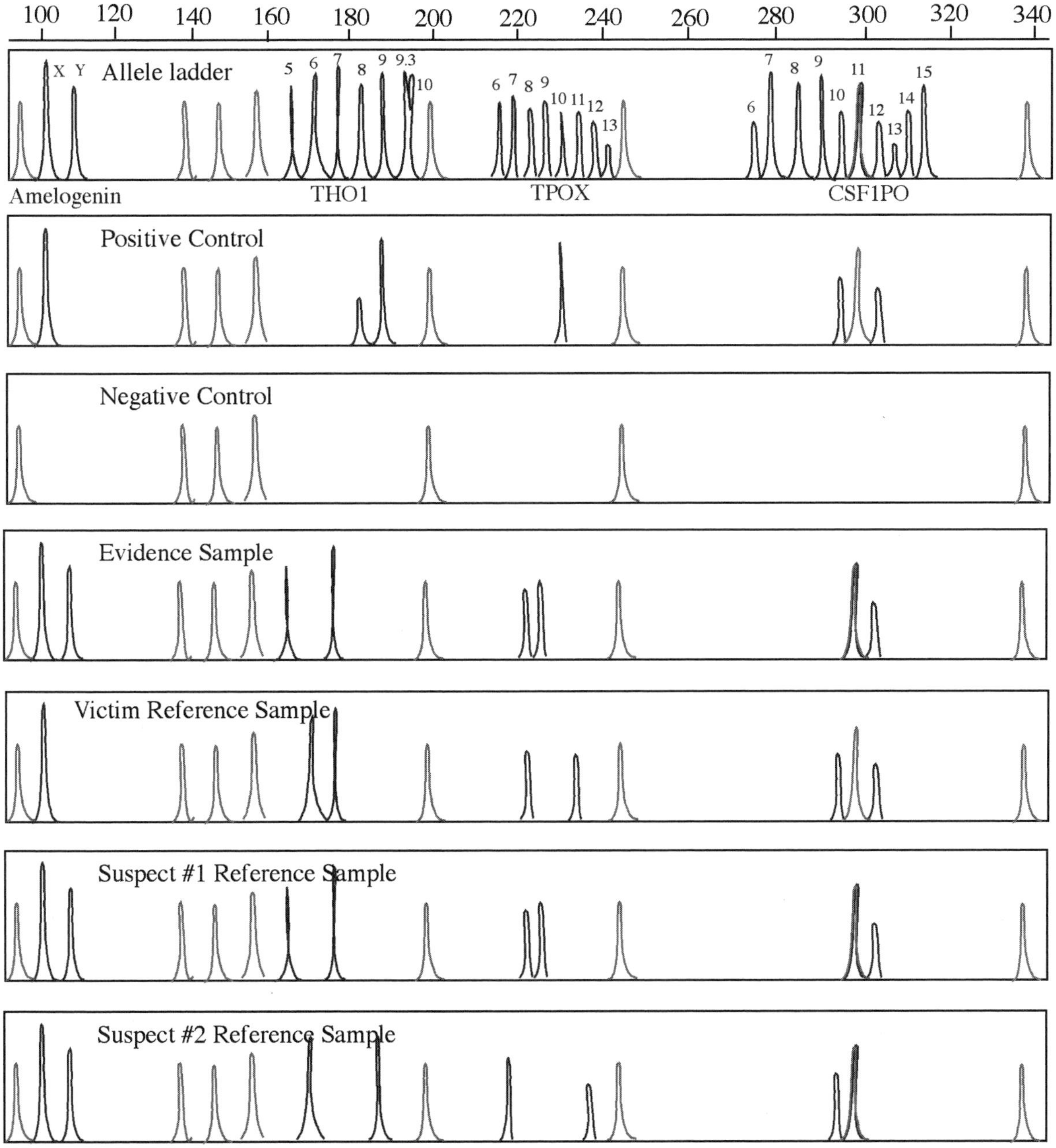

## Questions

1. Which suspect presents a profile compatible to the sample found at the crime scene?
    a. Suspect #1
    b. Suspect #2
2. There are only a few different numbers of repeats that are seen in our population—only 5 different TPOX STRS for example. By testing thousands of DNA samples, researchers know the distribution of these different STRS in the general population; those allele frequencies are shown in Table 25.1. Using these frequencies, one can determine the probability that someone else at random would have the same matching pattern. For example, what is the likelihood that someone else at random would have the same pattern of Matthew Hardman (a 5 and 7 repeat for the THO1 STR)?
    a. 1/200
    b. 1/206
    c. 1/600
    d. 1/1200
    e. 1/2600
3. What is the probability that someone else at random would have that same pattern of THO1 5 & 7, TPOX 8 & 9 and CSF1PO 11 & 12?
    a. 1/1600
    b. 1/1800
    c. 1/4800
    d. 1/121,600
    e. 1/43,200

**TABLE 25.1.**

Allele Frequencies for Common DNA Footprinting Markers.

| THO1 | | TPOX | | CSF1PO | |
|---|---|---|---|---|---|
| **5**: | 1/200 | **8**: | 1/2 | **9**: | 1/40 |
| **6**: | 1/4 | **9**: | 1/8 | **10**: | 1/5 |
| **7**: | 1/6 | **10**: | 1/18 | **11**: | 1/3 |
| **8**: | 1/7 | **11**: | 1/5 | **12**: | 1/3 |
| **9**: | 1/6 | **12**: | 1/20 | **13**: | 1/10 |
| **9.3**: | 1/3 | | | **14**: | 1/50 |
| **10**: | 1/100 | | | | |

## Web Version

Detailed teaching notes, the case PDF, and an answer key are available on the NCCSTS website at *sciencecases.lib.buffalo.edu/cs/collection/detail.asp?case_id=492&id=492.*

CHAPTER 26

# WHICH LITTLE PIGGY WENT TO MARKET?

## Bioinformatics and Meat Science

*Debra A. Meuler*

## Abstract

This case is based on a paper by Meer and Eddinger (1996) describing how one day their lab received a phone call from a local meat packing plant posing the very problem stated in the case. The case introduces students to basic genetics concepts, DNA structure, the technique of PCR, genetic databases, and the use of positive and negative controls during scientific investigations. It also teaches students the steps in the scientific process, from developing hypotheses to designing experiments and analyzing and interpreting data.


## Learning Objectives

- Gain experience in how science is done.
- Practice designing experiments.
- Analyze, interpret, and draw conclusions based on real data.
- Learn about polymerase chain reaction.
- Identify differences between the sexes and the genetic basis of sex determination.
- Become familiar with bioinformatics and genetic databases.

## Quantitative Reasoning Skills/Concepts

- Articulate complete and correct claims based on data.
- Use appropriate reasoning to support the validity of data-based claims.
- Create experimental designs to test hypotheses.
- Explore DNA analysis.
- Explore electrophoresis analysis.

## The Case Study

### *Part I: Pigs Is Pigs?*

Sue was busy doing what scientists do most of the time. She was waiting for something to happen. In this case the "what" was a sequencing gel. The phone rang. It was an old friend of hers currently working at the meat processing plant in town. He had a problem for her. He needed a way to determine if the pork he was using to make a new gourmet sausage came solely from gilts.

"Why do you care?" Sue asked. "What difference does it make what sex the meat came from? Pig meat by any other name is still pig meat."

"Not really," John replied. "Boar meat has a definite very disagreeable odor. The phenomenon is called boar taint. Having boar meat in the mix isn't a problem if you're making a product that is heavily spiced. The spices cover it up. But this new sausage recipe I'm working with has very few spices."

"I see what you mean. Having my breakfast smell bad doesn't sound too appetizing."

"My company pays top dollar for gilt meat," John continued. "But this last batch had a funny smell. I think it has some boar in it. I have no way of knowing if the distributor is cheating me. That's why I called you. I need a reliable, quick, and sensitive way to check if the meat that I'm receiving contains any boar meat."

Sue heard the timer go off telling her that the sequencing gel was done. She needed to finish the experiment and get the gel under film as soon as possible. John's problem would have to wait.

"Listen, John, I have to finish up some work here at the lab. But I'll call you back later and we can talk about it."

Sue got home late that night and decided to wait until the next afternoon to call John.

#### Questions

1. What is the specific problem John is asking Sue to help him with?
2. What information would Sue need to know before trying to solve the problem?

### *Part II: Boar Taint*

Sue's thoughts kept returning to John's problem throughout the day. She knew very little about pigs—only that she liked her brats boiled in beer and served with sauerkraut. She decided to do some research on boar taint on the internet before she called John the next day.

#### Questions

1. What is the difference between a gilt, a sow, a barrow, and a boar?

2. What causes boar taint?
3. What are some methods of detecting the chemicals causing boar taint in pork?
4. In mammals, how are males different from females?

## *Part III: Test Wanted*

The next day Sue called John. "Hi, it's me, Sue. I did some research last night on boar odor. I had no idea this was such a problem in the pork industry."

"Yeah," said John. Sue noticed he sounded a little tired. "There are a couple of research groups trying to figure out how to lower or eliminate the chemicals responsible for causing the odor. There are benefits in using intact males instead of barrows, namely lower feed costs and the meat is leaner. But the problem is that the meat stinks, literally."

"Isn't there some biochemical test you could use to detect for levels of skatole and 16 androsterone steroids in the meat?" asked Sue.

"Sure," said John. "I could send out samples of the meat and have a lab run it through a gas chromatograph or have an ELISA performed on it. But I want a test that is quick and sensitive."

"Well, let me think about it. I'll call you in a couple of days," said Sue.

"Thanks. I appreciate your help."

### Questions

1. Design an experiment that will show the presence of boar meat in a mixed sample, keeping in mind that biochemical tests are too slow and relatively insensitive.

## *Part IV: Sue's Solution*

Sue began to think about how she might detect the presence of boar meat in a mixed sample. Assaying for skatoles and male steroids was out since they can also be found in female tissue. She asked herself what else makes male tissue different from female tissue. Sue suddenly remembered her genetics. The one thing males have that females don't is the Y chromosome. She could use the presence of some gene on the Y chromosome as a marker for boar meat. The problem would be to detect the specific DNA. She then remembered her favorite television program—*CSI: Crime Scene Investigation*. She could use PCR to amplify the DNA. DNA is very stable. Even if the meat had been sitting around for a while or been cooked, there should be enough DNA to run a PCR amplification producing enough DNA to detect on a gel. Once you have the primer, PCR is relatively quick and moderately inexpensive.

### Questions

1. Generally, what genes are found on the Y chromosome?

2. Has the swine sex-determining gene on the Y chromosome been sequenced? Go to GenBank at *www.ncbi.nlm.nih.gov/entrez/query* to determine this. Select "nucleotide" and then enter "swine SRY gene." If the sequence is present, print a copy of it.
3. How does PCR work? What is the role of each item listed below in the process?
    a. Taq polymerase
    b. Primers
    c. Temperature cycling
4. How are primers selected and made?

## *Part V: Success?*

After finding the swine sex-determining region gene at GenBank, Sue selected two sequences to act as primers. She sent the sequence to a company in California and had them make the primers for her. Both primers should create a fragment 158 base pairs long. She ran a PCR reaction on samples of boar and sow meat as well as a mixture of both. The results are shown in Figure 26.1.

**FIGURE 26.1.**

Identification of Unique Sex-Determining Region Y Gene in Male Tissue.

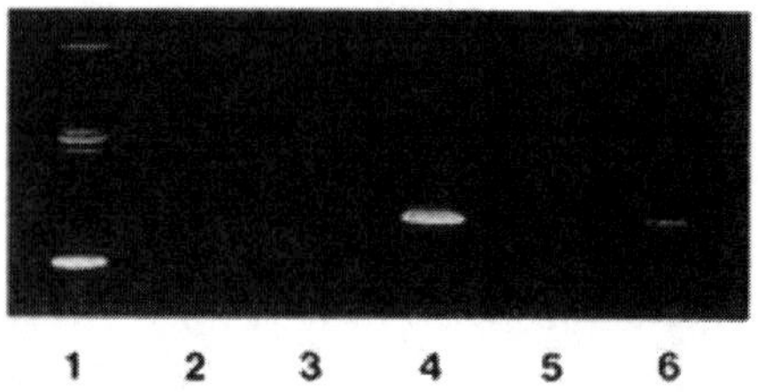


Presence of 158 bp sex-specific fragment from male tissue or sausage containing male tissue on 8% polyacrylamide gel. Lane 1: 123 bp DNA ladder, 123, 246, and 369 bp fragments from bottom to top. Lane 2: DNA omitted from the PCR reaction. Lane 3: Primers were omitted from the PCR. Lane 4: 158 bp fragment following pcr of boar tissue. Lane 5: PCR of sow tissue. Lane 6: PCR of sausage sample containing some male tissue.

## Questions

1. What do you conclude from Figure 26.1?
2. Why were lanes 1, 2, 3, 5, and 6 included in this experiment?

Sue was excited. The PCR amplification worked. She could detect the presence of the sex-determining gene in samples of boar meat but not in sow. She also saw the same size band after PCR of a sausage sample containing both boar and sow. Sue remembered that John needed a sensitive assay. She next wanted to know the sensitivity of her assay.

## Questions

1. Why does Sue want to know the sensitivity of her assay?
2. Figure 26.2 illustrates the results of such an experiment. What do you conclude from this figure?
3. Why were lanes 2, 3, and 4 included in this experiment?

**FIGURE 26.2.**

Sensitivity of PCR Reaction for Identifying Male Tissue in Mixed Tissue Samples.
Eight percent polyacrylamide gel showing bands from tissue samples using PCR following serial

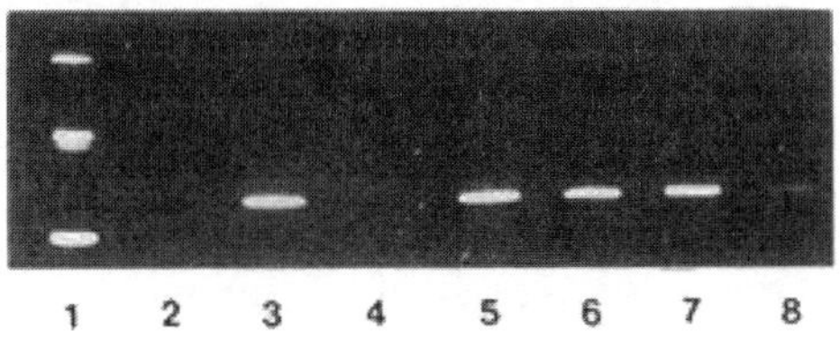


dilution. Lane 1: 123 bp DNA ladder; 123, 246, and 369 bp fragments from bottom to top. Lane 2: DNA omitted from PCR reaction. Lane 3: 158 bp fragment following PCR from boar muscle. Lane 4: PCR of sow muscle. Lanes 5–8: Boar muscle DNA diluted with sow muscle DNA at 1:10, 1:100, 1:1000, and 1:10,000 prior to PCR, respectively.

Sue was getting even more excited. Her calculations indicated that the sensitivity of her assay was down to a dilution of boar meat to sow meat of at least 1:10,000. She had one more question to answer before she could call John. She needed to know if processing the meat would affect the efficacy of PCR amplification of the swine sex-determining gene.

## Questions

1. Figure 26.3 (p. 250) illustrates the effect of spices and cooking on the efficacy of PCR to amplify the sex-determining gene. What can you conclude from this figure?
2. When Sue calls John with her results, do you think she has solved John's problem? Why or why not?

**FIGURE 26.3.**

Lack of Effect of Spices or Cooking on Efficacy of PCR to Amplify Male-Specific Region of DNA.

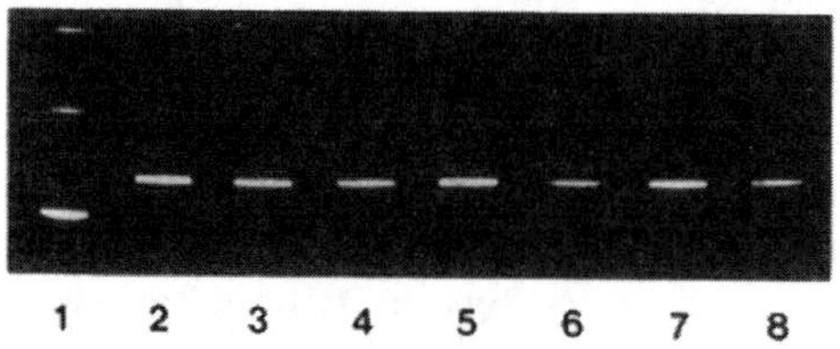


Eight percent polyacrylamide gel. Lane 1: 123 bp DNA ladder; 123, 246 and 369 bp fragments from bottom to top. Lane 2: 158 bp DNA fragment PCR amplified from male muscle sample. Lanes 3, 5, and 7 are from frozen boar muscle. Lanes 4, 6 and 8 are frozen bratwurst samples make with a mixture of boar and sow tissue. Lanes 3 and 4, samples cooked to 50°C for 15 min prior to PCR. Lanes 5 and 6, samples cooked to 70°C for 15 min prior to PCR. Lanes 7 and 8, samples cooked to 100°C for 15 min prior to PCR.

## *Assignment*

Your assignment is to write an abstract (summary) of Sue's results.

## Web Version

Detailed teaching notes (including a copy of the swine SRY gene sequence), the case PDF, and an answer key are available on the NCCSTS website at *sciencecases.lib.buffalo.edu/cs/collection/detail.asp?case_id=221&id=221*.

## References

GenBank. National Center for Biotechnology Information, National Institutes of Health. *www.ncbi.nlm.nih.gov*

Meer, D., and T. Eddinger. 1996. Polymerase chain reaction for detection of male tissue in pork products. *Meat Science* 44 (4): 285–291.

# CLASSIC EXPERIMENTS IN MOLECULAR BIOLOGY

*Robin Pals-Rylaarsdam*

## Abstract

This case study takes students through two classic experiments in molecular biology, namely, those by Griffith, Avery, McCarty, and MacLeod, which showed DNA to be the genetic material in *Streptococcus pneumoniae*, and the experiment by Meselson and Stahl, which demonstrated DNA replication to be semiconservative, as a way of reinforcing for students the nature of scientific discovery and the logic behind these findings.


## Learning Objectives

- Accurately describe the experiments performed by each group, observations made, and conclusions drawn.
- Articulate several possible outcomes/hypotheses for a given experiment, select the outcome that best fits the data collected, and explain why the other hypotheses are rejected in light of the data.
- Accurately answer questions regarding the evidence for semiconservative replication and the evidence for DNA being the genetic material in *E. coli.*

## Quantitative Reasoning Skills/Concepts

- Analyze and interpret qualitative experimental data, including sedimentation patterns in centrifugation experiments and mouse survival following various treatments with bacterial preparations.

## The Case Study

## Experiment #1: The Transforming Principle—Identifying the Molecule of Inheritance

### *Part I: Molecule of Inheritance*

If there is inheritance of traits from parents to children, or from "mother cell" to "daughter cells" in mitosis, then some*thing* must be passed from parent to child. We know today that this *thing* is DNA, in the form of chromosomes. However, someone needed to figure that out.

In the 1930s and 1940s, scientists were very interested in identifying the biochemical nature of the "transforming principle." The candidate molecules were DNA, RNA, and protein. These molecules were candidates because we knew that nuclei contained chromosomes, which are associated with phenotypes (think Morgan's fruit fly eye color experiments where eye color corresponded to the X- or Y-chromosome content of the fly cells), and isolated nuclei are composed mostly of protein, DNA, and RNA. Most scientists at the time were leaning toward protein being the genetic material because it is the most molecularly diverse of the three.

The investigations into the chemical nature of genetic material were initiated by one very important paper from 1928, written by Fred Griffith at the British Ministry of Health. Griffith was studying the bacterium *Streptococcus pneumoniae*, an important pathogen in the 1920s.

### Questions

1. Why would studying *S. pneumoniae* be an important topic in the 1920s? Some forms of *S. pneumoniae* cause disease (pneumonia), others don't. When grown on a laboratory plate, you can make a good guess about the pathogenicity (disease causing ability) of *S. pneumoniae* because *pathogenic* strains look shiny (smooth) due to a polysaccharide cell coat called a capsule. The capsule helps the bacteria "hide" from the immune system long enough to cause disease. *Nonpathogenic* strains lack the capsule and appear "rough" on a Petri plate. Generally these colonies are smaller, too.
2. Griffith used mice as his species for detecting the pathogenicity of the bacteria. Injecting mice with bacteria grown on petri plates either made the mice sick and killed them, or produced no disease. Fill in the diagram in Figure 27.1 below the mice predicting what you think will happen as a result of each injection (mice live or mice die).

**FIGURE 27.1.**

Predict What Griffith Will See in His Experiment.

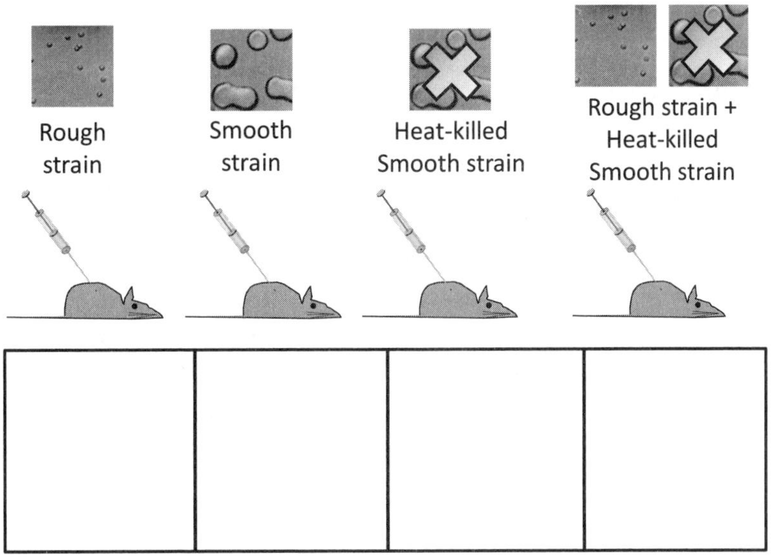


### *Part II: Results*

Figure 27.2 shows the actual results of the experiment.

**FIGURE 27.2.**

Griffith's Results.

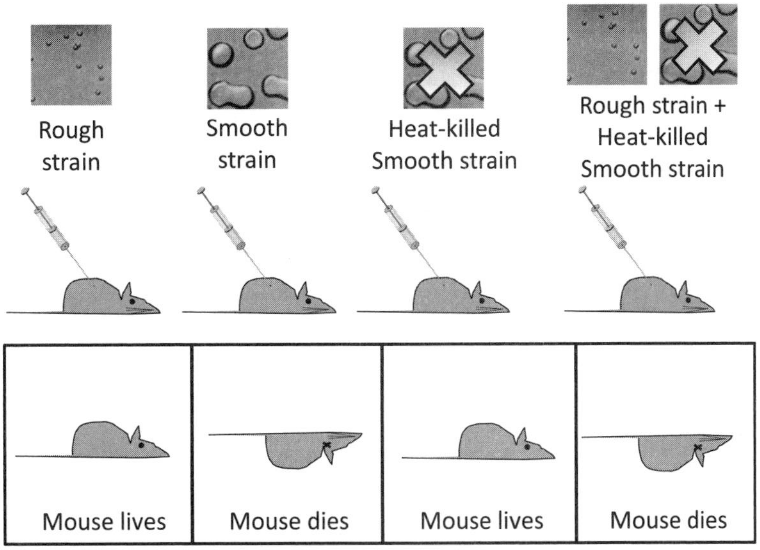

## Questions

1. Which of the four treatments are controls? Explain your answer.
2. Which of the results is unexpected?
3. What are *two* hypotheses that might explain the unexpected result? In other words, what might be going on in the system?

### *Part III: Enzymes as Tools*

The properties of the rough strain are its *phenotype*. In the experiment you just read about, the *phenotype* of the living rough strain changed from nonpathogenic to pathogenic. Scientists proposed that it changed because the *genotype* changed. The next set of experiments started with the hypothesis that the *genotype change* was due to some extra genetic material being added to the rough bacteria to change their *phenotype* to a smooth phenotype. The group of scientists who did the next set of experiments consisted of Oswald Avery, Colin MacLeod, and Maclyn McCarty. Their paper was published in 1944. These scientists had three tools to use in their experiments (in addition to the smooth and rough strains, and mice): (1) Protease, (2) DNase, and (3) RNase. All three of these tools are enzymes, as you can guess because their names end in "ase."

## Questions

1. Given the names of these three enzymes, what reaction do you expect each one to catalyze? Write your answers for each enzyme in the spaces provided below in Table 27.1.

**TABLE 27.1.**

Avery, McCarty, and MacLeod's Experimental Tools.

| Enzyme | Chemical Reaction Catalyzed |
|---|---|
| Protease | |
| DNase | |
| RNase | |

2. How could you treat dead smooth bacteria with these enzymes to determine whether DNA, RNA, or protein is the genetic material?

## *Part IV: More Results*

The scientists treated heat-killed smooth bacteria with either RNase, Protease, or DNase, then combined that reaction with living rough bacteria and injected mice with the mixture. The results are shown in Figure 27.3.

**FIGURE 27.3.**

Avery, McCarty, and MacLeod's Results.

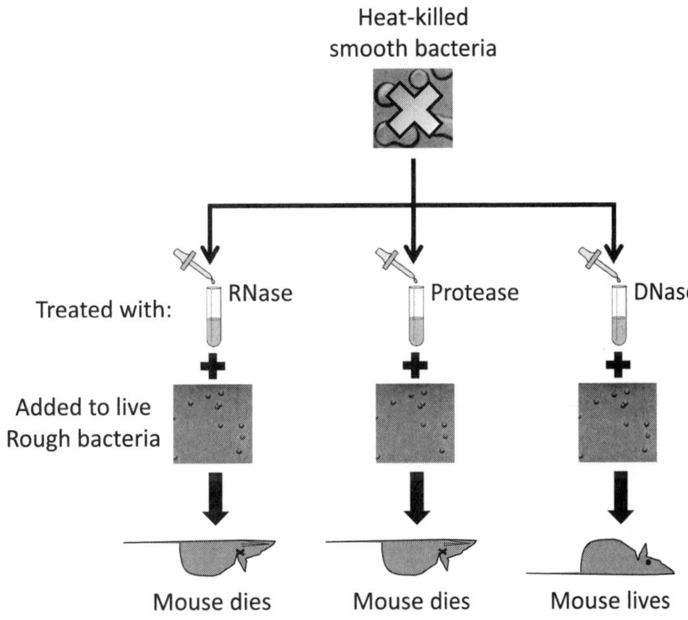


### Question

1. What conclusion can be drawn from these data?

## *Take-Home Assignment*

Address the following using a well-constructed essay paragraph. If you use diagrams, you must have text to thoroughly explain the diagrams rather than just drawing a picture.

*Describe the experiments by Griffith, Avery, McCarty, and McLeod that determined the role for DNA as the genetic material (include the logic behind the experiment).*

## Experiment #2: Meselson and Stahl Experiment—The Nature of DNA Replication

### *Part I: Three Possibilities*

How did you spend New Year's Day this year? In 1958, Matthew Meselson and Frank Stahl celebrated the first day of the new year by having breakfast with college friends in Chicago and passing a photograph around the table, not of a girlfriend or a new baby, but of the data behind what is sometimes called the "most elegant experiment in molecular biology"—the experiment that first demonstrated how DNA replication occurs (Judson 1996, p. 612). Others followed (and won Nobel prizes too) by giving us details about the enzymes involved, but Meselson and Stahl's experiment is so important and well designed that it has become necessary knowledge for one to be called an educated biologist.

Figure 27.4 shows three different possibilities for DNA replication. Only one really happens, but until Meselson and Stahl conducted their experiment, each of these was plausible. To the right of each diagram in Figure 27.4, write two or three sentences describing how the starting DNA molecule differs from the molecule after replication. Do this for each of the three postulated methods of replication.

**FIGURE 27.4.**

Three Possible Methods of DNA Replication.

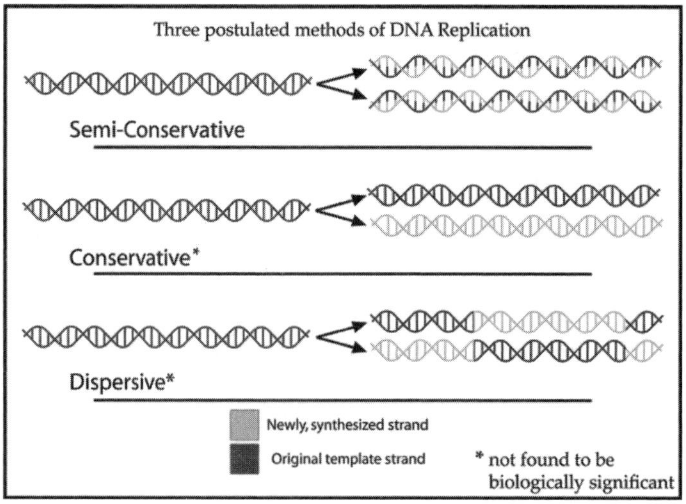


*Credit:* Original uploader was Adenosine at en.wikipedia; used in accordance with CC-BY-SA-2.5 license. *http://commons.wikimedia.org/wiki/File:DNAreplicationModes.png*

## *Part II: Nitrogen*

Meselson and Stahl had tools just as Avery, McCarty, and McLeed did. In this case, the tools were $^{14}N$ and $^{15}N$.

### Questions

1. Why is a nitrogen label a good tool for studying DNA?
2. What other molecules in a cell have nitrogen in them?
3. What's the difference between $^{14}N$ and $^{15}N$ at the atomic level?
4. What's the term for two atoms of the same element with different molecular masses?
5. Give an example of another element that has atoms of more than one molecular mass.

Bacteria in the laboratory can grow on plates or in broth cultures composed of precisely defined mixtures of chemicals. Meselson and Stahl grew bacteria in cultures containing only $^{15}N$ nitrogen for many generations so that the DNA was almost entirely composed of $^{15}N$-containing nucleotides. These chromosomes are denser than $^{14}N$ chromosomes, and by spinning chromosomes at very high speeds in a density gradient tube, Meselson and Stahl could tell the difference between the two kinds of chromosomes. Heavy chromosomes sank farther to the bottom of the tube, where the liquid was denser. Lighter chromosomes floated in the less dense liquid toward the top of the tube. This can be represented by the diagram in Figure 27.5. The blue lines represent the location of chromosomes in the tubes after centrifugation.

**FIGURE 27.5.**

Chromosomes Labeled With $^{14}N$ Versus $^{15}N$ Isotopes Sediment Differently in Cesium Chloride Gradients.

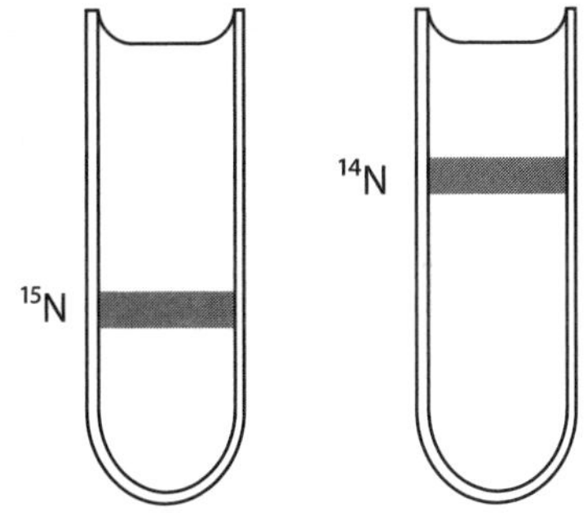


Controls

### *Part III: Results*

After growing the bacteria in $^{15}N$, producing bacteria with "heavy" chromosomes, they shifted the bacteria to growth conditions where only $^{14}N$ was present—making all the newly synthesized DNA from this less dense form of nitrogen. Figure 27.6 shows the results of their density gradients after exactly one generation of bacterial growth:

**FIGURE 27.6.**

DNA Collected From the First Generation of Cells Shifted to $^{14}N$.

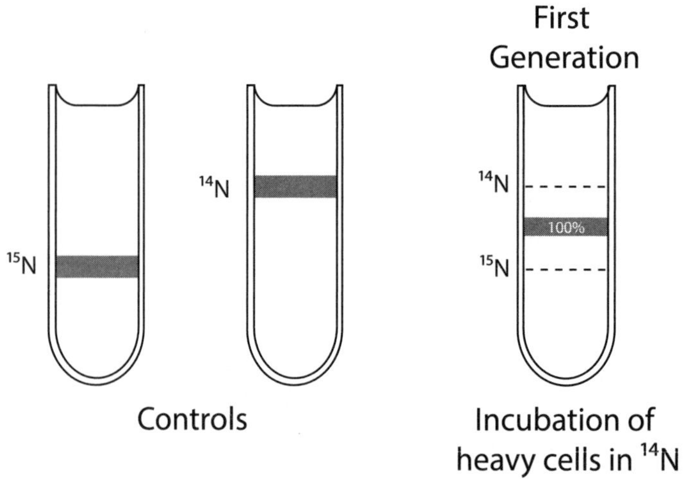


## Questions

1. Which of the three models for DNA replication are ruled out by this experiment?
2. What would the data look like if the model you ruled out was what was really happening? Include a diagram of a tube as part of your answer.
3. What could they do to tell which of the two remaining models is actually happening, using the tools that have already been described?

## *Part IV: Second Generation*

Figure 27.7 shows the results from the experiment of the second generation of cells grown in $^{14}N$.

**FIGURE 27.7.**

DNA Collected From the First and Second Generations of Cells Shifted to $^{14}N$.

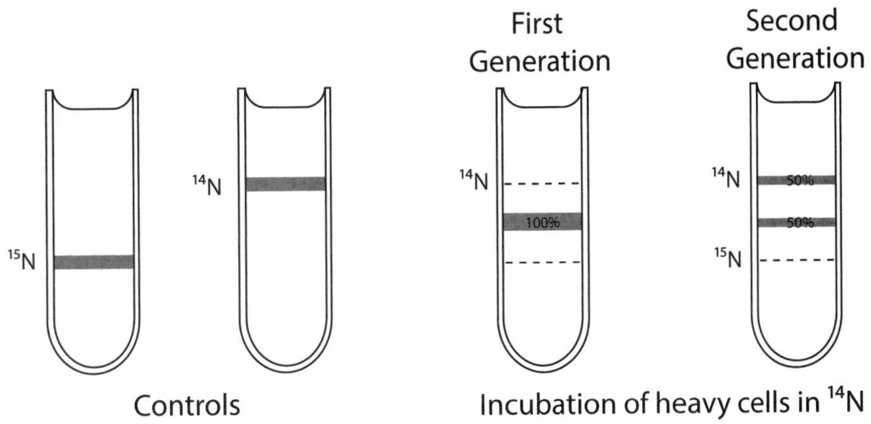


### Questions

1. Which model has now been ruled out by these results?
2. What would the data look like if this model was actually happening? Include a diagram of a test tube as part of your answer.

## *Take-Home Assignment*

Address the following question using a well-constructed essay paragraph. If you use diagrams, you must have text to thoroughly explain the diagrams rather than just drawing a picture.

*Describe in detail the chemical structure of DNA, how DNA is replicated, and the experiment by Meselson and Stahl that determined the method of DNA replication.*

## Web Version

Detailed teaching notes, the case PDF, and an answer key are available on the NCCSTS website at *sciencecases.lib.buffalo.edu/cs/collection/detail.asp?case_id=641&id=641*.

## References

Judson, H. F. 1996. *The eighth day of creation: Makers of the revolution in biology,* expanded edition. New York: Cold Spring Harbor Laboratory Press.

Meselson, M., and F. W. Stahl. 1958. The replication of DNA in *Escherichia coli. Proceedings of the National Academy of Sciences* 44: 671–682.

# SECTION VII

# EVOLUTION

# MY BROTHER'S KEEPER

## A Case Study in Evolutionary Biology and Animal Behavior

*Kari E. Benson*

## Abstract

In this case study, students interpret behavioral data with respect to evolutionary biology by examining the behavior of alarm calling in Belding's ground squirrel first reported by Paul Sherman in *Science* in 1977.


## Learning Objectives

- Develop testable hypotheses and interpret graphical information.
- Understand that natural selection does not (necessarily) act for the good of the species.
- Understand that natural selection can favor traits that do not directly enhance individual fitness.
- Understand that kin selection can explain many behaviors that seem otherwise maladaptive.
- Understand that humans are animals and that evolutionary strategies may be revealed in human behavior.

## Quantitative Reasoning Skills/Concepts

- Carry out basic mathematical operations.
- Interpret the meaning of simple statistical descriptors, such as error bars and trend lines.
- Use numerical evidence to formulate null and alternative hypotheses.
- Articulate complete and correct claims based on data.
- Create experimental designs to test hypotheses.
- Measure average percent of genes shared by common descent.

# The Case Study

## Part I: Hypothesis Development

Belding's ground squirrels (*Spermophilus beldingi*) are diurnal rodents. They live in subalpine meadows in the far western United States. Due to the extreme weather, the squirrels hibernate for seven or eight months of the year. The squirrels must enter hibernation with sufficient fat stores to survive this long hibernation. They spend their short active period by initially mating, then eating large quantities of food. They are primarily herbivorous, eating mostly seeds, flowers, and vegetation.

Adult females mate shortly after they emerge from hibernation. After mating, some males disperse to new groups and the others often return to hibernation before the young are born. The females establish territories within the social group and have between three and six pups. The pups emerge from their burrows when three to six weeks old and the juvenile males disperse (leave to join new groups) shortly after. The females typically remain in their natal (birth) group for life.

Paul Sherman (1977) studied Belding's ground squirrel behavior. The squirrels are subject to many dangers. Predators include coyotes, weasels, and raptors. Often, if a squirrel spots a predator, they will stand up on their hind feet and call out an alarm. When others hear the alarm, they quickly retreat to their burrows. Not all squirrels are equally likely to call.

### Question

1. Generate some hypotheses to explain why the squirrels call.

## Part II: Alternative Hypotheses and Predictions

What predictions do you have about the frequency of alarm calling for the hypotheses you generated in Part I? List them in Table 28.1.

**TABLE 28.1.**

Comparing Alternative Hypotheses.

| Hypothesis: | Who benefits? | When do they benefit? | Should all individuals call? | Group/predator response to call? | Immediate effect on caller? |
|---|---|---|---|---|---|
| | | | | | |
| | | | | | |
| | | | | | |
| | | | | | |
| | | | | | |
| | | | | | |
| | | | | | |

## Question

1. How can we discriminate between these competing hypotheses?

## *Part III: Experimental Results*

Not all squirrels call equally. See Figures 28.1 and 28.2.

**FIGURE 28.1.**

First Callers to a Predatory Mammal.

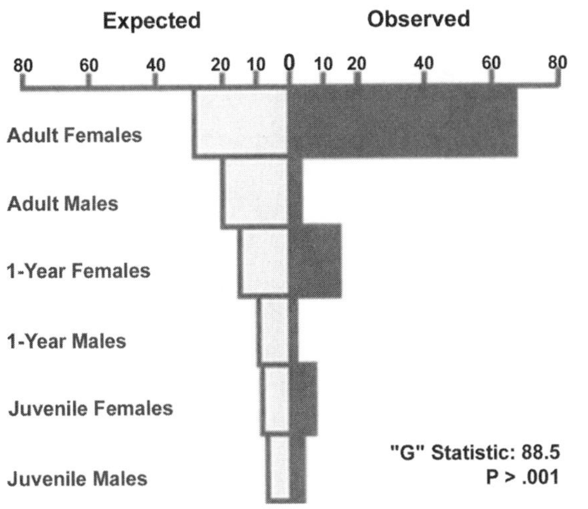


**FIGURE 28.2.**

All Callers to a Predatory Mammal.

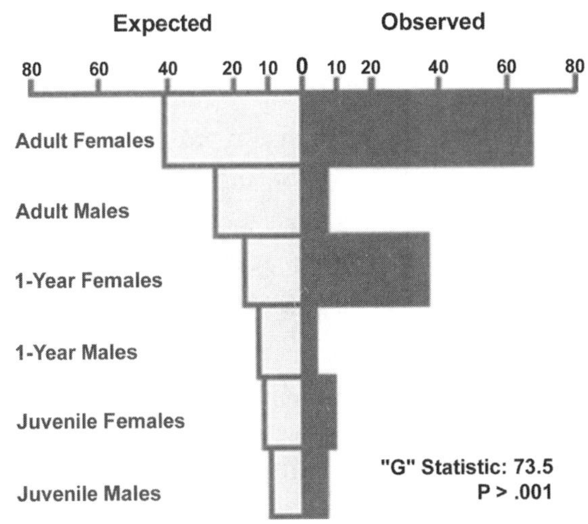


Figures 28.1 and 28.2 represent expected vs. observed frequencies of alarm calls across classes of Belding's ground squirrels drawn from 102 interactions with predators. Adapted from Sherman 1977.

### Question

1. What conclusions can you draw from these data?

## *Part IV: Sherman's Conclusions*

Females call disproportionately more often than predicted by their abundance. Adult females call more often than one-years or juveniles. Males call disproportionately less than predicted by their abundance.

### Questions

1. Why might this be?
2. *Advanced Questions:*
    a. How do these data compare to your predictions?
    b. Why would females call more than males?
    c. How should the proximity of relatives influence whether it is cost-effective to call?
3. Consider the following additional information: Females call more readily when they are close to other related individuals. Does this provide further support for the kin selection hypothesis?

## *Part V: Kin Recognition Mechanism*

The kin selection hypothesis requires that individuals can recognize kin. Sherman's data demonstrate that females are more likely to call when there are kin nearby.

### Questions

1. How might individuals recognize kin?
2. Can you provide some ways of testing whether a particular modality (call, smell, taste, and so on) is important in kin recognition?

## *Part VI: Other Squirrels*

There is another species of ground squirrel whose males behave differently. In this species (*Spermophilus tereticaudus*), males are more likely to alarm call before they leave their natal site, but remain silent after they disperse.

### Questions

1. Do these data support your current hypotheses about calling?

2. What predictions would you make if females dispersed and males remained in natal groups?
3. What predictions would you make if neither sex dispersed?
4. Why is it that one sex disperses from each of these groups?

## *Part VII: Economics of Kin Selection*

Hamilton (1964) proposed a mathematical means of interpreting whether individuals should help kin. The economic analysis incorporates several aspects of the situation.

First, the decision requires that you can recognize who is related to you and to what degree. In this case, Hamilton measures the percent of DNA that you would share with someone by common descent, which he calls relatedness (*r*). For example, you would share half of your genes with a parent by common descent. Thus, you would have a relatedness of 0.5 with either parent or with a full sibling; you would have a relatedness of 0.25 with a half sibling or a grandchild; and you would have a relatedness of 0.125 with a cousin. This is why the biologist J. B. S. Haldane purportedly stated that he would die for two of his brothers or eight of his cousins. You will need to know the relatedness between the donor and the recipient ($r_{recipient}$) and the relatedness between the donor and his or her offspring ($r_{offspring}$). Note that ($r_{offspring} = 0.5$) in typical diploid organisms.

Second, you have to know what it will cost you to help. For simplicity, Hamilton measured cost as the number of offspring that you won't have because you helped someone else. This is the cost of helping (*C*).

Third, you have to know how many more offspring your kin can have because you helped; this is the benefit of helping (*B*).

It is adaptive to help if: $\frac{B}{C} > \frac{r_{offspring}}{r_{recipient}}$

Thus, you can determine for a number of circumstances whether you should help your relative or not.

**Example:** You share a relatedness of 0.5 with your offspring and the same ($r_{offspring} = 0.5$) with a full sibling (one with whom you share a father and mother). If you can help some nephews, then $r_{recipient} = 0.25$. The benefit in the form of nephews must be greater than twice the cost to your own offspring for helping to be adaptive. That is, for every offspring you cannot have due to helping (this is the cost or *C*), anything more than an additional two nephews (this is the benefit or *B*) would satisfy the inequality. For example, this condition would be satisfied if $B = 2.5$ and $C = 1$.

Written mathematically, this would look like the following: $\frac{2.5}{1} > \frac{0.5}{0.25}$

This expression is correct. The left-hand part of the equation equals 2.5. The right-hand part of the equation equals 2. The left exceeds the right, so helping is adaptive through kin selection.

### Questions

1. Suppose there were a car wreck and you could only save one person, your best friend or your sibling. Whom would you save?
2. How many siblings would you have to save if helping forced you to give up one child?
3. How many nephews or nieces would you have to help if helping forced you to give up three children?

### *Part VIII: Applied Kin Selection*

Many recent articles demonstrate that decreased parental attention and increased child abuse are more common in stepchildren than for offspring that are genetically related to both caregivers.

### Question

1. How does kin selection explain these data?

## Web Version

Detailed teaching notes, the case PDF, and an answer key are available on the NCCSTS website at *sciencecases.lib.buffalo.edu/cs/collection/detail.asp?case_id=557&id=557*.

## References

Hamilton, W. D. 1964. The genetical evolution of social behavior. *Journal of Theoretical Biology*. 7: 1–52.

Sherman, P. W. 1977. Nepotism and the evolution of alarm calls. *Science* 197: 1246–1253.

# AS THE WORM TURNS
## Speciation and the Maggot Fly

*Martin Kelly*

## Abstract
At what point in evolution does a group of individuals become two distinct species? This case addresses that fundamental question by asking students to decide whether apple maggot flies are distinct as a species from hawthorn maggot flies. In making their decision, students examine the different models of speciation and consider the primary forces that cause evolutionary change.


## Learning Objectives
- Define evolution in the context of population genetics.
- Explain each of the five forces that cause evolutionary change.
- Describe three ways in which species can be characterized and clearly differentiated.
- Understand that speciation as a process is based on the same forces of evolution.
- Distinguish between allopatric, sympatric, and parapatric speciation.

## Quantitative Reasoning Skills/Concepts
- Carry out basic mathematical operations.
- Represent data in graphs.
- Use graphs to formulate predictions and explanations.
- Use numerical evidence to formulate null and alternative hypotheses.
- Articulate complete and correct claims based on data
- Use appropriate reasoning to support the validity of data-based claims.

## The Case Study

### *Introduction*
Hawthorn trees grow throughout North America and produce a small fruit that is eaten by a small fly larva. In 1864, apple growers discovered that an unknown maggot had started

feeding on apples. Through the years, hawthorn and apple maggot flies have progressively become more distinct. Presented below is evidence taken from the original scientific literature for you to consider and evaluate. From what may be incomplete and ambiguous data, try to answer the following two questions that at first glance may appear to be simple:

1. Do hawthorn maggot flies and apple maggot flies belong to the same species?
2. If not, and if apple maggot flies belong to their own species, what would be a biologically reasonable scenario for how the speciation occurred?

## *Facts about Hawthorn and Apple Maggot Flies (Rhagoletis pomonella)*

### The Organisms

The apple maggot fly (*Rhagoletis pomonella*) is native to eastern North America. It originally bred in the fruits of hawthorn trees. Apple maggot flies are about 5 mm long. The tip of a female's abdomen is more narrowly pointed than a male's (see Figure 29.1). Hawthorn and apple maggot flies are assigned to the same taxonomic species:

**FIGURE 29.1.**

Apple Maggot Flies (male on the left, female on the right).

- Hawthorn maggot flies and apple maggot flies are physically indistinguishable.
- There is no geographic isolation or physical separation between adult maggot flies.
- As host-races of the same species, these flies are not typically given different common names.

In fact, the genus *Rhagoletis* includes a set of four fly species that cannot be physically distinguished. Figure 29.2 displays the conventional classification.

### Maggot Fly Reproduction

- The female fly lays fertilized eggs into the fruit.
- Maggots (larvae) emerge from the egg, eat and grow, and pupariate where the last larval skin is retained and hardened to form the protective covering for metamorphosis.
- Metamorphing (pupariating) individuals develop into adult flies, emerge and reproduce.

## *Facts About Hawthorn and Apple Plants*

Both the hawthorn and the apple are woody plants belonging to the same taxonomic family (the Rose Family):

- Hawthorns are native to North America.
- Hawthorns are a large and complex group of trees and shrubs with over 50 species native to North America (northeastern and north-central). Hawthorns belong to the plant genus *Crataegus*.
- Most hawthorn species are identified by fruits that differ in size—for example, *C. marshalli* has a fruit that is 4.9 mm in diameter, while *C. pedicellata* has a fruit that is nearly four times larger in diameter (19.5 mm).

The apple is the most widely grown fruit in North America:

- Apples belong to the plant genus *Malus*. The taxonomic name *Malus domesticus* is preferred for the large-fruited, edible apple.
- Early European colonists brought both seeds and grafted apple trees to North America. Records of grafting desirable apple varieties onto wild rootstocks date back to 1647 in Virginia.

**FIGURE 29.2.**

Taxonomic Tree of Rhagoletis

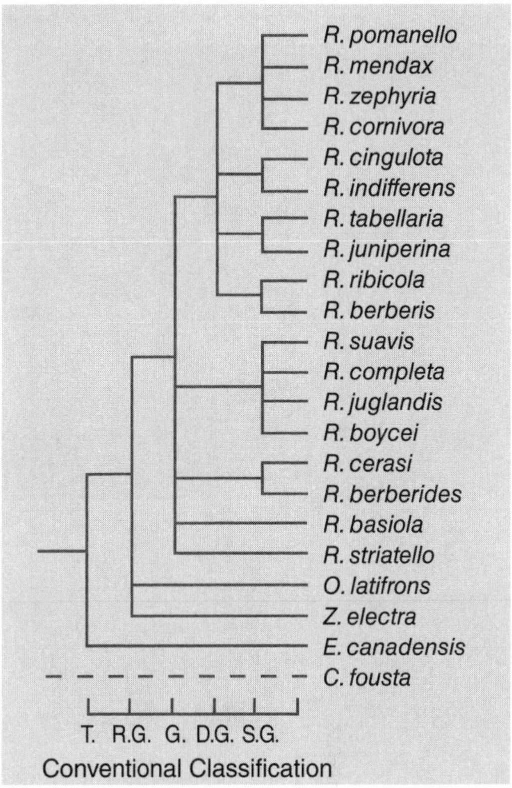


*Source:* adapted from Berlocher and Bush 1982).

In 1864 the Hawthorn maggot flies were first noted to infest apples grown in New York's Hudson River Valley:

- Maggot flies ultimately became a major fruit pest in northeastern United States and Canada.
- Thorough control of the maggot flies is needed to produce the highest quality and most marketable fruits.

Figure 29.3 (p. 272) compares the timing of fly emergence (solid and dashed lines) and fruit ripening (colored filled-in curves). Adult flies emerge from the chamber formed by the hardened larval skin (puparium) to reproduce before fruits are mature. Apple fruits ripen approximately one month earlier than hawthorn fruits, *but there is overlap* at the end of the apple fruiting season and the beginning of the hawthorn fruiting season. The female fly lays fertilized eggs into the ripe fruit. Maggots (larvae) hatch from the egg, eat fruit, grow, and pupate.

**FIGURE 29.3.**

Emergence of *Rhagoletis pomonella*

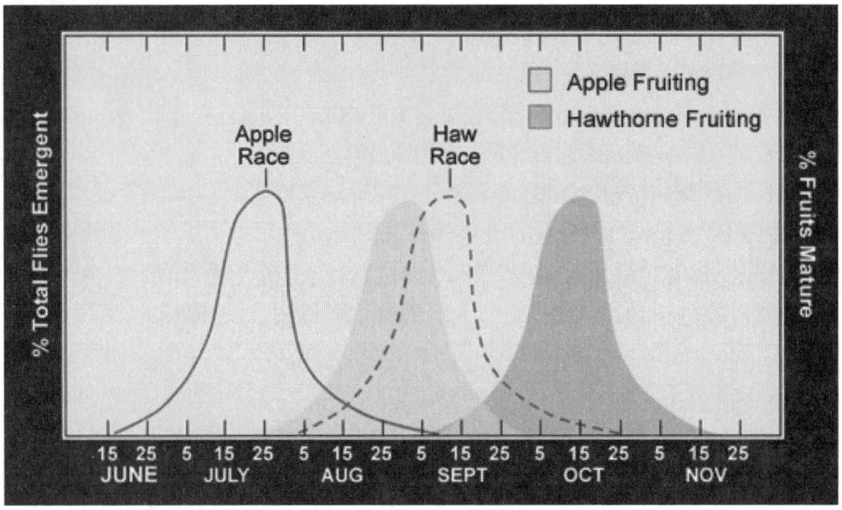


*Source:* adapted from Bush 1969

## *Fruit Characteristics*

Apples are significantly bigger fruits than hawthorns.

- The typical commercial apple fruit has a diameter of 2.75 inches (70 mm).
- The typical wild hawthorn fruit has a diameter of 0.5 inches (12.6 mm).

The larger fruits of apple trees provide 5.5 times more depth (based on diameter) to developing maggots than do hawthorn fruits.

- Parasitoid wasps can lay eggs into the maggot's body, with the wasp larvae ultimately killing the maggot.
- Apple maggots are better able to escape parasitoid wasps by burrowing deeper into the fruit than the wasp can penetrate with its egg-layer (ovipositor).
- Apple maggots bear 70% fewer parasitoid wasp eggs than do hawthorn maggots.

The larger fruits of apple trees provide 220 times more food (based on volume) to the growing and developing maggot than the smaller fruits of hawthorns.

- Apple maggot flies lay more eggs per fruit than do hawthorn maggot flies.
- Though the bigger apple provides more food (quantity), it does not provide better food (quality) to the growing maggot.
- The nutritional quality of hawthorn fruit is indicated by the better survival of both types of maggots in hawthorn fruits; 52% of maggot fly eggs survived in hawthorn fruits and 27% of maggot fly eggs survived in apple fruits.

- Caterpillars and weevils may also feed on the larger apple, reducing the quantity of food available to apple maggots.

## *Evolutionary Outcomes in Apple Maggot Flies*

- Fidelity to fruit type acts as a strong barrier to gene flow between the two types of maggot flies.
- There is only a 4–6% hybridization rate between hawthorn maggot flies and apple maggot flies.
- Hawthorn maggot flies strongly prefer to mate on and lay fertilized eggs into hawthorns.
- Apple maggot flies strongly prefer to mate on and lay fertilized eggs into apples.
- Hawthorn and apple maggot flies are genetically distinguishable (have recognizable genetic profiles).

### Questions

In your groups, address the following and list the evidence used to make your decisions.

1. What species concept should be used in this case?
2. Are apple maggot flies distinct as a species from hawthorn maggot flies?
3. Propose a biologically reasonable scenario that explains how apple maggot flies evolved.
4. How did you weigh the different pieces of evidence to reach a conclusion to questions (2) and (3)? What evidence was most important, what was least important, and so on?
5. What further information would you need to increase your confidence in the conclusions you reached?

## Web Version

Detailed teaching notes, the case PDF, and an answer key are available on the NCCSTS website at *sciencecases.lib.buffalo.edu/cs/collection/detail.asp?case_id=328&id=328*

## References

Berlocher, S. H., and G. L. Bush. 1982. An electrophoretic analysis of *Rhagoletis* (Diptera: Tephritidae) phylogeny. *Systematic Zoology* 31: 136–155.

Bush, G. L. 1969. Sympatric host race formation and speciation in frugivorous flies of the genus *Rhagoletis* (Diptera: Tephritidae). *Evolution* 23: 237–251..

# TROUBLE IN PARADISE
## A Case of Speciation

*James A. Hewlett*

## Abstract
Students apply principles of evolution they have learned in class to create their own story explaining the evolutionary history of a previously unknown species of rodent discovered on an island in the West Indies.


## Learning Objectives

- Understand the principles of evolution and classification, the concept of species, and what constitutes evidence in support of evolution.
- Develop a common name for a fictitious species of mammals and apply the rules of binomial classification to provide a scientific name.
- Apply concepts of micro- and macro-evolution to produce an evolutionary story for the fictitious mammals.
- Interpret simple data sets and make inferences and conclusions from that data.
- Produce data and/or evidence in support of an original evolutionary story of the student's own creation.

## Quantitative Reasoning Skills/Concepts

- Carry out basic mathematical operations.
- Use numerical evidence to formulate null and alternative hypotheses.
- Articulate complete and correct claims based on data.
- Use appropriate reasoning to support the validity of data-based claims.

## The Case Study

### *Background*
As an expert in the field of mammalian reproductive strategies, you have been hired by the Department of Nature and Island Resources of the West Indies. This organization is a

cooperative of several West Indies islands concerned with the loss of biological diversity on their island nations as tourism and development continue to grow. Scientists working on the island of St. Kitts and its sister island Nevis have uncovered what appears to be a previously undiscovered species of rodent.

Based on the original description of this animal, it was placed in a genus within the squirrel family. What you have been hired to do is to help save the population on St. Kitts, which is small and threatened by development. The population is so small that individuals are having difficulty finding mates and, in many cases, the reproductive seasons are being delayed by up to one year.

When you arrive in the region and begin your observations, you notice that the Nevis population is very healthy and could be used as stock for the recovery operation that you plan on the island of St. Kitts.

In your recovery plan, you bring animals from Nevis into the population on St. Kitts to bolster the population numbers, ensure the availability of mates, and increase the genetic diversity within the shrinking population. As a good scientist, you observe the reproductive behaviors of this animal in the field to ensure the success of your program. Within a very short time, you realize that your plan is failing. In the 240 attempts to bring a Nevis animal into the St. Kitts population, you are unable to observe a single successful reproductive event. Although these animals look identical, you are concerned that they are two distinct species. Your focus now becomes identifying the differences between the two populations. What follows is a brief review of the data you collected from your study.

**TABLE 30.1.**

Morphometric Data for the Rodent Populations on the Two Islands.

| St. Kitts Rodent | Nevis Rodent |
|---|---|
| Average weight: 83 g | Average weight: 86 g |
| Average length: 21.8 cm | Average length: 23.3 cm |
| Average hind limb: 7.8 cm | Average hind limb: 4.2 cm |
| Average forelimb: 4.2 cm | Average forelimb: 3.9 cm |
| Top speed: 2.2 meters/second (m/s) | Top speed: 0.8 m/s |
| Average leap height: 1.4 m | Average leap height: 0.4 m |
| Average gestation time: 29.3 days | Average gestation time: 42.7 days |
| Average time spent in courtship display: 12.6 seconds | Average time spent in courtship display: 21.3 seconds |

## *Assignment*

This case study describes a recovery program for a rodent population on the island of St. Kitts in the Caribbean. After reading the case study above, your job is to formulate your own story incorporating some of the details and data provided while also drawing on several evolutionary concepts studied in class and listed in Table 30.2.

There are no limitations on the details you can incorporate into your story, but it should follow some specific guidelines. Here are the guidelines for your story:

- It should be 600 words or less.
- It should incorporate the data supplied in the case study.
- It should incorporate at least three of the concepts from the concept list in Table 30.2. As you incorporate each concept, you must demonstrate its relevance to your story.
- It can be told in any form. For instance, one student presented the story as field notes collected from observing the animals in their natural habitat. Another student presented the story as a series of experiments and observations made by groups of scientists over hundreds of years. Be creative.
- It should account for the data on the organisms provided in the case study. It is acceptable to add more data as you develop your story as long as it fits into the patterns of the data provided.
- It can include graphics and illustrations. Be sure to cite the source and give credit for the material, including material taken from the internet.
- It should include a scientific and common name for the rodent populations. In developing these names, make sure you use the rules for binomial classification. In addition, make sure that you put the rodents into an existing genus. You come up with the species names.
- It needs a good title.

**TABLE 30.2.**

Concept List.

- Genetic drift
- Bottleneck effect
- Founder effect
- Gene flow
- Mutation
- Natural selection—Directional selection
- Natural selection—Stabilizing selection
- Natural selection—Diversifying selection
- Prezygotic reproductive isolation—Habitat isolation
- Prezygotic reproductive isolation—Behavioral isolation
- Prezygotic reproductive isolation—Temporal isolation
- Prezygotic reproductive isolation—Mechanical isolation
- Prezygotic reproductive isolation—Genetic isolation
- Postzygotic reproductive isolation—Reduced hybrid viability or fertility
- Allopatric speciation

Remember that you are developing an evolutionary picture of a rodent population using data supplied with the case study. Keep in mind that in an evolutionary story you will be describing events that may have occurred over very long time periods.

*Important:* When incorporating concepts from the "Concept List" into your story, you must elaborate on how they relate to your story. Simply including a concept word in your assignment is not acceptable. For example, stating that "the animals became two species because of genetic drift" is not sufficient. You must also explain how genetic drift works in this process.

## Web Version

Detailed teaching notes, the case PDF, and an answer key are available on the NCCSTS website at *sciencecases.lib.buffalo.edu/cs/collection/detail.asp?case_id=312&id=312*.

# PKU CARRIERS
## How Many Are in Your Hometown?

*David J. Grise*

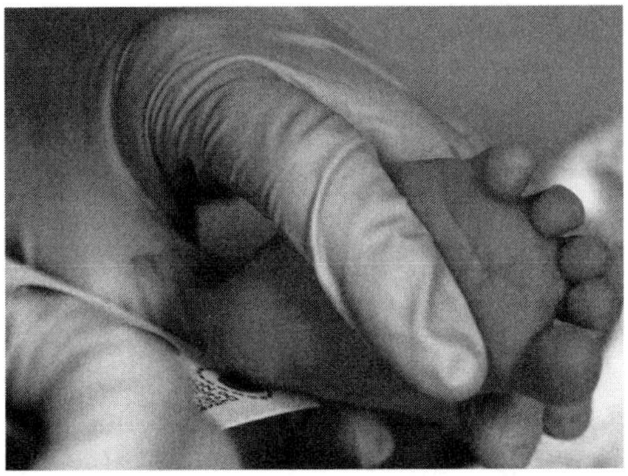


## Abstract
This case illustrates how a mathematical model can be used to address a biological question. Its primary goal is to introduce the Hardy-Weinberg model. After assuming a population is in Hardy-Weinberg equilibrium, students calculate the number of heterozygous individuals in a population.


## Learning Objectives

- Understand how a mathematical model can be used to address a biological question.
- Review basic genetics covered in class to this point.
- Understand that Hardy-Weinberg equilibrium is a null hypothesis (there will be no change in allele or genotype frequencies if no evolutionary forces are acting on the population).
- Learn what data need to be collected to use the Hardy-Weinberg equation to estimate frequency of carriers.
- Use the Hardy-Weinberg equation to calculate expected number of carriers.

## Quantitative Reasoning Skills/Concepts

- Carry out basic mathematical operations.
- Articulate complete and correct claims based on data.
- Use appropriate reasoning to support the validity of data-based claims.
- Create and interpret Punnett squares.
- Create and/or analyze family pedigrees.
- Interpret probabilities in Hardy-Weinberg equation.

## The Case Study

### *Part I: PKU*
Sitting in biology class one day, Jane was taking notes about traits determined by a single gene with a dominant and a recessive allele. She wasn't too interested because the example

used in class was seed color in pea plants. Although she would have rather been texting her friends about going to the beach near Corpus Christi later in the day, she wrote down that yellow is the dominant allele, the allele for green seed color is recessive to the allele for yellow seed color, heterozygotes have yellow seeds, blah, blah, blah. Thankfully, the clock made its way to 11:50 a.m., and she was free.

After class, Jane met some of her friends for lunch. Anna asked, "Jane, didn't you have baked potato and broccoli yesterday and the day before that too? Hey, you also have the same drink that you had the past couple of days. What is going on with that?"

"Just after I was born I was diagnosed with a condition called phenylketonuria, or PKU for short," replied Jane. "I don't understand the condition very well. My parents made me follow a special diet the doctors gave them. My diet has very little of the amino acid phenylalanine. Some nutrients are missing in my diet so I drink a can of this nutrient drink every day. Caitlin, read the warning on the back of that diet soda you are drinking."

"Why would there be a warning on my diet soda can?" asked Caitlin. "Oh, here it is! It says, *Phenylketonurics: Contains phenylalanine.*"

Jane replied, "If I have any of that stuff, I just can't think straight. When I first got here, I went off my diet. It was awful. I couldn't remember anything, I couldn't concentrate, and I couldn't pay attention. Biology was impossible when I was eating 'normal' foods. Now that I am back on my diet, biology is still a hard class, but it's not as bad as when I was eating 'normal' foods."

Mariela asked, "Jane, if you don't eat 'normal' foods, then what do you eat?"

"I eat things like I'm eating now," replied Jane. "I eat a lot of fruits, vegetables, low protein breads, and pasta. I have one of these phenylalanine-free formula drinks containing protein, vitamins, and minerals every day. My typical meal is a couple different types of vegetables and a baked potato."

"Does everybody in your family eat this diet?" asked Megan.

"No, my parents, brother, and sister don't have PKU, so they can eat 'normal' foods."

Amanda, Jane's best friend, said, "Hey, lab starts in 10 minutes, we better read the lab so we can answer the questions on the pre-lab quiz."

Later, Amanda called Jane and asked if Jane had started working on the questions they had to answer for class on Friday. Amanda normally didn't look at these questions until just before they were due, but because she was finding the course challenging, she took a look at the questions early. She read the first question to Jane: *Let's assume that earlobe shape in humans is determined by a single gene with two alleles. Two people with unattached earlobes have a child with attached earlobes. Which earlobe shape is determined by the dominant allele? Which earlobe shape is determined by the recessive allele?*

Hearing the question, Jane dropped everything she was doing and told Amanda she had to go do something and would call her back. It had suddenly occurred to Jane that maybe she was beginning to understand why she had PKU!

## Questions

1. What are Jane's symptoms when she eats foods containing the amino acid phenylalanine?
2. Given these symptoms, what organ is most affected when a person with PKU consumes the amino acid phenylalanine in their diet?
3. A person without PKU does not have any symptoms when they consume foods with the amino acid phenylalanine. Why might Jane have the symptoms she does when she consumes foods with phenylalanine?

Later that evening, after spending considerable time reading the text and searching the internet for information about PKU, Jane called Amanda and asked her to come over to her apartment so they could work on the questions for biology class that were due on Friday.

"Hi Amanda, I think I finally understand why I can't eat 'normal' foods!"

"What are you talking about Jane? I still can't understand dominant and recessive alleles. I need help with this."

"Amanda, that's it! I have two recessive alleles and you have at least one dominant allele. Because I have two recessive alleles, I can't make the enzyme phenylalanine hydroxylase (PAH)."

"Phenyl-what?" replied Amanda. "What does phenyl-whatever do and how does that explain anything about dominant and recessive alleles?"

"My parents are heterozygous at the gene locus for PAH so they can make PAH, which is the enzyme that breaks down phenylalanine. They both gave me a recessive allele. Because I have two copies of the recessive allele at the gene locus for PAH, I can't make PAH or break down phenylalanine. That's why I have PKU. When I eat phenylalanine, it just builds up and causes me problems."

"Really? I think I understand this, but I'm not sure."

"It's simple, Amanda. You can think of PKU as being due to a single gene for which there is a dominant allele and a recessive allele. If a person has a least one dominant allele, they do not have PKU because they can make an enzyme that breaks down phenylalanine. If a person like me has two recessive alleles, they can't make the enzyme and they have PKU."

"Great work, Jane, now we can easily answer the questions for Friday."

After class on Friday, Amanda and Jane told their biology professor that understanding the genetics of PKU helped them answer the questions that were due that day. Their professor, Courtney Jones, told them that they would determine the number of carriers for PKU in Corpus Christi later in the semester when they covered the Hardy-Weinberg Principle (also referred to as Hardy-Weinberg Equilibrium).

## Questions

Define symbols for the alleles at the gene locus for PAH and then answer the following questions:

1. What are the genotypes of Jane's parents?
2. What are the genotypes of Jane's brother and sister?
3. What is Jane's genotype?

## *Part II: Hardy-Weinberg*

"Today we will start discussing the Hardy-Weinberg Principle or Equilibrium," Dr. Jones said toward the end of class. "The Hardy-Weinberg Principle or Equilibrium is often used as a basis of comparison. It is a null hypothesis. The allele and genotype frequencies in a population will not change over time if no evolutionary forces are acting on that population. I am out of time today; please work on the Hardy-Weinberg question set for Friday."

Jane and Amanda got together on Thursday night to discuss the questions due the next day. The first question was about the data needed to determine the number of carriers in the population.

"Jane, what's a carrier?"

"My parents are carriers, Amanda. They don't have PKU because they have a dominant allele that produces PAH, but carry the recessive allele that doesn't make PAH."

"Hey, Jane, we know your parents are carriers. Can we count the number of carriers in the population and move on to the next question?"

"What are you thinking, Amanda? For most people, you can't know if they are a carrier or not."

"But, Jane, we do know if a person is a carrier or not. We know your parents are carriers. We can just count the number of carriers, and then divide by the number of people in the population to get the frequency of carriers and plug that number into the equation."

## Questions

1. Who is correct? Can Jane and Amanda directly count the numbers of carriers in a population? Why or why not?
2. Can Jane and Amanda determine any of the allele and/or genotype frequencies in the population just by counting? If so, which one(s)?

## *Part III: Carriers*

After determining that Jane is correct and that they cannot directly count carriers in the population, Amanda opened her notes from biology lecture. Dr. Jones had told them that the Hardy-Weinberg Equation, the mathematical expression of the Hardy-Weinberg Principle, can be stated as:

$(p + q)^2 = 1$ or as $(p^2 + 2pq + q^2) = 1$

"Jane, what the heck are $p$ and $q$?"

After consulting the text, Jane said, "I think I figured it out, $p$ and $q$ are allele frequencies. I think that in the case of complete dominance with two alleles, $p$ represents the frequency of the dominant allele, and $q$ represents the frequency of the recessive allele."

"Right, so with only two alleles, then $p + q = 1$. I still don't understand how this is helpful because we can't determine $p$ or $q$ just by counting people in the population."

"Amanda, is there another form of the equation, the one for genotypes?"

"Yes, here it is. I think $p^2$ represents the frequency of homozygous dominant genotype, $2pq$ represents the frequency of the heterozygous genotype, and $q^2$ represents the frequency of homozygous recessive genotype."

"That sounds right," said Jane. "And they add up to one because there are only three genotypes."

"But what do we do now?" asked Amanda.

"I don't know," replied Jane. "But we might want to start by determining if we know any of these five values. We know $q^2$."

"Right!" said Amanda. "We could count people with the recessive phenotype in Corpus Christi and divide by the total number of people in Corpus Christi and we'd have $q^2$."

"Exactly!" said Jane. "And because we know $q^2$ we can determine $q$. And if we know $q$, we can determine $p$. We are just about done with these questions!"

## Questions

1. Once Jane and Amanda know the frequency of the homozygous recessive genotype ($q^2$), how can they determine the frequency of the recessive allele ($q$)?
2. How can Jane and Amanda determine the frequency of the dominant allele ($p$)?
3. If 33 of the 300,000 people in Corpus Christi, Texas, have PKU, how many people are carriers (heterozygous) for PKU?
4. Dr. Jones mentioned that the allele and genotype frequencies in a population will not change over time if no evolutionary forces are acting on that population. To determine the number of carriers in a population, you make the assumption that no evolutionary forces are acting on the population. What are these evolutionary forces?

"Well, Amanda, what can we do with this information?"

"Jane, didn't you tell me that you would like to know the chance that you will have a child with PKU?"

"I would, but unless I marry someone with PKU, I don't know how to figure that out."

"Can we use the number of carriers in Corpus Christi to answer this question?"

"I don't know," replied Jane. "I think so, but I'm not sure. I have a 100% chance of passing on the PKU allele to my child, but how do I figure out the chance that my husband will be a carrier?"

"For the Corpus Christi population, we know that!" exclaimed Amanda. "The chance that your husband will be a carrier is the frequency of carriers. The chance that you will pass on the PKU allele is 1, the chance that your future husband will be a carrier is $2pq$, and the chance that he will pass on the PKU allele if he is a carrier is ½. Multiply them together and you have it."

"That makes sense to me," said Jane. "But could we determine the chance that you will have a child with PKU?"

"I don't know," said Amanda. "No one in my family has PKU, but I guess I could be a carrier."

"Well, we know the chance that you are a carrier is $2pq$. If you are a carrier, the chance that you pass on the PKU allele is ½. The same for your future husband: The chance he is a carrier is $2pq$ and the chance that he will pass on the PKU allele is ½. I think all we have to do is multiply all those together and we have an answer."

## Questions

1. Is their reasoning sound? Did they correctly calculate their chance of having a child with PKU? If not, what should they include in their calculations?
2. If Jane marries somebody in Corpus Christi without symptoms of PKU, what is the chance that she and her husband will have a child with PKU?
3. If Amanda marries somebody in Corpus Christi without symptoms of PKU, what is the chance that she and her husband will have a child with PKU?

## Web Version

Detailed teaching notes, the case PDF, and an answer key are available on the NCCSTS website at *sciencecases.lib.buffalo.edu/cs/collection/detail.asp?case_id=574&id=574.*

# SUPER BUG
## Antibiotics and Evolution

*Kristy J. Wilson*

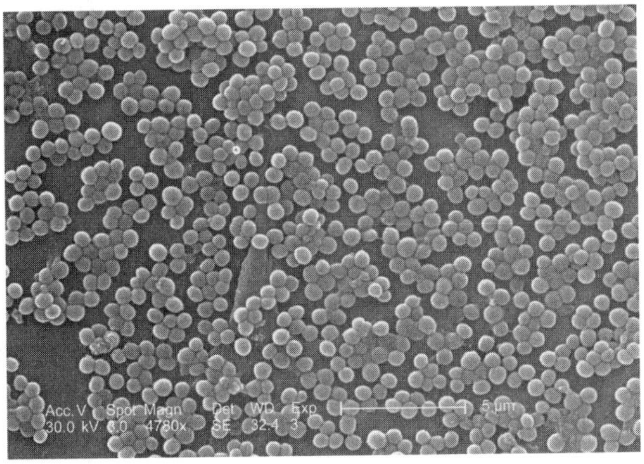


## Abstract
In this case study, students learn about the most common issues associated with antibiotic resistance and how these issues relate to evolution. In addition, students apply concepts of the evolutionary process to the case as they learn that evolution is not something that only happened millions of years ago, but is a dynamic ongoing process.

## Learning Objectives

- Demonstrate proficiency in the interpretation of graphs and charts.
- Apply evolutionary principles to a real-world scenario.
- Relate evolution to genetic changes and to predict what kind of genetic changes impact evolution.
- Analyze and discuss genetic diversity and its impact on evolution and predict what would happen to species without diversity.

## Quantitative Reasoning Skills/Concepts

- Carry out basic mathematical operations.
- Use graphs to formulate predictions and explanations.
- Articulate complete and correct claims based on data.
- DNA analysis (specifically looking at sequence information).

## The Case Study

### *Part I: The Rise of the Super Bug*
I was sitting in a hospital bay and I wasn't really worried. I get urinary tract infections all the time. It happens when you have Berger's disease, a type of auto-immune thing that affects the kidney, so that you have to get dialysis to do what the kidneys are supposed to

do. So getting urinary tract infections is no big deal. I had been to the doctor a couple of times already, but the pills he gave me didn't seem to be working. I was already here for my dialysis treatment, so I figured maybe the hospital doctors could give me something more powerful to help clear up the infection faster. I expected to get some IV antibiotics, sit around bored, and then be on my way. I was just visiting my cousins in India. Maybe I should have taken their offer and gotten some powerful antibiotics. It still amazes me that you don't need a prescription to get them over there; it would have made my life easier if they were so easy to get at home.

A nurse comes in briskly. "We're going to move you to your own room, honey."

I should be excited. You know, my own TV without all the noise and craziness just being in a curtained bay. But the nurse looks worried and she is pushing my bed along kind of fast. There is a ton of activity in the hospital bay I left as I see the other patients in the neighboring bays are being moved as well. What weirdness is this about? I'm getting a little worried.

"The doctor will be with you shortly," she says. But I don't believe that. Doctors take forever.

That's why I am surprised when he comes along 10 minutes later.

"OK, ahh … Sam," he says, consulting my chart. "We got your test results back and it looks like your bacterial infection is very serious."

OK, now I am really worried and maybe even a little bit scared because I just don't understand why this time is different and worse than the others.

*************

Yeah, so I guess I was the first U.S. patient with the New Delhi Super Bug. Instead of my normal stay in the hospital, I was there for weeks. I barely got to see anyone since I was quarantined. According to the doctors, I probably picked up the bacteria when I was getting dialysis at the hospital on my vacation in India. I really don't understand why my infection was a super bug. What exactly is a "super bug"? What makes infection with a super bug different from my other infections?

While I sat there in the hospital room, I couldn't watch any more daytime television, so I decided to do a couple of internet searches. I mean really; I'm not a pre-med student for nothing. So, Wikipedia first … it seems that a super bug is just a hyped up way of saying that the drugs used to treat the infection don't. These "super bugs" apparently have antibiotic resistance. Here's one of the "visuals" I found (Figure 32.1).

While I thought this information on antibiotic resistance was helpful, what exactly does this have to do with me sitting here forever? I Googled "Super Bug" and found a variety of news stories. Here's an extract from one of them:

*Doctors in India aren't surprised that the Super Bug probably originated there. Drug control there is poor and common antibiotics have become ineffective in India. Some reasons may be because people can buy powerful antibiotics over the counter, leading to overuse. They also take small doses and discontinue treatment in order to save money. There are no current antibiotics, nor any in development, that can kill New Delhi Super Bug on their own.*
—Vinny Ciancio (AccessRx)

**FIGURE 32.1.**

Exposure to Antibiotics Causes a Population Bottleneck Significantly Affecting Allele Frequency in the Population of Bacteria..

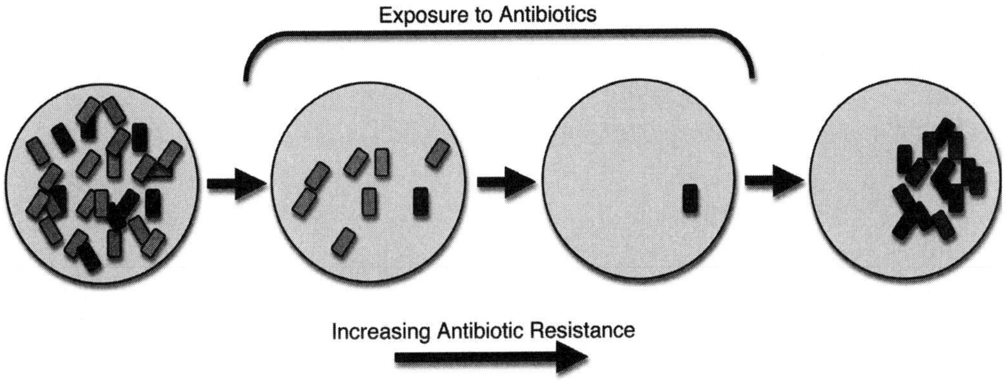


## Questions

1. What do you think could allow some of the bacteria to live even in the presence of antibiotics? (Hint: Are all the bacteria in a population the same? How might they differ?)
2. What are the biological, social, or cultural factors that may have influenced the increased resistance of this strain of bacteria to antibiotics? (i.e., What could have influenced the development of New Delhi Super Bug and influenced its spread?)

## Exercise

The acquisition of antibiotic resistance in certain bacterial species in a given location occurs over time. How does antibiotic resistance relate to evolution?

Form a group of four students. Define each of the principles of evolution listed on page 288. Then compare them to Sam's story of the antibiotic-resistant bacteria. Explain how bacterial antibiotic resistance demonstrates each principle. Designate one student in the group to report your findings to the rest of the class.

- Phenotype vs. genotype
- Diversity
- Allele and allele frequency
- Gene pool
- Selection or natural selection
- Population bottleneck
- Heritable traits
- Adaptation
- Population vs. individual
- Mutation
- Lateral gene transfer

## *Part II: Mechanism of Evolution*

"I know what a super bug is," I muttered to myself. It's simply a bacterium that is resistant to most or all of the drugs that could be used to treat it.

The boredom of just sitting here was really getting to me, so I kept reading my search results to find out how exactly a bacteria becomes resistant to antibiotics. Here's some of what I found:

> *Experts say that the infection is worth taking seriously, but the public health implications are uncertain. Multi drug-resistant bacteria have been around for decades. In fact, the so called "super bug" is not actually a bug at all. Instead, the drug resistance comes from a gene called NDM-1 that gets passed from one kind of bacteria to another. These genes have sparked even more concerns because they don't lie in the genomes of the bacteria themselves. Instead, they sit on small, circular pieces of DNA called plasmids, which can be passed between bacteria. What sets NDM-1 apart is that it lies on a plasmid that seems to move especially freely between bacteria, even if they are completely unrelated. That means the gene could move from an* E. coli *bacterium that causes urinary tract infections to other types of bacteria that cause pneumonia, salmonella, or cholera. With some 100 trillion bacteria on and in our bodies at all times, plasmids with the NDM-1 gene have many opportunities to spread. That can happen inside a person's gut, in the soil, or within water that contains fecal contamination.* —Emily Sohn *(Discovery News)*

Wow, the whole idea of bacteria passing DNA back and forth for antibiotic resistance is scary. One author I read described the situation perfectly as an "ongoing arms race between the bacteria that cause illnesses and the drugs designed to kill them." Since I had already done some reading about antibiotic resistance, I decided to write a paper on antibiotic resistance for my genetics class. Below are two pieces of data from primary research articles on NDM-1 or urinary tract infections that I found to use as references.

## Your Task

Examine the graphs and figures associated with the two experiments below and then answer the questions that follow.

## Experiment 1

Scientists examined how much antibiotic it would take to kill the bacterium *E. coli,* with and without the NDM-1 gene. The NDM-1 gene encodes an enzyme that breaks down antibiotics rendering them inactive. A graph of their results is displayed in Figure 32.2. The *x*-axis represents the specific antibiotic tested as well as the class of antibiotic that it belongs to. Each class of antibiotics has similar chemical structure and mechanism of action. For example, penicillin inhibits remodeling of the peptidoglycan cell wall of bacteria, which weakens the cell wall, making them susceptible to be lysed. In contrast, macrolides inhibit bacterial protein synthesis by binding irreversibly to the 50S subunit of the ribosome, inhibiting translocation of peptidyl-tRNA.

The *y*-axis represents the amount of antibiotics needed to kill the bacteria. It is represented as a percentage of the amount needed to kill the *E. coli* that does not contain NDM-1 gene (wild type). Thus for all the antibiotics, wild type is 100%. For example to kill the wild type bacteria it takes 1 µg/ml Piperacillin; in contrast, to kill *E. coli* with NDM-1 it takes over 256 µg/ml Piperacillin. Therefore, the percentage of wild type to kill the *E. coli* with NDM-1 is 25,600%. Please note that the *y*-axis is represented on a log scale.

**FIGURE 32.2.**

NDM-1 Plasmid Makes Bacteria Resistant to a Wide Range of Antibiotics.

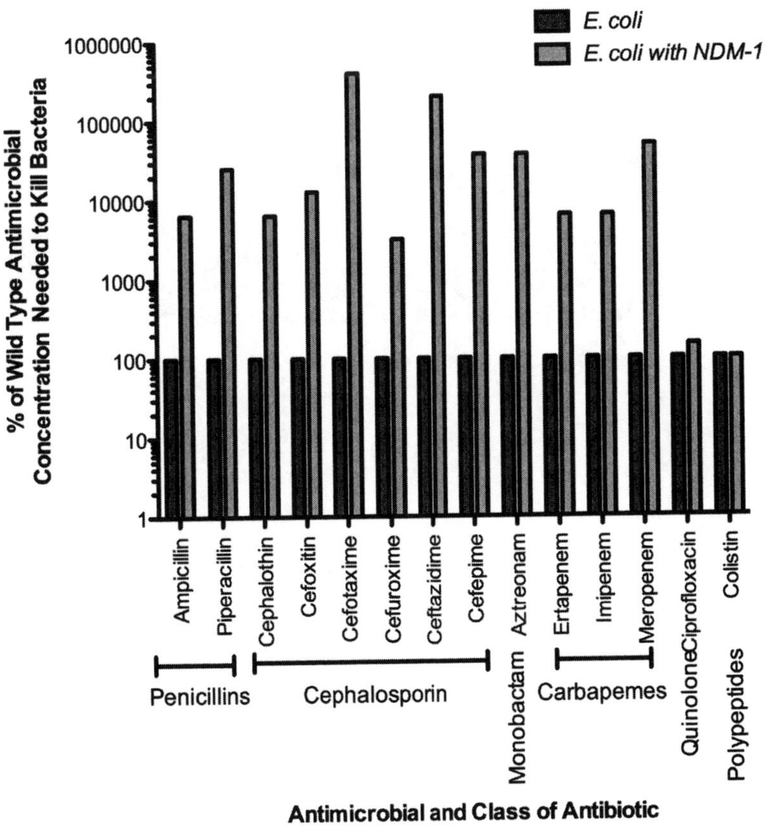

## Experiment 2

The mechanism of action of different antibiotics varies, but the quinolone class of antibiotics acts to prevent DNA replication. For bacteria to replicate their DNA, they need to separate the strands of DNA from each other. Two key enzymes help accomplish this task: DNA gyrase *(gyrA)* and topoisomerase IV *(parC)*.

Over a 14-year period, 828 *E. coli* isolates were collected from patients with urinary tract infections (UTI) similar to Sam's. Then these isolates were examined for quinolone-specific resistance and the presence of mutations in the *gyrA* and *parC* DNA sequences that gave *E. coli* quinolone resistance.

Table 32.1 describes these results from the randomly chosen isolates. The sequences of the *gyrA* and *parC* genes were known, so the sequences of the isolates were compared to the known sequence. The mutations found are described in the chart by the amino acid encoded by unmutated DNA, the position of the amino acid, and the amino acid that the DNA was mutated to. For example, *gyrA* has a Serine at position 83 with a DNA sequence corresponding to a TCA codon. The sequence of an isolate at the same position in the DNA was TTA. This is a codon for Leucine instead of Serine. Then the percentage of quinolone-resistant bacteria that contained this mutation is listed.

**TABLE 32.1.**

Location of Mutation Affecting Resistance to Quinolones

| *gyrA* | | | | *parC* | | | |
|---|---|---|---|---|---|---|---|
| Mutation | | | Resistant Isolates Containing Mutation | Mutation | | | Resistant Isolates Containing Mutation |
| Start Amino Acid | Position | Final Amino Acid | | Start Amino Acid | Position | Final Amino Acid | |
| Serine | 83 | Leucine | 100% | Serine | 80 | Arginine or Isoluecine | 93.6% |
| Aspartic Acid | 87 | Glycine or Asparagine | 98.7% | Glutamic acid | 84 | Valine | 56.4% |

Notice that the isolated resistant bacteria contain a very high percent of each mutation. Table 32.2 shows the relationship between the number of mutations in these two genes compared to resistance to quinolones where the percentage is the number of bacteria of each type that have that number of mutations. For example, of the nine isolates of antibiotic susceptible bacteria, 55.6%, or five, had no mutations.

**TABLE 32.2.**

Mutation Number Affects Resistance to Antibiotics

| Mutation Number | Susceptible (9 isolates) | Resistant (78 isolates) |
|---|---|---|
| 0 | 55.6% | |
| 1 | 22.2% | 1.3% |
| 2 | 22.2% | 2.6% |
| 3 | | 42.3% |
| 4 | | 53.8% |

## Questions

1. Examine the graph from Experiment 1.
    a. How many times more ampicillin does it take to treat *E. coli* that has NDM-1? (Hint: Convert the % of wild type to how many more times ampicillin is needed.)
    b. Would taking this much more be reasonable? (Consider that a normal dose is 1 pill.) How many pills would you have to take?
2. According to Experiment 2, how does the number of mutations affect resistance to quinolones?
3. How do you think the mutations in *gyrA* and *parC* cause resistance to quinolones? (Hint: Look at the amino acid numbers and remember that drugs need to bind the target.)
4. Which of the following would be more likely to increase the resistance of bacteria to more than one class of antibiotics: the mutations in *gyrA* and *parC*, or the expression of NDM-1? Why?
5. Explain the order of events concerning the development of antibiotic resistance in a population. (Events [not in correct order]: Exposure to antibiotics, bacteria population evolution, and random DNA mutations.)
6. As evolution is the change in allele frequency in a population over time …
    a. What does a bacteria need to do to influence the allele frequency in a population?
    b. When considering multicellular organisms, what kind of genetic changes will not impact evolution?

## Part III: Significance of Evolution Today

In the antibiotic arms race, it looks like the bacteria are starting to win, I thought. I wonder what would happen if there really was a super bug that nothing could treat? What if it was a bacterium that caused pneumonia or tuberculosis or cholera instead of just a urinary tract infection?

In my research, I found that the most important factor leading to antibiotic-resistant bacteria was the presence of antibiotics. I wondered if there was any way to decrease the exposure of bacteria to antibiotics to only when they are needed.

### Instructions

When thinking about evolution, many people assume that it is only something that happened millions of years ago and therefore is not important now. So, is evolution relevant today?

To explore this issue, you will create a chart and use it to discuss and record in your groups the economic, environmental, political, and medical issues associated with antibiotic resistance. Then, as a class, we will discuss the ideas or solutions that you propose for the growing problem of antibiotic resistance.

- Form a group containing one of the following: a journalist, a doctor, a politician, and a parent. The goal of each group is to compile a chart of the many factors that could influence antibiotic resistance like the example shown in Table 32.3.

**TABLE 32.3.**

Sample Chart.

| Medical | Political | Economical | Environmental |
|---|---|---|---|
| | A law would be needed to change antibiotic prescription disposal. | A new law or educational program would cost the government money. | Antibiotics flushed down the toilet or thrown in the garbage increase environmental antibiotic resistance. |

- If you are a doctor or politician or parent:
  - Individually examine the graph at the top of your page and look at the axes. What information does the graph contain? Use this information to write a few sentences about your conclusions.
- If you are the journalist:

   - See the chart example in Table 32.3 to understand how each fact that will be presented by the doctor, politician, or parent may be composed of medical, political, economic, and environmental factors.
- Work as a group to fill out your chart.
   - Take turns reading your conclusions from your graph and the facts at the bottom of the page.
   - Decide as a group which factors (medical, political, economic, and environmental) each conclusion represents.
   - Have the recorder write that information on the chart.
- After the chart has been completed, discuss as a group the question: *How should we reduce antibiotic resistance?*
- Pick a member of your group to present results of your discussion to the class.

## *Part III: Data for the Individual Roles in the Case*

### Doctor

In your role as doctor, examine the graph shown in Figure 32.3 and then write in your conclusions.

**FIGURE 32.3.**

Rate of Antibiotic Development Has Changed Over Time.

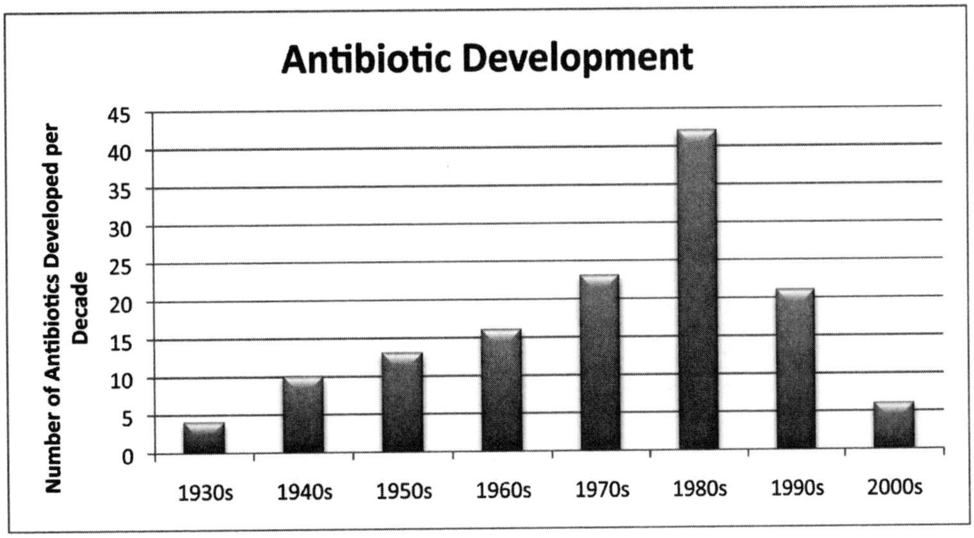

*Consider:*

- More than 70% of the bacteria that cause hospital-acquired infections are resistant to at least one of the drugs most commonly used to treat them.
- People infected with antibiotic-resistant organisms are more likely to have longer and more expensive hospital stays, increasing the burden on the healthcare system.
- New antibiotics are not profitable to develop. It takes around 500 million dollars and 12–15 years to develop and get a new antibiotic approved. Once the antibiotic is being used, resistance generally develops in 1–5 years.

## Politician

In your role as politician, examine the graph shown in Figure 32.4 and then write in your conclusions.

**FIGURE 32.4.**

Antibiotics Have Diverse Uses Beyond Treating Human Infections.

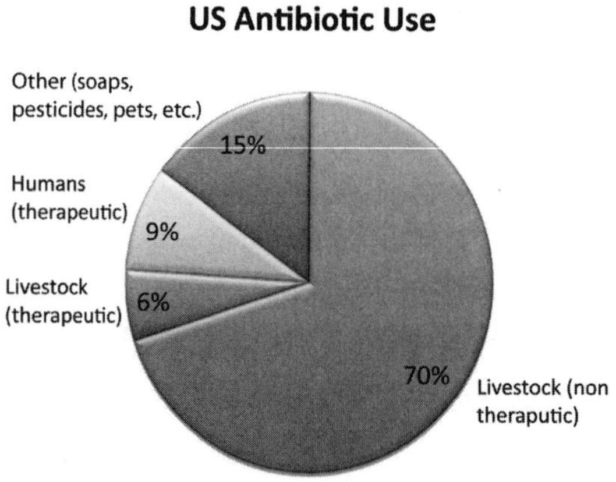


*Consider:*

- In 1950, scientists discovered that low doses of antibiotics make chickens grow faster than normal. Your constituents are heavily into agriculture and their livelihoods depend upon high yield.
- Reduced antibiotic use may lead to decreased productivity and increased food prices.
- Treating animals with antibiotics allows more animals to be raised on smaller amounts of land than animals not treated with antibiotics. Environmental

lobbyists argue that this treatment is inhumane and leads to greater antibiotic concentrations in the environment.

## Parent

In your role as parent, examine the graph shown in Figure 32.5 and then write in your conclusions.

**FIGURE 32.5.**

Percentage of Unnecessary Prescriptions of Antibiotics for Common Infections

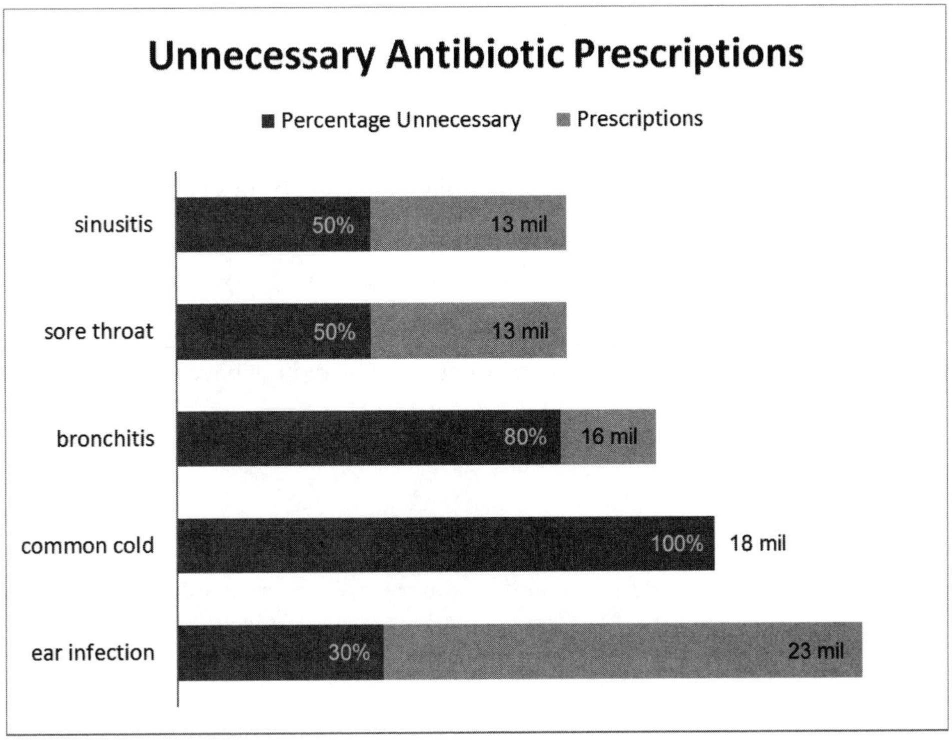


*Consider*

- Over 50% of patients don't finish their prescriptions. This allows partially resistant bacteria to live, so that next time the antibiotic does not kill the bacteria as effectively.
- Body soaps, household cleaners, sponges, and even mattresses and lip glosses are now packing bacteria-killing ingredients. These products can cause increased antibiotic resistance. Also, these products alter a person's microflora (normal bacteria that exist on skin and in digestive tract).

- Parents and patients often demand antibiotics for sickness even if it is unlikely to help. Antibiotics would be useless for infections caused by viruses for example. But if a doctor does not prescribe the antibiotic, the patient/parent can go to a different doctor. There are currently no laws in the United States regulating how doctors prescribe antibiotics.

## *Part IV: Checking Your Understanding*

*Exercise 1*: How does antibiotic resistance of bacteria demonstrate various principles of evolution? Make sure to use and underline the following terms in context: *selection, mutation, adaptation, bottleneck, fitness,* and *allele*. Limit your responses to one short paragraph.

*Exercise 2*: Where do antibiotics come from? What does their source have to do with evolution? Limit your responses to one or two paragraphs.

*Exercise 3*: Write one page on the role of population diversity in evolution. Be sure to address the following questions:

- What is population diversity? (Differentiate between phenotype and genotype.)
- Why is genetic diversity critical for evolution?
- What would happen to a population or a species if it did not have genetic diversity?
- In detail, how does a population become diverse? (Hint: Explain how mutations occur.)

## Web Version

The case PDF, detailed teaching notes, and an answer key are available on the NCCSTS website at *sciencecases.lib.buffalo.edu/cs/collection/detail.asp?case_id=594&id=594*.

# EXAGGERATED TRAITS AND BREEDING SUCCESS IN WIDOWBIRDS

## A Case of Sexual Selection and Evolution

*J. Phil Gibson*

## Abstract

In widowbirds, males undergo a dramatic change in plumage coloration and produce exceptionally long tail feathers during the breeding season; this change in appearance has facets of both intrasexual and intersexual selection. Students develop hypotheses and propose corresponding experiments and then are presented with data from actual experiments on sexual selection in widowbirds that they must analyze and interpret.


## Learning Objectives

- Explain the fundamental features of natural selection.
- Explain the process of natural selection in terms of sexual selection.
- Develop hypotheses for experiments testing intrasexual and intersexual selection.
- Interpret data from different experiments and then use those data to evaluate hypotheses and develop ideas for further experiments.
- Gain an understanding of trait variation among individuals.
- Be introduced to ideas regarding statistical testing.

## Quantitative Reasoning Skills/Concepts

- Interpret the meaning of simple statistical descriptors.
- Use graphs to formulate predictions and explanations.
- Accept or reject null hypotheses based on statistical tests of significance.
- Create experimental designs to test hypotheses.

# The Case Study

## Part I: Introduction

Natural selection is the evolutionary force that shapes the traits of a species in response to the various demands of its environment. Any process or event during the life of an organism that influences the number and quality of offspring produced by an organism due to a heritable trait(s) of that organism can act as a selective force. Selective forces can be produced by either the biotic or abiotic components of an organism's environment. Hence, natural selection is manifest as not a singular action, but rather as many different events occurring over the life of an organism. In this case study, the different and potentially conflicting manifestations of natural selection will be explored and studied.

### The Study Species

Widowbirds are small, finch-like birds in the genus *Euplectes*. They are striking members of the bird community in grasslands and shrubby savannas of southern and eastern Africa. This group is noted for the pronounced sexual dimorphism between males and females. During the non-breeding season, both male and female widowbirds have a brownish or buff coloration that blends with the grass and other vegetation. During the breeding season, however, males molt and produce black feathers on most of their body. Males also produce characteristic bright red and/or yellow epaulets and chevrons on their wings. Additionally, males of several widowbird species grow elaborately long tail feathers that can be up to half a meter in length.

During the breeding season, males secure and defend a territory from other males where they then build multiple nest frames. Males then perform a flight display that has a "bouncy rowing" appearance with loops and exaggerated wing beats to attract females to their territory. Females choose a male for breeding, line a nest frame in his territory with fine grass, and then incubate the eggs and feed the nestlings in that frame. After the breeding season, males molt to return to their pre-breeding coloration and appearance. Beyond initially building the nest frame, males do not participate further in raising their offspring. These elaborate behaviors and the striking seasonal sexual dimorphism in male widowbirds have provided researchers with an intriguing system in which to study how natural selection can shape traits of a species.

### Sexual Selection

The bright breeding coloration and long tails produced by male widowbirds are thought to be adaptations to attract the attention of female widowbirds. Reproductive systems in which individuals differentiate among potential mates and choose one based upon some characteristic(s) is a form of natural selection called sexual selection.

The fundamental idea of sexual selection is that choosing the best mate increases the probability of producing high-quality offspring who will pass on the parental genes to the next generation. Intrasexual selection occurs when members of one sex compete with one another for the opportunity to mate with members of the opposite sex or through actively securing and protecting a territory and its resources. Intersexual selection, frequently referred to as female choice, occurs when females choose among males based upon some criterion reflecting resources the male can provide or the quality of his genes.

### Concept Check

1. Evolution of reproductive characters and behaviors in long-tailed widowbirds has been shaped by natural selection. Develop hypotheses that could be used to test how intrasexual and intersexual selection could be shaping the evolution of traits in male long-tailed widowbirds.
   a. Hypotheses of intrasexual selection:
   b. Hypotheses of intersexual selection:
2. Explain the reasoning behind these hypotheses. How would natural selection be acting in them?

## *Part II: Truth in Advertising*

An important part of sexual selection in general and for long-tailed widowbirds in particular is that males need to signal their quality as a potential mate to the females.

### Concept Check

1. What are some of the possible signals of male quality in widowbirds and what information might they convey? What are the females choosing and why?
2. Develop an experiment that could be used to test the effectiveness of these signals in regards to the hypotheses of intrasexual and intersexual selection your group described previously.
3. While the signals given by males can indicate their quality, could they also be detrimental to the males? How?

## *Part III: The Handicap Hypothesis*

One idea that has been developed to explain the evolution of elaborate characteristics in males is called the *handicap hypothesis*. The handicap hypothesis proposes that females can assess the quality of a male by his ability to survive despite having a trait that could potentially be detrimental to his health. For example, exaggerated traits such as large horns on rams could be a hindrance to walking through thick brush or inhibit their ability to elude a predator. Similarly, while bright coloration indicates good health, it also increases visibility to predators. Widowbirds, particularly those that produce long tails, present excellent systems for evaluating the handicap hypothesis in sexual selection. As you consider the following studies, think about how they relate to the handicap hypothesis.

Researchers have conducted several studies to investigate the influence of coloration and tail length in widowbird mate choice and reproduction. Results of several experiments are described below.

## Epaulet Coloration Study

In a study of the red-collared widowbird (*Euplectes ardens*), researchers compared the brightness of the red epaulet among different males. They found that males with nesting territories tended to have redder epaulets than males without nesting territories. Among males with nesting territories, there was no significant relationship between the number of active nests (nest with a female and eggs) and the redness of the epaulets.

## Concept Check

1. How do you interpret the results of the epaulet coloration study in terms of sexual selection?

## Tail Length Study

In an initial field study, researchers compared the number of active nests and date of the first egg production in a nest among males with different tail lengths. Results of the study are given in Figures 33.1 and 33.2.

## Concept Check

1. What is the hypothesis being tested in this study?
2. Explain how the results either support or counter this hypothesis.

**FIGURE 33.1.**

Number of Active Nests for Males With Different Tail Lengths ($y = 0.038x - 4.84$; $F_{1,40} = 17.3$, $r^2 = 47.4\%$, $p < 0.001$). Data based on Pryke, Anderson, and Lawes 2001.

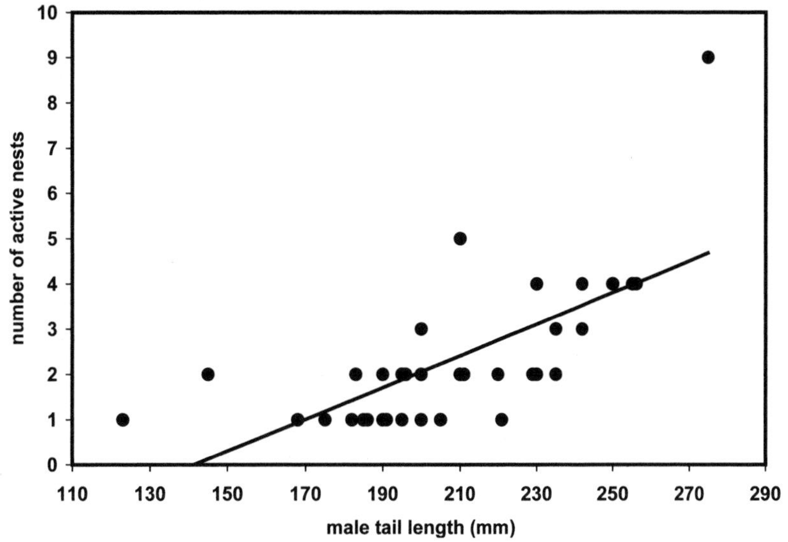


**FIGURE 33.2.**

Date of First Egg Laid in the Nest for Males With Different Tail Lengths. ($y = -0.085x + 27.32$, $F_{1,40} = 9.3$, $r^2 = 30.0\%$, $p = 0.0003$) Data based on Pryke, Anderson, and Lawes 2001.

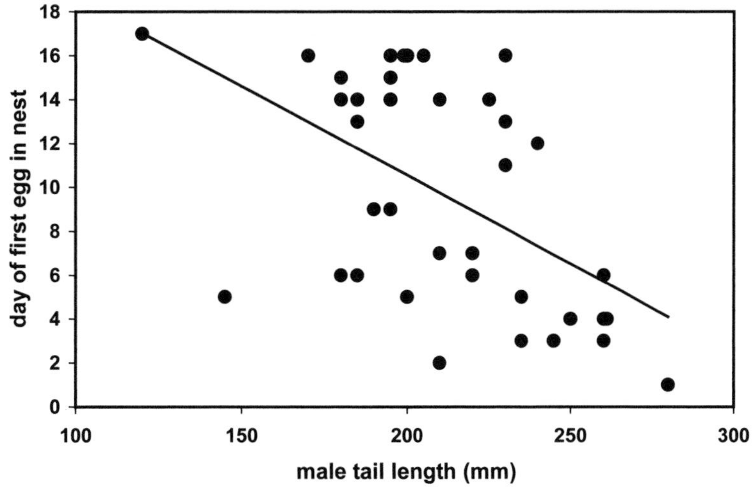

## Tail Length Manipulations

In a different study, researchers studied the long-tailed widowbird (*Euplectes progne*). They started by counting the number of active nests among four groups of nine male birds with similar tail lengths (Figure 33.3).

**FIGURE 33.3.**

Mean number of active nests (± standard error) for nine males in four different treatment groups before tail length manipulation. There are no significant differences in mean number of nests among groups. Data based on Andersson 1982.

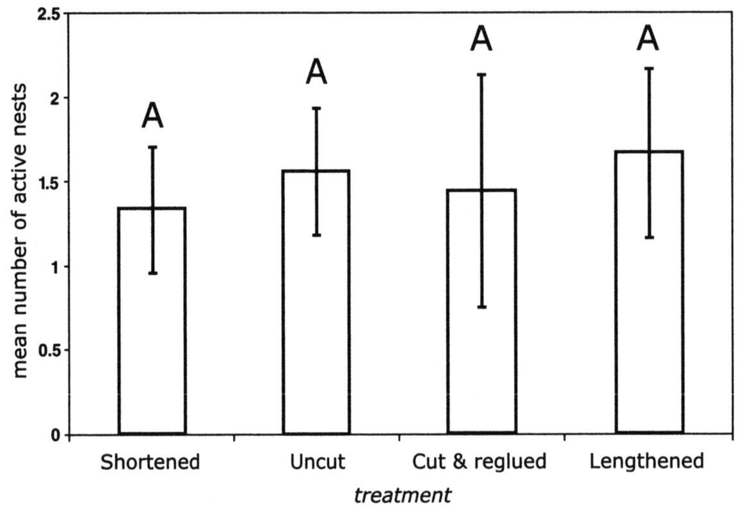


Next, researchers manipulated the four groups of males as follows:

- Group 1—tails shortened
- Group 2—tails uncut
- Group 3—tails cut and re-glued onto the male, length unchanged
- Group 4—tails elongated by gluing on the length cut from Group 1 males

The number of new active nests in the territories of males in the four groups after treatment is given in Figure 33.4.

**FIGURE 33.4.**

Mean number of new nests (± standard error) for nine males in four different treatment groups after tail length manipulation. Groups with different letters above them are significantly different from one another ($p < 0.05$). Data based on Andersson 1982.

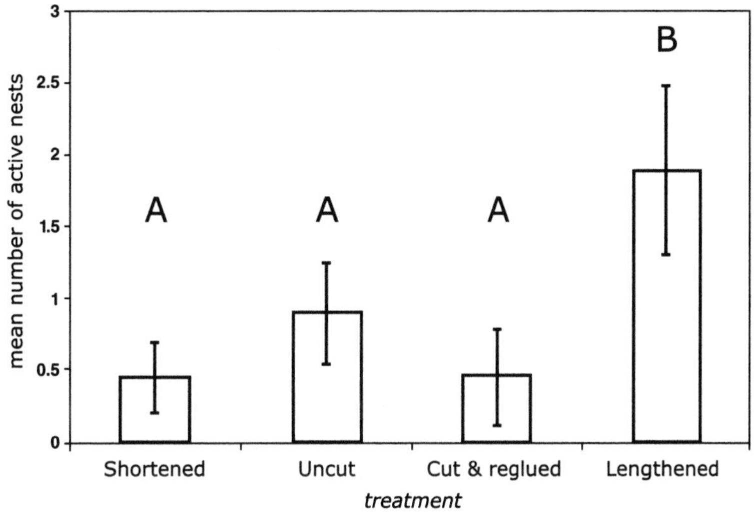


## Concept Check

1. How do you interpret the results of this experiment in terms of sexual selection?
2. What was the purpose of Groups 2 and 3 in this experiment?
3. Nothing in biology comes without a cost. Describe an experiment you could conduct to follow-up on the results of the tail length manipulation experiment to explore the potential costs of longer tail length in males. Do you think there is any evidence that natural selection has acted on the potential costs of long tails already?

## *Part IV: Longer Tails in a Short-Tailed Species*

Having conducted the studies described above in two long-tailed species, the researchers conducted a similar tail manipulation experiment in a closely related species, the red-shouldered widowbird (*Euplectes axillaris*). Although males in this species have distinctive breeding plumage colors, they do not produce a long tail. Data from this experiment are given in Figures 33.5 and 33.6 (p. 304).

**FIGURE 33.5.**

Number of males with different tail lengths in a population of red-collared widowbirds. Data based on Pryke and Andersson 2002.

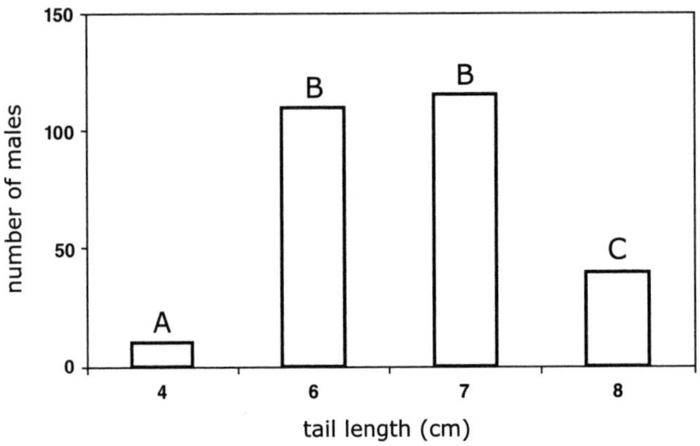


**FIGURE 33.6.**

Mean number of active nests (± standard error) in a population of red-shouldered widowbirds, which had tails shortened (6 cm), elongated (8 cm) or super-elongated (22cm). Groups with different letters above them are significantly different from one another ($p < 0.05$). Data based on Pryke and Andersson 2002.

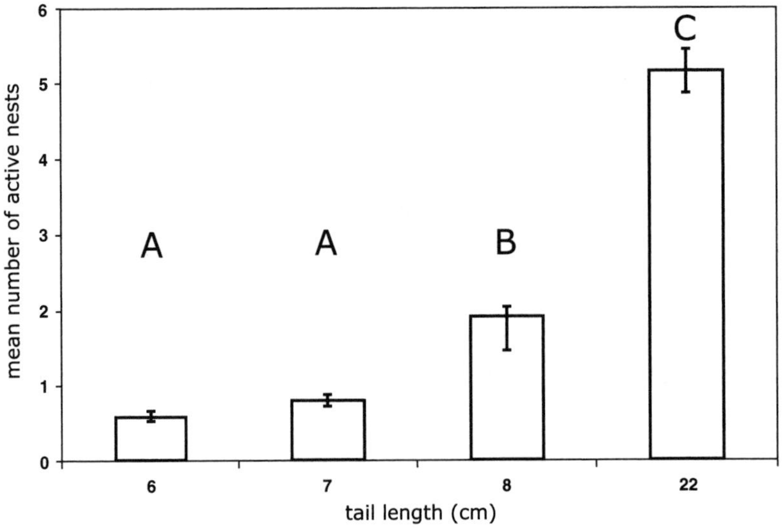

## Concept Check

1. What hypothesis was being tested in this follow-up study? Why was it necessary?
2. What do the data in Figures 33.5 and 33.6 show?
3. Do their results support their hypothesis? What do the results mean? Explain.

## Question for Further Thought

1. If long tail length is so important to female widowbirds, why don't male tails continue to get longer and longer?

## Web Version

Detailed teaching notes, the case PDF, and an answer key are available on the NCCSTS website at *sciencecases.lib.buffalo.edu/cs/collection/detail.asp?case_id=237&id=237*.

## References

Andersson, M. 1982. Female choice selects for extreme tail length in a widowbird. *Nature* 299: 818–820.

Pryke, S. R., and S. Andersson. 2002. A generalized female bias for long tails in a short-tailed widowbird. *Proceedings of the Royal Society of London Series B* 269: 2141–2146.

Pryke, S. R., S. Andersson, and M. J. Lawes. 2001. Sexual selection of multiple handicaps in the red-collared widowbird: Female choice of tail length but not carotenoid display. *Evolution* 55: 1452–1463.

## SECTION VIII

# PLANT FORM AND FUNCTION

# IS *GUAIACUM SANCTUM* EFFECTIVE AGAINST ARTHRITIS?

## An Ethnobotany Case

*Eric Ribbens, Barbra Burdett, and Angela Green*

### Abstract

Students read about a tropical population ecologist who is studying an unusual tree in the tropical forests of Central America and answer a series of questions designed to explore the process of screening and testing the medicinal value of plants identified as having potential health benefits.

### Learning Objectives

- Learn about the process required before a drug can be made available in Western medicine.
- Practice designing experiments and analyzing data.
- Consider the implications of somewhat ambiguous results and side effects in medicine.

### Quantitative Reasoning Skills/Concepts

- Formulate null and alternative hypotheses.
- Articulate complete and correct claims based on data.
- Use appropriate reasoning to support the validity of data-based claims.
- Interpret results comprising a mixture of qualitative and quantitative measurements.

### The Case Study

#### *Part I: Anecdotal Evidence*

Dr. Beth Tonoany is a tropical population ecologist who has been studying an unusual tree, *Guaiacum sanctum*, which once grew throughout the dry tropical forests of Central America as well as on some of the Caribbean islands. *Guaiacum sanctum* produces a wood called *lignum vitae*, and is known in Costa Rica and other Spanish-speaking countries as *guayacan reál*. The wood is extremely heavy because it contains extensive deposits of resin and it will sink if placed in water.

During World War I and II it was extensively harvested for use in the ship-building industry because the wood, which does not split easily, is self-lubricating, due to its high resin content. The wood is very durable and was in high demand for constructing bearing sleeves to support ship propeller shafts. It has also been used for making railroad ties.

Dr. Tonoany has been studying one of the last remaining populations of *lignum vitae* in the Palo Verde Nature Preserve in northwestern Costa Rica. Probably fewer than 100 trees remain in Costa Rica, most in the Palo Verde Nature Preserve. Her research has included tracking seedlings and saplings, locating and measuring adult trees, and interviewing some of the local people, Ticos, to learn about the tree's past history in Costa Rica. The tree, while rare now due to the dramatic conversion of tropical deciduous forest in Costa Rica into pasturelands and to selective logging of the tree for its valuable wood, was once more common, and many of the older Ticos remember that the saplings were used to make cattle switches because of the strong flexible wood in the saplings.

Interestingly, Dr. Tonoany has also heard from several Ticos that the tree also was used medicinally. Señora Milena Gonzalez, an elderly woman now living in Bagaces, told Dr. Tonoany that she remembered her grandmother "suffered from aches and pains in her legs" and would boil guayacan leaves in water to make an herbal tea she claimed made her aches go away. Señora Milena added that her grandmother said you had to keep drinking the tea for it to be effective, and that it was also necessary to have a pure heart. Señor Jorge Carrera, a retired cattle herder, remembered that Señor Lopez, who owned the ranch where he worked, would sometimes experience painful swellings of his big toe. He would apply a poultice of straw and cow manure to his foot, and drink a tea made by boiling guayacan wood in water. Señor Carrera insisted that in a day or two the swelling would disappear.

Dr. Tonoany became interested in these medicinal uses of *lignum vitae*. She spent some time in the library and discovered several key points about the medicinal uses of *Guaiacum sanctum*. For example the resin has medical value as a diaphoretic in treating rheumatism; it has been used in medicine as a laxative, for gonorrhea, for gout, and as a dentifrice, as well as in the treatment of syphilis. She discovered that the leaves of *Guaiacum officinale* contain several unique saponins and that scientist Dan Janzen found that a captive tapir refused to eat the leaves every time they were offered.

Dr. Tonoany encouraged her graduate student, Mabel Gailke, to determine if *Guaiacum sanctum* produces a chemical that has anti-inflammatory properties: "We have lots of anecdotal evidence that *lignum vitae* is useful in treating rheumatism, arthritis, and gout, but it's frustrating that there is absolutely no data to support these claims. I want you to design and implement a study that we can use to support or reject the idea that this species might be medically valuable."

## Questions

1. How should Mabel proceed? From talking with people around the department, she knows that for an initial trial she cannot work with humans, and due to budgetary constraints probably she will need to work with mice or rats. Design an experiment for her to implement.
2. *(Ethics question)* Does Dr. Tonoany need permission to harvest plant material from Costa Rica?

## *Part II: Rat Study*

Mabel Gailke designed a research project to test whether *Guaiacum sanctum* resin has an anti-inflammatory effect on rats, which was approved by the Biology Department.

Mabel's experiment tested the response of rat paws to swelling induced by carrageenan, a skin irritant. All rats were weighed, sexed, and, if possible, aged. The experimental rats were divided into six groups, balanced with representatives of various weights and equal ratios of males and females. After coating the left front paw of each rat with carrageenan to induce swelling, each of the six groups received a different oral treatment. One group was treated with a placebo, four groups were given *Guaiacum* resin in four different concentrations, and one group was treated with indomethacin, an anti-inflammatory drug used to treat arthritis. The *Guaiacum* resin was obtained by boiling leaves under reflux in 70% ethanol.

Inflamed joints were measured over an eight-hour period at hourly intervals after administration to compare swelling over time. Observations of behavior and side effects were logged at hourly intervals during the same eight-hour period. Results are shown in Table 34.1.

**TABLE 34.1.**

Effect of Drug Treatments on Paw Swelling and Frequencies of Side Effects

| Treatment | % Swelling After 8 Hours, ± 95% C.I. | Frequency of Lethargy | Frequency of Skin Irritation | Frequency of Hyperactivity |
|---|---|---|---|---|
| Placebo | 98.2 ±9.6 | 0.4 | 1.2 | 0.6 |
| Resin, 100 mg/kg | 95.4 ±12.7 | 0.9 | 3.2 | 0.2 |
| Resin, 200 mg/kg | 84.5 ±5.2 | 1.7 | 5.7 | 0.8 |
| Resin, 300 mg/kg | 76.3 ±4.6 | 2.6 | 6.3 | 1.3 |
| Resin, 400 mg/kg | 68.7 ±1.2 | 4.3 | 6.9 | 2.7 |
| Indomethacin, 2.5 mg/kg | 79 ±5.7 | 3.1 | 7.2 | 1.5 |

## Questions

1. What did Mabel find out about inflammation in rats treated with *Guaiacum* resin? Did using different dosages make a difference?
2. What strength of *Guaiacum* resin was most beneficial? Why?
3. In your opinion, which medication is better, indomethacin or *Guaiacum* resin? Why?
4. Including the behavior and side effects of taking *Guaiacum* resin, what is your overall opinion of the use of *Guaiacum* resin as an anti-arthritic medication?
5. Do you think *Guaiacum sanctum* will be a good candidate for marketing and further research? In other words, can this plant compete with drugs already on the market?
6. What do these results mean for human use of this plant for rheumatoid arthritis? Should studies be conducted in humans? If so, how?
7. Because this experiment did indicate that *Guaiacum* resin can be quite effective against inflammations, Dr. Tonoany and Mabel Gailke decided to collaborate with the nearby medical research clinic to test the effectiveness of *Guaiacum* resin on humans with severe arthritis. Design an experiment for the clinic to implement. Remember that this study should test whether *Guaiacum* resin has effects specifically on people with very severe arthritis.
8. *(Ethics question)* What concerns about intellectual property rights are raised in regard to this experiment?

## *Part III: Human Study*

Working with a local clinic, Dr. Tonoany and Ms. Geilke selected 20 individuals with severe arthritis from a set of volunteers to participate in a double blind study. All volunteers were severely crippled with arthritis, no longer found indomethacin an effective arthritis treatment, and were between the ages of 60 and 65. Fifteen were females and five were males. All volunteers were screened to ensure normal blood pressure, urinalysis, and erythrocyte levels, and all had the highest degree of complications due to arthritic joint swelling.

Half of the subjects were given *Guaiacum* resin at 400 mg/kg and half were given a placebo. Neither the doctor nor the patient knew who was receiving the resin and who was receiving the placebo. After one month, in addition to monitoring blood pressure, urine, and erythrocyte levels, x-rays of the most arthritic joint were examined and the degree of arthritic complications was categorized as A, B, C, or D, with D being the greatest degree of complications due to swelling of the joint. The results are shown in Table 34.2.

## Questions

1. What did the clinical study show?
2. Are the side effects a problem? Why or why not?
3. What are the limitations of the experimental design?
4. Dr. Tonoany has found that "probably fewer than 100 trees remain in Costa Rica, most in the PaloVerde Nature Preserve." What ecological concerns does this experiment raise?
5. Based on these results, what should Dr. Tonoany and her colleagues do next?
6. Is it realistic to test an unknown drug on humans after a single clinical trial?
7. *(Ethics question)* If it looks like this drug is potentially medically useful, should the native peoples be compensated for their trees and the information that led to the experiment?

## Web Version

Detailed teaching notes, the case PDF, and an answer key are available on the NCCSTS website at *sciencecases.lib.buffalo.edu/cs/collection/detail.asp?case_id=178&id=178*.

**TABLE 34.2.**

Effects of Guaiacum Resin on Arthritic Patients.

| Gender | Drug | Other | X-ray |
|---|---|---|---|
| F1 | resin | hair loss | A |
| F2 | placebo | 0 | D |
| F3 | resin | 0 | B |
| F4 | placebo | hair loss | C |
| F5 | resin | 0 | B |
| F6 | placebo | 0 | D |
| F7 | resin | hair loss | A |
| F8 | placebo | 0 | D |
| F9 | resin | skin rash | B |
| F10 | placebo | 0 | D |
| F11 | resin | 0 | C |
| F12 | placebo | nausea | C |
| F13 | resin | 0 | B |
| F14 | placebo | 0 | D |
| F15 | resin | 0 | B |
| M1 | placebo | 0 | C |
| M2 | resin | 0 | A |
| M3 | placebo | 0 | B |
| M4 | resin | skin rash | A |
| M5 | placebo | 0 | D |

CHAPTER 35

# I'M LOOKING OVER A WHITE-STRIPED CLOVER

## A Case of Natural Selection

*Susan Evarts, Alison Krufka, Luke Holbrook, and Chester Wilson*

## Abstract

This case explores the process of natural selection using white clover as an example. In general, two forms of white clover can be found around the world in various habitats. One type is able to produce cyanide in its leaves while the other is not. This variation within the clover species, along with the fact that cyanide production is paired with the production of a white stripe on the leaf, is used to teach the process of evolution through natural selection.


## Learning Objectives

- Understand the process of natural selection and the importance of environment-specific adaptations.
- Acquire an understanding of the concepts of *variation, natural selection, fitness, selection pressure, evolution,* and *adaptation.*
- Use these terms in a paragraph to describe the frequency of the two types of white clover.
- Predict the distribution of cyanogenic clover in given microhabitats.
- Gain experience with the scientific method and be able to propose hypotheses and justifications to explain the frequency of the two types of white clover.
- Design experiments to test hypotheses and describe data that would support these hypotheses.
- Understand and synthesize information from figures and tables.
- Be able to quantify the strength of selection and the relative fitness of the different clover forms in different habitats.
- Understand what values for strength of selection and relative fitness mean in terms of how selection is acting on these plants.

## Quantitative Reasoning Skills/Concepts

- Carry out basic mathematical operations.
- Use graphs to formulate predictions and explanations.
- Formulate null and alternative hypotheses.
- Articulate complete and correct claims based on data.
- Use appropriate reasoning to support the validity of data-based claims.
- Create experimental designs to test hypotheses.
- Calculate relative fitness and selection coefficients.

## The Case Study

### *Part I: "I'm Looking Over ..."*

White clover (*Trifolium repens*), a small perennial plant, is found throughout the world, and has two forms. One variant has entirely green leaves (*plain*) and the other has green leaves with a prominent white stripe (*striped*).

Both variants of white clover (plain and striped) are found along the coast of Long Island, New York. Most of Long Island is only a few feet above sea level. A series of low grass-covered hills separated by shallow depressions covers the area behind the oceanfront dunes. The shallow depressions reach to the water table, so they tend to be permanently moist year round and do not freeze in winter. Water drains away quickly from the low hills, which tend to dry out many times over the year and freeze in the winter. The habitat in the shallow depressions is more hospitable to molluscs (snails and slugs) that feed on clover. One type of clover is more common in shallow depressions while the other type is more likely to be found on low hills.

At the end of the case, we will come back to New York and ask you to predict which type of white clover is most abundant in each microhabitat. But first, let's consider the abundance of these two types of clover on a larger scale.

Figure 35.1 shows the relative frequency of white clover variants in Minnesota and North Carolina. Table 35.1 provides additional information on Minnesota and North Carolina.

**FIGURE 35.1.**

Relative Frequency of Plain and White-Striped Clover in Two Different Habitats.

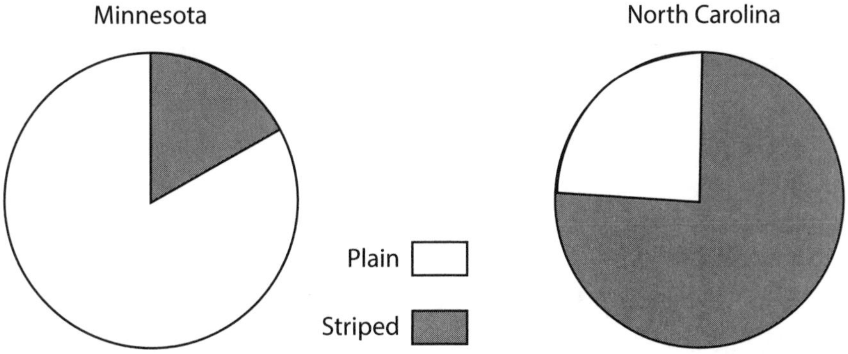


**TABLE 35.1.**

Physical and Ecological Factors of Typical Habitats in Minnesota and North Carolina.

| | Minnesota | North Carolina |
|---|---|---|
| Latitude | 43–49° N | 34–36° N |
| Mean elevation | 0.365 km | 0.213 km |
| Ave. monthly temp. range | −19.4° to 28.6° C | −2.6° to 31.3° C |
| High temperature | 45.6°C | 43.3°C |
| Low temperature | −51°C | −37 °C |
| Mean # days with high above 32°C* | 14 | 38 |
| Mean # of days with low below 0°C* | 154 | 75 |
| Ave. yearly precipitation | 66–76 cm | 107–117 cm |
| Presence of herbivores (molluscs such as snails, slugs) | smaller population, not present in winter | larger, more active population, present all year |

Data from Netstate.com and National Oceanic and Atmospheric Administration.
* Data for capital cities (St. Paul, Minnestoa, and Raleigh, North Carolina).

## Exercise 1

A habitat is defined as the place and conditions under which an organism lives. This includes physical factors such as temperature, soil type, availability of nutrients, and availability of moisture as well as biological factors such as presence of herbivores, competitors for nutrients, and pathogens. Using the information in Table 35.1, briefly summarize the habitat features for white clover in each state.

## Part II: Unlucky Clover

Some variants of white clover produce cyanide (CN), which is a powerful poison. Two gene products are required to produce active cyanide. One gene encodes an inactive cyanide-sugar complex that is stored in the plant cell's cytoplasm. The other gene encodes an enzyme that cleaves the sugar to activate the cyanide. This enzyme is stored in the cell wall. In general, striped clover contains cyanide; plain clover does not.

In consistent freezing temperatures, plant cell membranes (surrounding organelles and the cell itself) can burst. This is why the parts of plants above ground die back in colder climates. Root cells, however, are less likely to burst because they are underground and often store sugars, which protect the cell from freezing (just like antifreeze). This allows perennial plants to survive and grow again in the spring. Like the damage caused by freezing, herbivores can also damage plant cells. In the process of eating a leaf, herbivores destroy the membranes and organelles of the cells that make up the leaf.

### Exercise 2

a. Why do you think the two gene products are stored in different parts of the cell?

b. Suggest at least two ways these products might come together to make active CN in nature.

c. Suggest a reason that clover may produce cyanide. That is, what advantage does a plant gain by producing cyanide? Also suggest a possible disadvantage of producing cyanide. Or might there be no advantage?

d. It takes energy for an organism to produce a particular structure such as a stripe on a clover leaf that is otherwise plain. Why might cyanide-producing clover produce striped leaves?

e. To explore this idea a little further, consider the results of the hypothetical experiments shown in Table 35.2. In each situation, snails that have been taken from a wild habitat where both types of clover are present were put in a petri dish containing varying types of clover. How would you interpret each result? Fill in the table with your interpretations.

**TABLE 35.2.**

Interpretations of Results From Hypothetical Experiments Using Snails and Clover.

| Clover presented to snails | Snail response | Interpretation |
|---|---|---|
| plain leaves | eaten | |
| striped leaves and plain leaves | plain leaves eaten | |
| striped leaves | not eaten | |
| plain leaves painted with white stripe | not eaten | |

## Exercise 3

To understand why cyanide producing/striped clover is found at a higher frequency in North Carolina than in Minnesota, you must consider the "fitness" of each variant in the different habitats available in the two states. Fitness is determined by the ability of an organism to survive, grow, and reproduce in a particular habitat. You have probably heard the term "survival of the fittest," but if an organism is not able to also grow and reproduce, it will not be able to pass any of its alleles (genetic information) on to its offspring. An organism that has high fitness does well in its habitat and passes those favorable alleles onto its offspring when it reproduces.

Go back and review the habitats you described in Exercise 1 and think about the factors that would be important for plant fitness. Then list the ecological differences between North Carolina and Minnesota that might affect the fitness of each variant. In other words which factors might increase plant growth, survival, and reproduction in each habitat, and which factors might inhibit them?

We can express fitness and selection with numbers that tell us not only whether one organism has a higher fitness than another, but also the degree to which that organism is more likely to survive and reproduce than another organism. It is not always possible to make an absolute measure of fitness, but often we can measure relative fitness. For each type of organism, we take some measure related to fitness, such as the percentage of individuals of that type surviving to the next generation. We then divide the measures for each type by the highest value. Thus, the organisms with the highest fitness will have a relative fitness of 1.0, whereas other organisms will have some value less than 1.0, but no lower than zero.

Here is an example of how we can calculate relative fitness from a classic study by Bernard Kettlewell (Kettlewell 1955, 1956) on peppered moths (*Biston betularia*). The moths come in two forms (essentially dark and light), and Kettlewell studied them in two types of environments, polluted forests with trees with dark bark, and unpolluted forests with trees with light bark. He hypothesized that the color of the moth would determine how easily predators could spot it, such that dark moths should have a higher fitness in polluted forests, and light moths should have higher fitness in unpolluted forests.

To test this hypothesis, he marked moths of both types and released them into both environments. Sometime later, he collected moths from both environments and determined how many of the marked moths he recovered. Here are his results (Table 35.3).

**TABLE 35.3.**

Survival Rates of Dark and Light Moths in Unpolluted and Polluted Forests.

| | Unpolluted | | | Polluted | | |
|---|---|---|---|---|---|---|
| | Released | Recaptured | % Recaptured | Released | Recaptured | % Recaptured |
| **Dark** | 406 | 19 | 4.7 | 447 | 123 | 27.5 |
| **Light** | 393 | 54 | 13.7 | 137 | 18 | 13.1 |

How do you explain the fact that Kettlewell did not recover every marked moth? Based on the data, which moths had a higher fitness in the unpolluted forest? What about in the polluted forest?

Now we can calculate the relative fitness of each type of moth in each environment. We can treat the percent recaptured as a reflection of survival. In the unpolluted forest, the light moths are fittest, so we divide each percentage recaptured by the percentage of light moths recaptured, or:

Relative fitness of light moths = 13.7/13.7 = 1.0

Relative fitness of dark moths = 4.7/13.7 = 0.34

Calculate *relative fitness* for dark and light moths in the polluted forest.

One thing you might have noticed is that the difference between relative fitness of the fittest moths and the least fit moths is not the same for the unpolluted and polluted forests. This difference is called the strength of selection, or the selection coefficient(s). We can calculate this value for each environment. Here's the calculation for the unpolluted forest: Unpolluted forest: $s = 1.0 - 0.34 = 0.66$

Calculate $s$ for the polluted forest.

Since the unpolluted forest has a higher value for *s*, selection is stronger in the unpolluted forest than in the polluted forest. Describe what this means in terms of survival and reproduction of the moths in each environment.

## Part III: Investigating Clover Distribution

Now that you have considered the different habitats in which the white clover is found and the factors affecting fitness in clover, you will develop hypotheses to explain the observed distribution of plain and striped clover. A hypothesis is a tentative answer to a well-framed question. This means that one has developed an explanation of an event based on preliminary data, observations, and perhaps the work of other scientists. Scientists use observations and data to develop and justify their hypotheses. A hypothesis is presented as a statement, not a question, and must be both testable (there must be some way to test if it is valid) and falsifiable (it must be possible to show that an incorrect hypothesis is false).

### Exercise 4

Based on the data presented above and the differences in habitat between Minnesota and North Carolina, propose a hypothesis to explain each of the following: (a) the higher frequency of plain clover in Minnesota, and (b) the higher frequency of cyanide producing/striped clover in North Carolina. Justify the reasoning leading to each of your hypotheses. Be specific in terms of which variables (conditions) affect the frequency of each type of clover in each habitat. Remember to write your hypotheses as statements, not as questions.

### Exercise 5

Are your hypotheses the same for the different habitats? Explain why individuals or populations from the same species may show different traits in different habitats. Use the term "selection pressure" in your explanation. Selection pressure refers to the influence a particular factor has on the ability of an organism to survive and reproduce.

### Exercise 6

Once a scientist has formed a hypothesis, the next step is to test it with observations or experiments. Experiments should test only one variable at a time, and keep as many other factors as possible constant (which doesn't mean "unchanging," but only that they are the same for all experimental groups). Design experiments to test at least one hypothesis for each habitat.

### Exercise 7

For each of the experiments you proposed in Exercise 5, describe data that would support your hypothesis and data that would falsify your hypothesis.

## Exercise 8

Is there any reason you might expect selection to be stronger in one environment than the other?

Here are results of a hypothetical experiment looking at survival of the different types of clover at different locations (Table 35.4). Do these results support or refute your hypothesis?

**TABLE 35.4.**

Survival Rates of Plain and Striped Clover in Minnesota and North Carolina (based on a hypothetical experiment)

| | Survival | |
|---|---|---|
| **Variety** | **Minnesota** | **North Carolina** |
| Plain | 59% | 27% |
| Striped | 13% | 72% |

Calculate the relative fitness of each type of clover at each location. Calculate the strength of selection (s) at each location. Where is selection strongest?

## *Part IV: What Did You Learn?*

You have already thought about and used several concepts from evolutionary biology that aid in our understanding of how organisms adapt to their habitats. Now let's formally define them.

*Variation*: Differences among individuals of a species; different forms of the same trait.

*Natural Selection*: Differential survival and reproduction of individuals bearing different forms of the same trait.

*Evolution*: Genetic change in a population over time.

*Adaptation*: The evolution of a trait that increases the likelihood of survival and reproduction of an organism in a particular environment.

## Exercise 9

a. What are examples of variation in the clover?
b. Refer back to Figure 35.1 showing the relative frequency of plain and striped clover in Minnesota and North Carolina. Explain why there is variation in the frequency of each type of white clover between each of these areas.

c. Adaptation in the white clover means that over time there is an increase in the frequency of particular traits that would help individuals in that population of white clover survive and reproduce in that particular habitat. What are examples of possible adaptations in the clover? Remember, adaptations are specific to a particular habitat.

d. Comparing the white clover populations in Minnesota and North Carolina, what would you need as evidence that evolution has occurred?

e. Several factors may exert selection pressure on different traits in white clover in each habitat. What factor would you propose is exerting the strongest selection pressure on the production or nonproduction of CN in white clover in Minnesota? In North Carolina?

## Part V: Checking Your Understanding

### Exercise 10

Based on your understanding of the clover case and the definitions provided above, which of the following statements are true? Explain why each of the correct statements is true or correct each of the false statements to produce a true statement.

a. Natural selection can fully be explained by the phrase "survival of the fittest."

b. Variation is necessary for natural selection to occur.

c. Adaptation is defined with respect to local environmental conditions (e.g., heat, cold, rainfall, competitors, herbivores).

d. Natural selection acts on populations, not individuals.

### Exercise 11

a. Predict which variant of white clover would be most frequent in each of the microhabitats on Long Island (refer to Part I).

b. Write a paragraph that describes the distribution of clover in the microclimates of Long Island using the terms *variation*, *adaptation*, *natural selection*, and *evolution*. Be sure to fully describe each of these terms in your detailed paragraph.

## Web Version

Detailed teaching notes, the case PDF, and an answer key are available on the NCCSTS website at *sciencecases.lib.buffalo.edu/cs/collection/detail.asp?case_id=272&id=272*.

## References

Kettlewell, H. B. D. 1955. Selection experiments on industrial melanism in the Lepidoptera. *Heredity* 9: 323–342.

Kettlewell, H. B. D. 1956. Further selection experiments on industrial melanism in the Lepidoptera. *Heredity* 10: 287–301.

National Oceanic and Atmospheric Administration. NOAA National Data Centers Data Tables. *ols.nndc.noaa.gov/plolstore/plsql/olstore.prodspecific?prodnum=C00095-PUB-A0001#TABLES*

CHAPTER 36

# THE ECOLOGY OF *OPUNTIA FRAGILIS* (NUTTALL) HAWORTH

*Eric Ribbens*

1. Plant of *Opuntia fragilis*. 2. Flowering branch of *Opuntia rhodantha*. 3. Flowering joint of *Opuntia polyacantha*. (All natural size.)

## Abstract

This case is based on the author's own personal research on the fragile prickly pear cactus in Stearns County, Minnesota. The data described is a product of the work of several undergraduate students at St. Johns University, which partially funded this research. By simulating the process of doing science through its progressive disclosure format, the case encourages students to think about plant population ecology from an actual research perspective.

## Learning Objectives

- Explore aspects of basic plant population ecology.
- Think about research design.
- Simulate the process of doing science.

## Quantitative Reasoning Skills/Concepts

- Interpret the meaning of simple statistical descriptors, such as error bars and trend lines.
- Use graphs to formulate predictions and explanations.
- Articulate complete and correct claims based on data.
- Use appropriate reasoning (i.e., experimental design and/or statistics) to support the validity of data-based claims.
- Create experimental designs to test hypotheses.

## The Case Study

### *Part I: Your New Career*

Welcome to your new career as a plant population ecologist! As an ecologist, you are interested in how plants interact within a population, with other species, and with their surrounding environment. You have recently accepted a position at a university in central Minnesota and have been looking for an interesting plant species in the area to study. There is a county park being developed on 105 hectares of abandoned granite quarry land a few miles away from the university, and in a conversation you had recently with George, the Stearns County Parks Director, he mentioned that one of the plant species found in the parkland is *Opuntia fragilis*, the brittle prickly pear, which in his opinion should be on the Minnesota state list of endangered and threatened plant species.

You asked George to show you the population, and after walking through a scrubby red oak forest growing around piles of granite slag and water-filled quarries, you found an exposed granite outcrop about 20 meters long and 15 meters wide with several clusters of prickly pear growing along one edge of the outcrop. Immediately you fell in love with them. They are tiny, each joint about five centimeters long, bristling with spines, and sprawling over a mat of brownish moss growing in a crack in the granite. You quickly realized that this species might be an ideal organism to study—it is relatively easy to find and identify, quite rare, the population is completely isolated, with nice discrete boundaries, George would love to have you investigate the ecology of *Opuntia fragilis* at the park.

Now you are sitting in your office, your head bursting with ideas and questions. Where should you begin? You've already spent some time in the library and have some basic information. Particularly valuable was a book by Lyman Benson (1982), *The Cacti of the United States and Canada*. In this book, Benson refers to brittle prickly pear several times. The book has a range map showing that *Opuntia fragilis* is widely scattered across 25 states and five Canadian provinces. However, in most of those regions the populations are widely scattered and the plant is actually quite uncommon. You learn that *Opuntia fragilis* was one of the first four species of cacti collected from the U.S. interior, and was first collected by Thomas Nuttall on the shores of the Missouri River. *Opuntia fragilis* occurs up to latitude 58 degrees in northern Alberta and British Columbia, where winter temps can be –40° C. Benson proposed that its prostrate growth form and thickened pads are both adaptations to a cold climate. He reasoned that these traits were adaptive to cold because the low growth form means it is quickly covered by protective snow and thick pads provide a reduced surface-to-volume ratio. Both of these traits would reduce freeze damage.

Benson also mentioned that the dry fruits are capable of epizoochorous transportation (i.e., they get stuck in the fur of animals). In his opinion the wide northern range of *Opuntia fragilis* was caused by the easy fragmentation of the pads. Benson wrote, "The plains buffalo occurred in enormous herds, and their great hairy bodies would have been ideal for transporting the small cactus joints. The places where buffalo lay down probably included many plants of *Opuntia fragilis*." The cactus is common at the edges of "slick spots" formed on soils in eastern Montana and western North Dakota. These areas were probably buffalo wallows. The species flowers only sparingly in North Dakota. In Minnesota, *Opuntia fragilis* is scattered across the state, with most populations growing along the Minnesota River. The top central dot on Figure 36.1 shows the population in your county, but not in any other county within 80 miles.

**FIGURE 36.1.**

Approximate Distribution of *O. fragilis* in Minnesota. (Based on Ownbey and Morley 1991.)

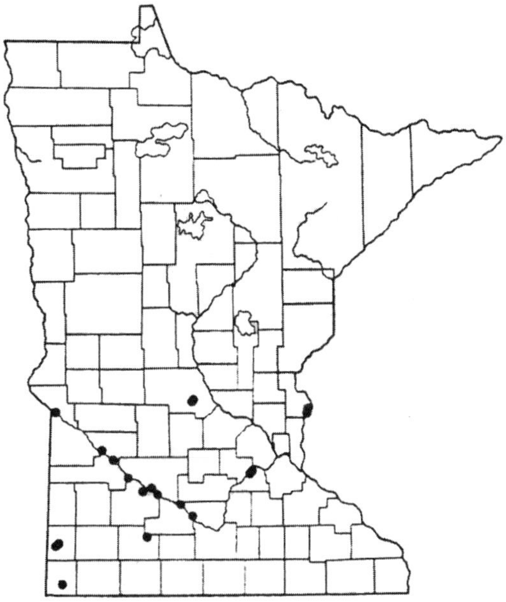

How should you begin your research? What questions do you want answered? What should you do to find the answers? Decide what your plans are and design your first summer of field work. Show your design to your instructor, and then proceed to Part II of the case.

## Questions

1. What kinds of questions do population ecologists ask?
2. Why don't we already know all we need to know about the ecology of *Opuntia fragilis*?
3. Why is it unusual to find a cactus species in the northern United States and Canada?
4. When populations occur in different regions, but not in the regions in between, we call that a disjunction. The scattered red dots in the upper Midwest on the map are disjunctions. Why are disjunctions interesting to plant ecologists?

5. What does it mean when we say *Opuntia fragilis* should be a threatened plant species in Minnesota?

## Part II: Your First-Year Plans

One of the most fundamental questions population ecologists want to answer is: *How big is the population?* You decide to answer this question for the population of *Opuntia fragilis* in the new quarry park. You want to know how many different plants there are as well as how many individual pads there are. You plan to survey the entire rock outcrop in the park, building a map of the locations of prickly pear, the rock outcrop segments, trees, and grassy vegetation. You will record the location of each individual and count the number of pads that the individual has produced.

A second question population ecologists want to have answered is: *How is the population structured?* This question involves answering several different questions, including: *How many individuals are there of each sex? How big are they? How old are they?* For your prickly pear, the questions are a bit simpler, because you have no way to determine how old an individual is and because prickly pears produce perfect flowers, with both male and female parts, which means that you will not have to keep track of separate sexes. Thus, you will be able to explore the population structure question by figuring out how big the plants are, which you can tell by counting the number of pads an individual has.

A third fundamental question in population ecology is: *How much does the population change from year to year?* You know that the number of individuals next year will be the number of individuals present this year, plus the number of new individuals produced, minus the number of individuals that die. Because the population is isolated, you don't have to worry about emigration and immigration. This question will take at least two years' worth of field work to answer. The first year you will need to gather initial population size data, and then develop a second year's census to provide a basis for comparison. You know that you will need to mark and carefully map the location of individual plants so that you can return the following year to determine whether each individual is a new plant, has died, or how much it has grown in size.

You realize that each *Opuntia fragilis* pad could be thought of as a separate individual, because you know that the pads can break off the parent plant and form a new plant on their own. This method of reproduction is asexual, producing genetically identical individuals. Therefore, you hope to be able to calculate population growth both in terms of the number of individual plants and the number of individual pads.

In addition, you know that *Opuntia fragilis* also can reproduce sexually by producing fruit. You decide that you want to watch for flowers, record how many flowers each plant produces, and revisit the site later in the year to determine which flowers have produced fruit. You will dissect some fruits to determine how many seeds each flower produces.

Finally, of course you plan to spend more time reading about this plant in the library, and you want to explore the region around the new park to see if there are other populations of *Opuntia fragilis* on nearby rock outcrops.

## Questions

1. Did your research plan cover each of the three fundamental questions of population ecology?
2. One of the challenges of being a scientist is deciding which questions are the most important and keeping your project small enough that you can actually finish it. What else could you be doing that is not included in the research plan described above?
3. What kinds of tools and supplies will be needed? Who is going to pay for them?
4. Does it matter that buffalo used to be found in Stearns County but have been eliminated long ago by hunting? What other animals might be important to the ecology of prickly pear? Should your research plan consider these questions?

## *Part III: Your First-Year Results*

You explored the region around the new park to see if there are other populations of *Opuntia fragilis* on nearby rock outcrops. You used topographic maps to find areas where rock outcrops could be found nearby, and you examined each rock outcrop. You found one previously undocumented population. Also helpful for this aspect of your research project was the university's retired botanist, Nick. Nick told you that there were several small populations growing on rock outcrops along a road near the park, and one large population on a granite hill about 15 miles away. One of the populations turned out to have been destroyed by a recent road expansion, but the others were still there. You added these populations to your research so that now you have four sites.

You surveyed the entire rock outcrop in each site and created a map of the locations of prickly pear, the rock outcrop segments, trees, and grassy vegetation (Figure 36.2, p. 330). You planned to record the location of each individual and count the number of pads that the individual has produced. However, you discovered that in several sites there were large clusters of prickly pear pads, one with more than 100 pads. In the clusters you were not able to distinguish individual plants. Therefore, you modified your original plans and marked the location of clusters without counting the pads within the clusters (remember a cluster may be one large or several smaller individual plants).

**FIGURE 36.2.**

Quarry Park. Gray areas are grassy. The black lines are cracks in the granite, and the long black object is a fallen tree. *O. fragilis* plants are marked with black circles.

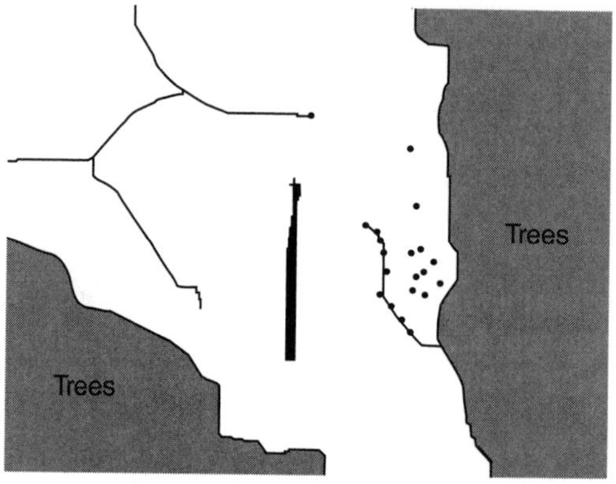


How big are the populations? You wanted to know both how many different plants there are and how many individual pads there are. Cold Spring Hill had the largest population of *Opuntia fragilis;* you found at least 230 plants. Your original site, Quarry Park, had the second largest population, with about 100 plants. A site on a small outcrop nestled into a woods, which you named the Woods Site, had only six individual plants, and a site on a small flat rock outcrop which you named the Table Site had only one large cluster covering about two square meters.

You also wanted to know how the populations were structured in terms of the size of each individual. The bar graph in Figure 36.3 shows for each possible number of pads how many plants you found with that number of pads, added up over the four sites. Note that several plants had more than 10 pads, and are included in the "10" column.

**FIGURE 36.3.**

Your First-Year Data.

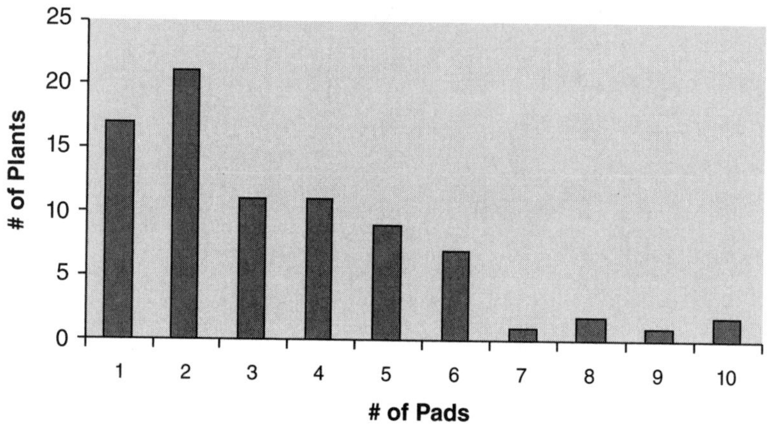

In June you watched for flowers. You planned to record how many flowers each plant produced and then revisit the site later in the year to determine which flowers had produced fruit. However, you discovered that only four flowers were produced in one entire population, one flower at another site, and two sites never produced any flowers! Furthermore, no fruits were formed. Therefore, your plans to observe the flowers and dissect the fruits had to be set aside.

## Questions

1. What does the map of the study site tell you?
2. What does the bar graph of plant sizes tell you?
3. What changes did you make in your research plans? Does the fact that you had to change your plans mean that you are a poor scientist?
4. In your library research, you discovered a research article by two Canadian scientists who studied *Opuntia fragilis* on rock outcrops in Manitoba and western Ontario. They reported that in their study sites, the brittle prickly pear only reproduces by fragmentation. Thus, no sexual reproduction is occurring in their populations, and the population expands by having individual pads break off and become established elsewhere on the site. This intrigues you because you also found no successful sexual reproduction. What are the implications for the population if it is only reproducing asexually?
5. In another article, the Canadians point out that isolated populations of *Opuntia fragilis* in Ontario are always located along rivers. The authors speculate that they were possibly spread by Native Americans, perhaps because they used the spines as fish hooks. Should you change your research plans to try to answer this question? If so, how would you change it? If not, why not?
6. What does it mean that no fruits were produced this year? Does it mean the population never reproduces sexually? What should you plan to do?
7. What should you do in the second year of research? Decide what your next research plan is.

## *Part IV: Your Second Year*

By carefully building maps of the populations and by repeating the survey, you had hoped to be able to calculate population growth both in terms of the number of individual plants and the number of individual pads. When you returned to each site, you discovered that your map of Quarry Park, your first site, was different enough from what you saw the second year that you were unable to determine accurately which pad was which. However, your other maps were designed more accurately, and you were able to relocate most individuals you measured last year. You counted the pads on each plant again, looked for new individuals, and watched for flowers again.

You found that between your first survey and the second, 7 of 136 plants died. You tracked a number of pads on the surviving plants. Of these, 37 pads disappeared, 82 produced new pads, and 251 stayed alive but did not produce new pads. You also found that the average plant size increased from 2.70 pads to 3.19 pads. You only found two flowers, and neither flower produced any fruit. You also discovered five plants, one with 12 pads, on the edge of the Quarry Park outcrop, which you had not mapped last year.

## Questions

1. Are the populations growing?
2. If you started with 370 pads and 37 pads disappeared, and if we assume that 75% of the disappeared pads eventually died, is the population growing?
3. Given the numbers in question 2, if we assume that the rate of disappearance is not influenced by the age of the pad, by the time 90% of the pads have died, how old are the survivors?
4. Why don't the flowers produce fruits (and thus seeds)?
5. What should you do about the five new plants you found?
6. What should you do next?

## Web Version

Detailed teaching notes, the case PDF, and an answer key are available on the NCCSTS website at *sciencecases.lib.buffalo.edu/cs/collection/detail.asp?case_id=183&id=183*

## References

Benson, L. 1982. *The cacti of the United States and Canada*. Palo Alto, CA: Stanford University Press.

Ownbey, G. B., and T. Morley. 1991. *Vascular plants of Minnesota: A checklist and atlas*. Minneapolis: University of Minnesota Press.

CHAPTER 37

# TOUGHER PLANTS

## Beating Stress by Protecting Photosynthesis in Genetically Modified Plants

*Robin Pals-Rylaarsdam and Monica L. Tischler*

### Abstract

This case introduces students to the scientific literature as they learn about how cold, heat, and salt can stress plants. They also learn that plants genetically engineered to produce glycine betaine, a modified amino acid, can withstand the environmental conditions that stress many agricultural plants.


### Learning Objectives

- Introduce primary sources of biological information.
- Begin to read and interpret basic graphs.
- Connect the primary literature to basic biology processes.
- Reinforce the steps of photosynthesis, particularly the light-dependent reactions.

### Quantitative Reasoning Skills/Concepts

- Interpret the meaning of simple statistical descriptors.
- Use graphs to formulate predictions and explanations.

### The Case Study

#### *Part I: Stress*

Alice and Todd looked out over their 25-acre plot of tomatoes. No doubt about it, the plants looked bad. This was their first harvest after graduating from the University of Florida and blowing all their graduation money on their local natural farm venture.

"I thought the irrigation system was all we would need. We should have majored in agriculture instead of graphic design," said Todd. "We set up a beautiful website, but we don't have anything to sell!"

With bills coming due and, worse yet, having to ask her parents for another loan, Alice decided to call the chair of agronomy at her alma mater to see if he could help. His secretary quickly referred her to the local agriculture extension office, where a cheerful extension agent answered the phone and agreed to drive out to the tomato farm.

## Question

1. What are the major stresses that agricultural plants face?

## *Part II: Glycine Betaine*

"Your plants are facing three environmental stresses out in the field," Florida State Extension Agent Dory told the would-be farmers. "Heat in the summer, frost even in our mild Florida winters, and salt from the irrigation that's been going on in those fields for decades. Have you considered planting a genetically modified strain of tomatoes that can help the plants survive these stresses?"

"But we want to be organic!" said Todd, horrified.

"Although the U.S. Department of Agriculture doesn't allow genetically modified crops to be labeled as organic, you can raise a crop without using pesticides or chemical fertilizers and still produce pesticide and chemical-free fruits and vegetables," advised Dory. "Most consumers worry most about the chemicals. There's been some really nice work done with using plants that make extra glycine betaine, a modified amino acid. I'll show you some papers from the peer-reviewed literature, where scientists communicate with each other after they make discoveries. Want to take a look?"

"Sure," said Alice. "What can this glycine betaine thing (Figure 37.1) do for our tomatoes?"

**FIGURE 37.1.**

The Structure of Glycine Betaine.

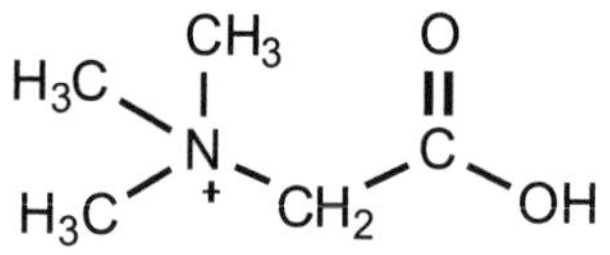


Glycine Betaine

## Questions

1. In Figure 37.2, what does wild type mean?
2. How is L1 different from wild type?
3. What does glycine betaine do for the leaves, flowers, and fruits in cold-exposed plants?

**FIGURE 37.2.**

Susceptibility to Cold Stress at Different Plant Stages.

Nine-week-old wildtype (a, c) and L1 transgenic plants (b, d), at stage when two or three flowers first opened fully, were incubated at 3°C for 7 days (16h daylight/8h dark), then transferred to a 25°C greenhouse. Leaves were observed after one day in the warm greenhouse (a, b), further flower development was observed after 2 weeks in the warm greenhouse.

*Credit:* Photos by the author Robin Pals-Rylaarsdam. This figure is intended to simulate Figure 6 in Park et al. 2004.

## *Part III: Photosynthesis*

"Those genetically modified plants look great," said Todd. "How does glycine betaine give them that protection?"

Dory showed them another figure from the paper (Figure 37.3). She asked them some questions so they could understand what they were looking at.

### Questions

1. What is the *x*-axis measuring?
2. What is the *y*-axis measuring?
3. What does WT mean?
4. What are L1 and L5?

"Those are the kinds of questions you ask for any graph you see in the scientific literature," said Dory. "But to understand the graph in Figure 37.3, we need to think a little more about photosynthesis. Do you know anything about that?"

Alice grinned. "We met and fell in love in Introductory Biology our first year of

**FIGURE 37.3.**

Effects of Chilling on Various Growth Parameters.

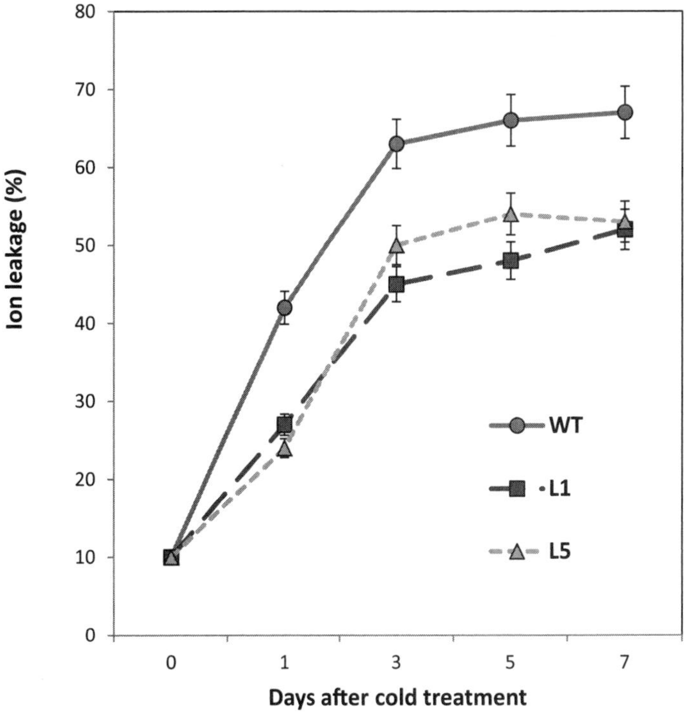


Five-week-old greenhouse-grown wild type and independent homozygous transgenic lines (L1, L5) were chilled (3°C) for 5 days, and then returned to a greenhouse.
*Credit:* Redrawn and adapted from Figure 5(g) in Park et al. 2004.

college," she said. "I think Todd would have flunked the course if I hadn't taught him all about photosynthesis."

Todd pulled a face. "That's not quite how I remember it, but yes, we used to know about photosynthesis pretty well," he said. "The graph measures ion leakage. How can that relate to photosynthesis?"

## Questions

1. Which photosynthesis process is most affected by ion leakage?
    a. Whether the cells can capture light
    b. Whether the Calvin cycle will function
    c. Whether ATP synthase will function
    d. Whether electrons will transfer from photosystem II
2. What trends can you observe in the graph in Figure 37.3? List at least two.

### *Part IV: Heat Tolerance*

"Wow, glycine betaine is great with potential frost damage. Maybe that late frost last spring is why our plants look so terrible," said Todd.

Dory nodded. "During the Florida growing season we have to worry about heat as well. Let me show you a study where glycine betaine helped with heat tolerance in plants (see Figure 37.4). This study is with tobacco plants, but it should apply to your tomatoes too."

## Questions

1. What is the *x*-axis measuring?
2. What is the *y*-axis measuring?
3. What are are two types of plants studied in this experiment?
4. Which process in photosynthesis produces oxygen?
5. What trends can you observe in the graph? List at least two.

**FIGURE 37.4.**

Effects of Heat Stress on Oxygen Production by PSII.

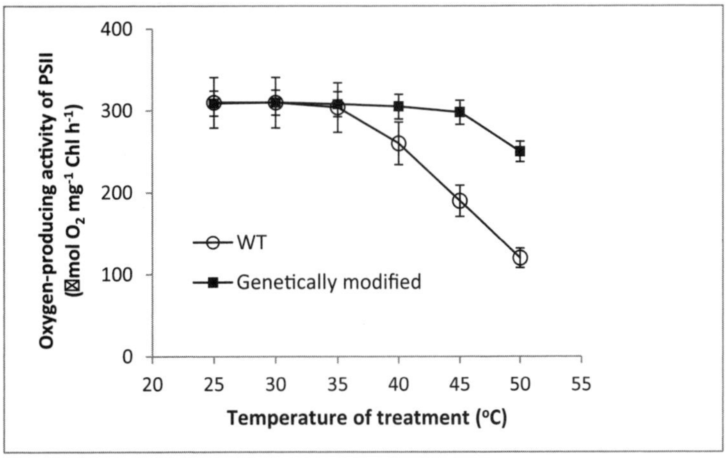


The graph shows changes in the oxygen-producing activity of PSII determined with thylakoid membranes isolated from leaves after exposed to different temperatures 25, 30, 35, 40, 45, or 50°C in the chambers for 4 h, in wild type and transgenic plants. The values are mean + SE of three independent experiments.

*Credit:* Redrawn and adapted from Yang et al. 2007.

## *Part V: Photosystem II*

"Why would heat change the activity of photosystem II?" asked Alice.

"Great question," answered Dory. "Let me show you what photosystem II looks like." Dory pulled up the ribbon diagram (Figure 37.5) of the structure of this huge protein complex. Cool, huh?"

**FIGURE 37.5.**

Structure of Photosynthesis II, PDB 2AXT.

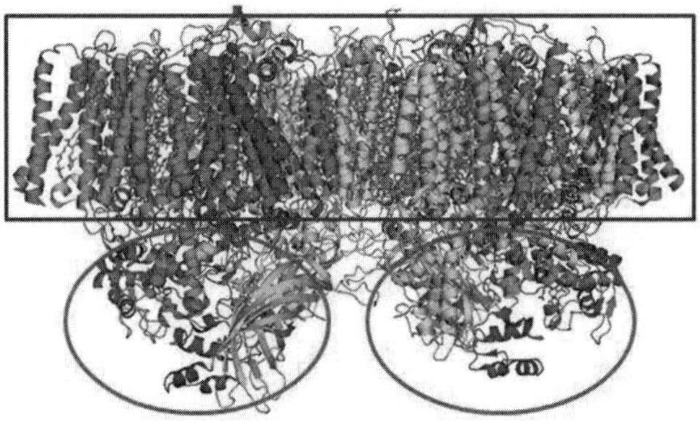

*Credit:* Modified from image by Curtis Neveus from Wikipedia at *en.wikipedia.org/wiki/File:PhotosystemII.PNG*.

Dory asked them:

"Do you know which part of the molecule goes through the thylakoid membrane?"

a. Box
b. Circles
c. Trick question—this is a big bunch of squiggles.

"I remember," said Alice. "Parts of a protein in the membrane are much more stable than those inside or outside of the membrane."

"Right," said Dory,

"So how does this explain why increased temperatures decrease photosystem II activity?"

a. Thylakoid membranes become more permeable to ions
b. The chlorophyll breaks down
c. The peripheral proteins lose their ability to bind to the transmembrane proteins
d. Water cannot bind to PSII to form oxygen.

## Part VI: Salt

"All right, now we know that the genetically engineered tomatoes can take heat and cold. We're set!" crowed Todd.

"Don't be too hasty, Todd. There's still one more potential stress on your tomatoes," warned Dory. "You've planted on a field that had been irrigated for many years. The water evaporates in the heat and leaves behind salt. If you lived in a cold climate you'd have to worry about salt runoff from the roads in the wintertime. At least that's not an additional problem for you guys."

"So is there any evidence that glycine betaine can help with salty soil?" asked Alice.

"Sure, let's take a look at this third paper," suggested Dory. "It's looking at isolated thylakoid membranes, but we can gain some good information from this one too" (see Figure 37.6).

**FIGURE 37.6.**

Effects of Betaine on the Dissociation of 18-(a), 23-(b) and 33-(c) kDa Extrinsic Proteins From PS2 Particles by NaCl.

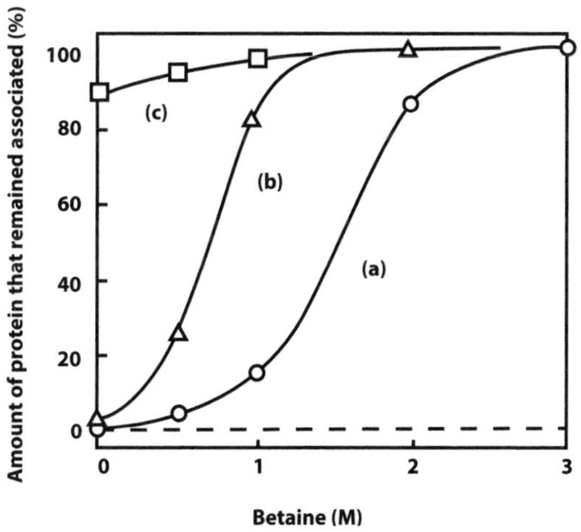


PS2 particles were incubated in media that contained 1.2 M NaCl, 0.3 M sucrose, 0.025 M MES/NaOH (pH 6.5) plus indicated concentrations of betaine.
*Credit:* Redrawn from Murata et al. 1992.

### Questions

1. What is the *X*-axis in Figure 37.6 measuring?
2. What is the *Y*-axis measuring?
3. What do lines a, b, and c refer to?
4. What trends can you observe in the graph in Figure 37.6? List at least two.

5. Which protein subunit of photosystem II is most stable and likely to be in the membrane?
6. Which protein subunit is least stable and likely to be a peripheral membrane protein?
7. What does glycine betaine do to protect photosystem II activity?

Todd and Alice decided to give the genetically modified tomatoes a chance. They would still need to ask her parents for a loan to tide them over, but they were hopeful that the next harvest would get them on the right track.

## Web Version

Detailed teaching notes, the case PDF, and an answer key are available on the NCCSTS website at *sciencecases.lib.buffalo.edu/cs/collection/detail.asp?case_id=658&id=658.*

## References

Murata, N., P. S. Mohanty, H. Hayashi, and G. C. Papageorgiou. 1992. Glycinebetaine stabilizes the association of extrinsic proteins with the photosynthetic oxygen-evolving complex. *FEBS Letters* 296 (2): 187–189.

Park, E.-J., Z. Jeknić, A. Sakamoto, J. DeNoma, R. Yuwansiri, N. Murata, and T. H. H. Chen. 2004. Genetic engineering of glycinebetaine synthesis in tomato protects seeds, plants, and flowers from chilling damage. *The Plant Journal* 40: 474–487.

Yang, X., X. Wen, H. Gong, Q. Lu and Y. Zhipan. 2007. Genetic engineering of the biosynthesis of glycinebetaine enhances thermotolerance of photosystem II in tobacco plants *Planta* 225 (3): 719–733.

# SECTION IX

# ANIMAL FORM AND FUNCTION

# THE 2000-METER ROW

## A Case in Homeostasis

*Nathan Strong*

### Abstract

The physically demanding sport of competitive rowing is the backdrop for this case study about homeostasis in which students follow the physiological changes that occur in an athlete competing in a 2000-meter race.


### Learning Objectives

- Relate the functioning of one system with another.
- Understand homeostasis as continuous process and not as a state.
- Illustrate cause-and-effect within the human body.

### Quantitative Reasoning Skills/Concepts

- Compare data before, during, and after a challenging athletic event.

If students are asked to graph and interpret the heart rate, respiration, and temperature data as part of the analysis process, then these as well:

- Carry out basic mathematical operations.
- Represent data in graphs.
- Use graphs to formulate predictions and explanations.

### The Case Study

Sixty minutes before the race, Jim was sitting quietly on the bank of the Schuylkill River. He was visualizing the race he was about to row. Two thousand meters of intense physical activity, pushing his body to the very limits of its capabilities. But sitting there, he was calm and relaxed, mentally willing his heart rate and respiratory rate down. He had done his stretching and warm-up exercises, but his heart rate was now just 65 beats per minute and he was breathing 12 breaths per minute. His body temperature was 37°C (98.6°F). He was well hydrated. His weight was 180 pounds.

That was an hour ago. Now, he was sitting in the bow seat of the Men's Varsity Eight. In lane 4 on the starting line, he could see two boats to his left and three boats to his right. The rowers all looked bigger than him and his crew, but then they always did. The starter on the shore was saying something over the loudspeaker, but Jim wasn't paying attention. He was concentrating on being ready and was listening to his coxswain. These last few seconds before the race were the most stressful—you could feel the tension in the air. He knew that all 48 rowers and even the six coxswains on that starting line were feeling the same as he was. He was sweating although the air was cool. His heart rate was now 85 beats per minute and he was breathing 18 breaths per minute. He felt a nervous excitement. His mouth was dry. He took one last sip of water.

"All hands are down," he heard the starter say. He tensed his muscles in his starting position. "Prêts … partez!" which was French for "Ready ... go!"

Three short strokes to get the 60-foot-long shell moving and then 20 strokes at maximum power. His crew was rowing 39 strokes per minute and water was flying everywhere. It seemed like he could hear everything—coxswains yelling, rowers grunting, oars and rigors banging. Mostly he heard himself breathing. He was putting all of his strength into each stroke, knowing that after those first 20, the pace and the power would come down some.

At the end of that first minute, Jim's heart rate was 201 beats per minute. He was taking two breaths per stroke, fast and forced. Their stroke rate was now 34 strokes per minute. He was sweating more now. His body temperature was 37.5°C (99.5°F). His muscles hurt—they felt like they were burning.

Three minutes later, they had traveled just over 1000 meters. They were still rowing at 34 strokes per minute. Jim tried to put himself in to a trance, shutting out the pain and the external distractions, concentrating on keeping the power up. He was giving each stroke about 80% of his maximum power. His heart rate was 180. His respiratory rate was also down slightly. His body temperature was 38°C.

With 250 meters to go to the finish line, Jim was sitting even with the bowman of the boat in lane 3. They were trading the lead with every alternate stroke. His cox was talking to the team, keeping them focused, getting them ready for the sprint. The crew next to them started to move—they were up one seat! He heard his coxswain call for what he was dreading—five strokes to bring it up for the sprint. He focused on a spot between the shoulder blades of his number two man and forced his muscles to respond. Thirty-seven strokes per minute, then 38 strokes.

Bow ball to bow ball, the winner of this race was going to be whichever crew got in the last stroke. As Jim crossed the finish line, six minutes and 58 seconds after starting and one-tenth of a second behind the triumphant crew in lane 3, his heart rate was 208 beats per minute. He stopped rowing and slumped over his oar, breathing nearly 80 times per minute but still not feeling like he could get enough air. It felt like his arms and legs were on fire. Sweat was pouring out of every pore of his body. He felt light-headed. His body temperature was 102°F.

Ten minutes later after a dejected row back to the docks, Jim's heart rate and respiratory rate were almost back to normal. His body temperature was still half a degree above normal. He felt drained of energy. He was still very thirsty. He had allowed himself only small sips of water on the row back. He weighed 176 pounds.

## *Your Task*

Working in your assigned study groups, each group will describe what is going on in Jim's body and why at each of the five moments described: on the starting line, one minute after the start, three minutes after the start, at the finish, and on the return trip to the dock. Specifically, what conditions are changing as a result of the race and what responses are made by the body to try to maintain homeostasis? What are the results of those responses? You should concentrate on changes in the nervous system, the respiratory system, the cardiovascular system, and the muscular system. But don't forget the endocrine system and the urinary system.

One suggestion would be for each student to take a body system or two and report to the group on the activities of those systems throughout the course of the race. Another approach would be for each student to take one of the five moments and describe the stresses encountered and the responses made.

Be sure that the answers to the questions below are included in your report, but your report should not consist only of the answers to these questions.

## Questions

*At the start*

1. What is responsible for raising Jim's heart and respiratory rate and stimulating sweating just before the race?
2. Why is the sympathetic division of the autonomic nervous system active just before the race?
3. What changes do you think are occurring in the digestive and urinary systems at this time?
4. What is happening to Jim's blood glucose levels just before the race?
5. Why is Jim's mouth dry?

*One minute in*

1. Rowing full speed is putting new demands on Jim's body. What are these new demands and how does the body respond to them?

2. What changes in Jim's muscles promote unloading of $O_2$ from hemoglobin for use by the muscle cells?
3. Why do Jim's muscles feel like they are burning?
4. What conflict is produced between Jim's need to keep his body cool and his need to remove nitrogenous wastes from his blood? What did he do before the race to help alleviate this conflict?

*At the halfway mark*

1. Since the end of the first minute, Jim has decreased the demands his muscles are making. How has he done this? And why has he done this?
2. What are the changes in his conditions as a result?

*At the finish*

1. Jim has stopped rowing and his muscles are now at rest. Why are his heart and breathing rates still so high?
2. Why is he sweating more now than during the race?
3. What changes have occurred to his blood chemistry since the start of the race? Think about glucose levels, pH, lactate levels, creatinine levels, and temperature.

*Back at the dock*

1. What changes have occurred in the last 10 minutes to allow Jim's heart and respiratory rates to come down?
2. Why is Jim four pounds lighter than at the start of the race?
3. What effect has this water loss had on his endocrine system?
4. Why did Jim only take sips of water after the race? What could happen if he drank as much as he wanted to?

## Web Version

Detailed teaching notes, the case PDF, and an answer key are available on the NCCSTS website at *sciencecases.lib.buffalo.edu/cs/collection/detail.asp?case_id=366&id=366*

# GIRL PULLED ALIVE FROM RUINS, 15 DAYS AFTER EARTHQUAKE

*Susan B. Chaplin*

## Abstract

This case examines the integrated physiological response to dehydration and starvation from the real-life report of a girl discovered 15 days after an earthquake devastated Port-au-Prince, Haiti, in 2010. From the meager scientifically relevant facts reported by newspaper accounts of the girl's condition, students work through the pathways of water loss from dehydration as they examine the multiple systems involved in homeostatic responses, and then calculate whether it is possible for a human to withstand 15 days without water.


## Learning Objectives

- Understand water balance from the perspective of avenues of water gain and loss and the movement of water between intracellular and extracellular compartments.
- Describe homeostatic mechanisms for regulating water balance, including osmoreceptors, ADH, and renal responses; renin-angiotensin-aldosterone system; and baroreceptors, vascular responses, and selective organ perfusion.
- Practice quantitative reasoning skills used to predict time of survival given data on rates of water loss.
- Explore potential water savings mechanisms unique to the Haitian girl that might have impacted her survival and differ from the response of non-indigenous or non-acclimated humans to the same stresses.

## Quantitative Reasoning Skills/Concepts

- Carry out basic mathematical operations.
- Articulate complete and correct claims based on data.
- Use appropriate reasoning to support the validity of data-based claims.

## The Case Study

### *Part I: The Facts of the Case*

I read the headlines, almost unbelieving. From all that disaster in Port-au-Prince, Haiti, in January 2010, a miracle occurred; someone was still alive, more than two weeks after the buildings collapsed around her. The paper reported that Darlene Etienne, a 17-year-old university student, was found in the rubble of a home near the university, very dehydrated, groaning weakly, but still conscious, with a very weak pulse and low blood pressure. Rescuers gave her oxygen and water and immediately evacuated her to a French military hospital ship for treatment.

"She was definitely within hours or perhaps minutes of death," said one rescuer. "It's exceptional that she managed to survive this long," said another. "In fact, it is rare for anyone to survive more than 72 hours without water, and no survivors have been documented in any earthquake after 14 days."

How did Darlene manage to survive? Was it due to her ability to conserve her body water, or did she somehow gain access to a meager supply of water while still buried?

Refer to the following website for information about dehydration, including the physiological characteristics associated with progressive states of dehydration: *Signs and Symptoms of Dehydration, www.symptomsofdehydration.com*, to help you answer the following questions.

### Questions

1. What are the physical signs and symptoms of progressive dehydration, such as Darlene might have experienced?
2. What do we know so far about Darlene's physiological responses to her prolonged ordeal?

### *Part II: Calculating Darlene's Water Balance*

The physiological consequences of Darlene's entrapment in the earthquake rubble were dehydration, starvation, and potentially heat exposure from daytime temperatures near 35°C (95°F) and high humidity. However, let's look first at just her ability to survive the dehydration of being buried for 15 days. First, we should consider where water is "stored" in the body that could be tapped during Darlene's prolonged entrapment.

### Questions

1. Based on Figure 39.1, list the major water compartments of the body, and explain how water moves between them. What is the 60-40-20 rule for body water?

2. Assuming that Darlene did NOT have access to water during her entrapment, how would her body begin to lose water? What are the specific avenues of water loss?
3. How might the body immediately begin to reduce those avenues of water loss in Question #4? What important physiological reflexes would minimize the rate of water loss from those specific avenues?
4. How would changes in blood flow to specific organs help Darlene resist dehydration? Consider how reduction of function in particular organ systems might help conserve water.
5. Calculation of Darlene's water loss—Enter answers in the spaces and table below as directed.
   a. Let's assume that Darlene weighs about 55 kg (~120 lb). Based on the 60-40-20 rule, how much total body water (in liters) does Darlene have?

      ______________________________

   b. Most humans can withstand only a 12% loss of total body water before they progress to clinical shock. The lethal body water loss for humans is 20% of total body water. Based on these estimates, how many liters of body water can Darlene afford to lose? 12% of total body water in liters: ____________________; 20% of total body water in liters: ____________________
   c. Data from published studies on women show that water loss varies as a function of age, weight, and environment. Values range from 2.7 L/day for young female adults (Sawha et al. 2005) to 3.3 L/day in active (but not exercising), young female students (Westerterp et al. 2010). How many days without water could Darlene survive at this rate of dehydration, assuming a maximum of 12% body water loss? Record your answer in Table 39.1.
   d. Are these water loss values (in 7c) of any use in predicting how much water Darlene might have lost per day? Justify your answer.
   e. The absolute bare minimum water loss possible for humans, with all compensating mechanisms in force, is about 1.2–1.4 L/day (approximately 6 cups of liquid). How many days could Darlene survive at this rate of water loss? Record your answer in Table 39.1 (p. 350).

**FIGURE 39.1.**

Body fluid compartments: Extra-cellular and intra-cellular body water compartments are exchangeable and together make up approximately 60% of the body mass.

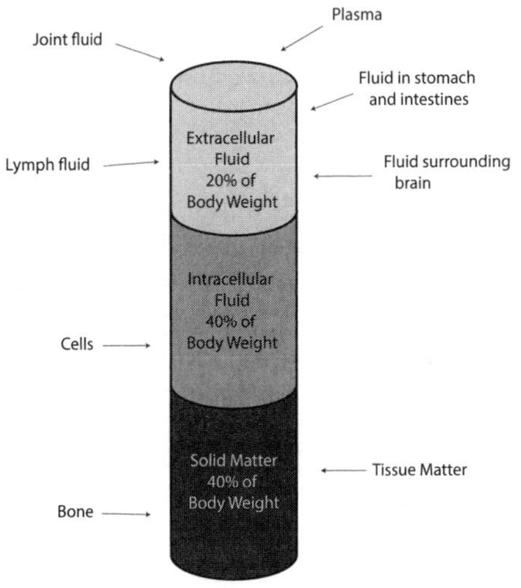

f. At the absolute minimal rate of water loss (7e) and maximal tolerance of dehydration (20% of total body water from 7b), how many days without water could Darlene survive? Record your answer in Table 39.1 below.

g. Now, based on these calculations, could Darlene have survived 15 days without water? Explain the basis for your answer.

**TABLE 39.1.**

Calculate Darlene's estimated survival time (in days) based on the parameters given in Question 5, and assuming conditions as stated below.

| Condition | Rate of Water Loss | Survival Time in Days |
|---|---|---|
| 5c. Average water loss for young adult females, 12% total body water loss | 2.7 L/day | |
| 5c. Average water loss during summer for European women (55 kg), 12% total body water loss | 3.3 L/day | |
| 5e. Absolute minimal water loss possible in humans, 12% total body water loss | 1.2–1.4 L/day | |
| 5f. Absolute minimal water loss possible in humans, 20% total body water loss | 1.2–1.4 L/day | |

## *Part III: Finding Other Explanations for Darlene's Survival*

Darlene's survival was indeed miraculous, but was it based in part on who she was, where she lived (Haiti), and the particular conditions to which she was exposed? Survival can sometimes depend on the smallest of advantages.

Refer to the following for information about dehydration: Sawka et al. 2005 and Westerterp, Plasqui, and Goris 2005.

### Questions

1. Would a middle-aged, northern European (or American) male tourist in Haiti have fared as well as Darlene? Are there physiological advantages of being a young female, born and raised in Haiti? Describe how these characteristics might have given her an advantage. In answering this question, consider the following:
    a. Could being buried in rubble in the warm, humid environment of Haiti have been an advantage for Darlene's survival? Explain how.

b. Does age, weight, or sex affect water loss or water requirements (see Sawha et al. 2005)?

c. Does the fact that Darlene was born and raised in Haiti matter? Describe the role that heat acclimation might play in her water balance.

2. Darlene survived a prolonged period of starvation, an additional physiological challenge for her body. Paradoxically, starvation might actually offset and/or minimize some water loss. How?

## *Part IV: An Answer?*

Some residents thought that Darlene had been trapped in a bathroom, where she was showering at the time of the earthquake. Darlene told rescuers she had a little Coca-Cola with her when the earthquake struck—but was there enough precious liquid for her to survive 15 days? From the newspaper article at the beginning of the case, we know that Darlene probably did not exhibit the maximal dehydration that would have resulted in her losing consciousness (i.e., >12% body water loss).

### Question

1. Based on your calculations above, how much water would Darlene have needed to consume daily to reduce the rate of her dehydration such that she lost a maximum of only 10% of her body water after 15 days?

## Web Version

Detailed teaching notes, the case PDF, and an answer key are available on the NCCSTS website at *sciencecases.lib.buffalo.edu/cs/collection/detail.asp?case_id=559&id=559.*

## References

Sawka, M., S. N. Cheuvront, and R. Carter. 2005. Human water needs. *Nutrition Reviews* 63: S30–S39. *www.dtic.mil/cgi-bin/GetTRDoc?AD=ADA435156&Location=U2&doc=GetTRDoc.pdf*

Signs and symptoms of dehydration. *www.symptomsofdehydration.com.*

Westerterp, K. R., G. Plasqui, and A. H. C. Goris. 2005. Water loss as a function of energy intake, physical activity, and season. *British Journal of Nutrition* 93: 199–203.

CHAPTER 40

# HOT AND BOTHERED
## A Case of Endocrine Disease

*Karin A. Grimnes*

## Abstract

This case follows the story of Carrie and her infant daughter Hayden who share similar symptoms: weight loss, metabolic abnormalities, and overactive endocrine glands as well as autoimmune complications. Students eventually determine that Graves disease is the underlying condition; however, the point of the story is less about the diagnosis and more about understanding the complex interplay of receptor, ligand, and feedback loops as well as how this interplay is complicated by receptor-based autoimmunity. Students interpret some simplified lab results and tie them to their physiological consequences.


## Learning Objectives

- Compose a simple hormone feedback loop between the pituitary and the thyroid glands and understand how it functions to maintain homeostasis.
- Determine how an autoimmune disease against cell surface receptors (such as Graves disease) can interfere with feedback loops to cause pathology.
- Gain more experience interpreting data and linking test results to physiological consequences.
- Understand how maternally produced antibodies (usually considered a benefit) can cause problems for a child before and/or after birth.

## Quantitative Reasoning Skills/Concepts

- Use numerical data to formulate null and alternative hypotheses.
- Articulate complete and correct claims based on data.
- Use appropriate reasoning to support the validity of data-based claims.

## The Case Study

### *Part I: A Well-Baby Exam*

Robert handled three-month-old Hayden's carrier and held open the door for his wife, Carrie.

"Any particular concerns about Hayden today?" asked Dr. O'Dell as they entered the examination room.

As she lifted Hayden from the carrier, Carrie said, "I don't think that Hayden is growing as fast as James did. And she might be running a slight fever."

Dr. O'Dell examined Hayden and checked her computer files. "Hayden's temperature is somewhat elevated, her skin is damp and her pulse is higher than I'd like."

She tilted the screen so both parents could see. "From this graph it appears that Hayden is falling behind her expected weight curve. Are you still breast-feeding her? Breast-fed babies tend to have slightly lower body weights."

"We shifted to formula after the first month, so that makes two months on formula now," replied Carrie.

"Does she eat well?"

"No problem with that. She's always hungry," Carrie answered, as Hayden pumped small fists in the air and screeched in agreement. "And fussy."

Robert added, "I'm worried about Carrie, too. She has some of the same symptoms as Hayden. And she's not sleeping well either."

Carrie smiled tiredly, pushing back a strand of hair. "Hot and bothered seems to be my middle name these days."

"Demands of a new baby can be exhausting, as you know. Some irritability can be expected," Dr. O'Dell glanced at Robert, "especially if you aren't getting enough sleep."

"Robert helps out," Carrie said quickly. "Lots of things bug me right now, that's all. I'm sure it's nothing."

"But it's got to be something," insisted Robert. "Carrie's always complaining about how warm the house is, and she's lost weight."

"Robert!"

"Carrie, I'm worried!"

Dr. O'Dell shifted from Hayden to examining Carrie. After collecting her vital signs, Dr. O'Dell manipulated the glands in Carrie's throat area and frowned. "You do seem to share several of Hayden's symptoms, like her elevated body temperature and rapid pulse, but I'm more concerned about this thyroid enlargement. How much do you know about the thyroid gland and how it operates?"

Both parents shook their heads as Hayden gurgled.

"Hayden wants to know too," Carrie said, trying to lighten the mood.

Dr. O'Dell smiled. "You know how much I like my patients to have background knowledge, but the thyroid situation is pretty complicated. I'll just stick to the main points today to get you up to speed. Okay?"

At their nods, she continued. "The regulation of the system starts when the hypothalamus in the brain releases TRH, or thyrotropin-releasing hormone. This TRH acts on the pituitary, causing that gland in turn to release thyroid-stimulating hormone. With me so far?"

"You mean this all starts in the brain, not in her throat?" Robert protested.

"Yes, the brain is an important player in hormonal control. For today, let's concentrate on the pituitary and the thyroid. The TSH released from the pituitary acts on the thyroid to help that gland release thyroid hormone, known as thyroxin, into the bloodstream. If your thyroid is overactive or enlarges around your throat, it produces too much thyroxin, and that can cause increased metabolism. A simple blood test for these hormones will help rule out thyroid problems."

Both parents were silent for a moment, thinking over what they'd learned.

Robert took Carrie's hand. "But this is easy to fix, right Doctor?"

Dr. O'Dell patted Carrie's arm. "Most cases have straightforward treatments."

A blood sample was taken from both Carrie and Hayden, and a follow-up visit was scheduled for a week later.

## Questions

1. What symptoms (in Carrie and Hayden) most clearly relate to an increase in metabolic rate?
2. Diagram the thyroid–pituitary relationship for a normal individual. Include the glands and several cells within each gland. High thyroxin levels are known to feed back to the pituitary, causing a reduction of TSH levels. Add this feedback loop to your diagram. Make sure you recognize the important role of the hypothalamus, even though it is not the focus of the case.
   a. Is the thyroxin feedback loop described above a positive or a negative feedback loop?
   b. Draw/label the cell receptors on the thyroid (and on the pituitary) necessary for feedback control.
3. Examine your thyroid-pituitary diagram. Remember that TSH is released at a constant, moderate level in order to maintain normal thyroxin levels in the blood.
   a. What would be the immediate result of high TSH level on thyroxin level?
   b. How would the feedback mechanism function to restore homeostasis after high TSH levels? Include receptor details.
   c. What would be the immediate result of low TSH level on thyroxin level?

d. How would the feedback mechanism function to restore homeostasis after low TSH levels? Include receptor details.

e. Summarize: Which of the two gland systems is considered to be "on" until it is turned "off"?

## *Part II: The Follow-up Visit*

"I have some interesting results to show you," Dr. O'Dell said as Carrie and Robert brought Hayden into the examination room. "Carrie, I didn't know that you participated in the study that Dr. Rasam, our endocrinologist, ran a few years ago."

"I wasn't sick," Carrie answered. "They asked for healthy volunteers, and they took a blood sample, but I wasn't chosen for the actual study." She sounded disappointed.

Dr. O'Dell smiled. "Dr. Rasam said they were overwhelmed by volunteers, so they couldn't use everyone. Luckily, your initial results were still in the database, so I was able to compare your recent data with the previous test. That will help us see any trends in the data over time. Take a look," she said as she swiveled the screen to show Carrie's results (Table 40.1).

**TABLE 40.1.**

Endocrine Test Results for Carrie.

| | Carrie 2 years ago | Carrie currently | Normal values |
|---|---|---|---|
| Thyroid hormone (thyroxin) | 6.0 ug/dL | 19.5 ug/dL | 4.5 – 12.5 ug/dL |
| Thyroid-stimulating hormone (TSH) | 1.03 mIU/L | 0.1 mIU/L | 0.3 – 3.04 mIU/L |

### Questions

1. Characterize Carrie's thyroid hormone and TSH levels over time.
2. Return to your thyroid-pituitary diagram.
   a. Assuming that TSH is the only factor involved, predict what TSH level (low, high) would be necessary to maintain her current thyroxin level.
   b. Consider Carrie's values (as high or low) in your diagram. What inconsistency is revealed by these data?
   c. Is Carrie's feedback system functioning normally? Explain.

## *Part III: Additional Testing*

Dr. O'Dell continued. "Low TSH levels should result in low thyroxin levels, not the reverse. Something seems to be stimulating the thyroid in the absence of TSH. When I saw your results, I spoke to Dr. Rasam and he suggested a special ELISA test on the blood sample I collected from you. The ELISA result indicates that Carrie shows early signs of Graves disease."

Both Carrie and Robert looked confused.

"Carrie, a subset of your immune system antibodies is mistakenly attacking your thyroid gland, causing an increase in hormone production. Common symptoms include insomnia, anxiety, fatigue, heat sensitivity, weight loss, and increased sweating. Your hair might get brittle, and your menstrual cycle might change."

Carrie nodded. "I've had all those symptoms."

"But this Graves disease can be cured, right?" asked Robert, holding Carrie's hand tightly.

"It's treatable, yes, but this autoimmunity is a lifelong problem that has to be carefully managed to avoid symptoms such as eye swelling or bulging often seen in Graves patients, as well as other complications."

### Questions

1. Consider the immunological involvement in this case, and the time frame over which it has occurred.
    a. Which antibody (Ig) class was produced first in this sequence of events?
    b. Which class is most likely involved in an ongoing autoimmunity situation?
2. Return to your thyroid-pituitary diagram. Explain the consequences to both thyroxin and TSH levels:
    a. if the auto-antibodies are against the thyroxin molecule.
    b. if the auto-antibodies are against the TSH molecule.
3. Does either scenario in Question 2 above fit Carrie's hormone data?
4. Anti-receptor antibodies can block hormone entry or stimulate the receptor (like original hormone). Use your diagram to explain the consequences to both thyroxin and TSH levels if the auto-antibodies:
    a. block the thyroxin receptors on the pituitary.
    b. stimulate the thyroxin receptors on the pituitary.
    c. block the TSH receptors on the thyroid.
    d. stimulate the TSH receptors on the thyroid.
5. Does any scenario in Question 4 fit Carrie's hormone data? What must be the problem in Graves disease?

6. Identify the type of hypersensitivity (by name and number) that Carrie is experiencing.

## *Part IV: Treatment Options*

Carrie was silent for a moment as she touched her daughter's hair. "What about Hayden?" she asked. "Does our daughter have this too?"

Dr. O'Dell pulled out another sheet of lab results. "Hayden's thyroxin levels were at the high end of normal during her newborn blood screen. Did anyone suggest a follow-up blood test?"

"No," answered Robert. "They said everything was fine."

"I'm afraid Hayden also has a problem, but one I hope is relatively easy to solve. Here's the data" (Table 40.2).

**TABLE 40.2.**

Endocrine Test Results for Hayden.

| | Hayden (newborn) | Hayden (3 mos.) | Normal values |
|---|---|---|---|
| Thyroid hormone (thyroxin) | 15.0 ug/dL | 22.2 ug/dL | 4.5 – 12.5 ug/dL |
| Thyroid-stimulating hormone (TSH) | Not performed | 0.3 mIU/L | 0.3 – 3.04 mIU/L |

## Questions

1. Which values for Hayden (of those given) are abnormal or borderline?
2. Given Carrie's diagnosis, what is the most likely source/cause of Hayden's problem?
3. How did the "active agent" enter Hayden? Give two possible routes.
4. If Carrie had continued to breastfeed, how would that have affected Hayden's problem?
5. For Hayden, Dr. O'Dell suggests three months of a low-dose anti-thyroid medication (such as methimazole) that will reduce her thyroxin production. Regular blood tests to monitor both thyroxin and TSH levels will be continued during this time.
   a. Why is short-term therapy (of several months duration) likely to work?
   b. Hayden's treatments would end about six months after her birth. Why is that number significant?

c. Will long-term therapy (years or lifetime) be needed? Why or why not?

d. Graves disease may have a heritable component. What future testing would you suggest for Hayden?

6a. Will this same therapy work for Carrie? What will happen as treatment progresses?

6b. What about general immunosupression as a treatment? Name a potential consequence.

7. Dr. O'Dell explains that Carrie may need to have treatments with a short-lived radioactive isotope of iodine that will accumulate in her thyroid gland along with the normal iodine concentrating there.

   a. What will these treatments accomplish?

   b. What will happen to antibody levels as a result? List the players and the general sequence of events.

   c. Why would thyroid hormone pills be prescribed after treatment is completed?

   d. Surgical removal of the thyroid gland (thyroidectomy) is rarely used to treat this problem. What would it accomplish here? Name a potential danger of this surgery (think anatomically).

8. Could Carrie's problem be solved by a thyroid transplant from a matching donor? Explain.

9. Autoimmunities are relatively uncommon. What usually happens to autoimmune antibody-producing clones during development?

## Part V: Final Outcome

Carrie elected to have the radioactive iodine treatment, rather than surgery. Her thyroid size and hormone level were monitored as the treatment progressed. Her thyroxin levels are now maintained by daily synthetic hormone medication. By six months of age, Hayden's metabolism, weight, and hormone levels are within normal ranges. Her hormone levels will be checked at regular intervals in the future, just in case Hayden inherited genes that might affect this system.

## Web Version

Detailed teaching notes, the case PDF, and an answer key are available on the NCCSTS website at *sciencecases.lib.buffalo.edu/cs/collection/detail.asp?case_id=606&id=606.*

# KEEPING UP WITH THE JONESES

*Philip J. Stephens*

## Abstract

This case focuses on Suzie, a determined young woman who is training hard for the upcoming figure skating season. Family dynamics combined with high aspirations of competing in the Olympic Games have negative consequences for her health. Students are presented with a variety of signs, symptoms, and medical data as well as a series of guided questions to research.


## Learning Objectives

- Understand female athlete's triad.
- Understand basic cardiovascular physiology.
- Learn about the effect of anorexia nervosa and malnutrition on the human cardiovascular system.
- Understand tissue microcirculation, involving filtration and reabsorption at the capillaries.
- Understand how malnutrition and low blood protein levels can induce edema.

## Quantitative Skills/Concepts

- Carry out basic mathematical operations.
- Use numerical data to formulate null and alternative hypotheses.
- Accept or reject null hypotheses based on statistical tests of significance.
- Articulate complete and correct claims based on data.

## The Case Study

### *Part I: The Accident*

Suzie Jones felt her heart pounding and the sweat dripping from her forehead as she ran the last mile through her neighborhood. She had left home at noon and had run around the high school track for what seemed like hours. She felt tired when she started, but found it pleasurable to drive her body to a point of exhaustion, believing that she could run forever on that warm spring afternoon. As a child, she had hated exercising, but now she found it helped clear her head and get her thoughts into perspective. Suzie felt light-headed as she rounded the corner for home.

"Funny," she thought. "Where's Mom's car?"

She saw a note taped to the garage door: *David's had an accident, come to the hospital ASAP.*

"This time next year I'll be able to drive," muttered Suzie as she started to run the mile to the hospital.

Suzie entered the emergency room and saw her mother sitting with her brother Dave's baseball coach.

"What happened?" asked Suzie.

Mrs. Jones looked at the coach and he answered: "A freak accident. Dave rolled his ankle as he was rounding first base. He hit the ground and we all thought that his leg was broken, but the x-rays proved us wrong. It's just a badly sprained ankle."

Suzie nodded her head in response as she walked the short distance to the water fountain. Just then, Mrs. Jones noticed one of the nurses and said to Suzie, "Isn't that your friend's sister at the nurse's station? Why don't you ask her how your brother is and how much longer this will take?"

"Mom, I've been running for hours and I smell. I look a mess. If it hadn't been for your note telling me to come right away, I would have showered and changed before coming here."

"Fine, Susan. We'll just wait then," replied Mrs. Jones, making her daughter feel guilty.

After about 10 minutes, a nurse called Mrs. Jones into the examination room, and after another 15 minutes she appeared with Dave, who was sitting in a wheel chair, awkwardly holding crutches. Suzie and the coach rose to meet them.

"I've given you a prescription for a more powerful analgesic than your regular over-the-counter pain medicine," said the doctor. Mrs. Jones held up the piece of paper and smiled at the young intern.

"Inflammation is caused by fluid moving from the blood and accumulating in the space between the cells. To minimize the inflammation of Dave's ankle, just remember PRICE—Protect, Rest, Ice, Compression, and Elevation. Call your family physician if his pain becomes severe," said the young doctor as he walked back to the examination rooms.

## Questions

1. What two parameters are responsible for creating the movement (filtration and reabsorption) of fluid across the capillary wall?

2. Draw a diagram of a capillary and label arteriole at one end and venule at the other. With pressure on the vertical axis, draw two lines to show how the two parameters (see question 1 above) vary along the length of the capillary.
3. Under normal circumstances, what components of the blood cross the capillary wall?
4. Cytokines, like histamine and leukotrienes, are secreted by damaged cells in Dave's ankle. How do these cytokines cause inflammation?
5. How does the application of ice to the ankle affect blood flow through the capillaries?
6. How does the removal of ice from the ankle affect blood flow through the capillaries and the cytokines?
7. How does compression, which is provided by an elastic (Ace) bandage wrapped around the damaged ankle, decrease inflammation?
8. How does elevation of the damaged ankle decrease inflammation?

## *Part II: The Next Morning*

Suzie joined her mother at the breakfast table while Dave sat in the den watching television.

"Cold, Suzie?" asked her mother.

"I am always cold these days," replied Suzie.

"I was thinking," said Mrs. Jones. "I didn't trust that doctor in the hospital yesterday. He was so young I wonder whether he has a medical degree. I would feel more comfortable if we had gone to Dr. Fay. I called her office, but the earliest appointment we could get is tomorrow. This flu outbreak is keeping them busy. They said that David should take your scheduled appointment today and that they can fit you in tomorrow instead. Why don't you have breakfast and you can come with us? You never know, they may be able to squeeze you in for your annual physical."

"Okay mom. But I already ate breakfast," said Suzie.

"When?" asked her mother.

"Oh, earlier," said Suzie vaguely. "I'll go get changed now."

Suzie was feeling resentful as she got up from the table. Her mother doted on her brother. He had always been their parents' favorite, no matter what Suzie did at school or with her ice skating. Her older brother always came first.

Just then they heard a moan from Dave in the den and the two women rose from the table. Suzie felt faint and passed out on the floor. Flustered over having to decide whether to tend to her son or to her daughter first, after a moment's hesitation Mrs. Jones took Suzie's feet and placed them on a chair, elevating her legs, and then went to her son to check on him.

Suzie slowly gained consciousness and cautiously sat on the chair. She sipped water from a glass on the table before standing up and walking to her room to change. In 10 minutes they were in the car and on their way to the doctor's office.

Suzie was tired of listening to her brother complaining to their mother about his ankle. She was hungry and felt like she had no energy, but tried to convince herself that her hunger would soon pass. When they got to the doctor's office, Suzie went to the nurse's station, but everyone was busy. Bored, she decided to stand on the scale and weigh herself and check her height.

The nurse appeared just as Suzie stepped off the scale. "Hi Suzie. We've been busy today. Sorry you had to wait," she said.

"Just passing the time by checking my weight and height," Suzie said as she pushed the metal sliders to their zero positions.

"So what was it?" asked Dr. Fay as she passed by the scale.

"Hi Dr. Fay, 5 foot 8 inches and 120," Suzie replied.

"I thought you were coming in for your physical today," said Dr. Fay.

"I was, but Mom said that Dave should see you because he hurt his ankle at practice yesterday. But I'll be in tomorrow for my pre-season physical," Suzie responded.

Sometime later, Suzie's mother and brother came back into the waiting room. Her mother seemed annoyed.

"These doctors stick together. She just repeated what that young hospital doctor said yesterday."

## Questions

1. What problems are there in Suzie's life, and does she exhibit any peculiar signs and symptoms?
2. Why did Suzie pass out when she stood up?
3. Why did Suzie's mother place Suzie's feet on a chair?
4. Why did Suzie feel as if she had no energy at the doctor's office?
5. Make an initial speculation about Suzie's condition at this time. Assuming that your speculation is true, what do you think the doctor will find in the results of Suzie's physical examination?

## *Part III: Suzie Sees the Doctor*

Suzie sat in the kitchen listening to the rhythmic sound of one of her mother's exercise machines next door. The sound stopped and a few minutes later her mother came into the kitchen with a towel around her neck.

"Do you mind going to Dr. Fay's by yourself this morning?" she asked. "David's still not himself, and all I do is sit outside and wait for you anyway. I'll drive you there and you can walk back. It's a nice day and I know you will enjoy the exercise."

"No problem, mom," Suzie replied.

"Your father comes home tonight from his business trip and I can use the extra time to clean up, so that he doesn't come back to a dirty house."

Thirty minutes later Suzie began her physical examination.

"You're supposed to take off your shoes when we weigh you," said the nurse as Suzie stepped off the scale.

"Shouldn't make too much difference," replied Suzie.

The nurse looked closely at Suzie's face as she waited for her to remove her sneakers before getting back on the scale.

The nurse adjusted the weights and the ruler.

"That's better. Now let's get your blood pressure," said the nurse.

Suzie sat on the chair and the nurse put the cuff around her right arm. Suzie felt the cuff squeeze around her arm and then a slow release as the cuff deflated. The nurse seemed puzzled, so she repeated the procedure and got the same values. She wrote the blood pressure on Suzie's chart.

Next Suzie felt the nurse repeatedly jab the inside of her right arm and then the sting as the nurse was finally able to draw blood.

"We meet again, young lady," said Dr. Fay as she entered the room. "So, an annual physical and a pre-season physical all rolled into one."

The doctor looked at the chart with only a few entries from the nurse, then said, "Okay, let's take a look."

When the physical was over Suzie looked in the mirror and caught Dr. Fay looking at her as she put on her sweats.

Dr. Fay had a pained expression on her face and asked, "Is your Mom waiting for you outside?"

"No, she's looking after Dave," Suzie replied.

"Your brother has an appointment with me tomorrow morning at 11. Why don't all three of you come in and see me. We'll have the results from your blood work by then, so we can kill two birds with one stone," Dr. Fay suggested.

"Can you at least give me the physical form so that I can skate? The first practice is tomorrow morning," Suzie pleaded.

"Sorry; I can't do that until the blood work comes in. Do you think that missing one practice will hurt?"

"I guess not," replied Suzie. "I'll explain to the coach that my brother is sick and Mom switched our appointments. Maybe he'll let me practice."

## Questions

1. What new signs and symptoms does Suzie exhibit that would concern you if you were the doctor?
2. Do you wish to make any further speculation about Suzie's condition at this time? Assuming that your speculation is true, what do you think the doctor will find in the results of Suzie's physical examination?

## *Part IV: Back to the Doctor's Office*

Table 41.1 provides some data from Suzie's physical:

**TABLE 41.1.**

Results of Physical Examination.

| Condition / Test | Normal | Suzie |
|---|---|---|
| Height | | 5 ft 8 in |
| Weight | | 105 lb |
| Blood pressure | 120/80 | 88/56 |
| Hematocrit | | 32 |
| RBC | | Pale and immature |
| Heart rate | 72 | 65 ectopic beats |
| Cardiac output | 4.5–5 L | 3.6 L |

After sending the nurse to the outer office to get the lab results on Suzie's blood, Dr. Fay turned to Suzie and her mother and said, "Suzie, before we discuss the results, you say that you run a lot?"

"That's right," replied Suzie, "This is my time to shine. I start competitions soon, and they run through the end of the year. I have always dreamed of getting to the Olympics, and my big chance is next February. From there, I could get a scholarship and go to college without being a burden to my parents."

"What do you drink after you exercise? Any sports drinks?" the doctor inquired.

"No, just water, I hate the taste of those drinks. They are too salty and I hate that sweet, sticky feeling it leaves in my mouth." Suzie became quiet and sullen, almost introverted.

"Who needs all of that sugar?" her mother asked.

"In this case, I think Suzie does," said Dr. Fay. "The results of her blood work will give us more information on that."

## Questions

1. Is Suzie's weight reasonable for her height?
2. Calculate the stroke volume of Suzie's heart, and compare it to that of a normal individual.
3. Why do you think her blood pressure is lower than normal? Does low blood pressure explain any of Suzie's signs and symptoms that you may have noticed?
4. Why is Suzie's hematocrit low, and why are her red blood cells pale and immature?
5. Compared with a normal, healthy person predict the level of the following in Suzie's blood (higher, same, lower): sodium, potassium, calcium, glucose, iron, and protein.
6. Do you wish to make any further speculation about Suzie's condition at this time?

## *Part V: Blood Results*

Table 41.2 provides the results of Suzie's blood work.

**TABLE 41.2.**

Results of Blood Work.

| Level | Normal | Suzie |
|---|---|---|
| Sodium | 136–145 mmol/L | 126 mmol/L |
| Potassium | 3.6–5.1 mmol/L | 2.4 mmol/L |
| Calcium | 4.2–5.3 mmol/L | 2.9 mmol/L |
| Fasting glucose | 65–95 mg/mL | 55 mg/mL |
| Iron | 50–140 ug/dL | 38 ug/dL |
| Protein | 6–7.8 g/dL | 3.9 g/dL |

The doctor continued, "There's no need to worry about your son, Mrs. Jones, the nurse will help him if he has any problems with his ankle. Now Suzie, I can't stress enough that the results of your physical examination show that you are in bad physical shape. I appreciate that you are driven to succeed, but as your doctor it's my duty to tell you that you are going about this in the wrong way."

"I feel great, doctor. I'm in the best shape I have ever been. I can run forever. So my blood pressure is a little low and I have had some fainting spells. Maybe I have been overdoing things lately and I'm a bit dehydrated. I am on the ice now, so I won't be running as much as I concentrate on skating," Suzie replied.

"I understand that, but I'm afraid that you're heading down the wrong road. When did you last have your period?" Dr. Fay asked.

"I don't remember. About a month ago," replied Suzie, avoiding eye contact with the physician.

"Perhaps a little longer? We didn't do a percent body fat test, but I would predict it is low. In fact, I would predict that your estrogen levels are too low to produce menses. Do you go to parties with your friends?" the doctor asked.

"She's lost interest in boys," replied Mrs. Jones. "She lives to skate."

The doctor nodded and continued, "I bet you're on a low-fat diet and your caloric intake is too low. It doesn't take a medical degree to see that you're underweight. You are starving yourself, Suzie, and your bones stick out. Sure, you have a nice sun tan because you're outside a lot, but look at your tan lines; your skin is pale and flaky."

"But I am almost there," exclaimed Suzie. "I still have fat under my skin."

"That's not fat. You're so malnourished that what you see as fat is, in fact, an edema; it's fluid. Your blood protein levels confirm that."

## Questions

1. Assuming that the ion levels in the blood plasma are similar to those in the interstitial fluid, what is the effect of low potassium levels on the membrane potential of Suzie's nerve and muscles?
2. Does this explain Suzie's slow heart rate and ectopic beats?
3. How does low plasma calcium level account for her decreased stroke volume?
4. What is the role of blood proteins in the movement of fluid between the blood and the interstitial space?
5. What would be the effect of low blood protein levels on the colloidal pressure?
6. How do low plasma protein levels produce edema?

## *Part VI: Conclusion*

"Suzie," said Dr. Fay. "This is serious. You are suffering from what is known as the female athlete's triad: a combination of disordered eating, loss of your period, and osteoporosis. Your rigid eating habits and strenuous training regimen have produced loss of menses, and if you keep going like this, you are likely to develop osteoporosis. I assume that you've heard of anorexia nervosa? I think that you are anorexic and your extreme exercise regimen is making things worse. I appreciate that a girl of your age is very aware of her body, and I don't think it's your fault entirely. I think that you are striving to please your parents, who seem to be pulled in other directions."

"We do our best, but it isn't easy with Dave. You know, we almost lost him when he was a baby," Mrs. Jones interrupted defensively.

"That must have been very hard on you at the time, but he's going into his senior year and will be away at college next year. When was the last time you sat down to dinner as a family or the last time you went to one of Suzie's competitions?" the doctor asked.

Mother and daughter looked at the floor.

Dr. Fay continued: "I am going to send you to a counselor, Suzie. I am also going to recommend that the entire family takes part so that all aspects of your problem can be addressed. You're a fine young lady who needs to take care of herself. Continue like this and you'll be in a hospital within a month. I already have enough data here in my hand to admit you to a hospital where they will monitor your food intake and feed you through a tube if necessary. However, I have known your family for years and believe that you'll do what is necessary to make things come out right in the end. Now, when are you coming back to see me?"

## Questions

1. What conditions make Suzie a candidate for anorexia?
2. Do you think the doctor's treatment is appropriate, or would you have admitted her into hospital?
3. When do you think Suzie should schedule her next visit to the doctor?

## Web Version

Detailed teaching notes, the case PDF, and an answer key are available on the NCCSTS website at *sciencecases.lib.buffalo.edu/cs/collection/detail.asp?case_id=339&id=339.*

# THE HUNGER PAINS
## Ghrelin, Weight Loss, and Maintenance

*Lynn M. Diener*

## Abstract
Many students are interested in the topic of weight loss and showing them some of the hormones that may impact weight loss and maintenance of weight loss is very engaging to them. Presented in a "Facebook-like" format, this case teaches students about hormones; in particular, it focuses on ghrelin—an amine hormone released by the stomach—and growth hormone, and explores the effect of sleep and diet on ghrelin.


## Learning Objectives
- Understand what hormones are and what they do, with a specific focus on ghrelin and growth hormone.
- Understand catabolism and anabolism.
- Explore the effect of sleep and diet on ghrelin.
- Make and interpret graphs.
- Critically assess a research study.

## Quantitative Reasoning Skills/Concepts
- Represent data in graphs.
- Interpret the meaning of simple statistical descriptors, such as error bars and trend lines.
- Use graphs to formulate predictions and explanations.
- Articulate complete and correct claims based on data.
- Use appropriate reasoning to support the validity of data-based claims.
- Create experimental designs to test hypotheses.

## The Case Study

### *Part I: You Look Fantastic!*

*Mallory Messner:* Hey Sara, it was great to see you during break! It's been way too long. And by the way, congratulations on the weight loss, you look fantastic. Do you mind if I ask how you did it?

April 5 at 1:32 pm Like

*Sara Finnegan:* Mal, it was great to see you too! Thanks for noticing the weight loss, it required a lot of hard work. I started exercising 5 days a week and restricting calories (eating smaller portions mainly).

April 5 at 1:45 pm Like

*Mallory Messner:* You'd think I would already have realized that there is no trick when it comes to weight loss, being a biology major and all–sigh–I just hoped maybe you had found some magic solution. Haha.

April 5 at 1:50 pm Like

*Sara Finnegan:* I gotta tell you though, I'm having a heck of a time keeping the weight off. It seems like I'm always hungry! You know, they always say that only 5% of people who lose weight ever keep it off long term. I'm hoping to remain in the 5% but right now I'm not so sure. =(

Have you heard about some hormone called ghrelin in any of your biology classes? I've been reading about it in the news lately, I wonder if it has anything to do with my struggles…

April 5 at 1:55 pm Like

*Mallory Messner:* Actually I do recall learning something about ghrelin in class. Let me take a look and get back to you. I'll send you an email!

April 5 at 1:57 pm Like

### Questions

1. Craft an e-mail from Mallory to Sara explaining some of the basics of ghrelin. Your e-mail should explain what a hormone is and what kind of hormone ghrelin is. It should also explore ghrelin's effect on growth hormone and metabolism. Feel free to use your textbook and reliable internet sources.

2. What is the effect of growth hormone on metabolism? Pay special attention to its effect on protein, bone, fatty tissue, and carbohydrates.
3. What does anabolic mean? What about catabolic? How would you classify growth hormone?

## Part II: Sleep Is Important

*Mallory Messner:* So ghrelin seems like an intriguing possibility, huh? Did you know that it's generally elevated in people after they lose weight? Even a whole year after they lost the weight!

April 5 at 6:03 pm Like

*Sara Finnegan:* Yeah, thanks for the email. I can't believe that a chemical like ghrelin can help to increase your appetite. And the fact that it's elevated in people after they lose weight, ugh!

April 5 at 6:09 pm Like

*Mallory Messner:* I found some other really interesting studies about ghrelin. How are you sleeping lately?

April 5 at 6:12 pm Like

*Sara Finnegan:* I'm a college sophomore, just like you, how do you think I'm sleeping?

April 5 at 6:14 pm Like

*Mallory Messner:* Haha, point taken. Well one study found some correlations with sleep and ghrelin levels. More sleep, less ghrelin! I found their data on the correlation between hours of sleep and BMI interesting as well.

| Hours of sleep | Average BMI | Standard error |
|---|---|---|
| 6.10 | 32.15 | 0.70 |
| 6.55 | 31.4 | 0.25 |
| 7.40 | 31.05 | 0.25 |
| 8.25 | 31.4 | 0.30 |
| 9.10 | 31.6 | 0.50 |

April 5 at 6:23 pm Like

### Questions

1. Make a line graph of these data. Don't forget to include error bars using the standard error. Identify and label the dependent and independent variables; this will dictate their placement on your graph.

2. Explain the trend you see in the data you graphed.
3. Using a ruler, show which error bars overlap and don't overlap on the graph.
4. Without knowing the results of any statistics done on the data, which data point(s) may be significantly different from each other based on the data provided? Which data did you rely on to come to your conclusion?
5. Knowing that less sleep means more ghrelin, what suggestions might you make to Sara if you were Mallory? What is a take-away message for this study?

## *Part III: Dessert for Breakfast*

*Sara Finnegan:* Maybe I need to start prioritizing my sleep just a little bit …

April 5 at 7:01 pm Like

*Mallory Messner:* Seriously! Me too … =) Another really fascinating recent study looked at the timing and composition of calories ingested, focusing specifically on breakfast. Are you familiar with those high protein diets?

April 5 at 7:04 pm Like

*Sara Finnegan:* Oh yeah, my roommate is trying to lose weight that way.

April 5 at 7:06 pm Like

*Mallory Messner:* Well researchers had one group of obese individuals eat a small (calorie-wise), protein enriched breakfast in the morning. The other group ate many more calories high in carbohydrates and enriched in protein. Both ingested the same number of calories over the course of the whole day, the differences were in the timing and quantity of fats, carbs and protein. The amusing part is that the second group of dieters also had dessert with every breakfast. =D

April 5 at 7:10 pm Like

*Sara Finnegan:* Seriously??? I'd love to start every morning with dessert. I bet I know who lost weight and who didn't.

April 5 at 7:13 pm Like

*Mallory Messner:* Seriously! And we're talking doughnuts, cake, chocolate bars. You might find the results surprising though. Here, take a look at the weight loss data. They were "dieting" from weeks 0 till 16. Week 16–32 was follow-up, when they were trying to maintain their weight loss.

| Low calorie breakfast | Dessert for breakfast | |
|---|---|---|
| ***Time (weeks)*** | ***average weight (kg)*** | ***average weight (kg)*** |
| 0 | 89 | 91 |
| 4 | 85 | 87 |
| 8 | 82 | 85 |
| 12 | 77 | 82 |
| 16 | 75 | 78 |
| 20 | 78 | 76 |
| 24 | 81 | 74 |
| 28 | 84 | 72 |
| 32 | 87 | 71 |

April 5 at 7:21 pm Like

## Questions

1. Make a line graph of the data above.
2. What is the trend the researchers saw? You should focus on which group lost more weight and had more successful weight loss maintenance.
3. Do you think Sara is surprised by the results?
4. Does ghrelin make you hungry or leave you feeling satisfied?
5. Knowing what you do about ghrelin, in which case do you think the researchers saw a greater decrease in ghrelin after eating?

## *Part IV: Easier Weight Loss?*

*Sara Finnegan:* Mal, that's a seriously cool study.

30 minutes ago Like

*Mallory Messner:* I know! And they saw all sorts of other things change in the dessert group. Levels of ghrelin decreased after meals, feelings of satiety (satisfaction) increased, and cravings decreased.

28 minutes ago Like

*Sara Finnegan:* Haha, maybe I'll try the dessert for breakfast diet to combat my difficulty in maintaining.

25 minutes ago Like

*Mallory Messner:* Well, it's only one study. I'm not sure I'd change your whole diet outlook based on one study, but the results are definitely compelling. There really is a lot left to learn about ghrelin and weight loss in general.

20 minutes ago Like

## Questions

1. Speculate about why the dessert for breakfast group saw decreases in cravings and increases in satiety.
2. Would you change your diet based on the study? What kind of evidence is necessary to make you "believe" a research study?
3. If you were doing research in this area, what would be your next step?

## Web Version

Detailed teaching notes, the case PDF, and an answer key are available on the NCCSTS website at *sciencecases.lib.buffalo.edu/cs/collection/detail.asp?case_id=655&id=655*.

# SECTION X

# HEALTH

CHAPTER 43

# MICHAEL'S STORY
## A Case Study of Autism

*Kristen N. Hausmann and Karen M. Aguirre*

## Abstract

Students engage in a variety of activities to learn about the possible "cause" of autism as well as its diagnosis and treatment. Designed to interest general biology students as well as students of psychology and health studies, this case is particularly useful for introducing students to the tasks and concerns of several kinds of biomedical professionals.


## Learning Objectives

- Compare normal and abnormal child development, especially with respect to autism.
- Encourage students' tolerance for ambiguity of explanation when it is inappropriate to accept a single hypothesis as true.
- Analyze and communicate information through visual displays, such as drawings, Venn diagrams, and graphs.
- Develop reasoning skills, particularly to learn to synthesize information from several sources and plan a course of action that is responsive to and appropriate in light of the information given.

## Quantitative Skills/Concepts

- Represent data in graphs and figures.
- Articulate complete and correct claims based on data.
- Use appropriate reasoning to support the validity of data-based claims.
- Recognize lack of correlation between two trends represented in curves.
- Appreciate the utility of Venn diagrams.

## The Case Study

### *Part I: Meet the Greens*

*Narrator:* As Mr. and Mrs. Green finished signing the papers to take their newborn son, Michael, home, the nurse said to them, "What a precious baby." The Greens couldn't have agreed more. Mr. and Mrs. Green went on to raise their baby as any caring parents would. At 23 months old, Michael was a healthy-looking boy. The Greens took him everywhere and encouraged him to explore his world. On the beach one day, Mrs. Green patiently held up a red pail and a shovel. "See, Michael," she said. "Pail. Pail. Pretty pail. Just say pail, darling." Michael stared past her, apparently watching Mr. Green, who was writing the child's name in the sand. That gave Mrs. Green an idea. Maybe "pail" was too hard. What about trying his own name again? "Look, that's your name." She pointed to herself and said "Mama." Then she pointed to the little boy and said "Michael. Say 'Michael,' honey." She stroked his hair. "Michael." The child continued to stare past her. Mrs. Green looked sad.

*Mr. Green:* "Oh well, he'll get it eventually. Some children take longer to learn how to speak than others."

*Mrs. Green:* "I don't know, he's almost two and he can't even speak common words. I've read and read, and made notes, and I even made a video the other day of Michael at the playground. I know you think I'm being too nervous, but I really think we should call Dr. Klotz and make an appointment for another checkup."

*Mr. Green:* "Well okay, if you think it might help."

*Narrator:* Mrs. Green wrote down all the symptoms that she had noticed in Michael that seemed to be a bit unusual for his age. She then called Dr. Klotz, Michael's pediatrician, and set up an appointment for the next day.

*Dr. Klotz:* "Come in Mrs. Green. Have a seat. And let's get Michael settled in the kid's corner. Fine. Now, what seems to be the problem?"

*Mrs. Green:* "Well, doctor, I know we've discussed this before, but now Mark and I both think something is wrong with Michael. He doesn't seem to be developing like the other children. We've set up play dates for the children within our neighborhood and he is very withdrawn. He doesn't seem to want anything to do with them. He also doesn't talk; he only uses gestures to tell us when he needs or wants something. I didn't think anything of it for a while, but he is going to turn two soon, and it just seems like something is wrong."

*Dr. Klotz:* "Go on. Tell me more about it."

*Narrator:* As Mrs. Green spoke about Michael's puzzling behaviors, Dr. Klotz observed both mother and child keenly. Mrs. Green repeated Michael's name frequently, and turned to smile at him, but the child did not respond and did not meet her gaze. The little boy sat quietly on a little chair gazing out the window. Beside him was a child's table full of colorful books and puzzles. Michael ignored them. Mrs. Green gestured frequently and wrung her hands. From time to time, she scratched a raw spot on her wrist. She appeared distracted and very troubled. Michael's father watched his wife and child unhappily, but it was difficult to discover what he thought by reading his expression.

*Dr. Klotz:* "Mrs. Green, how are you yourself feeling?"

*Mrs. Green:* "Oh, not too bad, Doctor. I have a little psoriasis. Sometimes it seems like it gets worse when I'm feeling stressed. And I do feel stressed. I'm so worried about my son."

*Dr. Klotz:* "What do you think is wrong with Michael, Mr. Green?"

*Mr. Green:* "I don't want to scare anyone, but I've been thinking maybe he's, well, slow."

*Mrs. Green:* "Michael is *not* slow!"

*Narrator:* For a moment, she seemed reluctant to go on.

*Mrs. Green:* "He has a cousin that was diagnosed with autism a while back. Could he be autistic?"

*Dr. Klotz:* "A cousin? Well, it seems that there is a genetic component to autism, but ..."

*Mr. Green:* "I've heard it runs in families sometimes."

*Dr. Klotz:* "Yes. And when you have twins, the incidence of both having autism is far higher if they are identical twins, rather than fraternal. But we don't know which genes are involved, whether there is more than one gene, and if it's the same gene or genes that are involved in each case."

*Mrs. Green:* "I don't understand that."

*Dr. Klotz:* "Well, suppose you get a cold. There are several different viruses that can cause what we call a cold. So, there's more than one possible causative agent—in other words, more than one way to get a cold. Sometimes you might have two different viruses at the same time in your upper respiratory tract, and they combine to cause multiple different cold symptoms. So, they are working together to cause that cold. And again, not every cold is alike. Sometimes your cold is mild, and sometimes it's a humdinger. Autism is a little like that. It can be mild, moderate, or quite severe. In fact, when it comes to autism, we usually talk about ASD, or an autism spectrum of disorders. Individuals with ASD have some common behaviors and challenges."

*Mr. Green:* "So, now you're saying it's viral? I thought you just said it was genetic."

*Dr. Klotz:* "No, no, I bring up the cold virus just as an analogy. Most researchers are looking at a dozen or so genes for proteins that may not be working properly in autistic children. But there are some people that think autism might be caused by a virus or viruses. And some people think it could be caused by environmental factors, like toxins, allergens, or pollutants."

*Mrs. Green:* "How about another type of environmental factor—how about poor mothering?"

*Dr. Klotz and Mr. Green:* "Not in this case."

*Dr. Klotz:* "There is very little support for that theory, even in general. But, we're putting the cart before the horse here. I told you to keep an eye on Michael last time you were here, and maybe make some notes. Well, from my observations, and what you've described today, it seems that Michael could possibly be autistic. But we're going to want to do some tests before we say that."

*Mrs. Green:* "What kind of tests?"

*Dr. Klotz:* "Behavioral tests, to see what he can and can't do. If it seems warranted, I'll recommend a pediatric neurologist who will investigate further and either rule out autism spectrum disorders or make a formal diagnosis and suggest a plan tailored to help Michael."

*Mrs. Green:* "Okay—anything we can do to help him. I just want him to grow and be as normal as he can be."

*Dr. Klotz:* "Let's try not to worry. Michael may not have autism. And if he does, it may very well be mild. And there are lots of things you can do to help a child with autism."

## Activities

*Activity I.1:* Make a growth chart showing the approximate age at which children reach developmental milestones like sitting up without support, reaching for objects, first words, first phrases, and other events. If you like, you may include infant, toddler, kindergarten pictures of yourself, or of a member of your family. With reference to your chart, answer the following question: Are Mr. and Mrs. Green's concerns about Michael's speech and social development well-grounded?

*Activity I.2:* Develop a list of behaviors associated with autism spectrum disorders.

## *Part II: What Causes Autism Spectrum Disorders?*

Mr. Green left Dr. Klotz's office with a bee in his bonnet. Over the next couple of weeks, while Mrs. Green methodically charted her observations of Michael in her notebook, he began a systematic study of the known causes of the autism spectrum disorders.

He found that scientists and doctors have lots of questions about the organic basis of the syndrome and many promising leads, but no definite answers. Studies have found the following possible causes.

### Activities

*Activity II.1:* Irregularities in some areas of the brain which can be detected by imaging techniques like MRI. Draw a picture of the brain showing the frontal and temporal lobes, amygdala, and cerebellum. Tell the function of these areas. How do you think abnormalities in these brain structures or in their functions could produce some of the symptoms of autism?

*Activity II.2:* Irregularities in levels or functionality of the neurotransmitters serotonin and GABA, or the presence of unusual alleles of several genes that encode proteins like shank3 and neuroligins, which are involved in formation and maintenance of synapses. Draw a generalized neural synapse and describe how neurotransmitters work at the synapse to connect one neuron to the next. Explain how inappropriate neural transmission could disrupt neural pathways and cause autistic behaviors.

*Activity II.3:* Influence of environmental factors like organophosphates and polychlorinated biphyenyls (PCBs); it is believed that the genetic makeup of autistic individuals may render them more sensitive to the presence of environmental toxins that affect neurophysiology. Explain how the release of high levels of environmental toxins could generate "clusters" of autism, similar to cancer clusters. Use a Venn diagram to show how genetic susceptibility inherited from both parents, along with environmental toxicity could produce autistic children.

*Activity II.4:* A link with vaccination against viral diseases, especially (i) MMR (measles-mumps-rubella), (ii) a set of vaccines that include the mercuric compound thimerosol as a preservative, and (iii) the practice of delivering multiple vaccines simultaneously to an infant, which, while efficient for the parents and health care people, might seriously weaken the juvenile immune system (Gerber and Offit 2009). While researchers continue to investigate a possible link between vaccination processes and autism, many scientists point to a recent study in the United Kingdom of the relationship between the practice of infant MMR vaccination and the rate of autism diagnoses. Look at the graph in Figure 43.1 (p. 384). What is the "take home message" of this graph (i.e., the main idea), and how does that message tend to disprove the idea that MMR vaccines are a cause of autism?

**FIGURE 43.1.**

Incidence of Autism and Prevalence of MMR Vaccination From 1988 to 1993.

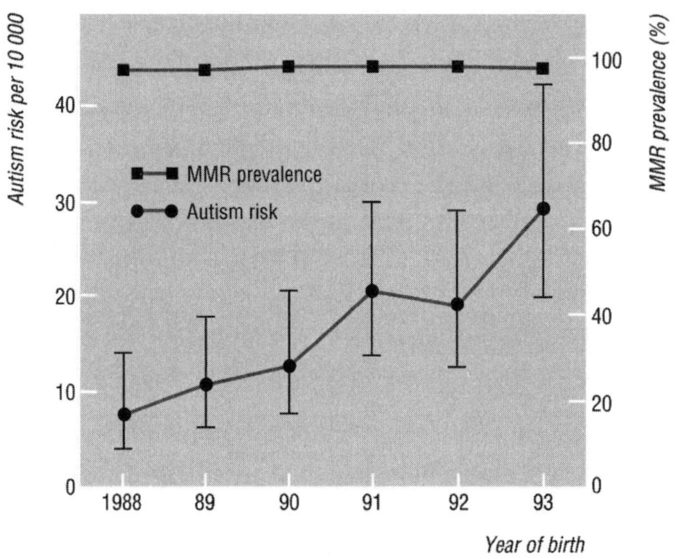


*Source:* Kaye, Malero-Montes, and Jick 2001.

Mr. Green read and read, and though his head was full of interesting ideas and hypotheses, his final conclusion could be summed up in his comment to Mrs. Green, "Well, dear, it looks like the doctors don't know what causes autism; they're trying pretty hard to figure it out though. But I guess that right now the best they can do is to detect the syndrome, describe each child's unique presentation of the disease, and figure out an individual treatment plan that is customized just for that child and his or her family."

## *Part III: Diagnosing Autism and Parent Education*

### Several Weeks Later

*Narrator:* Dr. Klotz compared Michael's speech and other behavioral skills to those expected for children his age and decided to refer the Greens to a pediatric neurology unit at a large regional teaching hospital and medical center. There, a specially trained multidisciplinary team gave the boy a comprehensive physical exam, with special emphasis on motor, coordination, reflex, and cognitive skills, as well as a hearing test. Blood was drawn and he was screened for several disorders that are sometimes associated with autism. Michael also received an EEG, which monitors electrical activity in the brain, and an MRI, which provides high-quality diagnostic images of the central nervous system.

## Activities

*Activity III.1:* The multidisciplinary team at the pediatric neurology unit included the following medical specialists. Select one professional from the list below, do some research, and prepare a presentation that describes: (i) the special area of expertise of that professional, (ii) what sort of training he/she receives, and (iii) how his/her measurements, observations, or analysis can contribute to the diagnosis of autism in a child. Think: Would any of these professions suit you?

- Neurologist
- Psychologist
- Speech/Language Pathologist
- Audiologist
- Radiologist
- Nurse Practitioner
- Pediatric Nurse
- Biomedical Laboratory Technician

*Narrator:* Dr. Katrine O'Rourke, a pediatric neurologist, met with her team, reviewed their results and suggestions and then asked her secretary to schedule an appointment with the Greens to discuss Michael.

*Dr. O'Rourke:* "Please have a seat."

*Mr. Green:* "Thank you, Doctor. Do you know if Michael is autistic?"

*Dr. O'Rourke:* "Mr. and Mrs. Green, first let me say that all tests for biochemical markers and illnesses that are frequently associated with autism were negative. No abnormalities were observed in his brain. However, our behavioral observations suggest that Michael is indeed autistic. So we have no definite physical cause here. In cases like Michael's, we say the child has idiopathic autism rather than primary autism. That means we're not sure what causes it. It could be one gene or many genes. It could be some substance from his environment. Or it could be an interaction between genes and environment."

*Mrs. Green:* "There's no cure for autism, is there? And since we can't see anything wrong with Michael, there's nothing to be done, right?"

*Dr. O'Rourke:* "You're right to say there's no cure. But you are wrong when you say there's nothing to be done."

*Mr. Green:* "Where do we start?"

*Dr. O'Rourke:* "There is someone I'd like you to meet. Let's go down the hall and visit with Mary Matthews. She'll be coordinating Michael's treatment team. Based upon Michael's specific needs, she'll make therapeutic recommendations to one of our programs or to other programs in your community. These will probably include individual or group therapies, speech and language therapy, and some training in social skills. And when the time comes, she'll help you to work with your school district to obtain specialized educational services that are appropriate.

## Activities

*Activity III.2:* Michael's treatment team also included a diverse group of psycho/social and education professionals. Select one professional from the list below, do some research, and prepare a presentation that describes: (i) the special area of expertise of that professional, (ii) what sort of training he/she receives, and (iii) how his/her measurements, observations, or analysis can contribute to a therapeutic plan for a child with autism. Think: Would any of these professions suit you?

- Social Worker
- Occupational Therapist
- Physical Therapist
- Child Psychologist
- Dietician

*Activity III.3:* When you have finished describing the roles of all of these professionals, take a few minutes to think about and describe the role of Michael's parents in his treatment.

## *Part IV: Choosing a Treatment Plan*

There are several types of treatments that Mr. and Mrs. Green must consider when selecting the types of treatments that are best for Michael. The social worker explained to them that the treatment plans are dynamic and are tailored to severity and the characteristics of the individual child with autism.

"Each child is different, and therefore must undergo different treatments. The treatments may change over short or long periods of time as Michael develops," explained Miss Mathews.

She went on to explain that there are several types of treatments and educational programs that the child can undergo. It is critical that each treatment is selected for the child according to his/her own weaknesses and strengths. Each child may have a different treatment, and while one treatment may work for one child, it may not for another. This will allow the child to move toward his/her own certain goals and for progress to be made.

## Activities

*Activity IV.1a:* There are educational programs available for children age 3 and under as well as programs for school-aged children. List specific programs that fall into each of these categories. Which educational program may be possible for Michael and why might his parents select that one?

*Activity IV.1b:* There are also many types of medical and dietary treatments available for children who have autism, each of which is selected according to each child's needs. What medications are available for children with autism? Some parents may have their child switch to a gluten/casein free diet. Why would this help the autistic child, and what precautions should be taken when switching diets?

## Objectives

- Compare normal and abnormal child development, especially with respect to autism.
- Encourage students' tolerance for ambiguity of explanation when it is inappropriate to accept a single hypothesis as true.
- Analyze and communicate information through visual displays, such as drawings, Venn diagrams, and graphs.
- Develop reasoning skills, particularly to learn to synthesize information from several sources and plan a course of action that is responsive to and appropriate in light of the information given.

## Web Version

Detailed teaching notes, the case PDF, and an answer key are available on the NCCSTS website at *sciencecases.lib.buffalo.edu/cs/collection/detail.asp?case_id=587&id=587*.

## References

Gerber, A. S., and P. A. Offit. 2009. Vaccines and autism: A tale of shifting hypotheses. *Clinical Infectious Diseases* 48 (4): 456–461.

Kaye, J. A., M. Melero-Montes, and H. Jick. 2001. Mumps, measles, and rubella vaccine and the incidence of autism recorded by general practitioners: a time trend analysis. *British Medical Journal* 322 (7284): 460–463.

CHAPTER 44

# BREAST CANCER RISK

## Using Real Medical Histories to Rank Genetic and Environmental Influences

*Michèle I. Shuster and Karen Peterson*

### Abstract

This case explores risk factors for breast cancer. After a preparatory reading assignment, students assess medical histories based on women with breast cancer and rank their overall risk for the disease as well as make recommendations for risk reduction.


### Learning Objectives

- Learn about various risk factors for breast cancer and to assess whether a risk factor is controllable or uncontrollable.
- Use provided clinical histories to assess the overall cancer risk of four different women, and then rank these women based on overall breast cancer risk.
- Make recommendations for each woman on how she should act to reduce her breast cancer risk.
- Defend a position on the merits and challenges of genetic testing while taking into consideration factors such as genetic discrimination, insurance issues, what to do with the information, interpersonal dynamics in a family with a strong history of cancer, cost, and so on.
- Make a "Health Change Checklist" articulating what personal health and behavioral changes you can make to reduce your breast cancer risk (or general cancer risk).
- For courses with a service-learning component, students could produce an informational pamphlet on breast cancer risk factors and how screening can be accessed in the local area.

### Quantitative Reasoning Skills/Concepts

- Represent data in graphs; instructors can ask students to graph the risk of breast cancer over various age groups, or by *BRCA1/BRCA2* mutation status.
- Articulate complete and correct claims based on data and use appropriate reasoning (i.e., experimental design and/or statistics) to support the validity of data-based claims; the case can support these concepts given that the role of DNA-based genetic testing, an evidence-based practice, can be incorporated and the fact

that the ability to evaluate risks and rank overall probability of breast cancer based on known risks are skills that rely on evidence-based critical thinking skills.

- Creating Punnett squares, DNA analysis, and the interpretation of family pedigrees could be incorporated into the case as extension activities.

## The Case Study

### *Introduction*

Breast cancer is the leading cause of cancer death for women in the United States. At the present time, the overall lifetime risk for a woman in the United States to develop breast cancer is one in eight (this means that approximately 13% of women in the U.S. will develop breast cancer in their lifetime). It is thus important for us to understand some of the risk factors for breast cancer, as well as some of the screening tests for breast cancer.

During this activity you are going to learn about some risk factors for breast cancer, evaluate the medical histories of several women with respect to their breast cancer risk, and then make some recommendations for how they might reduce their risk. To prepare for evaluating the medical histories, please read the following articles from the American Cancer Society:

- What Are the Risk Factors for Breast Cancer?
  *www.cancer.org/cancer/breastcancer/detailedguide/breast-cancer-risk-factors*
- Do We Know What Causes Breast Cancer?
  *www.cancer.org/cancer/breastcancer/detailedguide/breast-cancer-what-causes*

### Questions

1. How do age at menarche and age at menopause affect breast cancer risk?
2. What are the genes that are most commonly mutated in hereditary breast cancer? Approximately what percent of all breast cancers are hereditary?
3. How does a woman's weight influence her breast cancer risk?
4. If you were a physician taking a family history to assess breast cancer risk in a patient, what information would you want to know? Why would you want to know it?
5. How do pregnancy and HRT influence breast cancer risk?

### Profiles

Using the information in Tables 44.1–44.4 for the profile assigned to your group, discuss and circle the corresponding symbol for each aspect of her medical history indicating whether you think it decreases her risk for breast cancer (↓), increases her risk for breast cancer (↑), or has no impact (–) on breast cancer risk.

**TABLE 44.1.**

Profile for "Ana."

| | | | |
|---|---|---|---|
| Ana is a 64-year-old woman in generally good health. | ↓ | ↑ | – |
| She had her first child when she was 20. | ↓ | ↑ | – |
| She entered menopause at the age of 58. | ↓ | ↑ | – |
| She has been on hormone replacement therapy since entering menopause (for the past 6 years). | ↓ | ↑ | – |
| She has gained some weight since menopause. | ↓ | ↑ | – |
| Her mother had breast cancer diagnosed at age 37. | ↓ | ↑ | – |

**TABLE 44.2.**

Profile for "Paula."

| | | | |
|---|---|---|---|
| Paula is 71 years of age, and currently has a urinary bladder tumor, with metastases in the ovaries and possible involvement of one lymph node. | ↓ | ↑ | – |
| Paula had breast cancer at 22 years of age. She was treated with chemotherapy and bilateral (both breasts) mastectomy. At the time of her initial diagnosis and work-up, four positive lymph nodes were found. | ↓ | ↑ | – |
| Paula's sister was diagnosed with breast cancer three years ago, then ovarian cancer two and a half years ago. | ↓ | ↑ | – |
| Paula's mother died of lung cancer. | ↓ | ↑ | – |
| Two maternal uncles had pancreatic cancer. | ↓ | ↑ | – |
| Her maternal aunt had myeloma. | ↓ | ↑ | – |
| Her maternal grandmother has uterine cancer. | ↓ | ↑ | – |
| Paula's sister had genetic testing, and was found to have a BRCAI mutation. | ↓ | ↑ | – |
| Paula's sister has one daughter (Paula's niece). | ↓ | ↑ | – |
| After her sister's genetic testing, Paula had genetic testing, and the same BRCAI mutation as her sister was detected in Paula. | ↓ | ↑ | – |
| Paula has one daughter. | ↓ | ↑ | – |

**TABLE 44.3.**

Profile for "June."

| | | | |
|---|---|---|---|
| June is 58 years old. | ↓ | ↑ | – |
| She has been having "regular" mammograms (at two- to three-year intervals). | ↓ | ↑ | – |
| Her first period was at age 13. | ↓ | ↑ | – |
| She has had two pregnancies, resulting in two children, the first of which was at age 27. | ↓ | ↑ | – |
| She experienced menopause at age 51. She did not take hormone replacement therapy (HRT), but she used oral contraceptives for a total of four years in the past. | ↓ | ↑ | – |
| She has high blood pressure and high cholesterol. | ↓ | ↑ | – |
| She has low levels of thyroid hormones. | ↓ | ↑ | – |
| She also has "weak bones." | ↓ | ↑ | – |
| Her maternal aunt died of breast cancer in her 30s. | ↓ | ↑ | – |
| Her mother died of a brain tumor at age 39. | ↓ | ↑ | – |
| Her father is alive and well at age 84. | ↓ | ↑ | – |

**TABLE 44.4.**

Profile for "Nora."

| | | | |
|---|---|---|---|
| Nora is a 51-year-old, pre-menopausal woman. | ↓ | ↑ | – |
| Her last bilateral mammogram showed no evidence of a mass. | ↓ | ↑ | – |
| She had her first period at the age of 13. | ↓ | ↑ | – |
| She has had two pregnancies, each resulting in the birth of a child, the first of which was at age 32. | ↓ | ↑ | – |
| She used oral contraceptives for six years. | ↓ | ↑ | – |
| She has not taken any hormone-replacement therapy (HRT). | ↓ | ↑ | – |
| She smoked until age 26. | ↓ | ↑ | – |
| She consumes between 1 and 4 alcoholic drinks per week. | ↓ | ↑ | – |
| Her mother had breast cancer at 48 years of age, and now has lymphoma (at age 72). | ↓ | ↑ | – |
| Her maternal grandmother had breast cancer at age 47, and died of lung cancer. | ↓ | ↑ | – |
| Her paternal first cousin presently has breast cancer. | ↓ | ↑ | – |
| Her paternal aunt died "at a young age" from breast cancer. | ↓ | ↑ | – |
| Her father was of Ashkenazi Jewish heritage, and died of colon cancer at 66 years of age. | ↓ | ↑ | – |

## Web Version

Detailed teaching notes, the case PDF, and an answer key are available on the NCCSTS website at *sciencecases.lib.buffalo.edu/cs/collection/detail.asp?case_id=271&id=271*.

# A LIGHT LUNCH?

## A Case in Calorie Counting

*Brahmadeo Dewprashad and Geraldine S. Vaz*

## Abstract

This case makes connections between core concepts in chemistry and obesity-related factors. It tells the story of two friends and their underestimation of the calories they have consumed in a meal and their overestimation of the efforts needed to maintain a healthy body weight. Concepts covered include use of conversion factors, calculation of percentages and body mass index, and calculation of caloric values of different foods.


## Learning Objectives

- Use conversion factors to calculate the energy value of different foods.
- Inter-convert energy values given in calories and kJ.
- Calculate percentages.
- Calculate body mass index (BMI) and understand its use in categorizing individuals as healthy, overweight, or obese.
- Calculate the amount of calories burned during walking and understanding effective strategies for weight maintenance.

## Quantitative Reasoning Skills/Concepts

- Carry out basic mathematical operations.
- Articulate complete and correct claims based on data.
- Use appropriate reasoning to support the validity of data-based claims.

## The Case Study

### *Before Class*

A. Read the case story on pages 396–398.

B. Locate and read the following article: United States Department of Health and Human Services and United States Department of Agriculture. 2005. *Dietary Guidelines for Americans 2005. www.cnpp.usda.gov/Publications/DietaryGuidelines/2005/2005DGPolicyDocument.pdf*

C. Complete the Pre-Case Questions individually and submit two weeks prior to undertaking the case study in class. The assignment will be graded and returned to you at least a week before you undertake the case study. Also, attempt answering the case study questions as you will be required to share your responses with group members during the in-class case study session.

## In Class

D. Work in your assigned group and formulate responses to the Case Questions. Select a team member to moderate the discussions.

## After Class

E. Complete the Post-Case Questions and submit along with an individual write-up of answers to the case study questions.

## Case Story

"Look at this pair of jeans. Don't you think I will look good in them?" asked Elizabeth.

"They suit you. Go try them on, girl," encouraged Charonda.

Elizabeth went into the changing room. She emerged a few minutes later wearing a pair of jeans that was unbuttoned and clinging to her body. "What do you think?" she asked.

"Nice, but maybe a bigger size. Everyone is now going for baggy clothes," Charonda suggested diplomatically.

"No, this is my size! I'll lose a few pounds and they'll fit perfectly," Elizabeth countered adamantly.

"OK, take them. Anyway, I'm getting hungry, let's grab something to eat," Charonda suggested.

"There is a place next door we can get something quick. Let's have a light lunch so that we can pig out at Duane's party tonight. I just love the Caribbean food he serves!" Elizabeth replied.

"I'll order. What do you want?" Charonda asked.

"I love cheeseburgers! I gotta watch my weight and my cholesterol level now. Looks like the pounds came on over winter. What are you having? I'll follow your example, skinny girl," Elizabeth observed.

"Two slices of cheese pizza, a large garden salad, and an iced tea," Charonda replied.

"A diet iced tea, I bet," remarked Elizabeth.

"Nah, artificial sweeteners taste awful," Charonda replied.

"Yeah, nothing like the real stuff. I'll have the same, but I like spicy. Two slices of pepperoni pizza, a taco salad, and a grape soda for me. I love ranch dressing, but don't bring any for me ... too many calories," Elizabeth requested.

As they sat down to eat, Elizabeth looked around at the other diners and observed. "Crowded huh; salads seem to be popular today."

"Yeah, that time of the year. Doesn't hurt to lose the few pounds gained over winter—swimsuit season coming up," Charonda opined.

"Looks like I have to do that too. You know, I tried several times to lose weight but it is so hard," confessed Elizabeth.

"Yeah, I know it's tough," agreed Charonda.

"Look at that lady with the two kids in the corner table. Her plate is loaded with fried chicken and fries and she is so thin. Some people can load up on fats and never put on weight," observed Elizabeth.

"For class I was reading that we all have different metabolic rates; our hormone levels, weight, muscle mass, age and other factors determine how many calories we burn. To keep the same weight we have to eat about the same amount of calories we burn up. Calories are not the only thing to watch. You do watch your cholesterol intake and that's great. Trans fats and saturated fats aren't good either. Although that lady is skinny, the fried chicken and fries are not healthy choices, they have lots of saturated fats and maybe even trans fat," Charonda counseled.

Elizabeth nodded in agreement and then shifted the conversation to news about mutual friends during the rest of the meal. All the talk about diet and calories was making her feel depressed.

"That was good," Charonda observed as they got up to leave.

Elizabeth complained. "Yeah. You know, I wish I had as high a metabolic rate as you. Then I could enjoy food like you do. We eat about the same amount but I'm so much bigger than you. I always feel guilty after I've eaten something that I really love."

"Don't worry so much. We walked for about 30 minutes in the mall. I am sure we burned up about half of the calories we just ate," Charonda opined.

"We walked more like 40 minutes. I bet we burned up all the calories we ate. We should come to the mall and window shop more often. It is much more fun than working out in a gym," said Elizabeth.

Later that evening, Elizabeth was unpacking her shopping bag and decided to try on the jeans once again. She inhaled deeply and contracted her stomach as she cautiously put the jeans on. They still didn't fit! She gave them an upwards tug and exhaled in relief as the jeans moved up to her waist. However, despite all her efforts, she could not button them. She wondered how much weight she had put on since she last weighed herself. She unearthed the bathroom scale, climbed on it, and closed her eyes as she saw the needle racing across the scale. After a while, she opened her eyes and peered down at the needle. She exhaled in relief as it settled at the 200 lb mark. She plucked up enough courage to measure her waist. Her jaw dropped as she noticed the measurement.

"Ninety one inches? Can't be!" she exclaimed. As she looked closely, she noticed she had used the side of the tape that gave measurements in centimeters. She sighed in relief, turned over the tape, and re-measured her waist.

"Aha! Thirty four inches; not bad for someone who is 5 feet 4 inches and has a big bone structure. But I still have to lose a few pounds. I'll give up sugar from my diet until I lose 20 pounds, starting tomorrow. Tonight though is time for jerk chicken and rum cake!"

## Pre-Case Questions

1. Provide a very brief explanation of the following terms: (a) carbohydrate, (b) protein, (c) fats, (d) saturated fats, (d) trans fats, and (e) cholesterol.
2. The foods that we eat provide energy for the body. The energy value is usually measured in calories (cal), kilocalorie (kcal), and kilojoule (kJ). What is the relationship between these units?

## Case Questions

1. Use the information in Table 45.1 to determine the amount of calories in the food consumed by Elizabeth and Charonda. Did Elizabeth follow Charonda's example and consume a similar amount of calories during their "light" lunch? The caloric values of carbohydrates, fats, and proteins are 17, 38, and 17 kJ/g, respectively, and 1 calorie (cal) = 4.184 kJ.

**TABLE 45.1.**

Nutrition Facts of Lunch.

| | Elizabeth's Lunch | | | Charonda's Lunch | | |
|---|---|---|---|---|---|---|
| **Menu item** | **Pizza with pepperoni** | **Taco salad** | **Grape soda** | **Cheese pizza** | **Garden salad** | **Iced tea** |
| Amount | 2 slices (142 g) | 1 Serv. (261 g) | 12 fl oz (372 g) | 2 slices (126 g) | 1.5 cup (224 g) | 1 cup (8 fl oz) |
| Carbohydrate | 39.8 g | 26.6 g | 41.7 g | 41.0 g | 6.7 g | 20.4 g |
| Protein | 20.2 g | 17.4 g | 0 g | 15.4 g | 2.6 g | 0 g |
| Saturated Fat | 4.4 g | 6.0 g | 0 g | 3.0 g | 0.0 g | 0.1g |
| Polyunsaturated Fat | 2.4 g | 1.5 g | 0 g | 1.0 g | 0.1 | 0.6g |
| Monounsaturated Fat | 6.2 g | 4.5 g | 0 g | 2.0 g | 0 g | 0 g |
| Cholesterol | 28 mg | 5 mg | 0 mg | 19 mg | 0 mg | 0 mg |

2. Elizabeth is 200 lb and Charonda is 150 lb. An average person of 150 lb walking at a rate of two miles per hours burns about 240 Calories per hour while an average person of 200 lb burns about 320 Calories per hour. Did either Elizabeth or Charonda "burn off " the calories consumed with the walk they took? Assume that they walked at an average speed of two miles per hour for 40 minutes.
3. For a female age 19–30 with a sedentary lifestyle such as Elizabeth and Charonda, the estimated daily calorific need is 2000 calories. What percentage of this did they consume during lunch? Would you recommend a very large dinner for them if they wanted to restrict themselves to their calorific needs and they each had a breakfast of about 600 calories?
4. The body mass index (BMI) of an individual is used as an indication of weight-related health risks and is defined as weight in kilograms divided by height, in meters, squared. BMIs of 24 or less, 25–29.9, and 29.9 or over, respectively, indicate healthy weight, overweight, and obesity. In which category will you place Elizabeth?
5. How much weight does Elizabeth need to lose in order to be at a healthy weight?
6. Elizabeth has a sister Mary who has the same height and weighs 205 lb. However, Mary, who ran track in high school, is much more muscular. Elizabeth considered

giving the pair of jeans to Mary. However, she decided not to because she felt that the jeans would probably not fit Mary since she likely had a larger waist size than Elizabeth because although they had the same height, Mary was heavier than her. Calculate Mary's BMI. What do you think about Elizabeth's assumption about Mary's waist size?

7. A waist size >35 inches in females is associated with obesity related health risks. Fat located in the abdominal region is associated with a greater health risk than peripheral fat. What conclusions can you draw about Elizabeth's waist measurements?
8. It is recommended that one consume less than 10 percent of calories from saturated fats. Does the saturated fat content of the meal consumed by Elizabeth fall within these guidelines? The caloric value of fats is 38 kJ/g, and 1 calorie (cal) = 4.184 kJ.
9. It is recommended that one consume less than 300 mg/day of cholesterol. Is the amount of cholesterol in Elizabeth's meal at an acceptable level?

## Post-Case Questions

1. According to the U.S. Department of Agriculture (USDA), the average American consumes about 20 teaspoons of sugar that have been added to products such as cereals, soda, coffee, and ketchup. Make a list of all the food that you have eaten over a school day and estimate the amount of calories that you obtained that day from the sugar added to the food that you have eaten. When computing the calories, bear in mind that one teaspoon of sugar has 16 calories and that sugar is a carbohydrate and thus has a calorific value of 4 calories/g. Manufactured food products are usually labeled with the amount of sugar in the product. How does your added sugar intake for that day compare with that of the average American?
2. A reduction of 500 calories or more per day is a common initial goal in most weight loss programs. How many teaspoons of sugar would Elizabeth have to cut back on in order to reduce her intake by 500 calories per day? What do you think of Elizabeth's plan to remove sugar from her diet in order to lose weight?
3. What advice would you give to Elizabeth about the health risks associated with her weight?

## Web Version

Detailed teaching notes, the case PDF, and an answer key are available on the NCCSTS website at *sciencecases.lib.buffalo.edu/cs/collection/detail.asp?case_id=460&id=460.*

# PHARMACOGENETICS
## Using Genetics to Treat Disease

*Jeanne Ting Chowning*

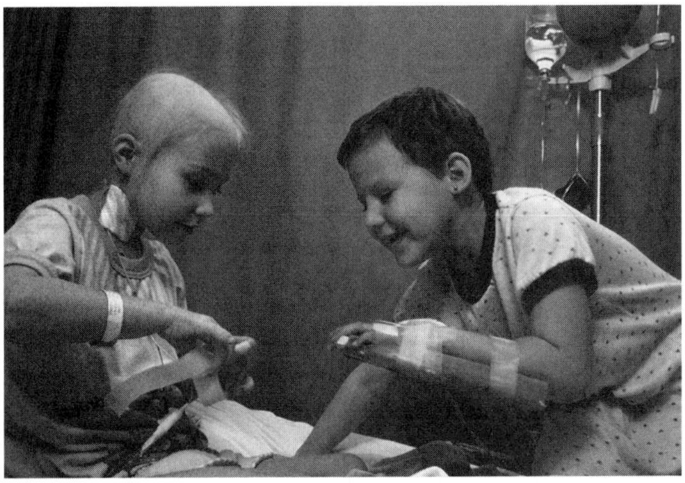


## Abstract
This case investigates the applications of genetics to medicine by exploring one of the first examples of a pharmacogenetic test to enter mainstream clinical practice. Through a scenario based on clinical observations, students learn about acute lymphocytic leukemia, as well as the wide range of individual responses to the drug used to treat it.


## Learning Objectives

- Be able to use scientific/case study data and interpret graphs in order to draw conclusions.
- Understand how individual genetic variation can impact medical practice and clinical outcomes, using the example of leukemia and thiopurine methyltransferase (TPMT).
- Be able to predict how polymorphisms in the gene for TPMT indicate courses of medical care for particular individuals.

## Quantitative Reasoning Skills/Concepts

- Carry out basic mathematical operations.
- Interpret graphs and use them to formulate predictions and explanations.
- Articulate complete and correct claims based on data.
- Use appropriate reasoning to support the validity of data-based claims.
- Biochemical pathway analysis.
- Analysis of relationship between genotype and phenotype.

## The Case Study

### *Part I: Acute Lymphocytic (Lymphoblastic) Leukemia*

It's called the children's ward. For two teenagers who have been recently diagnosed with leukemia, it seems insulting to have their lives hijacked by doctors and nurses with stuffed animals clipped to their stethoscopes.

Laura is a forward on her school soccer team and leads the league in scoring. For the last four months, she has been really tired, but nothing seemed really wrong until her legs became covered with bruises. Just pressing her fingers on her skin was practically enough to make a bruise. It didn't seem real when her doctor, Jane Ryder, diagnosed her with Acute Lymphocytic (or Lymphoblastic) Leukemia (ALL), or when she told her that ALL is the most common malignant (spreading) cancer found in children. She's 14 years old; she's not a child!

Beth is 13 and looks remarkably like Laura. Both have straight dark hair, large brown eyes, and tall slender builds. Beth has never been that athletic; she prefers reading and theater. She is hoping to be part of the drama team next year when she goes to high school, even though she'll only be a freshman. But she's been missing a lot of school because of one virus after another, lots of fevers and night sweats, then that rash in the fall. Now she is in a hospital, and it seems like the only people she sees are her parents, Dr. Ryder, and the nurses.

Laura and Beth both have ALL, which arises from the uncontrolled growth of immature lymphocytes (a type of white blood cell, or leukocyte). These cells, which are "stuck" in an early stage of development, become so numerous that they crowd out normal blood cells. Each year about 30 cases occur per million people, and most of those cases are in children ages 2–5 years. The cause of ALL remains largely unknown, although a small number of cases are associated with inherited genetic syndromes. Both girls are suffering from anemia (low blood cell levels), fevers, bleeding, and are pale and thin. Dr. Ryder has decided to treat them as inpatients, keeping them in the hospital while treating them with a "thiopurine" drug called 6-mercaptopurine (6-MP) known to be highly effective in treating leukemia. Thiopurines are very similar to the regular purine nitrogen bases such as adenine and guanine that make up DNA and RNA. The only difference is that thiopurines have an extra sulfur group attached to them. They are similar enough to a regular purine base that our cells convert them to nucleotides (with the addition of a deoxyribose sugar and phosphate). These modified thioguanine nucleotides (TGN) are then incorporated into DNA.

The TGN nucleotides interfere with DNA replication and stop rapidly growing cells like cancer cells from further growth. Unfortunately, they also block the growth of other fast growing cells needed for good health, like the cells in the bone marrow that develop into erythrocytes (red blood cells) and leukocytes. As with many drugs given as chemotherapy, it is important to give a high enough dose to prevent cancer cells from replicating, while avoiding damage. Too high a drug dose can be very toxic. Dr. Ryder knows that drugs are processed in various ways in the body. They must be absorbed by the blood, distributed throughout the body's tissues, converted or transformed into forms that are easier to eliminate, and then removed from the body. Dr. Ryder gives both girls the same dosage of the drug before leaving the hospital for the night.

While making her rounds over the next few days, Dr. Ryder sees Laura's vital signs plummet. Her anemia has worsened; her erythrocyte count is so low that her heart function could be compromised. Her fevers are spiking, and her breathing is becoming shallow and labored. She is not eating and is being hydrated intravenously. Her condition is life-threatening. In contrast, Beth's anemia has decreased, she is free of fever, and is actually showing signs of an appetite and boredom, good indicators of improved health. Dr. Ryder had not anticipated that the drug could act so differently in two individuals. Even as she looks at Beth's chart, she can picture Laura's body struggling to hold its own just two private rooms away. Dr. Ryder knows she must find out why her patients are responding so differently. But where should she start, and will she find an answer in time to help Laura?

## Questions

1. Suggest a reason why the drug might affect the two girls differently.
2. What tests might Dr. Ryder order to determine why the two girls are reacting as they are to the drug? Provide two or three appropriate examples of tests.

## *Part II: Enzyme Activity*

Dr. Ryder learns that the difference in patient reaction to the drug probably has something to do with how the drug is naturally metabolized in the body to be removed as waste. After searching the scientific literature, she learns that the drug 6-MP can be either converted to the active form, TGN nucleotides, or inactivated with the help of the TPMT enzyme (thiopurine methyltransferase) (Figure 46.1, p. 404). Within each patient who takes the drug, both processes are occurring and they compete with each other.

Since the therapy aims to harm rapidly replicating cells without overly impacting normal ones, it is important that excess drug is inactivated. Dr. Ryder decides to see how levels of the TPMT enzyme activity might vary between people.

She reviews the research papers that have been published about the TPMT enzyme and finds an interesting graph (Figure 46.2, p. 405) of the results of a study of 298 randomly selected Caucasian individuals; researchers conducting that study found the levels of TPMT enzyme activity shown in Figure 46.2.

## FIGURE 46.1.

Flow Chart Showing Activiation and Inactivation Paths of the Drug 6-MP.

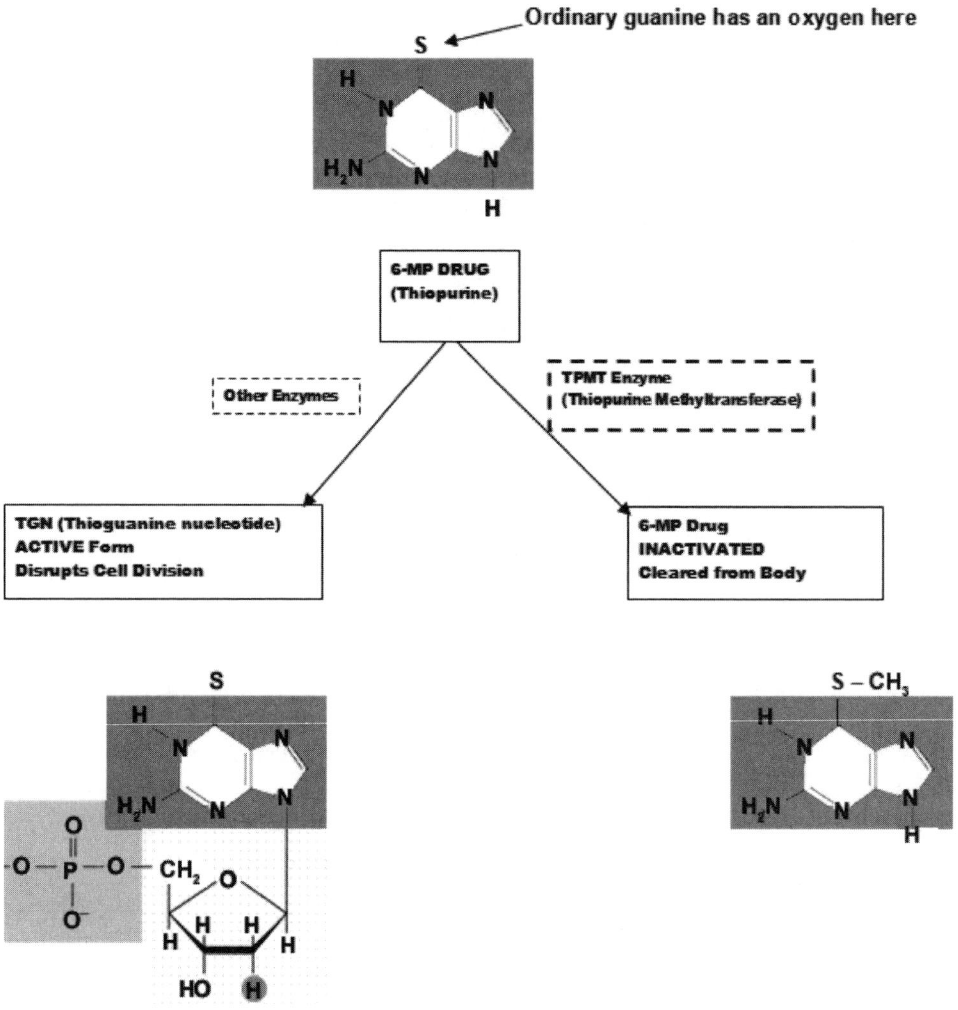

**FIGURE 46.2.**

Simplified Bar Graph Showing Results From a Study of 298 Randomly Selected Caucasian Patients.

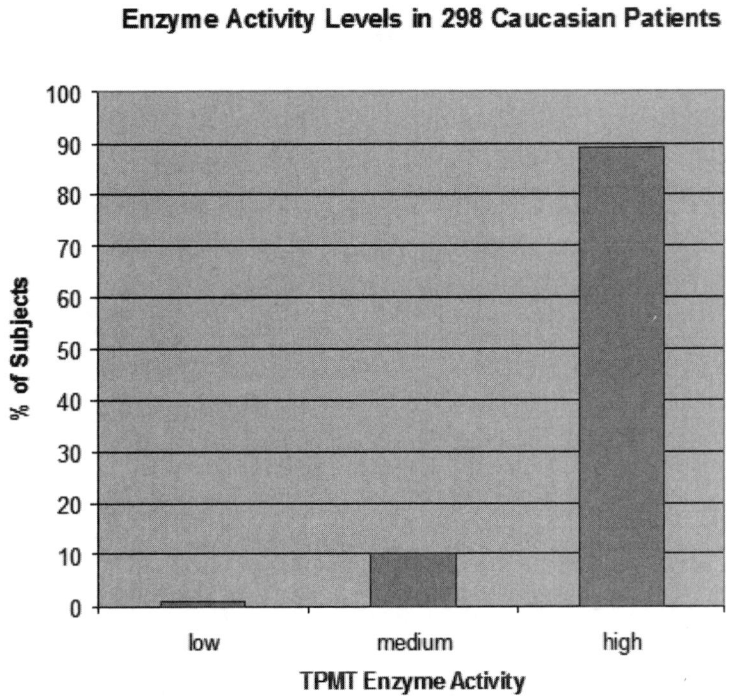


*Source:* Simplified graph patterned after the top panel of Figure 2 in Weinshilboum and Sladek (1980).

## Questions

1. If Dr. Ryder had 10 Caucasian patients in the next month, how many would you predict to have each of the TPMT enzyme activity levels, based on the graph in Figure 46.2?

    Low:

    Medium:

    High:

    Would you expect the actual/observed number of patients to be different? Why might there be differences?

2. Each individual inherits two copies of the gene for the enzyme, one from each parent. Dr. Ryder suspects that variation in enzyme activity level is controlled by two different versions (alleles) of that gene. Does the graph in Figure 46.2 (and

**FIGURE 46.3.**

RBC TPMT Frequency Distribution Histogram for 298 Randomly Selected Caucasian Subjects.

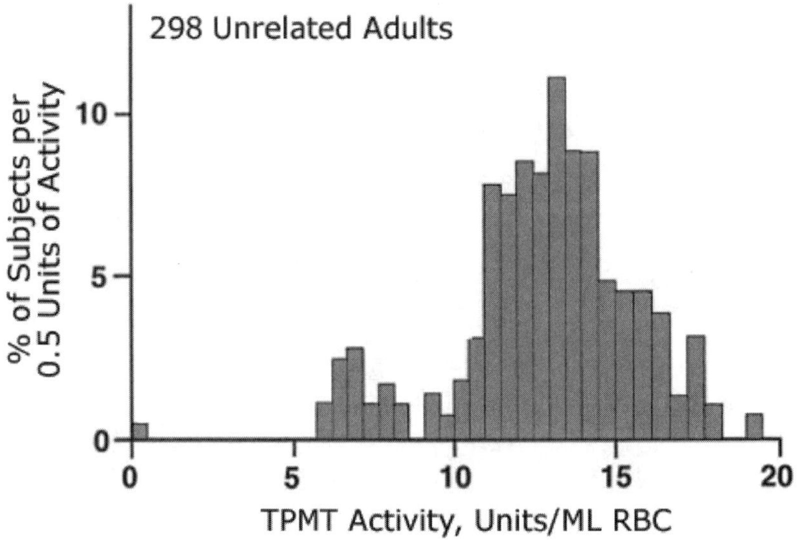


*Source:* Histogram drawn after top panel of Figure 2 in Weinshilboum and Sladek (1980).

the number of phenotypes) suggest that enzyme activity levels are based on a dominant/recessive or a co-dominant pattern of inheritance? Explain your answer.

3. Which bar in Figure 46.2 (low, medium, or high) represents individuals who might be homozygous for a "low enzyme activity'" version of the gene? Which bar represents individuals who might be homozygous for a "high enzyme activity" version of the gene? Which bar represents heterozygotes?
4. Answer the question: "How does enzyme activity level vary among the patients examined?" In your answer, be sure to include supporting data from the graph in Figure 26.2. Explain how these data support your conclusion.
5. Challenge question: The actual graph (Figure 46.3) showed much more detail. Why do you think that there is more variation between patients than shown in the simplified graph in Figure 46.2?

## *Part III: TPMT Enzyme Activity Levels*

Dr. Ryder tested Laura, who was very sick, and found that her TPMT enzyme activity level was extremely low.

### Question

1a. Why would individuals with the lowest level of enzyme get the sickest when they take the drug? Suggest one possible reason.

Investigating further, Dr. Ryder decides to look at drug levels in many patients who are all receiving the same standard doses of the thiopurine drug and compare them to enzyme levels. She compares the level of thioguanine nucleotides (TGN) created by the thiopurine drug to the body's level of TPMT enzyme in patients. The results are shown in Figure 46.4.

### Question

2. Describe the relationship between TPMT enzyme activity levels and TGN levels. Be sure to include supporting data from Figure 46.4.

**FIGURE 46.4.**

Scatter Plot of TGN Versus Enzyme Activity. Thioguanine nucleotide concentrations and TPMT enzyme activity levels in 95 children with Acute Lymphoblastic Leukemia (ALL) who were being treated with standard doses of thiopurine drugs.
*Source:* Modified from Lennard et al. (1990).

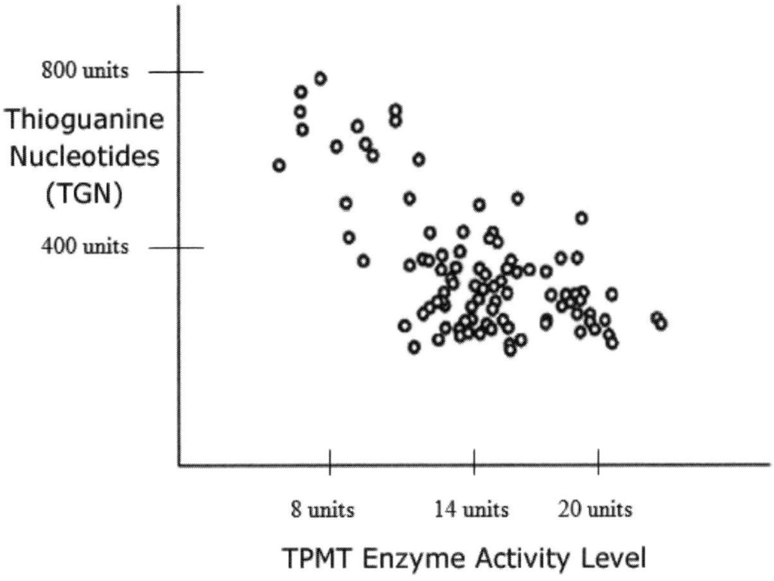

## *Part IV: Putting It All Together*

From her research, Dr. Ryder hypothesized that patients such as Laura (who became very sick upon receiving the drug) have very ***high/low*** TPMT enzyme activity and therefore very ***high/low*** levels of TGN nucleotides at normal doses. They easily became sick from the effects of the drug and could even die. These patients are ***homozygous / heterozygous*** for the version of the gene encoding ***high/low*** enzyme activity. A better drug dose for these patients is 1/10th the level of other patients.

Patients such as Beth with ***high/low*** TPMT enzyme activity had ***high/low*** levels of TGN nucleotides. These patients would do well with the drug, and in some cases might even need a larger-than-normal dosage for the treatment to be most effective. These patients were either homozygous for the version of the gene encoding ***high/low*** enzyme activity, or were heterozygous.

Based on Figure 46.2 in Part II, about 10% of the Caucasian population is ***homozygous/ heterozygous***.

### Question

1. In the paragraphs above, circle the correct answer (***high*** or ***low***, ***heterozygous*** or ***homozygous***).

## *Part V: SNPs and TPMT*

DNA techniques reveal that the TPMT gene is located on chromosome 6, is about 34 kilobases in length (34,000 DNA bases), and has 8 exons. An exon is a region of a gene that is present in the final functional transcript (mRNA) from that gene. The diagram in Figure 46.5 shows a representation of the TPMT gene, showing the exons as boxes. The first "wild type" is the most common version. In our case, the second version of the TPMT gene is associated with low enzyme activity (TPMT*3A) and has two single nucleotide polymorphisms (SNPs), or changes in single DNA nucleotide bases (from "G" to "A" in one case and from "A" to "G" in another) that result in different amino acids being inserted in the enzyme. This, in turn, affects the enzyme's function. Over 20 different gene variants have been found, three of which are shown in Figure 46.5.

**FIGURE 46.5.**

Selected Human TPMT Alleles. The wild-type human TPMT allele (TPMT*I) and variant alleles TPMT*3A, TPMT*3B, and TPMT*3C. Rectangles represent exons, with black coding areas and white untranslated regions.

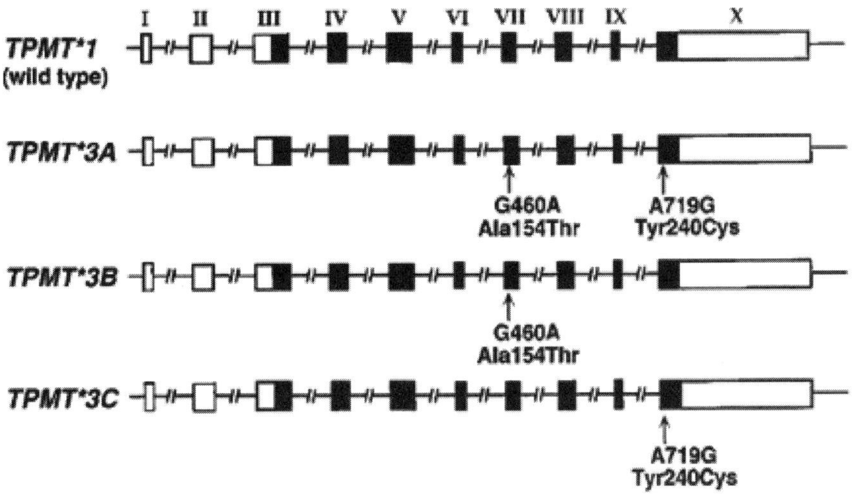


*Source:* Weinshilboum (2001).

## Questions

1. Dr. Ryder now has the ability to conduct a SNP genetic test on her patients to determine what level of drug they should get. A new patient on the ward, Kevin, is homozygous for TPMT*3A. Circle the area of the graph in Figure 46.4 in Part III that might likely corresponds to Kevin's TGN and enzyme activity levels. Explain why you circled that region.
2. What level of the drug (low, medium, or high) should Dr. Ryder give him? Explain your answer.
3. In your own words, summarize how knowing someone's TPMT DNA sequence could be used to determine what kind of medical care they should receive.

## *Postscript*

Dr. Ryder responded quickly to Laura's drug reaction. She discontinued the drug for Laura, and Laura's condition began to improve rapidly.

## Web Version

Detailed teaching notes, the case PDF, and an answer key are available on the NCCSTS website at *sciencecases.lib.buffalo.edu/cs/collection/detail.asp?case_id=247&id=247*

## References


Lennard L., J. S. Lilleyman, J. Van Loon, and R. M. Weinshilboum. 1990. Genetic variation in response to 6-mercaptopurine for childhood acute lymphoblastic leukaemia. *Lancet* 336: 225–229.

Weinshilboum, R. 2001. Thiopurine pharmacogenetics: Clinical and molecular studies of thiopurine methyltransferase. *American Society for Pharmacology and Experimental Therapeutics* 29: 601–605.

Weinshilboum, R. M., and S. Sladek. 1980. Mercaptopurine pharmacogenetics: Monogenic inheritance of erythrocyte thiopurine methyltransferase activity. *American Journal of Human Genetics* 32: 651–662.

# SECTION XI

# ECOLOGY AND BEHAVIOR

# THE DEAD ZONE

## Ecology and Oceanography in the Gulf of Mexico

*Kathleen Archer and Lauren Sahl*

## Abstract

This case focuses on the seasonal hypoxic area in the Gulf of Mexico known as the Dead Zone. It follows a fictional college student whose father is a commercial fisherman trying to make a living from the Gulf. Students learn about the biological and physical forces that produce, maintain, and eventually dissipate a low-oxygen marine hypoxic zone.


## Learning Objectives

- Understand the close integration of biological and physical influences on an aquatic environment and the outcome when nutrient inputs are elevated.
- Understand the structure of an aquatic food web.
- Understand the role of the microbial loop.
- Understand the role of salinity and temperature in creating water column density structure.
- Understand how the interaction between biological processes and water column structure can cause hypoxia.
- Read and interpret graphical data.

## Quantitative Reasoning Skills/Concepts

- Interpret the meaning of simple statistical descriptors.
- Use graphs to formulate predictions and explanations.
- Articulate complete and correct claims based on data.
- Use appropriate reasoning to support the validity of data-based claims.

## The Case Study

### *Part I: The Problem*

Bill sat at the kitchen table adding up last month's expenses from running his fishing boat. With his trawler he fishes for bottom fish from his home base in Terrebone Bay, Louisiana—snapper and grouper mostly. But for the last few summers he has had to boat farther and farther out from the Louisiana shore to get to decent fishing grounds. The additional fuel costs were killing him. He rubbed his tired eyes and tried running the numbers through his calculator again.

"Hi Dad," said his daughter Sue, walking into the kitchen. "How does it look this month?"

"Not so good," said Bill, tossing his pencil onto the table. "The fuel bills were higher than ever this summer. It's going to be tight for our finances. I wish I knew why the fish disappear near shore in the summer."

He privately worried about how he was going to be able to afford Sue's college tuition this fall. Maybe it was time to get out of the fishing business, except fishing was all he knew. Plus, all his money was tied up in his fishing boat and gear. Who would buy it now that fishing in the Gulf was so problematic?

Sue sat down at the table and toyed with the pencil. She knew about her dad's worries. "You know, Dad," she said, "I've been thinking. Let me talk with some of my professors at the university. Maybe I can get some information from them about what causes the fish to disappear, and whether anyone is working on a solution. Someone at school ought to know something."

Bill smiled at his daughter, even though he wasn't hopeful. "Good idea, kiddo," he said. "Maybe more people are working on this than we know. See what the professors can tell you."

Sue hurried across campus. She had an appointment with Professor Gracia in the biology department, and she was late. She rushed up the stairs of the biology building and knocked at his door.

"Come in," Professor Gracia called out. "You must be Sue. I'm glad you could make it before I had to leave. You are right in thinking that a number of scientists must be working on the problem you described," he said as he handed her a map of the United States. "Look here," he said, pointing to a region of the Gulf of Mexico just below Louisiana and eastern Texas. "See that shaded area? We call that the Dead Zone. During the summer there is very little in the way of marine macro-organisms there."

"Wow, I had no idea it was so big!" said Sue. "Do the fish actually die there?"

Professor Gracia started gathering up materials for his next class. "Some fish may die. Most of the fish and crustaceans that can leave the Dead Zone do so. It's called the Dead

Zone because the dissolved oxygen levels in the water get so depleted the water can't support life."

Sue could see that the far edge of the Dead Zone corresponded with the distance her dad had to boat to get to good fishing grounds. "Is anyone working on why the Dead Zone forms?" she asked.

"A lot of people are very concerned and are actively collecting data to help get to the bottom of the cause," said Professor Gracia. "I've got to get to class right now, but let's meet again. I have more information and data to share with you."

"That's sounds great," said Sue. "I'll talk to you soon."

## Part II: What Affects the Dissolved Oxygen Content of Water?

"Hey guys, look at these maps of the Dead Zone I got from Professor Gracia," said Sue, walking up to her friends sitting at the lunch table in the student cafeteria. "What I don't get is why this particular area should have such low dissolved oxygen concentrations."

**FIGURE 47.1.**

Map of the United States Showing Area of the Dead Zone in the Gulf Coastal Waters of Louisiana and Texas (Goolsby and Battaglin 2000).

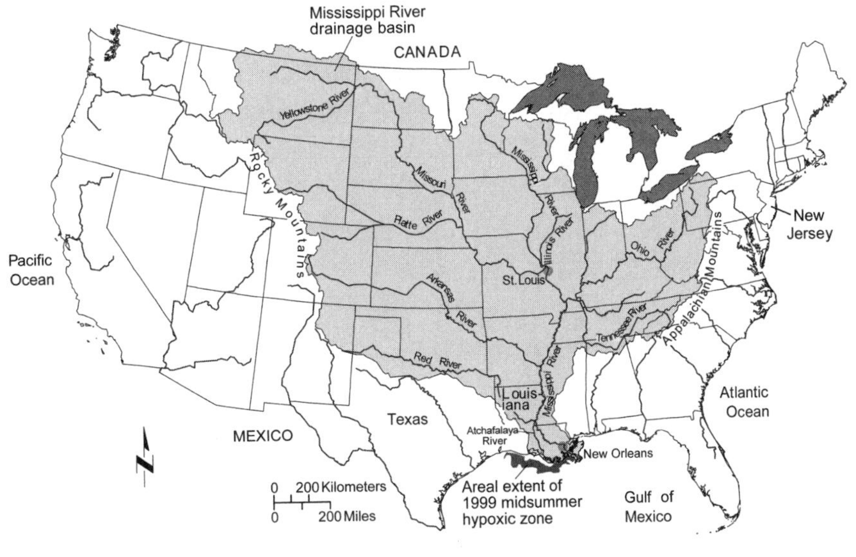


Figure 1. Mississippi River drainage basin, major tributaries, and areal extent of 1999 midsummer hypoxic zone.

**FIGURE 47.2.**

Detail of the Dead Zone (shaded) in the Gulf of Mexico. (Rabalais, Turner, and Scavia 2002. Copyright, American Institute of Biological Sciences. Used with permission.)

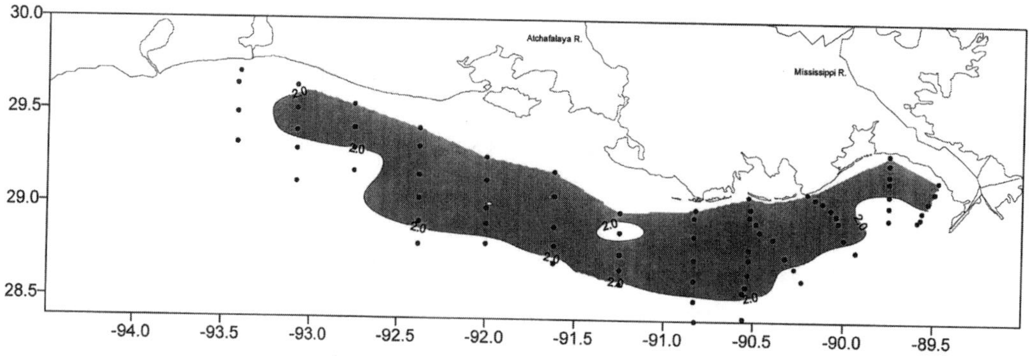


Sue handed the maps (Figures 47.1, p. 415, and 47.2) to her friend Paula, a physics major. Paula stopped eating her sandwich long enough to give them a look. "There must be some physical cause," Paula said. "I can't imagine anything else that could affect the dissolved oxygen content of water so dramatically."

"Oh, come on," said Sue's friend Zack. "Living organisms should have a huge impact—aren't all the fish busy consuming oxygen in the water?"

"Well, of course you would think of that, you're a biology major," said Sue. "But let's be systematic. What are all the physical and biological influences we can think of that could affect how much oxygen is dissolved in the water?"

## Questions

1. What physical forces or conditions affect the dissolved oxygen content of water?
2. What are the biological processes that can affect dissolved oxygen concentration?
3. What might cause each identified condition to fluctuate over the season?
4. If you had to choose, which of the conditions you've identified seem most likely to be the primary cause of hypoxia in the Gulf? Why?

## *Part III: How Do the Gulf Waters Change With the Seasons?*

"Thanks for meeting with me again," said Sue, shaking hands with Professor Gracia. "I'm hoping you can help me understand what's going on in the Gulf, what people think causes the low oxygen levels."

"I can sure get you started," replied Professor Gracia, pulling out some papers from the pile on his desk. "You know, the Gulf waters are very dynamic, changing dramatically with the seasons, and from the surface to the bottom. For example, the Atchafalaya and Mississippi Rivers carry enormous amounts of fresh water into the Gulf and the volume fluctuates with the season. Because the river water is fresh, it's less dense than the seawater, and tends to stay on the surface. The prevailing current near shore in the Dead Zone is from east to west, so the river water is carried from where the river empties toward western Louisiana and Texas.

"Here are some data that will be useful for you to look at showing some of the seasonal changes in temperature, salinity, and dissolved oxygen concentration (Figures 47.3 and 47.4). Scientists measure the temperature, salinity, and dissolved oxygen concentration of water by using a probe. The probe continuously measures these properties as it is lowered to the sea floor. The data are presented in graphs called station profiles. Here are some taken at different times from a station just off Terrebonne Bay."

Professor Gracia handed several station profiles and a water discharge graph to Sue, then glanced at his watch. "I'm afraid I've got to head off to a meeting, but why don't you take these profiles and spend some time with them. See what you can glean from the data."

"Thanks," said Sue. "I will."

**FIGURE 47.3.**

Salinity (Triangles), Temperature (Squares), and Dissolved Oxygen Concentration (Circles) at Various Depths, in Meters (0 = Surface). A station off Terrebonne Bay, Gulf of Mexico. (Modified from Rabalais, Turner, and Scavia. 2002.)

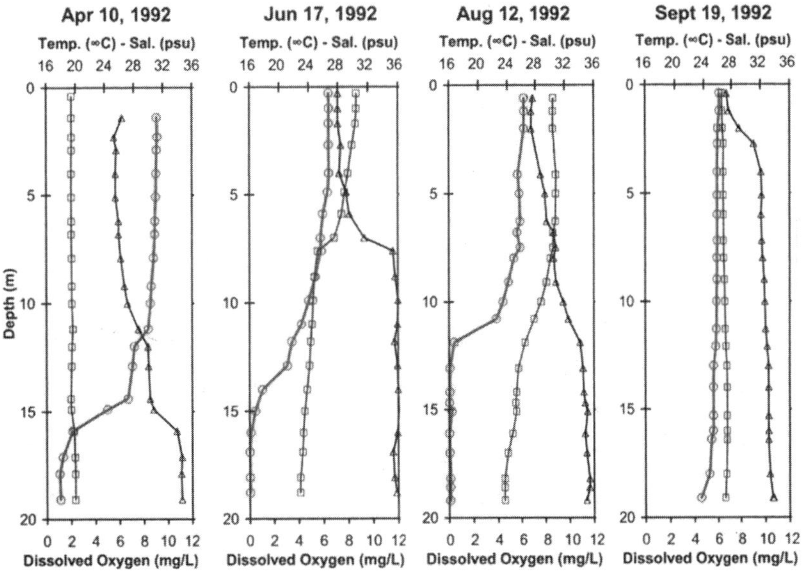

**FIGURE 47.4.**

Average Monthly Water Discharge From the Mississippi River for the years 1930–1992. (Modified from Walker 1994.)

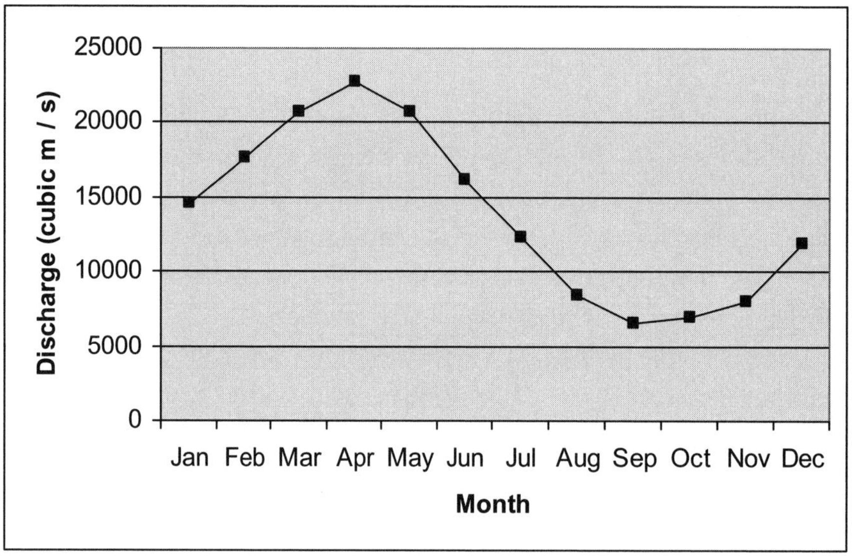


## Questions

1. What is the average temperature of water in the top 5 meters in April? In August? How do those values compare to the average temperatures at 15–20 meters for those months?
2. Typical seawater has a salinity of 35 psu (practical salinity units). In which month is the difference in salinity of surface and bottom waters the greatest? Why do you think the difference is the greatest at this time of year?
3. In which month is the salinity difference between surface and bottom waters the least? What reasons can you think of to explain why the surface and bottom water salinities become more uniform at that time?
4. Water that contains 2 mg oxygen per liter or less is termed hypoxic, since at that concentration many aquatic aerobic organisms are unable to survive. How does the depth at which hypoxia is observed change over time?

## *Part IV: How Do the Organisms Affect Dissolved Oxygen Concentration?*

After spending time looking over Professor Gracia's station profiles, Sue felt like she had a much better sense of the seasonal changes in the Gulf and the effects of freshwater on the salinity at different depths. Her friend Zack's comments about fish using up oxygen made her wonder just how much living organisms can affect the oxygen concentration in such a large body of water. She wondered about what organisms are present besides fish, shrimp, and seaweeds—organisms she already knew about. Sue had learned about food webs in her introductory biology course, so she was comfortable with the idea of primary producers, primary consumers, and predators. But what organisms were playing these roles in the Gulf, and could they realistically affect the oxygen concentration in the water?

She decided to do some legwork to figure out who the key players are, where they reside in the water column, and how much respiration they carry out using the basic ideas of a generalized food web to guide her. She listed these questions for herself:

## Questions

1. What group of organisms are the most important primary producers in the marine aquatic food web? How deep down in the water column can they be found?
2. What factors are the most important for controlling the growth of these organisms? That is, what limits their growth?
3. Why does the primary productivity in the Gulf of Mexico fluctuate over the year (see Figure 47.5)?

**FIGURE 47.5.**

Primary Production in the Gulf of Mexico in mg Carbon Assimilated Per Cubic Meter Per Day. No data were collected for July. (Modified from Sklar and Turner 1981.)

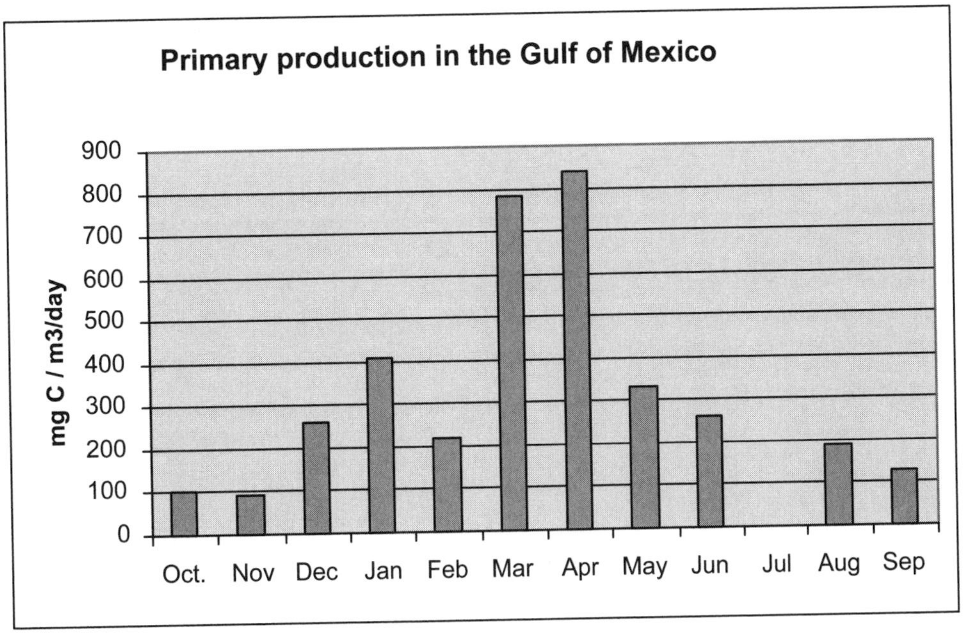

1. What are the major consumers in the Gulf of Mexico food web?
2. What are the remaining components of the food web in this area?
3. What groups are responsible for the greatest total amount of respiration (consumption of oxygen)?
4. At what time of the year does respiration rate peak (see Figure 47.6)? How does that compare to peak times of primary production? Why is there a lag between these two?

**FIGURE 47.6.**

Respiration Rates in the Gulf of Mexico at 18–20 m, Transect C6b. (Modified from Dortch et al. 1994.)

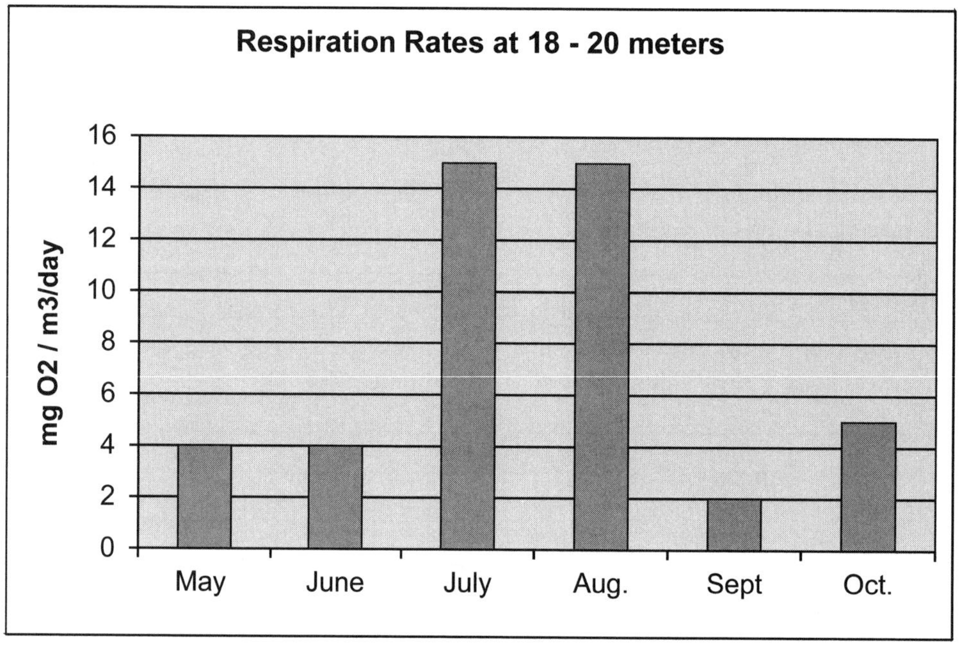


## *Part V: Why Does the Phytoplankton Population Increase?*

Sue could see that photosynthesis by the phytoplankton population increased sharply in the spring months, suggesting their populations had soared. Following the spring peak, photosynthetic rates declined as the population members died and respiration rates in the water rose dramatically. It made sense to Sue that the organic matter from dead phytoplankton was sinking, providing a rich food source for marine bacteria populations at the base of the water column. As the bacterial populations climbed, they depleted the oxygen available in the water, especially at the bottom of the water column. But why did the phytoplankton population explode in the first place? Sue knew that light and nutrients were the things most likely to limit growth. Day length was increasing in April and May when the populations climbed, but since the population crashed when day length continued to increase in June, light did not seem to be the cause. Nutrients seemed more likely to be the culprit, carried into the Gulf by the Mississippi River. This also made sense knowing that the prevailing current would carry nutrient-rich water from the river to the west of the Mississippi's mouth, exactly where the Dead Zone was located.

Nitrogen is commonly the limiting nutrient so Sue decided to confirm her suspicions by tracking down data on the monthly change in the nitrogen concentration of the Mississippi River (Figure 47.7).

**FIGURE 47.7.**

Monthly Discharge of Nitrate and Nitrogen From the Mississippi River Into the Gulf of Mexico. Values are normalized for the average annual value from 1978 to 1995. (Modified from Turner et al. 2005.)

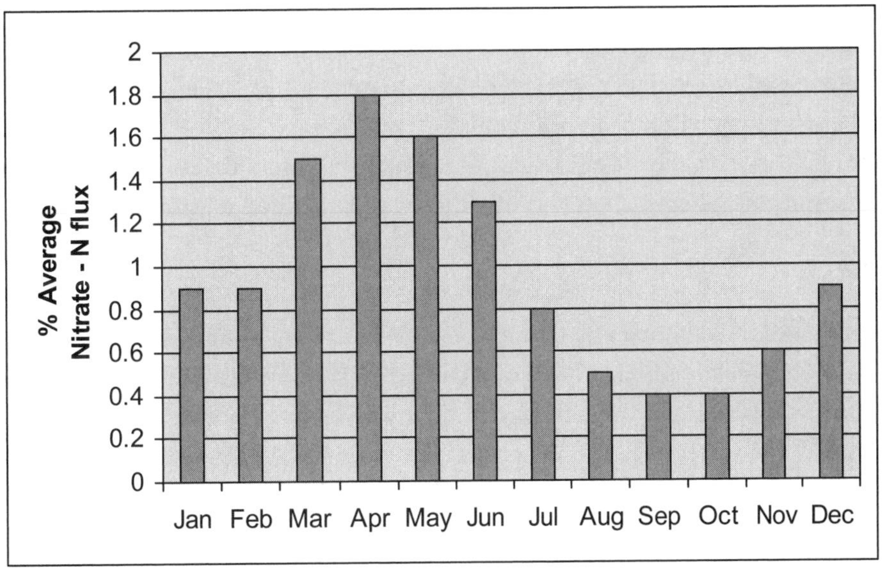


## Questions

1. What are the peak months for nitrate-nitrogen discharge from the Mississippi River into the Gulf?
2. How do the peak months for nitrate-nitrogen discharge compare to the peak months for phytoplankton primary production?

## Part VI: Why Is the Dead Zone a Seasonal Phenomenon?

"Hey Sue, can I join you?" asked Paula. Sue was sitting in the cafeteria, digging into her lunch.

"Sure, Paula. I'm excited—I actually have made some headway on my project to figure out what's happening in the Dead Zone," said Sue. "It looks like the Mississippi River water is carrying nutrients like nitrogen into the Gulf, and that in turn promotes a population explosion of photosynthetic plankton. Excretion of organic compounds from the phytoplankton, as well as their dead cells when they die, sink down, providing a rich source of food for heterotrophic aerobic bacteria. It's the bacteria that use up the oxygen in the water."

Paula picked at her salad. "Um, ok. But the Mississippi River flows constantly—why does the Dead Zone occur only in the summer? Your dad is able to fish much closer to shore in the late fall and into the winter. What makes the Dead Zone disappear then; what restores oxygen to the water?"

"Ah, Paula, you always manage to get right to the part I haven't figured out yet," said Sue. "I understand why the oxygen depletion happens, but I really don't know what restores the oxygen levels once they are low."

Sue thought back on the ways that dissolved oxygen enters the ocean. One or more of these processes must re-oxygenate the water for the Dead Zone to disappear.

### Questions

1. Does it seem likely that any of the seasonal changes noted in Part II, Question 3, re-oxygenate the bottom waters of the Dead Zone in the autumn and winter?
2. Recall that in the summer the water column in the zone of hypoxia is layered. Figure 47.3 in Part III shows that the river plume occupied the upper water column. This resulted in a low salinity surface layer, made warm by solar irradiance. Beneath the river plume was the Gulf water. This water had a higher salinity and was cooler. How do temperature and salinity affect the density of water? How does this affect the stability of the water?
3. Let's check your answers with a demonstration. Your instructor will queue up a film clip. Predict what will happen to the water when the barrier is removed from the tank, and explain why.
4. Observe the film clip. Did it confirm your prediction? If not, what did happen and why?
5. To mix a stable water column requires kinetic energy. Can you think of any processes that might supply this energy? Do any of these processes change in intensity with the seasons?
6. What makes the hypoxia disappear in the fall and winter?

## Part VII: Where Does the Nitrogen Come From?

"I'm impressed—you've put together most of the pieces of the Dead Zone puzzle," said Professor Gracia.

Sue blushed, but nodded, as they walked together toward his office. "Well, it really matters to my family, so I had a pretty strong motivation," she said. "I think I understand now why the Dead Zone is temporary, getting flushed out by the turbulence of fall and winter storms. The data on nitrogen carried in by the Mississippi show a sizeable increase in early spring when the river discharge rate is at its peak. That supports the bloom of phytoplankton, and the eventual population explosion of marine aerobic bacteria. They deplete the oxygen available in deeper waters, and form the Dead Zone in early summer. The one thing I haven't figured out is where the nutrients in the Mississippi river water are coming from, and why the Dead Zone was not a problem many years ago."

"I think your second concern, why hypoxia is a relatively recent phenomenon, is explained by this graph (Figure 47.8)," said Professor Gracia. "What do you notice about nitrogen discharge in the sixties versus the last decade?"

**FIGURE 47.8.**

Nitrate and Nitrogen (in Millions of Tons Per Year) Discharged Into the Gulf of Mexico From the Mississippi River. (Modified from Goolsby and Battaglin 2001.)

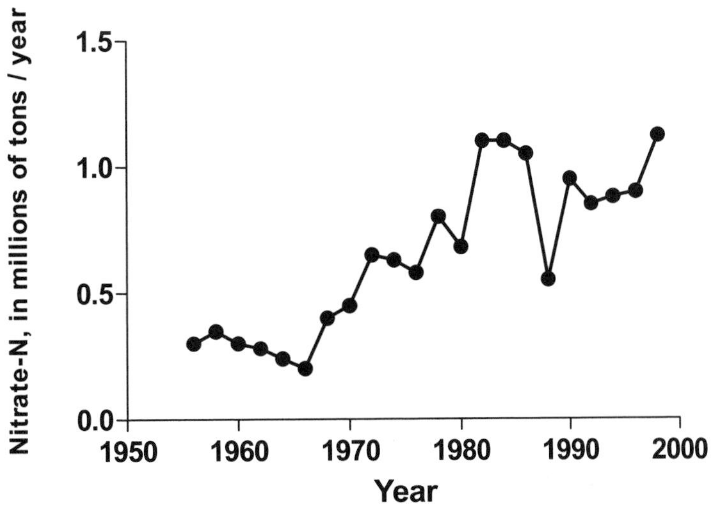


"I can see that nitrogen has increased, but what is the source of the nitrogen?" said Sue.

"That's probably the most controversial part of this whole problem," said Professor Gracia, opening his office door. He pushed some books off a chair and motioned toward it. "Here, have a seat. Most researchers, such as Nancy Rabalais and Don Goolsby, have argued that the most important source of nitrogen comes from the fertilization of farms on the land that drains into the Mississippi River. Nutrients not used by crops are washed into the river system and are carried downstream. The farming interests argue that you can't rule out the possibility that it comes from other sources. Here, take a look at this letter to the editor of the journal *Science* by Clifford Snyder, the Midsouth Director of the Potash and Phosphate Institute."

Professor Gracia pulled out a folder from his filing cabinet, and handed Sue a sheet.

"There are also no conclusive data that identify the sources of the nitrate and nitrogen that enter the Mississippi River and ultimately reach the Gulf. In the White House Committee on the Environment and Natural Resources (CENR) Topic 3 report, Goolsby and Battaglin (2000) used a statistical model to conclude that agriculture was the major source of nitrogen to the Mississippi River Basin. Their conclusion was not surprising, since inputs to the model were based on the assumption that many non-agricultural sources (for example, urban runoff and geological nitrate) were insignificant. Their estimates of discharge are simply proportionate to the tonnage of each input source in sub-basins of the Mississippi River Basin. River monitoring clearly indicates that major nitrogen loads come from the geographic area of the Corn Belt, but the sources remain unclear. This geographic area contains naturally rich soils of the prairies, as well as agriculture. The proportion of the nitrogen that comes from agriculture and the proportion of the agricultural nitrogen that arises from fertilizer use remain uncertain."

Sue read the letter quickly. "Snyder seems to be saying that while it's true the nitrogen is coming from the Corn Belt, it could be originating from the prairie soils, that we can't know how much is coming from the natural soil and how much is coming from added fertilizer. I guess it would be hard to tell exactly where a nitrogen molecule came from," Sue said.

"Okay," said Professor Gracia. "Now take a look at this data (Figure 47.9) from Don Goolsby and his colleagues, and see what you think."

## Questions

1. Which nitrogen source has added the greatest amount of nitrogen to the land in the Mississippi River Basin in the years since 1970?
2. Refer to Figure 47.8, which shows the increase in nitrogen carried by the Mississippi into the Gulf, and to Figure 47.9. Are the data in these graphs consistent with the idea that nitrogen naturally present in rich prairie soils is the source of nitrogen carried into the Gulf of Mexico? Why, or why not?

**FIGURE 47.9.**

Nitrogen Inputs to the 20-State Region of the Mississippi River Basin, in Kilograms of Nitrogen Per Hectare Per Year. Fixation refers to the nitrogen fixation that occurs in legume crops. (Modified from McIsaac et al. 2002.)

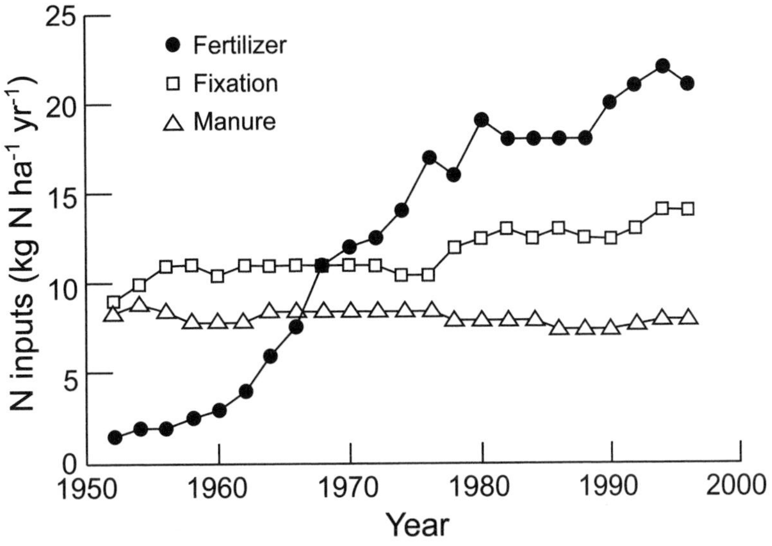


## *Part VIII: Conclusion*

When important scientific claims are made, there is typically a flurry of research and experiments, and a welter of different conclusions and interpretations. As data from different sources accumulates, however, it becomes clearer which interpretations are consistently supported, and which are not. Although a small minority of scientists continue to argue that the source of the nitrogen increase has not been proven, most scientists examining the data from numerous studies have concluded that fertilizer application in farms of the Mississippi River Basin are the source of nitrogen that leads to the Dead Zone. The problem has moved slowly from scientific debate to scientific consensus and into the arena of public policy and government action. The United States Geologic Survey released a report in January, 2008. Here is an excerpt from the accompanying news release which states unequivocally:

> "Nine states in the Mississippi River Basin contribute the majority of nutrients to the Northern Gulf of Mexico, threatening the economic and ecological health of one of the nation's largest and most productive fisheries. Excessive nutrients have resulted in a zone of low dissolved oxygen or hypoxia, caused by the growth of large amounts of algae. This can stress and cause death in bottom-dwelling organisms in the Gulf." (Alexander et al. 2008)

Now that the cause of the Dead Zone has been determined, state and federal agencies are looking for ways to reduce nutrient pollution from farmlands before it enters the Mississippi River system. Voluntary reduction in fertilizer application, restoring wetlands along waterways, and establishment of vegetated buffering zones to absorb nutrients before they enter rivers and streams are among the action strategies being pursued. The goal is to reduce the area of the Dead Zone to 5,000 square kilometers by 2015. This represents about 1/3 the average square area of the Dead Zone between 2003 and 2007. Achieving this goal will require overcoming many challenges, including reluctance of farmers to alter farming practices. In the meantime, small fishing operations near the Dead Zone will continue their struggle to survive.

## Web Version

Detailed teaching notes, the case PDF, link to a film clip, and an answer key are available on the NCCSTS website at *http://sciencecases.lib.buffalo.edu/cs/collection/detail.asp?case_id=217&id=217.*

## References

Alexander, R. B., R. A. Smith, G. E. Schwarz, E. W. Boyer, J. V. Nolan, and J. W. Brakebill. 2008. Differences in phosphorus and nitrogen delivery to the Gulf of Mexico from the Mississippi River basin. U.S. Geological Survey. http://*water.usgs.gov/nawqa/sparrow/gulf_findings*

Dortch, Q., N. N. Rabalais, R. E. Turner, and G. T. Rowe. 1994. Respiration rates and hypoxia on the Louisiana shelf. *Estuaries* 17 (4): 862–872.

Goolsby, D. A., and W. A. Battaglin. 2000. Nitrogen in the Mississippi Basin—Estimating sources and predicting flux to the Gulf of Mexico. *USGS Fact Sheet 135-00. http://ks.water.usgs.gov/pubs/fact-sheets/fs.135-00.html*

Goolsby, D. A., and W. A. Battaglin. 2001. Long-term changes in concentrations and flux of nitrogen in the Mississippi River Basin, USA. *Hydrological Processes* 15: 1209–1226.

McIsaac, G. F., M. B. David, G. Z. Gertner, and D. A. Goolsby. 2002. Relating net nitrogen input in the Mississippi River basin to nitrate flux in the lower Mississippi River: A comparison of approaches. *Journal of Environmental Quality* 31: 1610–1622.

Rabalais, N. N., R. E. Turner, and D. Scavia. 2002. Beyond science into policy: Gulf of Mexico hypoxia and the Mississippi River. *BioScience* 52: 129–142.

Sklar, F. H., and R. E. Turner. 1981. Characteristics of phytoplankton production off Bataria Bay in an area influenced by the Mississippi River. *Contributions in Marine Science* 24: 93–106.

Walker, N. D. 1994. Satellite-based assessment of the Mississippi River discharge plume's spatial structure and temporal variability. *OCS Study MMS 94-0053.* U.S. Dept. of the Interior, Minerals Management Service, Gulf of Mexico OCS Region, New Orleans, LA.

Turner, R. E., N. N. Rabalais, E. M. Swenson, M. Kasprzak, and T. Romaire. 2005. Summer hypoxia in the northern Gulf of Mexico and its prediction from 1978 to 1995. *Marine Environmental Research* 59 (1): 65–77.

# THREATS TO BIODIVERSITY
## A Case Study of Hawaiian Birds

*Sarah K. Huber and Paula P. Lemons*

### Abstract
Students learn about introduced species and how they pose a threat to biodiversity by analyzing the impact of introduced species on the native bird populations of the Hawaiian Islands.

### Learning Objectives
- Describe the characteristics of an introduced species that makes it more likely to become established in a new area.
- Describe the reasons that certain endemic species (e.g., Hawaiian birds) are particularly vulnerable to introduced species.
- Analyze data showing the direct and indirect effects of introduced species on endemic species.

### Quantitative Reasoning Skills/Concepts
- Carry out basic mathematical operations.
- Represent data in graphs.
- Use graphs to formulate predictions and explanations.
- Formulate null and alternative hypotheses using numerical evidence.
- Analyze data to test hypotheses.
- Articulate complete and correct claims based on data.
- Use appropriate reasoning to support the validity of data-based claims.

# The Case Study

## *Background Reading*

What is biodiversity? Defining biodiversity is a difficult and complex task that depends on the level of analysis used to categorize a region. At the ecosystem level, biodiversity may be defined as the number of biomes in a given region. At the organism level, biodiversity is the number of species in a given area. A third definition of biodiversity is based on genetic diversity. Yet another way to conceptualize biodiversity is to think of it as evenness. For example, evenness may consider the number of species in a given area relative to the total number in that area. Because biodiversity is defined in different ways and at different levels in biology, monitoring the biodiversity of a particular region can be a difficult task.

Regardless of how biodiversity is defined, there is little question that it is declining. Though most of the public's attention is focused on a few charismatic endangered species, such as the Northern spotted owl, the gray wolf, and the giant panda, these are only a miniscule fraction of the number of species that are threatened, endangered, or already extinct.

Biodiversity is threatened by disruptions to the natural ecosystem that limit the resources needed by an organism (e.g., light, water, food, or space) or alter how that organism interacts with other organisms (e.g., competition and predation). Two phenomena that create these types of disruptions include the establishment of *exotic*, or *introduced species*, and *habitat fragmentation*.

The establishment of introduced species threatens indigenous biota. Introduced species are brought to an area either intentionally or by accident and are not part of the native ecosystem. Although most introduced species fail to survive in a new habitat, some actually thrive and can out-compete native species, prey on native species, transmit exotic diseases, facilitate the spread of native diseases, hybridize with natives, and alter habitats.

Along with introduced species, habitat fragmentation may disturb native ecosystems. When people alter natural areas, for example, through agriculture or urban sprawl, the habitats needed to sustain native species are often eliminated. The remaining natural areas are left isolated. This process is referred to as habitat fragmentation. With habitat fragmentation, the direct loss of suitable habitat is not the only problem. Other, less obvious effects can also be important. For example, breaking up large populations into smaller ones that cannot remain self-sustaining may result in loss of genetic exchange among different populations, or increased edge effects. In the take-home exercise, you'll learn how the introduction of ungulates such as cattle, goats, or pigs by humans has led to habitat fragmentation.

But why should humans worry about introduced species, habitat fragmentation, or even extinction? Practically speaking, numerous species fulfill crucial ecological roles in our biosphere by recycling nutrients, producing oxygen, or pollinating plants, while other species are actual or potential natural resources that can be used for crops, fibers, and medicine. Reservoirs of genes for disease resistance can be found in the wild relatives of crop plants or domestic livestock. When the value of biodiversity is assessed in terms of ecology and resources, its importance to human health, the economy, social justice, and national security can be appreciated. Others argue that biodiversity should be preserved for ethical and aesthetic reasons.

Over the next two weeks you will examine the biodiversity crisis using the Hawaiian Islands as a case study. This archipelago is geographically diverse in size, elevation, and habitat type and is historically rich in biodiversity. Hawaii's flora and fauna are an example of how isolation can lead to adaptive radiation (the emergence, from a common ancestor, of numerous species to fill underused niches). This has produced many very specialized species, most of which are endemic, meaning they are found nowhere else on Earth. However, these species are particularly vulnerable to the effects of introduced species, habitat loss, and fragmentation. To put the magnitude of the problem in perspective, the Hawaii Natural Heritage Program tracks 30 vertebrates, 102 invertebrates, and 515 plants that are considered to be "critically imperiled globally." For comparison, in New Jersey, which is approximately the size of Hawaii, the Natural Heritage Program tracks 3 vertebrates, 14 invertebrates, and 21 plants that are "critically imperiled globally" or "imperiled globally." We will attempt to understand some of the reasons why, over the last several centuries, there has been a massive decline in Hawaii's biodiversity.

## *In-Class Exercise*

1. Examine the data presented in Table 48.1 (p. 430). How many of these species are currently extinct? What other trends do you notice? What factors might contribute to these trends?
2. One factor that leads to a decline in biodiversity is the introduction of non-native species. However, most species that are introduced to an area do not become established. What are some characteristics of species that might make them more likely to thrive in a new habitat?
3. Several species of large rats arrived to Hawaii as stowaways on ships. These rats live in a variety of habitats and eat a variety of foods, both plants and animals. Speculate about how these introduced rats could directly and indirectly affect native bird species.
4. Researchers hypothesize that several factors may affect the extent of predation by rats on birds. These factors include bird size, nesting site, and the amount of time young spend in the nest (duration of egg incubation and nestling period). Formulate one hypothesis and its accompanying null hypothesis about how one of these factors might affect predation.

a. Bird size
   - H1 (hypothesis):
   - H0 (null hypothesis):

b. Nesting site
   - H1 (hypothesis):
   - H0 (null hypothesis):

c. Incubation and nestling period
   - H1 (hypothesis):
   - H0 (null hypothesis):

**TABLE 48.1.**

Status of Native Birds Breeding in the Hawaiian Islands.

| Group | Species Known to Have Existed | Current Species | Endangered or Threatened Species | Number of Extinct Species |
|---|---|---|---|---|
| Seabirds | 22+ | 22 | 2 | |
| Herons | 1 | 1 | 0 | |
| Ibises | 2 | 0 | – | |
| Waterfowl | 11 | 3 | 3 | |
| Hawks | 3 | 1 | 1 | |
| Rails | 11 | 2 | 2 | |
| Stilts | 1 | 1 | 1 | |
| Owls | 4 | 1 | 0 | |
| Crows | 3 | 1 | 1 | |
| Honeyeaters | 6 | 2 | 2 | |
| Old World Flycatchers | 1 | 1 | 0 | |
| Old World Warblers | 1 | 1 | 1 | |
| Hawaiian Thrushes | 6 | 3 | 2 | |
| Honeycreepers | 45 | 20 | 9 | |
| **Totals** | 117+ | 59 | 24 | |

*Source:* Modified from Scott et al. 1988.

5. Examine the data given to you (in Table 48.2A, 48.2B, or 48.2C). Do the data support or refute your hypothesis?

**TABLE 48.2A.**

Predation by Rats (*R. rattus* and *R. exulans*) on Birds. Included in this table are the typical stages of life at which rats prey upon the species of bird listed, the population trends of each bird species since rats were introduced, and the size of each bird measured as the average length of male and female birds.

| Bird Species | Stage of life-cycle preyed upon | Effect on population | Size (cm) |
|---|---|---|---|
| *Diomedea immutabilis* (Laysan Albatross) | chicks | continuing coexistence with rats | 81 |
| *Diomedea nigripes* (Black-footed Albatross) | chicks | minor | 81 |
| *Pterodroma hypoleuca* (Bonin Petrel) | eggs, chicks | major decline | 30 |
| *Pterodroma phaeopygia sandwichensis* (Hawaiia Dark-rumped Petrel) | chicks | nearly 40% of eggs and chicks destroyed during 2-year study | 43 |
| *Phaethon rubricauda* (Red-tailed Tropicbird) | eggs, chicks | up to 65% and 100% losses of eggs and chicks respectively in some years | 102 |
| *Puffinus pacificus* (Wedge-tail Shearwater) | eggs, chicks | minor | 43 |
| *Fregata minor* (Great Frigatebird) | adults | minor | 94 |
| *Porzana palmeri* (Laysan Rail) | unknown | extinction | 15 |
| *Sterna fuscata* (Sooty Tern) | eggs, chicks | continuing coexistence with rats | 43 |
| *Sterna lunata* (Grey-backed Tern) | eggs, chicks | all young destroyed in one year | 38 |
| *Telespyza cantans* (Laysan Finchbill) | unknown | extinction | 19 |

*Source:* Modified from Atkinson 1985 and Pratt, Bruner, and Berrett 1987.

**TABLE 48.2B.**

Predation by Rats (*R. rattus* and *R. exulans*) on Birds. Included in this table are the typical stages of life at which rats prey upon the species of bird listed, the population trends of each bird species since rats were introduced, and the usual nest location for each species.

| Bird Species | Stage of life-cycle preyed upon | Effect on population | Usual nest situation |
|---|---|---|---|
| *Diomedea immutabilis* (Laysan Albatross) | chicks | continuing coexistence with rats | ground surface |
| *Diomedea nigripes* (Black-footed Albatross) | chicks | minor | ground surface |
| *Pterodroma hypoleuca* (Bonin Petrel) | eggs, chicks | major decline | burrows |
| *Pterodroma phaeopygia sandwichensis* (Hawaiia Dark-rumped Petrel) | chicks | nearly 40% of eggs and chicks destroyed during 2-year study | burrows |
| *Phaethon rubricauda* (Red-tailed Tropicbird) | eggs, chicks | up to 65% and 100% losses of eggs and chicks respectively in some years | ground surface |
| *Puffinus pacificus* (Wedge-tail Shearwater) | eggs, chicks | minor | burrows |
| *Fregata minor* (Great Frigatebird) | adults | minor | branches < 3m high |
| *Porzana palmeri* (Laysan Rail) | unknown | extinction | ground surface |
| *Sterna fuscata* (Sooty Tern) | eggs, chicks | continuing coexistence with rats | ground surface |
| *Sterna lunata* (Grey-backed Tern) | eggs, chicks | all young destroyed in one year | ground surface |
| *Telespyza cantans* (Laysan Finchbill) | unknown | extinction | on or near ground |

*Source:* Modified from Atkinson 1985.

**TABLE 48.2C.**

Predation by Rats (*R. rattus* and *R. exulans*) on Birds. Included in this table are the typical stages of life at which rats prey upon the species of bird listed, the population trends of each bird species since rats were introduced, and incubation and nestling periods for bird species. The incubation period is determined as the number of days from egg laying to hatching. Nestling period is determined as the number of days from hatching to fledging.

| Bird Species | Stage of life-cycle preyed upon | Effect on population | Incubation Period (days) | Nestling Period (days) |
|---|---|---|---|---|
| *Diomedea immutabilis* [1,4] (Laysan Albatross) | chicks | continuing coexistence with rats | 62–67 | 140 |
| *Diomedea nigripes* [1,4] (Black-footed Albatross) | chicks | minor | 62–67 | 165 |
| *Pterodroma hypoleuca* [2,3] (Bonin Petrel) | eggs, chicks | major decline | 48.7 | unknown |
| *Pterodroma phaeopygia sandwichensis* [1] (Hawaiian Dark-rumped Petrel) | chicks | nearly 40% of eggs and chicks destroyed during 2-year study | 50–55 | 115 |
| *Phaethon rubricauda* [3,4] (Red-tailed Tropicbird) | eggs, chicks | up to 65% and 100% losses of eggs and chicks respectively in some years | 40–50 | unknown |
| *Puffinus pacificus* [1,4] (Wedge-tail Shearwater) | eggs, chicks | minor | 48–63 | 60–90 |
| *Fregata minor* [1,4] (Great Frigatebird) | adults | minor | 51–57 | 166 |
| *Porzana palmeri* (Laysan Rail) | unknown | species extinct | unknown | unknown |
| *Sterna fuscata* [3,4] (Sooty Tern) | eggs, chicks | continuing coexistence with rats | 27–33 | 16 |
| *Sterna lunata* [4] (Grey-backed Tern) | eggs, chicks | all young destroyed in one year | 24–35 | unknown |
| *Telespyza cantans* (Laysan Finchbill) | unknown | species extinct | unknown | unknown |

Modified from Atkinson 1985.

1. Berger 1972
2. Grant et al. 1983
3. Harrison 1990
4. Niethammer, Magyesi, and Hu 1992.

## Take-Home Assignment

As you discovered in class, introduced small mammals like the black rat have devastated the bird populations of Hawaii through predation. However, grazing mammals such as pigs, cows, and goats also have contributed to the decline and extinction of Hawaiian birds. In 1778 and the years following, large numbers of these mammals were brought to the Hawaiian Islands for agricultural reasons on expeditions led by Captain James Cook and other sea captains. Since that time, many of these mammals have become feral (i.e., though once domesticated, they no longer depend on humans).

Your assignment, as a class, is to develop an understanding of the problems associated with the introduction of these ungulates (hoofed mammals) to the Hawaiian biota, specifically to native birds. We can categorize these problems as follows: (1) how ungulates affect the habitat of native birds, (2) how ungulates facilitate the spread and establishment of other introduced species, and (3) why Hawaii's birds are particularly susceptible to introduced species. During the next week, each group in your class will examine one of these aspects of the problem using information you get from references your instructor provides. Next week, groups will share their findings with the entire class.

- Group 1: How might the ungulates introduced to Hawaii affect the habitats of native birds?
- Group 2: How might the ungulates introduced to Hawaii aid in the establishment and spread of other introduced species?
- Group 3: What characteristics of Hawaii's endemic birds make them more vulnerable than other birds in Hawaii to species invasions like that of the ungulates described above?

## Web Version

Detailed teaching notes, the case PDF, resources for the take-home assignment, an answer key, and additional references are available on the NCCSTS website at *sciencecases.lib.buffalo.edu/cs/collection/detail.asp?case_id=449&id=449*.

## References

Atkinson, I. A. E. 1985. The spread of commensal species of Rattus to oceanic islands and their effects on island avifaunas. In *Conservation of island birds*, ed. P. J. Moors, pp. 35–81. Princeton, NJ: Princeton University Press.

Berger, A. J. 1972. *Hawaiian birdlife*. Honolulu: The University Press of Hawaii.

Grant, G. S., J. Warham, T. N. Pettit, and G. C. Whittow. 1983. Reproductive behavior and vocalizations of the Bonin Petrel (*Pterodroma hypoleuca*). *Wilson Bulletin* 95 (4): 522–539.

Harrison, C. S. 1990. *Seabirds of Hawaii: Natural history and conservation*. Ithaca, NY: Cornell University Press.

Niethammer, K. R., J. I. Megyesi, and D. Hu. 1992. Incubation periods for 12 seabird species at French Frigate Shoals, Hawaii. *Colonial Waterbirds* 15 (1): 124–127.

Pratt, D. H., P. L. Bruner, and D. G. Berrett. 1987. *A field guide to the birds of Hawaii and the tropical Pacific*. Princeton, NJ: Princeton University Press.

Scott, J. M., C. B. Kepler, C. van Riper III, and S. I. Fefer. 1988. Conservation of Hawaii's vanishing avifauna. *Bioscience* 38 (4): 238–253.

# THE WOLF, THE MOOSE, AND THE FIR TREE

## A Case Study of Trophic Interactions

*Gary M. Fortier*

## Abstract

Students study predator-prey dynamics in the Isle Royale National Park ecosystem drawing on data and findings from an article by McLaren and Peterson that appeared in *Science* in 1994.

## Learning Objectives

### *Analytical Objectives*

- Interpret graphical data.
- Identify unstated assumptions.
- Identify confounding effects from multiple factors.
- Produce testable predictions from hypotheses.
- Use data to support or refute competing hypotheses.
- Determine limitations imposed by experimental design.
- Assess the use of correlations in hypothesis testing.

### *Conceptual Objectives*

- Evaluate trophic level interactions:
  - › Determine whether predators can control prey populations.
  - › Determine the relationship between primary productivity and plant growth.
- Understand how primary productivity may be measured indirectly.
- Understand how ecological parameters, such as plant growth rates, may be measured indirectly.

## Quantitative Reasoning Skills/Concepts

- Interpret the meaning of simple statistical descriptors.
- Use graphs to formulate predictions and explanations.

- Use numerical evidence to formulate null and alternative hypotheses.
- Articulate complete and correct claims based on data.
- Use appropriate reasoning to support the validity of data-based claims.
- Create experimental designs to test hypotheses.
- Predict the relationships between multiple variables based on biological models.
- Determine the underlying assumptions of a model.
- Integrate data from multiple graphs.
- Distinguish between correlation data and experimental data.

## The Case Study

### *Part I: Introduction*

Isle Royale National Park, the largest island in Lake Superior, provides biologists with a fairly unique system for studying the interactions between different trophic levels. Isle Royale has a rather simple food chain consisting of producers and a single large herbivore that in turn has only a single predator, the gray wolf *(Canis lupus)*. The island had a large abundance of balsam fir *(Abies balsamea)* until the park was colonized by moose *(Alces alces)* that swam to the island in the early 1900s. After the establishment of this large herbivore, the balsam fir declined from 46% of the overstory in the 19th century to about 5% today. Nearby islands that are inaccessible to moose continue to have a large fir component in their forests; thus the decline of the fir on Isle Royale has been attributed to moose herbivory. Balsam fir is not considered optimal forage for moose but it can comprise up to 59% of their winter diet.

Over the last several decades, significant temporal fluctuations have been observed in the densities of the wolf and moose populations and the growth rates of balsam firs. Two hypotheses have been suggested to account for these fluctuations. The primary productivity—or "bottom up" hypothesis—suggests that plant growth is limited by the energy available to plants, which is determined in turn by temperature and precipitation. Additional plant growth means more forage is available—thus herbivores, and ultimately carnivores, should increase in abundance. Alternatively, the trophic cascade—or "top down" model—predicts that changes in one trophic level are caused by opposite changes in the trophic level immediately above it. For example, a decrease in moose abundance should produce increased plant growth if moose herbivory limits plant growth. Changes in primary productivity would only have a discernible effect on vegetation if higher-level interactions had been removed.

The Isle Royale ecosystem provides us with a good opportunity to test the predictions of these alternative hypotheses. Longitudinal data are available for each of the key variables, including annual plant growth, herbivore density, and carnivore density. The historical growth rates of balsam fir have been determined through tree-ring analysis. When herbivores remove large quantities of the foliar biomass, annual wood accrual decreases and ring widths are reduced.

Thus tree ring data allow us to estimate the intensity of herbivory over time. Moose and wolf populations have been censused for decades on Isle Royale, providing us with annual estimates of herbivore and carnivore densities. Long-term records are available for each trophic level in the Isle Royale ecosystem, providing the necessary data to evaluate both hypotheses.

## Questions

1. What type of correlation (positive or negative) would you expect to see between the population densities or growth rates of each trophic level in this system (fir/moose/wolves) under the primary productivity hypothesis?
2. What type of correlations would you predict under the trophic cascade hypothesis?
3. What would you predict as the effect of wolf removal on plant growth under each hypothesis?
4. What assumptions are made regarding the measurement of growth rates in balsam fir?
5. What assumptions are made regarding the long-term impact of moose herbivory on balsam fir?
6. Do these assumptions seem warranted?

## *Part II: Trophic System Data*

The data in Figure 49.1 (p. 440) include census information for the moose and wolf populations, ring width indices from firs on each end of the island, and actual evapotranspiration rates (AET) from April to October. The east and west ends of the island differ substantially in terms of climate and flora. The west end consists of hardwood forests with a higher AET rate and warmer, earlier summers relative to the boreal forests in the east. The AET rate varies with temperature and rainfall and serves as an index of the amount of water available for plant growth. This rate is strongly tied to primary productivity.

## FIGURE 49.1.

Population Parameters of the Isle Royale Ecosystem From 1958–1994.

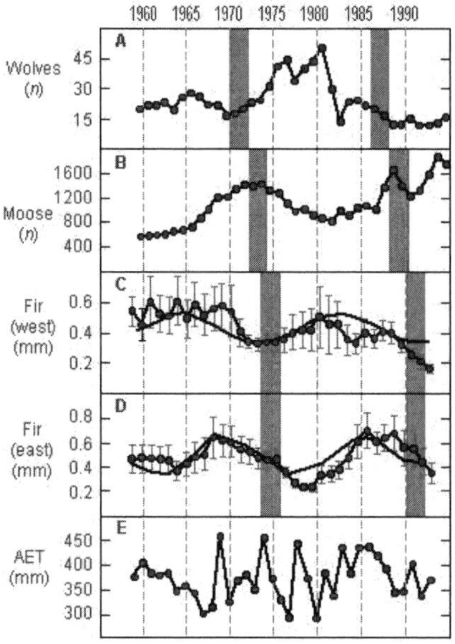


*Key:* Shaded areas signify periods of forage suppression that may be connected to interactions between herbivores and carnivores.

A. Population size of wolves each winter (based on aerial counts).

B. Population size of moose each winter (based on aerial counts and skeletal remains).

C. Ring-widths from the west end of Isle Royale, N=8.

D. Ring-widths from the east end of Isle Royale, N=8.

E. Actual evapotranspiration rates (AET), annual calculations based on data from April to October at a weather station 20 km from Isle Royale. AET is an approximation of primary productivity; it represents water availability as a function of temperature and rainfall.

*Source* Regraphed from information published in *Science* 226 (December 2, 1994): 1557.

## Questions

1. What is the purpose of each figure? Are there unclear terms or confusing aspects to any figure?
2. How do the maxima and minima of the ring-width indices correspond to changes in moose density? Does this support the primary productivity hypothesis, the trophic cascade hypothesis, or neither?
3. Do firs from either end of the island (east/west) respond the same way to changes in moose density? How can you account for any observed differences?
4. How do the maxima and minima of the wolves correspond to changes in moose density? How might you account for this relationship?
5. Which hypothesis is supported by the data on annual AET?

## *Part III: Ring Width Indices*

The local topographies for the two samples depicted next page are substantially different. The chronologies in Figure 49.2 (p. 442, part A) are from an east-end subsample of trees designated RH (Rock Harbor). This area contained an open-canopy section of previously disturbed boreal forest; it exhibits an increase in growth rates after a period of high wolf predation in the late 1970s. Figure 49.2 (part B) depicts a west-end subsample designated SS (Siskiwit Swamp). These fir trees are in a closed-canopy hardwood forest that has been heavily browsed by moose for some time.

## Questions

1. Are there any confusing aspects to the figures or caption?
2. The moose population peaked in the mid-1970s and then declined over the next decade. How did the trees at each site respond in the years following the peak? Are the results for these samples surprising given the larger data sets for tree ring-width on the previous page?
3. How should the difference in canopy cover affect growth rates? How will the height of the trees at each site affect their response to changes in primary productivity? The authors suggest that primary productivity was increasing during the late 1970s and most of the 1980s—does either ring-width index appear to reflect that change?
4. Which hypothesis do you feel is best supported by the ring-width chronologies above?
5. What final conclusions can you draw about the interactions between each trophic level on Isle Royale? Is control exerted from the top down, as suggested by the

trophic cascade model, or are interactions between trophic levels ultimately controlled by primary productivity?

6. Design an experiment that would allow you to clarify any ambiguities from Figures 49.1 or 49.2. Why might an experimental approach prove advantageous in this situation?

**FIGURE 49.2.**

Ring-Widths of Balsam Firs From Isle Royale.

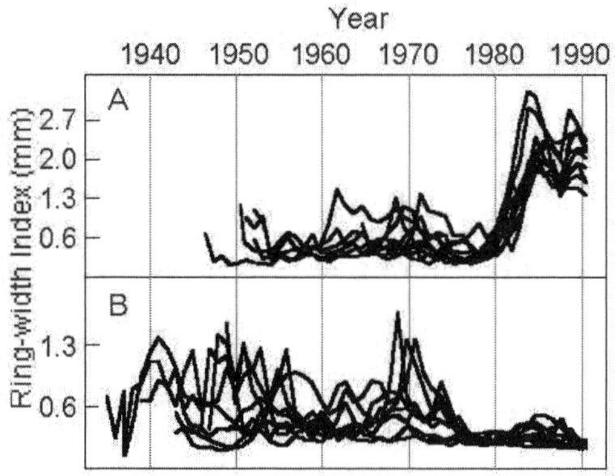


*Key:* Each line represents data from an individual tree harvested in 1992. Note that moose are able to browse as high as 3 m.

A. Location RH (N=10), firs from this area were 26–48 years old and exceeded 3 m in height during the late 1970s.

B. Location SS (N=9), firs from this area were 48–60 years old and were less than 2 m in height.

*Source:* Re-graphed from information published in *Science* 226 (December 2, 1994): 1557.

## Web Version

Detailed teaching notes, the case PDF, and an answer key are available on the NCCSTS website at *sciencecases.lib.buffalo.edu/cs/collection/detail.asp?case_id=453&id=453.*

## Reference

McLaren, B. E., and R. O. Peterson. 1994. Wolves, moose, and tree rings on Isle Royale. *Science* 266: 1555–1558.

CHAPTER 50

# MATHEMATICS IN CONSERVATION

## The Case of the Endangered Florida Panther

*Geffrey F. Stopper and Andrew G. Lazowski*

### Abstract

This case study teaches probability theory and transmission/population genetics through their application to the conservation of the endangered Florida panther.


### Learning Objectives

- Articulate some of the basic terms and concepts of transmission genetics, population genetics, and inbreeding.
- Understand how probability theory is essential in transmission genetics and population genetics.
- Apply probability to solve real-world problems.
- Write meaningful statements about probability.

### Quantitative Reasoning Skills/Concepts

- Carry out basic mathematical operations.
- Articulate complete and correct claims based on data.
- Use appropriate reasoning to support the validity of data-based claims.
- Interpret probabilities in Hardy-Weinberg equation.
- Calculate and interpret the relationship between population size and the magnitude of effect of genetic drift.
- Apply mathematics of population biology to inform decisions in conservation of endangered species.

## The Case Study

### *Part I: Endangered Species*

As human population sizes increase around the world, we are constantly changing, depleting, and fragmenting habitats of wild species. This habitat change and fragmentation is especially detrimental to large mammals that tend to require large habitable ranges in which to survive, are long-lived, and produce few offspring per year.

As of November 2010, in the United States alone there were 414 animal species listed as endangered (*www.fws.gov*), meaning that they are "in danger of extinction throughout all or a significant portion of [their] range" (United States Code, Title 16, Chapter 35). These include species of bears, deer, bats, wolves, seals, whales, and large cats (among many others). The group of large cats includes the interesting case of the Florida panther.

In the mid-1990s, the Florida panther had reached critically low levels, with only 20 to 30 animals remaining in the wild (Johnson et al. 2010; Packer 2010).

It turns out that mathematics is incredibly important in informing our understanding of the biological dynamics of these populations. Mathematical modeling can help us understand the likelihood of extinction in a threatened or endangered population, and is critical in our planning for their continued survival. Here we will investigate some of the important mathematical principles underlying our understanding of the genetics of animal populations, especially as those principles apply to conservation of endangered species, using the Florida panther as an example.

### *Part II: Basic Genetics*

All organisms have a set of genetic instructions by which they are built. These instructions are written in the language of DNA. The full set of instructions for any one organism makes up that organism's *genome*. This genome—the entire set of instructions—is found in every single cell of multicellular organisms (with the exception of a few types of cells).

In organisms, including humans and Florida panthers, the genome is made of many long strings of DNA called *chromosomes* (Figure 50.1). Each of these chromosomes has many genes. The genes are the specific sections of the chromosomes that are responsible for making proteins, and so it's the genes that control the vast majority of what happens in the organism developmentally and physiologically. Between these gene regions of the chromosome, there is a lot of DNA that is not part of any gene (Figure 50.1). Each specific gene is reliably found at a specific location, or *locus*, on a specific chromosome. Because the animal inherits one copy of each chromosome from its father and one copy of each chromosome from its mother, each animal has *two copies of each gene*.

**FIGURE 50.1.**

Schematic of a Hypothetical Animal Genome.

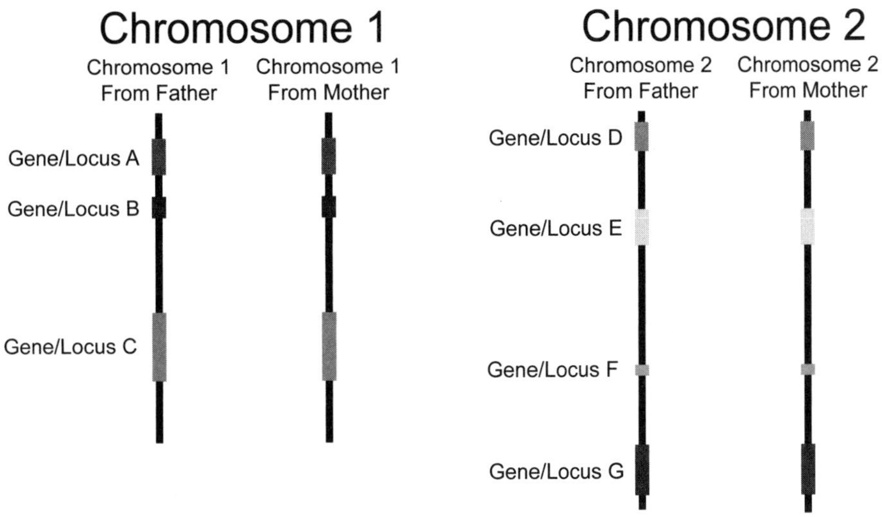


**Note:** For each chromosome there is a copy that is inherited from one's mother and a copy that is inherited from one's father. Note: In real animals, there are usually many more chromosomes, each chromosome contains many more genes, and a much larger portion of each chromosome is non-gene DNA than suggested here.

Within a population, each gene may potentially have many variant types of that gene. This assortment of types is the basis of the variability in many characteristics among humans, such as eye color, hair color, and height. These different types or varieties of genes are called *alleles*.

Because each individual has two copies of each gene, each individual can either have two of the same allele, or the individual can have two different alleles. An individual that has two of the same allele at a locus is called a *homozygote*, or is said to be *homozygous* for that gene (Figure 50.2, p. 446). An individual that has two different alleles at a locus is called a *heterozygote*, or is said to be *heterozygous* for that gene (Figure 50.2). This designation of the types of alleles an individual has at a locus is called its *genotype*.

**FIGURE 50.2.**

Zoomed View of Two Copies of Chromosome 1 (from top left of Figure 50.1).

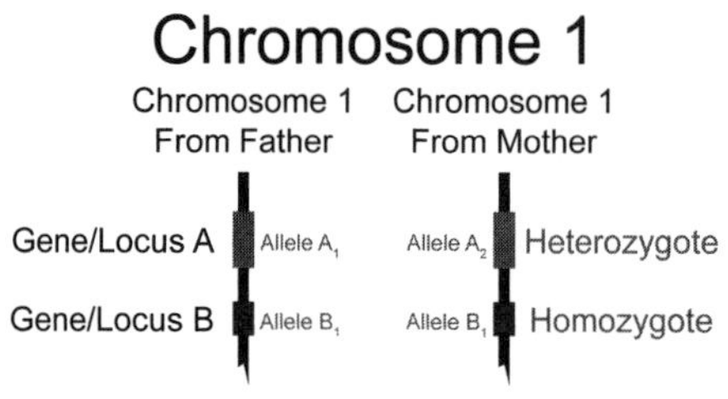


*Note:* Different allele designations at locus A ($A_1$ and $A_2$) show that this individual has inherited different versions (alleles) of the gene from its mother and its father at this locus. It is, therefore, called a heterozygote for gene A. At locus B, however, this individual has inherited the same version (allele) of the gene from both its mother and father ($B_1$ and $B_1$). It is homozygous for gene B.

When an individual reproduces, that individual makes new versions of each chromosome for its offspring. This new version of each chromosome is a hybrid of that individual's two copies of the chromosome that the individual inherited from its own parents. Each *gamete* (egg or sperm) receives one of these hybrid chromosomes from the parent. The result of this is that each gamete randomly receives one of the two alleles of each gene from that parent (Figure 50.3).

**FIGURE 50.3.**

Passing of Alleles Into Gametes.

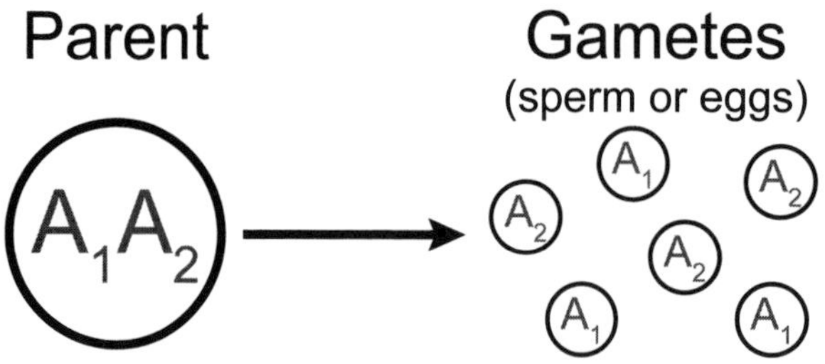


*Note:* For each gene/locus, a parent passes one of its two alleles into each gamete. Note that every gamete will receive one allele from each locus, but here we are focusing only on locus A.

## Question 1

Given that the passing of alleles into gametes is random, if we observe one gamete (egg or sperm) of an individual at a specific gene/locus:

a. What is the probability that the allele in that gamete is the one from the father of the individual making the gametes?

b. What is the probability that the allele in that gamete is the one from the mother of the individual making the gametes?

**WAIT**

When two animals—such as Florida panthers—reproduce to make an offspring, one gamete from the mother and one gamete from the father fuse, so that the offspring has two alleles for each gene/locus. It turns out that if we make a few assumptions about a population (e.g., that mate pairings in the parent generation are random, there is no mutation, and a few others), we can make an abstraction of the population that allows us not to worry about the specific pairings of alleles within specific individuals, and instead only pay attention to frequency (or proportion) of alleles in each population (Figure 50.4).

**FIGURE 50.4.**

Abstraction of a Population Represented as Only Alleles, Rather Than Individuals.

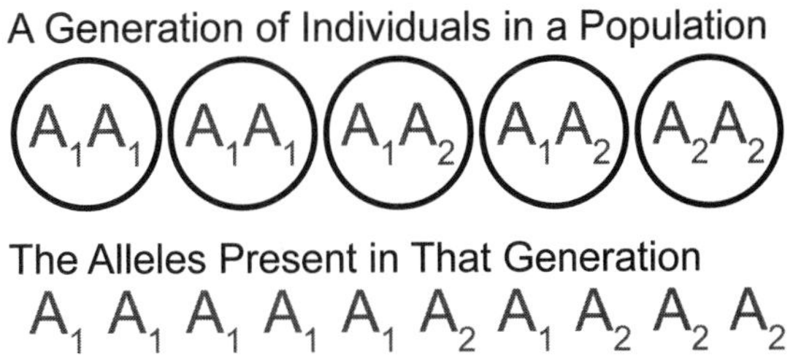


**Note:** The top row shows the allele pairings (genotypes) in individuals. The bottom row shows the alleles present in the population without respect to individuals.

## Question 2

a. In Figure 50.4, what is the frequency of Allele $A_1$ in the population (i.e., what proportion of the alleles at Locus A are of the type $A_1$)?

b. In Figure 50.4, what is the frequency of Allele $A_2$ in the population (i.e., what proportion of the alleles at Locus A are of the type $A_2$)?

**WAIT**

If we abstract the population to allele frequencies as above, we now have a lot of power to calculate the probabilities of certain genotypes in the next generation. Given our assumptions about random mating, we can say that every allele in individuals in the next generation is selected randomly from the alleles available in the parent generation. Consider the selection of allele $A_1$ a "success," therefore the selection of $A_2$ is considered a "failure." Each individual offspring samples twice (once for the allele inherited from each of its two parents) from the alleles that are available in the previous generation. So if $A_1$ and $A_2$ are present with equal frequencies in the parent generation, then the probability of "success" is equal to the probability of "failure," which is 0.5. The probability of having a homozygote for allele $A_1$ would be the probability of getting two "successes." The probability of having a homozygote for allele $A_2$ would be the probability of getting two "failures." The probability of having a heterozygote would involve getting one "success" and one "failure." Note that there are two ways of getting the heterozygote ($A_1A_2$ or $A_2A_1$).

## Question 3

Given that the population depicted in Figure 50.4 reproduces to make a generation of offspring and using the allele frequencies you calculated for that population:

a. What distribution can be used to calculate these probabilities?
b. What is the probability of an individual in the offspring generation being homozygous for $A_1$?
c. What is the probability of an individual in the offspring generation being homozygous for $A_2$?
d. What is the probability of an individual in the offspring generation being heterozygous?

**WAIT**

## *Back to the Florida Panther*

Now let's return to our population of Florida panthers. Our goal here, as with most species conservation efforts, is to keep the population from going extinct. From many biological studies, we know that the extinction of a population becomes more likely as a population becomes smaller. This is true for several reasons. One is the obvious fact that, in a population with few individuals, an environmental challenge to the population (e.g., a natural disaster or disease) is more likely to kill all of the individuals. But this is not the only reason that having a small population is bad for avoiding extinction.

There are two other significant reasons that small populations are bad for avoiding extinction:

1. Small populations are more likely to lose alleles due to genetic drift.
2. Small populations are forced into inbreeding.

## *Genetic Variation and Genetic Drift*

Small populations are more likely to lose alleles due to *genetic drift*. Genetic drift is change in allele frequencies due to chance. Species/populations that reproduce by having sex appear to benefit from having a great variety of alleles in the population (in fact, there's a good chance that sex evolved in order to increase genetic variation in the species/population). Genetic drift exhibits its effect primarily on alleles that are neutral (that is, they are not beneficial or detrimental to the population). The fact that allele frequencies can change due to randomness from one generation to another should be clear from the exercises you did above, where allele frequencies in one generation influence, but do not absolutely determine, allele frequencies in the following generation.

To illustrate genetic drift, let's focus on a specific gene/locus with neutral alleles. For any given allele at that locus, we can determine the probability that it will eventually disappear from the population. Because these alleles are inherited directly from an individual's parents, once an allele disappears from the population, it is gone forever (except in the incredibly unlikely event that it is re-created by another mutation, the probability of which is negligible and can be statistically ignored). We can also determine the probability that a given allele will eventually become the only allele for that gene/locus in the population. If it becomes the only allele, we say that it is *fixed*, or that it has reached *fixation*. It is important to realize that an allele reaching fixation in a population means that all other alleles at that gene/locus have been lost forever from the population!

For any given point in time, the probability that an allele eventually becomes fixed in the population is exactly equal to its proportion in the population. And the probability that it will disappear from the population is exactly one minus its proportion in the population.

### Question 4

Given the population we used in the example above, answer the following:

a. What is the probability that Allele $A_1$ eventually becomes fixed in the population?

b. What is the probability that Allele $A_1$ eventually disappears from the population?

c. What is the probability that Allele $A_2$ eventually becomes fixed in the population?

d. What is the probability that Allele $A_2$ eventually disappears from the population?

**WAIT**

Note that these above probabilities are true regardless of population size. But it turns out that population size has a drastic effect on *how quickly* an allele disappears or goes to fixation—the smaller the population size, the more drastically genetic drift affects the population by eliminating allelic variation from the population. As we discussed briefly above, and will discuss in more detail below, variation is generally good for a population, and so the loss of variation is bad for the population. This is important for our panther population, because the small population of panthers means that alleles across the entire genome will disappear quickly.

How drastically does the size of a population affect how quickly alleles are lost or fixed? There are two types of calculations that we can do to understand the effect of small population size.

First, we'll consider how the population size affects the probability distribution of alleles in the next generation. Suppose an allele has frequency $p_1$. We would like to see how much the allele frequency can change in the next generation. Let $p_2$ be the allele frequency in the second generation. This probability, $p_2$, is a random variable, so it has an expected value and standard deviation. One can show that the mean μ and standard deviation σ of this random variable are:

$$\mu = p_1 \text{ and } \sigma = \sqrt{\frac{p_1(1-p_1)}{2N}}$$

## Question 5

a. Suppose that the data are bell shaped. How much data lies within two standard deviations of the mean? Explain your answer.

b. Suppose that the allele frequency $p_1 = 0.5$ and the population size $N = 25$ (an accurate estimate of the population size of panthers in the early to mid-1990s). Now consider your percentage answer (from 5a above), *y*%. For that *y*% of cases, the allele frequency of $p_2$ is in what range?

c. Repeat the calculation in 5b above for population sizes 33, 100, and 1,000. What does an increased population size do to the range?

d. In words, summarize how population size affects the probability distribution of the trait in the next generation.

**WAIT**

Now let's consider how the population size affects the average rate at which alleles are lost from the population. Using the proportion of an allele in the population, *p*, we can also determine the number of generations it takes for an allele to become fixed or lost given the population size.

The average time to fixation is:

$$\overline{T}_{fixed} = \frac{-4N(1-p)\ln(1-p)}{p}$$

And the average time to loss is: $$\overline{T}_{lost} = \frac{-4Np \ln}{1-p}$$

## Question 6

a. Calculate the average time, in generations, to fixation of an allele that starts at proportion 0.4 in populations of sizes 25, 33, 100, and 1,000.
b. Calculate the average time, in generations, to loss of an allele that starts at proportion 0.4 in populations of sizes 25, 33, 100, and 1,000.
c. Calculate the average time, in generations, to loss of an allele that starts at proportion 0.1 in populations of sizes 25, 33, 100, and 1,000.

**WAIT**

So far we have focused on alleles that are neutral with respect to natural selection. That means that none of the alleles we have considered is either beneficial or detrimental to the population in comparison to the other alleles for that gene/locus. *But just because an allele is not beneficial to the organism now, doesn't mean it won't be beneficial in the future of an ever-changing dynamic environment.* This is one of the reasons that maintaining many alleles in the population is generally a good thing, and the high rate of allele loss in a small population is a bad thing.

There is one other significant reason that small populations run a greater risk when it comes to extinction. Understanding this reason requires that we now consider alleles that are currently beneficial or detrimental to the population, and this deals with the fact that *small populations are forced into inbreeding.*

## *Inbreeding*

You probably already have a sense that inbreeding is bad. There is a social stigma against inbreeding in our human species that is shared by essentially every human society in the world. But it turns out there is a clear biological basis for this stigma. Inbreeding is usually detrimental to the health of offspring. To understand why that is true, we need to return to our understanding of genes and alleles. Remember that *genes* make *proteins*. It is these proteins that make the traits of an organism. So if a trait is determined by a single gene, there are two alleles that could potentially contribute to that trait.

*How do these alleles interact to make the trait of an organism?*

The way a trait is determined by the alleles for a gene depends on how the alleles, and the proteins they make, interact with each other. Obviously, if an individual is homozygous for a gene/locus (i.e., having two of the same allele), that allele determines the trait. If an individual is heterozygous for a gene/locus (i.e., having two different allele types), there are two main possibilities: (1) The alleles can both contribute to the trait, or (2) the alleles can interact in such a way that only one allele determines the trait. This latter case is quite common, and is the case on which we will focus here. In this case, we call the one allele that determines the trait the *dominant* allele. The allele that does not contribute to the trait is called *recessive*.

This pattern of dominance and recessiveness is the basis of a major problem of inbreeding. Mutations in genes cause new alleles to come about, and these mutated alleles are often very bad for the individual organism. We call these bad alleles *deleterious*. If this new deleterious allele is dominant, it is very likely to negatively affect the individual's reproduction, so that an individual is less likely to survive and reproduce, and so the allele will not be passed on to future generations and will quickly disappear from the population. If the new detrimental allele is recessive, it will only affect the trait if there are two copies of the deleterious recessive allele. When an allele affects a trait, we say that allele is *expressed*. Therefore, a deleterious recessive allele is only expressed when it is present as a homozygote. The effects of this deleterious recessive allele are hidden when it is present in a heterozygote. These deleterious recessive alleles persist in populations and are rarely expressed unless they become very common in the population, because one of the deleterious recessive alleles must be inherited from each parent in order for it to affect the trait. So what we find in nature is that *many rare deleterious recessive alleles exist at many genes/loci in any population*.

Two close relatives are more likely to have the same genes than are two randomly chosen individuals in the population. So when two close relatives mate, the offspring tend to have more homozygous genes/loci than the offspring of randomly chosen mates—*inbreeding causes an increase in homozygosity*. This increase in homozygosity also means that *inbreeding causes an increase in traits determined by deleterious recessive alleles*.

Because the size of the Florida panther population is so small, all of the individuals are closely related and so are forced into inbreeding.

## Question 7

Let's calculate the effect of inbreeding on the expression of rare deleterious alleles.

a. Consider a rare deleterious recessive allele for a specific gene/locus. In this hypothetical population, the deleterious recessive allele exists at a proportion of 0.01. In an offspring with randomly chosen parents, what is the probability that the offspring will be homozygous for the deleterious recessive allele?

b. Now let's consider that the Florida panther population has 20,000 genes/loci (this is a reasonable estimate, and is about the number of genes that humans have). And let's assume that for every gene/locus there is a deleterious recessive allele that exists at a proportion of 0.01 in the population. If all mating is random, in the average offspring, how many of its genes/loci are homozygous for deleterious recessive alleles?

c. Now consider an off spring with full-sibling (brother and sister) parents. In this offspring, what is the probability that the offspring will be homozygous for the deleterious recessive allele? Note that full siblings share, on average, 50% of their genes. So, in order to calculate this, consider that one allele in an offspring is randomly inherited from the population. Then, given that the randomly inherited allele is the deleterious recessive allele, we can say that there is the normal chance of inheriting the deleterious recessive allele due to randomness, plus an increased chance that the other parent has the allele due to the fact that it is a full sibling of the other parent. This added increased chance must take into account that there is a 50% chance that the other parent has one copy of that allele due to relatedness, and the fact that that parent has two alleles, so there is a 50% chance they pass on that deleterious recessive allele if they have it.

d. Now consider the same mating of full siblings in a Florida panther population with 20,000 genes/loci where each gene/locus has a deleterious recessive allele that exists at a proportion of 0.01 in the population. On average, how many of the offspring's 20,000 genes/loci are homozygous for deleterious recessive allele?s

e. Compare the results of 7b and 7d above and explain what this means about the effects of inbreeding.

**WAIT**

Clearly inbreeding has a drastic effect on how many deleterious recessive alleles are affecting traits! This highlights yet another major problem of small population size, and an incredibly serious problem in conservation biology. Because inbreeding increases the likelihood of homozygosity, this last problem of inbreeding can be approximated by measuring the amount of homozygosity. If inbreeding increases, the average proportion of genes/loci that are homozygous in a species should also increase. Inbreeding can similarly be identified by a corresponding decrease in heterozygosity.

## Question 8

Summarize the three major problems with population size.

**WAIT**

We now have a good understanding of the problems that small populations pose for the conservation and preservation of species. This all adds up to the conclusion that, as the remaining numbers of a threatened species decrease, the probability of saving the population does not scale linearly with population size. Rather, as the population depletes, the per-capita effort needed to save a population/species must increase. The fact that it becomes increasingly difficult, per capita, to save a species as its population's size decreases, is termed the *extinction vortex* (Gilpin and Soulé 1986). This "vortex" tends to exhibit an increasing strength pulling the population toward extinction as the population size decreases.

If we look at data for the Florida panther population, we find lots of evidence of the existence of an extinction vortex. The increased presence of homozygous deleterious recessive alleles and the overall loss of alleles have serious effects on many characteristics of the panther population. One important trait is whether or not they have descended testes. During mammalian sexual development, testes descend from inside the body into the scrotum, and if testes do not descend, an animal is generally sterile. The failure of one or both testes to descend is known as *cryptorchidism*. Obviously a high proportion of sterile individuals will have an effect on the possibility of increasing population size. Another important trait is *atrial septal defects*. These are defects in chambers of the heart that complicate blood flow through the heart, making it more difficult to survive. An increase in heart defects will also obviously have an effect on the possibility of increasing population size. In this population of Florida panthers, these traits were measured over generations, as summarized in Table 50.1.

**TABLE 50.1.**

Occurrence Of Deleterious Traits in Florida Panther Population From 1970 to 1995, With Standard Errors Removed for Simplicity (Johnson et al. 2010).

| Heritage Group | Average Heterozygosity | Proportion of Males Cryptorchid | Proportion With Atrial Septal Defects |
|---|---|---|---|
| 1970–1984 | 0.231 | 0.33 | 0.33 |
| 1985–1989 | 0.208 | 0.50 | 0.16 |
| 1990–1995 | 0.190 | 0.63 | 0.21 |

## Question 9

Summarize the observed trends in the traits in Table 50.1.

## Question 10

It turns out that the Florida panther is closely related to a population of panthers (cougars) that still exist in Texas. In fact, the Florida population and the Texas population used to be part of one continuous population of panthers. So it is highly likely that they could and would interbreed. Based on the information available in the mid-1990s, some conservation biologists believed that the only way to save the population of Florida panthers would be to introduce several Texas cougars into Florida to revitalize the population of Florida panthers. Do you think this is a good idea? Also consider factors beyond probability that may influence society's decision on this matter.

**WAIT**

It turns out that conservation managers decided to introduce eight female Texas cougars into the population of Florida panthers in 1995 (hence the reasoning for our doing many of the previous calculations for population size 25 and 33). Aside from simply increasing population size, this increase in genetic variation had notable effects on important traits in the Florida panther, as summarized in Table 50.2.

**TABLE 50.2.**

Occurrence Of Deleterious Traits in Florida Panther Population From 1970 to 2007, With Standard Errors Removed for Simplicity (Johnson et al. 2010).

| Heritage Group | Total Number of Individuals Observed Over Time Period | Average Heterozygosity | Proportion of Male Cryptorchid | Proportion With Atrial Septal Defects |
|---|---|---|---|---|
| **Prior to Texas Cougar Introduction** | | | | |
| 1970–1984 | 33 | 0.231 | 0.33 | 0.33 |
| 1985–1989 | 37 | 0.208 | 0.50 | 0.16 |
| 1990–1995 | 62 | 0.190 | 0.63 | 0.21 |
| **After Texas Cougar Introduction** | | | | |
| 1996–1998 | 67 | 0.220 | 0.54 | 0.06 |
| 1999–2001 | 102 | 0.224 | 0.42 | 0.07 |
| 2002–2004 | 139 | 0.226 | 0.23 | 0.06 |
| 2005–2007 | 116 | 0.240 | 0.12 | 0.09 |

## Question 11

a. Summarize the change in the traits in Table 50.2 after the introduction of the Texas cougars.

b. After seeing these data, do you think the introduction of the Texas cougars was a good idea?

WAIT

## *Some Extra Panther Probability Problems*

### Question 12

Use the data in Table 50.2 to answer the following questions. While the "Total Number of Individuals Observed Over Time Period" is not necessarily the same as the population size (because it considers individuals present in the population over a time range rather than a specific point in time), it is highly correlated with the population size, and for our purposes we can use these numbers as the population sizes where needed.

a. Suppose in the early 1990s a doctor volunteers to help one panther with its atrial septal heart condition. She will help the first panther she finds that is in need of help. What is the probability that the first, second, or third panther she finds has this condition?

b. Suppose the son of the early 1990s doctor now volunteers his time to help one panther with this condition during the time period 2005–2007. He will help the first panther he finds that is in need of help. What is the probability that the first, second, third, fourth, or fifth panther he finds has this condition?

c. Interpret the difference in the results of the previous two problems.

d. In your calculations for the doctor and her son, did population size matter? If so, explain how you used the population size. If not, explain why it didn't matter, but mention the significance in terms of how the introduction of Texas cougars helped.

## Web Version

Detailed teaching notes, the case PDF, and an answer key are available on the NCCSTS website at *sciencecases.lib.buffalo.edu/cs/collection/detail.asp?case_id=693&id=693*.

## References

Gilpin, M. E., and M. E. Soulé. 1986. Minimum viable populations: Processes of species extinction. In *Conservation Biology: The Science of Scarcity and Diversity*, ed. M. E. Soulé, pp. 19–34. Sunderland, MA: Sinauer/Sunderland.

Johnson, W. E., D. P. Onorato, M. E. Roelke, E. D. Land, M. Cunningham, R. C. Belden, R. McBride, D. Jansen, M. Lotz, D. Shindle, J. Howard, D. E. Wildt, L. M. Penfold, J. A. Hostetler, M. K. Oli, and S. J. O'Brien. 2010. Genetic restoration of the Florida panther. *Science* 329: 1641–1645.

Packer, C. 2010. Genetics. A bit of Texas in Florida. *Science* 329: 1606–1607.

CHAPTER 51

# SEARCH FOR THE MISSING SEA OTTERS
## An Ecological Detective Story

*Mary Allen and Mark L. Kuhlmann*

## Abstract
Students learn how to apply ecological principles to a real-life ecological problem, namely, the decline in sea otter populations in Alaska. Students interpret data from graphs and tables and develop testable hypotheses as they work in groups to solve the mystery of the "missing" sea otters.

## Learning Objectives

- Be introduced to basic concepts of population and community ecology.
- Interpret data from graphs and tables.
- Practice developing testable hypotheses.
- Understand indirect effects in biological communities.
- Learn about sea otter, killer whale, and kelp forest ecology.

## Quantitative Reasoning Skills/Concepts

- Carry out basic mathematical operations.
- Interpret the meaning of simple statistical descriptors.
- Use graphs to formulate predictions and explanations.
- Use numerical data to formulate null and alternative hypotheses.
- Articulate complete and correct claims based on data.
- Use appropriate reasoning to support the validity of data-based claims.
- Create experimental designs to test hypotheses.
- Interpret tabular data.

## The Case Study

### The Problem

Sea otters are one of the few cute and cuddly creatures in the ocean. Visitors to the coast of the Pacific Northwest love to watch their antics as they float effortlessly on their backs among the floating fronds of kelp (large algae) or frolic with one another in play. They also have some human-like skills. Sea otters place rocks on their chests and crack mussels and clams on them, one of the few examples of tool use by animals other than primates. They also roll spiny sea urchins between their paws to make them easier to eat. It comes as a shock to many to find that this "poster child of marine near-shore ecology," as marine ecologist Robert Paine calls them, may be fighting for its survival in some areas of Alaska.

Dr. James Estes, a marine ecologist with the U.S. Geological Survey, and his coworkers recently found that the sea otter population in the Aleutian Islands of Alaska had crashed since 1990. Although wild animal populations always rise and fall to some degree, a decline of this size cried out to be explained. Dr. Estes and his colleagues began an ecological detective hunt to uncover the cause of the declining otter population. Their investigation would eventually lead to the culprit, revealing a huge slice of the complexity and scale of nature's interconnectedness: from the sea otter itself to the web of interactions among species in the community around it and to events occurring on vast scales in the open ocean of the North Pacific.

One reason that Dr. Estes and his fellow investigators could eventually come to grips with such a complicated story is that they had been studying sea otters and kelp forest communities across nearly 2,000 miles of Aleutian and Alaskan coast for nearly three decades. During this time, they tracked sea otters' patterns of movement using tags and surgically implanted radio transmitters. They had conducted regular counts of otters across the region, giving them a large-scale and long-term picture of otter population dynamics. By the late 1970s, the researchers had found that otter populations on many islands had recovered strongly from near extinction a century ago by the fur trade, and there was every expectation that they would continue to be robust. So when they began to find declining populations in the early 1990s, Dr. Estes was surprised and perplexed.

The decline in the sizes of sea otter populations inhabiting the Aleutian Islands, which was observed by Dr. Estes and his group, was indeed large. On some islands the sea otter populations declined by 90 percent in fewer than 10 years (see Figures 51.1 and 51.2)! What could cause such rapid decline in the number of otters in this island chain of Alaska?

Over the next several weeks, we will consider this problem from several perspectives. As we work to solve this mystery, keep in mind the following questions: What factors could be contributing to such a rapid change in the size of sea otter populations? Should we spend federal and state tax dollars to support scientists and others in their investigations of this problem? Are we wasting money on animals that are merely "cute and fuzzy," or might the loss of sea otters from the Aleutian Islands have effects on other organisms? To begin our search for answers, we first need to know something about sea otter biology and population biology.

## *Sea Otters*

The sea otter, *Enhydra lutris*, is the smallest marine mammal. Sea otters are distributed throughout the northern Pacific Ocean and are restricted to coastal regions because they collect their food (mostly crabs, clams, mussels, and sea urchins) from the ocean floor. They can remain underwater for only 30 to 90 seconds and so they inhabit areas where depths are shallow enough for short dives to the bottom. Once an otter brings food to the surface, it floats on its back, using its belly as a dinner tray. Otters often use rocks to smash open the hard shells of their prey, an activity that makes them unique among marine mammals.

Sea otters spend much of their time in water that can be as cold as –4°F. Consequently, they have evolved several mechanisms for maintaining a constant body temperature that is higher than that of their surroundings. Unlike other marine mammals (sea lions, for example), sea otters do not use an extra fat layer (blubber) to retain heat. Instead they have a double fur coat. The coat closest to the body of the otter, the underfur, is very fine and traps air. Heat released from the otter's body warms the trapped air, which serves as insulation.

**FIGURE 51.1.**

Changes in the Relative Abundance of Sea Otters at Several Locations in the Aleutian Islands, Alaska. (Redrawn from Estes et al. 1998)

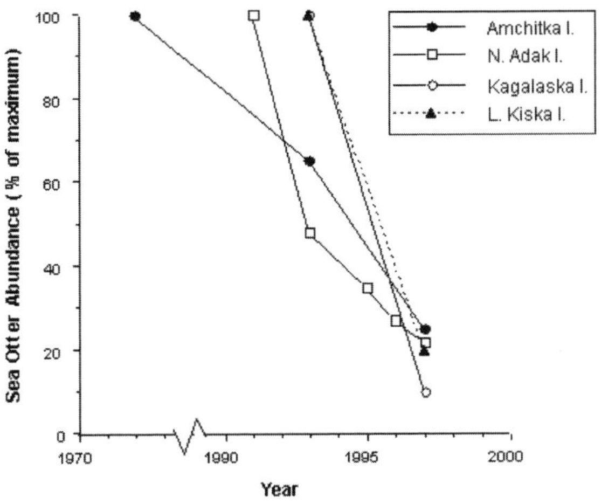


**FIGURE 51.2.**

Map of the North Pacific Ocean Showing the Aleutian Islands and Some Specific Sea Otter Study Sites (Estes and Duggins 1995).

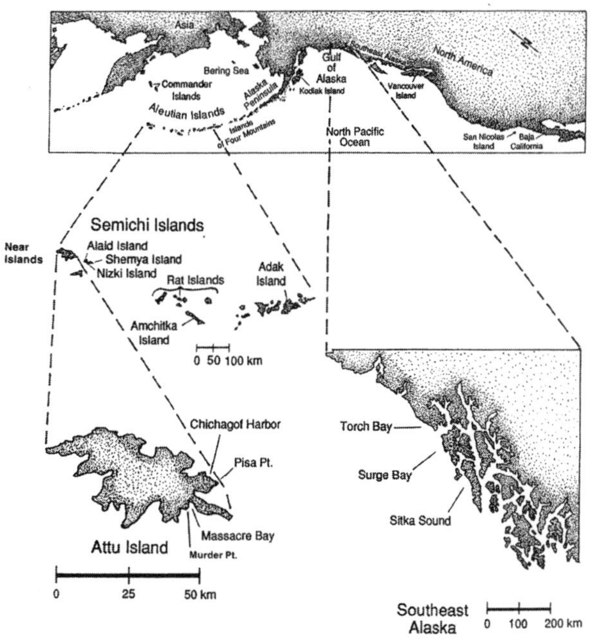

On top of the underfur are guard hairs, which keep the underfur dry. The guard hairs are much longer than those of the underfur and remain waterproof as long as they are clean, so sea otters spend 48% of the daylight hours grooming and cleaning their fur. This is the reason oil spills are so dangerous to sea otters. The oil coats the guard hairs and, since oil cannot be easily removed, the underfur becomes wet, losing its insulative qualities, and the animal dies of hypothermia.

In addition to their two coats of fur, sea otters also keep their body temperature constant by maintaining high metabolic rates. It takes a lot of energy to maintain high metabolic rates. Consequently adult sea otters must consume 30% of their body weight each day. A human weighing 150 lbs would need to eat 45 lbs of food each day to do the same!

Sea otters are social animals although they group largely by gender. A group of otters is called a "raft," probably because they spend much of their time floating on their backs. In Alaska the average size of an otter raft is 100 individuals. Males generally mix with a group of females solely for purposes of mating. Mating is rough business. A male grabs a female with his front paws and flips her, belly-up, onto his belly. The male bites the female's nose, holding onto her in this fashion during the 30 to 60 minutes of copulation. Newly mated females are easily distinguished by their bloody snouts. This proves to be advantageous for scientists studying sea otters, since particular females can often be identified by their distinctive nose scars. A female is pregnant for approximately five months and gives birth to a single pup. The pup will remain with the mother, initially nursing and later eating prey collected by the mother, until it is approximately 12 months old.

Sea otters used to be found all along the Pacific Rim coastline, from northern Japan, through the Kuril Islands (Russia), the Commander Islands (Russia), the Aleutian Islands (part of Alaska), and down the Alaskan, Canadian, and U.S. mainland coasts to the Baja Peninsula (see Figure 51.2). In the mid-1700s, Russians began hunting otters for their pelts, and by the late 1700s, the English and Americans had also entered this fur trade. Sea otters were hunted nearly to extinction over the next 100 years. In fact, America purchased Alaska from the Russians in 1867 hoping to gain a greater share of the sea otter fur trade. What America did not realize was that Russia was willing to sell the territory because the otter populations had been reduced to a level where it was no longer economically productive to hunt them.

Before the onset of hunting in the mid-1700s, the estimated number of sea otters worldwide was 300,000 individuals. By the end of the 19th century, the number of remaining sea otters had dropped to approximately 1,000 in Alaska and 20 in California. Hunting of these animals ended with the signing of the International Fur Seal Treaty of 1911. The sea otters that remained in the 1900s were scattered amongst 13 relict populations. Several of these populations died out while those in Alaska flourished. The single population remaining in California has grown slowly and at its peak in 1995 consisted of 2,400 individuals. Presently there are sea otter populations on the Kuril Islands, Commander Islands, Aleutian Islands, and small portions of the mainland coasts of Alaska and California. The total worldwide population is currently estimated to be 150,000 individuals.

## Part I: What Could Be the Cause of Decreasing Otter Numbers?

Around 1991, Dr. James Estes and his colleagues at the University of California, Santa Cruz, noticed that the otter populations they had been studying for over 20 years were beginning to shrink. Sea otter populations inhabiting several of the Aleutian Islands had declined as much as 90% in fewer than 10 years (Figure 51.1). What could cause such a sharp drop in sea otter numbers in this island chain of Alaska? Read the following excerpt from an article published in the *New York Times* (Stevens 1999) and see if you can determine where all of the missing otters had gone.

> *Could the otters simply have migrated from one part of the region to another? To find out, the researchers analyzed populations over a 500-mile-long stretch of the Aleutians from Kiska to Seguam …. By 1993 otter numbers in that whole stretch had been cut by half. Here the geographical scope of the research effort became critical; a smaller region would not have been large enough to reveal the decline. In 1997, they … found that the population decline had worsened, to about 90 percent….*
>
> *"That told us for sure it was a very large scale decline, but we were still trying to understand the cause," Dr. Estes said…." The researchers … ruled out reproductive failure. Their studies enabled them to keep track of how often otters gave birth and how many young survived, and this revealed that reproduction was continuing to re-supply the population.*
>
> *With other possible causes eliminated … mortality had to be the explanation. In the past, they had seen temporary declines in otter populations because of starvation, pollution or infectious disease. "In all those cases," Dr. Estes said, "we find lots of bodies. They get weak and tired and come ashore to die." This time not a single dead otter was found—a clue, he said, that "something really weird was going on."*

## Part II: What Predator Could Be Causing the Large Decrease in Otter Numbers?

### A. How Would You Test a Hypothesis?

Dr. Estes and his group hypothesized that increased predation by killer whales was the cause of the sea otter decline. This was an unusual idea, since killer whales and sea otters had been observed together in Alaska for decades with no obvious interactions occurring between them. The first time a killer whale was observed attacking a sea otter was in 1991. Nine more attacks were observed in the next seven years and it was these attacks that finally led Dr. Estes and his colleagues to propose their hypothesis. To test this hypothesis, the scientists needed to have information about the killer whale.

1. Make a list of the types of information about killer whales you believe the scientists might need to test their hypothesis that increased predation by the whales was the cause of the sea otter decline.
2. Describe two experiments that would allow you to test the hypothesis that increased predation by killer whales was the cause of the sea otter decline. Keep in mind the following key components of any good experiment: a control (something to which to compare the treatment), replication (do it more than once), and consideration of confounding factors (what might cause differences other than what you manipulate in your experiment?).

## B. What Do the Data Tell You?

Estes and his colleagues estimated the impact of killer whales on sea otter populations by comparing trends in population size and survival rates of individually marked otters between two adjacent locations on Adak Island – Clam Lagoon and Kuluk Bay. Kuluk Bay is on an open coast, so sea otters there are exposed to killer whales. In Clam Lagoon, the entrance from the open sea is too narrow and shallow for killer whales to get in. Based on Figures 51.3 and 51.4, what can you conclude about the effects of killer whales on sea otter populations? Why do you think the scientists both counted all the sea otters and did the tagging and radio tracking?

## C. Could Predation by Killer Whales Account for a 90% Decrease In Otter Numbers?

If increased predation by killer whales was the primary cause of the sea otter decline in Alaska from 1990–1996, as Estes and his group suspected, killer whales would have to have eaten 40,000 sea otters in six years! How many killer whales would it take to eat this many sea otters? We know that killer whales travel in groups ranging from five to 25 individuals. Would it take one such group or 100? This is an important question to answer to determine whether killer whale predation could account for all of the missing sea otters. Using data provided in Table 51.1 (p. 464), calculate how many whales feeding exclusively on sea otters it would take to eat 40,000 sea otters.

**FIGURE 51.3.**

Changes in Sea Otter Population Size Over Time at Clam Lagoon and Kuluk Bay, Adak Island, Alaska. Redrawn from Estes et al. 1998.

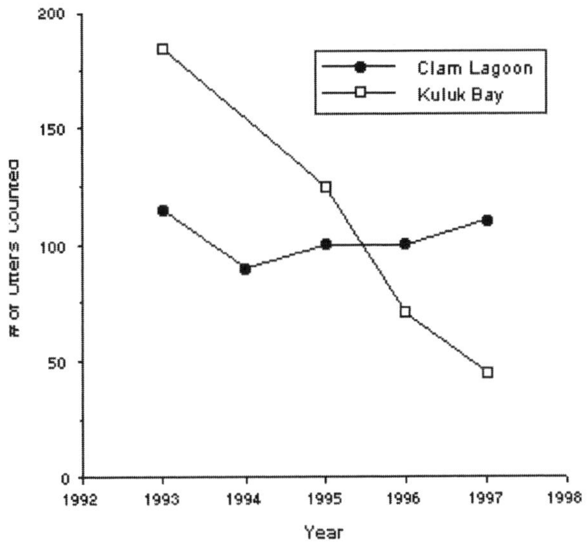


**FIGURE 51.4.**

Survival Rates of Sea Otters Individually Marked in 1995 With Flipper Tags and Radio Transmitters at Clam Lagoon and Kuluk Bay, Adak Island, Alaska. Redrawn from Estes et al. 1998.

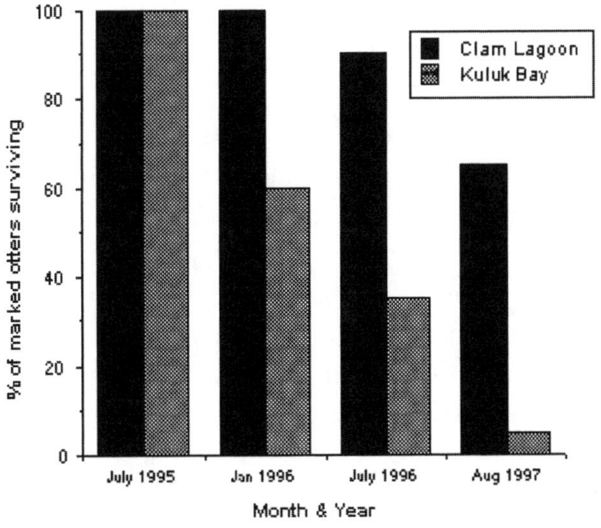

**TABLE 51.1.**

Killer Whale and Sea Otter Energetics

| Estimated number of Aleutian Island sea otters eaten, 1990–1996 | 40,000 |
|---|---|
| **Adult sea otters** | |
| Average caloric content | 1.81 kcal/gram wet weight |
| Average mass, male | 34 kg |
| Average mass, female | 23 kg |
| **Killer whales** | |
| Average field metabolic rate | 55 kcal/kg of whale/day |
| Average mass, male | 5,600 kg |
| Average mass, female | 3,400 kg |

## Part III: Why Are Killer Whales Eating Sea Otters Now?

All the evidence collected by Estes and his coworkers points to killer whales as the cause of the decline in sea otters: the increase in observed killer whale attacks on sea otters, the differences in sea otter survival and population trends at the two locations on Adak Island (Figures 51.3 and 51.4), and the energetic data (Table 51.1). Yet prior to the 1990s, killer whales and sea otters had co-existed peacefully for decades. What do you think has caused the killer whales to start eating sea otters? Discuss this question with your group and develop some working hypotheses to share with the class.

## Part IV: Who Cares if Otter Numbers Are Decreasing?

The data below are from a long-term and large-scale study of sea otters and kelp forest communities in southeast Alaska and the Aleutian Islands. Tables 51.2 and 51.3 compare sea urchin and kelp abundances in areas with and without sea otters (see Figure 51.2 for a map showing the locations). Although sea otters formerly were found at all of these locations, they were exterminated from most of their range by hunting during the 19th century. Amchitka and Adak Islands in the Aleutians were locations of some of the few remnant populations at the time otters were protected in the early 1900s. Sea otters were re-introduced to southeast Alaska in 1968–1971. That population expanded into Surge Bay by the early 1970s and into Torch Bay in 1985.

Table 51.4 (p. 467) summarizes data from several studies on the diet of sea otters. What do these data tell you about the role of sea otters in their community? How do you think the sea otters are affecting these two groups of species? What effects do you expect sea otters to have on the rest of the kelp forest community?

**TABLE 51.2.**

Abundance and Population Characteristics of Kelps and Sea Urchins at Two Locations in the Aleutians, Amchitka and Shemya Islands, in 1972 and 1987 (shown as means ± 1 standard error). The same four sites at Amchitka and two sites at Shemya were sampled in both years*. Sea otters were continuously abundant at Amchitka and absent from Shemya during the 15-year period (Estes and Duggins 1995).

| | Amchitka Island | | Shemya Island | |
|---|---|---|---|---|
| | **1972** | **1987** | **1972** | **1987** |
| **Kelp species (inds./0.25 m²)** | | | | |
| *Alaria fistulosa* | 1.6 ± 1.30 | 0.3 ± 0.22 | 0 | 0.5 |
| *Laminaria* spp. | 2.3 ± 0.49 | 3.9 ± 0.95 | 0 | 0 |
| *Agarum cribrosum* | 1.2 ± 0.61 | 0.5 ± 0.42 | 0 | 0 |
| *Thalassiophyllum clathrus* | 0.1 | 0 | 0 | 0 |
| **Total kelps** | 5.1 ± 0.66 | 4.7 ± 1.15 | 0 | 0.5 |
| **Sea urchins** | | | | |
| Maximum test diameter (mm) | 30.5 ± 1.34 | 27.3 ± 3.24 | 72.5 ± 0.71 | 70.5 ± 4.95 |
| Biomass (g/0.25 m²) | 45.1 ± 16.9 | 36.7 ± 15.0 | 368.2 ± 151.7 | 369.3 ± 14.3 |
| Density (inds./0.25 m²) | 27.9 ± 14.5 | 23.4 ± 7.5 | 50.0 ± 14.6 | 38.6 ± 1.4 |

*The 1972 data were obtained from 10 haphazardly placed 0.25 m² quadrats/site, the 1987 data from 20 randomly placed 0.25 m² quadrats/site.

**TABLE 51.3.**

Abundance and Population Characteristics of Kelp and Sea Urchins at Two Locations in Southeast Alaska, Torch Bay (1976–1978) and Surge Bay (1978 and 1988), shown as means ± 1 standard error. Sea otters were continuously absent at Torch Bay and present at Surge Bay during these time periods (Estes and Duggins 1995).

| | Torch Bay | | | Surge Bay | |
|---|---|---|---|---|---|
| | **1976** | **1977** | **1978** | **1978** | **1988** |
| **Kelps (inds./m$^2$)** | | | | | |
| Annuals* | 2.1 ± 1.39 | 0.2 ± 0.25 | 11.6 ± 6.69 | 2.1 ± 0.45 | 3.7 ± 2.34 |
| Perennials** | 0.1 ± 0.11 | 0 | 0.9 ± 1.14 | 48.4 ± 6.33 | 50.3 ± 7.46 |
| **Total** | 2.2 | 0.2 | 12.5 ± 5.56 | 50.5 ± 6.43 | 54.0 ± 9.33 |
| **Sea urchins (inds./m$^2$)** | | | | | |
| *S. franciscanus* | 3.6 ± 3.05 | 3.8 ± 2.55 | 4.9 ± 3.71 | 0 | 0 |
| *S. purpuratus* | 1.0 ± 0.75 | 2.3 ± 2.52 | 0.3 ± 0.41 | 0 | 0 |
| *S. droebachensis* | 3.4 ± 2.24 | 1.5 ± 0.95 | 0.2 ± 0.18 | 0.02 | 0.04 |
| **Total** | 8.0 ± 4.56 | 7.6 ± 5.78 | 5.4 ± 4.27 | 0.02 | 0.04 |

*Primarily *Alaria fistulosa* and *Nereocystis leutkeana*.
**Primarily *Laminaria groenlandica*.

**TABLE 51.4.**

Occurrence of Prey Items in Sea Otter Stomachs and Feces (Estes, Smith, and Palmisano 1978).

| **Source** | Wilke 1957 | Kenyon 1969 | Kenyon 1969 | Burgner and Nakatani 1972 | Barahash-Nikiforov 1947 | Williams 1938 |
|---|---|---|---|---|---|---|
| **Location** | Amchitka | Amchitka | Amchitka | Amchitka | Commander Islands | Western Aleutians |
| **Sample period** | 1954 | 1962–1963 | 1962–1963 | 1970 | 1930–1932 | 1936 |
| **Sample type** | Stomach | Stomach | Stomach | Stomach | Feces | Feces |
| **Sample size** | 5 | 309 | 309 | 49 | 500 | 70 |
| **Analysis** | **Percent of total volume** | **Percent of total volume** | **Percent of total number of prey item** | **Percent of stomachs containing food item*** | **Percent of total volume** | **Percent of total volume** |
| **Prey item** | | | | | | |
| *Annelids* | 0 | 1 | 2 | 2 | 0 | 0 |
| *Arthropods* | | | | | | |
| Crabs | 0 | < 1 | 4 | 22 | 10 | 4 |
| Others | 0 | 0 | 3 | 0 | 0 | 0 |
| Mollusks | 8 | 37 | 31 | 38 | 23 | 13 |
| *Echinoderms* | | | | | | |
| Sea urchins | 86 | 11 | 21 | 82 | 59 | 78 |
| Others | 0 | 0 | 16 | 0 | 0 | 0 |
| Fish | 6 | 50 | 22 | 44 | 7 | 3 |
| Others | 0 | < 1 | 1 | 0 | 1 | 2 |
| **Total** | 100 | 100 | 100 | – | 100 | 100 |

*Percent of total volume: carnivores 65 (including fish 62.2) and herbivores 35.

## Web Version

Detailed teaching notes, the case PDF, and an answer key are available on the NCCSTS website at *sciencecases.lib.buffalo.edu/cs/collection/detail.asp?case_id=167&id=167*.

## References

Estes, J. A., and D. O. Duggins. 1995. Sea otters and kelp forests in Alaska: Generality and variation in a community ecological paradigm. *Ecological Monographs* 65: 75–100.

Estes, J. A., M. T. Tinker, T. M. Williams, and D. F. Doak. 1998. Killer whale predation on sea otters linking oceanic ecosystems. *Science* 282: 473–476.

Stevens, W. K. *New York Times.* 1999. Search for missing sea otters turns up a few surprises. January 5.

# SECTION XII

# BIOSPHERE AND CONSERVATION

CHAPTER 52

# LIVING DOWNSTREAM

## Atrazine and Coliform Bacteria Effects on Water Quality

*Thomas A. Davis*

### Abstract

Water samples collected from a local river show statistically significant elevated levels of fecal bacteria and atrazine, one of the most commonly used herbicides in the United States. A hearing has been called by the county to investigate the cause of the contamination, possible effects on aquatic life in the river, and what can be done to prevent a recurrence. In the ensuing debate, students analyze and interpret data as they present the viewpoints of various stakeholders.

### Learning Objectives

- Discuss both sides of a contemporary environmental issue and see how science is involved in producing data and information that is vital to making a decision; as part of this, students write an essay that states their position and explains why they feel that way.
- Understand how the scientific method, equipment, data, and results are used to solve everyday environmental problems.
- Interpret scientific data in graphical or table form and apply it to help understand and solve an environmental problem.

### Quantitative Reasoning Skills/Concepts

- Interpret the meaning of simple statistical descriptors.
- Use graphs to formulate predictions and explanations.
- Use data to formulate null and alternative hypotheses.
- Articulate complete and correct claims based on data.
- Interpret the meaning of data from water sampling sites.

# The Case Study

## *Part I: The Problem*

Here are the facts: Recent water samples show high levels of fecal coliform bacteria and atrazine in the Turkey River, which flows through the Milford property. Levels were high on two consecutive sampling days three weeks apart. A hearing has been called by the county to investigate how this happened, what the possible effects are on aquatic life in the river, and what can be done to prevent it from happening again.

A water quality sampling team has been collecting data on fecal bacterial levels, atrazine levels, and macroinvertebrates every three weeks, as shown in Figures 52.1–52.3.

As shown on the map in Figure 52.4 (p. 474), County Road X goes across the north end of the property and the four-lane state highway (Highway 24) traverses the southern end of the farm, thus allowing sampling access from public land on highway right-of-ways.

**FIGURE 52.1.**

Atrazine Levels in Turkey River.

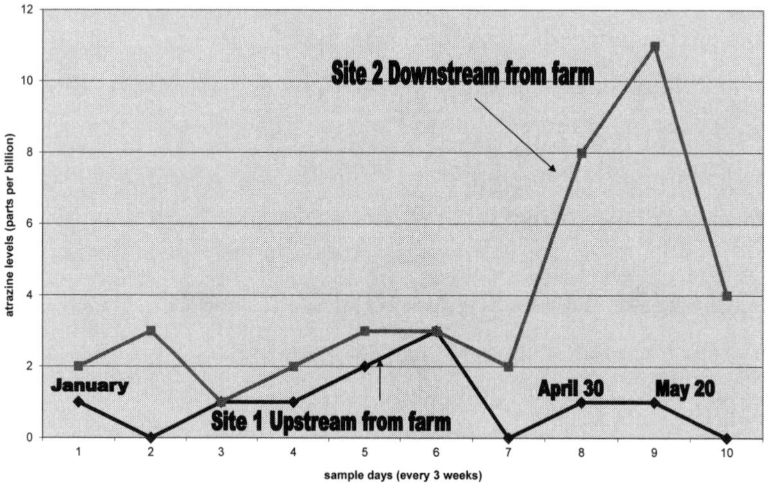

## FIGURE 52.2.

Species Richness of Aquatic Macroinvertebrates in Turkey River.

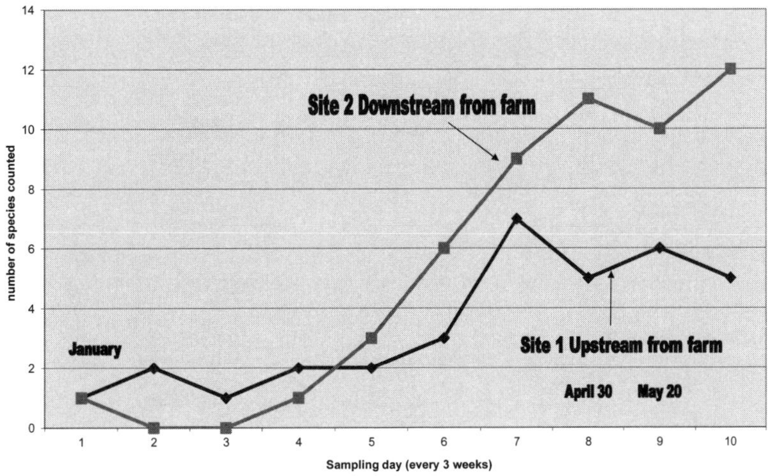


## FIGURE 52.3.

Fecal Coliform Bacteria in Turkey River.

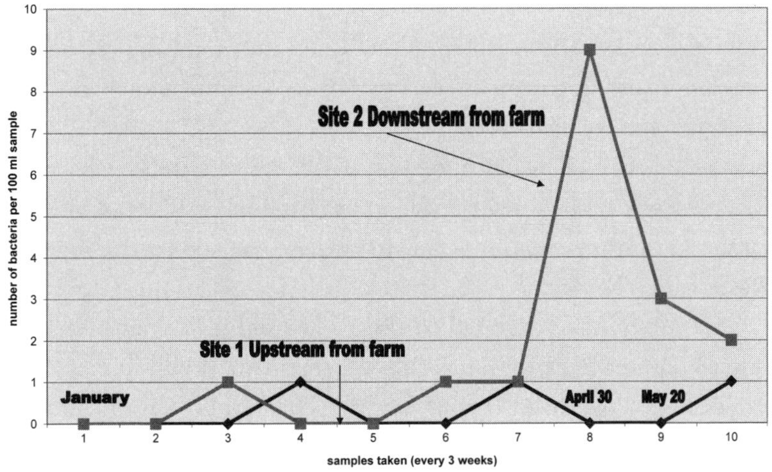

## FIGURE 52.4.

Map of Milford Farm Along Turkey River.

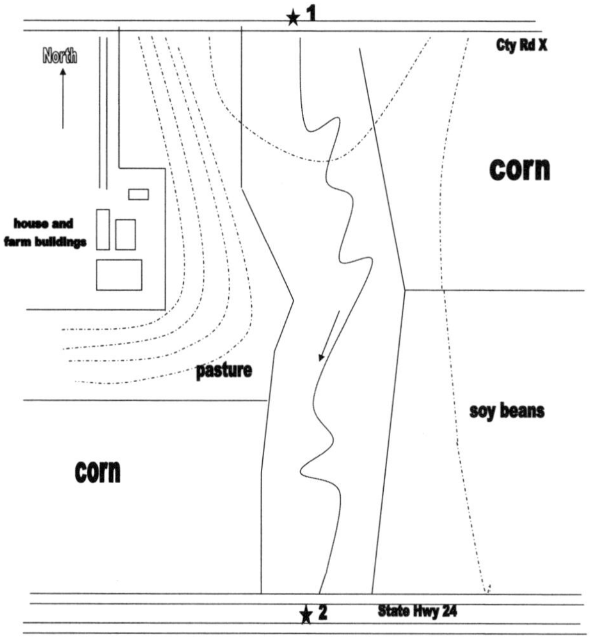


Dotted Lines are 20 ft contour lines; house and buildings sit up on a hill above the river; solid lines are fences; land on both sides of river has been planted with switchgrass as a buffer strip; stars indicate sampling sites – #1 is upstream from farm, #2 is downstream

This sampling process has been going on for eight years and has used similar sampling sites farther upstream and downstream, each of which have not shown any problems with high levels of atrazine or fecal bacteria.

Up to this point, there have been no effects of these levels on the brook trout population, which has a unique self-reproducing population in the Turkey River above and below the Milford property. Most trout found in local streams are stocked by the state's Department of Natural Resources. The debate will center on discussion of the meaning of the data, their source, what might have changed to cause elevated levels, and what the effects of these levels are on aquatic life and human life downstream. It will include the viewpoints of a number of stakeholders including the landowner's rights to apply atrazine to control weeds as well as the role of fisheries biologists and a water quality specialist to address the problem and future implications of high levels of bacteria and atrazine in the Turkey River.

The two sides of the debate are represented by:

- Side A: Fisheries biologists and local water quality program coordinator (and assistant).
- Side B: The landowners, atrazine salesperson, and county supervisor.

## The Roles

- *Brad and his assistant Brenda:* Iowa Dept. of Natural Resources and State of Iowa fisheries biologists
- *Samantha and her assistant Lou:* Local water quality monitor program coordinator and her assistant
- *Ben and Sandy Milford:* Landowner and his wife
- *Mary:* County Supervisor, head of zoning board
- *Suzie:* Atrazine salesperson

## Resource / Background Information

### Fisheries Biologists

As fisheries biologists with the state, with master's degrees in fish ecology, you have experience in developing fish habitat in streams and know what levels of certain pollutants can do to brook trout and macroinvertebrates. Be prepared to play the personality of your role: be a conservationist; be concerned and informed (you should know about the effects of chemicals on land and aquatic organisms); be stubborn; use your past outdoor field experience to help answer questions and present data. Try to make the landowners feel guilty that this contamination has occurred in a stream that many people have put time and money into to make it prime habitat for brook trout.

Information on the effects of fecal coliform bacteria on fish and aquatic life:

- *www.water-research.net/Watershed/fecalbacteria*
- *ga2.er.usgs.gov/bacteria/qanda.cfm*

### Water Quality Monitor Program Coordinator

The water sampling program and budget you oversee are sponsored by the Friends of the Turkey River and the National Wildlife Federation; you have a BS in water resources and an MS in natural resource management. Be prepared to play the personality of the role: be a conservationist: be concerned and informed (you should know about the effects of chemicals on land and aquatic organisms); be stubborn; use your past outdoor field experience to help answer questions. Don't be afraid to show other data from other sites that show how fecal bacteria and atrazine have had negative effects on stream biology.

Information on fecal coliform bacteria and water quality:

- *www.state.ky.us/nrepc/water/wcpfcol.htm*

Information on atrazine effects on water quality:

- *http://muextension.missouri.edu/explore/manuals/m00167.htm*

## Landowners

The Milfords, Ben and his wife Sandy, are farmers. They currently have 250 pigs and 50 stock cows. They raise soy beans and corn. They use some fertilizer and atrazine herbicide, which has helped them produce high-yield corn and beans for many years. They say they have respect for the land. Sandy does the bookwork and orders supplies. Both have agriculture degrees. Play the personalities of your roles: be farmers; be independent; skeptical; best way is your way; stubborn (of course I want to protect the quality of the land, but I need to feed my family too); ask other people to explain background of their data.

Information on farming practices to improve water quality:

- *www4.agr.gc.ca/AAFC-AAC/display-afficher.do?id=1193172134600&lang=eng*

## County Supervisor

Mary, the county supervisor, owns property adjacent to Mr. Milford but rents all of the land to some other farmer. She is an absentee landowner and lives in town 25 miles away. She is more concerned about the monetary value of her land and its crops than its ecological value. She is concerned about the high levels of these chemicals in "her" stream, but also knows that there are costs of doing business and tries to defend her "fellow" landowners in their actions.

Information on absentee landowners:

- *www.absenteelandowners.org/info-for-landowners*

## Atrazine Salesperson

Suzie knows all the facts about the successful use of atrazine in the past. She is aware of its danger to aquatic animals at higher levels and is also aware of the best ways to apply it safely; she has a BA in business. Suzie is known to get a bit testy when atrazine is described as a deadly chemical and its use is, in her view, unnecessarily criticized. She adamantly defends the use of atrazine as a safe, economically important herbicide that helps farmers be successful.

Information on atrazine information:

- *www.epa.gov/waterscience/criteria/atrazine/atrazinefacts.html*
- *http://extoxnet.orst.edu/pips/atrazine.htm*

# Web Version

Detailed teaching notes, the case PDF, and an answer key are available on the NCCSTS website at *sciencecases.lib.buffalo.edu/cs/collection/detail.asp?case_id=462&id=462*.

CHAPTER 53

# DO CORRIDORS HAVE VALUE IN CONSERVATION?

*Andrea Bixler*

## Abstract

This case focuses on conservation corridors as a means to reduce the problems of population size and isolation in a fragmented habitat. Students learn what a corridor is, consider how nature preserves and corridors function, and analyze data from an article on the use of corridors by various plant and animal species.

## Learning Objectives

- Know what a corridor is and how it might be useful in protecting endangered species.
- Apply an array of scientific principles, including those from population, community, and ecosystem ecology and population genetics, to solve a problem in conservation biology.
- Gain a greater understanding of techniques for censusing various species.
- Practice data interpretation.

## Quantitative Reasoning Skills/Concepts

- Interpret the meaning of simple statistical descriptors.
- Use graphs to formulate predictions and explanations.
- Articulate complete and correct claims based on data.
- Use appropriate reasoning to support the validity of data-based claims.
- Create experimental designs to test hypotheses.

## The Case Study

### *Part I: Introduction and Review of Relevant Biology*

In 2008, conservation groups filed petitions with the Supreme Court to stop the U.S. government from building a fence along the U.S.–Mexican border. The Court refused to consider the issue because of security threats. What was the environmental argument against the fence? While it was intended to stop drug smugglers and illegal immigrants from crossing the border, the fence would also restrict movement of endangered jaguars *(Panthera onca).*

Species that are endangered are found in very small numbers, often with very small geographic distributions. For an animal like the jaguar, which as an adult may weigh 45–115 kg (100–250 lbs.) and eats only meat, a large home range is necessary in order to locate sufficient food. They are known to move 2–3 km/day (1.2–1.8 mi), and even farther in the dry season.

Conservation groups charged that building an 1127 km (700 mi) fence along the southern border of the United States would make it more difficult for jaguars to cover the ground they need. Besides restricting their movements in search of prey, a barrier could prevent jaguars finding each other in order to breed.

## Questions

1. Why is it more difficult for top carnivores to obtain sufficient energy resources than it is for animals lower on the food chain?
2. What sorts of genetic changes are more common in smaller populations than large ones? Are these problematic and, if so, how?
3. What term or concept is used to describe the population size of breeding animals (not the total population size)? What factors discussed above might reduce the number of breeding jaguars below the total number?
4. Is it important for people to try to protect endangered species?

## *Part II: Nature Preserves and Corridors*

No one knows how many jaguars there are in the United States or Mexico, but it is doubtful there are enough to maintain a healthy population for long. And inbreeding and genetic drift make their population more susceptible to disease and environmental changes.

Obviously, nature preserves are ideal for protecting endangered species and their habitats. But it is not always possible to create adequate protected areas. As an alternative, environmentalists have suggested that elimination of barriers within the geographic ranges of endangered species might boost their survival through both greater habitat availability and increased genetic diversity. However, when there are no actual fences preventing species movements, there may still be human-made obstacles such as roads, urban sprawl, or agricultural areas. Exactly which of these might pose problems for a species depends on its particular needs.

Even when it is not possible to eliminate a fence, road, farm, or shopping mall, it may be quite easy to create a *corridor*, or area of habitat suitable for species to use in moving between natural areas. The importance of corridors has been widely reported in the conservation biology literature for decades now, and formed the basis of arguments in the case against the U.S. Border Fence.

## Questions

1. What does island biogeography theory suggest about the ideal design of a nature preserve? (Think of a preserve as a habitat island.)
2. What are some reasons why the number and size of nature preserves are limited? In your answer, consider what you know about both local and international pressures (social, economic, and political).
3. What are some examples of corridors that already exist where you live? They may not go by this name, but still serve the same function. (Think about areas where typical land use changes. For example, if you live in a farming community, are there unfarmed areas that could serve as corridors? If you live in a city, which areas are not built up and could they be corridors?)

## *Part III: Experimenting With Corridors*

From 1996 to 1998, Nick Haddad and several colleagues set about studying the effects of artificially created corridors within plantations of pine trees. The map in Figure 53.1 (p. 480) shows the 27 patches of open habitat the scientists created through the removal of trees. The patches are all 128 × 128 m in size (this amounts to 1.64 ha, about 4 ac, or about twice the size of a baseball diamond). Some of them are connected by corridors that are 32 m wide, ranging from 64 to 384 m in length.

Whether these patches and corridors seem large or small to you, the important thing is whether they seem large or small to the species Haddad et al. studied. There are butterflies that do not move more than 128 m in their lifetime. There are mice with home ranges of about half a hectare. And then there are animals like jaguars that have home ranges of at least 10 $km^2$ (4 $mi^2$). Obviously, butterflies would respond differently to the described study area than jaguars! Moreover, the type of habitat in the patches and corridors will only be suitable for certain types of organisms.

## Questions

1. How and why might animals move between habitat patches?
2. How and why might plants move between habitat patches?
3. As Haddad and colleagues point out, we often think of forests as "good" habitat (ideal for corridors), when they could be barriers. What sorts of species might Haddad and colleagues be studying for which pine forest can serve as a barrier?

**FIGURE 53.1.**

Corridor Experiment at the Savannah River National Environmental Research Park, South Carolina.

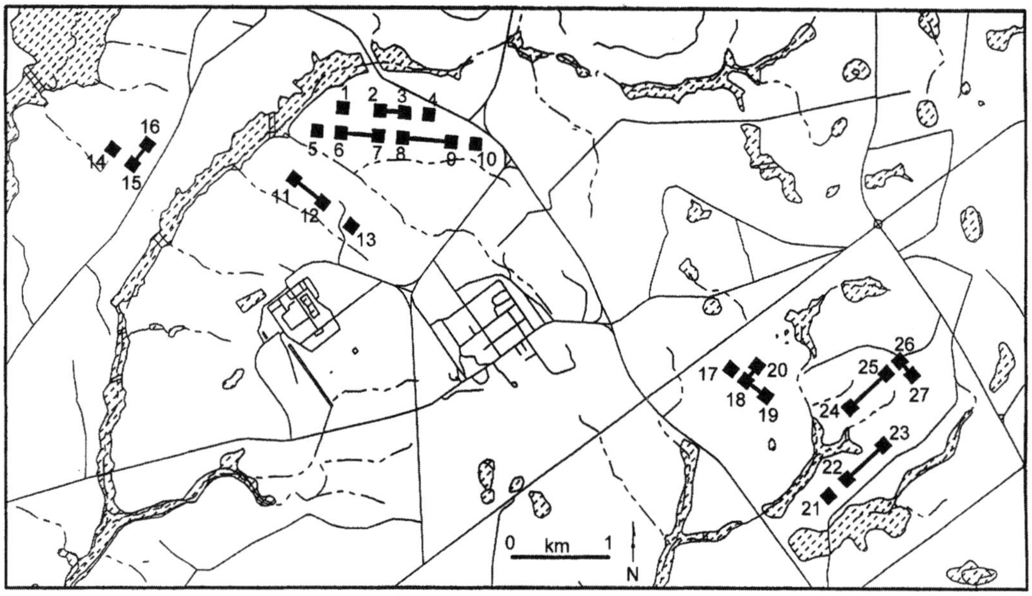


Black areas show patches (128 × 128 m, numbered 1–27) and 10 corridors (32 m wide, varying in length from 64 m to 384 m). Solid lines show roads, and stippled areas are ponds and streams. *Source:* Haddad et al., 2003.

4. What can you predict about the species Haddad and colleagues wanted to study, based on the size and vegetation of the habitat patches and corridors they used?
5. Examining habitat patches 14, 15, and 16, can you predict the type of comparison Haddad and his colleagues would make to determine whether corridors were important to the species studied? Specifically, what type of data would you collect, and in which patches, to determine whether corridors had an influence on the species of interest?

## Part IV: Methods and Results of the Study

Haddad and colleagues studied the movements of two species of butterfly, two small mammals, one bee species, four bird-dispersed plants, and the pollen of an additional plant. In each case, they determined whether the individuals were more likely to move via corridors; in other words, were they more often found in patches that were connected or unconnected to the center patch?

To collect data on these diverse organisms, they had to use a number of different techniques:

- Butterflies and bees were captured and individually marked; attempts were made to recapture them later.
- Hispid cotton rats were captured from locations 13 km or farther from the experimental area, radio-collared, released within habitat patches, and radio-tracked.
- Old-field mice were eliminated from three blocks of three patches; then marked mice were introduced to the center patch (e.g., patch 15) and attempts were made to recapture them in traps set in all nine patches.
- For two species of plants, members of that species already present were removed from the peripheral patches (e.g., patches 14 and 16) and any seeds found subsequently were assumed to have been brought by birds from the center patch.
- In the other two plant species, plants were not removed, but the seeds in the center patch were marked with fluorescent microspheres; these microspheres followed the same ingestion/excretion path as the seeds and allowed researchers to identify which seeds located in the peripheral patches were from plants in the center patch.
- For the pollination study, flowers in the center patch were dusted with fluorescent powder and presence of powder was observed on flowers in the peripheral patches. The single bee species observed pollinating 90% of these flowers was also marked and recaptured (as described in the first point above).

Figure 53.2 (p. 482) displays the data. Note that the statistical results are printed in the corner of each graph. Where it says "no analysis," there were insufficient observations of movement to conduct a statistical test.

## Questions

1. Briefly describe the overall pattern you see in the data.
2. For which species are the results significant?
3. Does your answer to Question #2 suggest any patterns among species types? For example, are plants different from animals or are butterflies different from bees? Describe the patterns and try to explain them according to the characteristics of the taxa involved.
4. Haddad and colleagues conclude that "In our study, we lack data on population viability and genetic diversity, and our dramatic increases in movement to connected patches strongly suggest, but do not demonstrate, the value of corridors."
   (a) Do you think this statement ("suggest, but do not demonstrate") is a fair assessment of their study? Explain your answer.

(b) What other data are the researchers suggesting they need to conclusively demonstrate the importance of corridors? Do you think they are right? For example, does knowing the level of genetic variability answer questions about long-term population survival?

(c) How could researchers collect these data? Give suggestions for several of the species in their study.

**FIGURE 53.2.**

Plant and Animal Movement Between Connected and Unconnected Patches.

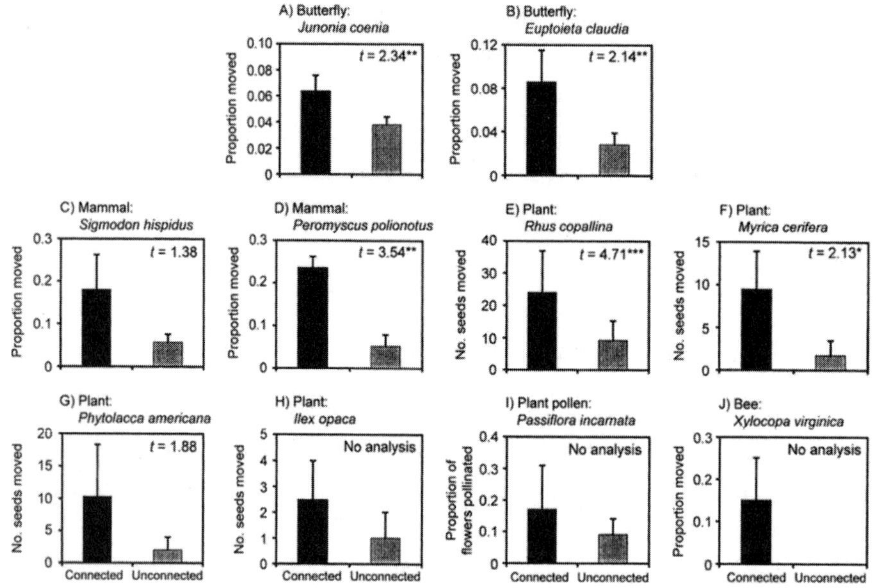


Panels (A)–(D) and (J) show the mean (+1 se) proportion of individuals that were marked in one patch and moved to a connected or unconnected patch. Panels (E)–(H) show the mean (+1 se) number of bird-dispersed seeds that moved from center patches to connected or unconnected patches. Panel (I) shows the mean (+1 se) proportion of flowers in connected or unconnected patches with fluorescent powder. Data for butterflies are adapted from Haddad, N. M. 1999, Corridor and distance effects on interpatch movements: A landscape experiment with butterflies, Ecological Applications 9:612–622. Asterisks indicate significance levels: *$P < 0.10$; **$P < 0.05$; ***$P < 0.01$.
*Source:* Haddad et al. 2003.

5. Based on what you know from the Haddad et al. study, what would be the effects of a border fence on the population of jaguars mentioned in Part I? Explain your thinking. Specify any additional information you need in order to make sound predictions.

## Web Version

Detailed teaching notes, the case PDF, and an answer key are available on the NCCSTS website at *sciencecases.lib.buffalo.edu/cs/collection/detail.asp?case_id=586&id=586*.

## References

Haddad, N. M., D. R. Bowne, A. Cunningham, B. J. Danielson, D. J. Levey, S. Sargent, and T. Spira. 2003.Corridor use by diverse taxa. *Ecology* 84 (3): 609–615.

Law, C., ed. 2003. Jaguar species survival plan: Guidelines for captive management of jaguars. *www.jaguarssp.com/Animal%20Mgmt/JAGUAR%20GUIDELINES.pdf*

CHAPTER 54

# THE WEALTH OF WATER

## The Value of an Essential Resource

*Melanie K. Rathburn and Karina J. Baum*

## Abstract

This case study, which focuses on the Cochabamba water revolt in Bolivia, is designed to encourage students to think about water as a limited natural resource. Students learn about the limited nature of freshwater and the impact that access to clean water has on people across all socioeconomic demographics.


## Learning Objectives

- Understand the limited nature of freshwater.
- Appreciate that access to clean water is an issue that does not make distinctions between developed and developing countries.
- Critically evaluate opposing views on water privatization.
- Calculate and analyze current data related to water consumption.
- Comprehend that individuals can play an important role in solving the water crisis.

## Quantitative Reasoning Skills/Concepts

- Carry out basic mathematical operations.
- Articulate complete and correct claims based on data.

## The Case Study

### *Part I: Spring Break*

After a long semester, Paul felt like he deserved a break. When his friend Sarah mentioned that she was traveling to Bolivia over spring break, he decided to go along. He had been taking Spanish as one of his courses at the university and thought this would be his chance to use his new language skills and to learn about a different culture. After reading a bunch of travel guides, they decided to start their trip in Cochabamba. The city is known for having a warm climate, excellent restaurants, the largest and most exciting market in Bolivia, and a vibrant nightlife. So they booked their tickets and off they went.

When they arrived, the people were friendly and hospitable, the food was incredible (a bit spicy, but great!), and the sights were unlike anything they had seen before. It was turning out to be a fantastic trip. One night at a cafe, Paul and Sarah ended up sitting at a table next to a group of Cochabambino University students. In his broken Spanish, Paul decided to strike up a conversation. They discussed all the great places to see in Bolivia. Sarah mentioned that she didn't want to just see the sights, but wanted to experience the culture of the region. Upon hearing this, one of the students, Maria, told them that the best way to learn about the people was to live with them. Maria invited Paul and Sarah to spend the weekend with her family. They jumped at the chance, and immediately checked out of their hotel.

The next morning, Sarah awoke to the smell of fresh baked bread. She was so excited to start this new stage of their travels. She decided to take a quick shower before she headed down for breakfast. It was so nice to be in such a welcoming home; it made Sarah think about her own family back in the United States. As she was showering, she heard a knock on the door.

"Are you almost done in the shower?" Maria asked.

"I just need five more minutes," Sarah responded.

Maria returned downstairs and told everyone that Sarah would need another five minutes.

"Five minutes … it's probably going to be another half an hour," Paul said jokingly.

Although Maria turned with a smile, Paul noticed the look of concern that passed between Maria and her mother. "Is anything wrong?" Paul asked.

"No, it's just that freshwater is limited in Bolivia, our delivery system is in disrepair and the little water we do receive is lost through leaks and rusty pipes. We have to be pretty careful with our water use."

"Why doesn't anyone fix it?"

"Didn't you hear what happened when our government tried to sell the public water system?"

Paul shook his head no as Maria began to tell him the story. "Cochabamba's economic prosperity relied on the mining industry. When this industry collapsed in the mid-1980s, there was no money to maintain the city's water system. The government felt that to deal with the problem they needed to privatize Cochabamba's public water supply and so they sold it to the multinational company, Bechtel. This privatization resulted in a dramatic increase in the cost of water. In Bolivia, many people live on less than $80 per month. With the new water rates, people were forced to choose between paying for water and feeding their families. For you to really understand what happened during the water crisis, why don't you read this article?"

Sarah came down the stairs and joined Paul and Maria as they sat down to read.

> LEASING THE RAIN: *The world is running out of fresh water, and the fight to control it has begun.*
>
> In April of 2000, in the central plaza of the beautiful old Andean city of Cochabamba, Bolivia, the body of Victor Hugo Daza lay on a makeshift bier. Daza, a seventeen-year-old student, had been shot in the face by the Army during protests sparked by an increase in local water rates. These protests had been growing for months, and unrest had also erupted in other parts of the country. The national government had just declared martial law. In Cochabamba, a city of eight hundred thousand, the third largest in Bolivia, a good part of the population was now in the streets, battling police and soldiers in what people had started calling la Guerra del agua—the Water War. Peasants from the nearby countryside manned barricades, sealing off all roads to the city. The protesters had captured the central plaza, where thousands milled around a tiled fountain and the catafalque of Victor Daza. Some of their leaders had been arrested and taken to a remote prison in the Amazon; others were in hiding.
>
> The chief demand of the water warriors, as they were called, was the removal of a private, foreign-led consortium that had taken over Cochabamba's water system. For the Bolivian government, breaking with the consortium—which was dominated by the U.S.-based Bechtel Corporation—was unthinkable, politically and financially. Bolivia had signed a lucrative, long-term contract. Renouncing it would be a blow to the confidence of foreign investors in a region where national governments and economies depend on such confidence for their survival. (Argentina's recent bankruptcy was caused in large part by a loss of credibility with international bankers.) The rebellion in Cochabamba was setting off loud alarms, particularly among the major corporations in the global water business. This business has been booming in recent years—Enron was a big player, before its collapse—largely because of the worldwide drive to privatize public utilities.
>
> For opponents of privatization, who believe that access to clean water is a human right, the Cochabamba Water War became an event of surpassing interest. There are many signs that other poor communities, especially in Third World cities, may start refusing to accept deals that put a foreign corporation's hand on the neighborhood pump or the household tap. Indeed, water auctions may turn out to test the limits of the global privatization gold rush. And while the number of populists opposing water privatization seems effectively inexhaustible—the leaders of the Cochabamba

rebellion included peasant farmers and an unassuming former shoemaker named Óscar Olivera—the same cannot be said of the world's water supply. There was a great deal more than local water rates riding on the outcome of this strange, passionate clash in Bolivia.

Excerpted from William Finnegan,
"Leasing the rain," *The New Yorker*, April 8, 2002.

## Questions

1. The people of Cochabamba were protesting the privatization of their water system because they felt that water is a basic human right. Do you agree with this belief or do you think water is a commodity that can be bought and sold? Keep in mind that even if it is a human right, there are costs associated with obtaining, purifying, and distributing water. Who do you think should pay for these cost? Where should the money come from?
2. The consequences of water privatization in Cochabamba grabbed the world's attention, and the views on this issue are diverse.

"Many people take water for granted: they turn on the tap and the water flows. Or they go to the supermarket, where they can pick from among dozens of brands of bottled water. But for more than a billion people on our planet, clean water is out of reach. And some 2.6 billion people have no access to proper sanitation. The consequences are devastating. Nearly 2 million children die every year of illnesses related to unclean water and poor sanitation—far more than the number killed as a result of violent conflict. Meanwhile, all over the world pollution, overconsumption and poor water management are decreasing the quality and quantity of water … The United Nations is deeply committed to this struggle. Access to safe water is a fundamental human need and a basic human right. And water and sanitation are at the heart of our quest to enable all the world's people, not just a fortunate few, to live in dignity, prosperity and peace."

—Kofi A. Annan, Former Secretary-General, United Nations
(*Human Development Report*, 2006)

"Indeed, privatization and commoditization have become so sanctioned as a fundamental solution to the water crisis that the International Monetary Fund, which provides loans to nations in trouble, frequently imposes water privatization as a condition in its lending agreements. The rationale for this is the IMF's belief that structural reforms of the local economy and social infrastructure … are essential for a country to improve its financial standing. Because companies are more skilled at managing a water supply than the local government—and are more motivated by hoped-for profits to succeed—water privatization, in the IMF's view, can improve the lives of a developing country's population. As a result of this assumption, recent multiyear IMF loans of upwards of $50 million each to some of the poorest countries in the world like Tanzania, Benin, and Rwanda specifically require that local water systems be turned over to private corporate interests."

—Jeffrey Rothfeder,
*Every Drop for Sale*, 2001

In light of the above statements, how should developing countries deal with the problems associated with a lack of clean, fresh water?

3. Bechtel is a multinational corporation and, like all corporations, the main goal is profit. Do you think Bechtel should profit from the management of a water system? If not, what should their incentive be? If so, what restrictions, if any, should be imposed?
4. Do you think Cochabamba's conflict is foreshadowing the future with more wars being fought over water? Can you think of other examples where access to water is being contested?

## *Part II: The Before and After*

On page 490 are actual water bills from the month before and after Bechtel took over the Cochabamba water system.

### Questions

1. Aguas del Tunari, the Bechtel subsidiary, claims that increased water consumption explains the price increase that Bolivians noticed in their water bills post-privatization. Compare the water bills on page 490. Does the amount of water use match Aguas del Tunari's claim?
2. What was the percent increase in the cost of water for this household?
3. Based on the average income for a Bolivian, what percent of their salary is dedicated to obtaining clean, freshwater?
4. Considering that the 2006 median U.S. salary for a dual-income household is $58,472 (U.S. Census Bureau), how much would you be spending on water? What would be your reaction if this happened to you?

**FIGURE 54.1.**

Pre-privatization Water Bil.l

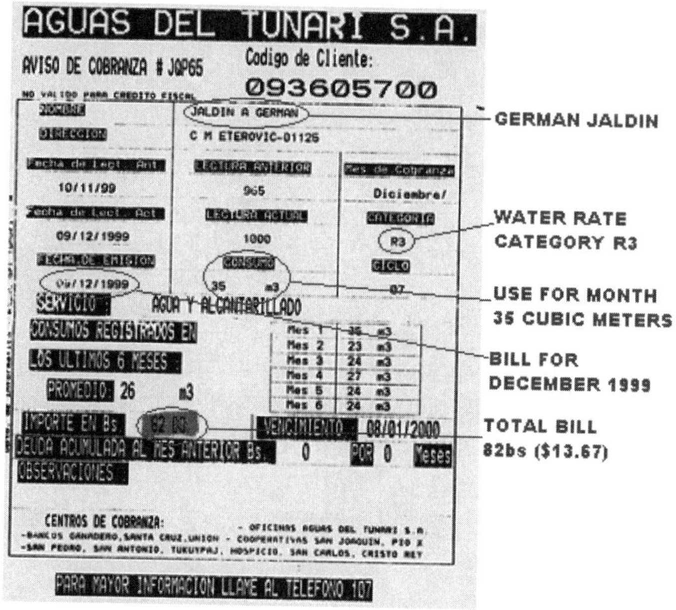


**FIGURE 54.2.**

Post-privatization Water Bill.

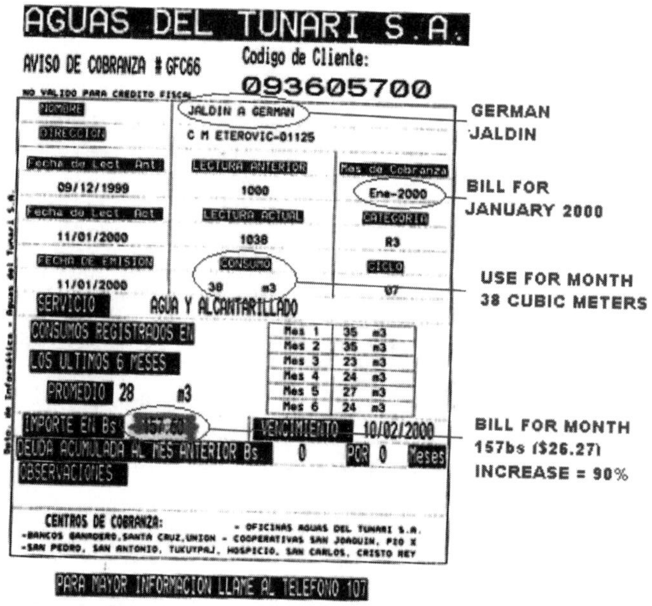

## Part III: Water and You

In 1992 the International Conference on Water and the Environment overwhelmingly ratified an agreement stating that water is not a public resource: it is a commodity. This position was again reinforced at the World Water Forum in 2000. Since then, water privatization has been promoted worldwide.

Water privatization is not just happening in developing countries. Suez Environnement is a French company that controls, maintains, and distributes water in over 120 different countries on five continents. In fact, private companies run many U.S. water systems. Although we live in a developed country, many places in the United States are running out of water. For example, in October 2007 Georgia declared a state of emergency as water resources declined.

This is not just an isolated incident; projections indicate that by 2025 the city of Atlanta will be completely out of water. This highlights the limited availability of this valuable resource and tells us that we need to be careful with our water consumption. Although the cause of these conflicts may differ in various parts of the world, the consequence is always the same: water is running out everywhere. In fact, the Former Chairman of the World Water Commission, Ismail Serageldin, predicts that the wars of the 21st century will be fought over water.

### Questions

1. What percent of the world's water is available as fresh drinking water?
2. What factors are responsible for the decline in freshwater worldwide?
3. The average American uses 480 gallons of water per week. Using Table 54.1 (p. 492) , calculate your own water consumption.

**TABLE 54.1.**

Water Use From Common Daily Activities.

| Activity | Water Loss* | Number of Times/Day | Total Gallons Used/Day | Total Water Use/Week |
|---|---|---|---|---|
| Hand washing | 1 gallons/min | | | |
| Showering | 2 gallons/min | | | |
| Bath | 50 gallons/tub | | | |
| Brushing teeth | 1 gallons/min | | | |
| Flushing toilet | 3 gallons/flush | | | |
| Laundry | 10 gallons/load | | | |
| Dish washing by hand | 5 gallons/load | | | |
| Drinking water | 1/16 gallons/glass | | | |
| TOTAL | | | | |

*Data from the USGS. Note that some quantities are provided on a per-minute basis.

4. Do you think it is necessary to reduce your water consumption? For each category listed above, what would you do to reduce your water usage? Are these realistic solutions?
5. Use your total water consumption per week to calculate your annual usage. (Hint: One year has 52 weeks.) Since the national average for water is $2.81/1000 gallons, use the median U.S. salary previously given to determine how much money you will be paying for water. Do you think this number represents the true value of water?
6. How would you communicate what you've learned today to your peers?

## Web Version

Detailed teaching notes, the case PDF, and an answer key are available on the NCCSTS website at *sciencecases.lib.buffalo.edu/cs/collection/detail.asp?case_id=219&id=219.*

# THE EFFECTS OF COYOTE REMOVAL IN TEXAS

## A Case Study in Conservation Biology

*Margaret A. Carroll*

## Abstract

This case presents published data on the effect of coyote removal in Texas. It was designed to help students understand trophic level relationships and the role of keystone species. Students interpret data presented graphically and predict how changes at one trophic level may affect populations and communities at other trophic levels.


## Learning Objectives

- Emphasize the importance of keystone predators.
- Demonstrate the difficulty of predicting the effects of ecological perturbations.
- Challenge students to interpret data that are presented graphically.
- Emphasize the importance of appropriate experimental controls.

## Quantitative Reasoning Skills/Concepts

- Interpret the meaning of simple statistical descriptors.
- Use graphs to formulate predictions and explanations.
- Formulate null and alternative hypotheses.
- Accept or reject null hypotheses based on statistical tests of significance.
- Articulate complete and correct claims based on data.
- Use appropriate reasoning to support the validity of data-based claims.

## The Case Study

### *Part I: Introduction*

The Plains of West Texas are part of a semi-arid ecosystem dominated by a mixture of shortgrass prairies and chaparral. The primary producers in the prairies include various species of grasses and other herbaceous flowering plants (forbs). The chaparral is dominated by a variety of shrubs including mesquite and yucca intermixed with grasses and forbs. The low-level predators, scavengers, and herbivores in this system include jackrabbits, cottontails, ground squirrels, and rodents (three species of rats, and seven species of mice). The mammalian mesopredators in this system are badgers, bobcats, skunks, and grey fox. The top-level predator is the coyote.

Humans often eliminate coyotes and other top predators from natural communities. Removal is generally aimed at increasing game populations, and protecting livestock, pets, and small children. Previous studies indicate that the effect of removing coyotes varies depending on the type of community from which they have been removed. You have received a request for proposals from The Nature Conservancy. The Conservancy wants to determine the effects of coyote removal in West Texas.

### Questions

1. What specific question do you intend to answer?
2. What type of experimental treatment and control will you use?
3. What variables do you intend to monitor?

## *Part II: Experimental Design*

Congratulations! Your proposal has been funded. Your final experimental design includes four 5,000-hectare (ha) sites—two control and two treatment (Figure 55.1). The communities in the control sites are similar to those in the treatment sites. All coyotes will be removed from the treatment sites and from a 5-kilometer (km) border around the sites. There will be no experimental manipulation in the control sites. You will monitor the animal community on all sites for one year prior to treatment and two years following coyote removal.

### Question

1. Make two predictions concerning the effects of coyote removal on the fauna of West Texas.

## *Part III: Mesopredators*

After monitoring the mesopredator populations for three years, you plotted the total abundance of badgers, bobcats, skunk, and fox found on treatment and control sites each year (Figure 55.2). Use these data to interpret the impact of coyote removal on the community of small mammalian predators.

**FIGURE 55.1.**

Location of Experimental Sites in West Texas. Sites 1 and 2 were the control sites. Coyotes were removed from sites 3 and 4 and from a 5-km border. (Henke and Bryant 1999.)

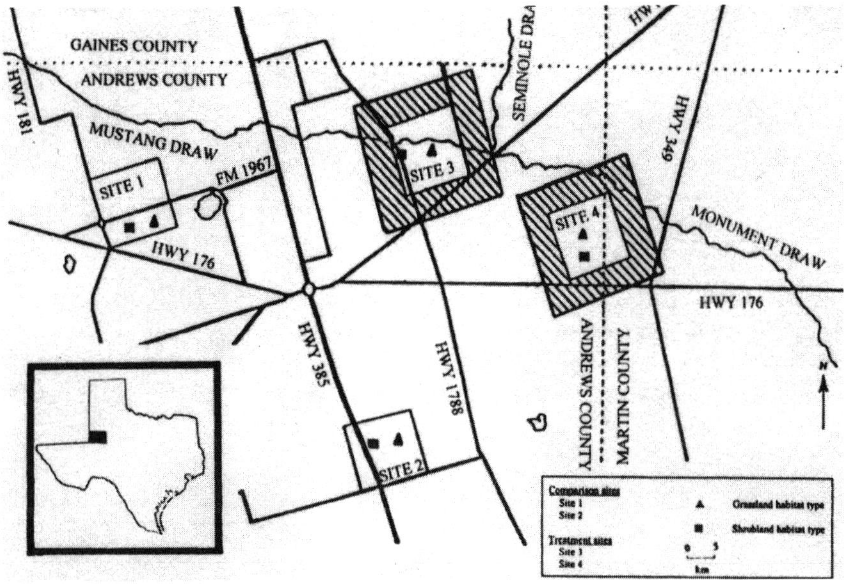


**FIGURE 55.2.**

Relative Abundance of Mammalian Mesopredators in the Experimental Sites Before and After Treatment. Error Bars represent one standard error. (Modified from Henke and Bryant 1999.)

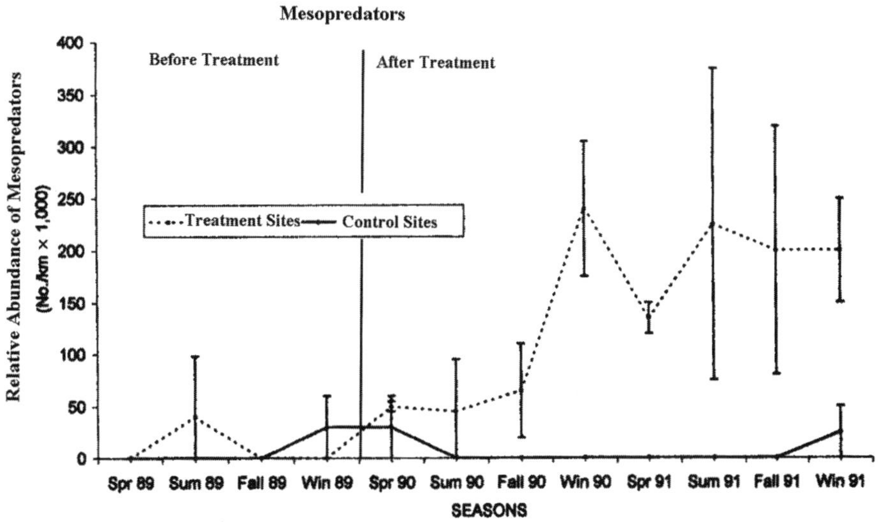

## Questions

1. What effect does coyote removal have on the mesopredator populations?
2. Predict what might have happened to the rodent populations as a result of changes in the mesopredator populations.

## *Part IV: Rodent Population Size*

You decide to analyze the data on rodent population size next. As a measure of population size, you compare the rodent biomass in grams per hectare in the treatment and control areas over the three years of the study (Figure 55.3).

**FIGURE 55.3.**

Biomass of Rodents in the Experimental Sites Before and After Coyotes Were Removed From the Treatment Sites. Error Bars represent one standard error. (Modified from Henke and Bryant 1999.)

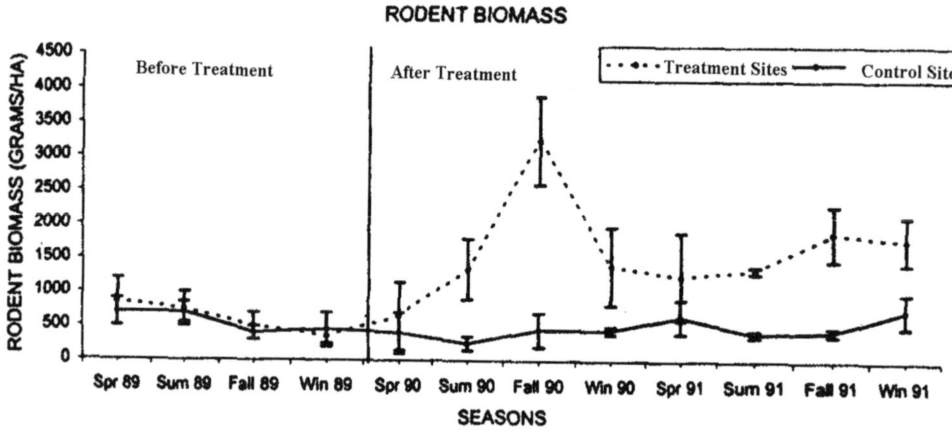


## Questions

1. What do you think is the primary factor controlling rodent population growth?
2. Given the changes in population size, what other changes might you expect in the rodent community?

## *Part V: Rodent Diversity*

When you look at the population size of individual rodent species, you realize that the Ord's kangaroo rat seems to be doing particularly well in treatment areas. Examine the data comparing the rodent diversity in the control and treatment areas before and after coyote removal (Figure 55.4).

**FIGURE 55.4.**

Diversity of Rodents in the Experimental Sites Before and After Coyotes Were Removed From the Treatment Sites. Rodent diversity was estimated using Simpson's Index. Error Bars represent one standard error. (Modified from Henke and Bryant 1999.)

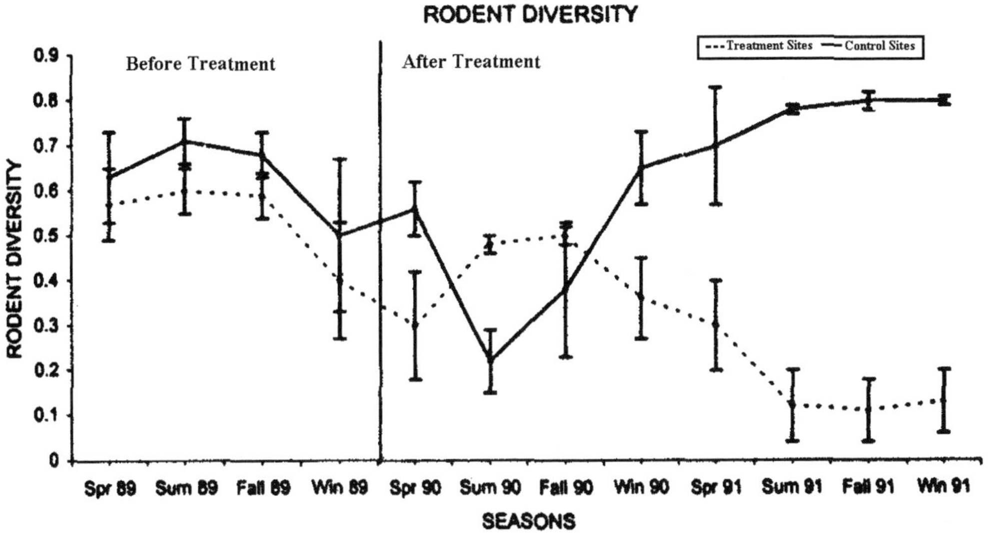


## Questions

1. In one sentence summarize the meaning of the graph shown in Figure 55.4.
2. How does the competitive success of Ord's kangaroo rat change in the absence of coyotes?
3. What term could be used to describe the role of the coyote in this community?
4. Propose one possible cause for the decline in rodent diversity in the control areas after treatment begins.
5. In your report to The Nature Conservancy, how will you summarize the impact of coyote removal in this community.

## Web Version

Detailed teaching notes, the case PDF, and an answer key are available on the NCCSTS website at *sciencecases.lib.buffalo.edu/cs/collection/detail.asp?case_id=438&id=438.*

## References

Henke, S. E., and F. C. Bryant. 1999. Effects of coyote removal on the faunal community in Western Texas. *Journal of Wildlife Management* 63: 1066–1081.

# LIST OF CONTRIBUTORS

Karen M. Aguirre, associate professor, department of biology, and associate dean, college of science, Coastal Carolina University, Conway, SC, PULSE Vision & Change Leadership Fellow

Mary Allen, professor and chair, department of biology, Hartwick College, Oneonta, NY

Jennifer Y. Anderson, RN

Kathleen Archer, associate professor, biology department, Trinity College, Hartford, CT

Karina J. Baum, AP biology, science department, Buckingham Browne & Nichols School, Cambridge, MA

Kari E. Benson, professor of biology and environmental science, and chair, biology department, Lynchburg College, Lynchburg, VA

Andrea Bixler, associate professor, biology department, Clarke University, Dubuque, IA

Jeffri C. Bohlscheid, science and technology manager, Food Group Technical Center, J. R. Simplot Company, Boise, ID

Peggy Brickman, professor, department of plant biology, The University of Georgia, Athens, GA

Barbra Burdett, associate professor, biology and anthropology, Lincoln College, Lincoln, IL

Margaret A. Carroll, professor, department of biology, Framingham State College, Framingham, MA

Merri Lynn Casem, professor, department of biological science, California State University Fullerton, Fullerton, CA

Susan B. Chaplin, Emeritus professor, department of biology, University of St. Thomas, Saint Paul, MN

Ling Chen, associate professor of chemistry, science department, Borough of Manhattan Community College/City University of New York, New York, NY

Barry Chess, professor, natural sciences division, Pasadena City College, Pasadena, CA

Jeanne Ting Chowning, Institute for Science and Math Education, University of Washington, Seattle, WA

Wilma V. Colon Parrilla

Thomas A. Davis, professor of biology, biology program, Loras College, Dubuque, IA

Susan M. DeSimone, associate in science instruction in biology, biology department, Middlebury College, Middlebury, VT

Brahmadeo Dewprashad, professor, department of science, Borough of Manhattan Community College, and doctoral faculty, graduate program in urban education, City University of New York, New York, NY

Lynn M. Diener, associate professor and biology chairperson, sciences department, Mount Mary University, Milwaukee, WI

Dustin J. Eno, former student, life sciences, Quest University Canada, Squamish, BC

Susan Evarts, horticulturalist, Minnesota Zoological Gardens, Apple Valley, MN

Gary M. Fortier, president, Animal Behavior Institute, Durham, NC

Dean Fraga, professor, department of biology, The College of Wooster, Wooster, OH

Michaela A. Gazdik, assistant professor of molecular biology, school of natural science and mathematics, Ferrum College, Ferrum, VA

J. Phil Gibson, associate professor, departments of zoology, botany, and microbiology, University of Oklahoma, Norman, OK

Angela Green, former student, department of biological sciences, Western Illinois University, Macomb, IL

Karin A. Grimnes, professor of biology, biology department, Alma College, Alma, MI

David J. Grisé, assistant professor, department of life sciences, Texas A&M University–Corpus Christi, Corpus Christi, TX

Kristen N. Hausmann, former student, department of biology, Coastal Carolina University, Conway, SC

Merle Heidemann, associate director, center for integrative studies in general science, Michigan State University, East Lansing, MI

Clyde Freeman Herreid, distinguished teaching professor, department of biological sciences, director, National Center for Case Study Teaching in Science, University at Buffalo, Buffalo, NY

Ky Herreid, web manager/editor, National Center for Case Study Teaching in Science, University at Buffalo, Buffalo, NY

James A. Hewlett, professor of biology/coordinator of biotechnology, science and technology department, Finger Lakes Community College, Canandaigua, NY

Luke Holbrook, professor, department of biological sciences, Rowan University, Glassboro, NJ

Sarah K. Huber, research assistant professor of biology and marine science, department of fisheries science, The College of William & Mary, Williamsburg, VA

Robert J. Huskey, professor emeritus, biology department, University of Virginia, Charlottesville, VA

Martin Kelly, assistant professor of biology, department of mathematics and natural sciences, D'Youville College, Buffalo, NY

Drew Kohlhorst, assistant director for curriculum development and evaluation, Center for Science Education, Emory University, Atlanta, GA

Alison Krufka, assistant professor, department of biological sciences, Rowan University, Glassboro, NJ

Mark L. Kuhlmann, associate professor, department of biology, Hartwick College, Oneonta, NY

Andrew G. Lazowski, assistant professor, department of mathematics, Sacred Heart University, Fairfield, CT

Celeste A. Leander, senior instructor, department of zoology, The University of British Columbia, Vancouver, BC

Paula P. Lemons, assistant professor, department of biochemistry and molecular biology, The University of Georgia, Athens, GA

Dennis Liu, head of educational media and outreach, department of science education, Howard Hughes Medical Institute, Chevy Chase, MD

Patricia A. Marsteller, director, center for science education, Emory University, Atlanta, GA

Giselle A. McCallum, former undergraduate student, life sciences, Quest University Canada, Squamish, BC

Debra A. Meuler, chair, natural sciences, and associate professor, biology department, Cardinal Stritch University, Milwaukee, WI

William Morgan, professor, department of biology, The College of Wooster, Wooster, OH

Stephen C. Nold, professor, biology department, University of Wisconsin–Stout, Menomonie, WI

R. Deborah Overath, assistant professor of biology, department of life sciences, Texas A&M University–Corpus Christi, Corpus Christi, TX

Robin Pals-Rylaarsdam, professor, department of biological science, Benedictine University, Lisle, IL

Karen Peterson, director, scientific career development, human biology division, Fred Hutchinson Cancer Research Center, Seattle, WA

Annie Prud'homme-Généreux, founding faculty, life sciences, and associate vice-president of research and administration, Quest University Canada, Squamish, BC

Melanie K. Rathburn, faculty of teaching and learning, department of general education, Mount Royal University, Calgary, AB

Eric Ribbens, professor, department of biological sciences, Western Illinois University, Macomb, IL

Lauren Sahl, professor, Corning School of Ocean Studies, Maine Maritime Academy, Castine, ME

Nancy A. Schiller, co-director, National Center for Case Study Teaching in Science, and librarian, University Libraries, University at Buffalo, Buffalo, NY

Patricia Schneider, professor, department of biological sciences and geology, Queensborough Community College / City University of New York, New York, NY

Patricia A. Shields, instructor, department of cell biology and molecular genetics, University of Maryland, College Park, MD

Michèle I. Shuster, associate professor, Department of Biology, New Mexico State University, Las Cruces, NM

Ann C. Smith, assistant dean, office of undergraduate studies, University of Maryland, College Park, MD

Philip J. Stephens, professor, department of biology, Villanova University, Villanova, PA

Richard C. Stewart, associate professor, department of cell biology and molecular genetics, University of Maryland, College Park, MD

Geffrey F. Stopper, assistant professor, department of biology, Sacred Heart University, Fairfield, CT

Nathan Strong, professor, department of chemistry and biological sciences, New Hampshire Technical Institute, Concord, NH

Monica L. Tischler, professor, department of biological science, Bendectine University, Lisle, IL

Gerald Urquhart, assistant professor, Lyman Briggs School of Science, Michigan State University, East Lansing, MI

Geraldine S. Vaz, attending physician, ambulatory care department, Jamaica Hospital Medical Center, New York, NY

Diane R. Wang, graduate student, biology, plant breeding and genetics, Cornell University, Ithaca, NY

Jacqueline Washington, associate professor of biology/chair, department of biology and chemistry, Nyack College, Nyack, NY

Chester Wilson, lab coordinator and greenhouse manager, biology department, University of Saint Thomas, Saint Paul, MN

Kristy J. Wilson, assistant professor of biology, school of mathematics and sciences, Marian University, Indianapolis, IN

Anne Zayaitz, associate professor, department of biology, Kutztown University, Kutztown, PA

# APPENDIXES

APPENDIX A

# EXPECTATIONS FOR MEDICAL SCHOOL STUDENTS

Excerpts from: Association of American Medical Colleges (AAMC) and Howard Hughes Medical Institute (HHMI). 2009. *Scientific foundations for future physicians: Report of the AAMC-HHMI Committee,* pp. 20–26. Washington, DC: Association of American Medical Colleges.

*Note:* The report differentiates between expectations deemed important for medical school education (these competencies are denoted by an "M" prefix) and those identified for entering medical students (denoted by an "E" prefix).

---

**Competency M8 – Apply quantitative knowledge and reasoning—including integration of data, modeling, computation, and analysis—and informatics tools to diagnostic and therapeutic clinical decision making.**
*Learning Objectives*

1. Apply basic mathematical tools and concepts, including functions, graphs and modeling, measurement and scale, and quantitative reasoning, to an understanding of the specialized functions of membranes, cells, tissues, organs, and the human organism, in both health and disease.

   Examples:

   - Interpret graphical representations of drug levels as a function of dosage and pharmacokinetics.
   - Given urine and serum creatinine levels, urine flow rate, height, and weight, calculate the estimated GFR (glomerular filtration rate).
   - Draw a graph of serum glucose levels after a meal, and explain how feedback mechanisms lead to damped oscillations in glucose levels.

2. Apply the principles and approaches of statistics, biostatistics, and epidemiology to the evaluation and interpretation of disease risk, etiology, and prognosis, and to the prevention, diagnosis, and management of disease.

   Examples:

   - Contrast relative risk and attributable risk as guides to clinical and public health decision making in cancer prevention.

- Compare information derived from confidence intervals and probability values in determining the significance of an association between estrogen treatment and cardiovascular disease.
- Explain methods used to adjust for confounding factors in determining the prognosis in HIV infection.
- Relate the characteristics of a diagnostic medical test to its ability to discriminate between health and disease given the prevalence of the disease.

3. Apply the basic principles of information systems, their design and architecture, implementation, use, and limitations, to information retrieval, clinical problem solving, and public health and policy.

   Examples:
   - Perform a search of PubMed or other bibliographic databases (such as PSYCHINFO, INSPEC, or Sociological Abstracts), using at least two Boolean connectors, on a clinical topic.
   - Explain the difference between an electronic medical record system and a computerized provider order entry system and their roles in patient safety.
   - Describe the uses and limitations of a clinical data warehouse as a research tool.
   - Explain the concept and importance of information system interoperability.
4. Explain the importance, use, and limitations of biomedical and health informatics, including data quality, analysis, and visualization, and its application to diagnosis, therapeutics, and characterization of populations and subpopulations.

   Examples:
   - Explain the difference between biomedical informatics and health care information technology.
   - Provide examples of how informatics can contribute to health care quality.
   - Explain the ways clinical information systems can fail.
5. Apply elements of the scientific process, such as inference, critical analysis of research design, and appreciation of the difference between association and causation, to interpret the findings, applications, and limitations of observational and experimental research in clinical decision making.

   Examples:
   - Contrast the value of evidence from observational versus experimental studies in determining the efficacy of therapeutic interventions.
   - Analyze the causal connection between dietary factors and coronary artery disease incidence.

- Using the same empirical data, provide arguments for and against routine PSA screening for prostate cancer.
- Recognize that human decision making generally weights only a limited set of factors at one time, and be able to use tools and methods that consider multiple factors and uncertainties.
- Recognize when patients are excluding important information in their decision-making processes.

Premedical students, no matter what their primary fields of study, should learn the major concepts and skills of science and mathematics, leaving to medical schools the task of building on this scientific foundation the further scientific competencies that provide them the ability to practice science-based medicine.

*Overarching Competency at the Time of Entry into Medical School*: Demonstrate both knowledge of and ability to use basic principles of mathematics and statistics, physics, chemistry, biochemistry, and biology needed for the application of the sciences to human health and disease; demonstrate observational and analytical skills and the ability to apply those skills and principles to biological situations.

**Competency E1 – Apply quantitative reasoning and appropriate mathematics to describe or explain phenomena in the natural world.**
***Learning Objectives***

1. Demonstrate quantitative numeracy and facility with the language of mathematics.

   Examples:

   - Express and analyze natural phenomena in quantitative terms that include an understanding of the natural prevalence of logarithmic/exponential relationships (e.g., rates of change, pH).
   - Explain dimensional differences using numerical relationships, such as ratios and proportions.
   - Use dimensional analysis and unit conversions to compare results expressed in different systems of units.
   - Utilize the Internet to find relevant information, synthesize it, and make inferences from the data gathered.

2. Interpret data sets and communicate those interpretations using visual and other appropriate tools.

   Examples:

- Create and interpret appropriate graphical representations of data, such as a frequency histogram, from discrete data.
- Identify functional relationships from visually represented data, such as a direct or inverse relationship between two variables.
- Use spatial reasoning to interpret multidimensional numerical and visual data (e.g., protein structure or geographic information).

3. Make statistical inferences from data sets.

   Examples:

   - Calculate and explain central tendencies and measures of dispersion.
   - Evaluate hypotheses using appropriate statistical tests.
   - Evaluate risks and benefits using probabilistic reasoning.
   - Describe and infer relationships between variables using visual or analytical tools (e.g., scatter plots, linear regression, network diagrams, maps).
   - Differentiate anomalous data points from normal statistical scatter.

4. Extract relevant information from large data sets.

   Examples:

   - Execute simple queries to search databases (e.g., queries in literature databases).
   - Compare data sets using informatics tools (e.g., BLAST analysis of nucleotide or amino acid sequence).
   - Analyze a public-use data set (e.g., census data, NHANES, BRFSS).

5. Make inferences about natural phenomena using mathematical models.

   Examples:

   - Describe the basic characteristics of models (e.g., multiplicative vs. additive).
   - Predict short- and long-term growth of populations (e.g., bacteria in culture).
   - Distinguish the role of indeterminacy in natural phenomena and the impact of stochastic factors (e.g., radioactive decay) from the role of deterministic processes.

6. Apply algorithmic approaches and principles of logic (including the distinction between cause/effect and association) to problem solving.

   Examples:

- Define a scientific hypothesis and design an experimental approach to test its validity.
- Utilize tools and methods for making decisions that take into account multiple factors and their uncertainties (i.e., a decision tree).
- Critically evaluate whether conclusions from a scientific study are warranted.
- Distinguish correlation from causality.

7. Quantify and interpret changes in dynamical systems.

   Examples:

   - Describe population growth using the language of exponents and of differential calculus.
   - Explain homeostasis in terms of positive or negative feedback.
   - Calculate return on investment under varying interest rates by utilizing appropriate mathematical tools.

**Competency E2 – Demonstrate understanding of the process of scientific inquiry, and explain how scientific knowledge is discovered and validated.**

*Learning Objectives*

1. Develop observational and interpretive skills through hands-on laboratory or field experiences.

   Examples:

   - Collect and interpret primary data for identification of mixtures of compounds.
   - Use reduced or partial data to construct three-dimensional representations (e.g., developing organic molecular models from written formulas or modeling a biological structure from analysis of serial sections).
   - Demonstrate ability to analyze and infer conclusions based on measurements made during laboratory assays or field observations.

2. Demonstrate ability to measure with precision, accuracy, and safety.

   Examples:

   - Consider the accuracy, precision, and reproducibility of primary data from laboratory results to properly analyze and draw conclusions, including the differences between random and systematic sources of error.

- Employ stoichiometric analysis to predict yield and use quantitative measurements to interpret experimental results.
- Be able to use a standard Material Safety Data Sheets (MSDS) to decide on appropriate personal protection and disposal techniques for use of a given chemical.

3. Be able to operate basic laboratory instrumentation for scientific measurement.

   Examples:

   - Employ appropriate instrumentation to measure electrical voltages and currents in simple circuits.
   - Use appropriate detectors and instrumentation to monitor radioactive decay.
   - Calibrate a balance.
   - Be familiar with instruments and approaches for major chemical and biochemical separation and purification techniques.
   - Identify major chemical or biochemical uses of analytical spectroscopic techniques, such as UV, visible and infrared absorption, fluorescence, mass spectrometry, X-ray, and NMR.

4. Be able to articulate (in guided inquiry or in project-based research) scientific questions and hypotheses, design experiments, acquire data, perform data analysis, and present results.

   Examples:

   - Be able to develop a project plan and report: generate a hypothesis, design a protocol with appropriate controls, consider control of relevant variables, collect and analyze quantitative data, draw conclusions, and present the results (e.g., as a scientific seminar, paper, or poster).
   - Be able to work within a team to plan and/or achieve a complex goal (e.g., a presentation or an experiment that draws on more than one scientific discipline).
   - Be able to read and analyze results presented in a paper from the scientific literature, to develop a hypothesis based on the results, and to describe experiments that test such a hypothesis.
   - Develop an exemplary design to achieve a goal, such as an electronic circuit, a molecular synthesis, or an enzyme assay.

- › Be able to explain what constitutes plagiarism in contexts of writing and presentation and how to avoid and prevent the falsification and fabrication of data.

5. Demonstrate the ability to search effectively, to evaluate critically, and to communicate and analyze the scientific literature.

   Examples:

   - › Use appropriate databases to find relevant literature on a topic, and be able to summarize and present the current state of knowledge.
   - › Evaluate papers in the literature with attention to weaknesses, such as in experimental design (e.g., confounding variables), logic, or conclusions.

APPENDIX B

# BIOLOGY EDUCATION TO PREPARE RESEARCH SCIENTISTS FOR THE 21ST CENTURY

*National Research Council*

Excerpts from: *BIO 2010: Transforming Undergraduate Education for Future Research Biologists* Committee on Undergraduate Biology Education to Prepare Research Scientists for the 21st Century, National Research Council (2003).

*Note:* The material below is excerpted from the report's Executive Summary and Introduction.

---

"The committee began its work in the fall of 2000. The report recommends a comprehensive reevaluation of undergraduate science education for future biomedical researchers. In particular it calls for a renewed discussion on the ways that engineering and computer science, as well as chemistry, physics, and mathematics are presented to life science students....

In contrast to biological research, undergraduate biology education has changed relatively little during the past two decades. The ways in which most future research biologists are educated are geared to the biology of the past, rather than to the biology of the present or future. Like research in the life sciences, undergraduate education must be transformed to prepare students effectively for the biology that lies ahead. Life sciences majors must acquire a much stronger foundation in the physical sciences (chemistry and physics) and mathematics than they now get...

Much of today's biomedical research is at the interface between biology and the physical, mathematical, or information sciences. Most colleges and universities already require their biology majors to enroll in courses in mathematics and physical science. However, faculty often do not integrate these subjects into the biology courses they teach...

## Quantitative Skills

The lack of a quantitative viewpoint in biology courses can result in students who are mathematically talented losing interest in studying the life sciences. While not all students who pursue an education in the biomedical sciences have an equal interest or predilection for mathematics, it is important that all students understand the growing relevance of quantitative science in addressing life-science questions.... Most biology majors take no more than one year of calculus, although some also take an additional semester of statistics. Very few are exposed to discrete mathematics, linear algebra, probability, and modeling topics, which could greatly enhance their future research careers. These are often considered advanced courses; however, many aspects of discrete math or linear algebra that would be relevant to biology students do not require calculus as a prerequisite.

While calculus remains an important topic for future biologists, the committee does not believe biology students should study calculus to the exclusion of other types of mathematics. Newly designed courses in mathematics that cover some calculus as well as the other types of math mentioned above would be suitable for biology majors and would also prove useful to students enrolled in many other undergraduate majors….

Incorporating mathematics, physical science, and emerging fields such as the information sciences into a biology curriculum is not easy, especially for faculty who do not consider themselves well versed in those topics.

One way to start is to add modules into existing biology courses. Throughout this report, modules are mentioned as a way to modify courses without completely revamping the syllabus. The committee uses the word "module" to mean a self-contained set of material on a specific topic that could be inserted into various different types of preexisting courses. For example, modules can provide opportunities to add quantitative examples or experimental data to a course. The modules would demonstrate the necessity of using mathematics and physical and information sciences to solve biological problems. Administrators, funding agencies, and professional societies should all work to encourage the collaboration of faculty in different departments and the development of teaching materials, including modules of the type mentioned above, that incorporate mathematics, physical science, or information science into the teaching of biology. The creation of new teaching materials is a significant undertaking. It will require a major commitment from college and university administrators and funders to be successful. Faculty must feel encouraged to spend the time necessary to dedicate themselves to the task of understanding the integrative relationships of biology, mathematics, and the physical sciences, and how they can be combined into either existing courses or new courses. In addition, faculty development opportunities must be provided so that faculty can learn from each other and from experts in education about the best approaches for facilitating student learning.

The following box presents a summary of the most important recommendations in this report…

## Recommendations

1. Given the profound changes in the nature of biology and how biological research is performed and communicated, each institution of higher education should reexamine its current courses and teaching approaches to see if they meet the needs of today's undergraduate biology students. Those selecting the new approaches should consider the importance of building a strong foundation in

mathematics and the physical and information sciences to prepare students for research that is increasingly interdisciplinary in character. The implementation of new approaches should be accompanied by a parallel process of assessment, to verify that progress is being made toward the institutional goal of student learning. Lists of relevant concepts are provided within the body of this report (pages 27, 32, 34, 37, 38, and 41).

2. Concepts, examples, and techniques from mathematics, and the physical and information sciences should be included in biology courses, and biological concepts and examples should be included in other science courses. Faculty in biology, mathematics, and physical sciences must work collaboratively to find ways of integrating mathematics and physical sciences into life science courses as well as providing avenues for incorporating life science examples that reflect the emerging nature of the discipline into courses taught in mathematics and physical sciences (page 47).
3. Successful interdisciplinary teaching will require new materials and approaches. College and university administrators, as well as funding agencies, should support mathematics and science faculty in the development or adaptation of techniques that improve interdisciplinary education for biologists. These techniques would include courses, modules (on biological problems suitable for study in mathematics and physical science courses and vice versa), and other teaching materials. These endeavors are time-consuming and difficult and will require serious financial support. In addition, for truly interdisciplinary education to be achieved, administrative and financial barriers to cross-departmental collaboration between faculty must be eliminated (page 60).
4. Laboratory courses should be as interdisciplinary as possible, since laboratory experiments confront students with real-world observations do not separate well into conventional disciplines (page 75).
5. All students should be encouraged to pursue independent research as early as is practical in their education. They should be able to receive academic credit for independent research done in collaboration with faculty or with off-campus researchers (page 87).
6. Seminar-type courses that highlight cutting-edge developments in biology should be provided on a continual and regular basis throughout the four-year undergraduate education of students. Communicating the excitement of biological research is crucial to attracting, retaining, and sustaining a greater diversity of students to the field. These courses would combine presentations by faculty with student projects on research topics (page 91).

7. Medical school admissions requirements and the Medical College Admissions Test (MCAT) are hindering change in the undergraduate biology curriculum and should be reexamined in light of the recommendations in this report (page 111).
8. Faculty development is a crucial component to improving undergraduate biology education. Efforts must be made on individual campuses and nationally to provide faculty the time necessary to refine their own understanding of how the integrative relationships of biology, mathematics, and the physical sciences can be best melded into either existing courses or new courses in the particular areas of science in which they teach (page 113).

...Among entering college students in the fall of 2001, 7% planned to major in a biological science (University of California et al., 2001). Only 2% of freshmen listed scientific researcher or college teacher as a probable career, 6% said physician, and almost 15% listed undecided.

Entering students encountered faculty who spent 57% of their time on teaching-related activities and 15% on research, although at research or doctoral institutions, and among full professors the amount of time devoted to teaching was lower (U.S. Department of Education, 2001). In the natural sciences approximately 86% of faculty reported lecturing as their primary method of instruction (U.S. Department of Education, 2001).

Revised teaching approaches that appeal more to students may encourage more talented undergraduates to consider scientific careers....

Throughout this report the committee uses the term "quantitative biology" to refer to a biology in which mathematics and computing serve as essential tools in framing experimental questions, analyzing experimental data, generating models, and making predictions that can be tested. In quantitative biology, the multifaceted relationships between molecules, cells, organisms, species, and communities are characterized and comprehended by finding structure in massive data sets that span different levels of biological organization. It is a science in which new computational, physical, and chemical tools are sought and applied to gain a deeper and more coherent understanding of the biological world that has strong predictive power...

## Mathematics and Computer Science

*RECOMMENDATION #1.5*

*Quantitative analysis, modeling, and prediction play increasingly significant day-to-day roles in today's biomedical research. To prepare for this sea change in activities, biology majors headed for research careers need to be educated in a more quantitative manner, and such quantitative education may require the development of new types of courses. The committee recommends that all biology majors master the concepts listed below. In addition, the committee recommends that life science majors become sufficiently familiar with the elements of programming to carry out simulations of physiological, ecological, and evolutionary processes. They should be adept at using computers to acquire and process data, carry out statistical characterization of the data and perform statistical tests, and graphically display data in a variety of representations. Furthermore, students should also become skilled at using the Internet to carry out literature searches, locate published articles, and access major databases.*

The elucidation of the sequence of the human genome has opened new vistas and has highlighted the increasing importance of mathematics and computer science in biology. The intense interest in genetic, metabolic, and neural networks reflects the need of biologists to view and understand the coordinated activities of large numbers of components of the complex systems underlying life. Biology students should be prepared to carry out *in silico* (computer) experiments to complement *in vitro* and *in vivo* experiments.

It is essential that biology undergraduates become quantitatively literate. The concepts of rate of change, modeling, equilibria and stability, structure of a system, interactions among components, data and measurement, visualizing, and algorithms are among those most important to the curriculum. Every student should acquire the ability to analyze issues arising in these contexts in some depth, using analytical methods (e.g., pencil and paper), appropriate computational tools, or both. The course of study would include aspects of probability, statistics, discrete models, linear algebra, calculus and differential equations, modeling, and programming.

## Concepts of Mathematics and Computer Science

### *Calculus*

- Complex numbers
- Functions
- Limits
- Continuity
- The integral
- The derivative and linearization
- Elementary functions
- Fourier series
- Multidimensional calculus: linear approximations, integration over multiple variables

## Linear Algebra

- Scalars, vectors, matrices
- Linear transformations
- Eeigenvalues and eigenvectors
- Invariant subspaces

## Dynamical Systems

- Continuous time dynamics—equations of motion and their trajectories
- Test points, limit cycles, and stability around them
- Phase plane analysis
- Cooperativity, positive feedback, and negative feedback
- Multistability
- Discrete time dynamics — mappings, stable points, and stable cycles
- Sensitivity to initial conditions and chaos

## Probability and Statistics

- Probability distributions
- Random numbers and stochastic processes
- Covariation, correlation, and independence
- Error likelihood

## Information and Computation

- Algorithms (with examples)
- Computability
- Optimization in mathematics and computation
- "Bits": information and mutual information

## Data Structures

- Metrics: generalized 'distance' and sequence comparisons
- Clustering
- Tree-relationships
- Graphics: visualizing and displaying data and models for conceptual understanding

## Additional Quantitative Principles Useful to Biology Students

### *Rate of Change*

- This can be a specific (e.g., per capita) rate of change or a total rate of change of some system component.
- Discrete rates of change arise in difference equations, which have associated with them an inherent time-scale.
- Continuous rates of change arise as derivatives or partial derivatives, representing instantaneous (relative to the units in which time is scaled) rates.

### *Modeling*

- The process of abstracting certain aspects of reality to include in the simplifications of reality we call models.
- Scale (spatial and temporal)—different questions arise on different scales.
- What is included (system variables) depends on the questions addressed, as does the hierarchical level in which the problem is framed (e.g., molecular, cellular, organismal).
- There are trade-offs in modeling—no one model can address all questions. These trade-offs are between generality, precision, and realism.
- Evaluating models depends in part on the purpose for which the model was constructed. Models oriented toward prediction of specific phenomena may require formal statistical validation methods, while models that wish to elucidate general patterns of system response may require corroboration with the available observed patterns.

### *Equilibria and Stability*

- Equilibria arise when a process (or several processes) rate of change is zero.
- There can be more than one equilibrium. Multiple stable states (e.g., long-term patterns that are returned to following a perturbation of the system) are typical of biological systems. The system dynamics may drive the process to any of these depending on initial conditions and history (e.g., the order of any sequence of changes in the system may affect the outcomes).
- Equilibria can be dynamic, so that a periodic pattern of system response may arise. This period pattern may be stable in that for some range of initial conditions, the system approaches this period pattern.

- There are numerous notions of stability, including not just whether a system that is perturbed from an equilibrium returns to it, but also how the system returns (e.g., how rapidly it does so).
- Modifying some system components can lead to destabilization of a previously stable equilibrium, possibly generating entirely new equilibria with differing stability characteristics. These bifurcations of equilibria arise in many nonlinear systems typical in biology.

### *Structure*

- Grouping components of a system affects the kinds of questions addressed and the data required to parameterize the system.
- Choosing different aggregated formulations (by sex, age, size, physiological state, activity state) can expand or limit the questions that can be addressed, and data availability can limit the ability to investigate effects of structure.
- Geometry of the aggregation can affect the resulting formulation.
- Symmetry can be useful in many biological contexts to reduce the complexity of the problem, and situations in which symmetry is lost (symmetry-breaking) can aid in understanding system response.

### *Interactions*

- There are relatively few ways for system components to interact. Negative feedbacks arise through competitive and predator-prey type interactions, positive feedback through mutualistic or commensal ones.
- Some general properties can be derived based upon these (e.g., two-species competitive interactions), but even relatively few interacting system components can lead to complex dynamics.
- Though ultimately everything is hitched to everything else, significant effects are not automatically transferred through a connected system of interacting components—locality can matter.
- Sequences of interactions can determine outcomes—program order matters.

### *Data and Measurement*

- Only a few basic data types arise (numeric, ordinal, categorical), but these will often be interconnected and expanded (e.g., as vectors or arrays).
- Consistency of the units with which one measures a system is important.

- A variety of statistical methods exist to characterize single data sets and to make comparisons between data sets. Using such methods with discernment takes practice.

### Stochasticity

- In a stochastic process, individual outcomes cannot be predicted with certainty. Rather, these outcomes are determined randomly according to a probability distribution that arises from the underlying mechanisms of the process. Probabilities for measurements that are continuous (height, weight, etc.), and those that are discrete (sex, cell type) arise in many biological contexts.
- Risk can be identified and estimated.
- There are ways to determine if an experimental result is significant.
- There are instances when stochasticity is significant and averages are not sufficient.

### Visualizing

- There are diverse methods to display data.
- Simple line and bar graphs are often not sufficient.
- Nonlinear transformations can yield new insights.

### Algorithms

- These are rules that determine the types of interactions in a system, how decisions are made, and the time course of system response.
- These can be thought of as a sequence of actions similar to a computer program, with all the associated options such as assignments, if-then loops, and while-loops.

### Using Computers

Many of the concepts above deal with types of analysis and modeling that require knowledge of computer programming. However, there is another aspect of computing that is important for the future research biologist: the use of computers as tools. Computer use is a fact of life for all modern life scientists. Exposure during the early years of their undergraduate careers will help life science students use current computer methods and learn how to exploit emerging computer technologies as they arise. As computer power continues to grow rapidly, applications that were available only on supercomputers a few years ago can now be used on relatively inexpensive personal computers. Computers are essential today for obtaining information from databases (e.g., genetic data from Genbank), establishing relationships (e.g., using the BLAST algorithm to quantitate the similarity of a given DNA or protein sequence to all known sequences), deducing patterns (e.g., clustering genes that are regulated in concert), carrying out statistical tests, preparing plots and other graphics for presentation, and writing manuscripts for publication. Furthermore, computers are playing a central role in the laboratory in controlling equipment, obtaining data from measuring devices, and carrying out real-time analysis (e.g., image acquisition in confocal fluorescence microscopy). Research biologists are increasingly acquiring and analyzing vast amounts of data (e.g., the degree of expression of tens of thousands of genes in multiple cellular states). They will need to be conversant with new theoretical and modeling approaches to come to grips with the interplay of many simultaneously interacting components of complex systems.

Many analyses of biological data can be accomplished with existing programs (e.g., BLAST). However, being able to modify or construct applications is necessary in many research areas. Learning how a computer application is developed provides students with insight into the software they use. Computer understanding can be taught by providing experiences in computer programming, teaching about computer algorithms, and how to construct simple simulations. This familiarity could be accomplished by exposing students to programming in higher-level languages such as Matlab, Perl, or C.

The Internet is increasingly becoming the primary source of information for life scientists. Databases in a variety of areas (e.g., genomics, global warming, population dynamics) provide integrative frameworks that are valuable for addressing important biological issues. Becoming fully conversant with databases such as the National Center for Biotechnology Information (NCBI) is important for all biology majors. NCBI's mission is to develop new information technologies to aid in the understanding of fundamental molecular and genetic processes that control health and disease.

Searchable databases at NCBI's Web site (*www.ncbi.nlm.nih.gov*) include Genbank (all publicly available DNA sequences), PubMed (access to more than 11 million Medline citations of biomedical literature, including links to full text articles), BLAST (Basic Local Alignment Search Tool for carrying out similarity searches of DNA or protein query sequences), Taxonomy (a wide range of taxonomic information at the molecular level), and Structure (database of three-dimensional structure of biological macro-molecules and tools for visualization and comparative analysis). Major model organism databases such as Fly Base (*www.flybase.org*) are useful, and The Interactive Fly (*sdb.bio.purdue.edu/fly/aimain/laahome.htm*) is a related learning tool.

Sites such as PubMed are essential for searching the literature and valuable for linking to full-text publications. Students should learn how to obtain different kinds of information from Web sites (e.g., DNA and protein sequences, atomic coordinates, phylogenetic relationships, functional anatomy, and biogeographic ecosystem data) and how to make information available to others over the Web (e.g., depositing new DNA sequences in Genbank). In addition, students should learn about mechanisms (e.g., peer review) of evaluating and increasing the reliability of information obtained on the Web.

An attractive option for quantitative literacy, mathematics, and computer science at some institutions might be the development of an integrated course to teach quantitative approaches and tools for research, as has been successfully developed at the University of Tennessee (see Case Study #4). This innovative two-semester course designed for life science majors replaces the traditional calculus course. It introduces topics such as the mathematics of discrete variables, linear algebra, statistics, programming, and modeling early in the course, to provide completely new material for well-prepared students. These topics are then connected to applied aspects of calculus. It should be noted that this course makes extensive use of graduate students in Tennessee's mathematical and computational ecology program. These graduate students are well positioned to explain the connections between mathematics and biology.

A two-semester quantitative course such as the one at Tennessee exposes students to many mathematical ideas but is too brief to provide much depth in many of them. A more intensive alternative would be a four-semester series. Two semesters could deal with calculus (single and multivariate), quantitative differential equations (including phase plane analysis), and the relevant elementary linear algebra, taught in the context of biological applications. A third semester might be on biostatistics, emphasizing different ways to analyze and interpret data. A fourth semester could include discrete math and algorithms and could be taught in the context of biological issues, including those arising in genomics.

Committee recommends:

A new mathematics sequence that exposes students to statistics, probability, discrete math, linear algebra, calculus, and modeling without requiring that a full semester be spent on each topic. A brief overview of these topics could be presented in two semesters, but a full introduction and the inclusion of more computer science would more likely take four semesters.

## CASE STUDY #4

### *Quantitative Education for Biologists*

**University of Tennessee**

This course sequence provides an introduction to a variety of mathematical topics of use in analyzing problems arising in the biological sciences. It is designed for students in biology, agriculture, forestry, wildlife, and premedicine and other prehealth professions. The general aim of the sequence is to show how mathematical and analytical tools may be used to explore and explain a wide variety of biological phenomena that are not easily understood with verbal reasoning alone.

Prerequisites are two years of high school algebra, one year of geometry, and half a year of trigonometry. The goals of the course are to develop the students' ability to quantitatively analyze problems arising in their own work in biology, to illustrate the great utility of mathematical models to provide answers to key biological problems, and to provide experience using computer software to analyze data and investigate mathematical models. This is accomplished by encouraging hypothesis formulation and testing and the investigation of real-world biological problems through the use of data. Another goal is to reduce rote memorization of mathematical formulae and rules through the use of software including Matlab and MicroCalc. Students can be encouraged to investigate biological areas of particular interest to them using a variety of quantitative software from a diversity of biological specialties.

In many respects, this course is more difficult than the university's science/engineering calculus sequence (Math 141-142) since it covers a wider variety of mathematical topics, is coupled to real data, and involves the use of the computer. Although the course is challenging, it has been designed specifically for life science students, and includes many more biological examples than other mathematics courses. It, therefore, introduces the students to quantitative concepts not covered in these other math courses that they should find useful in their biology courses. The main text is *Mathematics for the Biosciences* by Michael Cullen, which is extensively supplemented by material provided in class.

Each class session begins with the students generating one or more hypotheses regarding a biological or mathematical topic germane to that day's material. For example, students go outdoors to collect leaf size data. They are then asked: Are leaf width and length related? Is the relationship the same for all tree species? What affects leaf sizes? Why do some trees have larger leaves than others? Each of these questions could generate many hypotheses, and students can then go on to use Matlab to analyze the data sets they collect in order to evaluate the hypotheses. Some hypotheses do not relate to a biological area and are based on mathematics alone. For example, after linear regression is introduced, students are asked whether this regression can be reasonably used to determine the y-value for an x-value for which there are no data. This leads naturally to a discussion of interpolation and extrapolation.

As each topic is introduced, the instructor includes a brief description of how it relates to biology. This is often done by having a background biological example used for each main mathematical topic being covered, which can be referred to regularly as the math is developed. For example, in covering matrices, the material can be introduced with this example: "Suppose you are a land manager in the U.S. West, and you have satellite images of the land you manage taken every year for several years. The images clearly show whether a point on the image (actually a 500 m x 500 m plot of land) is bare soil, grassland, or shrubland. How can you use these to help you manage the system?" From this, the students develop the key notion of a transition matrix; the professor can then go on to matrix multiplication, and eigenvalues and eigenvectors for describing dynamics of the landscape and the long-term fraction in bare soil, grass, and shrubs.

Attempts are made to include real, rather than fabricated, data in class demonstrations, project assignments, and exams. For example, data of monthly $CO_2$ concentrations in the Northern Hemisphere can be used to introduce semi-log regression, and allometry data can be used for studying log-log regressions. Students are encouraged to collect their own data for appropriate portions of the course, particularly the descriptive statistics section. Scientific journal articles that use the math under study are also provided.

## Syllabus Math 151

- Descriptive statistics—analysis of tabular data, means, variances, histograms, linear regression
- Exponentials and logarithms, non-linear scalings, allometry
- Matrix algebra—addition, subtraction, multiplication, inverses, matrix models in population biology, eigenvalues, eigenvectors,
- Markov chains, ecological succession
- Discrete probability—population genetics, behavioral sequence analysis
- Sequences and difference equations—introduction to sequences and limit concept

## Syllabus Math 152

- Difference equations, linear and nonlinear examples, equilibrium, stability and homeostasis, logistic models, introduction to limits
- Limits of functions and continuity
- Derivatives and curve sketching
- Exponential and logarithms
- Antiderivatives and integrals

- Trigonometric functions
- Differential equations and modeling

Students are graded through weekly 10-minute quizzes, assignments based on the use of the computer to analyze particular sets of data or problems (some done in groups), three in-class exams, and a comprehensive final exam. The exams are generally not computer-based, focusing rather on the key concepts and techniques discussed in the course. Extra-credit opportunities require students to evaluate one of a wide variety of software programs available involving some area of biology. This requires becoming very familiar with the program, and writing a formal review of the software, in the same format as might appear in a scientific journal.

For more information: *www.tiem.utk.edu/~gross/quant.lifesci.html*

The panel suggested that all biology majors, not just future biomedical researchers, should be exposed to and develop a conceptual understanding for the idea of rate of change, modeling, equilibria and stability, structure of a system, interactions among components, data and measurement, stochasticity, visualizing, and algorithms…."

# RESOURCES FOR QUANTIFYING CASES
## Simulations, Games, and Data Sets

### I. Know/Need-to-Know Chart

A Know/Need-to-Know Chart is helpful in interrupted cases, allowing students to determine their current understanding of the problem and begin making predictions and considering additional information needed.

| Facts (What we know) | Questions (What do we need to know/Predict what will happen next) |
|---|---|
| Hypothesis (How do we move this case forward?) | Learning Issues (What do we not know/Want to know) |

### II. PhET Simulations

**URL:** *PhET.colorado.edu/*

**Overview:** PhET is designed as a collection of hands-on Java-based simulations and accompanying activities allowing users to experiment with a variety of concepts in physics, chemistry, biology, Earth science and other STEM disciplines as a means to visualize concepts at various levels. Biology simulations include curve fitting, color vision, density, eating and exercise, gene expression, membrane channels, molecular motors, natural selection, neuron, probability, radioactive dating, pH, reaction rates, optical tweezers, MRI, and several DNA-related simulations. Many have faculty-generated exercises that accompany them. See: *phet.colorado.edu/en/simulations/index*

**Note:** All simulations require Java 1.5 or higher; Sun Java can be downloaded free at *www.java.com/en/download*.

**Organization:** PhET is organized as a series of concept-related simulations and activities based on concept, type, educational level, and language. PhET also allows for searching for simulations and activities under the "For Teachers"→"Browse Activities" menu selection. Simulations can be found specifically using the "Play with sims" button on the home page. Simulations are then categorized by subject or grade level.

**Running a Simulation:** Once a simulation has been selected, it can be run either locally or using a web browser. Running locally: Simulations can be downloaded ("Download") and installed on a local computer to run at any time. Web Browser: Users can run simulations directly through their browsers using the ("Run Now!") button. Embed: Users also have the option to embed the simulation in their own website ("Embed").

**General Simulation Notes:** While each simulation is different, most simulations are composed of multiple activities related by a single concept. These additional simulations can be found as tabs within each primary simulation. Most simulations contain their own help and running instructions within the simulation itself; otherwise, help can be found on the simulation primary page.

**Simulation Resources:** Each simulation page contains a Teaching Resources section to help teachers/instructors get the most out of the simulation experience. In addition to Simulation Topics, and Sample Learning Goals, this section also contains links to additional teaching ideas, tips, activities and simulations categorized by suggested grade level and type. Finally, each simulation page contains information on Related Simulations and available translations.

**Help:** Additional resources and help can be found on the PhET homepage or simulation page including how to install and run PhET simulations on a local computer and any known software issues.

## III. BioQUEST Simulation Modules

**URL:** *bioquest.org/BQLibrary/library_result.php*

**Overview:** *The BioQUEST Library Online* contains peer-reviewed software simulations, tools, data sets, and other supporting materials from educators and developers engaged in education and research in science. The table below lists selected modules.

| Module | Description | Author(s) |
|---|---|---|
| 3-D FractaL Tree | Produces visualizations of tree forms based on data from specimens in the field or lab. | John Jungck, Jennifer Spangenberg, Noppadon Khiripet, Rawin Viruchpinta, Jutarat Maneewattanapluk |
| Action Potential Experiments | Demonstration/simulation laboratory for neurophysiology based on the "sodium theory." | Mark Bergland |
| Avida-ED | Tool for designing and performing experiments to test hypotheses about evolutionary mechanisms using evolving digital organisms. | Robert Pennock |
| BeeVisit | Interactive model of pollen transfer. | Barbara and James Thomson |
| BioGrapher | Excel front-end for AT&T GraphViz graphical visualization for undergraduate investigations. | Rama Viswanathan, Han Lai, Hlaing Lin, Khalid Qumsieh, John Jungck |
| BIRDD: Beagle Investigations Return with Darwinian Data | Collection of primary scientific data and supporting materials about the Galápagos Islands and Darwin's finches. | Frank Price, Sam Donovan, Jim Stewart, John Jungck |
| Cardiovascular Construction Kit | Allows students to design and construct wide range of cardiovascular systems. | Sarah Douglas, Daniel Udovic, Nils Peterson |
| Cardiovascular Function Lab | Simulation that explores how the heart performs as a blood pump. | Edward Crawford, Nils Peterson |
| Cell Differentials | Simulation randomly generates white blood cell images to provide users with visual recognition practice. | Donald Buckley, Deborah Clark<br>Karen Barrett, Lynn Gugliotti, JoAnne Morrica |
| Curacao | Computer program that simulates the sterile insect release method (SIRM) of pest population suppression. | Phil Arneson, Barr E. Ticknor |
| Developmental Selection | Research simulation that allows students to investigate the possible causes of incomplete embryo development in perennial legume fruits. | Donald Buckley, Martin Cohen |

*Continued*

| Module | Description | Author(s) |
|---|---|---|
| Environmental Decision Making | Tool for modeling and simulating three different ecosystems (ponds, grasslands, logging), including social and economic forces. | Elisabeth C. Odum, H. T. Odum, Nils Peterson |
| Epidemiology | Simulates spread of an infectious disease through a population. | Daniel Udovic, Will Goodwin |
| Evolve | Allows students to model evolution and get quick results from population genetics experiments. | Frank Price, Virginia Vaughan |
| Genetics Construction Kit | Simulation of a classic Mendelian genetics laboratory. | John N. Calley, John Jungck |
| Hypoxia Zone: Modeling Stratified Waters | Models effects of reducing nutrient loads to surface waters on microbial populations and oxygen levels. | H. T. Odum, Ethel Stanley, Elisabeth Odum |
| Java Demography | Simulates exponential growth in age-structured populations. | Daniel Udovic, Jasper Barber, Will Goodwin, Gordon Hennesy |
| Late Blight Life Cycle | Models the late-blight life cycle in potatoes. | H. T. Odum, Elisabeth Odum, Ethel Stanley |
| Lateblight: A Plant Disease Management Simulation | Allows students to manipulate the variables that affect the development of late blight. | Phil Arneson, Barr Ticknor |
| MacRetina | Simulates data from retinal ganglion cells in the eye to the brain. | Richard Olivo |
| Microbial Genetics Construction Kit | Simulates a microbial genetics laboratory. | John N. Calley, John Jungck |
| Molecular Genetics Explorer | Simulation of flower color in a hypothetical plant. | Brian White, Ethan Bolker |
| Peach | Simulates peach fruit and tree growth based on daily carbon gain, maintenance respiration and growth of fruits, leaves, and other structures. | Yaffa Grossman, Ted DeJong, Scott Vosburg |
| Pfiesteria Life Cycle | Simulation that allows students to manipulate environmental variables in a life cycle model of a normally benign dinoflagellate to produce an outbreak of its toxic form. | H. T. Odum, Elisabeth Odum, Ethel Stanley |
| Phylogenetic Investigator | Software package designed to facilitate creative problem-solving in phylogenetic analysis. | Steven Brewer, Robert Hafner |
| Resistan | Mechanistic simulation model of the process of selection of fungicide-resistant biotypes of a hypothetical fungal pathogen. | Phil Arneson, Barr Ticknor |
| Sampling | Computer tool designed to help biology students obtain a qualitative understanding of basic concepts related to estimation. | Daniel Udovic, Gordon Hennesy, Will Goodwin |

*Continued*

| Module | Description | Author(s) |
|---|---|---|
| Sequence It! | Simulation program that allows you to experience the art and logic of protein sequencing through experimentation. | Allen Place, Tom Schmidt |
| SimBio2 | Simulation of the Biosphere 2. | Elisabeth Odum, H. T. Odum |
| TB Lab | Simulated microbiology lab for exploring how the bacteria responsible for TB develop resistance to antibiotics. | William Sandoval, Brian Reiser, Renee Judd, Richard Leider |
| The Search for the Hereditary Molecule | Research lab simulation gives students control of the classic investigations that supported that DNA is the hereditary molecule. | Donald Buckley, William Coleman |
| Virtual Laboratory | Simulation program based on the Nobel Prize–winning Hodgkin-Huxley model for excitation of the squid axon. | Robert Macey<br>Tim Zahnley |
| Wine Modeling | Simulation that allows you to model the fermentation process and explore variables and their effects on winemaking. | Ethel Stanley, Elisabeth Odum, H. T. Odum, Virginia Vaughan |
| Winter Twig Key | Interactive visual key to dichotomous trees using winter twigs. | Ethel Stanley, Joseph Armstrong, Dent Rhodes |

## IV. BEDROCK

**URL:** *bioquest.org/bedrock/*

**Overview:** The Bioinformatics Education Dissemination: Reaching Out, Connecting, and Knitting-together (BEDROCK) Project, funded by the National Science Foundation (NSF), is aimed at integrating bioinformatics throughout the undergraduate biology curriculum using an inquiry-based approach in which students explore and analyze actual data in a way that recreates the experience of conducting research. There are over 150 participant projects as well as a number of problem spaces.

## V. ESTEEM—Excel Simulations and Tools for Exploratory Experiential Mathematics

**URL:** *bioquest.org/esteem/* and *bioquest.org/esteem/esteem_result.php*

**Overview:** A project of the BioQUEST Curriculum Consortium, the Biological ESTEEM Collection contains over 60 modules that relate to the mathematics behind biology. Microsoft's spreadsheet software Excel was chosen as a general development environment for the ESTEEM project because most biologists and mathematicians have it on their desktop computers, use it at least minimally for data collection, and find it fairly easy to operate. In addition, Excel is powerful enough to develop applications that involve matrix algebra, statistics, finite difference equations, and simple ordinary differential equations. Since parameters are easy to change in Excel and it is easy to import data from diverse and heterogeneous resources, the modules can be easily adopted, adapted, extended, and used by students engaged in a variety of biology and mathematics courses. In addition to a downloadable Excel (.xls) file, each module is supplemented with references to textbooks where the relevant biology and mathematics are introduced, the original sources of such models, current research articles that employ the models explicitly or derivatives of these models, and online related resources. In some instances, additional documentation, other software (particularly Java Applets and remotely run Web Mathematica applications), classroom-lab-field activities, science and mathematics education research references, and historical material are also provided.

## VI. Foldit: "Solve Puzzles for Science"

**URL:** *fold.it/portal/*

**Overview:** Foldit and EteRNA (described briefly in the section that follows) are multiuser computer games that allow students and the general public to participate in real science and learn how science works. Using these games, students can develop and test hypotheses. We are proposing that interested case writers develop cases that are entry point into these games.

Specifically, Foldit allows students to learn about protein structure and protein folding.

## VII. EteRNA: "Played by Humans, Scored by Nature"

**URL:** *eterna.cmu.edu/web/*

**Overview:** EteRNA allows players to participate in creating libraries of synthetic RNA designs. The goal is to develop new principles for "designing RNA-based switches and nanomachines—new systems for seeking and eventually controlling living cells and disease-causing viruses."

## VIII. A Word About Finding Data Sets

International and national agencies are a major source of biology-related data sets of all kinds. These agencies include the National Institutes of Health (NIH), the Centers for Disease Control and Prevention (CDC), the U.S. Geological Survey (USGS), the National Oceanic and Atmospheric Administration (NOAA), the U.S. Environmental Protection Agency, the U.S. Department of Human Health and Human Services, the World Health Organization (WHO), and many more. We recommend that you explore the websites of these organizations to see what kinds of readily available data sets they have. For help identifying statistical data of interest, we suggest you use FedStats at *www.fedstats.gov.*

FedStats is a sort of "one-stop shopping mall" for statistics published by the U.S. federal government organized by topic. The FedStats website also has a section called "MapStats" that provides socioeconomic profiles of states, counties, and Congressional districts; in addition, there are "Data Access Tools" with links to selective databases.

# INDEX

*Page numbers printed in **boldface** type refer to figures or tables.*

T